BUILDING A GREAT VICTORIAN CITY

LEEDS ARCHITECTS
AND ARCHITECTURE
1790–1914

EDITED BY
CHRISTOPHER WEBSTER

BUILDING A GREAT VICTORIAN CITY

LEEDS ARCHITECTS AND ARCHITECTURE 1790–1914

EDITED BY
CHRISTOPHER WEBSTER

PUBLISHED BY
NORTHERN HERITAGE PUBLICATIONS

IN ASSOCIATION WITH THE
THE VICTORIAN SOCIETY
The champion for Victorian and Edwardian architecture
WEST YORKSHIRE GROUP

Published by Northern Heritage Publications
an imprint of Jeremy Mills Publishing Limited
www.jeremymillspublishing.co.uk

in association with the Victorian Society West Yorkshire Group

First published 2011

ISBN 978–1–906600–64–8

Publication of this book was assisted by generous grants from the Paul Mellon Centre for Studies in British Art, the Leeds Philosophical and Literary Society and a generous donation in memory of David Crellin (1965-2006), formerly architectural adviser to the Victorian Society.

LEEDS PHILOSOPHICAL AND LITERARY SOCIETY

THE VICTORIAN SOCIETY
The champion for Victorian and Edwardian architecture

Front cover: Leeds, Cookridge Street, showing, on the left, shops by Brodrick (1864), Bakewell's Coliseum (1885) in the centre, and on the right, the corner of Brodrick's Mechanics Institute (1860-65). (*Ruth Baumberg.*)

Back cover: Leeds, Roman Catholic Cathedral of St Anne (J.H. Eastwood and S.K. Greenslade, 1901-4), seen from the entrance to the offices and warehouse of William Smith, 1840-7. (*Ruth Baumberg.*)

Frontispiece: Leeds, Old Medical School, Road (William Hill, 1890-4) (*Ruth Baumberg.*)

Dedicated to the memory of

COLIN CUNNINGHAM (1942-2011)
a great scholar of Victorian architecture

DEREK LINSTRUM (1925-2009)
who opened our eyes to the wonders of Leeds architects

and
TOM WESLEY (1941-2007)

ADEL

ROUNDHAY

CHAPEL ALLERTON

HEADINGLEY
CUM BURLEY

✝ Kirkstall
Abbey

POTTERNEWTON

BRAMLEY

LEEDS

ARMLEY

✝ Parish
Church

HALTON

WORTLEY

HOLBECK

FARNLEY

HUNSLET

BEESTON

River Aire

Township Boundaries

The Borough of Leeds showing the 'out
townships' as they existed through the
nineteenth century. Adel and Roundhay
were outside the borough.

Contents

PART TWO
THE DIRECTORY
BY THE AUTHORS, PLUS HUGH KERRIGAN

Abbreviations

BAL, *Directory*
British Architectural Library & RIBA, *Directory of British Architects, 1834-1900*, Mansell, 1993.

Beckwith
F. Beckwith, *Thomas Taylor, Regency Architect*, Thoresby Society, monograph 1, 1949.

CBC
Archives of the Church Building Commission, Church of England Records Centre, London.

Colvin
H. Colvin, *A Biographical Dictionary of British Architects*, 1600-1840, Yale U.P., 2008.

dem.
demolished

Felstead
A. Felstead *et al, Directory of British Architects, 1834-1900*, Mansell, 1993.

ICBS
Incorporated Church Building Society papers, Lambeth Palace Library, London.

Harper
R.H. Harper, *Victorian Architectural Competitions*, Mansell, 1983.

LAA
Leeds Architectural Association (1877-1883)

LYAS
Leeds and Yorkshire Architectural Society (1883 onwards)

LI
Leeds Intelligencer

LM
Leeds Mercury

LMA
London Metropolitan Archives

Linstrum, *Leeds*
D. Linstrum, *Historic Architecture of Leeds*, Oriel Press, 1969.

Linstrum, *WYAA*
D. Linstrum, *West Yorkshire Architects and Architecture*, Lund Humphries, 1878.

MB
minute book

Meth
Methodist

MNC
Methodist New Connection

MNC Mag
Methodist New Connection Magazine

NY
North Yorkshire

Pevsner, *Leeds*
S. Wrathmell, *Pevsner Architerctural Guides: Leeds*, Yale UP, 2005.

Pevsner, *WY*
P. Leach and N. Pevsner, *The Buildings of England, Yorkshire West Riding: Leeds, Bradford and the North*, Yale UP, 2009.

PM
Primitive Methodist

PTS
Publications of the Thoresby Society, Leeds

Trowell
F. Trowell, 'Nineteenth Century Speculative Housing in Leeds … 1838-1914', 3 vols, unpublished PhD thesis, University of York, 1982.

Trowell, TS
F. Trowell, Speculative Housing Developments in the Suburb of Headingley, *Publications of the Thoresby Society, Miscellany, Vol LIX, Part 1, 1983*.)

TS
Thoresby Society, Leeds

UMC
United Methodist

UMFC
United Methodist Free Churches

WM
Wesleyan Methodist

WY
West Yorkshire

WYASB
West Yorkshire Archives Service, Bradford

WYASL
West Yorkshire Archives Service, Leeds

WYASW
West Yorkshire Archives Service, Wakefield

Preface and Acknowledgements

CHRISTOPHER WEBSTER

In the summer of 1876, *The Architect* sent a reporter to Leeds to review the recent buildings in this rapidly developing town.[1] He began enthusiastically: 'There are few, if any, of our manufacturing towns that possess stronger attractions for an architectural visitor … Leeds … stands un-rivalled.' He proceeded to discuss Brodrick's 'beautiful town hall', as well as his Corn Exchange, Institute – 'no town … possesses so handsome a Mechanics Institute as Leeds – and the Oriental Baths, all of which 'display no common skill in architectural composition.' Of the recent churches, St Bartholomew, Armley – by Walker and Athron – and St Peter, Dewsbury Road – by William Perkin – were identified for praise. Among the Nonconformist chapels, Thomas Ambler's Oak Road Congregational Chapel stood out from many. As for the principal streets, Leeds excelled: 'scarce any commercial town in the kingdom can boast of such long avenues of fair architecture in varied brick and stone as Boar Lane, Wellington Street, [and] Park Row … afford.'

Twenty years later, a similar review appeared in *The Builder*.[2] Some of the same buildings were discussed and many new ones added: George Corson's School Board offices and Municipal Buildings, as well as his Grand Theatre, Chorley and Connon's Liberal Club and W.H. Thorp's Medical School. Of Park Row it concluded, 'it is not often that one meets with a modern city street which can show so large a proportion of buildings that are worth notice.'

That these articles were commissioned is hardly surprising: Leeds was, after all, one of the great provincial centres of the age. It had

1. *The Architect*, 1876, pp. 195-6; 250-1.

2. *The Builder*, 71, 1896, pp. 505-13.

witnessed industrial growth on an heroic scale and a not inconsiderable proportion of the ensuing profits had been devoted to architectural statements capable of proclaiming the town's achievements as well as its aspirations. What these articles clearly reveal is the extent to which this great centre of Victorian commerce and industry had been shaped by architects with Leeds offices. True, both writers also mentioned work by 'outsiders', but not much of it and, interestingly, the earlier article was decidedly lukewarm about the new Infirmary from Sir George Gilbert Scott's London drawing board.

In the century and a quarter which forms the focus of this book, a succession of exceptionally talented men who either grew up in Leeds, or moved to Leeds in the belief that it offered compelling opportunities, provided the town with almost all of its architectural requirements. Industrial growth provided the money to pay for stately new buildings and these Leeds-based designers rarely failed to satisfy their client's ambitions. Some, like the Bedford and Kitson partnership, Brodrick and Chantrell are reasonably well known, but others, for instance C.W. Burleigh, Percy Robinson and W.H. Thorp, emerge from the shadows as gifted individuals.

Terminating this study in 1914 certainly has historical neatness but, interestingly, it coincides with the pattern of architectural practice in the city: the careers of the great Leeds architects who are featured in the later part of this book did not survive into the 1920s and the major buildings of the inter-war period were largely the work of London firms.

What conclusions should we take from a study like this? It might be imagined that provincial architects would mainly work close to home as other towns had their own men. However, the book confirms that this was not always the case: those Leeds designers who had a particular Nonconformist denominational allegiance – for instance Thomas and Charles Howdill with the Primitive Methodists, and James Simpson with the Wesleyans – secured work over a huge geographical area. And an ambitious architect like Hill, eagerly entering secular competitions advertised in the professional journals, also travelled the length of the country to supervise his victories.

Stylistic preferences inevitably evolved and the book reveals a predictable chronological development; activity in Leeds was, to a considerable extent, a microcosm of English architectural history in this period. However, this study also reveals much about the development of architectural practice. Several of the architects at work in the third quarter of the nineteenth century – for instance Hill, Perkin and Backhouse and Thomas Shaw – produced huge numbers of working class, usually back-to-back houses. This was a sector of the market that both earlier and later men eschewed, as did their contemporary Brodrick. Yet Hill's involvement with the building type did not prevent him being almost as successful as Brodrick in securing major public buildings. Thomas Taylor emerges as one of the country's most important early designers of Gothic churches – and one just ahead of Thomas Rickman, usually credited as the pioneer – while John Clark, with few surviving buildings to maintain his reputation, is revealed as a Neoclassicist of exceptional ability.

Despite the proliferation of professional magazines and journals that helped disseminate both stylistic and practice-related issues, the period was still one of often profound regional differences. The response of the Leeds architects to national debates about the professionalisation of architecture (discussed in Chapter 9) confirms them as often ahead of their more conservative London colleagues. And while the recent book on Birmingham architects [3] reveals a whole series of turn-of-the-century practices in that city dominated by substantial domestic projects – often Arts and Crafts inspired – it was a branch of building activity which has few parallels in Leeds. At the same time, among the architects in Birmingham or Bristol,[4] there were none whose practices were dominated by Nonconformist chapels in the way that Leeds' Simpson or Howdills were. The emergence of the provincial architectural profession during the nineteenth century – in most cases, from nothing – is a fascinating story. The recent appearance of the 'Pevsner City Guides' is a welcome development and has done much to awaken interest in provincial buildings and confirm their quality. In addition, the Victorian Society's 'Powerhouses of Provincial Architecture' lectures and publication[5] have raised the profile of a succession of gifted individuals and addressed some wider issues. This is a subject which deserves to be more widely appreciated.

❦

My aim of producing the typescript for this book in a little over a year was ambitious, and would have been impossible had I not had the good fortune to be able to assemble a gifted team. The writers, for the most part already well known for their work on Leeds subjects or the period in general, have laboured diligently to accommodate my various pre- and proscriptions, and I am grateful to them for making my task as editor an enjoyable one. I have also been fortunate in securing the assistance of three others who have made major contributions to the project. Ruth Baumberg has worked tirelessly and cheerfully setting out to take innumerable photographs as well as being responsible for editing and arranging all the 330 images. Initially I had hoped to persuade Peter Hirschmann to join the writing team. With a modesty, entirely misplaced, he declined, but has proved to be at least as valuable in his role as Project Administrator and I am deeply indebted to him for taking on and efficiently managing a series of time-consuming, but

3. P. Ballard (ed.), *Birmingham's Victorian and Edwardian Architects*, Oblong for the Birmingham Group of the Victorian Society, 2009.

4. A. Gomme et al, *Bristol, an architectural history*, Lund Humphries, 1979.

5. K. Ferry (ed.), *Powerhouses of Provincial Architecture*, The Victorian Society, 2009. Of particular relevance is Geoff Brandwood's ground-breaking essay 'Many and varied: Victorian provincial architects in England and Wales' (Ferry, pp. 3-14) which provides a national context for many of the themes in this book.

essential, tasks that would otherwise have fallen to me. I had the good fortune to meet by chance Hugh Kerrigan who generously offered to devote literally weeks of his time to trawling through the Leeds newspapers in search of references to Leeds architects. The catalogues of work by men such as Brodrick, Perkin and Backhouse, and Shaw would have been much shorter without him.

Leeds is particularly fortunate in the resources it has for the architectural historian. The Central Library contains invaluable complete runs of many of the period's architectural journals and I am grateful to Moira Hainsworth and Sharon McIntosh for cheerfully carrying the heavy volumes for us. The library also contains many unique photographs and original illustrations and I am grateful to Rose Gibson for advice, and to Dave Sheard in the library's Photographic Department for supplying us with images. At the City Art Gallery, Christine Sitch and Ted Wilkins were especially helpful. We have made much use of the remarkable collections of the Thoresby Society and I am grateful to Anne Brook and Eveleigh Bradford for their assistance. Stephanie Davidson, Vicky Grindrod and the staff of the West Yorkshire Archives Service in Leeds have given a faultless service. Finally, Geoffrey Forster and his staff at the Leeds Library have answered many questions, found many obscure books and given us valuable assistance in scanning images.

I would like to acknowledge, with gratitude, assistance in various ways from the following: Geoff Brandwood, Peter Brears, Marcus Cooper, James Lomax, Alexander Robertson, Susan Webster and Graham West.

I am grateful to Simon Thurley for his stimulating Introduction.

Introduction

SIMON THURLEY   CHIEF EXECUTIVE, ENGLISH HERITAGE

Who, visiting the restored Tiled Hall at the City Library, dining in the Corn Exchange, or seeking respite in St Peter's Church, could fail to become just a little curious about the architects who left us with these impressive examples of their skills and the taste of their times? Colin Cunningham, Derek Linstrum and others have previously established the names of 'Town Hall Brodrick' and Chantrell, designer of Dean Hook's rebuilt parish church. But many of the architects featured in this book will be new to the reader. In the city centre the confident hand of Corson certainly deserves wider appreciation, as does the partnership of Bedford and Kitson, who set the standard for an educated and innovative approach to suburban housing. But the stories of each of the architects contributes to a fuller understanding of the growth of the Victorian city and the lives of its makers.

The construction of the M1 motorway may have cut a swathe of destruction through Leeds' southern suburbs, but the city centre itself has not suffered too badly from the Post-War love affair with the car and with novelty. Indeed, if one were wanting to recreate the ideal Great Victorian City, then most of the building blocks could be found in Leeds. Brodrick's Town Hall, of course, the embodiment of civic pride and a permanent cure for municipal status anxiety, would stand at the centre. Corson's Library and Thorp's Art Gallery would provide appropriate support. Scott's General Infirmary and Brodrick's Mechanics' Institute would cater for body and mind. Retail therapy could be provided by Leeming and Leeming's City Market Hall, Matcham's County Arcade, or along Blomfield's Headrow. Out on the edge, Armley Gaol by Perkin and Backhouse might stand as a sobering reminder that the Victorian city bred crime as well as capital.

A good portion of these outstanding buildings are not by local men, because Leeds, to its credit and continuing enjoyment, did not exclude outside talent as ruthlessly as other cities such as Bradford or Birmingham. But Leeds architects gave the city its character, populating it with schools, chapels, commercial buildings and houses. If, as Kevin Grady notes, the city's roads are a medieval inheritance that allows us to walk in the footsteps of many generations, the Victorian architects featured in this book have provided the city with the landmarks we use as we traverse the city. They lend substance, character and distinctiveness to the city's neighbourhoods. But more than this: in spite of some regrettable losses, a significant proportion of today's Leeds was designed and built by the Victorians. Their churches and chapels, civic buildings, shops, offices and homes remain in daily use. The city has a good recent record of restoration and adaptation, which has ensured that important historic buildings continue to meet modern needs while feeding our souls through the quality of their materials, their workmanship and their detailing.

This volume follows on the heels of a similar endeavour by the Birmingham Group of the Victorian Society, published in 2009. Such initiatives demonstrate that the voluntary sector is active across the country, catering to a lively interest in the history of our surroundings. The sharing of detailed and authoritative research is an act of generosity that many will appreciate, both curious citizens and future campaigners, for the protection of our familiar and valued heritage.

❀

PART ONE

THE MAJOR ARCHITECTS AND THE CONTEXT FOR THEIR WORK

Leeds, Central Library, Calverly Street,
central staircase (George Corson,
1878-84). (*Ruth Baumberg.*)

1. *From Medieval Borough to Great Victorian City*

KEVIN GRADY

1. *The Rise to the West Riding's Georgian Cloth Marketing Centre*

The visitor to the great Victorian city of Leeds in 1900 could perhaps be forgiven for being unaware of its considerable antiquity.[1] The more perceptive observer might have noted the Old Norse street names Briggate and Kirkgate and the clues demonstrative of an earlier manorial existence and indeed a medieval borough – Mill Hill, Boar [borough] Lane, and the Head Rows which marked the boundary between the medieval borough and the manor's open fields. In fact, for centuries the framework of central streets had been largely unchanged, as indeed it is today.

In the Middle Ages Leeds emerged as a small settlement of farmers and craftsmen with an important mother church at the heart of a large parish. The village clustered around the parish church with farmhouses extending up Kirkgate. The gradual movement of the centre to the west began in 1207, when the Lord of the Manor laid out the manorial borough or 'new town' consisting of the long broad street known as Briggate, which extended down to the bridge over the River Aire, with its thirty burgage plots on either side. Over the centuries the craftsmen and tradesmen of Briggate flourished, and what became one of the greatest market places in the north of England today remains the city's principal shopping street.[2] (2.1)

The 'in-township' of Leeds, that grew up around Briggate and Kirkgate had in its parish hinterland ten neighbouring hamlets, which

1. This brief survey of the development of Leeds from the Middle Ages to the Edwardian period is primarily drawn from the most comprehensive modern study of the city's history: S. Burt and K. Grady, *The Illustrated History of Leeds*, Breedon Books, 2002. It covers all the aspects of this chapter and provides extensive notes on sources and has a large bibliography. The other major thematic overall study of the city is D. Fraser (ed.), *A History of Modern Leeds*, Manchester University Press, 1980. Excellent articles on many different aspects of the history of the city can be found in the publications of the Thoresby Society (the Leeds Historical Society). The notes to this chapter aim to highlight only the most important works on the subjects discussed and provide the sources for direct quotations.

2. G. Woledge, 'The Medieval Borough of Leeds', *PTS*, XXXVII, 1945, pp. 288-309; P. Brears and K. Grady, *Briggate Yards and Arcades*, Leeds Civic Trust, 2007.

were to become substantial villages or 'out-townships'. In the sixteenth and seventeenth centuries the West Riding's woollen textile industry underwent great expansion during which Leeds grew considerably as a centre of woollen cloth manufacture. But the extensive domestic cloth manufacture in its out-townships and beyond enabled a thrusting and dynamic community of Leeds cloth merchants to spring up in the early seventeenth century and the town's rise to dominance as the marketing and merchant centre of the West Riding cloth industry began. In a bid to gain control over the local cloth industry, in 1626 its leading merchants obtained a Royal charter of incorporation creating the municipal borough of Leeds, the borough being co-extensive with the parish.[3]

3. For the development of the Leeds woollen cloth industry to 1830 see: H. Heaton, *The Yorkshire Woollen and Worsted Industries*, Oxford University Press, 2nd edition, 1965; R.G. Wilson, *Gentlemen Merchants: The Merchant Community in Leeds, 1700-1830*, Manchester University Press, 1971.

1.1: John Cossins, New and Exact Plan of the Town of Leeds, 1726. The continued dominance of the medieval street pattern is clear. At the north end of the Briggate marketplace on the east side, the ends of burgage plots of the former manorial borough can be seen.

1.2: Leeds, the Mixed (or Coloured) Cloth Hall, interior. Built in 1756-7, it was the town's largest cloth hall being 127 yards by 66 yards. It contained 1,770 clothiers stalls arranged in rows or 'streets'. (Plate in George Walker, *Costume of Yorkshire*, 1814.)

By the early eighteenth century, thousands of clothiers from the villages to the south and west flooded into Leeds, their packhorses carrying large quantities of cloth to be sold in its famous cloth market in Briggate. In 1720 Daniel Defoe described 'the large, wealthy and populous town of Leeds' and exalted in the remarkable size and importance of the market – a 'prodigy of its kind'.[4] Most of this cloth was dressed, cropped and, where appropriate, dyed in the town and the merchants sent it on to other parts of the country and the Continent for sale. Leeds became the service centre for the extensive hinterland that it dominated. The growing prosperity and commercial success of the town is celebrated in John Cossins', New and Exact Plan of the Town of Leedes, published in 1726 (1.1). The map shows the fine houses of the leading merchant families on its face and most prominently in its margins.

From 1700-1800 the town grew impressively. Its population increased from 6000 to 30,000, while that of the borough reached 53,000.[5] It became the sixth largest town in England. By the 1770s its affluent merchants handled one half of the woollen cloth exports of England, a remarkable one-sixth of the country's domestically produced exports. This astonishing growth was facilitated by the building of a series of ever larger market halls for the sale of cloth (1.2).

Contemporary panoramas and maps enable us to appreciate the growth of this extremely prosperous market town sitting on the gentle incline on the north bank of the River Aire. Even in the 1780s it still had the character of a large country town; its merchants and clothiers going about their business passed orchards and tenterfields, and pleasant street frontages with fine merchant houses.[6]

Despite the surge in its population growth in the last quarter of the eighteenth century, its inhabitants were largely housed within the existing bounds of the present-day shopping area of Leeds.

4. Daniel Defoe, *A Tour Through the Whole Island of Great Britain, 1724-26*, Penguin edition, 1971, pp. 500-05.

5. For these and subsequent population statistics see: C.J. Morgan, 'Demographic Change, 1771-1911' in Fraser [note 1].

6. The physical development of the town's streets and housing is brilliantly traced in Maurice Beresford's encyclopaedic work: 'East End, West End: The Face of Leeds During Urbanisation, 1684-1842', *PTS*, LX and LXI, 1988.

The burgeoning working classes lived in cottages built in the yards and folds of the centre or at Quarry Hill. From the 1780s the first streets of back-to-back houses were built in what was to become the 'East End' of Leeds. Initially, this posed no problem but soon the cramming of the rapidly growing workforce into these densely-built houses and yards, with an absence of sewers and adequate sanitation, was to create major public health problems.

From the 1760s some of the middle classes began to move to the socially segregated elegant terraces and squares of the Park Estate being created just to the west of the existing built-up area, and to the pleasant slopes on the northern fringe of the town centre. There was as yet no apprehension that in the decades to come the town would be engulfed by smoke and industry. As late as 1806 the *Leeds Guide* noted the attractiveness of this western extension to the town, particularly viewed from the hills south of the river:

> Perhaps the most pleasing view of Leeds is from the rising ground on the road to Beeston, from which the elegant buildings of Park Row, Park Place, the Cloth Hall, the Infirmary, and the different churches, may be seen to great advantage. The greatest length of the town is from West to East, and which taken from Park Place the western extremity, to its eastern termination, St Peter's Square, is about one mile and a half; from North to South it does not extend more than half a miles. [Beginning] our present survey at the west end of the town … Park Place is a very elegant range of buildings, with a South aspect which commands a very pleasing view of the country, particularly of the river Aire; all the houses are built in a very superior style and are principally inhabited by affluent merchants or gentlemen who have retired from business … On the north side is St Paul's Square, and though the houses are not equal to those in Park Place, they are all well built in the modern style. [Going east] we arrive at the Infirmary, which with the Mixed Cloth Hall form one side of a very extensive square … The West side is called East Parade, the North, South Parade and the East, Park Row; the whole of which consists of genteel, well-built houses.[7] (2.10)

In truth it was the Park Estate which gave Leeds any real claim to architectural pretension. While the core of the town to the east was a hive of commerce and domestic manufacture, apart from some churches and chapels and the third White Cloth Hall and Assembly Rooms of the 1770s, and merchants houses of distinction, its few other public buildings were decidedly unprepossessing; with the exception of Briggate, its streets were narrow and heavily congested.[8] The Moothall, rebuilt to the designs of William Etty in 1710 (2.1), awaited demolition, the Workhouse in Lady Lane was no object of beauty, while

7. J. Ryley, *The Leeds Guide*, Leeds, 1806, pp. 66-8.

8. The detailed information about the public buildings provided in Leeds discussed in this chapter is drawn from: K. Grady, 'The Georgian Public Buildings of Leeds and the West Riding', *PTS*, LXII, 1989 and for Victorian and Edwardian buildings from Burt and Grady [note 1].

the theatre in Hunslet Lane was 'barn-like'. But the town had potential. Reflecting on the condition of the older central streets, the *Leeds Guide* concluded optimistically that 'Leeds possesses the capabilities of becoming perhaps one of the handsomest towns in the kingdom.'[9]

2. *The Industrial Revolution (1790-1840)*

Following his 1828 visit, the German Prince Herman Ludwig Heinrich Furst von Puckler-Maskau recorded:[10]

> I reached the manufacturing town of Leeds just in the twilight. A transparent cloud of smoke was diffused over the whole space which it occupies, on and between several hills, a hundred red fires shot upwards into the sky and as many towering chimneys poured forth columns of black smoke. The huge manufactories, five stories high, in which every window was illuminated, had a grand striking effect. Here the toiling artisan labours far into the night, and that some romantic features might not be wanting in the whirl of business and illumination of industry two ancient gothic churches reared their heads above the mass of houses and the moon poured her silver light upon their towers, and seemed to damp the hard glare of the busy crowd below, with serene majesty.

Von Puckler's description, some twenty years after the publication of the *Leeds Guide,* paints a very different picture of the town. In the fifty years from 1790 the town's population grew dramatically, at least trebling from around 25,000 to over 88,000. The population of the parish and borough increased from some 40,000 to over 150,000. The town's fabric extended astonishingly but haphazardly. Francis and Netlam Giles' fascinating map of Leeds published in 1815 reveals the spread of new streets of houses beyond the tight confines of the medieval and Georgian core, and the appearance of factories. This development was entirely unregulated. As one contemporary commented, it was as if the town had had 'an earthquake for an architect'.[11]

Until the 1790s, and for some years yet to come, the West Riding woollen cloth manufacture was essentially a handicraft industry conducted in cottages and small workshops with only some preparatory processes and the fulling of cloth using waterpower. In 1789 there were no 'mills' in Leeds in the sense we understand them today. There were water mills which ground and crushed things and some large workshops where craftsmen made all manner of products (occasionally employing up to 30 or 40 people) but there were no large factories.

9. Ryley [note 7], p. 74.

10. Von Puckler, Muskau Prince, H.L.H., *Tour in Germany, Holland & England 1826, 1827 and 1828*, 1832, IV, p. 210.

11. *LM*, 1852. See Beresford [note 6], p. 231.

Leeds was already growing rapidly on the back of the huge increase of the handicraft manufacture of cloth when the first steps in its transformation into an industrial city began in the 1790s. The great entrepreneur Benjamin Gott created the world's first woollen mill which rapidly expanded to employ 1200 workers, with Gott becoming one of the twelve largest employers in England. Shortly afterwards the linen draper, John Marshall, pioneered the flax spinning industry in Leeds, at Holbeck just south of the River Aire. By 1803 his mills too employed over 1000 people and he had founded an industry. Close by in Holbeck Matthew Murray pioneered the Leeds engineering industry, making at his Round Foundry not only textile machinery but steam engines which already, by the 1790s, rivalled those of Boulton and Watt. In 1812 he made the world's first commercially successful steam locomotive.[12] (1.3) But the size of the enterprises of Gott and Marshall were quite exceptional: initially they had few imitators. It was not until the 1820s that the factory age came into full swing in Leeds. By then workers were flooding into the town at a dramatic rate. In the 1820s its population grew by almost fifty per cent. (1.4)

Crucial to the industrial and commercial expansion was the creation of good transport links.[13] In 1700 Leeds had become an inland port when the making navigable of the River Aire gave direct communication by water to Hull and thus to the Continent. In 1770 the commencement of work on the Leeds and Liverpool Canal

1.3: Industrial Leeds in 1829. Matthew Murray's locomotive pulls coal wagons from Middleton Colliery to the coal staithes on Meadow Lane near Leeds Bridge. Far left is Murray's Round Foundry and centre right Chantrell's Christ Church built 1823-6 for workers in the new industrial suburbs. (*Engraving by Nathaniel Whittock, from T. Allen, A New and Complete history of the County of York, I.T. Hinton, 1831, vol. 2, opp. p. 543.*)

12. The development of factory industry is described in E.J. Connell and M. Ward, 'Industrial Development, 1780-1914' in Fraser [note 1]. Important works are: W. B. Crump, ed., 'The Leeds Woollen Industry, 1780-1820', *PTS*, 1931 (regarding Gott); W. G. Rimmer, *Marshalls of Leeds: Flax-spinners*, Cambridge University Press, 1960; E. Kilburn Scott, ed., *Matthew Murray Pioneer Engineer*, privately published, Leeds, 1928.

13. For the development of transport facilities in Leeds see: R. W. Unwin, 'Leeds Becomes a Transport Centre', in Fraser [note 1]; P. L. Smith, *The Aire and Calder Navigation*, Wakefield Historical Publications, 1987; M. Clarke, *The Leeds and Liverpool Canal*, Carnegie Press, 1990.

extended this water communication to the west, and when the canal was completed in 1816 there was a direct link by water to America. Huge quantities of goods and raw materials, including coal and stone, were carried on these waterways, both bringing cargo to Leeds and enabling it to supply a large hinterland. The cheap transport for the goods it manufactured and traded in was invaluable. The extension of its turnpike roads was also of great importance. The coach journey to London, which took three days in 1760, had dropped to 21 hours by 1836. Leeds developed as a major coaching centre. In 1800 40 coaches left Leeds daily; by 1838 this had increased to a remarkable 130 departures to destinations all over the country.

Particularly because of its extensive international trade, Leeds acquired excellent financial and legal services experienced in handling large foreign trade transactions. Its banks were a good deal larger than the typical provincial banks, and were to be of major importance in the town's industrial growth and its success as an important financial centre in the years to come.[14]

The rise in population created a demand for larger and new types of public amenities. Greater affluence allowed such amenities to be accommodated in buildings of an architectural elegance and style hitherto seldom attained. Rising prosperity in the 1790s brought a flurry of church and chapel building with Salem Chapel, Hunslet Lane for the Independent dissenters (1791) and St Paul's Church, Park Square (1791-4), St James' Church, off Kirkgate (1794) and Albion

1.4: Factory girls flooding out of Marshall's flax-spinning mill in Marshall Street, Holbeck. Temple Mill comprised the weaving shed to the left covering 2 acres completed in 1840 and the office block to the right finished in 1843. Architect Joseph Bonomi, junior.

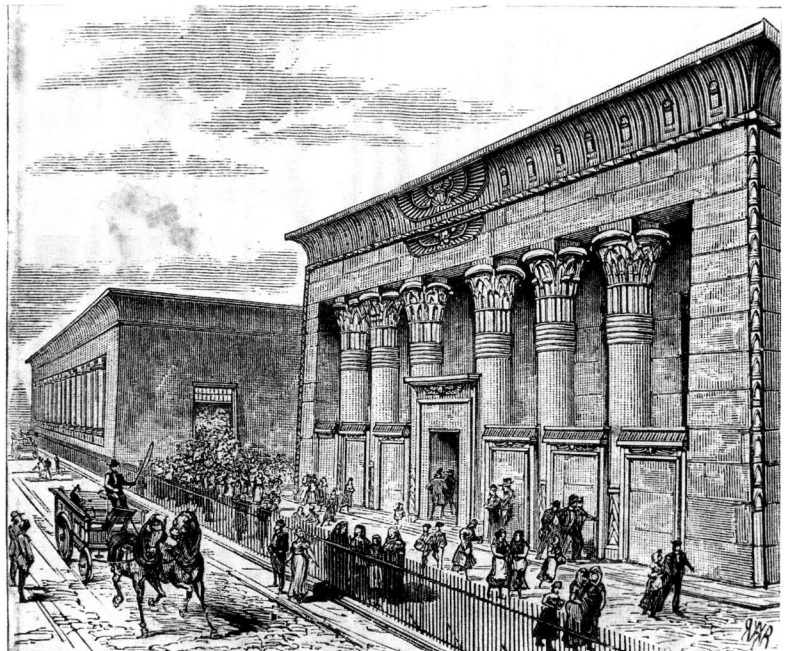

14. K. Grady, 'Commercial, Marketing and Retailing Amenities, 1700-1914' in Fraser [note 1].

Chapel, Albion Street (1796) for the Anglicans. For social purposes the Music Hall was built in Albion Street in 1790 which included an art gallery and exhibition rooms as well as its music saloon.

The provision of new amenities was relatively slow between 1800 and 1819, reflecting the problems created by the Napoleonic Wars. No doubt the hardships experienced in the cloth trade and the frequent disruption of trade with the Continent and America – and which also discouraged the building of mills – made civic leaders cautious. Extension and improvement was thought judicious for the time being. The Workhouse was enlarged, as was the Mixed Cloth Hall, while the parish church was substantially renovated and the Charity School rebuilt. But some parties were undeterred. A Methodist chapel was built in Albion Street in 1802, and the proprietors of the Leeds Library erected a handsome new building in Commercial Street in 1808. Indeed there were some bold initiatives. The medical facilities of the Infirmary were complemented by the building of the House of Recovery (a fever hospital) in Vicar Lane in 1802-04. Two important new schools also were founded: the Lancasterian School (1812) in Alfred Street off Boar Lane and the National School (1813) just off Kirkgate. The most imposing new building of the period was the Court House erected in Park Row (1811-13) (5.2). While mills were starting to be erected on the fringes of the town, a picture was beginning to emerge of a town whose principal central streets featured imposing public buildings.

By 1819, with the wars with France at an end, the caution and restraint of the early years of the century had begun to dissipate. A report on the outlook for Leeds noted a new mood afoot: 'There is an evident alteration taking place in the character of the people of Leeds. They are putting off in some degree that rudeness which is peculiar to them, enlightened pursuits are more cultivated, and the elegancies and comforts of life are more sought after.'[15] This new mood was manifested in the building of the Philosophical Hall (1819-21) in Park Row (6.2) and the Public Baths (1819-21) in Wellington Street (6.1). Thereafter a prodigious buildings boom ensued, taking off in 1823. The extent of church and chapel building was remarkable. First the 'Million Act Churches' – St Mary's, Quarry Hill (5.14), Christ Church, Meadow Lane (6.4), and St Mark's, Woodhouse (4.13) – were built between 1823 and 1826, in areas of working class housing. The Nonconformists were not to be outdone with the building of Queen Street Independent Chapel (1823-25), Brunswick Methodist Chapel (1824-25) (4.4) and a handful of chapels for other sects.

At the height of the boom in 1824-25, gripped by feverish excitement, townsmen felt that the *Leeds Guide's* optimism that Leeds might become one of the most attractive towns in the kingdom was

15. Hertfordshire Country Record Office, T4951, Report of surveyors to Earl Cowper on his Leeds estates, 1819.

1.5: Park Row in 1830. This was the most easterly street of the Park Estate. To the left, with the portico, is the Court House (1811-13) designed by Thomas Taylor and, to the right, the Commercial Buildings (1826-29), the magnificent merchants' exchange designed by John Clark. (*Engraving in Parsons and White, Annals of Leeds, 1830.*)

about to be fulfilled. In December 1824 the *Leeds Intelligencer* newspaper boasted that:

> There is perhaps hardly a town in England in which the passion for improvement is so strong as it is in Leeds. Scarcely a week elapses that we have not the pleasure to announce some project for improving and adorning the town … It is a rather curious coincidence that we have now erected or in contemplation three churches, three dissenting meeting houses, three markets, three bridges and streets innumerable.'[16]

Meanwhile, house building was going on at a tremendous rate. Dr John Simpson of Bradford in his diary for June 1825 recorded a meeting with Mr Oastler 'the old miser from Knaresborough'. 'The people of Leeds', Oastler warned, 'are building houses and streets on speculation, and have to borrow money from men such as myself. If trade becomes bad they will all be ruined!'[17]

The most striking feature of the mid-1820s was the absolute mania for building markets and commercial facilities. No less than four architecturally impressive market buildings, a merchant's exchange, and a wholesale fruit and vegetable and cattle market were provided[18] (1.5 and 1.6). At the same time, to accommodate the greatly increased volumes of freight the Aire and Calder Navigation Company constructed a magnificent new warehouse by Leeds Bridge and a new dock on the opposite side of the river (4.6).

The shocking nature of the commercial crash when it came at the tail end of 1825 cooled people's ardour for a while. However, the cyclical nature of the industrial economy was now established and the mid-1830s produced another boom, though not as frenetic as its

16. *LI*, 2 Dec 1824.

17. *Diary of Dr John Simpson of Bradford 1825*, Bradford, 1981, p. 61.

18. K. Grady, 'Profit, Property Interests and Public Spirit: the Provision of Markets and Commercial Amenities in Leeds, 1822-29', *PTS*, LIV, 1976.

1.6: The Central Market and Duncan Street (Francis Goodwin, 1824-7). (*Leeds Library and Information Services.*)

predecessor. Architects could now find employment on such projects as the Waterloo Swimming Baths (1833-34), erected near the Leeds and Liverpool Canal Basin, and the establishment of the Zoological and Botanical Gardens (1837-40) in Headingley. Religious fervour too overcame caution and numerous churches and chapels were built, most notably St. Patrick's Roman Catholic Church, York Road (1831-32), St Peter's Wesleyan Chapel, St Peter's Street (1834), Lady Lane Wesleyan Chapel (1835), St George's Anglican Church (1836-38), Mount Pleasant (now Great George Street) (7.15), St Ann's Roman Catholic Church, Park Terrace (1837-38) (4.3) and Oxford Place Associationist Methodist Chapel (1835). Such was the rate of change over this period that Francis and Netlam Giles' detailed town plan of 1815 was quickly superseded in 1821 by Charles Fowler's plan which in turn needed major revisions in 1826 and 1831. Fowler produced a new plan in 1844 and J. Rapkin in 1850 (1.7).

The growth of factory industry was now celebrated in prospects and panoramas of the town showing the rapid spread of mills and warehouses along the river and in the industrial townships of Holbeck and Hunslet on its southern banks, some requiring the services of architects, others those of millwrights.

To escape the smoke of industry which began to blow across the town centre from the west, in the early decades of the nineteenth century the middle classes of limited means largely confined their

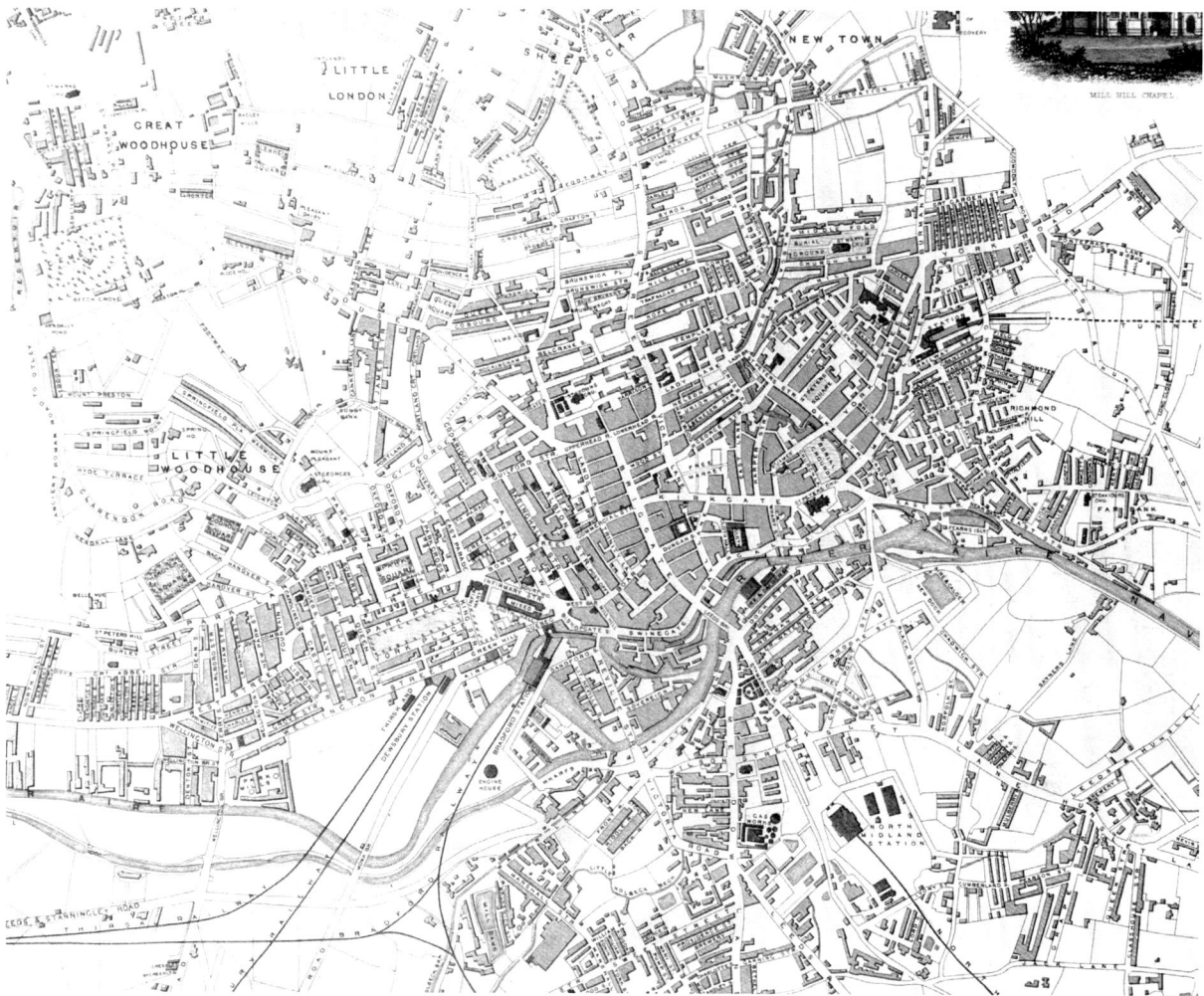

19. The extension of the fringes of the town and the early period and process of suburbanisation is described in: Beresford [note 6] and his chapter 'The Face of Leeds, 1780-1914' in Fraser [note 1]. The later phases of suburbanisation are microscopically studied in C. Treen, 'The Process of Suburban Development in North Leeds, 1870-1914' in F.M.L. Thompson, ed., *The Rise of Suburbia*, Leicester University Press, 1982.

moves to the northern fringes of the township. In contrast, many of the wealthy merchants, bankers and new industrialists went further north, taking leases on properties in the villages of Headingley, Chapel Allerton or Potternewton or on farmhouses with potential for improvement.[19] Recognising the potential of Headingley and Potternewton (commonly referred to as Chapeltown today) their aristocratic landowners became increasingly keen to exploit their estates there. The low density residential development of Headingley Hill began in the late-1820s with the building of mansions and villas of a superior character (4.8). Nevertheless, due to an extensive and sustained inflow of workers more than half of the population of the borough lived in the in-township until the mid-nineteenth century. Meanwhile, the population of what contemporaries began to refer to as the 'industrial suburbs' of Holbeck and Hunslet just south of the river also grew fast. Wortley and Bramley too expanded as centres of textile production. (1.8)

3. *Victorian Prosperity (1840 to 1870)*

The building of Leeds Town Hall in 1853-58 – an essay in civic pride, if ever there was one – symbolised the progression of Leeds from a large industrial town to a wealthy city.[20] This wealth was generated by the rapid expansion and diversification of the town's industry and commerce. Leeds enjoyed great prosperity in the middle decades of the nineteenth century, though it suffered greatly from the adverse effects of unregulated expansion and deteriorating environmental conditions. A massive increase in the population of the town from 88,000 to 178,000 between 1841 and 1901, and of the borough from 152,000 to 428,000, provided a huge supply of labour for the rapid expansion of the town's industries. Textile production still employed two out of every five workers in 1841. The flax industry continued to expand and at its peak in the 1850s employed 9,500 workers, though at no stage did it challenge the supremacy of wool. The introduction of steam-powered machinery for spinning woollen yarn from the 1820s and power looms from the 1840s finally drove all but a few domestic clothiers out of business. For both woollens and worsteds Leeds remained the principal centre for dyeing, finishing and marketing until at least the middle of the nineteenth century.[21] However, considerable

1.8: Tunstall's Fold, Mabgate, 1901. These working-class cottages were built in the 1790s on the edge of the town centre.

20. A. Briggs, *Victorian Cities*, Penguin, 1968, chapter 4.

21. Connell and Ward [note 12].

diversification was underway. From the mid-century the textile industry's share of employment was in relative decline. Engineering now took over in first place. By 1851 one in twelve men worked in engineering; 4,000 alone were makers of boilers. Outstanding amongst all the foundries and engineering works were the world renown makers of traction engines and locomotives. The leather industry took off from the 1820s; by 1870 it employed 20,000 workers. The town was the leading centre for production of sheep skins and the second largest centre for the production of hides. By 1890 100,000 pairs of boots and shoes were made in Leeds every week.

In the 1850s John Barran founded the Leeds ready-made clothing industry with the introduction of the band knife and the Singer sewing machine. By the end of the century almost one in four females worked in the clothing industry.[22] Many other industries prospered: brewing, chemicals, glass and pottery making, brick making, printing, coal mining, quarrying and transport. By the end of the century, Leeds could truly be said to be a city of a thousand trades and had one of the most diversified and dynamic economies in Britain. The town's role as a financial centre continued to flourish too. Its banks grew in number and stability, while in 1845 a Stock Exchange was established. The erection of its own premises in Albion Street in 1847-9 (4.2) meant that for many years Leeds was the only provincial town with a purpose-built exchange. Insurance companies were also strongly represented. By 1837, 35 companies had branches or representatives in the town; by mid-century this had risen to over 70.[23]

The ability to transport raw materials, goods and people locally, nationally and internationally was critical to the town's prosperity. It became one of the great railway centres of the Victorian age.[24] Three railway schemes were projected in the 1820s but were aborted because of the financial crash. However, in 1834 the Leeds to Selby line was opened taking goods to Selby where they could be loaded on to boats on the Ouse and reach Hull, thus totally avoiding the Aire and Calder Navigation. In 1840 the Leeds to Derby line was opened, providing a direct rail link to the Midlands and London. A year later the line to Manchester was completed.

When the Leeds and Bradford Railway opened in 1846 it built Wellington Station between the river and the canal basin, the first town-centre passenger station. The Midland Railway Company quickly obtained powers to run into the station. The Leeds-Thirsk Railway was opened in 1849 and ran trains into its own station (subsequently known as Central Station) on Wellington Street. By the 1850s thirty trains were leaving the town's stations every day. In the 1860s an enormous embankment and viaduct was built right through the centre of the town, linking the North Eastern Railway Company's Marsh Lane station on the north-eastern side of the town to a new station on the

22. The growth of the clothing industry is fully described in K. Honeyman, *Well Suited: A History of the Leeds Clothing Industry, 1850-1990*, Oxford University Press, 2000.

23. Grady [note 14].

24. For the coming of the railways see: Unwin [note 13] and Burt and Grady [note 1], pp. 140-142.

LEEDS from HOLBECK JUNCTION.

south side of Wellington Station, where City Station is today, with cavernous arched foundations built over the River Aire. The opening of the line centralised passenger facilities in the town. Thereafter the maps and panoramas of Leeds from the south show Leeds to be a town full of railway tracks, embankments, viaducts and stations. (1.9) Surprisingly, the railways did not wipe out the Leeds waterways; the links to Liverpool and Hull, and the places in between, remained of great value for carrying coal, stone and other heavy or bulky goods for which speed of delivery was not essential. The banks of the river and canal continued to be crowded with existing and new warehouses, mills and timber and coal wharves.

The novel task of governing a town whose population, buildings and industry were expanding at an extraordinary and unprecedented rate was formidable. There were no provincial precedents and the archaic and fragmented machinery of local government in Leeds creaked under the strain. When the reformed Leeds Corporation or Council met for the first time in December 1835 it had responsibility for little more than the finance and management of the police. While Parliament had reformed the municipal corporations in 1835, there had been no intention of establishing comprehensive authorities equipped to govern rapidly evolving towns like Leeds. It had only recently reformed the Poor Law to set up boards of guardians to deal with the poor; and it had passed numerous Improvement Acts to enable improvement commissions to regulate the built environment of particular growing towns. Municipal corporations in the past had played their main role in the administration of justice and law and order, and the principal aim of reform was to ensure that from now on this was done on a democratically elected basis. During the Victorian period, however, expediency and entrepreneurial spirit drove Leeds Corporation to widen the range of its activities until it had achieved a major influence over many facets of the town's life.[25] By the end of the century it provided gas, water, electricity supply and trams. It had

1.9: Leeds from Holbeck Junction. (*From the* Illustrated London News, *30 May 1868.*) This view looks north-east across the town showing the impressive array of railway tracks and viaducts running into the stations along Wellington Street. In the centre distance is Leeds Town Hall and immediately to its right the tower of St. Paul's Church, Park Square.

25. The activities of Leeds Corporation are fully described in B.J. Barber, 'Municipal Government in Leeds, 1835-1914' in D. Fraser (ed.), *Municipal Reform and the Industrial City*, Leicester University Press, 1982.

responsibility for environmental health; it had created parks, libraries, markets and other amenities and it had begun to tackle the problems of the slums. Here were opportunities for architects. The Borough Gaol was built in 1846-7, Kirkgate Covered Market 1857, the Corn Exchange completed in 1864 and, most famously of all, the Town Hall – a true centre of municipal government – was opened in 1858.

Amidst the teeming hoards of the great Victorian city, social casualties without family support were an inevitable consequence. Welfare provision on a scale previously unimagined was needed.[26] The Leeds Workhouse Board erected the very grand Moral and Industrial Training School, primarily for orphans, in the then airy situation of Beckett Street to the north of town in 1846-8 (19.35). Within a decade it had added an equally imposing neighbour, the Leeds Union Workhouse of 1858-61. The truly frightening cholera and typhus epidemics of the 1830s and 1840s, each killing hundreds of townspeople, made the need for large public medical institutions stark. The middle classes' spirit of benevolence and desire for self-preservation ensured that in 1846 a new House of Recovery was built in Beckett Street (19.36). Public dispensaries were also funded by public subscription, while in the 1860s the governors of the Leeds General Infirmary commissioned George Gilbert Scott to design the magnificent new Infirmary in Great George Street (1862-68) (18.12).

The needs of the soul were not to be neglected.[27] When the Queen Victoria came to the throne it was said that Methodism was 'the established religion' of Leeds. Indeed, the Church of England provided only eight of the 35 places of worship in the town. Because of the astonishing growth of numbers in the borough and the physical

1.10: Queen Victoria's procession passes down Woodhouse Lane on 7 September 1858 to the opening of the Town Hall. (*From the* Illustrated London News, *18 September 1858*.) The Queen was passing two recently built places of worship. The chapel on the left, with the pediment is the New Connexion Methodist Chapel (1857-8) and the church with the spire is St Columba's Presbyterian Church (1855-6).

26. Burt and Grady [note 1], pp. 162-3, 172-6.

27. For religion and places of worship see: N. Yates, 'The Religious Life of Victorian Leeds' in Fraser [note 1], and Burt and Grady [note 1], pp. 181-5.

extension of the town, substantial segments of the populations were unprovided with places of worship. Leeds was to enjoy a period of prolific church and chapel building in the coming years. When Walter Farquhar Hook became Vicar of Leeds in 1837 the Anglican fightback began. Architects must have rubbed their hands with eager anticipation as the religious denominations vied with each other for supremacy. Hook began with the rebuilding of the Parish Church and then moved vigorously on. By the time of his departure for Chichester in 1859 there were 18 town churches, 18 suburban churches and 21 Anglican day schools. From 1865 to 1901 the Leeds Church Extension Society continued his important work building another 25 churches. The other denominations, as a group, were equally prolific builders: the Methodists in their bewildering array of subgroups and the Baptists, and to a lesser degree the Unitarians, Presbyterians and Catholics. (1.10)

By 1851 the social segregation of the town's rapidly enlarging population was increasing as the middle classes escaped to the suburbs, leaving the workers behind in the industrial areas. In every decade after 1821 Headingley increased its share of the borough population. As the 1861 census report put it, 'The sanitary position of Headingley with Burley has induced a large portion of the mercantile community of Leeds to reside in the township'.[28] From 1850-70, large numbers of the middle classes managed to move out. 'Respectable terraces' with accommodation for one or two servants, though rarely with provision for a stable or carriage house, began to be built. Dwelling houses in the Hyde Park area just beyond Woodhouse Moor, for example, were taken mostly by tradesmen who had businesses in Leeds or professional men, who 'transacted business at offices in Leeds during the day and hoped to return home at night to quietness and peace'.[29] The suburbs began to grow rapidly, the availability of the omnibuses from the town to Headingley and Potternewton and Chapel Allerton from 1838 facilitating their growth.

The arrival of the 'respectable' terraces in Headingley drove the upper middle class still further afield in search of the genuine social seclusion of a mansion. In 1861 for example, William Brown built *Bardon Grange* in Weetwood Lane and the banker Henry Oxley built *The Elms* (now Oxley Hall). In the following year, the brewer F. W. Tetley commissioned George Corson to design *Foxhill*. *Spenfield*, near the reservoirs on the Otley Road, was designed in 1875 for another member of the Oxley family. Others went beyond the northern fringes of the borough, building mansions and large villas in Roundhay and Adel. Closer to the town centre, in what today we would regard as the Inner City, terrace after terrace of back-to-back houses was built.[30]

28. 1861 *Census Report*, Vol. I, p. 613, quoted in Morgan [note 5].

29. Treen [note 19], pp. 168-9.

30. For the story of the back-to-backs see: M. W. Beresford, 'The Back-to-Back House in Leeds, 1787-1937' in S. D. Chapman, ed., *The History of Working Class Housing: A Symposium*, David and Charles, 1971.

4. Transforming the City
(1870–1914)

An 1893 publication referred to Leeds thus:

> A town of the times is this great hive of workers, whose labours are for the welfare of mankind, and whose products have the whole wide world for their market … Though Leeds may lack the classic charm of Greece or Italy, or even the time-honoured dignity that reposes in our own ancient cathedral towns, she can place in the counterbalance her nine hundred factories and workshops, monuments of her wealth, industry and mercantile prestige.[31]

In the last decades of the nineteenth century Leeds industry and commerce surged ahead with great confidence and vitality. By the Edwardian era its workforce numbered over 200,000. Clothmaking, readymade clothing and engineering were its largest industries. It could still boast that over one-third of the country's woollen manufactures came from Leeds. Tailoring was now the largest single employer, occupying one in five. With 30,000 workers, engineering employed one-fifth of the male workforce. Leather and its associated industries remained very important. Transport and domestic service each employed one in twelve workers. The range of products made in Leeds was truly remarkable, including in addition printed matter, bricks, pottery, glass, chemicals, rubber, rope, screws, bicycles, musical instruments, clocks, and furniture.

Between 1871 and 1901 the population of the town grew from 139,000 to 178,000, while the borough grew from 259,000 to 429,000, and to 445,000 by 1911. Improved transport allowed more people to move out to the suburbs. The populations of the industrial townships of Hunslet and Holbeck continued to grow rapidly, with countless terraces of back-to-backs, while major new areas of population growth were Armley, Wortley and Bramley. Until around 1890 the growth of Chapel Allerton and Potternewton continued to be modest while the suburban growth of Headingley, with its horse buses and trams, continued strongly (1.11). In the 1890s, however, with the development and extension of the electric tramways, widespread growth of the northern suburbs began. Headingley lost its select middle-class status as terraced and even back-to-back houses were built there. The most spectacular transformation was in Potternewton which quadrupled in size between 1891 and 1911. The growth of the suburbs extended beyond the city boundaries, with Roundhay's population almost trebling between 1891 and 1911.

The last decades of Victoria's reign and the Edwardian period wrought a major transformation of the public face of Leeds. Increased

31. London Printing and Engraving Co., *The Century's Progress: Yorkshire Industry and Commerce,* 1893, p. 150.

wealth and aspiration enabled Leeds to acquire the style of a grand Victorian and Edwardian city. This was achieved by the combined efforts of public bodies and private enterprise.[32] The Council's role was greatly extended in these years, as we have seen, and to serve its needs – and to extend the cultural provision for the town's inhabitants – in 1884 the Municipal Buildings designed by George Corson next to the Town Hall were opened including the Central Library. In 1888 the City Art Gallery was added. Less glamorous but more vital was its provision of sewers and water supply, and gas and trams.

The voluntary sector's attempts to satisfy the demand for schools for the city's children were overwhelmed in the mid-Victorian period and it was the work of the Leeds School Board, elected in 1870 under Forster's Elementary Education Act, which remedied the problem. Its action was swift and impressive. By 1878 31 large schools capable of accommodating 19,000 pupils had been erected in the borough. In 1889 the noble Central Higher Grade School was opened on Woodhouse Lane. The achievement of the Leeds School Board was indeed impressive; when its responsibilities were passed to the Leeds Corporation in 1902, it handed over no less than 157 elementary schools, 2 higher grade schools, 4 Industrial Schools, and 5 Special Schools.

As the century progressed it was increasingly appreciated that provision for technical education was essential to the economic success of an industrial city. The creation of the magnificent Mechanics' Institute in Cookridge Street in 1860-65 (10.9) designed by Cuthbert Brodrick reflected this, as did the founding of the Yorkshire College (later the University of Leeds) in 1874 (18.15). The Yorkshire College's first purposed-built buildings were erected in College Road in the 1870s, and a splendid range of buildings was added, to the designs of Alfred Waterhouse, in subsequent years.[33]

32. Burt and Grady, [note 1], pp. 190-98.

33. For educational provision in Leeds see: W.B. Stephens, 'Elementary Education and Literacy' in Fraser [note 1] and Burt and Grady, [note 1], pp. 176-181.

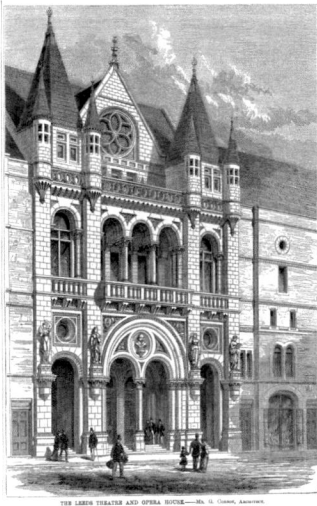

1.13: The Grand Theatre and Opera House, Upper Briggate (George Corson, 1876-8). (The Builder, *36, 1878, p. 1203.*)

Above all, the transformation of the city centre caught the eye.[34] Here the widening of streets, beginning with the ambitious Boar Lane Improvement Scheme of 1868-70 (1.12). The erection of imposing offices, warehouses, and commercial institutions brought a dignity and architectural impressiveness which hitherto the town had often lacked. The banks and larger insurance companies wished to demonstrate their financial stability by erecting impressive premises. These were clustered to such an extent in the vicinity of Park Row that by the 1890s that *The Builder* described it as the Pall Mall of Leeds.[35] The former coaching inns on Briggate and Boar Lane continued to provide important services but a new class of commercial and railway hotels was built. The Queen's, the Trevelyan Temperance Hotel and the magnificent terracotta Hotel Metropole were notable examples. New theatres (1.13) and restaurants were built which added a new flamboyance, gaiety and style to the city's streets. Most of all, it was in the provision of shops that the city reached new levels of quality and style (1.14). Rising real incomes and a growing population created more consumer spending and with the shortage of central street frontages, five impressive shopping arcades were built to extend retail provision; a virtual redevelopment of the shopping centre took place.[36] In 1877-78 Thornton's Arcade was built on the site of the Old Talbot Inn and Yard off Briggate. Its success encouraged emulators. Armistead and Procter built the Queen's Arcade on the site of the Rose and Crown Yard in 1888-89. This was followed by the Grand Arcade, promoted by the New Briggate Arcade Company in 1896-98 and the Victoria Arcade of 1898.

The widening of Vicar Lane and Duncan Street, in particular, now provided appropriately grand setting for new retail and office

1.12: Boar Lane on Market Day, 1872. The street's widening from 21 feet to 66 feet in the late 1860s encouraged the building of retail and commercial properties of a metropolitan character. (*Author's collection*).

34. Burt and Grady [note 1], pp. 190-96.

35. *The Builder*, 19 Dec 1896, pp. 510-12.

36. Grady [note 14], pp. 192-5.

developments of a high quality to match and even outdo those enabled by the widening of Boar Lane in 1868. These streets hitherto were little more than 20 feet wide and by being increased to 66 feet now achieved the scale appropriate to a big city. The largest and most sumptuous development was that of the County Arcade and the adjacent Cross Arcade, designed by Frank Matcham and built in 1898–1904 by the Leeds Estates Company, with frontages on both Briggate and Vicar Lane. (1.15) The most spectacular addition of all was the City Markets in 1902-04 (9.9), just a little lower down on the east side of Vicar Lane.[37] In February 1893 Leeds rejoiced in formally becoming a city and a decade later this was celebrated with creation of City Square which, with its grand statuary, gave Leeds one of the best civic spaces in the country.[38]

With complete justice the *Leeds Shopper's Guide* of 1909 could sing the praises of the remarkable transformation of the shopping and commercial area between 1875 and 1909:

No city in England can boast a more wonderful transformation than that witnessed in Leeds during the past two or three decades … The centre of Leeds has been practically re-carved and polished. Nearly the whole of the ramshackle property that skirted the east side of Briggate has been demolished, and on the site has been erected a class of shop property that would do credit to any city in the country. With the offices in Park Row, East Parade and South Parade almost equal improvements have been made, while for some time past there seems to have been a wholesome rivalry amongst the owners of shop property in Commercial Street to remodel their premises in the most up-to-date and withal artistic lines. Boar Lane, Duncan Street, and Vicar Lane reveal equally amazing individual enterprise.[39]

1.14: The Leeds Industrial Co-operative Society emporium, Albion Street (J.R. Connon, 1883-4), typical of the new generation of stylish retail premises. (The Architect, *21 June 1884*.)

1.15: Briggate and the County Arcade c.1900. The Leeds Estates Company's stunning redevelopment of the east side of Briggate 1898-1900 created the County Arcade, Queen Victoria and King Edward Streets – entirely new streets of elegant shops – new shops on Briggate and Vicar Lane, cafés and restaurants, and the Empire Theatre. (*Leeds Civic Trust collection*).

37. S. Burt and K. Grady, *Kirkgate Market: An Illustrated History*, privately published, Leeds, 1992.

38. M.W. Beresford, 'A Tale of Two Centenaries: Leeds City Charter and City Square, 1893', *University of Leeds Review*, vol. 36, 1993/94; G. Black, 'City Square and Colonel Harding', *PTS*, LIV, 1975.

39. Leeds Traders' Special Show Week brochure, *Shopping in Leeds*, 1909, p. 27. The visual transformation of the city is profusely illustrated in K. Grady and J. Stringer, *Edwardian Leeds in Postcards*, Leeds Civic Trust, 2004.

2. The progress of professional architects in eighteenth century Leeds

TERRY FRIEDMAN

Emerging from 'barbarism to a very high degree of elegance' was the optimistic verdict of the renown Yorkshire historian T.D. Whitaker in 1816 when reviewing Leeds's cultural status as expressed in its buildings.[1] It is especially poignant because though the town failed to enjoy the benefits of home-grown professional architects until the 1780s, one of the positive effects of this situation was the necessity in the case of major enterprises of attracting outsiders, particularly from the thriving centre of York, some twenty-four miles away, which witnessed a flowering of architectural design and technology stretching back into the early Middle Ages.

During the eighteenth century in England, and especially in the provinces, the architectural profession was not yet so clearly separated from the building trades as it was to become after the founding of the Institute of British Architects in 1834. John Soane, then the father of the profession and favoured as the leading candidate for the Institute's Presidency, had defined its parameters as early as 1788:

> The business of the architect is to make the designs and estimates, to direct the works and to measure and value the different parts; he is the intermediate agent between the employer, whose honour and interest he is to study, and the mechanic, whose rights he is to defend. His situation implies great trust; he is responsible for the mistakes, negligences, and ignorances of those he employs; and above all, he is to take care that the workmen's bills do not exceed his own estimates.[2]

1. In *Loidis and Elmete*, Robinson, Son and Holdsworth, 1816, p. 66.

2. *Plans Elevations and Sections Of Buildings*, Messrs. Taylor, 1788-89, p. 7. Soane was debarred from the post by the Royal Academy rules (Colvin, p. 963).

Soane's younger contemporary, Daniel Asher Alexander put it more bluntly: 'An Architect … conceives the design, prepares the plan, draws out the specification – in short, supplies the mind. The builder is merely the machine; the architect the power that puts the machine together and sets it going'.[3]

The first recorded professional architect to find employment in Leeds was John Etty (c.1634-1708), who in his capacity as H.M. Surveyor of York maintained close contact with Sir Christopher Wren (Surveyor of the King's Works, operating from the capitol), supplied large quantities of roof timber for St Paul's Cathedral during its final phase of construction, and also made repairs to the Viscount Irwin's mansion at Temple Newsam, outside Leeds. This work was continued by his son, William Etty (c.1675-1734) between 1710 and 1727, during a period when he was concurrently employed as John Vanbrugh's clerk of works at Castle Howard and also undertook consultative visits to London, which introduced him to the busy, post-Fire metropolitan building world.[4] The Ettys were also members of a 'parcel of artists' based in York which included the celebrated Leeds antiquary Ralph Thoresby, who was much involved in promoting prestigious building projects in the town. In one of the earliest records of its architectural appearance, 'A New & Exact PLAN of the Town of LEEDES, Survey'd by John Cossins' published in 1726-27 (1.1), it is described as 'Large Rich & Populous … accounted one of ye best … belonging to this County & … Particularly Famous for its Great Manufacture of Cloth'.[5] Scattered among the irregular medieval lanes are the prominent landmarks of the fourteenth century Parish Church in Kirkgate, St John and the Moot or Town Hall (both located in

2.2: W. Halfpenny. 'This Church is of my Invention for Leeds in Yorkshire', engraving. (*W, Halfpenny*, The Art of Sound Building, *1725.*)

2.1: Leeds, Moot Hall, Briggate, entrance façade (William Etty, 1710-11), with Andrew Carpenter's statue of Queen Anne, 1712-13, and later cupola, engraving by C. Heath, published 1 May 1816.

3. Quoted in Colvin, pp. 35-6.

4. Colvin, pp. 365-66. *The Wren Society*, Oxford University Press, XIII, 1936, p. 33, XV, 1938, pp. 25-46, XVIII, 1941, p. 68. C. Saumarez Smith, *The Building of Castle Howard*, Faber and Faber, 1990, pp. 61, 86, 124, 137-38, 147, 181-82. Pevsner, *Leeds*, pp. 282, 284, 289-90, C. Gilbert, 'Country House Paraphernalia at Temple Newsam', *Leeds Arts Calendar*, 56, 1965, pp. 7-8.

5. H. Murray, *Scarborough, York and Leeds The Town Plans of John Cossins 1697-1743*, Yorkshire Architectural and York Archaeological Society, 1997, Chapter 5.

6. WYASL, Leeds Pious Uses Committee 1664-1788, Pt. I, f.151.

7. Saumarez Smith [note 4], pl. 23. In combination with the figure of Queen Anne in the pedimented tabernacle, carved by Andrew Carpenter in London in 1712 and installed on 27 May 1713 amidst 'great rejoicing … a splendid procession and festival', which Thoresby claimed was 'generally esteemed … the best that was ever made, not excepting the most celebrated one in St Paul's Church-yard' in London, by Francis Bird (R. Thoresby, *Ducatus Leodiensis*, Leeds and Wakefield, 1715, p. 250. T. Friedman, 'A Noble Magnificent Statue', *Leeds Arts Calendar*, 72, 1973, pp. 5-13), the front also recalls the 1671 Royal Exchange in London (A. Saunders, ed., *The Royal Exchange*, The London Topographical Society Publication, No. 152, 1997, figs. 31, 46). Carpenter's marble statue is now displayed in Leeds Art Gallery.

8. Thoresby owned Andrea Pozzo's *Perspectiva Pictorum et Architectorum* (1693-1700), Colen Campbell's *Vitruvius Britannicus* (1715) and Bernard de Montfaucon's *Antiquity Explained* (1721) (S. Piggott, ed., *Sale Catalogues of Libraries of Eminent Persons, Antiquaries*, Mansell, 1974, pp. 5, 36-38). James Gibbs's *A Book of Architecture* (1728) and *Rules for Drawing The several Parts of Architecture* (1732) were advertised for sale in the *Leeds Mercury*, 6, 13 June 1738. It is worth noting that as the town prospered and grew, the *Intelligencer* attracted an increasing number of advertisements inviting its architect-readers to submit designs for proposed buildings further afield and even outside the county. For example, on 22 May and again on 5 June 1787, designs were sought for 'A New Church to be Built' at Blackburn (a job subsequently awarded to James Whittle of Manchester).

9. T. Friedman, *Church Architecture in Leeds 1700-1799*, TS, Second Series, Vol. 7, 1997, pp. 76-7, figs. 17, 19, 20.

10. Pevsner, *Leeds*, pp. 94-9. For a full account of Holy Trinity see Friedman [note 9], Chapter 3, which gives the cost as £5,463/12/5 (pp. 95-96).

11. Yorkshire Archaeological Society, MS. 10.

Briggate and dating to the seventeenth century) and Trinity Church in Boar Lane, while vignettes of residences of leading citizens frame an urban area defined by the River Aire to the south, the eastern start of the York Road, Towns End to the north and westward to the Presbyterian Meeting House at Mill Hill.

In 1710 Etty junior received his earliest important commission from the Leeds Pious Uses Committee to create a new, impressive main front to the Moot Hall (2.1), which was completed in 1711 at the cost of £210 and survived until 1826.[6] Its most striking architectural feature was the pair of giant order Composite pilasters, almost certainly the first local appearance of this standard Baroque motif, which would have been familiar to him from Castle Howard.[7]

A competition in 1722-23 for a new chapel-of-ease, the first in a hundred years, dedicated to the Holy Trinity, to remedy overcrowding in St Peter's and St John's, attracted participation from far afield. William Dickinson, formerly Wren's measurer at St Paul's and a co-surveyor to the Fifty New (or Queen Anne) Churches in London and currently Deputy Surveyor to the Dean and Chapter of Westminster, submitted a full-blown Baroque scheme. William Halfpenny, a carpenter and architect from Richmond, Surrey, offered a fashionable Palladian solution subsequently illustrated in *The Art of Sound Building* (1724), among the earliest of a growing number of architectural pattern books to find their way to the town, tell-tale evidence of its maturing sophistication (2.2).[8] This was the earliest expression in Leeds of a wholly Classical church, replete with novel features reflecting metropolitan *avant garde* trends, most notably the open colonnaded, pyramidal roofed tower, inspired by contemporary reconstructions of ancient Greek tomb architecture, and the idea of encasing the body of the church in an antique pseudoperipteral temple-like form (where the external giant pilasters are attached to the main perimeter walls).[9] This latter innovation also featured in William Etty's winning design (2.3), a solution well suited to a public building promoted by a no-nonsense, money-conscious mercantile community, which must have caused a stir in the town.[10] Indeed, when construction was launched in the Spring of 1723 a colleague informed Thoresby – a Dissenter – then visiting London, that this 'is better news to you than that of Ro[a]sting bishops'![11]

These civic advances coincided with a radically new approach to town house design, where the gable ends and stone mullion window frames of the previous centuries were abandoned in favour of a regular, symmetrical block with straight Classical cornices and wooden sashes (1.1). Of this new breed, three now vanished examples standout. John Atkinson's residence in Call Lane (shown on site in Cossins's plan), perhaps finished in 1717, was admired by Thoresby 'for the exquisite Workmanship of the Stone-work, especially the Dome, and for a

2.3: Leeds, Holy Trinity, Boar Lane
(William Etty, 1723-27), engraving by
S. Porter after Thomas Taylor. (*T.D.
Whitaker*, Loidis and Elmete, *1816,
opposite page 65.*)

painted Stair-Case, excellently performed by Mons Permentier, &
exceeds all in Town'. Jacques (or James) Parmentier was a French émigré
painter whose most celebrated work was the pair of grand pictures
covering Leeds Parish Church's chancel wall depicting *The Last Supper*
and *Moses and Aaron and the Giving of the Law* (*c.*1712-15, destroyed

12. Thoresby, *Ducatus* [note 7], pp. 79-80.
Friedman [note 9], pp. 20-23; Murray [note
5], pp. 69, 82-83.

13. Linstrum, *WYAA*, p. 96, pl. 57;
Linstrum, *Leeds*, p. 25. Etty subscribed to
J. Gibbs's *A Book of Architecture*, 1728.

14. Linstrum, *WYAA*, p. 96, pl. 56. Colvin,
pp. 1040-41. Murray [note 5], pp. 78-9.
The Leeds cornice and window derive from
Borromini's Oratorio di S. Filippo Neri and
Bernini's Palazzo Barberini in Rossi, pls.
35-6, 89, respectively. For Beninbrough see
K. Downes, *English Baroque Architecture*,
Zwemmer, 1966, p. 71, pls. 190-95.

*c.*1838), placed above the painted wood altarpiece attributed on stylistic grounds to Etty. This decoration and the resemblance of Atkinson's dome to Castle Howard suggests that the York architect may have been responsible for this imposing creation.[12] Etty may, too, have been the designer of Sheepscar Hall, the wealthy clothier Nathaniel Denison's residence on Hartley Hill (*c.*1725, later called Bischoff House, demolished 1968), with its uncommon overall ashlar facing, rustic-blocked (or 'Gibbs-surround') and pedimented windows.[13] Most striking was the cosmopolitan Towns End house of Robert Denison, *c.*1710-18, demolished after 1924 (2.4), built of red brick and stone-dressing with a central door and window, and a Doric cornice copied from D. de Rossi's *Studio D'Architettura Civile...di Roma,*1702 (2.5). Similarities to Beningbrough Hall, near York, leave little doubt that they share the same carpenter-architect, William Thornton (*c.*1670-1721). These examples more than ably competed with any contemporary townhouses in Yorkshire.[14]

During the 1730s and 40s progressive, grand scale domestic activity centred at Temple Newsam House, where the Londoner, Daniel Garrett (died 1753), protégé of the Architect-Earl of Burlington, remodelled

2.5: P. da Cortona. Garden entrance to Palazzo Barberini, Rome, 1628-39. (*D. de Rossi*, Studio D'Architettura Civile di Roma, *I, 1702, Pl. 51, detail.*)

2.4: Leeds, Robert Denison residence, Towns End, (attributed to William Thornton, c.1710-18), dem., photographed c.1880. (*Leeds Library and Information Service.*)

2.6: Leeds, Temple Newsam House, Picture Gallery (Daniel Garrett, 1738-46). (*Leeds Museums and Galleries.*)

the Jacobean Long Gallery into the present, glamorous Palladian-Rococo Picture Gallery and Library (1738-46), among the outstanding mid-Georgian interiors in the country (2.6).[15] In 1752 another metropolitan interloper James Paine (1717-89) designed Kirkstall Grange (now Beckett Park) at Headingley (2.7), a pioneer example of his innovative Palladian villa-with-wings,[16] while John Watson junior (died 1771), a surveyor of bridges to the West Riding of Yorkshire, erected the beautifully chaste Palladian Horsforth Chapel in north-west Leeds (1750-58, demolished 1884).[17] Curiously, both buildings failed to attract local followings.

In 1750 John Carr of York (1723-1807), soon to become the principal architect practising in the North of England during the second half of the century, burst forth as a designer of plain, economical, voguishly detailed late-Palladian town houses, later adopting Adamesque decoration of the sort found at Harewood House, just outside Leeds where he had worked. His townhouses in Boar Lane (1750-53), Kirkgate (1752-4) and Bridge End (by 1769), all vanished without trace, were likely to have resembled types erected elsewhere in the county.[18] The sole survivor in Leeds is Jeremiah Dixon's suburban villa called Gledhow Hall (1764-66, now flats), built on high ground

15. Pevsner, *Leeds*, pp. 288-89, pl. 155.

16. P. Leach, *James Paine*, Zwemmer, 1988, pp. 23, 58-9, pl. 28. Pevsner, *Leeds*, pp. 263-4, pl. 140.

17. Friedman [note 9], pp. 109-120, Appendix D, figs. 34-39.

18. B. Wragg, G. Worsley (ed.), *The Life and Work of John Carr of York*,, Oblong, 2000, pp. 170-72, figs. 9, 11, 18, 237.

2.7: Leeds, Kirkstall Grange (now Beckett Park), Headingley (James Paine, 1752). (*Author*.)

19. Carr's work at Gledhow Hall is not documented, but almost certainly by him on the basis of stylistic and circumstantial evidence. See Wragg [note 18], pp. 149-50.

2.8: Leeds, Gledhow Hall, Roundhay (attributed to John Carr, 1764-66). (*Ruth Baumberg*.)

to the north of town (2.8), with its emphasis on basic geometry, strict symmetry and multiple polygonal bays strategically placed to capture internally the maximum of daylight.[19] The model may well have been Plate 30 in Robert Morris's *Rural Architecture: Consisting Of Regular*

2.9: 'Elevation and plan of a house'.
(*R. Morris*, Rural Architecture, 1750,
pl. 30, *engraving by Parr after a design
by Morris*.)

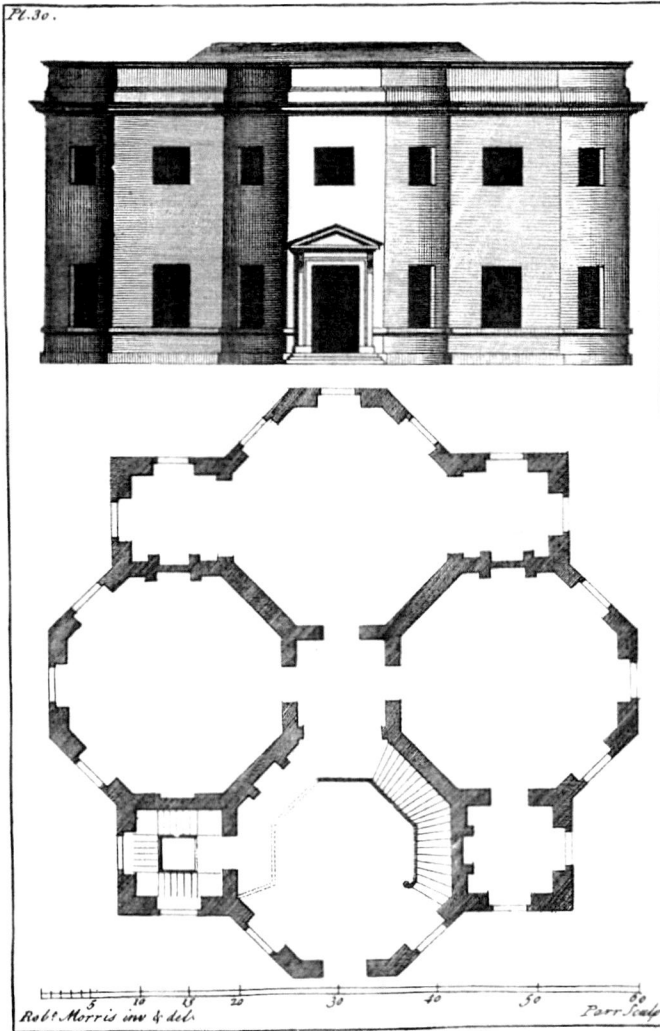

Designs in the Country, 1750 (2.9), applauded in the text for its
'Situation … on an Eminence whose Summit should overlook a long
extended Vale, and, if attainable, quite round the Horizon'.[20]

Carr was also involved in repairs and improvements to the Parish
Church in Kirkgate (1761-72, demolished *c.*1838) and St John,
Briggate (1764-66, remodelled 1884-98). He designed a new chapel
at Farnley, Leeds (1761-62, demolished 1884),[21] but his *chief d'oeuvre*
was the new General Infirmary (1768-92, demolished 1893), the first
of its kind in Leeds (2.10). Costing £4,599, and described in Edward
Baines's *The Leeds Guide* of 1806 as 'what such places ought to be –
plain, handsome and substantial'; the prison reformer, John Howard
praised it as 'one of the best Hospitals in the kingdom [with a] great

20. Pages 4-5. Pevsner, *Leeds*, pp. 12, 243.
D. Hill, *Turner and Leeds Images of Industry*,
Leeds Museums & Galleries, 2008, pp. 97-
103, pls. 86-91. Carr owned a copy of
Morris's *Select Architecture*, 1755 (Colvin,
p. 221). Gledhow was celebrated enough to
have been the subject of a watercolour by
J. M. W. Turner (engraved in *Loidis and
Elmete*, [note 1], opposite p. 131).

21. Wragg [note 18], pp. 34-6, 53-6, 120-
23, Appendices C-D, figs. 12, 40-1.

2.10: Leeds, General Infirmary (John Carr, 1768-92). (*T.D. Whitaker*, Loidis and Elmete, *1816, p. 84, engraving by J. Le Keux after Thomas. Taylor.*)

LEEDS INFIRMARY.

22. Both quoted in Baines, p. 45.

23. *LI*, 5 March 1771. Wragg [note 18], pp. 33, 44, 54, 60, 66, 68, 80, 172-73, figs. 25, 181.

24. Carr's local reputation remained secure for some time: *The Universal British Directory*, 2nd ed., Vol. III, 1790, p. 542, praised him as the 'architect of [the] fine house' at Harewood, then called Gawthorp Hall, 'whose great genius, taste, and skill in his profession, stand in no need of encomiums here'.

2.11: Leeds, New Assembly Rooms and Third White Cloth Hall, (attributed to William Johnson, 1775-77). (*Reconstruction by P. Brears.*)

attention to cleanliness',[22] while the *Leeds Intelligencer* reported that it was 'dedicated to mercy and Christian charity … to the great joy of every benevolent heart … the lower ranks of the people testified their gratitude by ringing the bells'.[23] Its heroic presence, with a Venetian windowed centrepiece repeated in the subtly projecting corner pavilions and arched windows recessed in linking blind arcades – all Carr leitmotifs – made a notable impact on the town.[24] The composition is

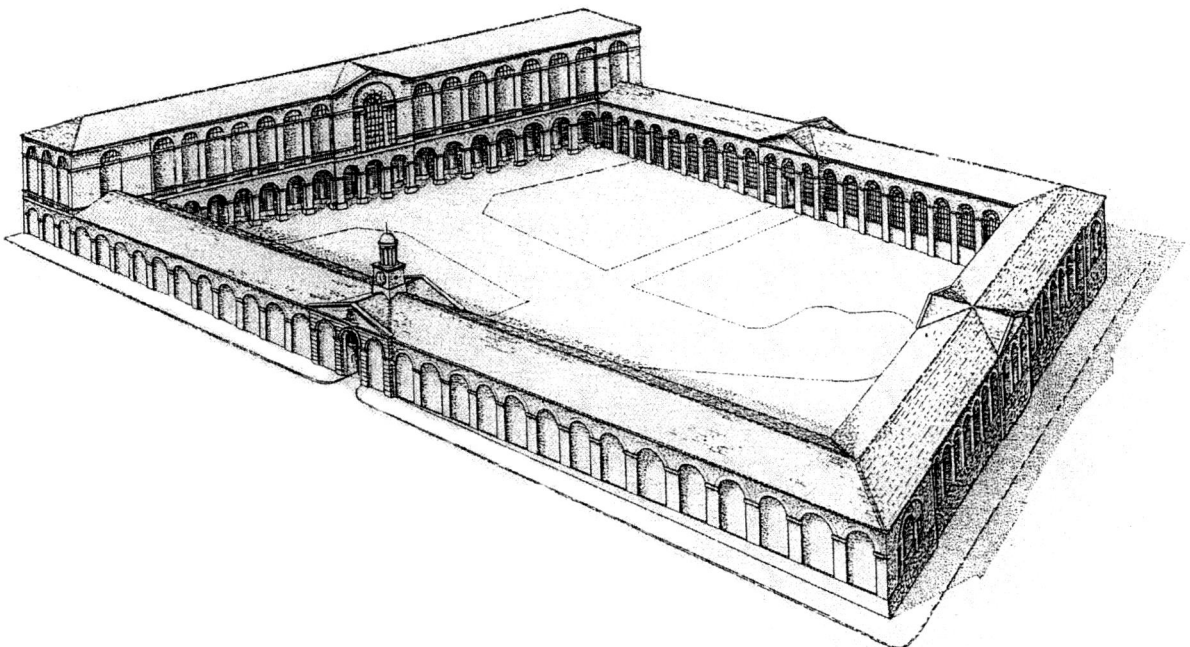

reflected in the White Horse Inn, Boar Lane (architect and date unknown, demolished 1869)[25] and in the New Assembly Rooms (1775-77), its upper storey windows illuminating the cardroom and ballroom overlooking a huge courtyard surrounded by the Third White Cloth Hall's 1,213 arcaded stalls, approached through a triumphal, three-bay, pedimented centrepiece, sections of which still survive (2.11).[26] As the domed cupola crowning the latter entrance was reinstated from an earlier Hall by 'Mr Johnson', presumably William Johnson, it is possible he was also the architect of this complex. At the time of his death in 1795 he had been employed for 'many years architect' at Temple Newsam House by Charles, 9th Viscount Irwin, who was involved with promoting the new hall.[27]

Johnson was, and remains, a shadowy figure, as demonstrated in a letter written by Sir John Russell of Leven Grove near Northallerton, North Yorkshire, dated 26 May 1775 concerning proposed alterations to 'so paltry a form' as Wapsbourne, Chailey in East Sussex, which might be erected by James Wyatt 'if my friend Johnson who I have employed before is dead' or 'I might employ a smaller creature to execute [it]'.[28] He was not alone among numerous members of the Leeds building trades capable of practicing as what was then called an 'Architect': that is 'a Master Workman in Building … who designs the Model, or draws the … Draught of the whole Fabrick; whose Business it is to consider the whole Manner and Method of the Building' as well as serving as a 'Superintendant', at the same time 'having a…Officinator whose Business is to chuse … and sort all the Materials from every

25. P. Brears, *Images of Leeds 1850-1960*, Breedon Books, 1992, p. 101. S. Burt and K. Grady, *The Illustrated History of Leeds*, Breedon Books, 1992, p.101.

26. P. Brears, 'The Leeds Assembly Rooms', *The Georgian Group Journal*, 1994, pp. 76-80. Both buildings were bisected by the North Eastern Railway Co's viaduct in 1864-65; the remaining parts are now occupied by commercial premises. Brears [note 25], p. 60.

27. 'On Friday last died after a lingering illness, Mr. Johnson, many years architect at Temple Newsham, near this town' (*LI*, 1 June 1795, p. 3). Linstrum, *WYAA*, pp. 284, 379. W. Johnson also received £14/19/3 'for valuing the previous Cloth Hall on the occasion of its demotion in 1789.

28. East Sussex Record Office, AMS 5440/25.

2.12: Leeds, Mixed Cloth Hall, 'South East Prospect' (John Moxson, 1756-68), dem. (*Engraving by R. Ledger after T. Atkinson, dated 22 August 1758. Leeds Library and Information Services SRQ 720.942 LIN*)

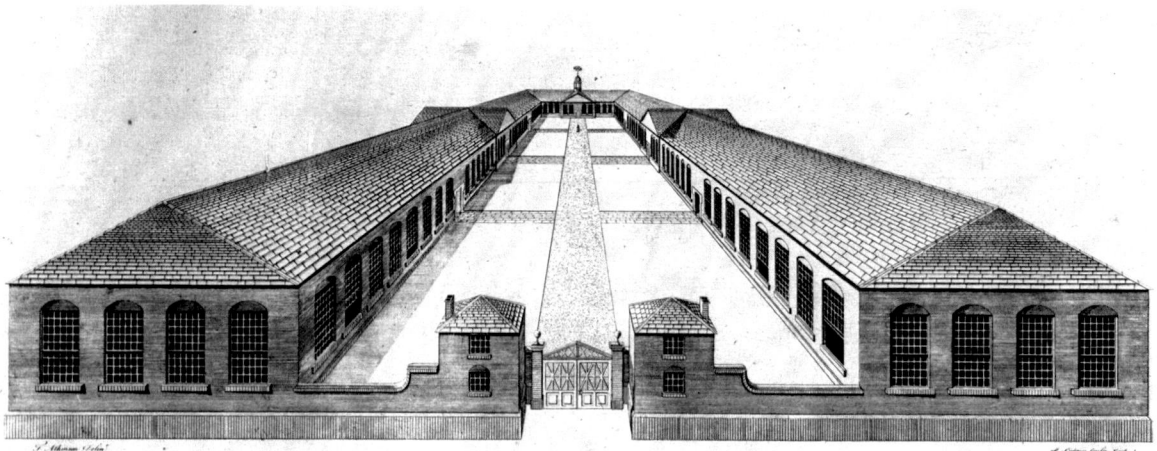

A South East Perspective View of the Mix'd Cloth Hall at Leeds in the County of York.
Erected by Subscription of the Clothiers, to whom this Plate is Dedicated, by their most Humble Servant Robert Ledger

particular Part of the Building', in other words a perpetually on-site clerk of the works, a man falling between the traditional craftsmen and the rising professional architect.[29]

Within this category could be included John Moxson (1700-82), Surveyor of Highways at Leeds, who was responsible for The Mixed Cloth Hall (1756-68, demolished in 1889) (2.12), a 480 foot long, single-storey, red brick complex, which thrilled a visitor in 1767 for being a 'spacious, grand Building and perhaps the largest Cloth Hall in Europe [with] 199 Windows [lighting] five long apartments'.[30] Around 1780 its forecourt was embellished with the addition of a more sophisticated octagonal domed Exchange (2.13) which closely resembled John Carr's mausoleum for the Leeds merchants Robert and William Denison, attached to Holy Rood, Ossington, Nottinghamshire (1782-84, demolished 1838) (2.14), and he may have been the architect of the Exchange as well.[31]

The decision in 1768 to site the Infirmary immediately north-west of the Mixed Cloth Hall established a strong, diagonal umbilical cord along West (subsequently Infirmary) Street linking the old town to the emerging West End, where new building schemes flowered under the next generation of architects. William Lindley of Doncaster (1739-1818), Carr's assistant and draughtsman, designed Nos. 5-7 Park Place (1777-78) as well as Denison Hall, Little Woodhouse (1768-88), an imposing, eleven bay, stone-faced mansion with a stately engaged Ionic temple frontispiece and elegantly appointed interiors.[32] Two local carpenters employed there also pursued careers as designer-developers. William Hargrave repeated the Denison pattern in red brick with stone

29. T. M. Russell, ed., *The Encyclopaedic Dictionary in the Eighteenth Century Architecture, Arts and Crafts*, Vol. 3, *The Builder's Dictionary* [1734], Ashgate, 1997, pp. 31-32, under 'ARCHITECT'.

30. The Revd Joseph Ismay, 'A Journey in May, 1767' (A. Heap and P. Brears, *Leeds Described Eyewitness Accounts of Leeds 1534-1905*, Breedon Books, 1993, p. 24).

31. Wragg [note 18], p. 189, figs. 48-9. Baines's *The Leeds Guide*, 1806, p. 57 called it 'a beautiful building'.

32. Colvin, p. 655. Wragg [note 18], p. 53. Pevsner, *Leeds*, p. 191, fig. 102. R. Hewlings, *Denison Hall, Little Woodhouse, Leeds*, unpublished notes on Denison Papers, University of Nottingham, citing tradesmen's names and costs.

dressing at Nos 17-19 Park Place (1788-1800) while William Lawrence erected more modest terraces in Park Square (1790-97), including his own residence at No. 10.[33] Nearby, Thomas Johnson (1762-1814), the first native-born professional architect to practice in Leeds, launched his career in the early 1790s with a striking, new, fashionable church dedicated to St Paul, the subject of Chapter 3.

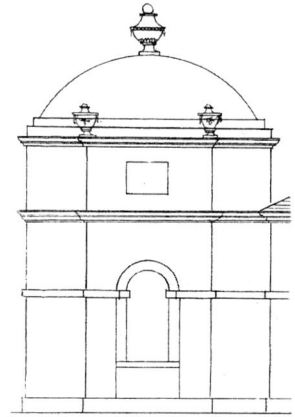

2.14: Ossington, Notts, Denison mausoleum (John Carr, 1782-4), dem. 1838. (*Pen and ink drawing by Carr, Nottingham University Library, Denison of Ossington papers.*)

33. Colvin, pp. 482-83, 636. Pevsner, *Leeds*, pp. 112-15, fig. 55. See also C. Webster, 'The Architectural Profession in Leeds 1800-50: a case-study in provincial practice' in *Architectural History*, Vol. 39, 1995, pp. 176-91.

3. *Thomas Johnson (1762-1814)*

TERRY FRIEDMAN

The closing years of the eighteenth century were an explosive moment in the history of Leeds architecture. The population had nearly doubled from 17,121 in 1775 to 30,669 in 1801.[1] The opening of the Leeds-Liverpool Canal in 1777 encouraged large scale factory development, and the town expanded tidily beyond its irregular medieval hub westward into former countryside to accommodate a rising mercantile middle class requiring new, fashionable residences together with their civic and religious amenities, as well as virgin land on which to erect their great textile spinning mills. A visitor reported in 1788 on 'a town of great trade ... the whole returns of the place could not be less than from five to seven millions a year', another in 1795 'in opulence ... the principal place of the West Riding [of Yorkshire] ... it bears a high rank among our manufacturing towns'.[2] This secular and industrial juxtaposition, a marriage that did not happen, for example, at the religiously more important archiepiscopal centre of York, or at Wakefield, the County Town, is poignantly evoked by a view in Humphry Repton's *Red Book* presented in 1810 to Benjamin Gott, then the leading Yorkshire woollen manufacturer, showing proposals for estate improvements at Armley, in the south-western suburb of the town. Perched on the brow of a steep hill is the celebrated garden-architect's suggested Neoclassical remodelling and enlargement of the existing residence overlooking Gott's Bean Ing, the first of the utilitarian mills (begun 1792, demolished 1960s), notable for its heroic presence, huge work-force and revolutionary Boulton and Watt steam-powered engines, located just beyond the recently laid out West End, an area

1. S. Burt and K. Grady, *The Illustrated History of Leeds*, Breedon Books, 1994, p. 258.

2. A. Heap and P. Brears, *Leeds Describ'd Eyewitness Accounts of Leeds 1537-1905*, Breedon Books, 1993, pp. 26-27; Pevsner, *Leeds*, pp. 13-15.

today defined by The Headrow, Park Row, Park Square and the River Aire.[3] It was in anticipation of capturing lucrative commissions from this newly prosperous clientele as well as from established wealthy landowners that the following advertisement appeared in the *Leeds Intelligencer* on 5, 12 and 19 June 1787:

Mr Thomas Johnson, *Architect*, Begs Leave to acquaint the Nobility and Gentry That after having been under the Inspection of JAMES WYATT, Esqr: of London, three Years, And having since resided in Rome, and seen all the principal Cities of Italy, with a View to Improvement in his Profession, joined to a Tour through France, humbly offers his Services in ARCHITECTURE, that Branch of Science being familiar to him. His wish is to give some Proof to his Employer, in uniting Taste with Oeconomy, and to join Elegance to Convenience.[4]

This marked the first occasion when a professionally trained architect (as defined at the beginning of Chapter 2) publicly announced his intention to set up practice in the town. Born on 8 May 1762, his address is given as Mill Hill (the area presently lying immediately to the east of Leeds Station below Boar Lane), strategically located on the border between the old town and the then newly expanding West End.[5] That Johnson most likely had been born in Leeds is suggested by the fact that his spinster sister, Dinah, still resided in the town in 1814.[6] In the autumn of that year Thomas died intestate and she was designated legal heir, suggesting that he may have been a bachelor or a widower.[7] No portrait is known. There is a paucity of documented work – perhaps as few as sixteen commissions received over twenty-seven years (1787-1814) – which at the time of this publication account for the survival of only 37 architectural drawings, the majority in the form of plans and none representing major enterprises. There are also his vague activities as an urban developer, suggested by the following advertisement which appeared on two occasions in the *Leeds Intelligencer,* on 31 August and 7 September 1795:

Capitol Building Ground.
WOODHOUSE LANE, LEEDS.
Very soon will be offered to SALE, in LOTS … situate on the North Side of Woodhouse-Lane extending from Black-Map Lane to Woodhouse-Bar … which from its Nearness to the Town, dry and healthful Situation, is very eligible for Building upon. – It commands most beautiful, picturesque, and extensive Prospects to the South, South-East, and South West. Plans and Particulars are now preparing, and will soon be ready for the Inspection of the Public …

3. C. Fox, *The Arts of Industry in the Age of Enlightenment*, Yale UP, 2009, p. 438, fig. 221; S. Daniels, 'Landscaping for a manufacturer: Humphry Repton's commission for Benjamin Gott at Armley in 1809-10' in *Journal of Historical Geography*, 7, no. 4, 1981, pp. 379-96; P. Brears, *Images of Leeds 1850-1960*, Breedon Books, 1992, p. 140. The residence was remodelled *c*.1818 by Robert Smirke, architect of The British Museum (1823-46), as the first Greek Revival mansion in West Yorkshire (Linstrum, *WYAA*, p. 82, pl. 44). V.M.E. Lovell, *Benjamin Gott of Armley House, Leeds 1762-1840 Patron of the Arts*, PTS, LIX, Pt. 2, No. 130, pp. 178-87. Bean Ing's unrecorded designer may have been Benjamin's older brother William Gott of Burley, Leeds (1745-1810), a bridge and canal builder (Colvin, p. 437), listed in *Bailey's Northern Directory*, 1781, p. 223, as an 'architect & engineer', the earliest published appearance of the term in respect to a local practitioner, though emphasis should be placed on the engineering aspect as his most prominent activity.

4. Page 1, dated 22 May 1787. For Johnson see Linstrum, *WYAA*, p. 379. Colvin, pp. 582-83.

5. He is listed in Binns & Brown, *A Directory, For the Town of Leeds*, 1800, p. 33 as 'Johnson – , architect, Mill-Hill', in George Wilson, *A New and Complete Directory For the Town of Leeds*, 1807, p. 30, *The Leeds Directory, For 1809*, p. 42, and Wardle & Bentham, *The Commercial Directory, For 1814-15*, p. 73 as 'Johnson Thomas, *Architect*, Mill hill'. In the first two of these he is the only architect listed in Leeds, but in Wardle and Bentham he is joined by Benjamin Jackson of Kirkgate, William Lawrence of Park Square and Thomas Taylor of Commercial Street.

6. 'Miss Johnson the Sister…sole Exer of the late Thos. Johnson', dated 5 October 1814 on verso of a Leeds Bank receipt of 25 July 1809 (The Leeds Library, album of bills etc.).

Inquiries may be made of Mr. Thomas Johnson, Architect in Leeds. August 28th. 1795.[8]

However, neither drawings nor specification can be traced and probably no subsequent construction involving Johnson took place. Nor does this take into account an indeterminate, now long vanished group of modest terrace and cottage properties developed in the East End (1799-1805), which may have been his bread-and-butter.[9] To this should be added the probability of works which have vanished altogether without trace, as well as the apparently unaccountable lean last six years of his life, when no specific architectural activity is recorded, though there is the tantalizing advertisement placed soon after his demise in the *Intelligencer* by the architect Lawrence Ingram, who

> Begs Leave most respectfully to solicit the Patronage of the Nobility, Gentry and Others in this Neighbourhood, in the above Profession, and on Account of the Death of Mr. Johnson, for those Friends who have employed him in that Line, he would be glad to finish any Plans not executed by him; and their further Favors would also be most gratefully acknowledged.[10]

However, so far none of these latter have been identified and, therefore, Johnson is likely to remain something of a mystery, though his was by no means an undistinguished career.

An architectural education and early career

Trained at the Royal Academy Schools in London, where he was admitted on 5 July 1782, age 20, and awarded the Silver Medal later in the same year,[11] he was, as we learn from his 1787 press advert (see above), placed under the 'Inspection', that is, tutelage, of one of Britain's leading architects, James Wyatt.[12] Then, following in his master's footsteps, he sojourned in Italy and toured France during 1785-87.[13] Though nothing is known about who Thomas met or what buildings he examined, and influences can probably never be indisputably demonstrated, the uniqueness of a Leeds-born architect studying in Italy in the eighteenth century must be taken into account. Some notion of his activities may be provided by the experiences of his fellow Yorkshire-born, RA Schools-trained architect, Willey Reveley, traveling contemporaneously, who among much else made a close inspection of the second century AD Temple of Antoninus and Faustina in the Roman Forum, later converted into the church of S. Lorenzo in Miranda, a transformation which Johnson was to enact in one of his major new works (3.6), as we shall see.[14] When he returned to settle in

7. Colvin, p. 582. 'Johnson Diocese at York deceased intestate as it is asserted was granted to Dinah Johnson, spinster his sister She having been first Sworn &c. before the Surrogate aforesaid (Saving &c.) Sworn under £1000 and Bond is entered' (Borthwick, DAB Jan 1768-September 1822, Ainstie 1814 (microfilm 1161), November 1814). He should not be confused with a Leeds plasterer of the same name working 1772-96 (T. Friedman, *Church Architecture in Leeds 1700-1800*, Publications of The Thoresby Society, Second Series, Vol. 7, 1997, pp. 136, 140, 154), who also resided in Mill Hill (*Leeds Directory*, 1790, p. 539), nor with Thomas Johnson, the Warwick architect (Colvin, pp. 581-2).

8. Page 2.

9. M. Beresford, *East End; West End*, PTS, 1988, pp. 178-79, 476. Some of these buildings may be recorded in photographs (Burt and Grady [note 1], pp. 102, 116).

10. *LI*, 15 Aug 1814, advert dated 8 August 1814, giving Ingram's address as No.1 Trinity Lane.

11. S. C. Hutchison, 'The Royal Academy Schools, 1768-1830', *Walpole Society*, Vol. 38, 1962, p. 146, no. 419.

12. During the years of Johnson's association, 1782-85, Wyatt (1746-1813) designed Kentish Town Chapel, London, Heveningham Hall, Suffolk and the Darnley Mausoleum, Cobham, Kent, among much else (Colvin, pp.1175-89; T. Friedman, 'James Wyatt's Earliest Classical Churches', *The Georgian Group Journal*, 1997, pp. 56-70).

13. He is listed as a 'Gians' (an English Protestant), age 23, residing in Rome in Easter 1785 in the Via Babuino, near the Spanish Steps, then the centre of the British artistic community, and on 2 November 1786 as an arrival in Venice, where Wyatt had trained (J. Ingamells, *A Dictionary of British and Irish Travellers in Italy 1701-1800*, Yale UP, 1997, pp. 560, 1025).

14. Reveley (1760-99) was in Italy 1784-88 (Colvin, pp. 856-57; Ingamells [note 13], p. 807). J. B. Ward-Perkins, *Roman Imperial Architecture*, Penguin, 1981, p. 125, pl. 60.

Leeds in 1787 there would have been the immediate benefit of gaining an advantageous foothold through William Johnson (died 1795), presumably either his father or a close relative, an elusive local builder-architect who worked for the Ingrams of Temple Newsam House and may have designed the New Assembly Rooms in The Calls (2.12). Opened in 1777 'by the most brilliant appearance of general company' and attended by '200 ladies and gentlemen of the first rank and fashion in the county' on the occasion of the 1790 Archers Ball,[15] they were precisely the people to whom Thomas hoped to offer 'Proof' of his talents. It is clear that the majority were drawn from close-knit West Riding manufacturing and clerical communities.

There is good reason to believe that chief among these early clients was the Revd Miles Atkinson (1741-1811), for whom Thomas designed his major Leeds building, St Paul, Park Square (1791-93, demolished 1906). Miles was the son of Revd Christopher Atkinson, rector of Thorp Arch, and brother of the celebrated cleric poet William Atkinson. Another brother, Johnson Atkinson, D.L., M.D. of Leeds, had married Elizabeth Busfield in 1765 and on the death of her uncle in 1772 assumed the surname of Busfield and resided at Myrtle Grove, Bingley, to the north-west of Leeds beyond Bradford.[16] When, in 1793, Johnson sought the job of designing the proposed General Infirmary at Sheffield (which he failed to secure), he used a letter of recommendation from Busfield (discussed below) which drew on the evidence of work already undertaken for himself and other members of the family.[17] It cannot be coincidental that Busfield and three further

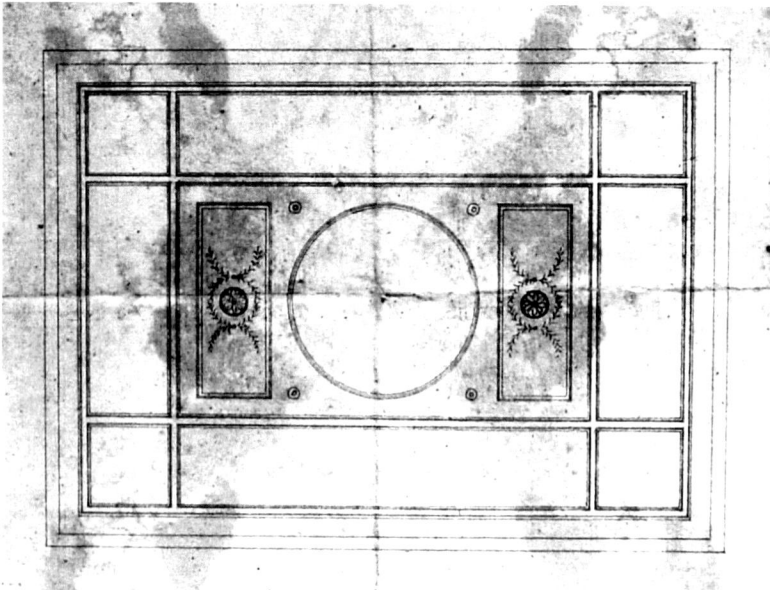

3.1: Foxholes Hall, Lancs, design for a 'Stair Case Ceiling' (Thomas Johnson, 1791). (*Courtesy of Hugh Pagan Ltd.*)

15. P. Brears, 'The Leeds Assembly Rooms', *The Georgian Group Journal*, 1994, pp. 77-78, quoting the *LI*, 17 June 1777 and the *LM*, 2 November 1790. See this publication, Chapter 2.

16. *Oxford Dictionary of National Biography*, Oxford U.P., 2004, Vol. II, pp. 840, 850; *Burke's Landed Gentry*, 18th edn, Vol. I, p. 270. 'J.A. Busfield…his Brother, the Rev. William Atkinson … both Poets' are associated with others as a 'Junto' in E. Baldwyn, *Remarks on the Oath, Declarations, and Conduct of Johnson Atkinson Busfield, Esq.*, G. Kearsley, 1791, pp. 61, 68-9.

17. Busfield's recommendation following the competition announcement (Sheffield Archives, NHS, 17/2/1/9); Johnson's contribution is untraced.

3.2: Foxholes Hall, Lancs, 'Elevation of the North Front' (Thomas Johnson, 1791). (*Courtesy of Hugh Pagan Ltd.*)

18. In 1787. His younger brother Edward Markland was partner in the firm of Markland, Cookson and Fawcett, who owned Bank Mills, Leeds (Beresford [note 9], pp. 241-42, 244; information from Hugh Pagan).

19. For example, the dining room ceiling at Heveningham (J. M. Robinson, *The Wyatts An Architectural Dynasty*, Oxford UP, 1979, pl. 46). The drawings representing ground, chamber, attic and cellar plans, south, north and east elevations, vestibule, staircase, ceiling, drawing and dining rooms, library, chamber floor and roof carpentry, signed 'T Johnson', 'T. Johnson Archt' or 'Thos Johnson Archt', with detailed 'Estimate of a new House to be built at Foxholes, near Rochdale, for John Entwisle Esqr', signed 'Thomas Johnson / May 3rd 1791 (Sotheby's, 26 April 1990, lot 391; in 2011 in the possession of Hugh Pagan Ltd, PO Box 354, Brockenhurst, Hampshire, SO42 7PS, UK). Hall built 1792-93 to modified scheme probably by Johnson (*The Victoria History of the Country of Lancashire*, Constable & Co., 1911, 5, p. 227; C. Hartwell, *et al.*, *The Buildings of England Lancashire: Manchester and South East*, Yale UP, 2004, p. 602).

Johnson clients – Dr William Hey of Leeds, Revd W. H. Coulthurst of Halifax and John Entwisle of Foxholes in Lancashire (actually John Markland, a member of a prominent Leeds cotton spinning and wool scribbling firm who assumed the Entwisle name on inheriting the property from a distant cousin)[18] – were among the subscribers to *Practical Sermons, By the Late Rev. Miles Atkinson, A. B. Vicar of Kippax, Minister of St Paul's, and Lecturer of the Parish Church of Leeds. To which is Prefixed A Short Memoir of the Life and Character of The Author,* London, 1812.

Johnson's earliest autographed works, dated 3 May 1791, for a new mansion near Rochdale called Foxholes Hall, his only known commission outside Yorkshire, is unique for its comprehensiveness: a folio of 26 large presentation drawings including plans, elevations, details and technical renderings, accompanied by a detailed estimate, which itemizes the use of 'Higgins Stucco' (presumably one of the many then fashionable artificial wall treatments) and '4 Ionic Capitals', priced £10, Johnson's favourite Classical order, with the total bill given as £583/1/3. The decorative plasterwork (3.1) reveals a predilection for simplified Adamesque Neoclassicism in the manner of James Wyatt.[19] The north elevation study features an austere treatment of regimented windows (3.2), made even more sparse in execution (3.3), indicative of a major crossroads in late-Georgian domestic architecture. The modern Roman *avant garde* which had so dazzled older, provincial followers of Robert Adam has been rejected in favour of the

3.3: Foxholes Hall, Lancs as built 1792-93, pre-1970 demolition photograph (Thomas Johnson, 1791-3). (*Link4Life, Local Studies, Rochdale, E21 (27009), 3020.*)

conservative Neoclassical repertory of Wyatt, who expressed a preference for the 'very good architecture at Venice by Palladio' (the influential Renaissance architect).[20] At the same time Johnson embraced John Soane's current precepts, voiced in his *Plans Elevations and Sections Of Buildings* (1788-89), in which 'foreign absurdities' were replaced by a 'well-contrived and ingenious design, where beauty, elegance and convenience unite',[21] the very language employed in Johnson's 1787 advert, with an additional stress on 'Oeconomy' commensurate with a nation about to go to war with France, and demonstrated in Soane's wings at Malvern Hall, Warwickshire (3.4).

3.4: 'The Perspective View of the Alterations and Improvements' to Malvern Hall, Warwickshire (John Soane, 1783-6). (*J. Soane*, Plans Elevations and Sections of Buildings, *1788-89, pl. 6.*)

20. K. Garlick and A. Macintyre, eds, *The Diary of Joseph Farington*, Yale UP, 1983, III, p. 918.

21. Page 5. The wealthy Leeds merchant, John Denison of Ossington, Nottinghamshire is listed among the subscribers. For Soane (1753-1837) see Colvin, pp. 962-71.

The full-height canted central bay, specified in the 1791 estimate as the 'bow room', which may not have been realized at Foxholes, reappeared by 1793 as among 'several little Things' Johnson did for Busfield at Myrtle Grove, to up-date an otherwise standard two storey, nine bay, featureless ashlar block the client had erected in 1770-72, which was greatly altered in the nineteenth century and now functions as Bingley Council Offices.[22]

In 1793 Johnson responded to an advertisement concerning a projected new Royal Infirmary at Sheffield, which was unusual in requesting 'Persons as may be willing to offer their Services to prepare Plan and Estimates and to superintend the Erection ... to send their Terms sealed up ... on or before the 21st day of February' and 'to do this before they give themselves any Trouble in drawing any plans &c & to send such Recommendations from any places where they may have been employed as may enable the committee to form a general opinion of their professional Character.'[23] No drawings were offered since this prestigious job was awarded to another Wyatt-trained

22. Pevsner, *WY*, p. 125; E. E. Dodd, *Bingley A Yorkshire Town Through Nine Centuries*, Harrison, 1958, pp. 86-7. The central block is reminiscent of John Carr's early Yorkshire houses, a number of which feature full-height canted bays (B. Wragg, *The Life and Work of John Carr of York*, ed. G. Worsley, Oblong, 2000, pls. 5-6, 37, 87, 107). The Tuscan pedimented central door and somewhat awkward (and subsequently altered) flanking wings may also be part of Johnson's contribution. Of the interior, an original staircase with Adamesque Neoclassical plasterwork survives. Baldwyn's *Remarks* of 1791 (see note 16) refers to 'The splendid ornament of Myrtle-Grove' (p. 62).

23. See Catalogue.

3.5: Leeds, Nos. 39-40 Park Square (Thomas Johnson, 1795-97). (*Ruth Baumberg*.)

architect, Birmingham-based John Rawstorne.[24] However, Busfield's 12 February 1793 letter of recommendation emphasized that the design 'would both do himself credit & perfectly satisfy his Employers' on the grounds that Busfield had 'known [Johnson] long – he has done several little Things for me in the Line of his Profession – has had the whole & sole Direction in building a House for my late mother, another for my Brother at Leeds … in all these … Concerns he has given compleat satisfaction both with Respect to Abilities Attention & strict Probity'.[25] Of Jane Atkinson's house nothing is known.[26] Miles's vicaral residence at No. 9 Park Square, erected following the signing of a site lease on 1 March 1789 and, therefore, perhaps Thomas's earliest work, survives but with its façade altered in 1908.[27] Larger, still extent variations were erected at Nos. 39-40, on the north side of Park Square, during 1795-97 (3.5).[28]

24. R. Harman and J. Minnis, *Pevsner Architectural Guides Sheffield*, Yale UP, 2004, pp. 16, 283, pl. 165. Sheffield Archives, [note 17].

25. Sheffield Archives, [note 17], addressed to Rev James Wilkinson, a member of the building committee.

26. Jane, wife of Revd Christopher Atkinson, was the daughter of William Johnson of Old Hall near Kendal, Westmorland (*Oxford Dictionary of National Biography*, Oxford UP, 2004, vol. II, p. 850).

27. See Catalogue.

28. See Catalogue.

3.6: Leeds, St Paul, Park Square, (Thomas Johnson, 1791-93), dem. 1905. (*Leeds Library and Information Services, 436*.)

Leeds commissions

A significant part of Busfield's 1793 assessment was based on Johnson being 'at this Time not only the Architect but has the entire conduct & superintendence of the new Church which my said Brother is building' in Leeds, that is, St Paul, Park Square (1791-93, demolished 1906), the most substantial new church erected in the town in over sixty years (3.6). His starting point was an Antique Ionic *tetrastyle* pseudoperipteral temple (in which a series of giant order pilasters enwrapped the rectangular body) from which a lofty steeple rose at the west end of the roof, an amalgamation of Pagan and Christian which had fascinated English architects since the early eighteenth century, as famously interpreted by James Gibbs at St Martin-in-the-Fields in London, and which, as noted above, had enticed Reveley to study the Christianised Antoninus and Faustina.[29] Johnson cleverly tailored the ancient model to the specific needs of the urban site by concentrating identical engaged pedimented temples on both west and east ends. The latter, facing towards town, featured prominent entrances in each of the outer bays, which led to lobbies on either side of a full height apsidal-shaped chancel, thence into the galleried nave. This composition was repeated at the west front, with the middle bay serving as a semi-independent baptistery. Long south and north elevations, the latter facing towards the verdant open space of the Square, abrogated entirely the giant pilasters, relying instead on flat, astylar surfaces of uniformly repetitive, unframed windows bracketed by single, slightly projecting corner bays emphasized by *oeil-de-boeufs*, niches, panels and urns, crowned by a continuous frieze and cornice without architrave. Costing £10,000 to build, on its consecration in 1793 the church was described as 'finished … in a proper and commodious manner'.[30]

Johnson returned to this simple vocabulary in the interior of the Roman Catholic Chapel, Lady Lane (1793-94, demolished), the first such purpose-built place of worship in Leeds, where extrovert architectural expressions of Papist devotion, despite the Catholic Relief Act of 1791, were still held in deep suspicion by the Establishment. Though a Protestant, his studies in Italy undoubtedly would have held him in good stead with the client, to whom he charged £278 for supplying a design and supervising construction at a cost totaling £1,500.[31]

In the mid-1790s Johnson entered a brief period of more robust architectural creativity which is particularly demonstrated by two notable surviving buildings. No. 1, Albion Place, Leeds (1793-95), built for Dr William Hey, the celebrated one-eyed surgeon, was the most superior new residence in the town center (3.7),[32] with its central entrance framed by Tuscan columns *in antis* and a keyed arch over the fan-light. This design reveals his alertness to current Neoclassical

29. Friedman [note 7], pp. 150-51, fig. 51, and T. Friedman, *The Eighteenth-Century Church in Britain*, Yale UP, 2011, Chapter 21.

30. Borthwick, Reg. 38, f. 289r. For the cost see K. Grady, 'The Georgian Public Buildings of Leeds and the West Riding', *PTS*, LXII, no. 133, 1987, p. 163.

31. See Catalogue. The exterior, which is likely to have been extremely modest, is unrecorded.

32. On 6 July 1793 William Walker transferred the 'Conveyance of a piece of Ground in Albion Street' to Hey (WYASL, WYL 160 75/5/1); the house was insured for £1,000, stables and coach house for £20 (Beresford [note 9], p. 168).

3.7: Leeds, Dr William Hey's residence, No 1 Albion Place, now Leeds Law Society (Thomas Johnson, 1793-95). (*Ruth Baumberg*.)

pattern books in a bid to introduce greater domestic refinement in Leeds,[33] and marked a trenchant sculptural presence on an otherwise conventionally late-Georgian façade. This treatment was developed further at Holy Trinity, Halifax (1795-8) (3.8), where the doubling of the Ionic pilasters across the upper story and the boldly projecting, pedimented centrepiece with recessed quarter-engaged columns frame a more deeply set, tripartite window raised on a rusticated basement which is punctured by a lunette window. While innovative in the context of Yorkshire church design of the period, it perhaps turns to James Wyatt's older brother Samuel's Trinity House, Tower Hill, London.[34]

Johnson's direct dependence on the work of his master is epitomized by the Commercial Street façade of The Leeds Library (1805-08), an entirely new building type in Leeds. It was founded in 1768 as a proprietary subscription library and continues today as the oldest extant example in Britain. It is his major surviving work in the city (3.9). The reading rooms occupying the upper stories are monumentalised by Ionic giant order pilasters rising from a rustic arcaded basement and the whole façade recalls Wyatt's Oriel College Library, Oxford (3.10).[35]

33. For example, John Soane's Langley Park, Norfolk lodges (1786) in *Plans Elevations and Sections of Buildings*, 1788, pl. 23.

34. Friedman [note 7], pp. 155–6, pl. 54. Given incorrectly to J. Oates (T. Allen, *A New and Complete history of the County of* York, London, 1831-32, V, p. 385). D. Stillman, *English Neo-classical Architecture*, Zwemmer, 1988, II, pl. 295.

35. G. Tyack, *Oxford an architectural guide*, Oxford UP, 1988, pp. 186-87.

3.8: Halifax, Holy Trinity, Harrison Road
(Thomas Johnson, 1795-6). (*Author.*)

3.9: Leeds, The Leeds Library,
Commercial Street (Thomas Johnson,
1807-08). (*Engraving by J. Le Keux after
T. Taylor, in T. D. Whitaker,* Loidis and
Elmete, *1816, opposite p. 86.*)

3.10: Oxford, 'The New Library at Oriel College' (James Wyatt, 1788-89). (*Courtesy of Geoffrey Tyack.*)

In the library design, Johnson went further towards achieving simplicity by compressing the volutes of the capitals and abandoning altogether the architrave of the entablature as well as the cyma reversa, dentil and ovolo of the cornice (an idiosyncratic abbreviation which he had earlier employed at St Paul's). Unusually well documented for this date, yet never before studied in detail, its building history throws invaluable light on the processes of promoting public edifices at a crucial moment in the development of Leeds commercial architecture.

The Library's *Minute Book* reveals that on 3 September 1804 it was agreed to build a 'New Library Room' under the direction of a committee chosen from among its subscribers, who were instructed on 25 February 1805 to select 'a proper situation' and 'determine upon Plans and Estimates' for the above as well as a 'House for the Librarian' to be financed by issuing forty shares at £50 each. On 17 August Johnson, as part of his property development portfolio, advertised in the *Leeds Mercury* the sale of two large freehold plots in 'an airy, healthful and pleasant Situation' in Commercial Street.[36] On 1 November it was agreed that the 'Front ... be faced with Stone' and twelve days later one of the subscribers, John Howarth, offered a 'Plan' (untraced) which was immediately returned with 'thanks'; on the same occasion other members were encouraged to submit schemes, yet it was also 'definitively settled, Mr Johnson be requested to furnish the Plan' (also untraced). Fortuitously, the committee included two earlier clients: Revd Miles Atkinson, who had promoted St Paul, Park Square (1791-93), and Dr William Hey, for whom Johnson designed the nearby Albion Place residence in 1793. On 16 July 1806, a nine-man subcommittee was 'fully empowered to receive & to adopt plans, & to cause to be erected such Buildings as may to them seem best suited to

36. Advertisement dated 15 August 1805, p. 2 (Beresford [note 9], p. 170). For a general history see F. Beckwith, *The Leeds Library 1768-1968*, The Leeds Library, 1994.

37. The Leeds Library, *Minute Book 1800-1879*, ff. 1-8, 10-13. For Howarth see Beresford [note 9], p. 310.

38. Cawood mason £669/3/6, Gledhow and Co. bricklayers £629/6/-, Woodheads joiners £1, 204/0/6, Curtis slater £106/8/-, Brown glazier £291/14/-, Briggs plumber £65/7/-, Heaps plumber, £5/7/-, Simpson water pipes £7/15/-, Waggitt plasterer £270/4/6, Nelson whitesmith £64/5/-, Reynolds and Paley £50/7/6, Cawood and Sons iron founders £52/17/-, Garland alterations £4/1/-. Some of these are familiar names among local builders.

the purpose of this Situation, and to the capabilities of the ground purchased provided the whole Sum expended does not exceed five thousand Guineas'.[37] The printed 'New Library Building Account' for 1805-09 records a total expenditure of £5,078/4/10, including payments of £105 to 'Mr. Johnson, (Architect)', and the full complement of builders.[38] In the same document Thomas Johnson is listed as no. 45 of the 92 who subscribed £50 each. On 1 September 1809 he signed a receipt for £2/10/0 as 'Interest due to me'[39] and on 25 April 1810 sanctioned an expenditure of £36/11/1½ for minor improvements to the fabric undertaken during the previous year by Richard Woodhead & Co.[40] He also provided a modest residence for the librarian, Mrs Mary Robinson, at the rear of the building.[41]

Remarkably, though having nothing to do with our architect, in 1807-8 while the basement shops were being prepared but before the Library officially opened, William Bullock of Liverpool temporarily rented the upper floor for the public display of his 'MUSEUM of Natural and Foreign Curiosities, Antiquities, and various Productions of the fine Arts', which opened on 28 December 1807. According to a press advertisement 'The ROOM is fitted up in the most fashionable

39. The Leeds Library, album of bills and receipts. On 12 July 1817 Braithwaite & Son supplied '1 Man 2 Days whitewashing &c Geting Scaffolding' and '3 Stone of flake white' presumably for external paint work.

40. The Leeds Library, loose MS with work itemized dating 21 Jan.-30 Dec. 1809.

41. See Catalogue. Perhaps the (now demolished) semi-detached extension shown on Thomas Ambler's 'Plan of Present Building', 1877 (The Leeds Library, archives).

3.11: Cawthorne, nr Barnsley, SY, All Saints, 'Plan B, proposing to rebuild the Body of Cawthorne Church' (Thomas Johnson, 5 April 1805). (*Sheffield Archives, Sp St 60736.*)

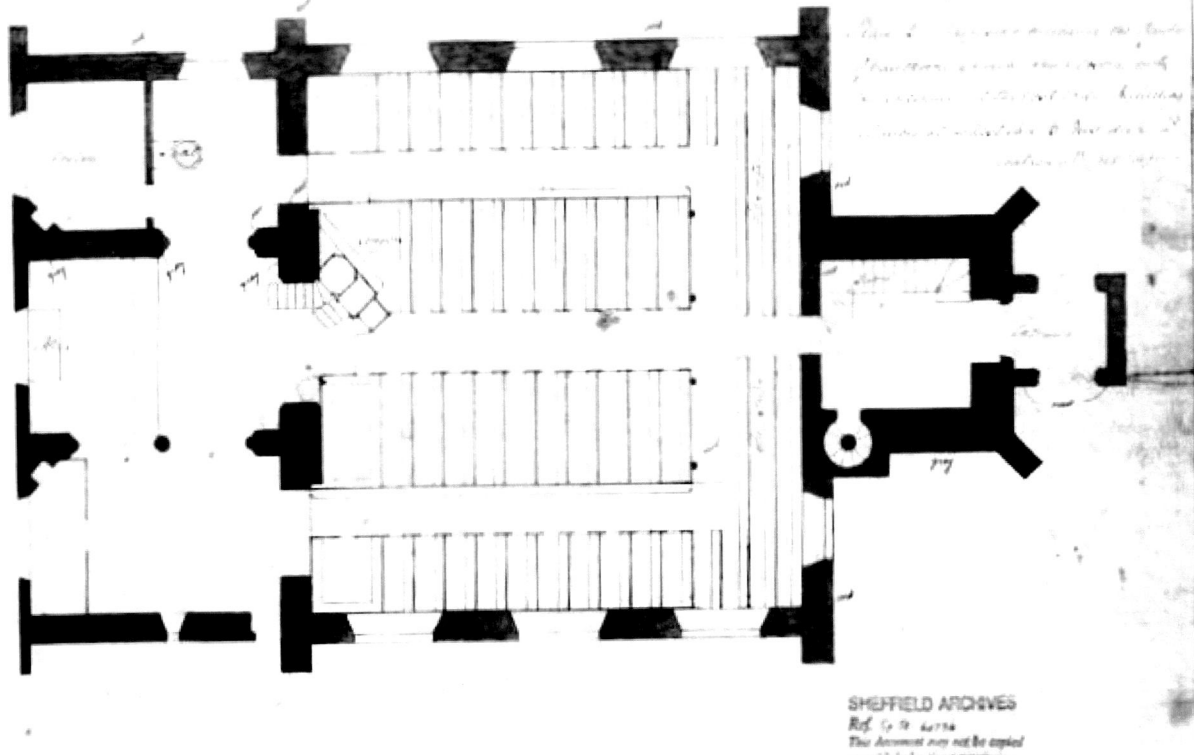

Egyptian Stile … from the Proprietor's Manufactory in Liverpool'.[42] This significantly predates Bullock's more celebrated London attraction, the Egyptian Hall in Piccadilly (1811-12), and was one of the earliest internal applications of this stylistic phenomenon in Britain.[43]

Johnson also explored various medieval forms. In 1805 he proposed 'to rebuild the Body' of All Saints, Cawthorne, near Barnsley. A set of signed and dated plans (3.11), unfortunately without elevations, shows the retained thirteenth century fabric (chancel, north chancel aisle and west tower rendered in grey wash) with a new south chancel aisle, north and south aisles and entrance porch in red wash, featuring buttresses, splayed windows, a west gallery and an engaged column attached to a chancel pier. This marked an early, more archaeological attempt to marry old and new which was distinctly at odds with the then common practice of imposing Classical improvements on ancient Gothic structures, what Horace Walpole aptly condemned as the 'bastard breed'.[44] Whatever actually got built, for no graphic evidence survives, was swept away in 1828 and 1875-80.[45]

A 'Cottage, for the Work People' (3.12) for Newland Park near Wakefield, enclosed in a 5 April 1808 letter to the client, Sir Edward Smith, Bart., is the only known instance in his *oeuvre* of a rustic *cottage orné*, complete with a three-centred pointed arch door protected by a Tudor label hood-mould, double-light mullion windows and thatch roof.[46] The type, which had recently become widely fashionable in Britain, corresponds closely to patterns published in Charles

42. 'To Cash received of Mr. Bullock Rent of Library, for his Museum', £63 (The Leeds Library, 'New Library Building Account' (1808-09), printed). *LI*, 28 Dec. 1807, Vol. LV, p.1. See also R. D. Altick, *The Shows of London,* The Belknap Press, 1978, Chapter 18; C. Wainwright, intro., *George Bullock Cabinet-Maker,* John Murray, 1988.

43. The Egyptian Hall, Nos. 170-73 Piccadilly, London, 1811-12 by P. Robinson, the Great Room re-styled in 1819 by J. B. Papworth; see also John Foulston's Public Library, Devonport, Plymouth, 1823 (J. S. Curl, *Egyptomania The Egyptian Revival: a Recurring Theme in the History of Taste,* Manchester U.P., 1994, pp. 156-61, pls. 110-11, 113-14; Colvin, p. 879); see also M.P. Costeloe, *William Bullock Connoisseur and Virtuoso of the Egyptian Hall: Piccadilly to Mexico (1773-1849),* Bristol, 2008, pp. 34, 36. I am grateful to Timothy Stevens for this last reference.

44. To Richard Bentley, September 1753 (W.S. Lewis (ed), *Correspondence,* Yale UP, 1837-38, XXXV, p. 150. For a detailed discussion of this phenomenon see Friedman [note 29], Chapter 17.

45. The fabric was partly rebuilt by T.W. Atkinson (born in Cawthorne 1799) in 1828-29 (Colvin, p. 79; L. Butler, ed., *The Yorkshire Church Notes of Sir Stephen Glynne (1825-1874),* Yorkshire Archaeological Society, 2007, p. 143; C.T. Pratt, *A History of Cawthorne,* David and Heywood, nd., pp. 68, 88, 115-17).

46. See Catalogue.

3.12: Newland Hall, nr Wakefield, 'Mr. Johnson's Plans of the Cottage for the Work People', detail (Thomas Johnson, 5 April 1808). (*John Goodchild Collection, Local History Study Collection, Wakefield, Newland MS, DB.*)

3.13: 'Designs for Cottages' in Charles Middleton, *Picturesque and Architectural Views For Cottages, Farm Houses and Country Villas*, 1793, pl. 1, detail, no. 1.

47. J. Archer, *The Literature of British Domestic Architecture 1715-1842*, MIT Press, 1985, pp. 564-66. Numerous examples of Tudor hood mouldings are illustrated in R. Elsam, *An Essay On Rural Architecture*, 1803.

48. Photographs of ruined farm buildings and gate piers in John Goodchild Collection (see Catalogue). Mr Goodchild informs me that there is neither ordnance nor physical evidence of the cottage.

49. Pevsner, *Leeds*, p. 191, pl. 102.

50. A group of drawings: 'Ground Plan of Wings proposed to be added to Sewerby House', 'Elevation of the Bows', both signed 'Leeds July 26th 1807 Thos Johnson Arch', 'Ground plan of proposed alterations at Sewerby House', 'Chamber Plan', first floor plan, 'West side of the West Wing', all unsigned but in Johnson's hand for the house and stable block in Hull History Centre, Lloyd-Graeme, UDDLG/x/30/912.

Middleton's *Picturesque and Architectural Views for Cottages, Farm Houses, and Country Villas* (1793), described as 'inhabited by the poorer sort of country people … chiefly built of slight materials … generally inhabited by persons in the service of the family on whose estate they are erected … composed of stone, brick, or timber, stuccoed or rough cast, and covered with thatch' in which 'a parlour, kitchen, pantry, and scullery…with lodging rooms over…are rooms required' (3.13).[47] Though apparently not realized, Thomas turned to another Middleton scheme published in the same book, under 'Farm Houses', for a cluster of barns, stables, cowsheds, pigcotes, yards and a carpenter's shop for Newland, dated 23 April 1807.[48]

His addition to the early Georgian central block of Sewerby Hall, Bridlington in East Yorkshire of a pair of plain, two storey, bow-fronted wings (1807-08) looks back to William Lindley's Denison Hall in Leeds (1786).[49] The studies (3.14) are mainly interesting as a demonstration of technical skills: here he recommended making 'a gruve…behind the Window head of the East Bow to receive the upper square of the lower sheet when thrown up. As a a a a', and treating the wooden cornice 'painted like stone'. While Sewerby adds little to the progress of Johnson's *oeuvre*, it is significant that the client, John Graeme, favoured his admittedly conservative solution to an alternative scheme by an unknown hand featuring clumsy Baroque baubles and ill-proportioned Classical temple frontispieces.[50]

Johnson's legacy is not easily determined. St Paul's enjoyed no local progeny. Nos 9, 39 and 40 St Paul's Square are among the earliest examples of fashionable townhouse design which his slightly older contemporaries, William Lindley and William Hargrave, were also developing at the same time. His repetitive bay system on the Leeds Library front marked the beginning of regular, urban, mercantile planning in the emerging western expansion of the town. Its direct influence is evident in at least two noteworthy surviving Leeds buildings of indeterminate dates, neither of which have identifiable designers. Both were first illustrated in *Charlton & Archdeacon's Directory of the Borough and Neighbourhood of Leeds* (1849-50). The seven bay, three storey, red brick block of J.W. Clark's West Riding Carriage Manufactory (now the Great George Street approach to

3.14: Sewerby Hall, East Yorks, 'Elevation of the Bows', detail (Thomas Johnson, 26 July 1807). (*Hull History Centre, UDDLG/x1/30/911.*)

3.15: Leeds, G. W. England
(previously Bullman and Son) Cabinet
and Upholstery Manufacturer, 31
Commercial Street, architect and date
unknown. (Charlton and Archdeacon's
Directory of the Borough and
Neighbourhood of Leeds, 1849-50, p. 12,
detail, courtesy of The Leeds Library.)

51. *LM,* 15 June 1831, p. 3, reported that
'flames raged with such force that the roof of
[the] entire front of [the] building fell in',
causing £5,000 worth of damage
(information courtesy of Geoffrey Foster).

52. Colvin, pp. 86-7, 118-9, 711-2.

53. Pevsner, *Leeds,* pp. 112-3, 192, pls. 55,
57, 102; Wragg [note 22], p. 53.

54. Page 32.

55. Cusworth resided at 2 Mill Hill
(E. Baines, *Directory, General and
Commercial, of the Town & Borough of Leeds,
For 1817,* p. 184.)

56. Pp. 18-9.

Millennium Square) is a near replica of the Library. And no. 13 Commercial Street (3.15), located directly opposite the Library, is the last survivor of what may have represented a common early nineteenth century business premise in the expanding town. The façade is framed by plain, giant order Tuscan pilasters, supporting a hallmark abbreviated entablature. However, it is unclear whether the extent and manner of the reconstruction after a serious fire in 1831 was little more than a partial rebuilding to restore the previous form of the premises occupied by Robert Bullman and Son, upholsterers, the earliest recorded owners, or a complete reconstruction to a different design.[51]

Thomas Johnson maintained a respectable but unspectacular practice. In this respect he differed little from other provincial architects of the period – one brings to mind Joseph Badger of Sheffield, William Belwood of York and Charles Mountain Sr of Hull, to name but a few based in Yorkshire.[52] Johnson's special significance for the progress of architecture in Leeds lay in that his earliest endeavours of the 1790s already displayed evidence of a radical shift in taste away from the increasingly unfashionable Adamesque Neoclassicism of Carr and his local followers – Hargrave, Lawrence and Lindley[53] – to embrace an unprecedented, up-to-date Soanian simplicity, as the verdict of J. Ryley's *The Leeds Guide,* 1808, makes amply clear: 'very elegant and stately [where] Plain beauty unites with strength in a modern style of architecture [which] does honour to the age in which it was reared'.[54] This foreshadowed the next generation of local architects, particularly Johnson's pupil Joseph Cusworth,[55] and R.D. Chantrell. It is what Edward Baines, author of *The Leeds Guide* of 1806, meant when he observed 'Every year has witnessed an increase of buildings having started into existence, with a rapidity which instantly afford matter for astonishment ... Within the last thirty years the town has increased to more than double its number of inhabitants, and is annually augmenting in its dimensions, as well as improving in the quality of its buildings ... LEEDS possesses the capabilities of becoming perhaps one of the handsomest towns in the kingdom'.[56]

The author is grateful for assistance from Geoffrey Foster, John Goodchild, Nicola Herbert, Hugh Pagan and Angela Speight.

Catalogue

LEEDS, No. 9 Park Square (east side), new residence for Rev Miles Atkinson, 1789 (?), altered 1908. (Sheffield Archives, NHS 17/2/1/9.)

FOXHOLES HALL, Wardleworth, Lancashire, new residence for John Markland, drawings 1791, built 1792-93 to modified scheme probably by Johnson; demolished 1970. (26 working drawing in the possession of Hugh Pagan Ltd, Hampshire, in 2010.)

LEEDS, St Paul (C of E), St Paul's Square, 1791-93, for Rev Miles Atkinson and Christopher Wilson, Bishop of Bristol, dem. 1906. (Sheffield Archives, NHS 17/2/1/9.)

BINGLEY (WY), Myrtle Grove, additions for Johnson Atkinson Busfield, before 12 February 1793. (Sheffield Archives, NHS 17/2/19.)

UNIDENTIFIED HOUSE for J.A. Busfield's mother, before 12 February 1793. (Sheffield Archives, NHS 17/2/1/9.)

SHEFFIELD, The Royal Infirmary (WR), 29 January 1793 competition launch. (Sheffield Archives, NH 17/2/1/17; Johnson's contribution (17/2/1/9), if any, untraced.)

LEEDS, Roman Catholic Chapel, Lady Lane, for Fr Albert Underhill, priest, 1793-94, dem. (Friedman [note 7], pp. 164-67.)

LEEDS, No. 1 Albion Place, residence, consulting rooms and service blocks for Dr William Hey, 1793-95, now offices. (Beresford [note 9], p. 168.)

HALIFAX, Holy Trinity, Harrison Road, 1795-98, for Rev Henry William Coulthurst. (*LI*, 17 August 1795.)

LEEDS, Woodhouse Lane, 'Plans and Particulars…now preparing' for a 'Capitol Building Ground… Inquiries may be made of … Thomas Johnson, Architect', untraced and probably unexecuted. (*LI*, 31 August 1795.)

LEEDS, Nos. 39, 40 Park Square, 1795-97, lease developed by Thomas Johnson, 1795-7. (Beresford [note 9], pp. 148-49.)

LEEDS, Quarry Hill, Mabgate, Union St., multiple ownership of cottage properties, 1799-1805, dem. (Beresford [note 9], pp. 178-79, 476).

CAWTHORNE, nr Barnsley, All Saints (C of E), proposed additions to medieval fabric, *c.*1805. (Sheffield Archives, Sp St 60736; WYASL, RD/AF/2/6/8.)

LEEDS, The Leeds Library, Commercial St., 1805-08. (The Leeds Library, *Minute Book 1800-1879*, ff. 1-6; printed 'New Library Building Account', album of bills, receipts).

LEEDS, 'House for the Librarian' (Mrs Mary Robinson), behind Commercial Street, 25 February 1805, dem. (The Leeds Library, *Minute Book 1800-1879*, ff. 7-8.)

NEWLAND HALL, nr Normanton (WY), 'Johnson's Plan for a Blacksmiths Shop & Carpenter's Shop' and various farm buildings, for Sir Edward Smith, Bart. 20 May 1807, dem. (John Goodchild Collection, Local History Study Centre, Wakefield, Newland MS, DB.)

SEWERBY HALL, nr Bridlington (EY), proposed additions of wings to early Georgian house for John Graeme, 1807-8. (Hull History Centre, Lloyd-Graeme, U DDLG/x1/30/911.)

NEWLAND HALL, nr Normanton (WY), 'Mr. Johnson's Plans of the Cottage for the Work People … proposed to be built at Newland Park' with signed and dated letter, 5 April 1808, for Sir Edward Smith, Bart., prob. unexecuted. (John Goodchild Collection, Local History Study Centre, Wakefield, Newland MS, DB.)

Misattributed Work

RASTRICK (WY), St Matthew, 1796-98, attributed variously to Johnson, P. Atkinson, C. Watson (Linstrum, *WYAA*, p. 192, pl. 147), though by J. Whittle of Manchester (Colvin, p. 1113).

4. The Architectural Profession in Leeds, 1800–1850

CHRISTOPHER WEBSTER

The subject of this chapter – the architectural profession in the late-Georgian and early-Victorian town – has a crucial sub-text: how did it come to be established and why did it grow so quickly? There was, after all, only one resident architect in Leeds in 1800 while the *Directory* of 1853 lists twenty-three firms or individuals offering their services. It raises interesting questions: why was there such a rapid increase in demand for the architects' services; from where did these men come; what were they employed to do; what training had they undertaken and is it reasonable to think of them as 'professionals' at all; what sort of status did they enjoy in the town? All these and other questions will be examined as a means of establishing the context for the working lives of the book's first group of nineteenth century architects.[1]

On one level, the growth of the architectural profession in Leeds was part of a national pattern; a study of (say) Manchester, Birmingham or Liverpool would produce broadly similar conclusions. It was during the eighteenth century that the profession established itself in London, principally building churches or working for wealthy land-owning families. According to Frank Jenkins, it was during the second half of that century that the profession emerged as 'something approaching … the pattern which we accept today.'[2] By around 1800, architects' services could be found in most of the county towns like York and Derby – still largely working for 'old' money – and by the early nineteenth century the provision was gradually spreading to the industrial centres like Leeds. The simple explanation for the establishment and growth in the profession in Leeds was that it was an

1. See also C. Webster, 'The Architectural Profession in Leeds, 1800-50: a case study in professional practice' in *Architectural History*, 38, 1995, pp. 176-91. That article includes not only more examples of the issues discussed in this chapter but also more detailed references.

2. F. Jenkins, *Architect and Patron*, Oxford U.P., 1967, p. 91.

4.1: Leeds, Commercial Buildings (John Clark, 1825-9). (*Engraving by John Lucas after a drawing by Clark, Thoresby Society.*)

integral part of the process of industrialisation; industrial prosperity produced a rapidly expanding population and created a demand for new buildings for worship, business, leisure and housing. And significantly, industrial prosperity provided the money to pay for them. Indeed, it produced the money to pay not just for plain, functional structures, but opulent ones capable of proclaiming their owner's status and Leeds' aspirations as a provincial powerhouse; this was, after all, an age when a town's status was inextricably linked to the quality of its architecture. And such ambitions were fulfilled most effectively by the services of a competent architect rather than a pretentious builder with a modest understanding of architectural design. With the exception of a handful of major buildings – some of which are discussed in Chapter 2 – most of the town's eighteenth century buildings were 'designed' by the tradesmen who erected them without any need of an architect's services. The better quality masons or joiners, aided by a well established series of pattern books published specifically to guide them, were generally able to produce a sound, if unremarkable, house or row of shops. However, in the building boom that followed the end of the wars with France, bigger, more complex structures were increasingly required and ones which displayed a sound knowledge of the latest stylistic fashions (4.1). The reign of the tradesman/designer was giving way to that of the professional architect.

The Statistics of the Leeds Profession

It will be helpful to begin by considering the statistics of the profession, based on the various *Directories* for Leeds which appeared every few years – although at irregular intervals – from a variety of publishers. The directory for 1798 fails to record Thomas Johnson's presence although he is listed in that for 1800. He was still the sole architect in the 1809 directory, but he was joined by three others in 1814, there were six in 1822, six in 1830, ten in 1837, eleven in 1843, thirteen in 1847, nineteen in 1851 and twenty-three by 1853.[3] A total of forty-one architects practised in the town either independently, or in partnership, during this half century. The provision is relatively modest before Waterloo, but there is rapid expansion in the 1830s, and even more after 1840. In addition, there are a small number of men who in various documents referred to themselves as 'architect', but, mysteriously, never appeared in a directory.[4]

How did these forty-one practitioners reach a position where they could claim membership of the profession? At the top of the quality pyramid were men like Thomas Taylor (arrived *c.*1806) and R.D. Chantrell (arrived 1819) who had undergone a thorough training in the office of a leading London architect and who chose to establish a practice in Leeds after winning a major competition in the town, and in the belief that it offered further rewards. In this category could also be placed John Clark who came from Edinburgh (arrived late 1820s) as well as Thomas Johnson who returned in 1787, having probably grown up in Leeds, discussed in Chapter 3. Between them, this quartet secured the great majority of the choice jobs that arose in the town in the first half of the century, and from their offices graduated a number of men who subsequently set out in independent practice. From Johnson's came Lawrence Ingham and Joseph Cusworth, from Taylor's, Lees Hammerton, and from Chantrell's J.P. Percy, R.W. Moore and Thomas Shaw;[5] John Child worked for both Taylor and Clark. With the exception of Child and Shaw, who went on to produce some impressive work, none of them appear to have been either especially talented or successful, but it might reasonably be assumed all of them had received instruction in the design and execution of a building project, and had had instilled in them some understanding of the architect's duties.

At the bottom of the pyramid were several men from the building trades who aspired to the greater status that the title 'architect' implied and elevated themselves accordingly. The most audacious case is that of William Lawrence. He was employed by the Doncaster architect William Lindley as a carpenter/joiner at Dennison Hall in 1786-8 (see Chapter 2) and subsequently designed and built several substantial, neat but unremarkable terraced houses in Park Square in the 1790s,

3. A comprehensive set of the relevant directories can be found in the Reference section of the Central Library, Leeds.

4. In this category could be placed Lees Hammerton, who had probably been an assistant to Thomas Taylor and completed several of Taylor's churches following the architect's death. A ' Mr Timperley' of Leeds submitted a set of drawings for the Leeds Public Baths competition in 1819.

5. Chantrell's protégées form an interesting group. Percy described himself as 'for some years assistant to Mr Chantrell', Moore was 'the late pupil of Mr Chantrell' and Shaw had been Chantrell's clerk of works throughout the rebuilding of Leeds Parish Church (1837-41). Having been an assistant, pupil or clerk of works was clearly seen as a suitable preparation for an independent career.

describing himself as 'carpenter, joiner and architect' on the leases.[6] He appears at this time in the directories as a 'joiner and cabinet maker', but in the editions of 1809, '14 and '16 he re-branded himself as 'architect'; his elevation was announced in the *Leeds Mercury* of 17 January 1807 when he informed

> his numerous Friends that he has declined the Business of Joiner and Carpenter … [and] begs Permission to offer his Service to the Public as an ARCHITECT, SURVEYOR and VALUER OF BUILDINGS, and to inform them, that he intends carrying out the Business of RAFF-MERCHANT [7] on his premises in Simpson's Fold, and shall be happy to receive a Share of their commands.

Also employed at Dennison Hall was the carpenter William Hargreaves who went on to design and build 17-19 Park Place, Leeds (*c.*1788-1800), almost identical to Lindley's mansion's façade, but rendered in brick with stone dressings, as well as other houses in the Park estate.[8] A similar pattern was subsequently followed by James Simpson (see Chapter 8). He worked as a joiner through the 1820s and early '30s while undertaking some architectural projects, but announced his membership of the profession only in 1837, apparently without any real training or office experience. Clearly this was no

6. M. Beresford, *East End, West End*, Thoresby Society, 1988, p. 474.

7. A Raff Merchant was an importer of foreign timber.

8. Beresford [note 6], p. 474.

4.2: Leeds, Stock Exchange, Albion Place (Hurst and Moffatt, 1847-9), one of several impressive buildings by this Doncaster practice which had a subsidiary office in Leeds. (*Leeds Library and Information Services.*)

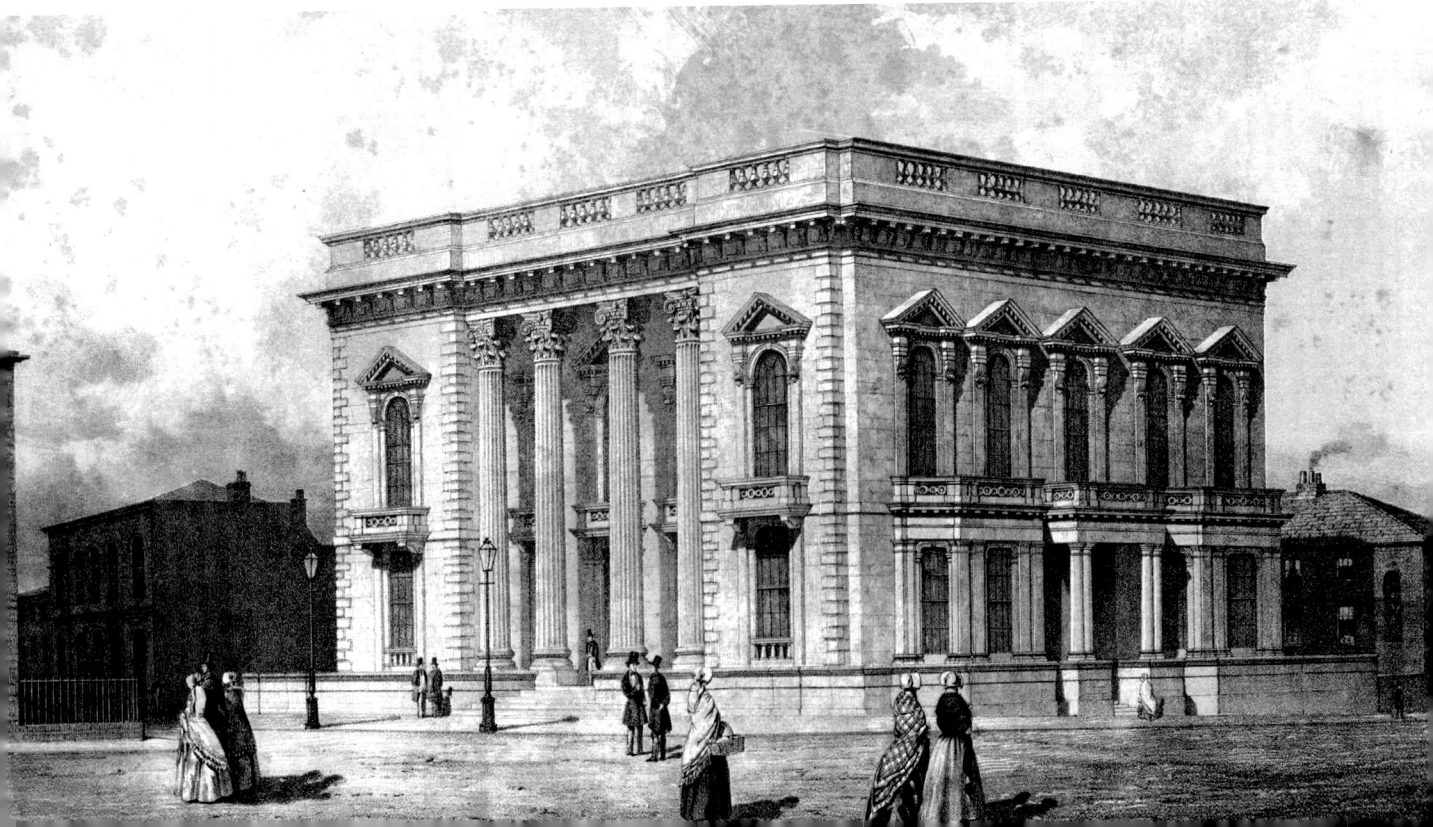

handicap and subsequently he enjoyed a hugely successful career designing Nonconformist chapels throughout the north and midlands. Even more remarkable is the case of Elisha Backhouse who trained with Benjamin Jackson in what was, essentially, an estate agent's business. He went on to form a partnership with William Perkin that dominated the profession in Leeds and the surrounding area in the middle years of the century. The duo far surpassed Brodrick for the sheer quantity of work that passed through their office, even if they could not match his artistic inventiveness.

Although Leeds was the largest and most prosperous of the West Yorkshire towns, and therefore the one that offered the greatest opportunities for a successful career, it appears only one of the forty-one architects began his career in one of the lesser towns, but graduated to Leeds. This was Perkin – whom we have just encountered – who moved from Wakefield in the early 1830s [9] and went on to have a glittering Leeds career in partnership with Backhouse. The Doncaster firm of Hurst and Moffat operated a subsidiary office in Leeds through the 1840s and secured several jobs in the town (4.2), although a similar enterprise by the York firm of R.H. and S. Sharp in the early '40s appears to have brought little reward for the brothers.[10]

What did it mean to be a provincial architect?

Although all the forty-one men practising in Leeds were listed in the directories as architects, there was no consistent understanding of what the title implied in this period. The next issue therefore concerns terminology. Nationally, such allied professions as surveying, land measuring and engineering were often associated with architecture; even rent collecting and the curing of smoking chimneys might be tasks lumped in with the designing of buildings.[11] And at a time when what we now refer to as 'estate agency' had yet to emerge, the selling and letting of land and buildings was invariably handled by a man who adopted the designation 'architect'. So far as our forty-one Leeds men were concerned, certainly some were architects in the sense that we would understand the word today: they had undergone a thorough training, ran reputable offices and seem to have offered a reliable service to the public; crucially, they did not mix the design and supervision of a project with the supply of materials or labour to execute it (see Chapter 2). Within this category can be placed Taylor, Chantrell and Clark. However, even at this end of the profession, links to the lower end of the allied activities can be found, for instance on at least one occasion Chantrell is known to have advertised the sale of a property.[12] The next tier of the profession is, perhaps predictably, more diverse. Benjamin Jackson – in practice from 1814 to his death in 1836 – is known to have produced a small number of modest designs, but

9. He first appeared in a Leeds *Directory* is 1834.

10. Colvin, pp. 915-6.

11. The issue of how architecture might best be established as a noble profession, clearly separated from the more mundane, but associated activities, was one that exercised many architects at this time. See C. Webster, *R.D. Chantrell (1793-1872)*, Spire Books, 2010, pp. 46-8.

12. E.g. *LI*, 28 June 1827.

frequently advertised the sale or letting of residential and commercial properties. He also included surveying among his expertise. He produced a road-widening scheme and incompetently supervised alterations to Hunslet Chapel.[13]

Joseph Cusworth also produced some designs for new buildings or alterations, but seems to have been more active as a surveyor and in the 1817 *Directory* describes himself as an 'architect and land surveyor'. He undertook repairs, surveys and road-widening for the Leeds Improvement Commissioners.[14] John Child had been the clerk of works for the Commercial Buildings (see Chapter 7) and must have believed this represented an adequate preparation for a professional career as he opened his own office around 1830. He designed a number of buildings, including the impressive St Anne's Roman Catholic church (4.3), but also sold building materials, let houses, offered his services as a surveyor to the Improvement Commissioners and superintended the construction of a 'reservoir, well and cesspit.'[15] J.P. Percy referred to himself in the 1820s as 'architect and civil engineer', John Cliff, in 1845 used the style 'architect, surveyor and valuer', and in 1851 James Philips described himself as 'architect and land surveyor'.[16] And there were others who occasionally designed a building, but chose an alternative professional title. For instance, Charles Fowler appeared in the 1820s and '30s directories as 'Land Surveyor' or 'Building Agent' and only from 1845 as 'Architect', whereas Josuah Major was always 'Landscape and Architectural Gardener'. Perhaps most significantly, throughout this half-century, countless newspaper advertisements appeared inviting designs for a proposed new building which started 'To Architects and Builders … '

4.3: Leeds, St Anne (RC), Park Row (John Child, 1836-8), an accomplished design by a relatively minor Leeds architect. (*Leeds Library and Information Services.*)

4.4: Leeds, Brunswick Chapel (Joseph Botham, from Sheffield, 1824-5), one of the most elegant of the many Nonconformist chapels built in the town in the first half of the nineteenth century.

13. Webster [note 1], p. 189, note 19.

14. WYASL, DB 197/241.

15. *LI*, 7 Sept. 1844.

16. *LI*, 1 Feb 1827, 28 June 1845, 25 Oct. 1851.

4.5: Leeds, Mill Hill Chapel (Unitarian), Park Row (Bowman and Crowther, (1847-8). Edward Oates, a member of the building, felt it necessary to appoint an architect from within Unitarianism and this Manchester practice had already produced some esteemed chapels for the sect. (*Vignette from J. Rapkin, Map of Leeds, 1850.*)

4.6: Leeds, Aire and Calder Navigation warehouse, Call Lane (Woodhead and Hurst of Doncaster, 1827-8), a seven-storey industrial edifice which was soundly proportioned and elegantly detailed, despite its awesome scale. (*T. Allen*, A New and Complete History of the County of York, *vol. II, 1831, opp. p. 542.*)

as if the two callings were synonymous in the context of architectural composition. As late as the middle of the century, an architect might emerge from an unlikely background. J.W. Hugall had been in business as a Leeds wine merchant before proclaiming himself an architect 'which was more in accordance with his taste'. He asserted 'I have been an architect since 1847. Before that I was an amateur.'[17] He went on to secure a modest reputation as an antiquary and church restorer.

This issue leads logically to the next: which buildings were designed by an architect who then supervised their erection, and which were

17. *LM*, 29 June 1850.

simply 'produced' by a builder? Basically, the more prestigious the building, the greater was the likelihood of an architect's involvement. Thus in this period, all the churches were designed by architects, and probably most of the Nonconformist chapels too (4.4; 4.5), although some chapels do not have an architect's name attached to them. A large market would certainly be erected from an architect's design, a row of shops probably would be and a single shop might be, although in 1842 Clark – still among the town's principal architects – was paid a modest 3 gns to alter a shop front. There is some evidence of architects designing industrial buildings too (4.6; 7.4), and logic would tend to suggest such huge projects were unlikely to be undertaken without professional supervision. The town's housing stock more than tripled between 1801 and 1851, rising from 6,882 to 21,215.[18] But how many

18. M. Beresford, 'the Face of Leeds, 1780-1914' in D. Fraser (ed.), *A History of Modern Leeds*, Manchester U.P., 1980, p. 73.

4.7: Leeds, Headingley Castle, off Headingley Lane (John Child, *c.*1843-6), a rare example of a large villa whose architect is known, but only because the first owner – Thomas English – chose to record details of the castle's erection in a stained glass window lighting the staircase: 'Johanas Child Arch. Leeds 1846'. (*Ruth Baumberg.*)

4.8: Leeds, Buckingham House, Headingley Lane (1830s), one of many substantial north Leeds villas which is clearly the work of an architect rather than a builder, although its designer is not known. (*Ruth Baumberg.*)

of the 14,000 new houses were designed by architects? The number of known architect-designed houses only just reaches double figures (4.7). This statistic has more to do with the very limited survival of records of private house building rather than because architects shunned their design. Indeed, it is likely that a significant proportion of the working lives of our architects was devoted to domestic dwellings – especially in the cases of the substantial detached villas in Headingley, Chapel Allerton and Potternewton – although rarely can the historian now do more than make reasoned attributions (4.8).[19] Generally, architects were not concerned with working-class housing,[20] a point underlined by the 1822 *Directory*. Here in the list of 'Professions and Trades' is 'Joiners and House Builders',[21] as though the two activities were synonymous. In reality, the men listed were tradesmen/developers, and certainly not architects.

How did the Leeds architects – at whatever level of the profession they occupied – keep abreast of metropolitan stylistic and professional debates? The first relevant journal was the monthly *Architectural Magazine* which had a five-year lifespan from 1834, and from 1843, weekly editions of *The Builder* and simultaneously other, similar, magazines transmitted current thinking. However, for other parts of this half century, maintaining familiarity with the latest fashions and technological innovations was more difficult. A number of largely un-illustrated magazines aimed at the general, but well-educated, reader – for instance the *Quarterly Review, Gentleman's Magazine* and *Westminster Review* – regularly carried articles about architecture, but they were essentially theoretical, aimed at the interested gentleman, and would have been of limited value to the average architect. Nevertheless, these would have been readily available at the various Leeds newsrooms for a small subscription. Most importantly, there were several

19. A number of publications have linked John Clark's name to these houses, although this writer could find no documentary evidence beyond those listed in Chapter 7.

20. However, there are exceptions. In 1832 Clark designed 'cottages' in Sheepscar, Leeds. WYASL, DB 197/287 and 197/292. Interestingly, the situation was reversed in the second half of the century, see Chapter 9.

21. E. Baines, History, *Directory and Gazetteer of the County of York ...* , Baines, 1822, p. 116.

booksellers who carried, or could order, current architectural pattern books. A typical advertisement was one from T. Inchbold, whose shop was 'under the Moot-Hall'. It was addressed 'To Architects', and included all the latest volumes from the London publisher, 'J. Taylor's Architectural Library'.[22]

Over what geographical area did the Leeds men work?

The third question concerns the geographical spread of Leeds' architectural services. Here the pattern is relatively clear: the second-rate talent – mainly those combining building design with allied activities – rarely strayed beyond the town's boundaries; the services of the more talented, 'professional' architects could be sought much further afield. This was especially true where the architect had a specialism. Thus Taylor and Chantrell, both of whom concentrated on ecclesiastical work at a time when they had few professional rivals for this type of commission, worked throughout West Yorkshire and into the neighbouring counties. John Clark, adept at the production of Classical public buildings and substantial villas, secured commissions in Bradford, Harrogate, Doncaster and Hull, produced designs – perhaps unexecuted – for buildings in Berwickshire and Manchester, and entered the Houses of Parliament competition in 1835, producing a proposal for the most expensive and prestigious project of the age. Simpson's exceptional ability as a chapel designer brought him commissions throughout Yorkshire and into several northern and midlands counties. There appears to have been a fairly rigid pattern of architects producing places of worship for only one denomination. Thus Taylor and Chantrell seem to have worked only for the Church of England, Simpson for the Nonconformists and Child largely for the Catholics.

By the middle years of the century, architectural services had become more widely available throughout the region, yet the prominent Leeds firms of Perkin and Backhouse had a huge practice supplying the full range of building types and secured work over a large area, although its ecclesiastical work was entirely for the Anglicans, apart from one Nonconformist chapel as the partnership was establishing itself.

To what extent did architects from London or other provincial towns secure work in Leeds? The simple answer is 'rarely'. The issue is discussed fully in Chapter 18, but some facts are relevant here. Of more than one hundred commissions for religious and public buildings in the town in the first half of the nineteenth century,[23] only a handful did not provide employment for a Leeds firm. Clearly the prizes on offer were sufficient to tempt architects from all over the country to enter Leeds competitions, but the town's building committees remained remarkably loyal to the men with Leeds offices. Was this simply Leeds

22. *LI*, 8 May 1820.

23. Netlam and Francis Giles' plan of Leeds of 1815 lists forty-eight churches, chapels and public buildings, whereas Charles Fowler's 1844 map listed 205. However, many of these were modest conversions of late-eighteenth century terraced houses to create banks or offices.

chauvinism, or should we conclude that, at a time when the profession generally was not always held in high esteem, there were distinct advantages in having easy access to the designer should problems occur either during or after a building's erection? Even the competition for a relatively modest project like the Public Baths in 1819 produced twelve entries, several from eminent men: six were from London – including Decimus Burton and James Elmes – and others came from Thomas Rickman from Liverpool, York's Watson and Pritchet, and Doncaster's Linley, Woodhead and Hurst. The winner, Chantrell, had recently settled in Leeds. The 1835 competition for the town's new cemetery attracted seventeen entries from a dozen towns and cities; three came from Leeds, including the winner, Clark.[24] Of the sixteen new or rebuilt churches in the parish of Leeds before 1850, eleven were by Leeds firms, and before 1842, seven out of eight were by them, despite several London architects seeking ecclesiastical work in the town. However after 1842, beginning with J.M. Derick's St Saviour's, a series of metropolitan architects enjoyed some success, including G.G. Scott (St Andrew's, 1844) (18.4) and William Railton (Holy Trinity, Meanwood, 1848-9) (4.9). It was, no doubt, the appearance of *The Ecclesiologist* (from 1841) and the birth of the Yorkshire Architectural Society (1842) that made the local committees more circumspect when it came to choosing an architect for a new church; employing a London man who came with a solid reputation as a *church* architect might avoid the censure of the newly confident army of amateur critics, emboldened by groups like the YAS. The launch of *The Builder* in 1843 and the more-or-less concurrent spread of the railway network also contributed

24. The Cemetery committee meeting of 5 August 1833 resolved to advertise the competition in the two Leeds papers plus the *Manchester Guardian*, *Liverpool Times* and 'Birmingham's best newspaper'. (LU SC MS 421, no. 33.)

4.9: Leeds, Holy Trinity, Meanwood (William Railton, 1848-9), one of a number of impressive 1840s Leeds churches by London architects. (*Leeds University Library, Special Collections.*)

to a growing national pattern of architectural awareness at the expense of local traditions and loyalties.

The 1825 competition for the Commercial Buildings – discussed more fully in Chapter 7 – also involved London architects, but it deserves examination here for a different reason: its method of rewarding its entrants. Usually, competitions for new public buildings were open to all and offered rewards for what were judged the best two, or sometimes three, designs. Prizes of 20 gns and 10 gns – with perhaps 5 gns as a third prize – was typical in the 1820s.[25] The winner could anticipate that he would also be employed to supervise the erection of his design, for which he would be paid (usually) 5% of its cost, although, as we shall see, this did not always happen. But to procure a design for the Commercial Buildings, the committee invited six architects to enter a closed competition for which each negotiated a fee; the cost was staggering. Of the three unsuccessful London entrants, Goodwin was paid £120, while Barry and Salvin each received £100. The two local men, Chantrell and Taylor received 50 gns apiece, and Clark, the winner, received no prize beyond the standard 5% of the £30,000 construction bill. The competition element of the project therefore cost the shareholders an eye-watering £425.[26] Even the 1824 competition for the massive York prison complex – which cost £195,000 to construct – offered a prize of only £100 for the countless drawings such a large project would have required.

So far, this essay has been concerned with projects mainly financed by industrial wealth. However, old-established, landowning families also prospered in this period and often engaged in building. An examination of the architects they employed is an issue that will repay attention. Even the best of the Leeds architects – despite their generally sound reputations – secured almost no employment with this group. The explanation is surely concerned with the social separation that existed between old and new money. The situation is neatly explained by William White, writing in 1837:

> Though Leeds was formerly connected with some of the principal families of the West Riding, some of whom made it their place of residence, others sustained offices in its Corporation and others interested themselves in the transactions of its affairs, it has long been totally abandoned by the aristocracy. Three distinguished noble families reside within a few miles of it [at Harewood, Temple Newsam and Methley] but are seldom seen in its streets; the independence of manufacturing wealth being inconsistent with both the pride and dignity of rank.[27]

25. These were the prizes offered for designs for the new Public Rooms in Wakefield in 1820 (*LM*, 13 May 1820). Later on, for the 1847 restoration of St Mary, Scarborough, £50, £30 and £20 were offered (*LM*, 20 March 1847).

26. The building accounts are in TS, Library Drawer B.

27. W. White, *History, Gazetteer and Directory of the West Riding*, White, 1837, p. 496.

4.10: Oulton, near Leeds, St John (Rickman and Hutchinson, 1827-9), an expensive church, paid for by John Blayds of Oulton Hall, designed by the country's best Gothic exponent of the decade. (*Leeds Library and Information Services.*)

The successful Leeds industrialists were certainly wealthy, but their middle-class status could not be denied and their rise had produced a reciprocal retreat of the upper classes. One way in which old money could exercise its perceived superiority was in its employment of architects: an architect associated with industrial wealth was, *ipso facto*, likely to be denied work for landowning families. Thus, within fifteen miles of Leeds, all the major country house work went to London offices: Bretton Hall was extended by Jeffrey Wyatville (*c.*1815), Methley Hall was substantially remodelled by Anthony Salvin (1830-6), Decimus Burton enlarged Grimston Park (1840) and Charles Barry modernised Harewood (1843).

The architectural ambitions of those members of Leeds' industrial elite who wished to elevate themselves to the ranks of the rural or suburban gentry reveals a more complex pattern of employment. Benjamin Gott, perhaps the most successful of the early-nineteenth century mill-owners, employed the eminent London architect Robert Smirke to remodel Armley House (*c.*1818) and used Humphrey Repton to lay out his gardens a decade earlier (18.1). Yet when Gott wished to add a family chapel to his local church in Armley (1823-5), he employed Chantrell. Chantrell was also used for rebuilding the entire church in the 1830s – supported by Gott –and, almost certainly, it was Chantrell who designed the school and almshouses in Armley for which Gott paid. But in 1833, seeking to alter nearby Wyther Grange for his son John, he went to C.R. Cockerell in London.[28] At around the same time as their Armley work, Smirke and Repton were also employed at Oulton Hall, a few miles south of Leeds, for John Blayds whose money came from a Leeds banking family. In 1827, he decided to build a church on his estate and again went to a figure of national importance: Thomas Rickman (4.10). However, for his new stable block in 1837, he went to Clark, by this time the principal architect in Leeds, but two years later, when he wanted to enlarge his house, he returned to a Londoner. Smirke had more or less retired, but his younger brother Sydney was offered the job. Finally, when a fire destroyed much of the house in 1850, reconstruction was placed in the hands of the prominent Leeds firm Perkin and Backhouse.[29] Clark was also employed to create the two most ambitious suburban villas for Leeds' industrial wealth in the 1830s – Meanwood Hall (7.13) for Christopher Beckett, a banker (c.1834) and Gledhow Grove (7.12), for John Hives, a flax spinner (1835-40). The only identified case where a Leeds architect worked for 'the landed interest' comes in Chantrell's extensive project to complete Rudding Park, near Harrogate (after 1824-*c.*1835). This was for Sir Joseph Radcliffe, 2nd baronet, whose wealth just about qualified as 'old money'. A further indication of the class divide is that there are no known instances of any Leeds architects being employed in York – only twenty-four miles away – a city that

28. John Goodchild MSS, Gott Box 1, letter, 31 Dec. 1835.

29. For Oulton, see Giles Worsley, 'Oulton Hall', *Country Life*, 17 Sept. 1987.

still prided itself as the county town, with all the overtones of a social centre for the landed aristocracy and gentry that is implied by the designation. There is one notable exception: following the disastrous fire at York Minster in 1829, it was Chantrell from Leeds rather than any of the eminent York architects, who accompanied the archbishop as he toured the ruins.[30]

What was the architects' status in Leeds?

The final area of enquiry seeks to establish the status – both socially and as providers of a professional service to the public – that was enjoyed by the architects who worked in Leeds in this period. At least some of them can be identified as respectable members of the middle class: five owned shares in the Leeds Library; probably three were members of the Leeds Philosophical and Literary Society; four were members of a Masonic Lodge; two served as Commissioners for the Leeds Improvement Act and one was a churchwarden. However, despite these trappings of respectability, the profession's public reputation was not always secure. Writing to the *Intelligencer's* editor in 1848, after more than twenty years' successful practice in the town, John Clark, clearly in disgruntled mood, felt obliged 'to bring

30. The post-fire inspection was given substantial coverage in the London *Morning Post*, 9 Feb. 1829 and *The Standard*, 9 Feb. 1829, as well as in a range of provincial papers, including the *Bury and Norwich Post*, 11 Feb. 1829 and *Newcastle Courant*, 14 Feb. 1829. All quoted Chantrell's survey of the damage and his estimate that rebuilding would cost £60-70,000. However, there is no indication Chantrell received any paid employment in connection with the subsequent restoration.

4.11: Leeds, Briggate, showing the Corn Exchange by the little-known Leeds architect Samuel Chapmen who won the 1826 competition. It replaced William Etty's demolished early eighteenth century Moot Hall (2.1). Facing it is a neat block of four shops which might have been by any of the town's 1820s architects. (*T. Allen*, A New and Complete History of the County of York, *vol. II, 1831, opp. p. 537.*)

4.12: Leeds, Commercial Buildings, one on Clark's competition drawings which shows the Newsroom, 1825. (*Thoresby Society*.)

prominently [to] the public attention, and to expose the evils of the hollow, mis-called system of competitions which has unhappily gained a footing in Leeds as well as elsewhere, – a system as injurious to architecture and its professors as it is disgraceful to all who sanction it.'[31] Two decades earlier, Taylor too hinted at his dissatisfaction with this system of securing a design; in answer to rumours he had submitted a scheme for the proposed Corn Exchange (4.11), he replied that his ecclesiastical commissions kept him too busy to make 'plans for speculation.'[32] Perhaps Taylor's attitude is understandable as only a few months earlier he had entered the competition for the Commercial Buildings in Leeds (4.1, 4.12), only to discover that the winner – Clark, an architect then unknown in Leeds – had, apparently, been selected *before* the competition was announced.[33] Thus, whatever the drawbacks of the system, Clark had initially done rather well out of it and it seems his 1848 complaint was prompted by his failure to win any of four recent competitions he entered. Nevertheless, Clark's grumbles cannot be dismissed merely as pique; it was a system ripe for abuse as the following cases illustrate.

In 1820, it was announced that Leeds was to have three new churches financed by the 1818 Church Building Act (4.13). These were to be huge buildings with big budgets and the jobs were eagerly sought. One of the trio of successful architects was C.A. Busby from London. Busby was an associate of Francis Goodwin – also London-based – who had earlier been so successful at securing work from the Act's commissioners that they questioned his ability to manage simultaneously so many projects throughout the country, and concluded he should have no more for the time being. Unwilling to

31. *LI*, 26 Feb. 1848. This concerned the competition for the proposed Leeds Industrial Schools. For further correspondence on the issue see *LI*, 4, 11 and 18 March. Equally damaging for the profession's standing was the publicly aired fallout over the Leeds Gaol competition, discussed in Webster [note 1], p. 186.

32. *LI*, 8 Sept. 1825.

33. For a full account, see Beckwith, p. 69.

4.13: Leeds, St Mark, Woodhouse (Atkinson and Sharp, 1823-5). This York firm secured one of the three big-budget projects awarded to Leeds by the Church Building Commission. (*Leeds University Library, Special Collections.*)

see these prizes slip through his fingers, Goodwin induced other architects to submit his designs as their own, on condition the fee would be divided between them. Busby subsequently claimed Goodwin had proposed such an arrangement for the Leeds church and that when the Leeds local committee invited architects to meet it, Busby was shocked to find another architect who also had three sets of plans prepared by Goodwin and another with a letter of introduction from him, each unknown to the other.[34]

There appears to have been skulduggery over the selection of an architect for the new Central Market in 1824[35] (1.6) and for the 1835 competition for the new Workhouse, William Perkin's winning design was eventually sidelined – as was that of the winner of the second prize – and a plan by a 'favourite candidate [Clark]' was 'approved by the parish authorities.'[36] However, the most outrageous case – and one fully rehearsed before the *Intelligencer's* readers – concerned the new Borough Gaol at Armley (4.14) The 1843 competition for this big budget project[37] was won by Hurst and Moffat of Doncaster, with Perkin and Backhouse placed second. The guardians were unwilling to pay the usual 5% commission for such an expensive building and as Hurst and Moffat were equally unwilling to compromise, Perkin and Backhouse were invited to erect Hurst and Moffat's design – which, by this time, had received the approval of the Secretary of the Home Department in London – the guardians claiming that, having paid the winning architects their prize, the plans were rightfully theirs. Worse still, the Inspector of Prisons suggested additional accommodation was desirable, so Perkin and Backhouse were invited to submit a fundamentally new design with a larger budget. Clark – one of the unsuccessful entrants – not unreasonably enquired publicly why all the other entrants were denied the chance to submit revised schemes.[38]

34. The episode is recounted in M. Port, 'Francis Goodwin (1784-1835)' in *Architectural History*, 1, 1958, p. 66.

35. C. Webster, *R.D. Chantrell (1793-1872) and the architecture of a lost generation*, Spire Books, 2010, pp. 94-6.

36. *Architectural Magazine*, 2, 1835, pp. 484-5.

37. 'About £40,000', according to the *Directory of Leeds … and the Clothing District*, William White, 1853, p. 18. In 1843, such a sum would build ten substantial churches.

38. *LI*, 26 Aug., 11 Nov. 1843; 11 March 1848.

Nevertheless, and despite the unsavoury dealings just discussed, by the middle of the century there existed in Leeds what we can reasonably understand as a coherent group of men calling themselves 'architect' and offering a service which the public could identify. During the decades covered by this chapter, the emergence of the profession, its establishment and its growth can be understood in a number of different contexts. Certainly it was a part of the wider move towards 'professionalisation' in the nineteenth century which is confirmed by the parallel increase of (say) accountants, insurance brokers and lawyers. But the expansion of the architectural profession can also be explained by its having subsumed a wide range of more or less allied occupations which ranged from assessing rents and selling curtains at one extreme, to surveying and civil engineering at the other. No doubt it was the superior status which the term 'architect' implied, with its overtones of intellectual and artistic ability, along with implication of taste and connoisseurship, and the chance of fame and wealth, that encouraged

4.14: Leeds, Borough Goal, Armley (Perkin and Backhouse, 1843-7). (*Leeds Library and Information Services.*)

4.15: Leeds, New Wortley National School and Master's house (C.W. Burleigh, 1848). This was one of a large number of new schools erected in the 1840s and 1850s. (*Leeds Library and Information Services.*)

those lower down the ladder to adopt the title architect. And at a time when a career could be established just by renting an office, placing a brass plate on the door and announcing one's 'arrival' in Leeds in a newspaper advertisement, perhaps those whose claim to membership of the profession had little foundation can be forgiven their presumption. Certainly there were some who failed as they appear to have received no commissions at all.[39]

The third compelling explanation for the profession's growth is that it came to be seen as an essential component in the building process. Even for blunt Yorkshire businessmen, the extra 5% the architect charged was deemed value for money. It provided a fashionable design at a time when even a modest project could be seen as an 'ornament' to this aspirational town; perhaps more significantly, it was seen as the best way to police the worst excesses of the building trades and protect the interests of the client. Especially if the client was a public body or committee, the rule by the middle of the century was clear: where public money was being spent on, for instance, a school (4.15), a market or a place of worship, the services of an architect were essential to manage the project, control the finances and thus ensure transparency.

It might appear, then, that by the middle of the century, the architectural profession was firmly established and the account of its development complete. However, as we shall see in Chapter 9, several issues remained to be addressed in the second half of the century: college-based architectural education, regulation of the profession, and the need for a recognised body to represent the interests of architects. And as the town continued to prosper, both the centre and suburbs would see radical building projects, several of which necessitated the demolition of buildings from the first half of the century.

39. The 'Births, Marriages and Deaths' columns of the local papers contain countless references to the rites of 'Mr A. Name, architect' as if it was a positive designation like 'gentleman'.

5. *Thomas Taylor* *(1777 or 8 – 1826)*

CHRISTOPHER WEBSTER

Thomas Taylor[1] was the second London-trained architect to establish a successful practice in Leeds. However, unlike his predecessor Johnson who is now largely forgotten – despite a handful of impressive buildings – Taylor's reputation survived the battering of the Victorians and he now occupies a discernable, if modest, role on the Gothic Revival stage. He was a pioneer as a designer of churches that were of exceptional quality in the second and third decades of the nineteenth century. St Lawrence, Pudsey (1821-4), his biggest surviving church, is a remarkably stately building.

In 1811, he placed the following advertisement in the *Leeds Intelligencer*:

THOMAS TAYLOR, *ARCHITECT FROM LONDON*, begs leave to inform the Nobility and Gentry of the County of York, that his Designs having been approved for the New Court House, in Leeds, this, with his other Engagements in the County, will render him stationary in Leeds, where he will be happy to receive the Commands of those who may Occasion for his Professional Services, in which he flatters himself enabled to give every Satisfaction, as during a Period of Eight Years Practice under Mr James Wyatt, the present Surveyor-General, he was in the Habit of making Plans, Elevations and Sections, for executing some of the most distinguished Buildings in the Kingdom, and from Five Years Practice under Mr Andrews, builder of eminence in London, previous to being with Mr Wyatt, he is enabled to calculate Estimates upon an unerring Principle. And

1. Taylor was the subject of a monograph by Frank Beckwith in 1949, an almost unique occurrence for a late-Georgian provincial architect at that time. Its writer produced an impeccable piece of research, trawling a huge range of sources for the facts of Taylor's life and work. However, writing at a time when little work had been done on this, then unfashionable, period of architectural history, not unreasonably he struggled to contextualise adequately Taylor's work, and seemed to have lacked the confidence to make more than very limited praise of his subject's achievements. Nevertheless, the book contains much valuable factual information which need not be repeated here. F. Beckwith, *Thomas Taylor, Regency Architect, Leeds*, Thoresby Society, 1949.

farther trusts from having made careful Studies of all the superior French Buildings, he is enabled to arrange Architectural Decorations in a superior Style; Specimens of which may be seen in several distinguished Mansions in this Neighbourhood … [executed] during the Six years he has been in Yorkshire.[2]

The advertisement raises a number of questions: what might he have done while in Wyatt's office; what experience had he had of France; what were these 'unerring Principles' for preparing estimates; what brought him to Yorkshire and what had he done in the previous six years? All these issues will be addressed presently.

On the face of it, the advertisement supplies the key biographical details of his pre-Leeds life, and Beckwith,[3] not unreasonably, concluded the following: he joined Mr Andrews in 1791 or 2 – aged 13 or 14 – moved to Wyatt in 1796 or 7 and eight years later – around 1805 – moved to Leeds where he had spent the six years prior to 1811. It all fits! However, the *Catalogues* for Royal Academy shows, where Taylor exhibited regularly, place him in Wyatt's office by 1792. If he stayed for eight years, he would have left by 1800 or perhaps earlier, and there is thus an unexplained five year gap before he arrived in Leeds,[4] and if he was born in 1778 – as his obituary suggests – did he really enter Andrew's employment aged only eight? A partial explanation is that he was older than his friends who supplied information for the obituary thought, but this does not explain the entire post-Wyatt period.[5] But at whatever his age when he entered Andrews' employment, it is reasonable to conclude an apprentice in a trade as common as building would be unlikely to move far from the parental home, and this suggests Taylor was a Londoner.

In the context of his subsequent career, especially his pioneering Gothic churches, it is rewarding to consider what he would have learnt in Wyatt's office, especially as we now know he was there through the 1790s whereas Beckwith believed him to have arrived four or five years later. Wyatt had an exceptionally busy practice, but was, apparently, disorganised and un-businesslike, and relied on a large number of assistants who just about managed to keep the business from disaster. He had spent five years studying in Italy and his early work can be located in the mid-Georgian Classical tradition, but later he was equally adept with Gothic, and designed some of the earliest Gothic Revival mansions. He was also was an early restorer of cathedrals. While Taylor was in his office, he was engaged on restorations at Salisbury, Hereford, Durham and Ely cathedrals, St George's Chapel, Windsor, and was erecting the seminal Gothic palaces Belvior Castle (Leics), Ashridge (Herts) and Fonthill Abbey (Wilts). All these commissions would have familiarised Taylor with the repertoire of Gothic and so far as the design of churches was concerned, a rare Wyatt essay in this genre – at East

2. *LI*, 9 Sept. 1811.

3. Beckwith [note 1], pp. 11-12.

4. The R.A. *Catalogues,* in which he was always listed as 'Painter' not architect, give his addresses as follows: various London addresses, 1792-8; Oxford, 1799; various London addresses, 1800-9. He gave a Leeds address only in 1810, although he exhibited Yorkshire scenes in 1808 and '9. No address was given for 1811, the last year he exhibited at the R.A. (A. Graves, *The Royal Academy of Arts … Exhibitors*, E.P. Publishing, 1970, vol. 3, pp. 340-1.)

5. Taylor's obituary (*LI*, 30 March 1826) records his age as 48 and implies birth around 1778.

6. A. Dale, *James Wyatt, Architect 1746-1813*, Basil Blackwell, 1936, pp. 84–5.

7. I am grateful to Geoffrey Forster for this information which arose in a conversation he had with the usually reliable Professor Maurice Beresford.

8. He appears in the 1809 *Directory*, but is not in that for 1807. However Beresford notes him in Leeds by 1802. M. Beresford 'The Birth of Commercial Street' in *The Dial: The Leeds Library Magazine*, 3, 1993, p. 7.

5.1: Thornhill, WY, St Michael, The Saville Chapel, engraving by W. Smith after a drawing by Taylor. (*T.D. Whitacker*, Loidis and Elmete, *Robinson, Son and Holdsworth, 1816, opp. p. 320.*)

Grinstead in Sussex – was completed around the time Taylor entered the office. Its details – as we shall see – constantly reappear in Taylor's work. Antony Dale, Wyatt's first biographer, notes the master was 'forced at great expense to employ draughtsmen to visit the celebrated monastic and baronial structures of England and to make detailed drawings of their decoration,'[6] and Taylor's talents were almost certainly exploited in this way, a point that will be addressed shortly.

What brought Taylor to Yorkshire? The 1811 advertisement is silent on the issue. Perhaps Taylor had been involved with Wyatt's Ripon Town Hall (1798-9), or had been sent to York to record the Minster's details. And it has been suggested[7] that Jonathan Taylor, a land surveyor with an office in Commercial Street, Leeds, from around 1800,[8] was Thomas's brother.

What employment did Taylor receive in Leeds from 1805? There is scant evidence of architectural commissions, but plenty that he was

busy as an artist: he was talented, prolific and successful. The Leeds based Northern Society for the Promotion of the Fine Arts organised its first exhibition in 1809 and others followed at irregular intervals.[9] From the beginning Taylor was a loyal supporter showing large numbers of paintings[10] as he had done earlier at the Royal Academy.[11] These included landscapes and what might have been 'fancy pictures' in the George Morland tradition,[12] but the biggest group were architectural. They provide clear evidence he visited Northern France where he drew modern as well as medieval structures,[13] but they were primarily of British medieval buildings produced while in Wyatt's employment, as well as views of Yorkshire abbeys and major churches no doubt largely produced after 1805. From what little information survives concerning sales, it seems Taylor was held in high esteem.[14]

It is surely significant that, at the start of 1810, when Taylor joined a Masonic lodge, he chose to record his profession as 'artist' rather than architect.[15] It is thus likely that much of first few years in Leeds was spent in this capacity. Revd T.D. Whitaker chose Taylor as the principal supplier of illustrations – others were commissioned from Turner – for his magisterial *Loidis and Elmet* and *Ducatus Leodiensis*, both of which were published in 1816 and are known to have been the product of many years preparation.[16] (2.3; 2.10; 3.9; 5.1) Although some of Taylor's fine plates show modern buildings, many more illustrate the area's medieval churches in a series of outstanding atmospheric perspective views – most engraved by John le Keux, generally regarded as the finest of the period's engravers – comparable with those that appeared in John Britton's many superbly illustrated volumes. Especially impressive are his views of Kirkstall Abbey and the interior of the Saville Chapel at Thornhill, near Dewsbury, both in *Loidis*.

Taylor even had ambitions to publish his own book of illustrations of Yorkshire's rich medieval past. In a pamphlet he published in 1813[17] he included the following:

> In [Liversedge church] I have ... followed the most simple Gothic style to be met with in Churches and Monastic Buildings in this county; and, I believe, the County of York can, in this respect, vie with any other district in the United Kingdom. I offer this observation with a degree of confidence and pride; as being the result of visits and numerous architectural drawings, which I have made of these buildings during the eight years I have been in Yorkshire. These drawings are intended for a publication of the Monastic Architecture of this county [and] of course have been attended to in an architectural way, in preference to the *tout ensemble* which has been the general mode of portraying these valuable relics of our ancient, and certainly original style of architecture.[18]

9. For the Northern Society, see T. Fawcett, *The Rise of English Provincial Art*, Clarendon Press, 1974, pp. 168-70.

10. Taylor exhibited at the exhibitions in 1809, 1810, 1811, 1822, 1823 and 1826. Copies of the Society's *Catalogues* are held in Leeds Central Library.

11. He exhibited a total of 58 items at the Royal Academy from 1792 to 1811, missing only 1807. Graves [note 4].

12. For landscapes, 1809, no 62 was 'Pontaberglasslyn' [Pont Aberglaslyn, Gwynedd] and items 167 and 169 carried the same title 'A Cottage Scene'. Probably these were the same two paintings as items 183 and 184 in the 1810 exhibition which had the same title.

13. In 1809 he showed 'View of Paris' (no. 174), in 1810 'Sketch of the City of Amiens' (no. 190), in 1811 ''Sketch of the Pantheon, Paris' (no. 193) and in 1822 'View of the Pantheon at Paris' (no. 179).

14. Taylor's 1822 exhibit, no. 205, 'Interior of the Cathedral at York showing the Screen and Choir' was bought by the leading collector John Sheepshanks. (For Sheepshanks, see F. Davis, *Victorian Patrons of the Arts*, Country Life, 1963, pp. 74-9.) Taylor's 1823 exhibit, no. 54, 'York Cathedral, view of Transept', was sold for £20 putting it among the most expensive works on show. By way of contrast, Anthony Salvin's 'Bambrough Castle', no. 33, sold for just 4 gns.

15. Taylor joined the Lodge of Fidelity in Leeds on 29 January 1810. A. Scarth and C.A. Brown, *A History of the Lodge of Fidelity*, Beck and Inchbold, 1894, p. 210.

16. Beckwith [note 1] refers to them as 'published at long last', p. 39.

17. Taylor's pamphlet formed part of Revd Hammond Roberson's *An Account of the Ceremony of Laying the First Stone of Christ's Church, now building in Liversedge*, privately printed, 1813, pp. 63-71.

18. Roberson [note 17].

The passage implies Taylor had exceptional knowledge of these buildings, but even more interesting is his proposed mode of delineation. It is assumed that by *'tout ensemble'* Taylor meant perspective views where landscape was an important ingredient, and that by intending to show them in 'an architectural way', he implied they would be in plan, elevation and section. The project must have been abandoned, but had the book appeared it would have been ground breaking. Britton had already published several volumes in his *Architectural Antiquities* series (1807-26) and had in preparation the *Cathedral Antiquities* series (1814-35), all of which had a number of architectural drawings alongside the perspective views. However, Britton's market was clearly antiquarian rather than the architectural and only in later volumes does he appear to identify potential sales to architects. Closer to what Taylor had in mind were F. MacKenzie and A. Pugin's *Specimens of Gothic Architecture … at Oxford*, of 1816[19] and in the 1820s, Pugin's solo effort, *Specimens of Gothic Architecture*,[20] but Taylor would have been well ahead of these writers. Yorkshire's monastic remains had to wait another thirty-one years until Richardson and Churton illustrated them.[21]

An intriguing advertisement appeared in the *Mercury* in 1816 advertising 'Three Novel, Interesting and Popular LECTURES on the ARCHITECTURE and other REMAINS of England and Wales as connected with the earliest periods of our National History, illustrated with a considerable number of large Drawings, from Aboriginal, Roman, Saxon, and Norman remains in Britain.'[22] They were organised by Edward Baines, but the lecturer is not recorded. Could it have been anyone but Taylor, especially as the advertisement mentions Welsh buildings, a topic largely overlooked by the period's antiquaries, but something that featured in several Taylor paintings?

Taylor's secular work

Of the 'several distinguished mansions in this neighbourhood' in Taylor's 1811 advertisement, nothing specific can be linked to him, although there are a number of country houses from the first decade of the century with which he might have been associated, for instance Rudding Park, near Harrogate, begun in 1807, and attributed by Hussey to 'the Wyatt school'.[23] Taylor's known early employment in Leeds – apart from the repairs at Leeds Parish Church, to which we will turn presently – is entirely artistic and antiquarian, but his move into the mainstream of architectural practice was confirmed by his appointment to build the new Leeds Court House in 1811. A public meeting in February 1809 resolved to apply for an Act of Parliament for a new courthouse and prison which was secured in only a few months.[24] The site, at the bottom of Park Row in what is now City

19. Published by J. Taylor.

20. Two volumes, 1820-2, published by Nattali.

21. W. Richardson and E. Churton, *The Monastic Ruins of Yorkshire*, 2 vols, Robert Sunter, 1843.

22. *LM*, 10 Feb. 1816. The lectures were to take place on 20, 21 and 22 February.

23. C. Hussey, *English Country Houses Late Georgian*, Antique Collectors' Club, 1984, p. 74.

24. The details can be found in Beckwith [note 1], p. 18-20.

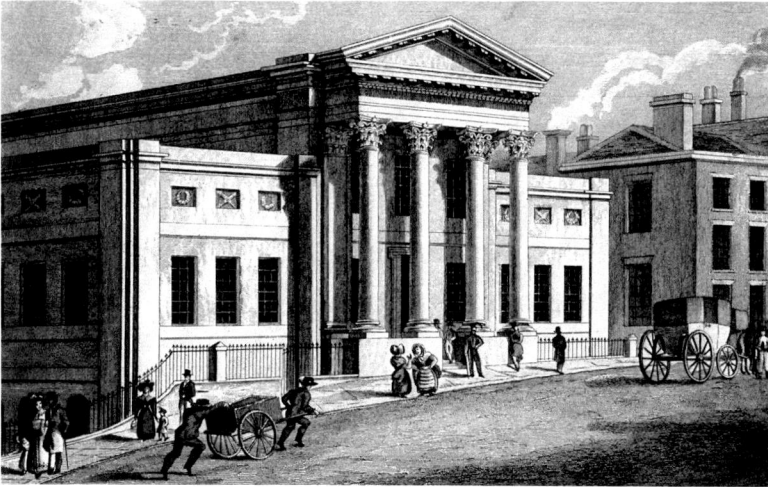

5.2: Leeds, Court House (Thomas Taylor, 1811-13). (*T. Allen*, A New and Complete History of the County of York, *I. T. Hinton, 1829-31, vol II, opp. p. 529.*)

Square, was announced in late 1810, Taylor was appointed in mid-1811 and invited tenders in August. The career shift from artist to architect corresponds with Taylor's appearance in the 'Architects' lists in the local *Directories*: he does not appear in the 1809 volume but is in the next one, published in 1814. It places his office in Commercial Street where it remained for the rest of his career.

The Court House was a handsome building distinguished by a *tetrastyle* Corinthian portico and plainer wings,[25] but architecturally it was a building of little originality that might suggest it was an early – perhaps the first – executed work of its author (5.2). The 'extra' (lower) storey of the side elevation is not satisfactorily resolved with the two-storey principal façade, an issue high-lighted by the awkwardly detailed, apparently baseless, corner pilasters. Nevertheless, it was an important statement of Leeds' aspirations as a regional centre, it was enthusiastically reported in the newspapers, and it announced Taylor's ambitions as a serious challenger for Johnson's architectural crown. Further secular commissions soon arrived in his office, indeed there was almost a decade which runs from the start of construction on the Court House – a time when Johnson seems not to have been much engaged in the town – to the early 1820s – by which time Chantrell was comfortably established – when Taylor had only limited competition. Inevitably, private commissions were rarely recorded but he must have designed several of the villas, terraces and commercial buildings constructed in Leeds in this period.

At a time when architects' estimates were widely believed to wholly unreliable, Taylor's ability 'to calculate estimates on an unerring principle'[26] was likely to have much enhanced his status. His methodology can be seen in the surviving archives of the Church Building Commission; whereas most architects' estimates comprise

25. A detailed description can be found in *LM*, 9 Oct. 1813, and repeated more-or-less verbatim in the 1817 *Directory ... of Leeds*, reprinted in Beckwith [note 1], pp. 20-1.

26. Quoted above, *LI*, 9 September 1811.

only global sums for (say) carpentry or masonry, Taylor's include huge amounts of detail. Usually he enumerates the quantity of each component, its unit price and thus the actual cost of every single item of the labour and materials in a particular project, involving many pages of manuscript.

In the post-Waterloo drive for better educational provision, Taylor successfully secured many of the available commissions, including all four in Leeds. Invariably, budgets were exceedingly tight and he developed a pared down 'Tudor' repertoire which at least gave a modicum of historical resonance to the façades. The first was the Lancastrian School, Leeds, for which he produced a design in October 1811 – 'much admired for its elegant simplicity' – and 'offered his services to undertake the architectural department gratuitously.'[27] Joseph Lancaster's system was enthusiastically supported by dissenters and the new institution seems to have galvanised Anglicans to offer an alternative: a National School. Again, Taylor was to be the architect. The building, which stood on the site of the old Tythe Barn in Kirkgate, west of the parish church, opened in February 1813 and cost £1,208-6-6d.[28] In considering how best to arrange the proposed institution, the Leeds committee 'made frequent applications to other [provincial societies] and sent Mr Taylor … to Durham to inspect the admirable schools, conducted there, under the superintendence of Rev. Bowyer … and to take plans of their furniture and arrangement.'[29] Further rejuvenation of educational provision soon followed: the Charity School, which had stood since 1726 in St John's churchyard, was rebuilt by Taylor in 1815-17 in a 'beautiful Gothic style'.[30] Remarkably, the building survives as Age Concern's Leeds base. Finally, the Grammar School, Leeds' premier educational establishment, was 'greatly enlarged'[31] under Taylor's guidance in 1822 which, among other things, included the east porch and elegant bell turret[32] (5.3). Taylor

27. *LM*, 5 October 1811, reporting a public meeting. The school stood in Alfred Street, near the present railway station. It cost £2,092. Further details can be found in T.D. Whitaker, *Loidis and Elmet*, Robinson, Son and Holdsworth, 1816, pp. 73-4.

28. The cost is given in Beckwith [note 1], p. 27, although he gives no source for the information.

29. *LM*, 15 May 1813, included in the school's First Report. See also Whitaker [note 27], p. 74.

30. *LI*, 30 Dec. 1816.

31. T. Allen, *A New and Complete History of the County of York*, I.T. Hinton, vol. II, 1831, p. 517.

32. WYASL, DB/197/196. Taylor was paid £25-10-0 for 'repairs' in 1823, but this might refer to a separate job. WYASL DB197/2.

5.3: Leeds, Free (Grammar) School, alterations including porch and clock turret by Taylor, 1822.

also designed a new National School for Birstall, opened in 1819 (5.4), and used the same design for the school at nearby Liversedge.[33] He also designed a National School for girls, finished by January 1824, adjacent to his new church in Sheffield.[34]

Another feature of northern industrial towns in this period was the desire to improve facilities for commerce, industry and marketing; sometimes buildings of considerable extent were the result.[35] An early example was announced in 1812 and concerned 'Intended Improvements on the River Aire' in Leeds. Merchants and others were informed that a substantial plot of land between the Calls and the river 'containing about 8,000 yards', was to be sold as a whole or on 'Building Leases, subject to a plan already assigned, for the erection of Warehouses, Wharfs, with the Excavation of a Basin, with a Carriage Road from … Kirkgate.' The plans were to be seen at Mr Taylor's office.[36] A decade later, a broadly similar project emerged in Rochdale where Taylor was highly regarded following his work on the local parish church. A consortium proposed a new market place for the town and an advertisement invited tenders for 'Removing certain buildings in the Town' and 'carrying into Execution the Approved Design' according to plans prepared by Taylor.[37] An 1825 *Directory* confirmed 'a new market place has just been completed.'[38]

33. *LM*, 17 April 1819.

34. Beckwith [note 1], p. 54, quoting Allen [note 31].

35. Somewhat ironically, Beckwith tends to group these as 'minor work', perhaps because he saw them as a diversion from the more serious ecclesiastical commissions.

36. *LM*, 9 Sept. 1812, repeated on 3 Oct. 17 Oct. and 14 Nov. It also appeared in *LI*, 28 Sept. 1812.

37. *LM*, 1 February 1823.

38. E. Baines, *History, Directory and Gazetteer … of Lancashire*, Wales and Co., II, 1825, p. 534.

5.4: Birstall, near Leeds, former National School (Thomas Taylor, 1819). *(Author.)*

Schemes like these could lead to extensive building, but to what extent was Taylor likely to be involved? Although generalities might be misleading, a likely scenario is this: an individual or group of developers seeking to 'improve' an area would engage an architect initially to confirm their ambitions were practical and to produce drawings of the proposed development. However, the architect had a second essential function: the more impressive he could make the finished project appear – through elevation drawings or, best of all, seductive perspective views – the more likely it was to attract buyers or investors and thus succeed as a speculation. Yet while his designs had to be stylish, they needed to be capable of realisation without incurring excessive cost. By putting his name to a project and inviting potential buyers to his office, ostensibly to ask practical questions, the architect hoped that purchasers would subsequently appoint him for as much of the scheme as they planned to develop personally. However, only rarely did purchase commit a speculator to carry out a specific design and often, once contracts were signed, a purchaser was free to build as he pleased – using whatever architect he wanted – within only fairly general parameters. The development of the area around what is now Commercial Street in Leeds usefully illustrates the point. In 1802 it was advertised for sale, sensibly divided into suitable-sized building plots. Plans were to be seen on Thomas Johnson's office (see Chapter 3) and he must have anticipated some employment from it. Certainly he was appointed for the Leeds Library's new edifice that was erected on the street in 1807-8, but it was Taylor who designed the Union Bank which faced it. Tenders for the bank were invited in November 1812 and its shell was completed in only seven weeks, much to the delight of the partners, one of whom was Thomas Nicholson who was either about to commence a major programme of building, or perhaps had already started it, on the huge estate in Roundhay which he acquired in 1803.

Who was Nicholson's architect at Roundhay? It is an issue that has long exercised Leeds' architectural historians, much of the confusion stemming from the statement in *Goodall's Illustrated Royal Handbook to Roundhay Park* – published in 1872 to commemorate the official opening of the estate as a publicly owned park – that 'the mansion was erected from the designs of Mr Clark of York'.[39] This can easily be refuted: John Clark (see Chapter 7) did not arrive in Leeds until well after the buildings were completed, and anyway was not from York. A map of the estate dated 1825 – interestingly by Jonathan Taylor, Thomas's putative brother who had also surveyed the estate in 1803, soon after purchase – shows all the main buildings, including the mansion (5.5), stable block (5.6), workshops, cottages, gate lodges on Wetherby Road and the 'castle', to have been completed. It seems likely they had already stood some time as an account of 1807 refers to

5.5: Leeds, Rounday Park Mansion (attrib. Thomas Taylor, c.1815) (*Ruth Baumberg.*)

Nicholson being in the process of 'embellishing [the estate] at no small expense', a letter of 1816 states 'The Nicholsons are completely settled in their new House', and a publication of 1927 notes 'Thomas Nicholson built the Mansion in 1815'.[40] Given these dates, it is conceivable that Nicholson's architect was Thomas Johnson (Chapter 3), but since it was Taylor that built Nicholson's bank, and in 1824 was appointed by Nicholson's half-brother Stephen – Thomas died in 1821 – to build the church in a corner of the estate, it is logical to conclude he oversaw the rest of the extensive Roundhay project. Certainly this fits very comfortably with Taylor's 1811 puff, quoted above: probably Roundhay was one of the 'distinguished mansions of the neighbourhood … that would render him stationary in Leeds.' There is a further useful piece of evidence: the folly known as 'The Castle' is a remarkably impressive structure for an item of mere garden ornament. But what are the possible sources? Interestingly, the arrangement of a gate flanked by two massive circular towers is not typical of Yorkshire's medieval castles, but examples can be found in both Canterbury and North Wales, two places known to have been visited by Taylor on his sketching trips for Wyatt.[41] Roundhay's mansion is an assured Classical essay that exploits the rich Roman vocabulary that Wyatt had developed and, presumably, instilled in his pupils. Many of Roundhay's details

40. These three items are quoted in N.R. Hurworth, *Thomas and Elizabeth Nicholson, the Quaker Founders of Roundhay Park*, privately published, 2005. I would like to acknowledge much valuable assistance from Dr Hurworth on various aspects of Roundhay. His sources are: L. Howard, *Journey Through the West Riding and Cumberland in 1807*, LMA ACC/1017/1397; LMA ACC/1270/15; H. Lupton, quoted in *St John's Roundhay, Centenary Souvenir*, 1927, p. 14.

41. *Catalogues* from both the RA and Northern Society confirm Taylor's visits to these two locations.

can be traced back to Wyatt, for instance the decoration on the elegant stone mullions in the tripartite windows, and the internal decoration. The main façade of the stable block is also a sophisticated composition. Its cupola incorporated an unusual feature: the eight diminutive columns which support the dome are not joined by a conventional circular entablature but a series of arches, a likely source for which was John Carr's chapel at Farnley (1761) on the south side of Leeds.

The land Thomas Nicholson acquired in 1802 was only approximately half the estate put up for sale; the other 'half' was bought by Samuel Elam. While Nicholson saw his acquisition as providing a magnificent home for his family, Elam bought as an investment and was keen to sell parcels of land for development. The 1825 map, mentioned above, shows a number of substantial villas already built, including Eller Place and Fearneville. Might Taylor have been employed for these too? Sadly, no records of have been traced although it is known that Taylor completed North Hill for Stephen Nicholson in 1824-5[42] and would have been a logical choice of architect for Springwood (now

42. Although the property was 'new roofed', extensive work awaited completion, including the offices and landscaping. Taylor invited tenders in *LI*, 4 Nov. 1824.

5.6: Leeds, Rounday Park stables (attrib. Thomas Taylor, c.1815). (*Ruth Baumberg.*)

Frazer House) which Stephen subsequently erected for his sisters-in-law,[43] both of which were built on what had been Elam's land.

Despite Taylor's increasing commitment to church work, discussed below, the secular side of his practice remained vibrant. In 1825 he was one of six eminent architects[44] invited to submit proposals for the new Commercial Buildings in Leeds, envisaged as a Classical palace for the town's business community and with a huge budget. After much deliberation, Taylor's design was placed second – John Clark was the victor – and our knowledge of it is confined to a brief, far from enthusiastic, account in the *Intelligencer*. 'Taylor's [design] they would be less inclined to recommend. The lantern which surmounts it like a Chinese wart is quite out of keeping with massive solidity of the elevation and the upper row of windows or rather port holes in the front are also striking eye-sores. The internal disposition of rooms has much to commend it.'[45]

Throughout the first third of the nineteenth century, as architects struggled to define the precise service they were qualified to provide, various adjuncts to building design might well have been offered by the profession. Thus we find Taylor selling or letting an 'excellent family house', cottages and other houses at Holbeck Moor in 1813.[46] He advertised the sale of 'Building Land in Bow Lane, facing Albion Street' in 1816[47] and in 1817 was seeking a tenant for 'Pasturing for Milk Cows in Hunslet'.[48] When to these prosaic activities are added Taylor's documented secular works, he emerges as an accomplished, successful, but essentially unremarkable late-Georgian architect. However, in one fundamental respect, Taylor is of exceptional significance in the story of English architecture: as a pioneering church designer.

Taylor's ecclesiastical work

By the middle decades of the nineteenth century, finding an architect capable of producing an impressive Gothic church was not difficult, but a generation earlier, it would have been a real problem. In the early years of the century, the 'modern style' was set firmly within the Classical tradition and a haphazard system of architectural education, supplemented by a series publications which explained rudimentary principles of composition and illustrated the details of the Classical orders, ensured all but the most inept designer could produce an acceptable 'Grecian' composition. But understanding the structures of the Middle Ages took the intellectual challenge to an altogether higher plane: it was clear Gothic didn't conform to the carefully chronicled principles of Classicism, but at the same time, Gothic's own principles defied identification. No wonder most architects shunned the style. Taylor was not only a rare exception, but one would be hard-pressed to identify *any* English architect who could demonstrate a comparable

43. The lease which Stephen Nicholson granted to his relatives is dated September 1826 and refers to the house as 'a newly erected mansion'. WYASL DB39/22. *Ex inf.* Neville Hurworth.

44. The others were Chantrell from Leeds, Charles Barry, Francis Goodwin and Anthony Salvin from London and the otherwise unknown John Clark from Edinburgh.

45. *LI*, 30 June 1825.

46. *LM*, 31 July 1813.

47. *LM*, 24 Feb. 1816.

48. *LM*, 19 April 1817.

THOMAS TAYLOR (1777 OR 8 – 1826)   91

commitment to the style around 1810, and by 1820, only Thomas Rickman had, arguably, surpassed him as an authority. As a Gothic specialist, Taylor is of national importance and before his sudden death in 1826, he dominated the region's ecclesiastical work.

From where did this extraordinary interest arise? Mention has already been made of Taylor's extensive travels recording buildings and their details for James Wyatt's exploitation. The paintings he exhibited confirm he visited the cathedrals of Rochester, Canterbury and Amiens (France), major churches Stamford (Lincs) and Oxford as well as castles in Warwick, the Isle of Wight and North Wales; and subsequently in Yorkshire, he visited many of the county's monuments. These expeditions are, surely, the key to Taylor's own understanding of Gothic. Significantly, Taylor's earliest recorded architectural commission is in this style: repairs to Leeds Parish Church (1809-12). 'The South Side has been in a great degree new-built. The large South window exhibits a beautiful specimen of Gothic architecture from the designs of that ingenious artist, Mr Taylor of this place … '[49] Again he is referred to as 'artist' rather than architect, and seems to confirm he was known primarily at this time for his paintings.

The second key ingredient in Taylor's emergence as a pioneer Gothic architect is the Revd Hammond Roberson, of Healds Hall, Liversedge, in the parish of Birstall, near Leeds, who engaged Taylor to design his

49. *LI*, 11 May 1812.

5.7: Liversedge, WR, Christ Church (Thomas Taylor, 1811-16). A finished building has simple pitched-topped pinnacles instead of those shown here. (Engraving after a drawing by Taylor in H. Roberson, *An Account of the Ceremony of Laying the First Stone of Christ's Church, now building in Liversedge*, privately printed, 1813.)

new church at Liversedge, probably in 1811, but perhaps earlier,[50] and paid for it himself (5.7). Roberson became the perpetual curate there and later a prebend of York. He was a remarkable character, widely seen as the model for the Revd Matthew Helstone in Charlotte Bronte's *Shirley*, 'inflexibly Anglican and immovably Tory'.[51] From his own published work – as well as Bronte's – comes a picture of a man who believed passionately in arresting the spread of Nonconformity in his locality by the presence of a vibrant Established church, and who adhered firmly to the liturgy and rubrics of the *Book of Common Prayer*.[52] For Roberson, one of the objections to Nonconformity seemed to be the lack of structure and consistency in its services, while the Church of England offered clear principles. It also offered a sense of continuity and history. 'The numerous [churches that] our pious ancestors … left us demonstrate their knowledge of nature, their judgement, their skill, their tastes and their devotion.' They are much more conducive to piety than modern buildings of 'just symmetry and proportion where everything is neat, decorous and solemn.'[53] Conversely, he believed Taylor's design 'forces upon our recollection the judicious piety of our fathers. This style of building is perfectly distinguished from everything that is mean or insignificant. When executed with simplicity, it is chaste and decorous, and yet conveys suitable ideas of grandeur.'[54] Only once, at the end of the sixty-two page pamphlet, does Roberson use the word 'Gothic', but it is clear he sees the style as the perfect confederate for the form of service he worked tirelessly to promote. For Taylor, this alliance with Roberson – probably the most dynamic cleric in the West Riding before the arrival of Dr W.F. Hooke at Leeds in 1837 – proved to be invaluable; commissions for other new churches and substantial reconstructions of older ones soon followed.

Liversedge is a remarkable church for its date. It has a long chancel, the nave is divided from the aisles by arcades which support clerestories, the roof avoids the flatness found so often in the early nineteenth century and inside it is open with arched ribs and no tie beams, seating was on benches rather than in box pews, and despite Roberson's claim of economy, the external decoration is far from parsimonious. Its features also formed the basis of Taylor's entire ecclesiastical output until the early 1820s.

What were the likely sources? The key features of the finished church – the overall plan and proportions, the buttresses, their cappings and the embattled parapets – can all be traced back to Wyatt's rebuilding of East Grinstead Church, Sussex (1789–92), a job perfectly timed for Taylor's arrival in the office. Only the tracery has changed, Wyatt's sophisticated Perpendicular was replaced by a range of 'Y' patterns, perhaps for economy, but conceivably no Yorkshire mason could be found capable of executing more complex patterns.

50. Tenders were advertised in April 1812, but it is likely that Roberson had been contemplating the project and arranging his finances to pay for it, for some time. *LM*, 12 April 1812.

51. Beckwith [note 1], p. 25.

52. In his *Address* at the Liversedge foundation stone laying [note 17] Roberson announced his church would be 'built for the celebration of Divine Worship according to the rites and forms prescribed by our excellent national Church Establishment.' (p. 6.) And in the *Prospectus* for the new church which he published in 1811, he refers to the importance of 'the Doctrines, the Sacraments, the Rites and Ceremonies of the Established religion be[ing] faithfully and duly administered.' (Quoted in Beckwith [note 1], p. 94.)

53. *Account* [note 17], p. 24.

54. *Account* [note 17], p. 29.

5.8: Pudsey, Leeds, St Lawrence (Thomas Taylor, 1821-4). (*Ruth Baumberg.*)

5.9: Pudsey, Leeds, St Lawrence (Thomas Taylor, 1821-4). (*Ruth Baumberg.*)

With the design successfully completed and widely praised, Taylor used it with only modest variations in the numerous commissions for new churches over the next decade including: Christ Church, Bradford (1813-15); St Mary, Luddenden, West Yorkshire (1816-17); Holy Trinity, Huddersfield (1816-19); St Lawrence, Pudsey, Leeds (1821-4) (5.8; 5.9); St Philip, Sheffield (1822-8); Christ Church, Attercliffe, Sheffield (1822-6); St John, Dewsbury Moor (1823-6) (5.10). The churches in this list include large and small, some with clerestories, some without, but the basic repertoire was unchanged.

In the early 1820s, Taylor developed a second adaptable model. It consisted of a nave without aisles or clerestory, a tower with broach spire and lancet windows; the most remarkable feature was the inclusion of north and south transepts, each lit by a trio of windows, the central one of which rose higher than the flanking ones. The transepts gave visual interest to the exteriors and provided additional accommodation around the pulpit, but Taylor was almost alone in departing from the Commissioners' preferred parallelogram. Taylor used the design on a large scale at Holy Trinity, Ripon (1826-7) (5.11; 5.12) and on a much smaller scale at Christ Church, Woodhouse, Huddersfield (1823-4), St John, Roundhay, Leeds (1824-6) (5.13) and St Peter, Earlesheaton, Dewsbury (1825-7).

The obvious departure from these two models is St Mary, Quarry Hill, Leeds (1823-6), although it is not dissimilar to the Liversedge type. Perhaps Taylor was keen to impress in his adoptive town and channelled a larger than usual proportion of the budget to external decoration. He specified panelling for the upper stages of the tower and substantial intermediate pinnacles on each of its four sides to produce an almost Perpendicular appearance, somewhat at variance with the Early English windows of the nave and chancel (5.14). He also

5.10: Dewsbury, WY, St John, Dewsbury Moor (Thomas Taylor, 1823-7). (*Author.*)

developed a curiously decorated parapet, horizontal on the north, south and west sides, but pitched at the east (5.15). And had he lived to build the huge new church in Travis Street, Manchester – where he was appointed in 1823 – it would have had been broadly similar to Pudsey, but with the addition of a spire like Ripon's to create a monumental edifice.

Alongside these new churches were numerous repairs, extensions and new galleries for others including: St Bartholomew, Colne, Lancs (repairs, 1815); St Chad, Rochdale, Lancs (repairs, 1815-16); Holy Trinity, Ossett, West Yorks (extension, 1821); Gildersome Chapel, Leeds (new gallery, 1821-2); Holy Trinity, Littleborough, Lancs (new gallery, 1822-3); St Peter, Birstall, Leeds (alterations, 1824); St Luke, Heywood, Lancs (enlargement, probably unexecuted, 1824). Taylor's commitment to these sorts of alterations is underlined by his 1816 proposal to publish '*AN ADDRESS to the CLERGY of Great Britain …* on the possibility of repairing Ancient Parochial Churches and Chapels

5.11: Ripon, NY, Holy Trinity (Thomas Taylor, 1826-7). (*Anon.*, The Tourist Companion … Ripon, *Langdale*, 1833.)

5.12: Ripon, NY, Holy Trinity (Thomas Taylor, 1826-7). (*Anon.*, The Tourist Companion, *Langdale*, 1833.)

in their original Style in Preference to the incongruous Matter generally introduced in the Repair of ancient Edifices and frequently at much greater Expense … '[55] It seems not to have been completed, but even this astonishing prospectus places Taylor in a unique position in the fledgling movement to establish Gothic as the most appropriate style for Anglican worship, a movement largely shunned by the architectural profession.

55. *LM*, 13 July 1816.

5.14: Leeds, St Mary, Quarry Hill
(Thomas Taylor, 1822-6). (*Leeds
University Library, Special Collections.*)

5.13: Leeds, St John, Roundhay (Thomas
Taylor, 1824-6). (*Leeds Library and
Information Services.*)

We can only speculate on what Taylor would have achieved had he
not died, apparently in his late forties, in March 1826.[56] During his
lifetime he enjoyed an enviable reputation, especially among those who
shared Roberson's vision of Gothic as a necessary adjunct to a revival
of Anglicanism. Dr Whitaker noted Taylor's 'perfect conception of old
English models'[57] and Edward Vernon, Archbishop of York, who
consecrated Taylor's Holy Trinity, Huddersfield and St Mary,
Southowram in 1819, considered them 'perfect examples of what we
need … nothing can be better or more truly church-like than their
external appearance or their internal arrangements in every way.'[58] Thus
Vernon 'confidently … recommended [Taylor] to the attention of the
Commissioners' and urged them to employ him for Pudsey's proposed
new church. R.D. Chantrell, writing to his former master Soane in
1821 noted 'the designs of Thomas Taylor have given great satisfaction
to the Archbishop and other exalted ecclesiastics.'[59] Much later,
Chantrell wrote of Liversedge that it was 'one of the best formed
modern churches of plain character, having a spacious chancel, nave,
and side aisles, vestries on each side of the chancel, a western tower,
and open roofs.'[60] But the most remarkable aspect of Taylor's reputation
is that, to a significant degree, it survived the proselytising of the

56. *LI*, 30 March 1826.

57. Whitaker [note 27], p. 250.

58. Letter to the CBC, 26 Oct. 1819, CBC,
Pudsey file, 16,039.

59. Sir John Soane's Museum, Private
Correspondence, XV.A. 32.

60. *Builder*, v, 1847, p. 301. Open roofs
had been an aspect of church design that
Chantrell had championed.

61. A. Trimen, *Churches and Chapel Architecture*, Longman *et al*, 1849, p. 83.

62. Published by Thomas Richards.

5.15: Leeds, St Mary, Quarry Hill (Thomas Taylor, 1822-6).

Ecclesiologists. Andrew Trimen considered Taylor 'foremost in the rank of those who successfully promoted … the ancient ecclesiastical style', a truly extraordinary opinion for 1849.[61] Taylor is the only Leeds architect to be included in the Architectural Publication Society's magisterial *Dictionary of Architecture*, 1870.[62] It was an honour denied even to Brodrick.

Catalogue

LEEDS, St Peter, repairs to south side, 1808-12, dem. (T. Allen, *A New and Complete History of the County of York*, I.T. Hinton, 1829-31, vol ii, p. 498; *LI*, 11 May 1812.)

LEEDS, Court House, 1811-13, dem. (E. Baines, *History, Directory and Gazetteer of the County of York*, Baines, 1822, vol i, p. 19.)

LEEDS, Lancastrian School, Alfred Street, 1811-12, dem. (*LI*, 21 Oct. 1811.)

LIVERSEDGE, WY, Christ Church, 1811-16. (H. Roberson, *An Account of the Ceremony of Laying the First Stone of Christ's Church, now building in Liversedge*, privately printed, 1813.)

LEEDS, proposed riverside development off Call Lane, c.1812. (*LI*, 28 Sept 1812.)

ROTHWELL, Leeds, St Mary, repewing. (Beckwith [note 1], p. 30.)

LEEDS, National School, High Court Lane, Kirkgate, 1812-13, dem. (*LM*, 25 April 1812.)

LEEDS, Union Bank, Commercial Street, 1812-13, dem. (*LI*, 23 Nov 1812.)

BRADFORD, Christ Church, 1813-15, dem. (Beckwith [note 1], pp. 31-2.)

COLNE, Lancs, St Bartholomew, repairs, 1815. (*LI*, 31 July 1815.)

LEEDS, Charity School for Girls, St John's Yard, 1815-16. (WYASL 160/197/6/1.)

ROCHDALE, Lancs, St Chad, repairs, 1815-16. (*LI*, 3 July 1815.)

LUDDENDEN, WY, St Mary, 1815-17. (*LI*, 11 Dec 1815.)

SOUTHOWRAM, Halifax, WY, St Anne, 1815-19. (*LI*, 6 May 1816.)

HUDDERSFIELD, WY, Holy Trinity, 1816-19. (*LI*, 8 July 1816.)

LITTLEBOROUGH, Lancs, Holy Trinity, 1818-20. (*LI*, 23 Feb 1818.)

BIRSTALL, nr Leeds, National School, 1819. (*LM*, 17 April 1819.)

LIVERSEDGE, WY, National School, 1819. (*LM*, 17 April 1819.)

LUDDENDEN, WY, St Mary, further work, 1819-22. (ICBS, file 00197.)

LIVERSEDGE, Christ Church, new gallery, 1819-25. (ICBS, file 00114.)

OSSETT, WY, Holy Trinity, additions, 1820-6, dem. (*LI,* 30 April 1821; ICBS, file 00257.)

PUDSEY, Leeds, St Lawrence, 1821-4. (CBC, file 16039.)

LITTLEBOROUGH, Lancs, new gallery, 1821-4. (ICBS, file 00325.)

GILDERSOME, Leeds, St Peter, new gallery, 1821-7, dem. (ICBS, file 00330.)

LEEDS, Free School (Grammar School), enlargement inc. porch and turret, 1822. (WYASL, DB/197/196.)

LITTLEBOROUGH, Lancs, parsonage house, 1822-3. (*LM*, 12 Oct. 1822.)

SHEFFIELD, St Philip, 1822-8, dem. (CBC file 20883.)

ATTERCLIFFE, Sheffield, Christ Church, 1822-6, dem. (CBC file 20886.)

LEEDS, St Mary, Quarry Hill, 1822-6, dem. (CBC file 20548.)

ROCHDALE, Lancs, Market Place, unspecified work, 1823. (*LI,* 23 Jan 1823.)

SHEFFIELD, National School for Girls, 1823-4. (Beckwith, p. 54.)

BIRSTALL, WY, St Peter, new gallery, 1823-4. (ICBS, file 00491.)

HUDDERSFIELD, Christ Church, Woodhouse Hill, 1823-4. (*LI*, 31 July 1823.)

DEWSBURY, WY, St John, Dewsbury Moor, 1823-7. (CBC, file 18158.)

DEWSBURY, St Peter, Hanging Heaton, 1823-5, subsequently altered after a fire. (CBC, file 18158.)

MANCHESTER, new church, Travis Street, 1823-6, subsequently built to designs of Atkinson and Sharpe. (CBC, MB 10, p. 398; *LI*, 2 Feb 1826.)

LEEDS, unspecified work for Pious Uses Committee, possibly for a house at The Bank, 1824. (WYASL, Free School Accounts.)

LEEDS, North Hill, Roundhay, completion of unfinished house for Stephen Nicholson, 1824-5. (*LI*, 4 Nov. 1824.)

LEEDS, St John, Roundhay, 1824-6. (*LI*, 23 Sept. 1824.)

HEYWOOD, Lancs, St Luke, enlargement, 1824-30, perhaps unexecuted. (ICBS, file 00532.)

LINTHWAITE, Huddersfield, new church, 1825, unexecuted. (CBC MB 17, p. 185.)

NETHERTHONG, nr Huddersfield, new church, 1825, unexecuted. (CBC MB 17, p. 185.)

DEWSBURY, St Peter, Earls Heaton, 1825-7, dem. (CBC, file 18158.)

HUDDERSFIELD, plans prepared for converting an Independent Meeting House to an Anglican church, 1826, probably not executed. (CBC MB 20, p. 252.)

LOCKWOOD, Huddersfield, possibly produced plans for new church, 1826. (*LI*, 20 March 1826.)

RIPON, NY, Holy Trinity, 1826-7. (*LI*, 3 Aug. 1826.)

Attributed

LEEDS, Roundhay Park, mansion, stables, gate lodges, folly etc, for Thomas Nicholson, before c.1820.

HUDDERSFIELD, Woodhouse, parsonage house, c.1823-4.

LEEDS, Springwood (now Fraser House), Roundhay, for Stephen Nicholson, c.1825-6.

6. *Robert Dennis Chantrell (1793–1872)*

CHRISTOPHER WEBSTER

Robert Dennis Chantrell[1] was the third man to assume the title of Leeds' principal architect in the late-Georgian period and like Taylor, he came from London tempted by the employment opportunities the expanding town offered. Chantrell's ambitions were well served in Yorkshire and he enjoyed an enviable reputation as a church architect – 'one of the first architects in all the North of England',[2] according to the Bishop of Ripon – before returning to London in 1847 where he passed a long semi-retirement as an eminent antiquary, scholar and something of an elder statesman of the profession.

Chantrell was born in Newington, south London, in January 1793,[3] the son of Robert Chantrell (1765-1840) and Mary Ann, née Dennis (1776-1829). Robert was a gifted and successful entrepreneur with interests in a range of businesses which took the family to various cities in Continental Europe, and our young architect had a remarkable childhood moving through Germany and Belgium before settling, at the age of 12, in Bruges. At the opening of the nineteenth century it was, and remains, a city famous for its rich architectural heritage; half a century later, Chantrell was to write enthusiastically about the tall, 'picturesque gables ornamented with arches and tracery … On entering the ancient town … we are reminded of the olden times … '[4] Perhaps it was a precocious interest in these surroundings that prompted Robert to think of a career in architecture for his son, and in 1807, aged fourteen, Chantrell returned to London to begin seven years of articled pupilage with John Soane, arguably the greatest architect in England at that time. What made Robert think of Soane to educate his son? It

1. For Chantrell, see C. Webster, *R.D. Chantrell (1793-1872) and the Architecture of a Lost Generation*, Spire Books, 2010.

2. Church of England Records Office, Papers of the Church Building Commission, Golcar file.

3. The precise date of his birth is not recorded, but he was baptised on 24 January 1793. London Metropolitan Archives, P92/MRY/14.

4. RIBA Archives, MS SP.12, no. 17.

is known that Robert had, from the beginning of the century, been acquiring major works of art in war-torn Europe, some he kept for his own extensive collection, but other pieces he sold to collectors in England. It is likely Soane was one of his clients, but whatever the link between them, the choice of Soane was a most fortuitous one for young Chantrell. Soane usually had no more than four or five pupils at any one time and these young men enjoyed what was, without doubt, the most thorough architectural education available in England at this time.

During the seven years Chantrell was in his office, Soane was at the height of his powers, engaged on those buildings which are now assessed as his best: the Bank of England, Chelsea Hospital, the Picture Gallery and Mausoleum at Dulwich and his own house, 13 Lincoln's Inn Fields. Perhaps more significantly, Soane had jut been appointed Professor of Architecture at the Royal Academy which must have made him focus even more closely on the question of what an aspiring architect needed to understand. The pupils assisted by preparing the huge number of diagrams which illustrated the lectures and the extensive reading Soane undertook before writing the lectures[5] must have informed the pupils' syllabus in the office. Soane meticulously stored the office records, including the Day Books, and it is now possible to see what Chantrell did on each day over these seven years. It was a conservative course which involved study of the Classical orders, the major monuments of Greece and Rome, and the key European buildings of the previous 300 years. However, the syllabus went only so far as the work of William Chambers (who died in 1796). It contained nothing of the vibrant turn of the century Classical *avant garde* and – particularly significant for the way Chantrell's career was to develop – nothing at all about the architecture of the Middle Ages.

We might reasonably conclude that Soane considered that there were four components in the ideal education: articled pupilage, an acquaintance with the standard works of architectural theory, experience on a building site, foreign travel. When Chantrell left Soane's office in January 1814, on his 21st birthday, he had undertaken the first two. However, the wars with France effectively precluded travel and anyway, he had other plans: two weeks later he married Elizabeth Caroline Boham at St Mary Magdelene, Bermondsey.[6] The couple went on to produce four sons and four daughters, all of whom survived into adulthood.

Much less is known about the next two years of Chantrell's life. He lived in a number of different houses in Crown Row, Walworth, in properties probably owned by his father, and appeared in a London *Directory* in the 'Architects' section,[7] but there is no evidence he secured any commissions. It seems likely he was working for a surveyor in the middle years of the decade,[8] the ideal means of acquiring the third of

5. See D. Watkin, *Sir John Soane, Enlightenment Thinking and the Royal Academy Lectures*, Cambridge U.P., 1996.

6. This was on 12 February 1814. London Metropolitan Archives, P71/MMG.

7. Underhill's *Triennial Directory of London, Westminster and Southwark … for the years 1817,1818 and 1819*, probably compiled in 1816.

8. For an explanation, see Webster [note 1], pp. 67-8.

Soane's four components in the ideal curriculum. Then, in 1816, he moved to Halifax.

> WILLIAM BRADLEY, Architect, acknowledges with sincere gratitude to his Friends the liberal Encouragement he has experienced during a term of nearly Eighteen Years' Practice, and begs Leave to inform them that in Consequence of the flattering Prospect he has of future Patronage, has engaged as an ASSISTANT, Mr. Chantrell, of London, a Gentleman of considerable Ability in his Profession and who was articled to the justly celebrated and highly esteemed Architect, John Soane Esq. This, he trusts, will evince his ardent Desire through additional Assiduity and Facility, to merit Support.'[9]

9. *LM*, 23 March 1816. The author is very grateful to Hugh Kerrigan for alerting him to this fascinating piece of information which, unfortunately, appeared too late for inclusion in his *Chantrell*, [note1].

10. Linstrum, *WY*, p. 372.

11. The Baths were situated in Wellington Street and were demolished in 1857. Although the office was opened after winning the competition, the decision to move to Leeds was taken before his victory was announced. Webster [note 1], p. 274.

6.1: Leeds, Public Baths, Wellington Street (R.D. Chantrell, 1819-21). This crude illustration, from the Bath's *Shareholders' Handbook* for 1837-8, is the only known illustration of the building.

Arrival in Leeds

What brought Chantrell into contact with Bradley – an apparently disreputable[10] minor Halifax architect – is not clear, but while there he would have become acquainted with Yorkshire building practices. He would also have learnt of the remarkable industrial and mercantile growth taking place in Leeds and appreciated the employment possibilities that this would generate. He opened his office in The Saddle Yard, Briggate, on 15 March 1819, just 11 days after winning the competition for the Leeds Public Baths[11] (6.1). Two months later, he was announced as architect for the new hall for the Leeds Philosophical and Literary Society (6.2). He had made a triumphant entry into the town.

Construction of these two important Classical public buildings – the town's first since Taylor's Court house of 1811-13 – appears to have progressed smoothly over the next two years, and brought him into contact with the two buildings' subscribers and committees, which, in turn, brought more work. The patronage of William Hey and Benjamin Gott – both subscribers to the baths and members of the Phil and Lit's council – usefully illustrates the point. For Hey he designed a block of four shops in Commercial Street in 1820, and beginning in 1823, Chantrell undertook a whole series of jobs for Gott in Armley where he lived. Also in 1823, Chantrell secured one of the biggest commissions in his career, the new South Market in Leeds. It was an outstanding design, the most compelling part of which was the striking circular 'cross' at its centre in the form of a Neo-classical temple (6.3).

In his first four years in Leeds, Chantrell had secured all three of the new public buildings in the town, despite competition from numerous accomplished architects from London and other provincial towns. He had also obtained several other commissions and must have looked forward confidently. However, in 1824, as the South Market neared completion, an ominous cloud appeared on the horizon. Matters first reached the public stage in connection with the proposal to build the Central Market, in Duncan Street. Apparently Chantrell was chosen as the architect for what would have been the most expensive building of his career, but clearly there was a subsequent disagreement with the committee and the job was passed to Francis Goodwin (1.6). It seems those prominent townsmen who had initially promoted Chantrell had now turned against him and when, in 1825, a closed competition was held to provide a design for the new Commercial Buildings (a competition won by John Clark, see Chapter 7), the *Leeds Intelligencer*

6.2: Leeds, Philosophical and Literary Society Hall, Park Row (R.D. Chantrell, 1819-21. Watercolour by Chantrell. (*Leeds City Museum.*)

claimed that it was widely believed that this was a prize Chantrell had had no chance of winning.[12] The South Market was to be Chantrell's last public building.

Chantrell's importance in the bigger picture of Leeds architecture was not as a designer of Classical public buildings despite the quality of the three projects discussed above, but for his church work in the Gothic style. Indeed as a pioneer Goth, Chantrell occupied a place on the national stage, not just on that of Leeds. His first new church was Christ Church, Meadow Lane, an edifice awarded to Leeds by the Church Building Commission and largely financed by parliamentary funds. The Commissioners had no stylistic preferences and delegated such matters to the local committees. In the north of England there appears to have been little debate; from the beginning, they wanted Gothic. These were lucrative commissions and there were several ambitious architects roaming the country in an attempt to seduce committees with dazzling Gothic designs and unrealistically low

12. For the Central Market, see *LI*, 7 July 1825. For the Commercial Buildings, see *LI*, 30 June 1825, 7 July 1825.

6.3: Leeds, South Market (R.D. Chantrell, 1823-4), drawing by Chantrell. (*Thoresby Society, Leeds.*)

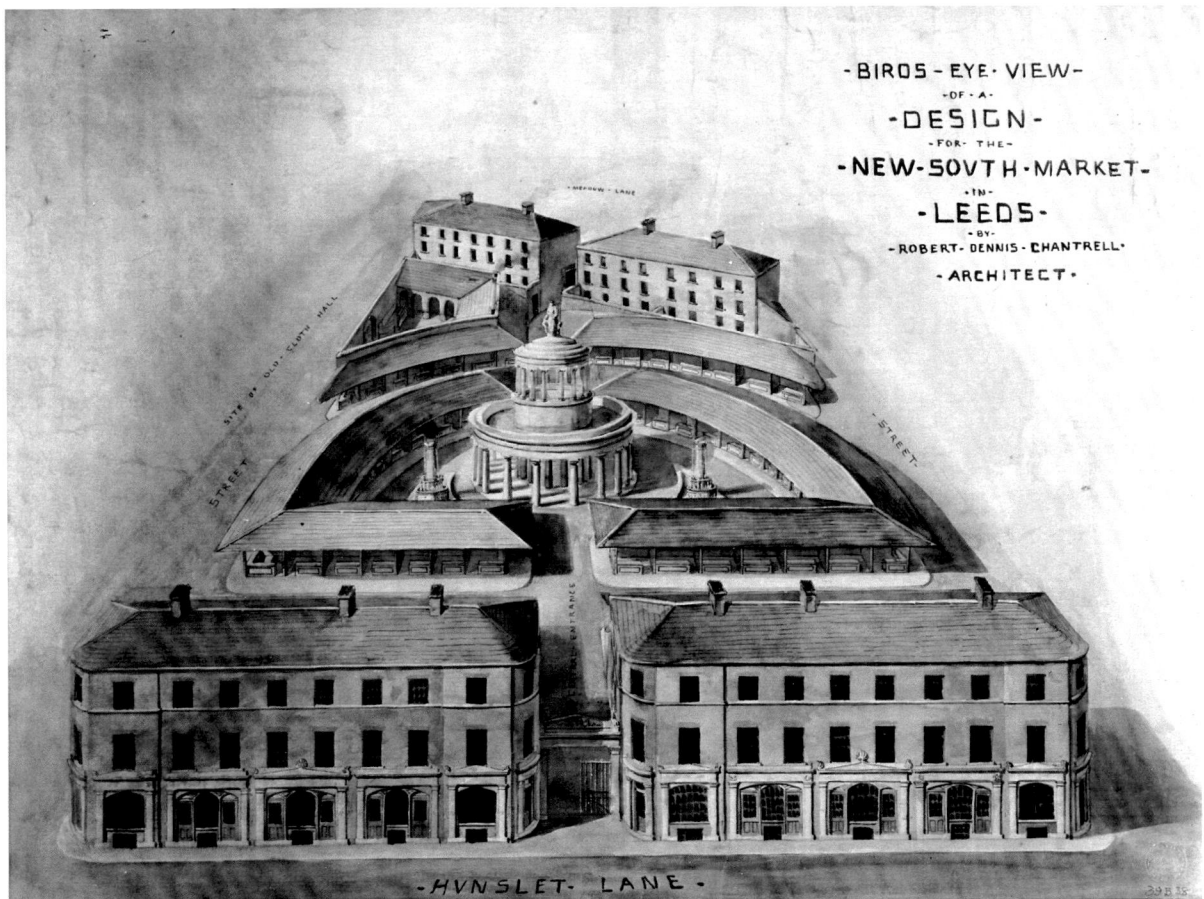

budgets. If Chantrell was to succeed in this competitive arena, he would have to refine his understanding of the style quickly, a style, let us not forget, about which Soane had taught him probably nothing.

It was in November 1820 that the *Intelligencer* reported that Leeds had been awarded three new churches from the Commissioners' funds and invited architects to submit designs; the time limit was subsequently extended to 1 March 1821. We might imagine Chantrell, seated at his drawing board, pondering the challenge: how best to design a big church and provide it with a convincing Gothic dress? In desperation, he wrote a revealing letter to Soane. 'I take the liberty of applying to you for advice … I should wish to present a Grecian or Roman design, but the objections to them, made by the Local Committee, would be so strong that I fear my labour would be entirely lost, still I must say that I consider the present a firm opportunity for restoring the best examples of Greece and Rome.' Earlier in the letter he wrote, 'I expect to be strongly opposed by some persons in this and the neighbouring towns who have submitted to the county mania for plain Gothic works.'[13] 25 years later, an article he published in *The Builder* included, 'though generally well grounded in Greek and Roman architecture [the architects of the Gothic churches of the 1820s] found themselves called upon to construct works utterly at variance with Greek and Roman principles; and having no time to study or collect data were required at once to compose works in the unfamiliar style.'[14]

The result of his deliberations, Christ Church (6.4), is an exceptionally accomplished design; that Chantrell acquitted himself so well in this, his first Gothic design, tells us much about his ability. Perhaps it reveals much about his training too; Soane had sidestepped the Middle Ages in his pupils' education, but he had equipped them with the skills necessary to understand the importance of sound proportions and massing. Once these were established, the application of appropriate Gothic details was relatively straight forward, and by no means an insurmountable challenge thanks to a steady stream of useful books of adaptable details published after Waterloo.[15]

1826 saw the consecration of Christ Church – a cause of much celebration locally – and an on-going stream of praise for its designer: 'As [it] was the first of parliamentary churches founded in Leeds, so it is the first in architectural beauty and does great credit to the architect, R.D. Chantrell,'[16] was not untypical. 1826 also saw the sudden death of Thomas Taylor (see Chapter 5), the region's principal ecclesiastical architect. Taylor's demise could hardly have come at a more useful time for Chantrell. Chantrell must have realised that having lost the support of those who had once promoted him in the highly partial world of architectural competitions would limit his future prospects for secular commissions, precisely the types of building for which Soane had prepared him. But churches, where he could work for the rationally

13. Sir John Soane's Museum, Private Correspondence, xv, A, 32.

14. *Builder*, v, 1847, p. 300.

15. For instance, F. Mackenzie and Augustus Pugin, *Specimens of Gothic Architecture consisting of doors, windows, buttresses and pinnacles … selected from Ancient Buildings at Oxford etc*, J. Taylor, 1816; Thomas Rickman, *An Attempt to Discriminate the styles of Architecture of England*, Longman, 1817; Augustus Pugin and E.J. Willson, *Specimens of Gothic Architecture selected from various Ancient Edifices in England* , Nattali, 1821-2.

16. *Walks Through Leeds*, J. Heaton, 1835, p. 104.

6.4: Leeds, Christ Church, Meadow Lane (R.D. Chantrell, 1821-6).

6.5: Netherthong, near Huddersfield, All Saints (R.D. Chantrell, 1826-30), unsigned drawing. (*Leeds University Library, Special Collections.*)

17. N. Scatcherd, *A Dissertation on Ancient Bridge Chapels*, Longmans, 1828, p. 46.

18. *Morning Post*, 9 Feb. 1829. Thomas Rickman noted in his diary for 9 Feb. 1829 that he had been informed that 'Chantrell is the Cathedral Surveyor so there is no likelihood of any [employment] at York.' (Rickman's Diary, Jan–June 1829, RIBA Drawings and Archives, RiT/2.) I am most grateful to Geoff Brandwood for this information. And Colvin noted in the first two editions of his *Biographical Dictionary* that Chantrell 'became surveyor to York Minster', although a search of the Minster archives produced nothing to confirm this as an official appointment.

motivated Commissioners, applying objective criteria, might be much more congenial and he would have known that church work had provided Taylor with a good living.

Clearly Christ Church had impressed the paymasters and soon six further jobs came from them, the maximum allowed for any one architect under the Commissioners' rules. These churches – at Lockwood and Netherthong (6.5) near Huddersfield, in the Leeds suburbs of Holbeck, Kirkstall (6.6) and Morley, and at New Mills in Derbyshire – must have kept him busy into the early 1830s. All had budgets much smaller than Christ Church's but each is an accomplished essay and, interestingly, different from the others. It appears that, having realised the vast range of details to be found in the medieval past, he was keen to use as many alternatives as possible. To satisfy his curiosity, there is evidence he made visits for the purpose of studying medieval remains; some of his sketches he worked up into finished watercolours which he exhibited in the 1830 and 1834 exhibitions of the Northern Society for the Encouragement of Arts, in the society's rooms next to the Music Hall in Albion Street, which Chantrell had altered in two projects during the 1820s. Indeed, so much of a Gothic specialist did he quickly become that in the late '20s his opinions were quoted in print by the noted local antiquary Norrisson Scatcherd.[17] Rather more significantly, following the calamitous fire at York Minster in 1829, it was Chantrell who accompanied the archbishop as he toured the ruins – as well as offering indications of likely rebuilding costs – rather than any of the established York architects.[18] However, the job of reconstruction eventually went to the prestigious London architect Robert Smirke.

6.6: Kirkstall, Leeds, St Stephen (R.D. Chantrell, 1827-9). (*Leeds Library and Information Services.*)

Between the consecration of Holbeck church in January 1832, and the commencement of the Leeds Parish Church project, late in 1837, Chantrell undertook a range of projects and the Classical tradition was not entirely abandoned. In *c.*1830-2, he designed a truly remarkable tower for Hunslet Chapel (6.7), his most overt tribute to his former master, although one might reasonably question how this cutting edge design was received by the worshippers at this nondescript, mainly 1744, brick chapel of ease. In 1834 he discreetly rebuilt the wings of Taylor's 1811-13 Court House and between 1824 and c.1835, he completed Rudding Park, near Harrogate. The latter was undertaken 'with the utmost discretion in the manner of the original design' and it is now impossible to identify the extent of Chantrell's contribution. However, the tradesmen's bills amounted to more than £11,000, a figure for which almost a complete new house could have been built, and his work must have been extensive. In 1834, he exhibited 'A country house now in progress in a neighbouring county',[19] but this has not been identified. Indeed, we know little about Chantrell's domestic work. There are odd references to unidentified houses, but the only one that can, with any certainty, be associated with him is Armitage Bridge House, near Huddersfield, 1828. Its elevations are entirely typical for its time, but it had a remarkable 'starfish' ceiling in one room – based on several by Soane – although this is now destroyed.

19. Northern Society for the Encouragement of Arts, *Catalogue*, 1834, p. 22.

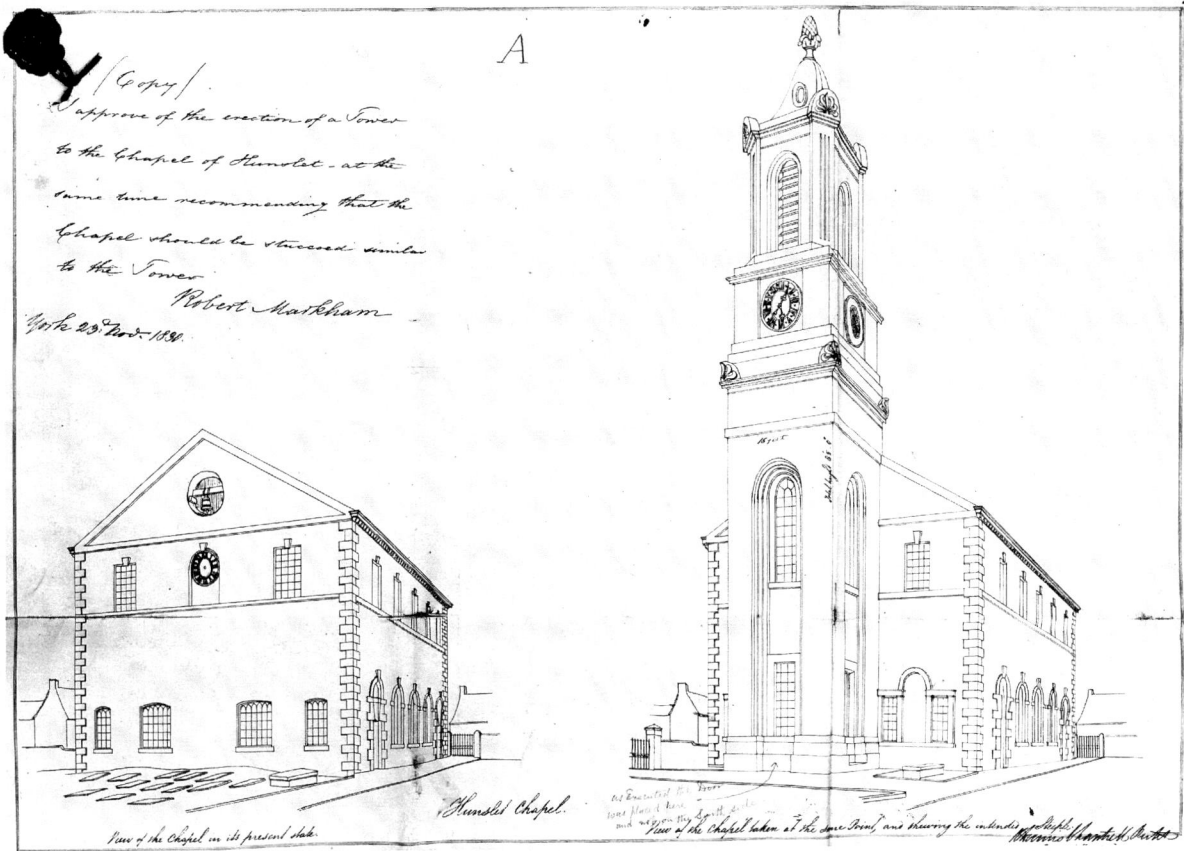

6.7: Hunslet, Leeds, Hunslet Chapel, 1744 and later, tower added by Chantrell, 1830. (*WYASL.*)

It seems Chantrell was not above minor jobs and throughout his career supervised a series of small-scale alterations and repairs, for instance at: the Free (Grammar) School, Leeds (1824); Feather Hill School, Woodhouse, Leeds (1832); the Leeds Library (1821, 1828, 1835). He was especially in demand for alterations to churches, including adding galleries at, for instance, Christ Church (1836) and St Mark's Leeds (1832-3; 1836-7).

In the early 1830s he undertook an interesting restoration at All Saints, Pontefract (1831-3) and produced an unexecuted scheme for rebuilding part of St Oswald's, Guiseley (1830-3) (6.8). Had it been completed, the new north aisle would have blended perfectly with the existing medieval work and the drawings reveal Chantrell's remarkable understanding of Gothic's principles,[20] a subject quite beyond the comprehension of most architects at this time. He rebuilt the little chapel at Headingley, Leeds (1836-8) but his most compelling design of the mid-decade was Christ Church, Skipton (1835-9) (6.9). The importance of the church is not so much in its elevations as in its plan as the latter anticipated many of the liturgical developments of the

20. See ICBS, file 01472.

6.8: Guiseley, nr Leeds, St Oswald, Chantrell's proposed new north aisle for this medieval church, 1832. (*Lambeth Palace Library*.)

1840s associated with the Cambridge Camden Society and the Oxford Movement, fundamentally concerned with a 'Higher' form of Anglican liturgy. The driving force behind the project was Christopher Sidgwick, from the Skipton mill-owning family, who wanted 'a true Christian edifice [and oversaw] the internal arrangements.' It was his 'object … to make it precisely conformable to what was designed by the

6.9: Skipton, Christ Church (R.D. Chantrell, 1835-9). (*Roger Hatfield.*)

Reformers of the Church of England [so as] to render it easy for the officiating minister to observe the Rubrics to the strictness of the letter. His readings on the subject [were] extensive.'[21] The church had a long chancel, raised on four steps, and had a reading desk 'arranged so that the minister can look to the people when addressing them in the absolution, etc, and look from them when praying.'[22] All the seats – whether rented or free – were uniform open benches. This might all seem unremarkable, but for a church of the late '30s, it was revolutionary. Sidgewick was well connected with the leading progressive clergy in the county, several of whom would soon found the Yorkshire Architectural Society, and Chantrell was perfectly placed to exploit these connections.

The rebuilding of Leeds Parish Church (1837-41), initially a relatively modest proposal to re-order and increase accommodation, was a project that lifted Chantrell's career to a new level (6.10). Its importance cannot be overestimated, and not just for the architect's reputation. It was the biggest new church in England since Wren's St Paul's, a building predicted by the Higher end of the Anglican community to be a beacon for the long-awaited drive to reclaim the industrial towns from the grip of Nonconformity, and a physical manifestation of the theological revisions of the Oxford Movement. At the re-dedication in September 1841, the *Intelligencer* was, predictably, euphoric but there was much national interest too. The *Church Intelligencer* caught the mood: 'We trust we shall have no more churches built in the bald and beggarly style of dissenting meeting-houses, unworthy of God and discreditable to those who build them, but in

21. *LI*, 28 Sept. 1839, repeated almost verbatim in *Gentleman's Magazine*, 147, 1839, p. 532.

22. *Ibid.*

6.10: Leeds, Leeds Parish Church (R.D. Chantrell, 1837-41).

the manner of the magnificent church at Leeds which stands as a noble monument to the taste, the sterling Christianity, and old-fashioned piety and spirit of Churchmanship of the town.'[23] The Revd G.A. Poole, a prolific author of books and articles on church architecture, an advocate of Tractarian arrangements, and a commentator whose opinions should be considered seriously, also published immediately after the consecration: 'The completion of the Parish Church of Leeds – the stately and appropriate beauty of this noble pile – and the deeply religious and ecclesiastical tone which pervaded the ceremony of its consecration, may … be mentioned without apology, as having more than local interest, and promising no limited or transient effects on the ecclesiastical architecture of this kingdom.' Later in the book, Poole noted 'the encouraging signs of a few beautiful and appropriate edifices, yet wearing the freshness of youth … gives … hope'. Singled out as examples were Newman's chapel at Littlemore, Rickman's Hampton Lucy and Oulton, but 'noblest among the noble [is] the Parish Church of Leeds.'[24] Praise indeed.

Even before the Parish Church was finished, a steady stream of ecclesiastical commissions was arriving at Chantrell's office. There were new churches at Lothersdale (1837-8), Farnley Tyas, nr Huddersfield (1838-40), Poole, nr Otley (1838-40), Batley Carr (1839-41), Shadwell, Leeds (1839-42) (6.11), Cowling, North Yorkshire (1839-45), Honley, nr Huddersfield (1840-4), Leven, East Yorkshire (1840-5). In addition, there were numerous alterations and repairs elsewhere. Two of these were of exceptional importance. In 1838, Chantrell was asked to repair the west gable of the remarkable Norman church at Adel and later he re-roofed the chancel. The work at Adel was modest in terms of cost, but it was important in that the ancient church was seen

23. *Church Intelligencer*, 11 Sept. 1841.

24. G.A. Poole, *The Appropriate Character of Church Architecture*, T.W. Green, 1841, pp. iv, 12. For Poole, see Webster [note 1], pp. 338-9.

6.11: Shadwell, Leeds, St Paul (R.D. Chantrell, 1839-42). (*Leeds University Library, Special Collections.***)**

regionally as an object of special antiquarian significance and, subsequently, Chantrell was able to publish articles and deliver lectures about the projects. He was now not just a designer of new churches, but a pioneer in the context of sympathetic restorations. The project also brought him into contact with the Lewthwaites, a clerical family soon to become prominent in the Yorkshire Architectural Society, founded in 1842. Within months of its inception, Chantrell was a member of its committee – only the second architect to be nominated – and, initially, a very active one.

The second of these repair jobs could hardly have been more different. On the night of 19 July 1839, a fire devastated the roof of the cathedral of St Saviour in Bruges. This was seen not simply as a regrettable accident, but a national disaster. Chantrell's family had by now achieved considerable status in the city and two of his brothers had important political and mercantile connections. One of them, William, secured the commission to rebuild the roof. William had no architectural training, but could count public works among his many business interests. From the beginning of the project, it seems clear that William was relying on his brother in Leeds to supply the necessary architectural input, while he acted as project manager. Completion was achieved in an impressive 12 months and, amid the celebrations at the unveiling, Chantrell presented his proposal for completing the damaged tower, an exuberant 100 foot Romanesque crown that would sit on the existing 150 foot stump (6.12). Although later in the nineteenth century, a small, select band of English architects was involved with major Continental churches and cathedral competitions – for instance, Burgess, Scott and Street – Chantrell was the first English architect to work on a Continental cathedral.

The rededication of Leeds Parish Church brought Chantrell considerable prestige and 1842 was to bring a further facet to his fame. It was in this year that he claimed to have discovered the 'lost' principles of Gothic composition, the set of rules by which the proportions of the plans, elevations and details of the great medieval churches were calculated. The idea that a single set of rules was kept secret within Masonic lodges and was used throughout Europe is now discredited, but it had considerable currency in the nineteenth century. Major architects, including C.R. Cockerell, R.W. Billings and Edward Cresy, contributed to the subject and the theories of all of them were discussed in great detail in the various editions of the influential *Encyclopaedia of Architecture*, edited by Wyatt Papworth, that appeared throughout the second half of the century. Chantrell gave lectures on the subject and published his findings for an eager audience.

He was able to apply his discovery – or 'system' as he termed it – to his churches of the mid-'40s, and they form an impressive, though disparate, group. They include those at Rise, EY (1844-6), King Cross,

6.12: Bruges, Belgium, Cathedral of St Saviour. Chantrell's 1847 drawing showing the recently completed tower with the unexecuted west ends to the two aisles. (*Groeninge Museum, Bruges.*)

Halifax (1844-7), Armitage Bridge, nr Huddersfield (1844-8), Middleton, Leeds (1845-6) (6.13), Leeds, Bean Ings (1845-7) (6.14) and Keighley (1845-9) (6.15). The designs are assured and convincing and differ considerably from his churches of the '20s and '30s. However, one might reasonably question how far their sophistication is dependent on Chantrell's new-found 'system' of proportions, and how far they are the result of the Camdenian revolution that demanded steeply pitched roofs, long chancels and the details of a pre-Reformation heritage. Whatever the answer, Chantrell was among the first architects in the country to provide churches in which the new liturgical imperatives could be fully enacted.

After Leeds

At the beginning of 1847, at the age of 54, Chantrell announced he was leaving Leeds and moving to London, although several Yorkshire buildings remained unfinished.[25] He had been a big fish in the Leeds architectural pond, but it was in the capital that the real luminaries of the profession were based. However, there is no evidence that he returned to London to seek commissions, rather he appears to have

25. It seems he had some reliable clerks of works to supervise them and made frequent train journeys from London to inspect progress.

6.13: Leeds, Middleton, St Mary (R.D. Chantrell, 1845-6) and vicarage (1845-9).

6.14: Leeds, St Philip (R.D. Chantrell, 1845-7).

sought to capitalise on his status as an antiquary and a scholar of medieval architecture. It was an audacious move, but in 1847, following the deaths of Rickman and Cottingham, Chantrell might – with some justification – have believed himself to be in the very top echelon of a select group of antiquarian-architects. Initially, all went well. He delivered a lecture on 'The Ancient Roof ... of Adel' at the Institute of British Architects, and it was published later in 1847; in May that year he was elected as an ordinary member of the IBA's Council and the following month he gave a second lecture at the IBA on 'The Geometric System Applied by Medieval Architects to the Proportions of Medieval Structures', subsequently published in *The Builder*. The following year saw the publication of the proceedings of the Archaeological Institute's 1846 York conference which included Chantrell's paper on the Leeds cross. However, this scholarly momentum was not maintained, although there was one more important professional development. In 1849, Chantrell joined the Committee of Architects of the Incorporated Church Building Society. The committee was established the previous year and comprised twelve of country's leading church architects. They met monthly to inspect the schemes submitted with grant applications, and, individually, they travelled to inspect progress on site. Chantrell had the dioceses of York and Ripon. After a career spent altering and extending churches that had been the recipient of grants, Chantrell was perfectly placed to assess the merit of the proposals of others. And there, in the company of the Brandon brothers, R.C. Carpenter, Benjamin Ferry, Anthony Salvin, G.G. Scott and others, Chantrell diligently fulfilled his responsibilities for the next 14 years. He really had become one of 'the great and the good' of the church building world.

Probably in late 1862, he moved to Eastbourne and, somewhat reluctantly, retired from the committee. He was 69 and this marked the end of his professional life. The 1850s had seen a small number of projects undertaken for old friends; the last of them, in Suffolk, for a Huddersfield patron who had retired to the county, was completed in 1861. He continued his membership of the RIBA until 1868. The last decade of his life was spent near Brighton.

Chantrell's wife died in 1863 and in 1867, aged 74, he married again. His new wife was Mary, née Dear, a painter, 45 years his junior, a woman with whom, it seems, he had enjoyed a long, adulterous relationship. In 1869, they had a daughter Marian. He died on 4

6.15: Keighley, St Andrew (R.D. Chantrell, 1845-9).

January 1872, just before his 79th birthday, at the Queen's Hotel, Norwood, Surrey.

While in Leeds, Chantrell was an active supporter of a number of institutions, based both in Leeds and elsewhere. He was an early member of the Leeds Phil and Lit, although his membership lapsed in the late '20s following a disagreement about his bill, and he rejoined in 1839. During the 1840s he delivered a number of lectures for the society on architectural topics. He was a member of the Leeds Library by 1828, in 1835 he served as a Commissioner for the Leeds Improvement Act, and in 1837 he was on the provisional committee for the newly formed Leeds Zoological and Botanical Gardens. In 1836 he was elected a Fellow of the Institute of British Architects, one of the first architects from the provinces to join. To mark the occasion, he presented a copy of Palladio's *Il Quattro Libri delle Architectura* to its library and the following year gave his first London lecture explaining the method of stone quarrying used in Leeds. Also in 1837 he became a Freemason, joining the Lodge of Unanimity in Wakefield before transferring to the Lodge of Fidelity in Leeds. He was an early member of the Yorkshire Architectural Society and within months of its inception in 1842, had been promoted to its committee. The following year he joined the Cambridge Camden Society (later the Ecclesiologists) and in 1844 or 5 he joined the recently formed Archaeological Institute of Great Britain and was a member of its Architecture Committee at the time of its 1846 conference in York when he also delivered a paper about the 'Ancient Pillar' discovered while the old Leeds Parish Church was being demolished. Following his move to London, he became an Ordinary Member of IBA's Council and from 1849-63 he was a member of the Architects' Committee of the ICBS.

Did he ever abandon the taste for Classicism instilled in him by Soane? We shall never know, but – at least initially – it seems his reinvention as a Gothic exponent was largely opportunistic. I suspect he remained a Classicist to the end as his compelling, if incongruous, Soanian tower at Hunslet and his stunning Baroque extravaganza to replace the storm-damaged spire of Holy Trinity in Leeds (1839-40) would seem to confirm. How should he be remembered? Certainly, he produced the most important church of the early-Victorian period anywhere in the country and should be noted as the first architect to work on a Continental cathedral. He produced a succession of good churches, the best of which were exceptional for their date, and he was one of the country's few architects who could perform consistently well when faced with the challenges of Gothic. His reputation would have been assured had not the Ecclesiologists marginalized his achievements along with those of the rest of his generation as a means of promoting their own highly subjective agenda.

Catalogue

Comprehensive details of 144
documented commissions and 11
attributed ones can be found in
Webster [note 1]. The following is a
list of the major projects.

LEEDS, Public Baths, Wellington Street,
1819-21, dem. (*LI*, 5 April 1819.)
LEEDS, Philosophical and Literary
Society Hall, 1819-21, dem. (*LI*, 17
May 1819.)
LEEDS, Christ Church, Meadow Lane,
1821-6, dem. (CBC, file 20548.)
LEEDS, the South Market, 1823-4,
dem. (*LI*, 28 August 1823.)
RUDDING PARK, NY, alterations,
after 1824-c.1835. (WYASL,
Radcliffe of Rudding II/399, 400.)
LOCKWOOD, Huddersfield,
Emmanuel, 1826-30. (CBC,
file15548.)
NETHERTHONG, nr Huddersfield,
All Saints, 1826-30. (CBC, file
15548.)
KIRKSTALL, Leeds, St Stephen, 1827-
9. (CBC, file 18274.)
NEW MILLS, Derbyshire, St George,
1827-31. (CBC, file 18103.)
HOLBECK, Leeds, St Matthew, 1827-
32, spire later. (CBC, file 17593.)
GLOSSOP, Derbyshire, All Saints,
rebuilt nave, 1827-32, dem. (ICBS,
file 00456.)
ARMITAGE BRIDGE, Huddersfield,
Armitage Bridge House, 1828. (C.A.
Hulbert, *Annals of the Parish of
Almondbury*, Longman, 1882, pp.
275-6.)
MORLEY, Leeds, St Peter, 1828-30.
(CBC, file 15678.)

HUNSLET, Leeds, St Mary, new tower,
1830-2, dem. (WYASL,
RDP44/75.)
PONTEFRACT, WY, All Saints,
restoration, 1830-3. (ICBS, file
01347.)
GUISELEY, WY, St Oswald, alterations,
1830-3. (ICBS, file 01472.)
BRAMLEY, Leeds, Bramley Chapel,
alterations and extension, 1833.
(ICBS, file 00413.)
ARMLEY, Leeds, St Bartholomew,
largely rebuilt, 1833-4, dem. (ICBS,
file 00256.)
SKIPTON, NY, Christ Church, 1835-9.
(ICBS, file 02047.)
HEADINGLEY, Leeds, St Michael,
1836-8, dem. (WYASL,
RDP39/86.)
LOTHERSDALE, nr Skipton, Christ
Church, 1837-8. (ICBS, file 02173.)
LEEDS, Leeds Parish Church, 1837-41.
(ICBS, file 02293.)
ADEL, Leeds, rebuilt bellcote, 1838-9;
new chancel roof, 1843. (R.D.
Chantrell, 'Observations on the
Ancient Roof of the Church at Adel'
in *Yorkshire Architectural Society
Papers*, 1845, reprinted 1887.)
FARNLEY TYAS, nr Huddersfield, St
Lucius, 1838-40. (*LI*, 3 March
1838.)
POOL, WY, St Wilfred, 1838-40.
(ICBS, file 02028.)
LEEDS, Holy Trinity, added top 3 stages
of tower, 1839-40. (*LI*, 2 Feb.
1839.)
BATLEY CARR 1839-41. (ICBS, file
02590.)
SHADWELL, Leeds, St Paul, 1839-42.
(*LI*, 5 Oct. 1839.)
COWLING NY, Holy Trinity, 1839-45.
(CBC, file 15542.)

BRUGES, Belgium, Cathedral of St
Saviour, restoration following fire
and termination to tower, 1839-47.
(C. Webster and A. Van den Abeele,
'A portentous mass of bastard
Romanesque frippery' in
Architectural History, 42, 1999, pp.
284-92.)
HONLEY, nr Huddersfield, St Mary,
1840-4. (ICBS, file 01484.)
LEVEN, EY, Holy Trinity, 1840-5.
(ICBS, file 02784.)
DENHOLME GATE, WY, St Paul,
1843-6. (ICBS, file 03257.)
RISE, EY, All Saints, 1844-6. (*Builder*,
3, 1845, p. 585.)
HALIFAX, St Paul, King Cross, 1844-7,
dem. (ICBS, file 03474.)
ARMITAGE BRIDGE, Huddersfield, St
Paul, 1844-8, subsequently rebuilt
following a fire. (ICBS, file 03527.)
MIDDLETON, Leeds, St Mary, 1845-
6, spire removed 1939. (ICBS, file
03514.)
LUND, EY, All Saints, rebuilt chancel,
1845-6. (A. Steel, *History of All
Saints Church, Lund*, privately
printed, n.d., unpaginated.)
LEEDS, St Philip, Bean Ings, 1845-7,
dem. (CBC, file 20547.)
KEIGHLEY, WY, St Andrew, 1845-9.
(ICBS, file 00818.)
FANGFOSS, EY, St Martin, *c*.1849-50.
(ICBS, file 04114.)
BARMBEY, EY, St Catherine, rebuilt
nave and chancel, 1850-2. (ICBS,
file 04227.)
PEASENHALL, Suffolk, St Michael,
1860-1. (*Builder*, 19, 1861, p. 621.)

7. John Clark (1798–1857)

CHRISTOPHER WEBSTER

John Clark came to Leeds from Edinburgh in the late 1820s, probably just before his thirtieth birthday. Despite the huge amount of building going on in the Scottish capital after Waterloo, he seems to have designed little there, but he was at least able to immerse himself in the city's unique interpretation of Neoclassicism and which, as we shall see, he studied diligently. With its heady blend of majesty and swagger, alongside obvious references to the past glories of Athens and Rome, it was a style perfectly suited to the aspirations of a fast-growing industrial town like Leeds, keen to stamp in the minds of visitors and residents alike that it was a powerhouse of commerce and manufacturing, but one equally committed to culture and refinement. It was hardly surprising that he was received so warmly in West Yorkshire. Unlike Taylor and Chantrell who were Gothic church builders of regional importance, Clark's forte lay in secular work and as a Classicist he was of exceptional ability. Yet there is a second important theme to this essay: it is a salutary story of a fall from grace. In the last decade and a half of his life he received few choice commissions.

Clark was born in Edinburgh on 3 July 1798[1] and so would have spent the mid-late 1810s learning his craft. He could not have chosen a better time or place to study architecture as the post-Waterloo capital witnessed a staggering amount of construction designed by a remarkably gifted succession of architects. He must have trained in the office of one of these great men like William Burn, Gillespie Graham, Thomas Hamilton or W.H. Playfair as his work relies much on 'the Edinburgh style', but no records have been traced which place him in

1. This appears in Clark's will: Edinburgh Sheriff Court Wills, Sc70/4/54. It seems he came from a middle-class family which owned property in Castle Terrace. His sister Charlotte was one of many partners in the Edinburgh and Glasgow Bank. (*The Scotsman*, 20 February 1847.)

7.1: Edinburgh, No1, Castle Terrace (John Clark, 1824). (*Jill Turnbull.*)

any particular office. On the other hand, the central area of the city, where building activity was concentrated, was so compact that a diligent student might easily keep abreast of the work of all the leading architects. By 1823 he had set up in independent practice at 1, Roxburgh Street, Edinburgh, on the eastern fringe of the New Town, and from 1825 he was at St Cuthbert's Glebe, Lothian Road,[2] in a house he had just built.[3] It is a handsome structure, four storeys with rusticated basement, compact attic and two floors articulated by giant antae (7.1). It is an assured work for a young designer, but very much in the manner of those architects listed above who dominated the city's architecture around 1820.

There is no record of Clark building anything else in Edinburgh; while there was much work being carried out, there was also no shortage of talented architects and it seems Clark was determined to cast the net widely when seeking commissions. In April 1824, he entered a competition for an 'Institution in Bolton' to contain an 'Exchange, News Room, Committee Room, Library and Reading or Lecture Room', following an advertisement which appeared in

2. *Edinburgh and Leith Post Office Directory*, 1823-24, p. 153; 1825-26, p. 35.

3. The house now has the address 1, Castle Terrace. See J. Gifford *et al*, *The Buildings of Scotland: Edinburgh*, Penguin, 1984, p. 263. *The Scotsman* for 27 August 1825 includes: 'VALUABLE PROPERTY TO BE SOLD OR LET. Several Houses in that large and substantial built Tenement, lately erected at the foot of Lothian Rd. and fronting Princes Street ... Also, the North self-contained HOUSE in the same tenement [details of rooms] These houses have been built in the best manner, under the immediate inspection of the proprietor, Mr John Clark, architect ... ' I am most grateful to a number of people in Scotland who assisted me with my quest to find out about Clark's Edinburgh years. They include Graham Leake, Joe Rock, Jill Turnbull and David Walker.

Edinburgh's *Scotsman*.[4] About the same time, he entered a competition for a similar building in Rochdale.[5] Although he was successful in neither, he at least had the satisfaction of securing second place and thus a premium. However, in the 1825 competition for the Leeds Commercial Buildings (4.1; 4.12) he emerged as victor, and this was his entrée to the West Riding.

Arrival in Leeds

Most unusually, this was a 'closed' competition in which six architects were invited to submit designs for which they were each paid a fee instead of the chance of winning a prize. Alongside Clark, the six comprised Chantrell and Taylor – the principal Leeds architects – plus Charles Barry, Francis Goodwin and Anthony Salvin, three successful London architects in the early stages of their careers, all of whom had a connection with the area.[6] The interesting question is how did Clark come to be involved? More intriguingly, according to Alderman Hill, one of the Commercial Buildings' shareholders, negotiations had been proceeding with Clark for some time prior to the official selection of the winning design.[7] Indeed, Clark was even given the opportunity to re-work his design in order to answer some early criticism and reduce its cost – principally be substituting a dome for the tower – with the *Intelligencer* not unreasonably asking why 'the privilege [was not] extended to all.'[8] The saga reveals much about the nature of secular competitions and of Clark's willingness to be complicit in a very dubious system. But whatever the efficacy of the selection process, Clark's building was unquestionably impressive.

Surviving images of the building reveal little of the challenge presented by the exceptionally awkward site which Clark overcame, but not by reducing it to something closer to a rectangle as some of the competitors did. Rather he used almost every available inch of the site and conceived a design which had no 90° corners and, in effect, six different elevations. (The rear elevation appears on the extreme right hand side of 4.5.) The composition relied heavily on his Scottish background: the elevations to Park Row and Boar Lane are based on Edinburgh's St Bernard's Terrace (James Milne, 1824) while the curved centre is taken from the corner of Blenheim Place and Leith Road (William Playfair, 1821). It was a stunning overture to a decade of successes in which he 'show[ed] his Classical taste and prov[ed] his title to be a son of modern Athens.'[9]

It is not clear at what point Clark decided to settle in Leeds. He gave his address as 'Edinburgh' in the advertisement that invited tenders for the Commercial Buildings in January 1826[10] and continued to appear in the Edinburgh *Directories* until 1830.[11] His will[12] suggests a long-term association with the city and it is likely he made return visits

4. *Scotsman*, 7 April 1824.

5. Edinburgh's *Caledonian Mercury* on 10 July 1824 noted: 'We understand that at a public competition at Rochdale … a premium was awarded to Mr John Clark, architect of this city, for a design made by him of a building proposed to be erected there for commercial and public purposes. We have had very lately occasion to take notice of the same gentleman having, in similar manner, had a premium adjudged to him at Bolton.' A similar article appeared in *Scotsman*, 7 July 1824. The Rochdale project was the Commercial and Public Rooms for which designs were invited in *LM*, 15 May 1824. Clark's Bolton submission was for the Exchange and News Room, a competition won by Richard Lane of Manchester.

6. Goodwin had recently completed the Central Market in Leeds, Salvin exhibited with the Northern Society in the early '20s and Barry's Manchester work would have been known across the Pennines.

7. This account can be found in F. Beckwith, *Thomas Taylor, Regency Architect*, PTS, 1949, p. 69, although it is not clear where he found the Hill assertion. Indeed, the *Intelligencer* was of the opinion that Goodwin was the front-runner (23, 30 June 1825).

8. *LI*, 7 July 1825.

9. From Clark's obituary, *Building Chronicle*, May 1857, pp. 197-8.

10. *LM*, 28 Jan. 1826. Unusually tradesmen were to submit their estimates to the company's solicitors, Messrs Smith and Morritt in Leeds, and only contact Clark in Edinburgh for 'more details'.

11. He was listed in the annual *Edinburgh and Leith Post Office Directory* from 1823-1830. His final appearance was in the volume for 1829-30, probably compiled early in 1829.

12. Edinburgh Sheriff Court: Will SC70/4/54 and Inventory SC70/1/96.

regularly to maintain friendships and he would, surely, have kept a keen eye on architectural developments in the Scottish capital. His first appearance in the Leeds *Directories* also occurred in 1830,[13] although in that year he exhibited at the Northern Society for the Encouragement of Arts 'A view of a house proposed to be built by a Gentleman in Berwickshire'[14] which confirms he had not entirely severed his links with Scotland. His clerk of works at the Commercial Buildings was John Child who went on to have a credible career as an architect, and perhaps he was left in charge for long periods of time. At some point in the late 1820s, he made the decision to be based in Leeds, probably encouraged by the Commercial Buildings' shareholders who were certainly pleased with the progress of their new edifice and well placed to promote Clark in the region. One of them, George Banks, a very successful stuff merchant and former mayor, engaged Clark early in 1828 to design a mansion for an estate near Doncaster he had just purchased,[15] and to which we will return later. A succession of important secular commissions followed and for at least a decade, 'he had, perhaps, the best practice in the town'.[16]

Clark could hardly have wished for a better advertisement for his talents than the Commercial Buildings: it was, after all, the most expensive public building ever erected in the area – a magnificent mercantile palace – and its users were the region's business elite. But there was another very significant factor in Clark's favour: at a time when architects' estimates were 'everywhere vilified as things in which no confidence can be placed',[17] his reliability in this respect received an important boost. In the 'Local Intelligence' section of the *Mercury* in 1829, under the heading COMMERCIAL BUILDINGS, LEEDS, the paragraph continued, 'It rarely happens that an architect's estimate approaches so nearly the actual expense as that of Mr Clark's for this edifice … about 5% on the whole amount including furnishings and fees.'[18] It was a rare achievement and proclaimed an attribute at least as valuable to a potential patron as virtuosity at the drawing board.

Despite a succession of fine buildings, we know little about the architect: he appears to have played no part in the town's affairs and seems not to have joined professional or antiquarian societies that would hint at his interests. Furthermore, the nature of his work – almost entirely private commissions either for individuals or groups of speculators – means that almost none of his business correspondence has survived, unlike the situations for Taylor and Chantrell, whose ecclesiastical patrons were more diligent record keepers. Constructing an account of his career must rely heavily on the buildings he erected, the evidence of which suggests a man of outstanding ability, able to work in a variety of styles and capable of supplying a thriving industrial region with all its architectural needs. Clark, who remained a bachelor, initially took lodgings 'at Mrs Goodall's, Park Lane',[19] but by *c.*1830

13. *Directory of the Borough of Leeds*, Parson and White, 1830, p. 173.

14. Exhibition *Catalogue*, p. 25.

15. T. Friedman, *Joseph Gott Sculptor*, Leeds City Art Galleries, 1972, p. 73. Two drawings, one of which was signed and dated Jan. 1828, were in private hands in 1972, but cannot now be traced. Banks was a member of the Building Committee for the Commercial Buildings.

16. The quotation comes from a letter from the Leeds architect William Perkin in a publicly conducted spat with Clark about the conduct of several architectural competitions in the town. (*LI*, 4 March 1848.)

17. *LI*, 26 Feb. 1848.

18. *LM*, 7 March 1829.

19. *LM*, 25 March 1826.

7.2: Leeds, Free (Grammar) School, new library and master's house (John Clark, 1830). (*Watercolour by Walter Braithwaite, Leeds Library and Information Services.*)

he was living at 4 Park Square, moving to number 8 in 1834 and by 1839 to number 6, where he remained to his death. His two spinster sisters Charlotte and Isabella mainly lived with him; the third sister Elizabeth married a 'Mr Wilson' and remained in Edinburgh. The Leeds *Directories* place his office in the Commercial Buildings, in various addresses in Park Cross Street, but, unusually, these are interspersed with Park Square suggesting that, for long spells, he worked from home. There is no specific evidence of assistants, although it is unlikely he ran the office alone, and in August 1840 he advertised for a pupil.[20]

He entered the competition for the Huddersfield Dispensary, advertised in February 1829,[21] but did not secure any of the premiums. However, in 1830 he was appointed to build a new library and master's house for Leeds Free (Grammar) School (7.2). Although Clark's career in the 1830s is dominated by a series of magnificent Grecian essays, it is interesting that his second Leeds job was in a quite different style: Tudor. This was a logical choice for the Free School. The original structure dated from the seventeenth century and it was the style used by Taylor for his alterations in 1823 (5.3). The library was a modest three bay composition, enlivened by an elaborate niche over the central door and a substantial oriel window in the gable end. While the details were readily available in a series of pattern books,[22] Clark is nevertheless to be commended for his compositional skills.

Also in 1830, he submitted three alternative schemes for a tower for the Anglican chapel at Hunslet. This was a modest Georgian structure in a simple Classical style and it is likely Clark's designs would have followed this pattern, but the drawings have not survived. The job eventually went to Chantrell, but Clark's involvement reveals his

20. *LM*, 8 Aug. 1840.

21. *LI*, 5 Feb. 1829. He was noted as a competitor in *LI*, 26 March 1829. The competition was won by John Oates.

22. For instance: A. Pugin, *Specimens of Gothic Architecture*, Nattali, 1821; P. Nicholson, *The New Practical Builder*, Kelly, 1823, especially plate XIV.

7.3: Bradford, Independent College, Undercliffe (John Clark, 1831-4). (*Bradford Local Studies Collection.*)

7.4: Leeds, Bank Mills for Messrs Hives and Atkinson (John Clark, 1831-3). (*Ruth Baumberg.*)

willingness to chase modest commissions while he awaited grander ones. The wait would not be a long one.

The triumphs of the 1830s

In 1831 he was appointed to build Undercliffe College near Bradford,[23] a training college for those entering the Independent ministry,[24] the foundation stone of which was laid on 20 June (7.3). It was Clark's second major Yorkshire building and another assured Classical composition, although more orthodox than the Commercial Buildings.

Also in 1831, Clark was engaged to build Bank Mills for Messrs Hives and Atkinson, a substantial five-storey, twenty-one bay flax mill on the north bank of the River Aire in Leeds (7.4). The brick structure is largely utilitarian, but it follows the Classical principles of proportion and is dignified by some stone details including a full entablature. Knowledge of Clark's involvement comes only from his obituary, but suggests architects might well have been much more involved in the erection of industrial buildings than is often supposed. In many ways, the employment of an architect made good sense: while a display of architectural fashion was of little importance to its owner, the efficient management of such a huge building project certainly was and even for a hard-nosed Yorkshire businessman, an extra 5% in architect's fees probably appeared to be a sound investment. A decade later he built a vast flax mill complex for John Wilkinson in Hunslet and erected a warehouse in Wellington Road, Leeds, for William Hey (1834-5).

By the early 1830s, Clark's abilities had come to the attention of the Harrogate entrepreneur John Williams who identified the need for more refined bathing facilities in the town. His first project was the

23. I am grateful for information about this project from John Ayres, Susan Raistrick and George Sheeran.

24. The Independents had, since the late eighteenth century, operated a college at nearby Idle. The catalyst for the new premises seems to have been the 1829 legacy of two estates from a Mrs Bacon of Bradford, one of which was to be the site of the college while the other would provide an income for its maintenance. See *Congregational Magazine*, n.s. vol. viii, 1831, pp. 445-6; 581-92; J. James, *The History and Topography of Bradford*, Longman *et al*, 1841, p. 228-9.

7.5: Harrogate, Royal Chalybeat Spa, Ripon Road (John Clark, 1835). (*Author's collection.*)

Victoria Baths in Low Harrogate which opened in 1832. Like other buildings for bathing at this time, it would have been a long, single storey structure and Classical in style, although no image of it seems to have survived.[25] The commercial success of the Victoria Baths prompted others to enter the market and seeking to maintain his supremacy, Williams embarked on his most ambitious project: the Spa Rooms on Ripon Road, opened in 1835. Again he turned to Clark, but this time with a huge budget and a desire for a building of monumental scale. Clark was equal to the task and a massive Greek Doric temple was the result (7.5). The source of the design is the plates of *The Antiquities of Athens* by Nicholas Stuart and Nicholas Revett, published in parts from 1762, but thanks to various new editions, still the late-Georgian period's most comprehensive and accurate account of ancient Greek structures, and one that had had a huge influence in Edinburgh.

The Spa Rooms consisted of three relatively plain walls but with the conspicuous gable end of the road frontage dignified by a *hexastyle* portico, an idea broadly taken form Stuart and Revett's 'A Doric Portico

25. Late nineteenth century photographs exist, but show the building following significant changes in the 1870s that included a reduction in size and modifications to its façade. I am grateful to Malcolm Neesom for this information.

7.6: Leeds, General Cemetery, Woodhouse Lane, chapel (John Clark, 1833-5). (*Ruth Baumberg.*)

7.7: Leeds, General Cemetery, Woodhouse Lane, entrance gate, exterior (John Clark, 1833-5). (*Ruth Baumberg.*)

at Athens', (Book I, Chapter 1, plates I-VI). However, the portico itself is studiously based on that of The Temple of Theseus (Book III, Chapter I, plate III.) The one unorthodox feature is the arrangement of the frieze: the Theseus metopes were probably omitted for economy, but the arrangement of the triglyphs – doggedly out of vertical alignment with the columns – is harder to explain, although it was unlikely to have troubled the average visitor.[26]

In between these two Harrogate jobs, Clark won the competition for the Leeds General Cemetery on the edge of Woodhouse Moor, a project first announced in 1833. The result is, arguably, Clark's finest design, an imaginative composition in which the layout of the ten acre site exploits picturesque principles, and where the two main structures reveal Clark's Classicism at its most sophisticated. It is a project that deserves careful analysis. The central temple (7.6) again draws on Stuart and Revett, this time the Temple of Ilissus (Book I, Chapter II, plates I-VI) with its characteristic corner Ionic capitals and diminutive pilasters at the ends of the side walls. The closed end included stylised wreaths from the frieze of the Choragic Monument of Thrassylus (Book II, Chapter IV). However the most compelling aspect of the whole composition is the entrance lodge which incorporated houses for the Registrar and Sexton at either side of the gate. It is a work of stunning originality within the context of the Classical tradition. The most obvious precedent is the *Propylea* or gateway to Athens' Acropolis, once again set out with impeccable detail by Stuart and Revett (Book II, Chapter V),[27] but here handled quite differently, perhaps a reflection of Thomas Harrison's *Propylea* at Chester Castle (1808-15). The exterior is a blank, window-less box (7.7), composed of massive blocks of stone which befits the ensemble's function, with a tunnel-like

26. There were respectable precedents for this sort of arrangement, for instance in Soane's work.

27. Details like the scrolls that support the entablature of the gates inner face follow closely from some of the illustrations in W. Wilkins, *The Civil Architecture of Vitruvius*, Longman *et al*, 1812, especially Section 1, Plate 10.

entrance incorporating a pair of widely spaced Doric columns. These, unusually, are fluted only at the very top and bottom, direct copies from those of the temple at Delos (Book III, Chapter X, plate I), and set between a pair of *antae*. The tunnel's exit is, like the Athens model, quite different from its entrance with a central rectangular carriage opening flanked by smaller pedestrian ones. It is the lodge's inner face which is the most innovative aspect of the whole cemetery design (7.8), especially the giant pilasters which are without capitals and have a vertical inner face, but a sloping outer one. Also highly unusual are the side faces of the two houses with their sloping-sided panels. What are the possible sources for this remarkable composition? – certainly not the pages of *The Antiquities of Athens*. Clark's brand of Neoclassicism is here much more eclectic and the often staid idioms of the Greek Revival are invigorated with subtle nuances of Egypt, the latter widely seen as a style with appropriate associations for death.[28]

In the mid-1830s, Clark was appointed to build two Leeds banks. The first, the Trustee Savings Bank[29] (1834) had an awkward, irregular site on two relatively narrow streets, the limitations of which Clark overcame commendably (7.9). It included a substantial entablature between the upper two floors in the Edinburgh manner, but incorporated arched-topped openings at ground floor to reflect the growing influence of a national shift to Roman sources. Surviving images obscure much of its detail, but it appears to have shared aspects of the Cemetery's lodges' innovative exploitation of pilasters. The second bank – the Yorkshire District Bank (1836) – was on the prominent junction of Boar Lane and Bishopgate Street (7.10). The site was not only ideal for a monumental composition, but gave Clark the opportunity to stamp his authority at the opening of one of the town's major thoroughfares as it was, conveniently, directly opposite

7.8: Leeds General Cemetery, Woodhouse Lane, entrance gate and lodges, view from inside the complex (John Clark, 1833-5). (*Ruth Baumberg.*)

28. Clark's Egyptian influence is subtle and quite unlike that of (say) Joseph Bonomi at Temple Mills, Leeds (1838-43). Basically, he takes some of the novelty of the Egyptian idioms but reinterprets them as though they were Grecian. It is an idea with few precedents. C.H. Tatham's Mausoleum at Trentham, Staffordshire (1807-8) is the most obvious example. Perhaps a more compelling argument can be made for a link between the lodge's pilasters and those on the entrances gateways of Thomas Hamilton's Edinburgh High School (1825-9), although the latter are on a much smaller scale.

29. It was situated on the corner of Bond Street and Basinghall Street. It was demolished in the mid-twentieth century.

7.9: Leeds, Trustee Savings Bank, Bond Street (John Clark, 1834), dem. (*Leeds Civic Trust Picture Collection.*)

his Commercial Buildings; the view quickly became the subject of commercially produced prints. The bank's composition – apparently a circular, domed temple set within a plainer trapezoid – cleverly overcame the limitations of the steeply sloping site. Yet again Stuart and Revett provide the source: both the basic form and the species of Corinthian order come from the Temple of Lysicrates (Book I, Chapter IV).

The middle of this decade saw Clark engaged on a staggering amount of work which included mansions for two of Leeds' wealthiest citizens: John Hives – for whom Clark had already built Bank Mills – and Christopher Beckett, as well as new stables at Oulton Hall. For Hives he built Gledhow Grove (1835-40), another assured Grecian composition with what had become by this time predictable Clark motifs: a portico taken from the Temple of Nemesis at Rhamnus, the windows' architraves are from the Erectheion and the principal entrance's frieze from the temple of Thrassyllus (7.11). The side elevation has a bold, semi-circular, single storey bay. The skyline of the mansion and gate-lodge are enlivened by a myriad of chimney pots in the form of squat Ionic columns. But perhaps the most interesting aspect of the project is not the mansion but its stable block, where Egyptian influence is even more overt than at the cemetery. Its central feature is the clock tower with slightly tapering sides, highlighted by a plain torus moulding and crowned by an simple Egyptian cornice (7.12).

7.10: Leeds, Yorkshire District Bank, Boar Lane, (John Clark, 1836), dem. (*Author's collection*.)

30. The work involved a substantial extension to an existing property, and a re-facing of some of the older house.

7.11: Leeds, Gledhow Grove, Chapel Allerton (John Clark, 1835-40). (*Leeds Library and Information Services.*)

Beckett's house, Meanwood Park (*c.*1834),[30] is similar in size but radically different in appearance. This is a remarkable design, an early example of the national shift in Classical fashion from Greek to Italian Renaissance (7.13). What is fascinating here is that the details remain largely Grecian and from the usual sources, but the overall effect is

7.12: Leeds, Gledhow Grove, Chapel Allerton, stables (John Clark, 1835-40). (*Ruth Baumberg.*)

much more in keeping with sixteenth century Rome. The innovative features – most obviously the projecting bracketed cornice, the deep balconies and the parapet – fit surprisingly comfortably with the Grecian repertoire and the result is a building of great originality, several years ahead of most examples of this fashion, although Loudon was an advocate of the style by 1833.[31]

Yet another bold stylistic shift can be seen at St Catherine's, a substantial house near Doncaster for the Leeds industrialist Joseph Banks who bought 1,300 acres from the Loversall Hall estate in 1827 to establish himself as a landowner (7.14). Alongside his business interests, Banks was a supporter of a number of Leeds institutions – including the Northern Society for the Encouragement of the Fine Arts – and was one of the principal patrons of the Leeds sculptor Joseph Gott.[32] Clark was first engaged in 1828 and it is not clear whether the completed house corresponded to the 1828 design or was fundamentally revised; neither is it clear precisely when it was finished, although Banks appears to have been in residence by 1838 and still active in Leeds until 1837. The style is Tudor. It repeats elements of Clark's 1830 Leeds Free School design, but might also have relied on several Tudor mansions in Scotland by William Burn from the early 1820s[33] which could, in turn, provide a clue to the issue of Clark's architectural education.[34] Despite its novelty in Clark's output, the result was no less accomplished than the Classical houses.

The extensive stable block at Oulton was for John Blayds, probably even more wealthy than either Hives or Beckett. Blayds – like his father, also called John – sought to proclaim his perceived importance through the employment of a succession of London architects for other jobs and this commission represented something of a coup for Clark.

While on the crest of this wave, in 1836 Clark even secured the job of designing St George's church in Leeds (7.15), a privately funded

31. See J.C. Loudon, *An Encyclopedea of Cottage, Farm and Villa Architecture*, Longman *et al*, 1833, pp. 946-63, although none of the examples are much like Meanwood. A more convincing precedent is the garden façade of Barry's Travellers' Club, London (1830-2), but would Clark have known it?

32. Friednam [note 15], pp. 31-3; 73.

33. For instance: Blairquhan, Ayrshire, 1820 or Ratho Park, Midlothian, 1824. The style's popularity in Scotland seems to date from William Wilkins' Dalmeny House, West Lothian, 1814–17.

34. Details might also have come from Loudon [note 31], pp. 920-46, esp. p. 922.

7.13: Leeds, Meanwood Hall (John Clark, c.1834). (*Ruth Baumberg*.)

7.14: Doncaster, St Catherine's (John Clark, c.1828-38). (*Leeds Museums and Galleries, Henry Moore Institute.*)

project in the fashionable west end of Leeds whose shareholders would have included many of Clark's contented supporters. It was a mark of his standing that he secured the commission even though he had never designed a church before – although he had supervised repairs at Bradford's medieval parish church – and Chantrell, with many accomplished churches to his name by then, could only manage second place. The result reveals Clark's limited understanding of the principles of Gothic composition and a cavalier approach to mixing, somewhat incongruously, the different stylistic sub-divisions of the medieval past. In many ways, it usefully illustrates the 'want of mature knowledge [of Gothic]'[35] that would be pilloried unmercifully by critics only a few

35. ICBS, file 04359. The writer was describing a church by the York architect J.P. Pritchett, but language like this was commonplace by the early 1840s.

years after its completion. It was a big 'preaching box' with a shallow chancel at the east end – all in a dour Early English idiom – but with an elaborate, Decorated spire at the west end, bristling with pinnacles and crockets. It cost £11,000 and held 1,500 worshippers.[36] The project was partly to be financed by the sale of burial vaults below the church and under a substantial terrace running along the south side.[37] The latter is uncannily similar to the arrangement at Burn's St John, Prince's Street, Edinburgh (1815-18), a building on the axis of Clark's front door in Castle Terrace. The 1838 opening was enthusiastically reported in the *Intelligencer* – it was Leeds' first privately funded new church – but, interestingly, it included no reference to its architect.

Given the ineptitude of the St George's design, the quality of his concurrent work at St John's in Leeds might come as a surprise. The latter was consecrated in 1634, an almost unique example of a church from this turbulent period of English history and a late example of Gothic's survival. Clark's commission was to rebuild the tower which he did with little regard to its predecessor, but the result displays considerable sensitivity to the features of the rest of the church.

In the midst of all these successes, it will be instructive to review the totality of Clark's known output as a means of establishing the kind of work that passed through the office of a leading provincial practitioner in the closing years of the Georgian era. Alongside the major projects reviewed above, we know Clark continued to court yet more business. Around the middle of the decade he entered a competition for 'A Public Building in Manchester' – presumably unsuccessfully – and he was appointed to design the Wilberforce Memorial Column in Hull (1834-5).

36. W. White, *Directory … of Leeds*, White, 1853, p. 19.

37. The idea of selling vaults and adding the terrace seems to have been agreed long after construction had started. See *LI*, 30 Sept. 1837.

7.15: Leeds, St George (John Clark, 1836-8). (*Leeds Library and Information Services.*)

Most notably, he was one of the ninety-seven entrants in the 1835 competition for the new Houses of Parliament, the biggest building project the country had ever witnessed. The competition rules specified the style had to be Gothic or Elizabethan; Clark's was, apparently, Gothic.[38] At the other extreme he undertook work for the Leeds Pious Uses Committee whose responsibilities included the management of a portfolio of properties which financed various town charities. His tasks included the surveying, building or repairing of various humble cottages; a little later he charged 3 gns for alterations to a shop belonging to William Hey.

The 1840s: professional decline

By 1840, just fifteen years after winning the Commercial Buildings competition, and a mere ten years after formally taking up residence in Leeds – and despite achieving so much – his career was set on a decidedly downward trajectory; he remained in practice a further fifteen years but did little of note. Two sets of circumstances need to be addressed. Firstly, as an architect who had come to rely on employment by individuals and shareholders, his fortunes were susceptible to the whims and partialities of his potential masters. It would surely have been naïve to assume a process whereby committees of unqualified shareholders judged competitions – 'that convenient medium for the gratification of private and political animosities' in the wonderfully pithy words of the *Mercury*[39] – could be guaranteed to produce objectivity. Initially it was a system that had served him very well as it seems the conduct of the Commercial Buildings competition was by no means beyond question and that of the Leeds Workhouse competition – discussed below – certainly involved skulduggery. But in the 1840s he became a victim of the system, just as Chantrell had been marginalized in the mid-1820s. In addition, it seems Clark's temperament made him a poor loser and his fondness for writing letters to the editors of the local newspapers to discredit the committees who had overseen his competitive failures can only have exacerbated an already uncomfortable situation. Indeed, throughout his career, there are hints he was not an easy man with whom to do business.[40] It is an interesting vignette of provincial practice. We need to return to 1835 – while Clark still carried all before him – and the competition for a new Workhouse for Leeds. Its announcement[41] specified a budget of £10,000. Eleven architects from around the country entered, Clark's design was deemed the best but had to be excluded as its cost was calculated at £12,000, and the premiums were thus awarded to William Perkin of Wakefield (*q.v.*) and 'Mr Austin of London'. However, these designs were soon sidelined and a plan by a 'favourite candidate [Clark]' was 'approved by the parish authorities' and forwarded to the Poor Law

38. Colvin, p. 252.

39. *LM*, 16 July 1825.

40. Accompanying his entry for the Leeds General Cemetery competition in 1833 he wrote, 'I shall be glad to submit [my design] to the committee on the usual condition of any competition I have ever entered … that if not approved of it is to be (?)immediately returned, and if approved then I am to have the management of carrying it into effect.' (LU SC MS421 161/13.)

41. *LI*, 24 January 1835.

42. The story is told in a letter, probably from Perkin, in *Architectural Magazine*, 2, 1835, pp. 484-5.

43. See *LI*, 21 Feb; 9 May; 16 May; 12 Sept; 14 Nov; 28 Nov 1846; also *LM*, 16 May 1846.

44. See *LI*, 26 Feb; 4 March; 11 March; 18 March 1848.

45. *LM*, 26 Feb 1848.

46. WYASL DB/197, committee minutes.

47. *Builder*, II, 1844, p. 289. The cost 'will not be less than £3,000'.

48. *Building Chronicle*, May 1857, pp. 197-8. This is part of a laudatory obituary, repeated more or less verbatim in *Caledonian Mercury*, 7 May 1857.

49. *LM*, 22 Oct 1859.

Commissioners in London.[42] In the end, the Commissioners doubted it could be erected even for £20,000 and as they considered this too large a sum to expend, the project was temporarily suspended. Clark, sensibly, refrained from comment at this stage. However, following his failure to secure either of the generous premiums for the huge Leeds Prison project in 1843 and his rejection in the 1846 competition for the Industrial Schools – where he was one of only four entrants – he was moved to write to the editor of the *Intelligencer*. There followed a public exchange with Perkin – by then in partnership with Elisha Backhouse – whose practice was in the ascendancy. Clark succeeded in making some apparently valid points, but while Perkin seemed to emerge with a degree of dignity, Clark can have gained few friends among the closed circle of those who made up the committees of the various Leeds public buildings.[43] The issue flared again in 1848 when Clark crossed pens with Perkin and Backhouse about competitions, rehearsing his earlier grumbles about the prison among other things and implying he had been a competitor for the 1845 Stock Exchange building.[44] The *Mercury's* editor was less tolerant than the *Intelligencer's* and cutting short Clark's letter added, 'Mr Clark proceeds to complain of the unfair manner in which architects are too often treated … but as we have on former occasions laid his views on this point before the public, we must decline inserting this repetition of them.'[45] Nevertheless, Clark's rant continued in the rival paper. It was an undignified swan-song.

The story of Clark's career in the 1840s is a very different one from that of the '30s and in 1842 he offered his services as a surveyor to the Leeds Improvement Commissioners,[46] surely an act suggesting a degree of desperation. In the decade much of his known work centres around the unlikely location of Rawdon, a village about 7 miles west of Leeds. Here Robert Milligan, a Congregationalist whom Clark must have known from the Independent College at Undercliff, was able to provide a number of modest commissions. There was at least a massive mill in Hunslet and a substantial new church at Rossington near Doncaster, paid for by 'James Brown Esq of Leeds' who owned the estate.[47] However, it was a sad end to what had once been a glittering career. He died in 1855, aged 57 'after a protracted illness of eight years'[48] which would seem to explain his apparent retirement in his late forties. His sister Charlotte continued to live in the Park Square house, but his office furniture and effects were sold in 1859.[49]

Catalogue

In the following list, BC refers to Clark's obituary in *Building Chronicle*, May 1857, p. 197.

EDINGBURGH, 1 Castle Terrace, 1824. (*The Scotsman*, 27 Aug 1825; J. Gifford *et al*, *The Buildings of Scotland: Edinburgh*, Penguin, 1984, p. 263.)

ROCHDALE, Lancs, Commercial and Public Rooms, premiated competition entry, 1824. (*Caledonian Mercury*, 10 July 1824.

BOLTON, Lancs, Exchange and News Room, premiated competition entry, 1824. (*Caledonian Mercury*, 10 July 1824.

LEEDS, Commercial Buildings, 1825-9. (*LM*, 31 Oct 1829.)

HUDDERSFIELD, Dispensary, unsuccessful competition entry, 1828. (*LI*, 26 March 1829.)

DONCASTER, St Catherine's, Balby, a private house for George Banks, 1828-38. (Friedman [note 15], p. 73.)

BERWICKSHIRE, unidentified house, *c*.1830. (Northern Society for the Encouragement of the Fine Arts, Leeds, *Exhibition Catalogue,*1830.)

LEEDS, Free (Grammar) School, new library and master's house, 1830. (WYASL DB/187/263.)

LEEDS, St Mary, Hunslet, submitted 3 alternative designs for new tower, none executed, 1830. (WYASL RDP45/57.)

LEEDS, Bank Mills for Messrs Hives and Atkinson, 1831-3. (*BC*)

BRADFORD, Independent College, Undercliffe, 1831-4. (J. James, *The History and Topography of Bradford*, Longman *et al*, 1841, pp. 228-9.)

HARROGATE, Victoria Baths, 1832. (*BC*)

LEEDS, cottages at Sheepscar for Borough of Leeds, 1832. (WYASL DB/197/287.)

HULL, Wilberforce Memorial, 1834-5. (*Hull Packet*, 5 Dec. 1834.)

BRADFORD, Cathedral, reconstruction of s. side, 1832-3. (*LI*, 4 Oct.1833.)

LEEDS, cottages in Marsh Lane for Borough of Leeds, 1833. (WYASL DB/197/292.)

LEEDS, General Cemetery, Woodhouse Lane, 1833-5. (LU SC MS 421.)

LEEDS, Trustee Savings Bank, Bond Street, 1834. (*BC*)

LEEDS, Meanwood Park, remodelled, for Christopher Beckett, *c*.1834. (*BC*; *LI,* 7 June 1834.)

LEEDS, warehouse in Wellington Road for William Hey, 1834-5. (WYASL, DB75/19.)

LONDON, Houses of Parliament, unsuccessful competition entry, 1835. (Colvin, p. 252.)

HARROGATE, Royal Chalybeat Spa/Spa Rooms, 1835, (*BC*)

LEEDS, Workhouse, unexecuted deign, 1835. (*LI*, 24 Jan 1835; 19 March 1836.)

MANCHESTER, unexecuted design 'for a public building', *c*.1835. (*Catalogue of Leeds Public Exhibition*, 1839.)

LEEDS, Gledhow Grove, Chapel Allerton, for John Hives, 1835-40. (*BC*)

LEEDS, Yorkshire District Bank, Boar Lane, 1836. (*BC*)

LEEDS, St George, Mount Pleasant, 1836-8. (*LI*, 22 Oct. 1836.)

LEEDS, St John's, repairs and rebuilding of tower, 1836-8. (*LI*, 26 Nov. 1836.)

OULTON, Leeds, Oulton Hall, stables, for John Blayds, 1837. (WYASL, 333/153.)

LEEDS, Little Woodhouse estate, inc. Woodhouse Square, Clarendon Road and Hyde Terrace, proposed development, working with land surveyor S.D. Martin, 1839. (*LI*, 2 March 1839.)

LEEDS, two houses in Woodhouse Square, now Waverley House, 1840. (WYASL DB5/38.)

LEEDS, two houses in Hyde Terrace, 1840. (WYASL DB5/38.)

LEEDS, Potter Almshouses, Raglan Road, *c*.1840. (*BC*)

LEEDS, Hunslet Mill for John Wilkinson, 1842. (*BC*)

LEEDS, Mr Hopkinson's shop, Commercial Street, alterations to shop front, for William Hey, 1843. (WYASL DB75/19.)

ROSSINGTON, nr Doncaster, St Michael, 1843-4. (*Builder*, 2, 1844, p. 289.)

RAWDON, nr Leeds, British Training School, 1844-5. (*LM*, 23 Aug. 1845.)

BATLEY CARR, nr Dewsbury, parsonage, 1846, (Nettleton Paper, WYASL, 376.)

RAWDON, nr Leeds, Benton Park Congregational Chapel, alterations, 1846. (*LM*, 31 Oct. 1846.)

LEEDS, Industrial Schools, unsuccessful competition entry, 1846. (*LI*, 9 May 1846; *LM*, 28 March 1846.)

RAWDON, house for Robert Milligan, 1847. (Nettleton Papers, WYASL 376.)

Unidentified location, 'Gatekeeper's Cottage for Mr Brown Esq.', *c*.1847. (Nettleton Papers, WYASL 376.)

APPERLEY BRIDGE, house for J. Richardson, 1848. (Nettleton Papers, WYASL 376.)

8. *James Simpson (1791–1864)*

IAN SERJEANT

James Simpson was a local man from humble origins yet he had a remarkable career which brought him considerable prestige. He was known, primarily, as a Nonconformist[1] chapel builder, and his is a revealing story of the way an ambitious tradesman could rise to the rank of architect, in this case building a practice that stretched across much of Northern England. It is also an instructive example of the way in which patronage could be an essential ingredient in career transformation.

Simpson was born in 1791 in Aberford, a village ten miles east of Leeds. He was the fourth of five sons of John Simpson and Sarah Tingle who married in 1780.[2] Although his father was initially a labourer, the family prospered and rose to become well-connected Wesleyans. Simpson established himself as a joiner around 1820[3] giving an address of 11 Hope Street, Leeds, and is known to have worked in that capacity during the construction of Leeds' Brunswick Chapel (1824-5) where his brothers John and Thomas were trustees. Other relatives, including his nephew, John Raynar, a prominent Leeds solicitor, were trustees of chapels elsewhere in Leeds. Another nephew was the Revd William Simpson, for a time a Wesleyan missionary in India. James Simpson's brother John, and John's sons Morris and Edward, were founders of the shoe firm Stead and Simpson. Clearly Simpson was well placed to exploit family connections and at a time when the Wesleyans were dynamic chapel builders, he was perfectly positioned to secure commissions. Yet his success was based on more than nepotism; while the Wesleyans provided much employment in and around Leeds, his

1. Although Methodism does not consider itself to be Nonconformist, for ease of expression in this essay it is included within this general term.

2. Wesley Historical Society, Online Dictionary of Methodism. www.wesleyhistoricalsociety.org.uk/ Dictfr1.html

3. He first appears under the heading 'Joiners and House Builders' in Baines' 1822 *History, Directory and Gazetteer of … York*, but is not listed in the town's previous *Directory* in 1818.

practice stretched well beyond it, suggesting he had quickly developed a solid reputation.

What training did Simpson obtain? A Thomas Simpson of Aberford, who was almost certainly one of James' older brothers, enlarged the local church in 1821[4] and re-roofed a neighbouring church ten years later.[5] Perhaps James received some instruction from him. Certainly the time he spent as a joiner for the accomplished Sheffield architect Joseph Botham at Brunswick – which represented, at the time of its construction, the most sophisticated chapel design in the area – must have taught Simpson a great deal. It might also have inspired him to seek a higher calling. Even before the woodwork was completed there, he branched out to undertake his first job as an architect, at Beulah Street Wesleyan Chapel in Harrogate, in 1824. A major factor in his appointment was that his brother Thomas was one of the Trustees.[6] A steady stream of commissions followed; Simpson's career re-orientation was perfectly timed to capitalise on the post-Waterloo surge in chapel building.

When the dynamic Dr Hook arrived in Leeds in 1837 to take up his appointment as vicar of the huge parish, he noted it was a hotbed of Nonconformity: 'Methodism grew and flourished; Methodism alone kept pace with the rapid and enormous increase of population in the northern manufacturing towns, and struck its roots deeper and deeper year by year into the affections and understanding of the people.'[7] By way of confirmation, the 1815 map of Leeds[8] lists fifteen chapels for the various denominations; this had more than doubled to thirty-one by the time of the 1831 map[9] and the 1853 *Directory*[10] records forty. Other northern towns could demonstrate parallel increases. There was indeed work to be had by a reliable architect. And there is a further interesting aspect to the story of religious architecture in this period: patronage tended to be kept close to home. Certainly there are exceptions, but generally it was understood that the priority for a building committee was to find an architect from their own community. This leads neatly to the final factor in Simpson's favour: there seems to have been no prominent Nonconformist architect in Leeds; Botham, as we have seen, had come from Sheffield and the York architect J.P. Pritchett secured many chapel appointments throughout West Yorkshire, but was be no means universally admired.[11]

Simpson's career

1834 has in the past been given as the date of Simpson's shift from tradesman to architect – the date of St Peter's Street Chapel, Leeds – but a recently rediscovered document[12] places his elevation ten years earlier, when he erected a chapel in Harrogate. It was a modest project, costing only £900,[13] but it graphically reveals how the transition from

4. ICBS, file 00309. Thomas (1784-1846) was subsequently recorded as a 'painter and sign-writer', and obtained the contract for painting some of the new stations on the Leeds-Manchester railway which opened in 1841. (Wesleyan Historical Society website [note 2].)

5. *LI*, 17 March 1831. The church is at Saxton.

6. Minutes of Trustees Meetings, North Yorkshire Records Office.

7. W.R.W. Stephens, *The Life and Letters of Walter Farquhar Hook*, Richard Bentley, 1879, II, p. 370.

8. Netlam and Francis Giles, *Plan of the Town of Leeds*, 1815.

9. Charles Fowler, Plan of the Town of Leeds, 1831.

10. William White, *Directory… of Leeds*, White, 1853, p. 20.

11. Pritchett received much public censure for his Philosophical Hall in Huddersfield in 1840, e.g. *LM*, 12 Sept. 1840.

12. Letter from Simpson to the Wesleyan Chapel Building Committee, 20 Jan. 1837, reproduced in its Minute Book, Methodist Property Office Archive.

13. Letter [note 12].

tradesman to architect could be made. Given his subsequent success, he must always have been diligent and reliable. He would also have been more literate than his fellow builders. Perhaps he impressed Botham and with a nudge from his brother Thomas who had earlier supervised at least one construction project, he only needed to convince the Harrogate trustees. It was a humble beginning for what was to be a glittering career. These trustees must have been satisfied as four years later he was appointed to design and supervise the new Wesleyan chapel at Spen Valley, some ten miles south-west of Leeds. This is a convenient point to consider the issue of how Nonconformist trustees selected architects for their projects. Whereas the designers of substantial secular public buildings were usually chosen *via* a publicly advertised

8.1: Various chapels by James Simpson (*Author*).

LEEDS, OXFORD PLACE 1835

CHAPEL ALLERTON, LEEDS, 1836

HUNSLET, LEEDS, LOW ROAD, 1836

HUNSLET, LEEDS, CENTENARY, 1839

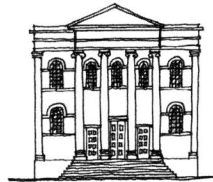

HULL, KINGSTON, 1840

BURNLEY, LANCS, HARGREAVE STREET, 1840

BARNSLEY, PITT STREET, 1846

KEIGHLEY, TEMPLE STREET, 1846

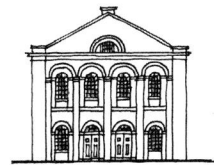

LEEDS, RICHMOND HILL, 1848

OLDHAM, MANCHESTER STREET, 1850

ASHTON-UNDER-LYNE, STAMFORD STREET, 1851

BATLEY, HICK LANE, 1861

competition, and more informal competitions were used by local committees intending to build Anglican churches using substantial Church Building Commission grants, it seems chapel building was organised rather differently. Finance came partly from gifts, but usually a loan would be needed and this would be obtained by the trustees in the same way a group of businessmen might borrow to build a row of shops. The selection of both bank and architect followed a similar pattern: the trustees sought the best arrangement for their congregation, but decisions were reached informally. The experience and advice of others in the denominational circuit was crucial.

It was a further six years before Simpson's next commission, St Peter's Street, in Leeds, again for the Wesleyans, which he began in 1834. From here onwards, the pace of new commissions accelerates remarkably, but what employment had he attracted earlier? It is unlikely that his first two chapels fully occupied him. Presumably, he continued to take work as a joiner and it was under this designation that he appeared at this time in the *Directories*.

During the next five years (1834-9) he secured a remarkable twelve jobs – almost all for the Wesleyans – most of which were for substantial new buildings, but all were in, or very close to, Leeds. Oxford Place (8.1), subsequently re-fronted, was the biggest and most prominent.

8.2: York, St Saviourgate Chapel, exterior (James Simpson, 1839). (*Ruth Baumberg*).

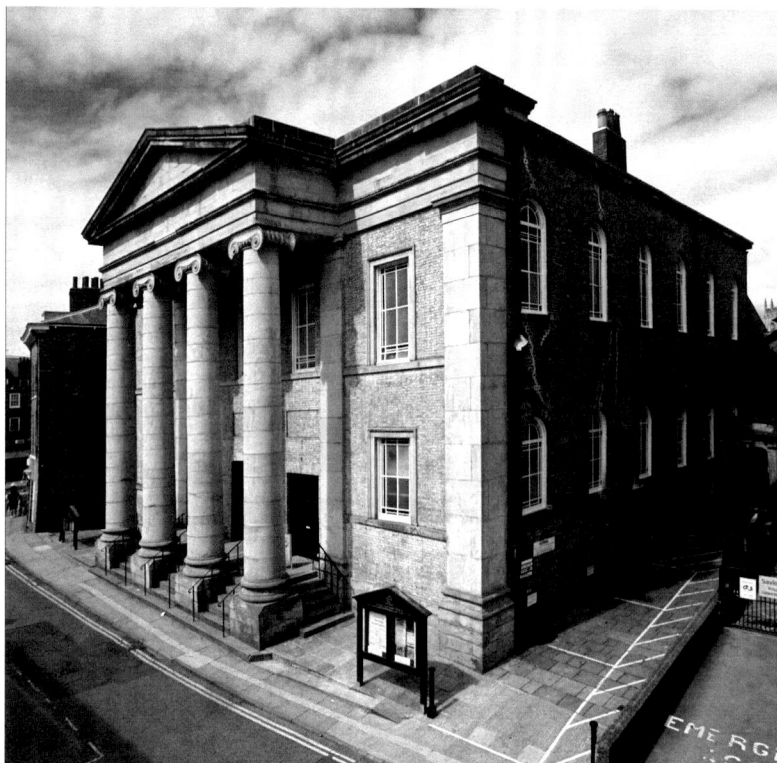

8.3: York, St Saviourgate Chapel, interior
(James Simpson,1839). (*Ruth Baumberg*).

Then, in 1839, came the commission for the St Saviourgate Wesleyan Chapel in York (8.2; 8.3), his most expensive and, with its impeccably detailed *tetrastyle* Ionic portico, his most impressive chapel so far. From here onwards, his fame spread and soon he would be working over an area that was vast in the context of a provincial practice at this time. By the early 1840s he had jobs in Lancashire and Derbyshire, and within a decade he could be credited with chapels in Cheshire, Nottinghamshire (8.12), Staffordshire and Wales.

Although Simpson's reputation rests on his large practice as a designer of chapels, he occasionally undertook other commissions, especially in the early years of his career. In 1844 he supervised the erection of a wall to surround the Market Place in Leeds. In the same year he designed a 'dwelling house, Schoolroom and offices near the Wesleyan Chapel, Meadow Lane',[14] Leeds, perhaps on land owned by the chapel, and he was often responsible for other buildings associated with chapels such as houses for ministers and caretakers, as well as the more usual day and Sunday schools. Generally these were constructed at the same time as the chapel but occasionally, as at Stony Lane, Eccleshill (1854), the schoolroom was added later (1858). There is also a tentative attribution in the most recent edition of the *West Riding* Pevsner of warehouses at 23-35 Cookridge Street, Leeds, erected 1840-1847, for the woollen cloth merchant William Smith.[15]

14. *LI,* 24 Feb; 1 June 1844.

15. Pevsner, *WY,* p. 447

He was still working at the time of his death in 1864, aged 73. During his career he designed at least sixty-four chapels, a staggering achievement considering the apparent absence of any sort of architectural training.

Simpson's office

As we have seen, Simpson's first appearance in the Leeds *Directories* comes in 1822 when he was listed as a 'Joiner'. Interestingly, and despite sound evidence he had begun to design chapels soon after, it is not until 1837 that he is listed in the 'Architects' column of the local *Directories*[16] with an office in his house at 41, Trafalgar Street, from where he continued to practise for the rest of his career. His reluctance to join the architects earlier is noteworthy; while there are several instances of men offering their services as an architect in the pages of a directory without, apparently, having any experience at all, examples of the contrary are rare. We might conclude the stream of pre-1837 chapel commissions was sufficient to keep him busy and perhaps the cut and thrust of a conventional practice offered no attraction to him. But why, then, did he change his mind in 1837, in the middle of the busiest period of his career? It seems unlikely he sought more work. The answer is surely concerned with status.

We might imagine him, while involved with his first handful of chapels, making a somewhat awkward transition from joiner – albeit a talented one – to the man in charge of the whole project. And perhaps for these early jobs, he undertook the joinery work too, arriving on site in his work clothes, only putting down his tools to explain a complex detail to a colleague and make routine inspections. At the same time, he must have been aware of the formation of the Institute of British Architects in 1834, an event attended by considerable debate both inside and outside the profession, much of it rehearsed in the period's journals, especially the country's first one devoted to architectural matters, the *Architectural Magazine* (1834-8). Debate centred not so much on stylistic issues as on the service architects provided to the public and how it could best be regulated to ensure the public's confidence. An advertisement in (say) 1827, seeking a design for a new edifice would often begin 'To Architects and Builders' as if both groups were equally capable of producing a competent design. But ten years later, the distinction between trade and profession would not be wasted on anyone connected with the building industry. If Simpson wanted to be taken seriously, he needed to reinvent himself as an architect. And such a transformation was surely not a matter of indifference to his paymasters; employing an architect to design their new chapel, rather than a tradesman, brought prestige to both the individual congregation and the denomination as a whole.

16. *Piggott's Directory of Leeds*, Piggott, 1837, p. 41.

James' son John (born 1831) initially trained with his father and, according to family tradition, also in London.[17] John appears to have joined James in the practice in the early 1860s, although there was to be no question mark over John's professional status; the end of his indentures were perfectly timed to capitalise on Brodrick's arrival in Leeds and by 1855 he was working as an assistant to one of the greatest talents of the age. Certainly he helped the master prepare the exquisite drawings for the Lille Cathedral competition in 1855-6 and, according to Brodrick's biographer, 'possibly Simpson was working in [his] office until it closed in 1869.'[18] However, this is unlikely. Advertisements for tenders in the early 1860s refer to 'Simpson and Son' and John might have been the John Simpson 'architect, Bradford'[19] who erected a handful of buildings in the early-1860s; certainly he was in independent practice in Leeds by 1868, using his father's old office.[20] John assisted in the completion of his father's last two chapels, at Gargrave and Gildersome (8.10) in 1864-5. The firm of Simpson and Son continued through the 1860s and John only appears in *Directories* in his own right from 1870. Among his designs are Bardon Hill, Leeds (1873-75), a Gothic mansion for his cousin Thomas Simpson, and Weetwood Manor and Weetwood Villa (now Leeds University's Oxley Hall).[21]

Although few records survive to assist an assessment of Simpson's professional skills, the letter quoted at the end of this essay suggests he was methodical, thoughtful and a diligent record keeper. The influential *Wesleyan Magazine* noted that York's Centenary Chapel 'was finished … six weeks before the expiration of the time specified in the contracts.'[22] It also praises his design. It was publicity beyond price; architectural beauty might be a matter of personal preference, but few trustees would be unconcerned about the efficient oversight of their project. Simpson must quickly have acquired an enviable reputation for delivering what his clients expected as both a project manager and as a provider of sound, efficient designs.

The architectural context

George Dolbey observes that as Methodism became more established there was an increasing awareness of architectural dignity and proportion, and he notes a correlation between this development and the emergence of architecture as a distinct profession.[23] While one can point to a number of sophisticated designs for chapels as far back as the middle of the eighteenth century, even in the early nineteenth century employing an architect was relatively rare, and there is no shortage of examples of chapels designed by their minister or a builder who was a member of the congregation. A combination of this absence of architectural expertise coupled with a constrained budget naturally

17. L. Simpson, 'James Simpson's Chapels', in *Leeds and Yorkshire Topic,* February 1982, pp. 38-39. The article, written by his great-great-grandson, notes he received instruction 'as an artist and architect, firstly under the Leeds drawing master, William Ripley-Robinson, and then in London.' No artist with this name is listed as an exhibitor in any of the northern or major London shows in the first part of the century, although a William Robinson from Leeds exhibited 'portraits and landscapes' at various prestigious London venues between 1822 and 1854. (A. Graves, *A Dictionary of Artists,* 1901, reprinted, Kingsmead Press, 1984, p. 237.) An accomplished self-portrait is the Leeds City Art Gallery's collection. There is no more information about the London training.

18. Linstrum, *WYAA*, p. 384.

19. e.g. *LM*, 14 Jan. 1860 or 19 April 1862.

20. *LM*, 24 Dec. 1867; 11 Jan 1868.

21. Linstrum, [note 18].

22. *The Wesleyan Magazine*, Dec. 1840, pp. 1041

23. G. Dolbey, *The Architectural Expression of Methodism: the first hundred years,* Epworth Press, 1964, p. 124.

produced a series of often utilitarian buildings. However, from the beginning Nonconformists recognised the importance of architecture; a flamboyant display was never on their agenda, but architectural dignity certainly was. And efficient planning in which all could hear the preacher was a seminal concern. In this respect, a number of arrangements were explored. The Octagon Chapel, Norwich (1750s),[24] the octagonal Unitarian Chapel, Paradise Street, Liverpool (1791),[25] the vast Surrey Chapel, London (1783) and the oval First Presbyterian Church in Belfast (1781-3) are just some of the many successful alternatives to the rectangle. Indeed, the *Minutes of the Methodist Conference* of 1770 specifically recommended the octagon as 'best for the voice, and on many accounts more commodious than any other',[26] and John Wesley recorded his enthusiasm for Belfast's arrangement after preaching there in 1789.[27] We will return to Simpson's approach to planning later.

His emergence as an architect in the mid-1820s gives him a central place in the development of Nonconformist architecture. The main denominations were becoming well established, and recruiting adherents in large numbers; there was an increased realisation of the importance of architectural elegance and, crucially, many congregations had the funds to pay for it. The repeal of the Corporation and Test Act in 1828 gave the vote to many Nonconformist citizens. This change in status certainly gave them confidence to compete with the Establishment, not just socially and politically but architecturally too. The old deference to the Anglican Church in terms of architectural expression was completely overturned and competition became acceptable, if not desirable in some quarters. Birmingham's prolific Methodist architects Crouch and Butler explained this neatly: 'as Nonconformists drew to themselves more of the better-to-do people, and as culture and refinement grew up among them, they felt unconsciously the ugliness of the "box" type of building'.[28] In the early years of the nineteenth century, they had a virtual monopoly on building, but following the passing of the 1818 Church Building Act, a series of big, expensive and showy Anglican churches began to appear; architecture became an important weapon in the battle for new recruits.

By the mid-1820s, the preferred form for Yorkshire chapels was already established; the Wesleyan chapel in Meadow Lane, Leeds (1816), the designer of which seems not to have been recorded, is a typical example: big, rectangular and Classical. It was a type later given more sophisticated facades by J.P. Pritchett who was responsible for the chapel work that passed through the office of Watson and Pritchett of York and who secured several important jobs with which Simpson, surely, would have been acquainted. Two other likely influences on Simpson need to be addressed. Firstly, there were developments in London, at the heart of the Wesleyan movement; as with so many other

24. See T. Friedman, 'The Octagon Chapel, Norwich' in *The Georgian Group Journal*, 13, 2003, pp. 54-77.

25. Designed by John Walmsley. Illustrated in *Lancashire Illustrated*, Fisher, Son and Jackson, 1831, p. 73.

26. D. Stillman, *English Neo-Classical Architecture*, II, Zwemmer, 1988, p. 442.

27. Quoted in Stillman [note 26], p. 446.

28. Crouch, J and Butler, E. *Churches, Mission Halls and Schools for Nonconformists*, Buckler & Webb Ltd, Birmingham, 1901, p. 21.

aspects of architectural fashion, new ideas spread out from the capital to the provinces. William Jenkins, who was both a Methodist minister and a trained architect, is generally credited with taking as a model John Wesley's revered City Road Chapel (1777-8) in London and reworking it. 'The outstanding figure in Methodist building' was Colvin's assessment of him.[29] But, as Dolbey asserts, the origins of City Road owe more to the plan of an Anglican auditory church than to early dissenting meetinghouses which were generally limited in scale, vernacular in style and without architectural pretension.[30] Jenkins' contribution was a series of chapels, usually of brick with stone dressings, rectangular in plan with gabled end walls, which relied on their proportions and carefully thought-out, but economical, detailing – often circular topped windows set in blank arches – and a pared-down Classical vocabulary. Typical examples are Carver Street Chapel, Sheffield (1804) and St Peter's Street Chapel, Canterbury (1811). His national status means it is probable that his designs would have been illustrated in publications which circulated among Wesleyans, setting a standard to which other chapel designers and ambitious chapel trustees could aspire.

The second likely influence on Simpson at the start of his career was W.F. Pocock's *Designs for Churches and Chapels*, first published in 1819.[31] A third edition came out in 1835 and the book's plates continued to be consulted beyond the middle of the century. This pioneering work was the first pattern book to be devoted to its subject. Although it aimed to appeal to both sides of the Protestant divide, its influence was much greater among Nonconformist builders and Pocock was, himself, a committed Wesleyan.

We can thus see Simpson setting out on his architectural career with Pritchett, Jenkins and Pocock for guidance, but at the same time the enterprise of chapel building was sufficiently young to be open to new ideas. Once Simpson had learnt the rudiments of his craft, and the confidence to experiment, there was scope for innovation. Superficially, his chapels have much in common: with a handful of Gothic exceptions discussed below, all are Classical and almost all of these are rectangular. Although Pocock had illustrated impressive semi-circular and octagonal schemes, Simpson seems not to have been tempted by them. However, he did adopt Pocock's suggestion of a segmental curve for the wall facing the pulpit – which he considered to be the best of all the alternatives[32] – at Centenary, York (1839-40) and Kingston, Hull (1840) (8.1). The parallelogram was virtually ubiquitous and thus if ever there was an opportunity for an architect to re-use a favoured model, this was surely it. However, an obvious feature of Simpson's work is the remarkable – perhaps even obsessive – variety of its Classical details.

29. Colvin, p. 573.

30. G. Dolbey [note 22], pp. 51-52.

31. A facsimile reprint is available from Spire Books, 2010.

32. W.F. Pocock, *Designs for Churches and Chapels*, Taylor, 1819, p. 10.

The concept of a standard plan capable of reproduction was one that occurred to the Wesleyan Chapel-Building Committee in 1837 and it advertised, probably in the *Wesleyan Methodist Magazine*, to invite specimen designs. Simpson's response is printed in full at the end of this essay. In précis, he makes the following points: although he had already built a number of chapels, he 'could never make the same plans do for two Chapels; because there are so many local prejudices to contend with' and 'because there is much truth in the statement that plans should be made to suit the ground'. He proceeds to catalogue the issues of differences in local materials and building traditions, and the inevitability of one set of trustees requiring accommodation that differed slightly from another. He ends with the only statement known in which he expresses his philosophy of design. In assessing his first ten chapels, he believed them to be 'plain, but not mean. There is nothing to offend a correct judgement, although one might wish for more ornament. There is a good form and figure, and there only wants a more splendid dress'.

How did a combination of these influences, practical requirements and constraints manifest themselves in Simpson's chapels? An analysis of some of his major compositions will repay attention.

Simpson's Classical chapel designs

Yeadon of 1834 (8.4) – the earliest of Simpson's chapels for which an image has survived – was severely plain. Was this result of a frugal budget? – possibly, but its architect's limited experience is a much more likely explanation. The symmetry of its principal façade and serried

8.4: Yeadon, Chapel Hill Chapel, exterior (James Simpson, 1834). (*WYASL*.)

8.5: Chapel Allerton, Leeds, chapel, exterior (James Simpson, 1836). (*Author.*)

ranks of windows are the only nod towards the Classical rules; its gable almost has enough detailing to suggest a pediment, but not quite. In short, its entrance front lacks articulation. However, Simpson learnt quickly. Just a year later, he produced Oxford Place chapel in Leeds (8.6) and a year after that, the accomplished Wesleyan chapel at Chapel Allerton, Leeds (8.1; 8.5). Oxford Place, with 2,600 seats, was big and at a cost of £5,300, it represented a very considerable project. Critics might still have used the word 'plain', but Simpson's increased understanding of the Classical tradition is evident. Relatively minor details like the building's neat stone cornice and string course between the storeys are incorporated to good effect. The entrance front is much enlivened by a pair of carefully proportioned Tuscan door-cases, enclosing double doors with semi-circular fan-lights. Chapel Allerton (1836) reveals another giant stride forwards. Although much smaller in size, its main façade is remarkably elegant. Here the relative narrowness of the front produces a more satisfying height to width ratio and the verticality is much assisted by the two strong lines produced by the slight projection below the pediment to suggest a portico in the best Palladian tradition. The single entrance is not unlike those at Oxford Place, but attached columns, as opposed to pilasters, help

8.6: Leeds, Oxford Place Chapel, interior shortly after completion. (James Simpson, 1835). (*Leeds Library and Information Services.*)

emphasise the third dimension. Of course, there was no shortage of post-Waterloo pattern books[33] to instruct an aspiring architect early in his career, and it has much in common with one of Pocock's plates, yet this transformation from Simpson's drawing board in a mere two years is surely indicative of his inherent ability.

Simpson's next chapel – Low Road, Hunslet (1836) (8.1) – reveals a significant innovation, although in most respects this modest sized chapel is unremarkable and the rendering to the front elevation later.

33. For instance, A.G. Cook's hugely popular *The New Builder's Magazine* with six editions from 1817 for Hogg and Co., or Peter Nicholson's equally influential *The New Practical Builder*, Kelly, 1823.

8.7: Leeds, Lady Lane Chapel (James Simpson, 1840). (*Ruth Baumberg, courtesy of the TS.*)

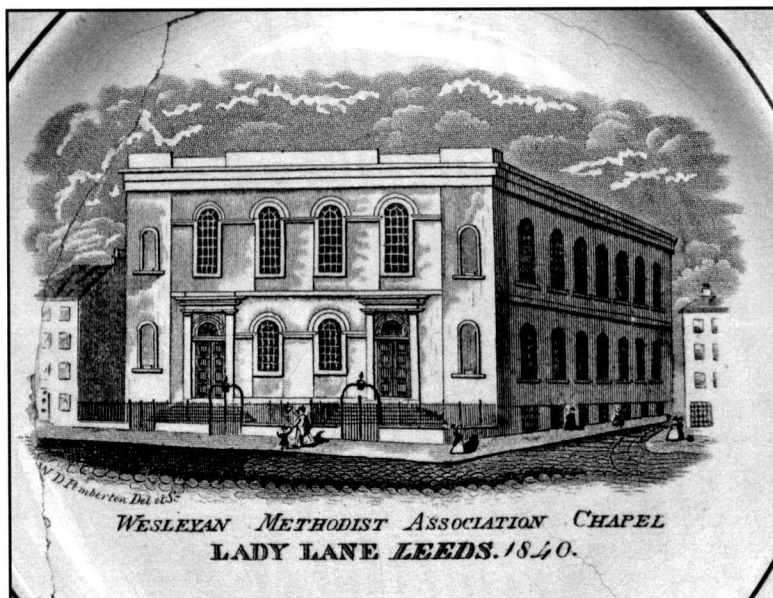

WESLEYAN METHODIST ASSOCIATION CHAPEL
LADY LANE *LEEDS.* 1840.

For efficient ingress and exit, a pair of principal doors was a common chapel format, arranged with varying degrees of success in a three or five bay Classical façade; Simpson takes the idea one stage further with the bold concept of an elevation with an *even* number of bays. Four or six bay chapels are not entirely without precedent, but this became one of most common features of subsequent Simpson designs, for instance the nearby Hunslet Centenary chapel (1839) (8.1).

This takes many of the ingredients of Oxford Place, but the addition of the pediment, the slight advance of the centre four bays, and the imaginative treatment of the blank outer bays – with some reliance on Pocock again – produces a composition of considerable elegance. Lady Lane Chapel in Leeds (8.7) of the following year is, on one level, merely a variation on the theme, but its differences reveal Simpson's virtuosity when using a handful of intrinsically unremarkable elements.

8.8: Morley, Queen Street, chapel, exterior (James Simpson, 1861). (*Ruth Baumberg*.)

The real crown among his early chapels must go to the Centenary Chapel in York (1839-40), built – like many others – to celebrate John Wesley's 1738 conversion. The stated intention of the trustees was to build a new 'cathedral chapel worthy of the city of York'.[34] The total cost was £7785 including £500 for the organ installed the following year. The *Wesleyan Magazine's* extensive account following the opening noted its construction 'under the judicious management of Mr. James Simpson of Leeds, the architect (of whose good taste and economical plans very much may be said) … It is lofty, and well-lighted, and admirably adjusted in its proportions … The end is circular which adds greatly to its beauty.'[35] It is a graphic account of what Simpson could achieve with a generous budget: a *tetrastyle* Ionic portico, corner pilasters and full entablature, the whole raised on a basement to complete the stately composition. A similar scheme was used at Hull the following year, where even the side elevations are carefully articulated, but to avoid repeating the earlier design, York's rectangular windows take on semi-circular tops. Longholme, Rawtenstall (1840-1) is yet another variation on this theme. The Wesleyan chapel in

34. Quoted in Central Methodist Church *Welcome Leaflet.*

35. *Wesleyan Magazine*, Dec. 1840, pp. 1041 and 1044. The curved wall facing the pulpit, combined with raked seating, gives an amphitheatre-like effect, Pocock's 'the figure of a parallelogram, with a portion of a circle at the extremity, which comes nearest to the form here recommended.' (Pocock [note 32], p. 10.)

8.9: Morley, Queen Street, chapel, section (James Simpson, 1861). (*From an original drawing by James Simpson, Methodist Property Office Archives.***)**

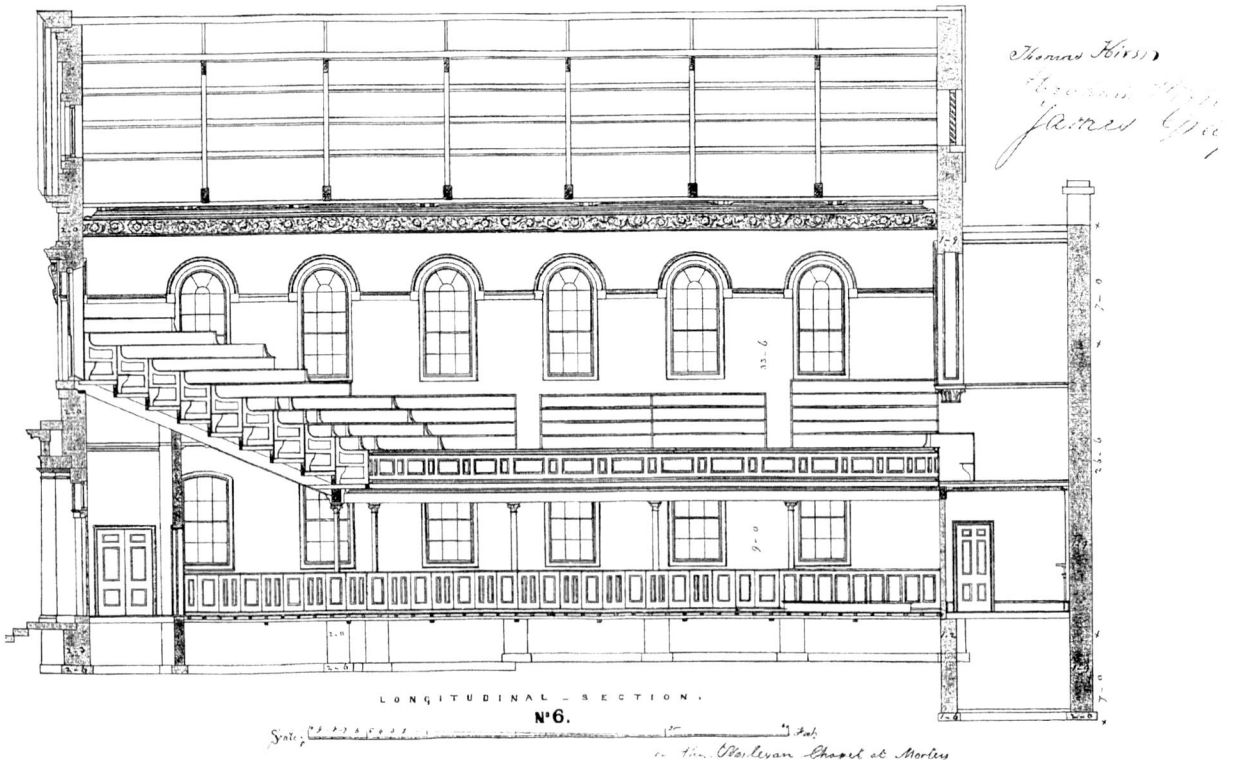

LONGITUDINAL - SECTION.
N° 6.

8.10: Morley, Gildersome Chapel, exterior (Simpson and Son, 1865). (Author.)

Burnley (1840) (8.1) is a further original composition from Simpson's basic repertoire, this time enlivened by massive panelled pilasters at the edges of the façade, borrowed yet again from Pocock.

The remaining twenty-four years of his career might reasonably be termed his 'maturity'. Although from the 1840s his Classical chapels are easily recognised, he continued to refuse to repeat a design, although there are many common features. A double entrance set in a four-bay façade – with or without a pediment – appears to have been his favoured model, but other features reveal the gradual development of his stylistic ambitions. The details of the porches, windows or oculus, for instance, seem always to vary. Bold Street, Warrington (1850), Priory Street, York[36] (1856) (8.11) and Queen Street, Morley (1861) (8.8; 8.9) are typical. But Simpson was inventive to the end and at Gildersome, Leeds (1865) (8.10), he demonstrated he had lost none of his ability to wring new life out of the standard formula.

Simpson's Gothic work

If the discussion of Simpson's output ended here, his would have been a career of exceptional importance in the story of Nonconformist architecture. There is, though, a further chapter to the story: his Gothic schemes. Although fewer in number, the best are, arguably, even more radical than his Classical ones.

The Wesleyan minister Frederick Jobson produced a series of papers advocating a preference for the Gothic style. Jobson had trained as an

36. The development at Priory Street included classrooms, lecture hall, kitchen, day school and houses for the minister, schoolmaster and caretaker at a total cost of £16,000.

8.11: York, Priory Street Chapel, exterior (James Simpson, 1856). *(Ruth Baumberg.)*

architect under the antiquary Edward James Willson of Lincoln, best known for the letterpress which accompanied Augustus Pugin's *Specimens of Gothic Architecture* (1821-3) and *Examples of Gothic Architecture* (1828-36). Jobson's papers were finally published as a book entitled *Chapel and School Architecture* in 1850. Echoing the younger Pugin, he argued that Gothic was the only true Christian architecture

8.12: Newark, Barnby Gate Chapel, Nottinghamshire, (James Simpson, 1846). *(Paul Swinney.)*

8.13: Headingley, Leeds, chapel, exterior
(James Simpson, 1845). *(Ruth Baumberg.)*

and that Classicism was pagan.[37] Not all were appreciative of Jobson's schemes. *The Builder* complained ' … the designs which it gives are mostly of indifferent character (all of one type, and that a common one).'[38] By the middle of the century, Gothic had eclipsed Classicism for the Anglicans but the Methodists and Baptists were more conservative and 'continued to build large Classical chapels throughout the nineteenth century,'[39] and the *Wesleyan Magazine* noted 'Some Gothic structures have not proved economical' and feared that excessive ornament might 'leads men into the temptation of vying with others in decorative as well as architectural taste.'[40] Jobson's 'Model Wesleyan Chapel' – a design by James Wilson of Bath – is, in essence, the auditory plan with a Gothic external form.[41]

But for Simpson Gothic was nothing new. He had already designed Headingley, Leeds (1844) (8.13; 8.14) and Summerseat, (8.15; 8.16) near Bury (1845) in the Gothic style well before Jobson published his influential book and only shortly after Pugin's *True Principles of Pointed or Christian Architecture* appeared. In view of the timescale it seems most unlikely that Jobson influenced Simpson but conceivably, Simpson influenced Jobson. Earlier Gothic chapels are not hard to find, and Pocock illustrates several. Simpson's innovation is in producing Gothic of a quality that just about vies with the best of the contemporary Anglican churches in terms of its accurate detailing. Indeed, Headingley, the first Gothic Nonconformist chapel in Leeds,

37. F.J. Jobson, *Chapel and School Architecture,* (1850, reprint), WMHS Publications, 1991, p.15.

38. *Builder,* 8, 1850, p. 469.

39. C. Stell 'Nonconformist Architecture and the Cambridge Camden Society' in C. Webster and J. Elliott (eds), *'A Church as it should be': the Cambridge Camden Society and its influence,* Shaun Tyas, 2000, p. 327.

40. *Wesleyan Magazine,* October 1859, p. 985-991.

41. Jobson [note 36], pp. 83-88.

8.14: Headingley, Leeds, chapel, interior
(James Simpson, 1845). *(Ruth Baumberg.)*

8.15: Summerseat, near Bury, Rowlands
Chapel, plan (James Simpson, 1844).
*(From an original drawing by James
Simpson, courtesy of Bury Archives
Service.)*

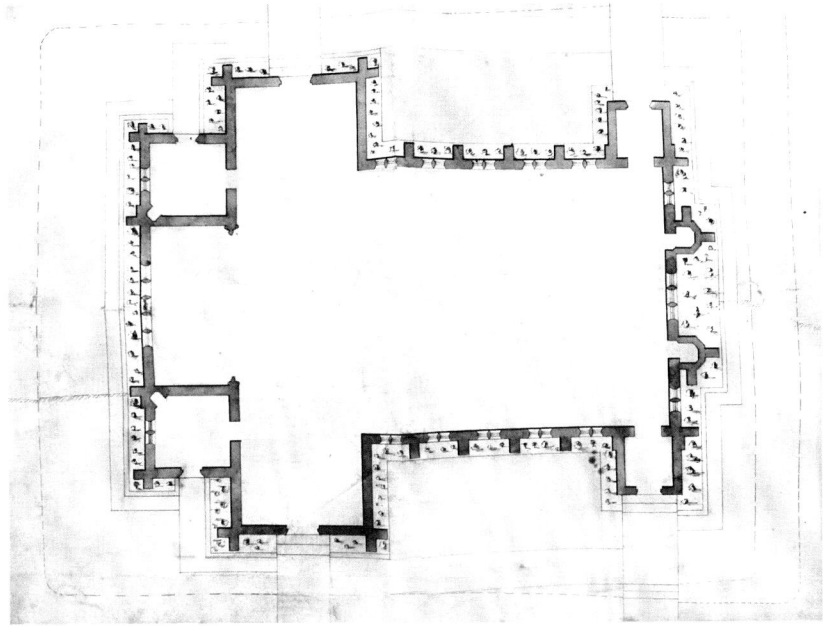

8.16: Summerseat, near Bury, Rowlands
Chapel, exterior (James Simpson, 1844).
(Courtesy of National Monuments Record.)

should be commended for its antiquarian accuracy while, at the same time, remaining faithful to its Nonconformist function. Summerseat is even more remarkable, identified by Stell as Methodism's 'grandest Gothic chapel'.[42] Here the detailing is lavish, built, with no expense spared, by the local manufacturer, John Robinson Kay who had previously engaged Simpson to design the Wesleyan chapel in Burnley. The chapel even included a chancel and transepts, yet its wide, aisle-less nave could never be mistaken as a church for the Establishment.

Conclusion

The best of Simpson's chapels are among the finest of their type and not unreasonably, he has been described as 'the greatest Methodist architect of the nineteenth century'.[43]

Perhaps his principal achievement was to be able to produce a succession of chapels, each different from its predecessors, and fully reflecting stylistic fashions that moved from Georgian Palladian, Greek Revival and Italianate, with just an occasional flirtation with Gothic, yet efficiently provided for a form of service that hardly changed at all. The countless Simpsonian chapels that abound in the north of England, built during and for a long time after his own career, is his ultimate accolade.

I gratefully acknowledge the assistance given by Colin Dews and Dr Chris Wakeling for access to notes and records in their possession. In particular, Colin Dews answered dozens of questions, gave me numerous contacts and allowed me to copy illustrations from his extensive collection.

Appendix

James Simpson – letter to Wesleyan Chapel-Building Committee, 20 Jan. 1837.

Dear Sir,

Since reading the advertisement of the Chapel Building Committee and your letter in the Magazine, I have had conversation with a gentleman here, on the subject of Chapel Plans. His object was to get a number of complete plans lithographed, and send them to the Committee. Perhaps I did wrong in refusing to enter into the project. My reasons were such as these. For some years back, I have built a number of Chapels, and yet could never make the same plans do for two Chapels; because there are so many local prejudices to contend with, in getting Trustees to adopt plans which have in them different constructions to those usually adopted by Builders at the place; and

42. C. Stell, *Nonconformist Chapels and Meeting-houses in the North of England.* HMSO, 1994, p. 73.

43. K. Powell and C. de la Hay, *Deserted Sepulchres,* SAVE Britain's Heritage, 1983, p. 8.

because there is truth in the statement that plans should be made to suit the ground, and local materials to be worked into it; (and Model plans cannot be made so), then they think the whole must be defective and wrong.

The Poor Law Commissioners have adopted the same plan you are about to do; and when leave to build workhouses was granted, they sent a Model Plan. Some of those I have seen, and think them as good as it is possible to make plans for any place; but nearly in every instance an Architect is employed to make Plans embodying all that the Commissioners require, and adapted to the Ground and the Local Materials. Now the Commissioners require the altered plans to them [sic] before they are acted upon; so they control and refuse every thing in such altered plans which they deem superfluous with the authority of an Act of Parliament.

Now, would Trustees submit their improved Plans to your revision? And if they did, can you or any man say what is superfluous? I assure you, that to give an opinion on a Plan to be executed at a place one has not seen, is exceedingly difficult. I say this from my own experience. It is not Plans that are wanted. There is now all over the kingdom plenty of good chapels of which the Plans cannot be mended. The thing to be now avoided, and where the great expense occurs, is in the execution of the Plan where it has to be carried out by what are termed the Working Plan and Drawings. Take for instance, Wesley Chapel in Leeds. The Plan is good, and if to build now, would not be much altered, so far as the Plan is concerned. Yet it cost £7/10/0 per sitting; and now the Chapel might be built on the same Plan, and you would see no difference, for £2.5.0 per sitting. From my own experience, I should think there is not much fear that in future Chapels will be built which shall ever require aid from the Chapel Fund; and where they are likely to be in good circumstances, not much notice is taken of the Building Committee. We had got Oxford Place Chapel half built when the permission to build came; and the same I have known in other places.

There is much embarrassment caused by Trustees beginning to build on data and calculations they do not abide by. One Chapel I am now employed on, was to cost £3000, and would have cost no more, but that, in its progress, it was thought desirable to enlarge the School; then to build a House; then to enlarge the Chapel; now to build another House; so that, in the end, the expense will be £6000. Nor does it appear to me that you can control such proceedings.

Below is an Abstract of the cost of ten Chapels selected as an average of the cost of all that I have built. When information is wanted on the cost and accommodation of a Chapel, I refer to it; and now find in it correct data to work upon. They are all good substantial Buildings. Those which have Schools or Vestries below, I think it not possible to exceed for convenience. They are plain, but not mean. There is nothing to offend a correct judgement, although one might wish for more ornament. There is a good form and figure, and there only wants a more splendid dress.

I have addressed this to you on account of former acquaintances, as I have had some doubt whether it might be of any use to the Committee. If you think it will, you are welcome to make what use of it you may think proper; and any other information you think I can give, I shall be happy to do so at any future time.

Yours respectfully,

James Simpson

[The letter includes the following table]

1. Basement divided into rooms, classes etc.

2. Basement, Schools, let to Com [?] for £20 p.a.

3. Basement, Schools and Vestries

4. Basement, Schools

5. Basement, Schools let for £15 p.a.

	Inside dimensions in yards	Total no. of sittings	Addn'l no. of free sittings	Total cost of everything within the walls	Cost per sitting	Cost per square yd on the floor	Addn'l cost of fence, palisade, drainage, paving	Avge rate the sittings are let at	Actual annual income	Annual expense of lighting cleaning repairs etc	Notes
St Peter's Leeds, Meth	32x24	2500	1000	£4200	32/-	£5.1.0	£350	5/-	£325	£105	
Oxford Place Leeds, Meth	32x25	2600	950	5300	40/9	6.11.0	600	6/6	658	165	1
Belgrave, Leeds. Ind.	30x21	1600	250	3700	45/- *	6.0.0	564	6/6	455	125	2
Yeadon, Meth.	17x19	845	124	1300	31/6	4.0.0	96	3/6	117	25	
Hightown	15x15	650	96	1025	31/6	4.10.0	110	4/-	96	24	
Harrogate	15x15	634	50	900	29/-	4.0.0	open	4/-	70	21	
Hunslet, Bapt.	14x16	650	100	1160	36/-	4.6.0	145	4/6	70	21	3
Holbeck, Rant.	14x12	510	150	1050	41/-	6.0.0	Open	3/-	70	21	4
Chapel-town, Meth.	14 ½ x12	520	150	1100	42/-	6.2.0	75 school and fence	3/6	70	21	5
Kirkstall, Meth.	12x12	500	130	800	32/-	5.10.0	250	3/6	70	21	

* The pews on the floor are all 42in wide, which accounts for the increased cost per sitting

Catalogue

Abbreviations

Letter: Simpson's letter to the Wesleyan Chapel-Building Committee, quoted above.

RCHME 1: C. Stell, *Nonconformist Chapels & Meeting-houses in Central England*, RCHME, 1986.

RCHME 2: C. Stell, *Nonconformist Chapels & Meeting-houses in the North of England*, RCHME, 1994.

Wakeling: C. Wakeling, *The Architecture of Nonconformist Churches during the Victorian and Edwardian Years*, unpublished Ph.D. thesis, University of East Anglia, 1993-4.

WM: *Wesleyan Magazine*

EH: *English Heritage*

WCC: minutes of Wesleyan Chapel Committee, Methodist Property Office Archives, Manchester.

Wes: Wesleyan

WMA: Wesleyan Methodist Association

Cong: Congregational

MNC: Methodist New Connexion

PM: Primitive Methodist

Ind: Independent

HARROGATE, Beulah Street Chapel (Wes), 1824. (Letter.)

SPEN VALLEY, WY, Hightown Chapel, (Wes), 1828. (Letter.)

LEEDS, St Peter's Street Chapel (Wes), 1834. (Letter.)

YEADON, Chapel Hill Chapel, (Wes), 1834. (Letter.)

WORTLEY, Leeds, Bell Chapel (proprietary), new gallery, 1835. (WYASL, signed drawings.)

LEEDS, Oxford Place Chapel, (Wes), 1835. (Letter.)

KIRKSTALL, Leeds, chapel (Wes), 1835. (Letter.)

LEEDS, Belgrave Chapel (Cong), 1836. (LM, 18 April 1835.)

HUNSLET, Leeds, Low Road Chapel (Baptist), 1836. (Letter.)

CHAPEL ALLERTON, Leeds, chapel (Wes), 1836. (Letter.)

LEEDS, Meadow Lane Chapel, extended and altered, 1837. (WYASL, chapel accounts, receipts.)

MORLEY, Leeds, Queen Street Chapel, enlargement (Wes), 1837. (LM, 11 March 1837.)

BRADFORD, White Abbey Chapel (Wes), 1837. (LM, 26 Aug. 1837.)

HOLBECK, Leeds, Princes Field Chapel (PM), 1837. (Letter)

HUNSLET, Leeds, Centenary Chapel (Wes), c.1839. (LI, 9 March; 6 April 1839.)

YORK, St Saviourgate Chapel (Wes), c.1839. (LI, 6 July 1839.)

SCARBOROUGH, Queen Street Chapel (Wes), c.1839-40. (LM, 5 Oct 1839.)

BOSTON, Lincs, Red Lion Street Chapel (Wes), 1839. (B. Moore, *History of Wesleyan Methodism in Burnley and East Lancs*, Gazette Printing Works, Burnley, 1899, p. 121.)

BURNLEY, Lancs, Hargreave Street Chapel (Wes), 1840. (Moore, *op. cit.*, p. 120.)

WOODHOUSE, Leeds, Woodhouse Street Chapel (Wes), 1840. (LI, 4 March 1840.)

LEEDS, Lady Lane Chapel (WMA), 1840. (*Kelly's Leeds Directory*, Kelly, 1886 p. xi.)

HULL, Kingston Chapel (WMA), 1840. (LM, 1 Feb. 1840.)

LOFTHOUSE, nr Wakefield, chapel (WMA), 1840. (LI, 2 May 1840.)

RAWTENSTALL, Lancs, Longholme Chapel (Wes), c.1840-1. (LM, 29 Aug. 1840.)

BACUP, Lancs, Mount Pleasant Chapel (Wes), 1841. (*Centenary Souvenir of Mount Pleasant Chapel 1841-1941*.)

DERBY, King Street Chapel (Wes), 1841. (*WM*, Dec. 1841.)

LEEDS, Park Lane, warehouse, 1843. (*LM*, 19 Aug 1843.)

LEEDS, wall to enclose Market Place, 1844. (LI, 24 Feb. 1844.)

LEEDS, house, schoolroom and offices, nr Wes. Chapel, Meadow Lane, 1844. (LI, 1 June 1844.)

KEIGHLEY, Lees Chapel (Wes), 1844. (EH, list description)

SUMMERSEAT, nr Bury, Rowlands Chapel (Wes), 1844. (Minutes of Trustees' meeting, Bury Archives Dept.)

HEADINGLEY, Leeds, chapel (Wes), 1845. (LM, 15 June 1844.)

KNOTTINGLEY, nr Pontefract, Ropewalk Chapel (Wes), 1845. (*Centenary History*, 1945.)

BRAMLEY, Leeds, enlarged chapel (Wes), 1845. (Wakeling.)

BARNSLEY, Pitt Street Chapel (Wes), 1846. (RCHME 2, p. 232.)

HAWORTH, WY, West Lane, chapel (Wes), 1846.

KEIGHLEY, Temple Street Chapel (Wes), 1846. (RCHME 2, p. 282.)

BIRSTALL, nr Leeds, St John's Chapel (Wes), 1846. (Colin Dews.)

HUNSLET, Leeds, Hunslet Road, chapel (MNC), 1846. (LI, 7 Feb. 1846.)

NEWARK, Notts, Barnby Gate Chapel (Wes), 1846. (RCHME 1, p. 160.)

LEEDS, Hanover Place Chapel (Wes), 1847. (RCHME 2, p. 288.)

WORTLEY, Leeds, Greenside Chapel (Wes), 1846-7. (LM, 11 April 1846.)

LEEDS, Richmond Hill Chapel (Wes), 1848. (*Kelly's Leeds Directory*, Kelly, 1886 p. xi.)

PONTEFRACT, Horsefair Chapel, enlargement (Wes), 1849-50. (LI, 29 Dec. 1849; 1 June 1850.)

LEEDS, Woodhouse Street Chapel (Wes), 1849. (WYASL, Trustees' Accounts.)

WEST BROMWICH, Hill Top Chapel (Wes), 1849. (Wakeling.)

IDLE, Bradford, Upper Chapel (Ind), 1849-50. (*LI*, 21 April 1849.)

IDLE, Bradford, Wesleyan School, 1849 (*Bradford Observer,* 9 Sept 1849.)

PONTEFRACT, minister's house (Wes), 1850. (*LM*, 16 June 1850.)

WILSDEN, Wesleyan School, 1850 (WYASL records)

WARRINGTON, Bold Street Chapel (Wes), 1850. (RCHME 2, p. 150-1.)

OLDHAM, Manchester Street Chapel (Wes), 1850. (Wakeling.)

BURNLEY, Red Lion Street Chapel (Wes), 1851 (Moore, *op. cit.,* p. 128.)

ASHTON-UNDER-LYNE, Stamford Street Chapel (Wes), 1851 (Colin Dews.)

LEES, Zion Chapel (MNC), 1853. (W. Walker, *Builders of Zion, c.*1920)

ECCLESHILL, Stony Lane Chapel (Wes), 1854 (English Heritage, list description)

KEIGHLEY, Wesley Place, Wesleyan School, 1854 (WYASL records)

COLLINGHAM, nr Newark, Notts, High Street Chapel (Wes), 1855 (Colin Dews.)

KEIGHLEY, Devonshire Street Chapel (Cong), 1855. (W.R. Marchbank, *100 Years of Progress*, 1956, p. 23.)

YORK, Priory Street Chapel (Wes), 1856. (*WCC,* 1856, p. 39.)

WREXHAM, Bryn-y-ffynnon Chapel (Wes), 1856 (A. Palmer, *History of the Town and Parish of Wrexham*, 1893, reprinted 1997 by Bridge Books, pp. 72-3.)

ALTRINCHAM, Bowdon Chapel (Wes), 1856 (Wakeling.)

CULLINGWORTH, Wesleyan School and Master's residence, 1856 (WYASB.)

NEWCASTLE-UNDER-LYME, Ebenezer Chapel (MNC), 1857 (RCHME 1, p. 215.)

LEEDS, Wesleyan school and master's house, Pottery Fields, 1857. (*LM*, 1 Aug 1857.)

LEEDS, minister's res. nr MNC chapel, Hunslet Rd, 1858. (*LM*, 27 Feb. 1858.)

BRADFORD, Eccleshill, school (Meth. Free Church), 1858. (*LI*, 24 July 1858.)

ROCHDALE, Union Street, Wesleyan school, 1858 (*LM,*31 August 1858)

HUNSLET, Leeds, Wesleyan schoolroom, 1859-60. (*LM*, 31 Dec. 1859.)

MIDDLETON, Market Place Chapel (Cong), 1859. (RCHME 2, p. 117.)

OLDHAM, Greenacres Road Chapel (Wes), 1860. (RCHME 2, p. 121.)

RIPON, Coltsgate Hill Chapel (Wes), 1860-1. (*LI*, 5 Oct. 1861.)

BATLEY, Hick Lane Chapel (Wes) 1861. (Colin Dews.)

OLDHAM, Brunswick Chapel (Wes) 1861 (J. Beever, *A History of Oldham Churches,* Neil Richardson, 1997, p. 29.)

MORLEY, Queen Street (Wes), 1861. (RCHME 2, p. 293.)

Simpson and Son

RIPON, det. villa, stables and out-buildings, c.1862-3. (*LM*, 8 Nov 1862.)

KEIGHLEY, Wesley Place Chapel (Wes), c.1862-3. (*LM*, 27 Dec 1862,)

SHAW, St Paul's Chapel (Wes), 1863. (EH, list description.)

GARGRAVE, nr Skipton, Chapel (Wes), 1865. (*Centenary Brochure,* 1865-1965.)

MORLEY, Gildersome Chapel (Baptist), 1865. (RCHME 2, p. 294.)

John Simpson

LEEDS, house and shop, North Street, c.1866. (*LM*, 28 March 1866.)

LEEDS, 16 houses in Bellevue Road, c.1867. (*LM*, 4 May 1867.)

LEEDS, 10 houses [where?], c.1867. (*LM*, 22 June 1867.)

LEEDS, schools for St John the Evangelist [?Holbeck], c.1867. (*LM*, 24 Dec 1867.)

FARSLEY, Leeds, Baptist chapel, c.1868. (*LM*, 10 March 1868.)

9. The Architectural Profession in Leeds, 1850-1914

JANET DOUGLAS

Besides continuing many of the themes discussed in Chapter 4, the availability of more extensive primary sources allows for answers to questions that could hardly be raised for the earlier period. Also it is in the second half of the nineteenth century that the professionalisation of architectural practise was undertaken seriously in the provinces with a view to replacing the prevailing individualism by a more collective outlook and identity. A third difference is that the social and cultural context in which architects worked was being transformed not only by economic changes but also by the rise of the local state and the accelerating process of suburbanisation which facilitated a massive rebuilding of city and town centres.

The building of Leeds Town Hall marked a pivotal moment in the development of architecture in Leeds, not merely because it brought the talented Cuthbert Brodrick to the town but because it also ushered in a set of discourses which articulated new perceptions about the built environment. Handsome buildings celebrated the wealth, taste and power of the town and it was widely believed that the moral order itself would be elevated and refined by beautiful streets and buildings.[1] In August 1850 the influential *Leeds Mercury,* spurred on no doubt by Bradford's plans for St George's Hall, depreciated the fact that the town was aesthetically stunted and that there was not

1. *The Builder,* 9 Aug 1845, argued that 'the architectural embellishment of a city is of much greater consequence in forming the character of a people than some hasty thinkers nowadays recognise'.

a single edifice … except our places of worship, deserving to be shown to a stranger as an ornament to the town either from its architecture or from it containing monuments or works of art deserving admiration. It cannot be denied that this is a discredit to Leeds.

The article continued by pointing out that without such buildings, 'the population will inevitably suffer in regard to taste, refinement and public spirit'.[2] Six months later the Leeds Improvement Society was formed 'to promote architectural and other public improvements in the town' and although it only existed for three years, during that time it championed the cause of the Town Hall and lobbied the Corporation for street widening schemes and the appointment of a smoke inspector. Dr John Heaton, the secretary of the society argued that 'we are naturally inclined to live up to things of beauty by which we are surrounded. Let a town once possess a single building which is an architectural ornament to it, and all the meaner edifices will be put to shame, and will begin to pall on the taste of the people'.[3] Heaton's optimism although not entirely misplaced, was slow to bear fruit; faced with local authority parsimony and the profit-seeking indifference of the many of the town's entrepreneurs, leaders of the town's architectural community continued to complain about the ugliness of Leeds well into the twentieth century.[4]

It was in the period 1851-1911 that the numbers employed in manufacturing industry first manifested a slight decline and commensurately the service sector began to increase in size bringing with it a new demand for premises for banks, insurance companies, offices, shopping and leisure facilities. To flaunt their wealth and attract customers, proprietors dressed up their new specialised premises 'in decorations borrowed from palaces and cathedrals'.[5] A restructuring of the central core of the town to accommodate the new businesses was made possible by increasing numbers of wealthier citizens moving to more pleasant environments in the suburbs. Addressing the first general meeting of the Leeds Architectural Association in 1877 – a group to which we will return later – its president, George Corson, recalled the time when he first came to Leeds in 1849 'from Woodhouse Moor to Great George Street you might walk through fields and the Moor itself was not hemmed in as now by houses on both sides. To dwell at Far Headingley in those days, was to live, like a hermit … and to think of building a house at Weetwood or Adel was sheer insanity'.[6] By the closing decades of the century the lower middle classes and even the better-off working class were following the example of bourgeoisie in seeking domestic comfort in the suburbs and according to Trowell's research, of the 46,506 new dwellings erected between 1876-1914, only 4% were detached or semi-detached villas.[7]

The taste for extravagant display, the belief that *more represents more*, gradually began to transform such utilititarian buildings as warehouses and factories. The arrival of the railways revolutionised the way

2. *LM*, 3 Aug 1850. St George's Hall (1851-3) was designed by the eminent Bradford firm of Lockwood and Mawson.

3. T. Weymiss Reid, *A Memoir of John Deakin Heaton, MD of Leeds*, Longmans Green and Co., 1883, pp. 45, 122.

4. For example, in 1902 Thomas Butler Wilson, President of the Leeds and Yorkshire Architectural Society complained that 'owners and builders seem to have a *carte blanche* for ugliness' (LYAS *Green Book* 1901-2), whilst Percy Robinson, seven years later noted 'the conspicuous lack of beauty in our town' (LYAS *Green Book* 1908-9). The records of the LYAS, including the annual reports, *Green Books*, committee minutes books, are held by WYASL.

5. A. Hamilton Thompson, 'Architecture in Leeds', *PTS*, 37, pt II, 1945, p. 67.

6. *LM*, 1 Nov 1877.

7. Trowell, TS.

THE ARCHITECTURAL PROFESSION IN LEEDS, 1850-1914   161

manufactured goods were marketed with the result that a warehouse district emerged close to the town's stations, its streets lined with lavish *palazzi*. Commenting on Alf Cooke's new printing works (1878-81) (12.10; 12.11), designed by Thomas Ambler, the president of LAA, James B. Fraser pointed out in 1881 that:

> It has hitherto too much been the custom of manufacturers and employers of labour generally, to relegate the planning and erection of workshops to a respectable and trustworthy builder thereby saving considerably as they imagine, in the matter of the Architect's commission. These hard-headed, money-making men are now apparently finding out the long-worked for experience of the Architect is worth paying for from a purely economic point of view, but if a slight additional expenditure beyond the requirements of the bare walls and square hole order of Architecture is required the ultimate result is the cheerfulness of his place of business, the better health of his employees and the improved appearance of his native or adopted town.[8]

The second half of the nineteenth century was also marked by the diminution of the *laissez-faire* rhetoric and policies that had characterised early industrial capitalism: unfettered physical and social development was tempered by the burgeoning powers of local authorities and the various apparatuses of the Poor Law and the School Boards. Such institutions of the local state not only required their own premises, but in the case of the borough councils, introduced regulatory regimes which paved and sewered urban areas, organised water, gas and later electricity supplies, widened public thoroughfares and towards the end of the century, demolished slum housing. Such changes all impacted on the working lives of architects. In Leeds the Improvement Act of 1866 established a detailed code of building by-laws which controlled the width of streets and pavements, established 'the bye-law back-to-back house' and insisted that all building plans must be deposited with the local authority for its approval. Besides recording the name of the owner, such plans also had to include the name of the person who had drawn up the plan, and three years later elevations and sections were required for all new buildings. According to Trowell, it was these regulations which vastly expanded the opportunities for architects in the town. His sample of building plans deposited between 1866 – 1914 showed that 87% of all drawings were signed by people calling themselves 'architects'.[9]

8. James B. Fraser, *Annual Report* of the LAA, 1880-1, WYASL.

9. Trowell, TS, pp. 97-101.

The number of architects and their social backgrounds

The unparalleled demand for buildings stimulated in part by the reorganisation of urban space meant that in the second half of the century there was an increasing need for people to design them. White's 1853 *Directory* for Leeds lists the names of 23 architects, by 1861 there were 31 and these figures rose dramatically in the years after 1870. By 1875 forty-eight architects were working in the town, ten years later there were 70 and their numbers peaked by the end of the century at 78.[10] Correspondingly there was also a massive increase in the number of building workers from just over 4,000 in 1851 to 14,725 in 1901.[11] As pointed out in Chapter 4, there was a hierarchy amongst architects: in the premier division were the famous names with city-centre practices in Albion Street and Park Row who not only worked on grand buildings in Leeds but also attracted commissions or won competitions outside the town. After 1876 it was these men who became office holders in the Leeds Architectural Association (LAA) and later the Leeds and Yorkshire Architectural Society (LYAS).[12] Below them were lesser names but still with city-centre practices and membership of the LAA or LYAS (9.1). Then there were the architects listed in the street directories who practised in the suburbs, and finally at the bottom of the hierarchy, were the men listed in the directories as surveyors or builders but who on planning applications styled themselves 'architect'. According to an anonymous 'Resident of Leeds' writing to *The Architect* in 1870,

10. Trowell, TS, pp. 104-110; M. Beresford and R. Unsworth, 'Locating the Early Service Sector of Leeds: The Origins of an Office District' in *Northern History*, XLIV, 2007, p. 1.

11. W.G. Rimmer (1967), Occcupations in Leeds, 1841-1951, *PTS*, L, 1967.

12. The Leeds Architectural Association was formed in 1876, changed its name to the Leeds Architectural Society in 1881 and in 1883 became the Leeds and Yorkshire Architectural Society. In 1914 it changed its name again becoming The Leeds and West Yorkshire Architectural Society and then in 1928 The West Yorkshire Society of Architects.

9.1: Armley, Leeds, St Bartholomew (Walker and Athron, 1872-8). It is indicative of the quality of the best of the men practising in Leeds that this church, outstanding by any standards, is by a firm that would normally be assessed as not in the town's 'premier league'. (*Leeds Library and Information Services.*)

the town possesses nearly fifty architects … The majority have received no liberal education or professional training of any sort, but have been brought up, in the first instance, to some building trade, or have assumed the title of architect solely on the strength of a smattering obtained at one of the local schools of science and art. Few of them ever travel beyond the confines of their own borough, sketching is almost entirely neglected, and for literature the professional weekly journals usually suffice. Into the hands of these gentlemen most of the work drifts, partly from the inability of the public to distinguish between false and genuine art, and in a great measure owing to the unscrupulous lengths to which many resort for the purpose of gaining practice.[13]

Who were these men and where did they come from? Derek Linstrum's 'Select Biographical List' of architects in his *West Yorkshire Architects and Architecture* includes the names of forty-four architects practising in Leeds in the second half of the nineteenth century. It has proved possible to trace the family backgrounds of all but three of them.[14] Based on their fathers' occupation, twenty-seven architects came from middle class backgrounds and fourteen were born into working class families, whilst the three sons of builders are difficult to categorise without knowing the size of their fathers' businesses. Then as now the term 'middle class' covered a wide range of income levels and social status. Men like Edward Birchall (1838-1903) (*q.v.*), Francis Bedford (1866-1937) (*q.v.*) and Sydney Kitson (1871-1937) (*q.v.*) were born into very wealthy local families though it is worth noting that none were eldest sons. Six of our sample were the sons of architects, three the sons of ministers of religion and the remainder included a variety of paternal backgrounds: woollen merchants, a teacher, a surgeon, an author, a land surveyor; whilst an important figure in the local architectural profession, Thomas Butler Wilson (1859-1942) (*q.v.*) was the son of a decorative plasterer who employed nine men and nine boys. In some instances, only a generation separated these men from the working classes, for example Henry Perkin (1847-1925) was the son of an architect, William Belton Perkin (*q.v.*) who built up a large practice in the town in partnership with Elisha Backhouse (*q.v.*), but his grandfather had been a master mason in Wakefield. Paternal occupation in terms of those architects who hailed from the working classes also varied, for example George Frederick Bowman (1860-1920), the son of a tailor, was brought up in the crowded Rotation Office Yard in the town centre, William Beever's father was a cloth finisher of Burley Road and Thomas Winn (1818-1908), the son of a Woodhouse builder, had himself began life as a bricklayer. Daniel Dodgson (1872-1904) was brought up by a widowed mother who kept a beer house and is an architect not listed by Linstrum, Walter Hobson

13. *The Architect,* IV, 1870, p. 337.

14. This study is based only on a group of highly select architects. Far more time would be needed to investigate the family backgrounds of the lower echelons of the profession and without relevant documentation, it might prove difficult even then to track down family details. The evidence used for the analysis is drawn from census material supplemented in the case of those born in Leeds by the addresses of their family home. Full details are unavailable for Charles Walklett Burleigh, William Hill (senior) and Thomas Shaw.

(1856-1916), was the son of a stone mason, became a pupil of Thomas Ambler (*q.v.*) and served as vice-president of LYAS from 1886-1901. Lower league architects – the ones described by *The Architect's* correspondent – probably shared these humble origins but because their working lives were spent on humdrum work, little is known of their biographical details. What this research does demonstrate is that whilst over half our sample came from middle class backgrounds, the profession was still a relatively open one and offered opportunities for upward social mobility which meant that someone like Percy Robinson (1868-1950) (*q.v.*) could begin his life in the slums of the town's West End and end his days in leafy Cliff Road, Headingley.

In terms of place of birth, 73% of the architects named by Linstrum were born in Leeds and five, including William Hill senior (*q.v.*), came from neighbouring towns in the West Riding. Clearly there were advantages to training and then working in one's home town. Apart from local patriotism ('local architecture for local people'), many of the subsequent chapters of this book demonstrate that commissions often depended on individual Leeds patrons, and it was far easier as 'an insider' to become embedded in the complex of local social networks

9.2: Askham Richard, nr York, Askham Grange, for Sir Andrew Fairbairn, formerly of Leeds (Chorley and Connon, 1885-6). (*Author.*)

Plan 50   Askham Hall

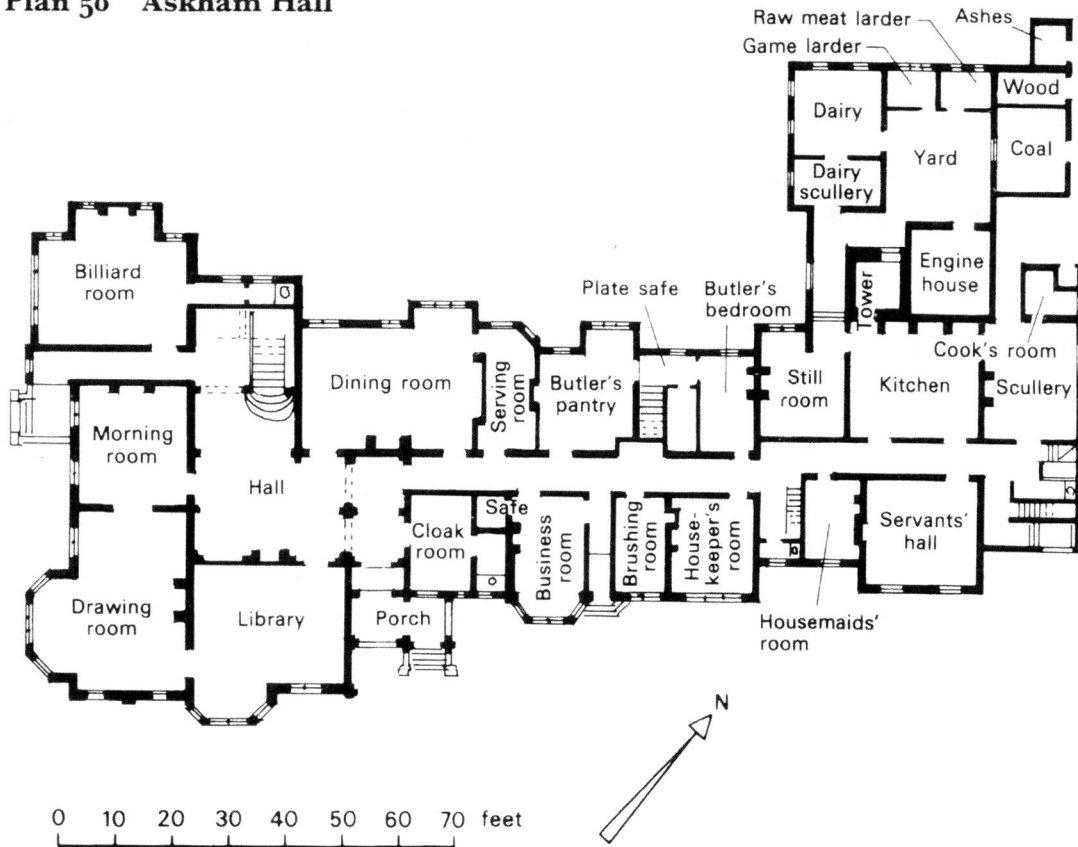

9.3: Askham Richard, nr York, Askham Grange, for Sir Andrew Fairbairn, formerly of Leeds (Chorley and Connon, 1885-6), ground floor plan. (*J. Franklin, The Gentleman's Country House and its Plan*, *Routledge, 1981*.)

responsible for the building of churches, chapels and hospitals as well as the mansions for Leeds industrialists who chose to retire to the country (9.2 & 9.3). Amongst those who came from further afield were the two most prestigious architects practising in the town in the second half of the nineteenth century: Cuthbert Brodrick (1822-1905) (*q.v.*) who was born in Hull and opened his office in the town in 1853 after winning the competition to design Leeds Town Hall; and George Corson (1829-1910) (*q.v.*) who hailed from Dumfries and followed his brother William Reid Corson to Leeds in 1849. Brodrick and Corson were not the only newcomers. The re-ordering of the town and the job opportunities this offered attracted such men as Richard Adams (1840-1904) (*q.v.*) from Wisbech, Cambridgeshire, William Bakewell (1839-1925) (*q.v.*) who spent his early years in Hampstead and Charles Walklett Burleigh (*q.v.*) who was born in Oxfordshire. William Landless (b.1847) for example, was born in Perth, trained in Glasgow and came to Leeds in 1887 to work as clerk of works on Birchall and Kelly's Higher Grade School and was then appointed architect to the Leeds School Board in 1889.

Architects and the Process of Professionalisation

It is a measure of the degree to which we take the notion of 'the professions' for granted that the term is often used when historically-speaking it is inappropriate. Historians and sociologists agree that professions in the sense that we use the word today emerged in the late eighteenth century and proliferated with the coming of industrial society, and that professionalisation is *a process* rather than a phenomenon with fixed beginnings and ends.[15] Professionalism has been defined as an occupational strategy directed at the achievement of upward collective social mobility, and once achieved it is concerned with such issues as occupational closure, remuneration and status. A key element in the acquisition of professional status is the establishment of a professional organisation that attempts to regulate entry and standards of practice through a system of formal education and statutory registration. Amongst sociologists there is no explanatory consensus about professionalisation: some regard it as progressive and benign, an integral part of an increasingly complex division of labour designed to generate high levels of expertise, ethical standards and protection for vulnerable clients. For others it represents, in the words of Bernard Shaw, 'a conspiracy against the laity',[16] a strategy to augment power and for the pursuit of self-interest.

Personal rivalry for commissions has resulted in architecture being a particularly fractious profession. Although the founding of the Institute of British Architects in 1834 is usually regarded as a key development, even in 1871 only 9% of 5,662 men who described themselves as architects in the census of that year, were members of what had become the Royal Institute of Architects (RIBA), a figure which had only increased to 15% by 1901.[17] Although control over training and registration are crucial weapons in the armoury of any profession, vested interests within the RIBA produced a virtual paralysis on these matters.[18] One of the reasons for its inaction was the schism between those who regarded architecture as a fine art related to other aesthetic practices, and those who saw the architect's role as a professional designer-manager, and who favoured both a compulsory and rigorous examination system and state-sanctioned registration.[19] Voluntary examinations had been introduced by RIBA in 1863 and in 1882 to become an associate member of the Institute one had to pass its examinations but this was not to extend to those seeking fellowship of the RIBA. In Leeds, the LYAS actually lobbied the RIBA on this matter in order to ensure that 'membership of the Institute have the same weight with the public that attaches to the College of Surgeons and other bodies'.[20] In 1884 the Society of Architects (SOA) was formed in London to press for state regulation of the architectural profession and speakers were sent round the country to agitate for

15. For historical studies of professionalisation , see H. Perkin, *The Rise of Professional Society*, Routledge, 1989; P. Corfield, *Power and Professions*, Routledge, 1995. Sociological texts include T.J. Johnson, *Professions and Power*, Macmillan, 1972; M.S. Larson, *The Rise of Professionalism*, University of California Press, 1977; K. Macdonald, *The Sociology of the Professions*, Sage, 1995. On the architectural profession, see Barrington Kaye, *The Development of the Architectural Profession in Britain*, Allen and Unwin, 1960; M. Crinson and J. Lubbock, *Three Hundred Years of Architectural Education in Britain*, Manchester U.P., 1994.

16. Bernard Shaw, *The Doctor's Dilemma*, 1906.

17. Trowell, TS, p. 105.

18. The Architectural Association was founded in 1847 in order to augment pupilage education whilst it was the Society of Architects that was established in 1884 to spearhead the campaign for registration.

19. N. Shaw & T.J. Jackson (eds), *Architecture: A Profession or An Art?*, John Murray, 1892. Crinson & Lubbock [note 15], p. 57, hint that class differences may well have contributed to the division between 'the art architects' and 'the professional architects'.

20. *LM*, 11 Nov 1884.

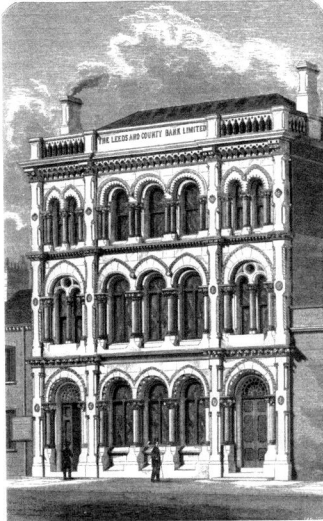

9.4: Leeds, design for the Leeds and County Bank, 4 Park Row (Lockwood and Mawson, c.1864). It is a mark of the rivalry that existed between the neighbouring towns that Bradford firms – even Lockwood and Mawson with many exceptional buildings to their credit – obtained almost no work in Leeds. (The Builder, 22, 1864, p 495.)

change. Although within the RIBA there were members who supported registration, many of the best-known national architects for a variety of divergent reasons opposed any involvement by the state. Amongst them was Norman Shaw who in a letter to Reginald Blomfield, wrote 'it must be war now and no quarter'.[21] Slowly as the RIBA grew in numbers and provincial architects ('country members' as they were charmingly called) became more influential in its affairs, the campaign for state registration increased in strength though it was not until 1931 that the first Architects' Registration Act was passed by parliament.

Professionalisation in Leeds: (1) The Leeds Architectural Society and the Leeds and Yorkshire Architectural Society

As we will see the divisiveness of the issues discussed above resonated in provincial architectural societies such as the Leeds Architectural Association, the forerunner of the Leeds and Yorkshire Architectural Society which was established at the end of 1876. The first provincial architects association had been founded in Liverpool in 1835 to be followed by Manchester (1837), Bristol (1850) and Nottingham (1862), and but for a quarrel between George Corson and William Henry Thorp (1852-1944) (q.v.), the LAA would have been formed in 1874. The substance of their disagreement was whether Bradford architects should be admitted to the new society (9.4). Corson was in favour whilst Thorp was not and without Corson's approval, wrote to the architects in Bradford informing them of their exclusion.[22] Despite the personal animosity this caused, the inaugural meeting of the Leeds Architectural Association was finally held in December 1876 in the Philosophical Hall on Park Row, George Corson was elected its president and William Thorp its secretary (9.5). The declared purpose of the LAA was to forge 'a professional bond for mutual aid and the advancement of their art'.[23] A more detailed account of the purposes of the association was given by one of its early vice-presidents, J. Wreghitt Connon (q.v.), in 1883. According to Connon 'their first objective was to promote the technical education of architectural students, their second objective was the fostering of fraternal feelings amongst architects' and their third 'the gaining of aid and sympathy of those outside the profession';[24] three years later his partner, Charles Chorley (q.v.), reminded members of LYAS of 'the pre-eminent importance of collective action and the pressing need for setting aside individual advantages for the general good'.[25]

These objectives must be understood in the light of the situation experienced by the town's elite architects. The dire portrayal of the majority of the town's architects in the letter from 'A Resident of Leeds', quoted above, also included a denunciation of the cut-throat competition which existed between them:

21. Oxford Dictionary of National Biography, http://www.oxforddnb.com/public/themes/96/96544-content.html?articleid=96544&back

22. The Bradford Society of Architects was established in 1874.

23. LAA, Annual Report, 1876-7.

24. LM, 11 Dec 1883.

25. LM, 19 Oct 1886.

9.5: Leeds, Philosophical Hall, Park Row, the location for the LAA's inaugural meeting (built R.D. Chantrell, 1819-21, refaced and extended, Dobson and Chorley, 1861-2) dem.

Professional etiquette can hardly be said to exist … One gentleman advertises in a local newspaper his readiness to make special arrangements when required; another announces his willingness to allow a reduction in terms of work designed for a charitable or religious object … The large practice of one gentleman is notoriously sustained by heavy commissions to estate agents and others for introducing business, and even levying blackmail from contractors is by no means unknown. Under such circumstances as these, how is it likely that architecture can flourish?[26]

At the LYAS Annual Dinner in 1884, George Bulmer reminded his audience that 'when he joined the profession fifteen years ago, it struck him that architects were on anything but friendly terms with each other'.[27] All this was very far from any professional ideal: little sense of corporate identity; a lack of competence; dubious professional ethics. It was all a long way from the respectability that would ensure the trust of the public.

The first general meeting of the Leeds Architectural Association in January 1877 was attended by eighty people – only 8% were members of RIBA but those present must have included surveyors, civil engineers etc.[28] Fifty-seven men paid the ten shillings and sixpence to join the new society. A year later there were seventy-seven members of LAA, in 1879 there were eighty-six members, making the society the third largest in the provinces. However, numbers fell back in the 1880s but rose eventually to 115 in 1898 – a third of whom were also members of RIBA. The association held fortnightly meetings during the winter months with lectures on historical and technical subjects; during the summer months there were excursions on Saturdays to both historic and newly erected buildings, in the case of the latter often accompanied by their architects. The numbers attending lectures varied depending

26. *The Architect*, 4, 1870. p. 337.

27. *LM*, 16 Dec 1884.

28. Trowell, TS, p. 106.

on their subject matter and fame of the speaker; ordinarily attendance was between 15-30 but 43 turned out to hear Aldam Heaton speak on 'Beauty in Colour and Form' whilst Agnes Garrett attracted an audience of 80 for her talk on 'Interior Decoration and Furniture'.[29] The LAA gradually built up its own library located in its early home in Brodrick's Leeds Institute. For students there was a sketching club and a series of prizes intended to raise their aspirations. Each year from 1877 the LAA organised a *conversazione* attended usually by approximately 300 people, 'the great and the good' of the town whereby it was hoped to influence and impress. The Association was also in regular communication with other provincial architectural societies exchanging information and mounting joint campaigns. For example, in March 1879 LAA received a communication from the Liverpool Architectural Association concerning Greenock Municipal Building Committee's decision to pay 4% remuneration rather than the customary 5%; Leeds sent a letter of disapproval, as did other provincial architectural societies.[30]

Presidential addresses at the annual general meetings and the annual *soirees* provide a register of the changing concerns of the LAA and LYAS. Although Connon might reassure guests at the LYAS's annual dinner that 'architectural societies had not been formed merely from selfish motives',[31] one of their purposes *was* to protect the material interests of their members. Following the LAA's letter to Greenock, the association held a general discussion about its own members complying with a list of charges to be adopted by the society. A year later a special meeting was held to discuss the RIBA's schedule of charges which the members accepted.[32] In the cause of united action the LYAS was quite prepare to discipline its own members when it came to their misdemeanours. For instance in 1887, when it was discovered that a former LYAS president, Edward Birchall, had offered to do work for the Leeds School Board at less than the customary 5% commission, the Society was quick to respond by asking him to withdraw from the LYAS.[33] The situation was undoubtedly made worse by the fact that an article in the *Leeds Mercury* stated that Birchall's undercutting of the rate of commission was not at all unusual and that this was recognised by the public; Birchall and Kelly's mistake was to be found out![34] Edward Dodshun, the LYAS secretary, wrote to *The Architect,* the local press and the RIBA explaining the reasons for the Society's drastic action: 'the three and half percent commission which they have agreed to accept' was, in the Society's view, insufficient 'to allow an architect to even obtain the barest means of livelihood' and would have the effect of 'seriously lowering the honour and standing of architects'.[35] Although John Kelly responded to these accusations in the *Leeds Mercury,* the LYAS remained resolute and Birchall was forced to admit that he had made 'a grave error of judgement'.[36] In 1893 another

29. In 1875 Agnes Garrett and her cousin, Rhoda Garrett set up the first all-female interior design company which won many high profile commissions.

30. LYAS Minute Book 1877-88, WYASL, WCL 1632 1/1.

31. *LM*, 16 Dec 1884.

32. On 5 Feb 1880. Minute Book [note 30].

33. At this time Edward Birchall was in partnership with John Kelly, the former partner of Richard Adams who had been the architect to the School Board. Kelly was not a member of LYAS so there was little the society could do about his role in the affair.

34. *LM*, 1 Aug 1887.

35. *LM*, 10 Aug 1887.

36. *LM*, 1 Nov 1887.

member, Walter Hanstock, was excluded from LYAS for selecting a motto in the baths competition which disclosed his identity.[37]

Other matters which exercised Leeds architects, and affected their remuneration, were the system of architectural competitions and the employment of non-Leeds architects to carry out work which they regarded as rightfully theirs. Although the foundation of many successful careers, competitions became increasingly unpopular amongst the profession in the second half of the nineteenth century. There was a growing belief that it took little real talent to turn out a fanciful drawing capable of seducing a lay client, but years of experience to produce a sound design capable of being implemented within the budget. Abuses were so frequent that it often seemed that competitions were at best a lottery and at worst, a complete sham as illustrated by the unsavoury episode of the Leeds Institute competition. Brodrick had been awarded the first prize but *The Builder* disagreed with the building committee's choice which they felt had been a prejudiced one, 'it is moreover, no secret as to who are the authors of the majority of the designs, and whilst examining the plans for this criticism, we invariably heard the spectators speak of the designs of Mr So-and-So'. Worse was to follow, the muck-racking journal also discovered that for some inexplicable reason the designs had not been sent to George Gilbert Scott who had been appointed to advise the committee.[38] Although the RIBA appointed a committee to investigate the abuses of the competition system in 1871, and the following year drew up a code of conduct for the promoters of competitions, irregularities continued. Much of George Corson's opening address to the members of LAA, in October 1879, was devoted to competitions: 'Competition', he remarked, 'was good, although its working out was often very bad. There was no confidence to be placed in a fair adjudication by the promoters unless they employed an architect of some standing as an assessor and agreed to abide by his decision'. Having listed the kinds of irregularities that occurred, he cited his own experience with regard to the competition for the design of Roundhay Park. Awarded the first prize of 200 guineas which barely covered his costs, the implementation of the scheme had been carried out by the Borough Engineer who had largely disregarded his winning design. The whole exercise had been in Corson's view, an utter waste of time and money (9.6). In this instance the prize-winning architect had not been entirely left out of pocket, but not all architects were so fortunate.[39] George Bulmer recounted his experience of competitions in a letter to the *Leeds Mercury* in 1884. The promoters of the competition for the Leeds and County Conservative Club had appointed George Corson as assessor and he had awarded the first prize to Bulmer, with the second and third prizes going respectively to Chorley and Connon, and Smith and Tweedale. However, when the Club House Company announced the results of

37. On 5 August 1893, WYASL, WYL 1632 1/2.

38. D. Linstrum, *Towers and Colonnades: the Architecture of Cuthbert Brodrick*, Leeds Philosophical and Literary Society, 1999, pp. 67-71.

39. *LM*, 31 Oct 1879; LAA, *Annual Report*, 1878-9.

9.6: A view from George Corson's winning design for the Roundhay Park Competition 1873. (*Steven Burt,* An Illustrated History of Roundhay Park, *Steven Burt, n.d., p. 33.*)

the competition, they had awarded the first prize to Smith and Tweedale and commissioned them to carry out the work.[40] Perhaps it was Bulmer's experience that prompted Edward Birchall, then president of LYAS, to repeat Corson's criticisms of the competition system adding that 'architects were beginning to show an indifference towards entering competitions'.[41]

The open competition system did of course mean that outside architects might secure commissions in Leeds which is probably why many members of the LYAS preferred a system of closed competitions – that is competitions limited to those working within the town. It is quite clear from a host of comments that many architects resented outsiders receiving local commissions (9.7, 9.8 and 9.9). For example Henry Walker (1846-1922) speaking appropriately at the annual *conversazione,* felt that:

40. *LM,* 6 Sept 1884.

41. *LM,* 4 Nov 1884.

9.7: Leeds, Leeds and Yorkshire Assurance Company offices, Commercial Street/Albion Street (W.B. Gingell, 1852-5). This, the earliest purpose-built office block in Leeds, was designed by a Bristol-based architect. (*Leeds Library and Information Services.*)

9.8: Leeds, former Midland Bank, City Square (W.W. Gwyther, 1899). By the end of the century, many national companies had their own in-house, usually London-based, architects to produce their buildings. (*Leeds Library and Information Services.*)

It was deplorable that the services of their local architects were not better appreciated at home. Could it not be wondered at when there was rarely a work of any importance to be put up in Leeds but that an architect from a distance was called in to do the work and carry off the pay. Now as regarded public works, so long as there was anyone practising in the town, competent and of good repute, it was only fair that the work should be kept at home, unless it could be shown that a better design could be had or money saved by going elsewhere.

The audience's response was a hearty 'Hear, Hear'![42] In September 1882, it was recorded in the LAS's Minute Book that 'the subject of the proposed new church at Headingley has been brought up and the employment of [London-based] Mr Pearson RA as architect. A circular protesting against the engagement of architects who are not townsmen

42. *LM*, 9 Dec 1880.

in so many of our important buildings has been drawn up by Mr Connon and meeting with approval, it was decided to send a copies of the same to the incumbent of the church and the church wardens.'[43] (9.10) Just as in earlier years there had been rivalries between architects and builders, so by the closing decades of the nineteenth century, there were constant complaints about the Borough Engineer usurping the role of the architect. For example in 1898 Corson reminded the Borough Council that he was 'no architect and its time you kept him busy in his own department'.[44] Although the LYAS would never have accepted that they were pursuing a policy that was tantamount to 'a closed shop', they lobbied with considerable zeal for work to be given to local architects, for instance in 1904 writing to the Guardians of Leeds to impress upon the Board, 'the claims of Architects practising in the city to a share of Architectural work promoted by the Leeds Union'.[45] Having welcomed the City Council's decision of 1909 to confine the Training College Competition to local architects (9.11), three years later the LYAS despatched a delegation to the local authority to remind it that 'corporation work should be given to local practising architects as in the past'.[46]

The LAA and LYAS were also public campaigning organisations, often critical of the local authority while offering expert advice about relevant matters. As early as 1879 Corson was complaining about advertising hoardings,[47] and displaying a disregard that would be unthinkable today, the Society advised the Council to demolish the Coloured Cloth Hall of 1756,[48] (1.2) though it worried on a number of occasions about the dire condition of Kirkstall Abbey.[49] A concern

43. Meeting on 4 Sept 1882. WYASL, WYL 1632 1/1.

44. K A. Jones, 'The West Yorkshire Society of Architects, 1876-1976' in *Yorkshire Architect*, 1976, p. 8.

45. On 8 Aug 1904. WYASL, WYL1632 1/3.

46. 30 Oct 1909 and 22 Feb 1912. [note 45].

47. *LM*, 31 Oct 1979.

48. *LM*, 11 Dec. 1883.

49. *LM*, 14 Nov. 1888.

9.9: Leeds, City Market (John and Joseph Leeming, 1902-4). The Leeming brothers were based in Halifax and, no doubt, secured the Leeds market as a result of their recently completed market in Halifax. (*Leeds Library and Information Services.*)

which echoed down the years was the setting of the Town Hall – 'one of the noblest buildings in England' according to Corson, and he exhorted the council 'to get rid of' the wretched buildings which surrounded it.[50] In 1880 the society unsuccessfully objected to the cast-iron fountain from Kirkgate Market being re-erected in Victoria Square writing to the press that it was 'an outrage to good taste … it is not a work of art, the material of which it is constructed rendering it unfit to be placed in such an important position'.[51] (9.12) In 1901, the LYAS wrote to the *Leeds Mercury* offering their services in the redesign of Victoria Square and a year later noted that whilst it welcomed the commissioning of Queen Victoria's Memorial Statue, it really did necessitate the redesigning of the public space in front of the Town Hall.[52] In October 1886 the president, Charles Chorley, delivered a scathing attack on 'the erratic and aimless' brief issued by the council committee responsible for the competition for the erection of a new art gallery.[53] Using the local press as their mouthpiece, the LYAS criticised the new Post Office in City Square – designed by the Post Office's London-based architect Henry Tanner – for being not 'sufficiently imposing for the site' (9.13). More generally, over many years the LYAS were joined in battle with the local authority over the design of City Square sending delegations to meet with the Council Building Committee and Colonel Harding himself, and producing drawings and a model of their own recommendations.[54]

For over 40 years various presidents bemoaned the piecemeal development of the town and the lack of planning with the consequence that the LYAS welcomed the 1909 Town Planning Act. It was not however until late in the nineteenth century that leading figures of the society spoke out against the back-to-back housing in which the majority of the local population lived. In 1891 W.H. Thorp

9.10: Headingley, Leeds, St Michael (J.L. Pearson, 1884-6). (*Fine Art Photographs of Leeds, Rock Brothers, n.d.*)

50. Jones [note 44], p. 8.

51. 20 April 1880, WYASL, WYL 1632 1/1.

52. T.B. Wilson, 'Scrapbook and Newspaper Cuttings', Special Collections, Leeds Metropolitan University.

53. *LM*, 19 Oct 1886. The competition was won by a leading member of LYAS, W.H. Thorp.

54. Colonel Harding, for a time a member of the Borough Council, was the promoter and a major financier of the City Square project. Meetings of: 19 Feb 1894, 24 Feb 1896 and 26 Mar 1896. WYASL, WYL 1632 1/3.

9.11: Headingley, Leeds, City of Leeds Training College (G.W. Atkinson and others, after 1910). (**Yorkshire Observer, 5 Oct 1910.**)

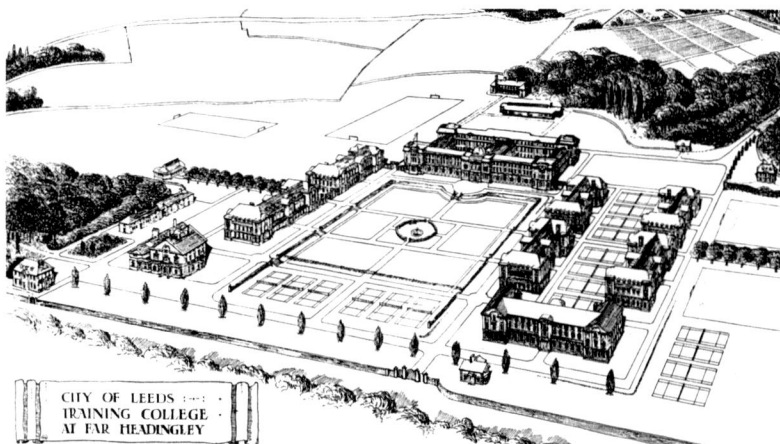

CITY OF LEEDS :–: TRAINING COLLEGE · AT FAR HEADINGLEY

9.12: Leeds, the Market Fountain re-erected in Victoria Square in front of Brodrick's Town Hall, c.1880. (*Leeds Civic Trust.*)

informed members that during his attendance at the International Congress of Hygiene and Demography, it had come as 'a great surprise … that in an important town like Leeds such dwellings should be permitted'.[55] Six years later at a dinner to celebrate the 21st anniversary of the Society, Corson criticised the Corporation for 'its building apathy and addiction to unhealthy back-to-back houses', and advised that 'you should be building new villages for the workers in the clean air around the city'. It is a measure of the growing influence of the LYAS that the Council's response was to appoint a special committee to investigate the local architects' proposals.[56]

Professionalisation in Leeds (2): the development of architectural education

As mentioned earlier, the issue of competence and credentials play a crucial role in any professionalisation project. The traditional system of training by pupillage was something of 'hit or miss' affair, 'scrappy' in the words of Alexander Crawford who, in the late-1870s, expressed support for RIBA examinations, as well as calling for local college-based courses in architecture.[57] Established in 1846, a Government School of Design under the auspices of the Leeds Mechanics Institute, had from the outset offered classes in technical and architectural drawing

55. *LM*, 24 Nov 1991.

56. Jones [note 44], p. 8. Perhaps the reason for LYAS' tardiness on this issue was that many of its members, even its leading members, were involved in the design of back-to-back houses. See Trowell TS.

57. LAA, *Annual Report*, 1877-78.

9.13: Leeds, Central Post Office, City Square (Henry Tanner, 1896). (*Fine Art Photographs of Leeds, Rock Brothers, n.d.*)

which were examined by government inspectors.[58] Yet despite the RIBA's compulsory examination system introduced in 1882, Charles Chorley in his presidential address of 1886, pointed out that:

> The architectural student could no longer plead ignorance of the curriculum to be followed in preparing for his calling in life. That had now been carefully laid down by the Royal Institute of British Architects and it could not be too often or strongly impressed upon the coming race of architects that in the near future no one could hope to be held in esteem by the public, or consider himself qualified for the pursuit of the profession of architecture, who had not, by successfully passing the examination, qualified himself for admission into the circle of the Institute. It was to be regretted that the Leeds' students had not yet shown themselves fully alive to the duty which lay before them of preparing for taking this examination.[59]

A year later Chorley, clearly driven to distraction by student indifference, came to believe that the only remedy was 'the legal registration of architects preceded by examination'.[60] In 1892 F.H. Simpson and C.B. Howdill (*q.v.*) developed further courses in architectural and building construction within the School of Art,[61] and seven years later 33 students were attending these classes following a syllabus which included the history of architectural styles, architectural design, building construction and drawing.[62]

For Thomas Butler Wilson at the beginning of the twentieth century, 'the battle cry' remained that of education and he pointed out how different the situation was abroad, 'all these countries felt that the

58. A.D. Garner, 'The English Mechanics Institutes: the case of Leeds 1824-42' in *History of Education*, 13, no 2, 1984.

59. *LM*, 19 Oct 1886.

60. *LM*, 1 Nov 1887.

61. The School of Design became the School of Art in 1852. For details on C.B. Howdill see D.C. Dews, 'Thomas and Charles Howdill: Leeds Primitive Methodist Architects, *Victorian Society West Yorkshire Group Journal*, 1979.

62. Linstrum [note 38], p. 44.

interests of the community and the State demand the efficient education of the student of architecture'.[63] But where in Leeds was such educational programme to be located? In the early summer of 1902, Butler Wilson held exploratory interviews with the Leeds Institute of Science and Arts and with Professor Bodington, the Vice-Chancellor of the Yorkshire College (later Leeds University). The latter was enthusiastic and promised a chair of architecture, but there were two problems as far as LYAS was concerned: any course of education in the college must be academic in terms of its philosophy and content; the College lacked the funds to establish any such course in the near future. Wilson and the LYAS were of the opinion that so important was the matter of a proper architectural education that it must begin 'at once' and so detailed negotiations were started with the Leeds Institute leading to a School of Architecture being established in 1902 under the auspices of the School of Art with a curriculum based on that of the Architectural Association in London.[64] In 1904 the first full-time staff were appointed but LYAS members remained active in the life of the new school, giving guest lectures, conducting site visits and offering 'crits'. By 1911 the School of Architecture offered courses to all levels of the RIBA's examinations. Lengthy negotiations led by Sidney Kitson, president of LYAS between 1910-12, ensued until in 1915 the RIBA recognised the Leeds' courses and granted its successful students exemption from the Institute's intermediate exams.[65]

Professionalisation in Leeds (3): the battle for registration

To what extent Leeds practitioners were divided over the issue of architects' registration is difficult to establish with any certainty. Registration was certainly a more pressing matter for provincial architects whose status and livelihood was more insecure than London-based architects and LYAS members saw the RIBA's hostility to registration as part of a more general pattern of neglect of their interests.[66] In June 1887, at a special meeting on the issue, a resolution was passed — proposed by William Henry Thorp and George Bulmer — recording that 'the members of LYAS strongly approve of the principle of the legal registration of architects and would heartily welcome its introduction'.[67] Although the LYAS was hopeful that the RIBA might take the lead over the question of registration, in this they were disappointed and therefore in May 1888 it made a grant of ten guineas towards the expenses of a registration bill promoted by the Society of Architects.[68] The failure of 1888 bill did not deter the Society of Architects, and in April 1889 they wrote to the LYAS inviting the secretary to a meeting to consider a new submission. A month later the society received details of their amended legislative proposals but this was quickly followed by a request from the RIBA not to respond to

63. LYAS, *Green Book*, 1902-3.

64. 12 June 1902, 10 July 1902, 24 July 1902. WYASL, WYL 1632 1/3.

65. D. Boswell, *Arts with Crafts, in Behind the Mosaic: One hundred Years of Art Education*, Leeds Museums and Galleries in Collaboration with Leeds College of Art and Design, 2003.

66. In his lecture on the RIBA in November 1884, Wreghitt Connon explained that the reason for its indifference was because 'there was insufficient representation of provincial members and the neglect of their interests is a result of the overwhelming influence of London on the Council'. *LM*, 18 Nov 1884.

67. 27 June 1887, WYAL WYL 1632 1/1

68. *LM*, 1 May 1888.

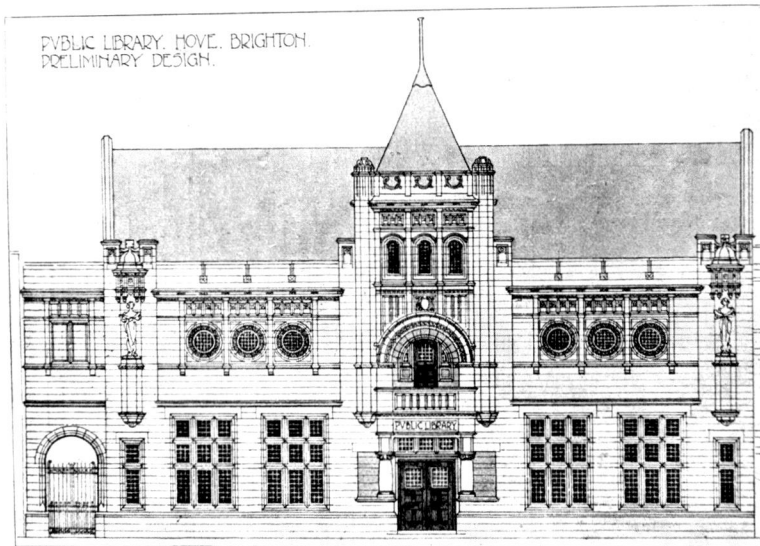

PVBLIC LIBRARY. HOVE. BRIGHTON.
PRELIMINARY DESIGN.

SoA until it received a further communication from the institute. The RIBA eventually wrote recommending opposition to the bill and the LYAS agreed to concur with this recommendation.[69] This seeming change of heart may have been an effort to curry favour with the RIBA as the LYAS was anxious to formally affiliate with RIBA, something accomplished in June 1891. However, the issue of the legal registration of architects did not disappear from the LYAS agenda. In 1900 the Society of Architects promoted a third bill and whilst the president of the LYAS, W. Carby Hall, revealed that he personally had 'mixed feelings' about the bill, he also pointed out that 'England is practically the only country where Architecture is not a registered profession' and that he was well aware that many other members were in favour of legislation.[70]

One of those who supported legal registration was Butler Wilson. If George Corson had been the guiding light of the LAA and LYAS in the nineteenth century, then Wilson occupied a similar role in the years before and after the First World War.[71] In his presidential address of 1903-4, he declared that registration had the support of the vast majority of architects in Leeds though there were some opponents.[72] Earlier in the year he had contacted the presidents of all allied societies proposing that a conference be arranged on the issue of legal registration. The conference was duly held in January 1904 and thirteen provincial societies voted in favour of registration.[73] In a spirit of openness, the LYAS organised a debate on legal registration on 6 February 1904 between W. Howard Seth-Smith and Professor Beresford Pite. For the former, registration was a way of ensuring that architects were properly qualified which would raise the standard and

9.14: Hove, Sussex, Public Library, winning competition entry (W.A. Jones and Percy Robinson, 1905). This was one of three national architectural competitions won by the partnership. (*Academy Architecture, 34, 1908, p. 22.*)

69. LYAS, *Annual Report*, 1890-1.

70. LYAS, *Annual Report*, 1899-1900; *LM*, 13 Nov 1900.

71. Wilson was President of LYAS 1901-2, 1902-3 and 1903-4; subsequently he was the LYAS Secretary and also held several positions after 1914..

72. LYAS, *Green Book*, 1903-4.

73. 3 Feb 1903, 16 Jul 1903 23 Dec 1903. [Note 64]. The thirteen societies were Aberdeen, Birmingham, Bristol, Cardiff, Dundee, Ireland, Leeds, Liverpool, Manchester, Northern, Nottingham, Sheffield and York.

status of the profession, whilst Beresford Pite argued 'architects should be free and endeavour to cultivate high ideals and an independent standard of artistic aims and professional conduct'.[74] In the three-hour discussion that followed, G.G. Bulmer asserted that 'in three-quarters of their work, there was no scope for artistic souls'.[75] Oglesby, Howdill, Perkin and Chapman all spoke in favour of registration and Pite's only supporter on this occasion was Sidney Kitson. Both Wilson and the next president of LYAS, G.B. Bulmer, became members of the RIBA's Registration Committee in 1907, and by 1911 even Kitson, despite his earlier opposition to registration, announced that he was now in favour.[76] Still the RIBA prevaricated, and it was announced to LYAS members in April 1913[77] that the situation within RIBA was 'unfavourable for further progress'. The struggle was to continue well beyond the period covered by this book and this missing link in the process of professionalisation was not to be achieved until the 1930s.[78]

Conclusion

'The Provincial' in English culture has come to be associated with a lack of sophistication and narrow-minded insularity,[79] and is rooted in the expectation that anyone with talent must eventually succumb to the lure of London. Weymiss Reid writing in 1883, was critical of how 'local reputation must acquire the stamp of metropolitan approbation before it is thought worthy of notice', but he believed that 'the time may come when the archaeologist of a future age will look for the best specimen of the buildings of the present age, not to the Law Courts or Houses of Parliament but to some provincial towns where the hurry and rush of life have not been as great as in the capital.[80] Others 'in the

74. [Note 64].

75. T.B. Wilson [note 52].

76. LYAS, *Green Book*, 1911-12.

77. 24 April 1913 [note 64].

78. The 1931 Registration Act granted RIBA responsibility for architectural training but the power to bestow the title, 'Registered Architect' was give to a special Architects Registration Council. In a second piece of legislation in 1939 registration was passed to the RIBA.

79. The term 'provincial' first came into common parlance in the last decade of the eighteenth century and from the beginning had negative connotations.

80. Reid [note 3], pp. 21 and 83.

9.15: Portsmouth, Guildhall (William Hill, 1886-90). Hill secured commissions in many parts of England, although this was his most impressive building. (*Colin Dews.*)

Town Hall, Portsmouth

North clearly believed that the nineteenth century belonged to their region',[81] and that the provinces were morally superior to the metropolis with an energy and vitality that London lacked. Metropolitan condescension has tended to demote provincial architects to the second-rate and as a result there have been few serious studies of their work.[82] Although Leeds architects mostly worked close to home, they did not do so exclusively as many of the subsequent chapters of this book demonstrate. In some instances they were successful in architectural competitions (9.14 and 9.15), on other occasions it was the geography of family connections,[83] patronage networks or religious allegiances which produced commissions far beyond Leeds. Francis Bedford might leave Leeds in 1903 for London but few before or after him were tempted to make the same move perhaps because in the words of Sydney Kitson, Bedford's former partner, 'the happiest architects are the Provincial Architects, for they usually have a greater range and variety in their work and have more varied lay interests than is possible to Londoners … nor does it seem needful …that the design of Provincial Architects should be measurably inferior to that of their London brethren'.[84]

Presidents of the LAA and LYAS

1877-8	George Corson	1896-7	William Watson
1878-9	Alexander Crawford	1897-8	George Corson
1879-80	Alexander Crawford	1898-9	George Corson
1880-1	Henry Walker	1899-1900	W. Carby Hall
1881-2	Henry Walker	1900-1	W. Carby Hall
1882-3	J. B. Fraser	1901-2	T. Butler Wilson
1883-4	Edward Birchall	1902-3	T. Butler Wilson
1884-5	Edward Birchall	1903-4	T. Butler Wilson
1885-6	J.W. Connon	1904-5	G.B. Bulmer
1886-7	C.R. Chorley	1905-6	G.B. Bulmer
1887-8	C.R. Chorley	1906-7	H.S. Chorley
1888-9	Henry Perkin	1907-8	H.S. Chorley
1889-90	Henry Perkin	1908-9	Percy Robinson
1890-1	W.H. Thorp	1909-10	Percy Robinson
1891-2	W.H. Thorp	1910-11	Sidney Kitson
1892-3	G.B. Bulmer	1911-12	Sidney Kitson
1893-4	G.B. Bulmer	1912-13	Albert E. Kirk
1894-5	E.J. Dodgshun	1913-14	Albert E. Kirk
1895-6	E.J. Dodgshun	1914-15	G.K. Bowman

81. D. Russell, *Looking North*, Manchester U.P., 2004, p. 28.

82. The Victorian Society, recognising this lacuna, has organised two conferences on provincial architects, and published the proceedings of the first as K. Ferry (ed), *Powerhouses of Provincial Architecture 1837-1914*, Victorian Society, 2009.

83. A surprising example of the importance of family networks is Shipton Court in Oxfordshire, a Jacobean manor house which was bought by Frederick Pepper who had the interior of the house completely remodelled and added a residential wing and service block. The architect was G. Bertram Butler of Leeds who just happened to be Pepper's brother-in-law.

84. LYAS, *Green Book*, 1910-11.

10. Cuthbert Brodrick (1821–1905)

COLIN CUNNINGHAM

Three mighty buildings effectively set the tone of mid-Victorian architecture in Leeds. They are all the work of one architect, Cuthbert Brodrick, who won the competition to design the town hall as an unknown young man in 1852. The three heroic structures, the Town Hall (1852–8), the Corn Exchange (1860–2) and the Mechanics Institute (1860–5, now the Leeds City Museum), are also his greatest works, and rightly place Brodrick among the finest of Victorian architects. Yet he is only known to have built some 35 buildings, most of those in Leeds, Hull or other parts of the East Riding. It is a surprisingly small *oeuvre*, and, though one or two more works may yet be attributed to him,[1] makes it a surprise that he reached such eminence. How did it come about that a man who was capable of designing such great buildings, and with such assurance, failed to attract clients by the dozen? And why did such early promise not develop into a full-blooded career?

Brodrick is certainly an enigma. The late Derek Linstrum, whose biography will remain the standard portrait of him for years to come, combed through all the available papers; and the result, as he freely admitted, was only a partial picture.[2] Yet there can be no doubt of the superb quality of his great buildings, although he never became one of the established masters among architects from the provinces such as Waterhouse, ten years his junior, or Paley & Austin with their extensive Lancashire practice. He evidently made a comfortable living. He was able to abandon architecture at fifty and retire to France, where he lived in some style at Le Vésinet near Paris and devoted his time to painting.

1. Advertisements in the *LI* for 20 Oct 1860 and 23 Feb 1861 call for tenders for a House and Stables at Weetwood near Leeds, which could mean either one or two houses, though advertisements for tenders suggest they are likely to have been built. The same paper (5 Nov 1853) mentions a font by Brodrick in St Mark's Woodhouse. (I am grateful to Hugh Kerrigan for bringing these items to my attention.)

2. D. Linstrum, *Towers & Colonnades: The Architecture of Cuthbert Brodrick*, Leeds Philosophical and Literary Society, 1999. This detailed biography includes a full list of Brodrick's known works and designs.

LEEDS NEW TOWN HALL.

He lived to the ripe old age of 84, and died in 1905. Yet he must surely go down in history as 'Town Hall Brodrick' the nickname he acquired for his first and greatest commission. He remains an enigma because he has left remarkably little in the way of records. No diaries and few letters survive. His sketchbooks are lost except for a few loose pages; and these together with some finely drawn presentation drawings and the working drawings for the town hall are virtually all there is to go on.[3] With no family to preserve his name he has only the buildings to speak for him. But speak for him they certainly do.

First the Town Hall (10.1-6). It is enough to demonstrate the full genius of its architect. The commission came to Brodrick at the end of only his first decade in practice. He had been trained in the office of H.F. Lockwood in Hull, which he joined at the age of fifteen. As soon as he was qualified he went, as did many young architects, for a one-year tour on the Continent, returning to set up in practice in 1845. There is a hint of a fierce independence here, in that he turned down the offer of a partnership with his former master for the freedom to work on his own. But the beginnings were slow. A bare nine commissions in Hull or neighbouring Hessle were his only work for seven years, until his design for the Leeds Town Hall was judged the winner in the competition. This was his first major commission outside his native Hull; and it was to be his masterpiece.

Competitions were a common method of selecting architects for important buildings in the nineteenth century. Brodrick had already tried his hand with a design for the Fish Market and Corn Exchange

10.1: Leeds, Town Hall, Brodrick's alternative design for the tower of 1853. (*Leeds Library and Information Services.*)

3. The sketches and presentation drawings are preserved in the in the RIBA Drawings and Archives. The working drawings for the town hall are in WYASL.

in Hull, but without success. The Leeds competition was a greater matter altogether. Only sixteen designs were submitted but the town council had persuaded Sir Charles Barry to act as assessor, which gave the competition considerable status. And Brodrick's victory has a major coup. When his name was announced, the town council sought reassurance from their assessor as to whether such a young man could do the job. He told them firmly that: '[although] previous to the competition he was not aware that such an architect existed, but he was perfectly satisfied that the Council might trust him with the most perfect safety'. This was some accolade, since Brodrick was only twenty-nine when he made the drawings. And Barry added that: 'after what he had seen of the drawings, he felt sure there was sufficient talent and genius in the architect to carry out anything which an architect could be required to do'.[4]

Civic pride was involved from the very start – Linstrum points out it was Bradford's 1851 decision to build St George's Hall that galvanised Leeds into action – and the town hall for Leeds was to be quite the grandest building affordable. Arguments over cost resulted in the commission being given for a design without a tower, a two-story structure whose colonnaded facade continued around the sides and rear in a repeated pattern of pilasters and three-quarter columns. No public building so huge had been erected in the town before. It has almost as large in footprint as Marshall's gigantic flax mill in Holbeck.[5] But the town hall was built with all the ornament needed to impress, in the best part of Leeds, and far surpassed even the chimney of Temple Mills in height. What Brodrick designed was an immense rectangle with recesses on its east and west sides. This plan was soon enlarged, with extra offices to fill the recesses, making the resulting rectangular mass even more dominant.

There are plenty of precedents for a such a use of Classical columns, for instance the *Neues Museum* in Berlin or the Paris *Bourse* or even Tite's Royal Exchange in London, completed a bare eight years before.[6] However, it is the muscularity of this version and the sheer insistence of the encircling columns that gives Leeds Town Hall its unforgettable grandeur. Work began in late autumn of 1852. The fortunate survival of extracts from the Clerk of Works diary[7] gives a clear insight into the attitudes of the architect. He was evidently determined to have the best quality of work. There are constant complaints of poor workmanship, poor quality stone, insufficient through stones. Perhaps the problems arose because no grand building on this scale had been built in Leeds; and the builders, Messrs Atack and Musgrave, were presumably more used to building mills. On one occasion Brodrick summoned Mr Atack to the site to demonstrate the failure and Atack 'promised to square the stones a little better and also to do the walling to the specification.'[8] Only a couple of months later the problems recurred and Musgrave

4. Quoted in A. Briggs *Victorian Cities*, Penguin, 1968, p. 163.

5. Temple Works, Holbeck, built for John Marshall to the designs of Joseph Bonomi the younger and James Combe between 1838 & 1843, described as the largest single room in the world.

6. Berlin *Neues Museum*, Karl Frederick Schinkel, 1825-30; Paris, *Bourse des Valeurs*, Alexandre-Théordore Brongniart, 1825; London, Royal Exchange, Sir William Tite, 1844. See Linstrum [note 2], pp. 23-5 for a discussion of potential sources for this design. Linstrum stresses the likelihood of French Beaux Arts inspiration on the grounds that Brodrick was much impressed with Paris on his Continental tour and later chose to live in the city.

7. WYASL, LLd1/4/42/3/3[c] 'Extracts from the Journal of the Clerk of Works Scheduled in the Answer of Cuthbert Brodrick No 8 Miscellaneous Papers'. The extracts were evidently prepared with a view to Brodrick's case against Samuel Atack for bankruptcy which, for a time, threatened the completion of the building.

8. Journal [note 7], Wednesday 9 Nov 1853.

10.2: Leeds, Town Hall, elevation of tower, contract drawing, 1856 (*WYASL, LLD/1/3/42/1/3/2*).

(who appears to have been the partner on site) 'objected to the dressing of so much of the face of the rubble walling generally and the expensive manner in which [he was] required to execute the wall.'[9] A year later 'Mr Brodrick was so dissatisfied with the Rawdon Hill stone being used for cornice in small entablature that he took a hammer & destroyed a cornice stone to prevent it being used on the Building (for that purpose).'[10] There were certainly difficulties securing enough stone for so huge a building; and the Clerk of Works notebook mentions no less than 33 different quarries, though it is possible that not all of them actually supplied stone.[11]

Yet for Brodrick one has the distinct impression that quality of workmanship was only the means to an end. Appearance was all. He

9. *Ibid.*, Saturday 28 Jan 1854.

10. *Ibid.*, Friday 16 March 1855.

11. See C. Cunningham *A Study of Town Halls of the 18th & 19th Centuries and the Reflection of Civic Pride in Public Buildings*, unpublished PhD thesis, University of Leeds, 1973 p.123, note 105. Twenty-two of the quarries mentioned are known to have supplied stone for Leeds Town Hall.

10.3: Leeds, Town Hall, detail of vase on parapet. (*Author, 1973.*)

would meticulously redesign details. Once he 'gave instructions to alter the cornice of entablature to a drawing by way of improvement in appearance';[12] and a little later 'to have a portion of the main cornice &c made of wood & fixed on the Building so as he might be able to judge of the general effect.'[13] And there was always the matter of the tower. Linstrum has pointed out that there is every probability that Brodrick designed a tower even before building started.[14] Influential supporters were also keen on the addition of a tower and lobbying began at the very outset. At an early stage the foundation walls were enlarged so that one could be added. This throws an interesting light on Brodrick's approach to design. The massive supporting piers of the tower meant that he had to abandon his grand entrance. Out went the open hall with a screen of columns leading to the great hall. Out also went a more open version with screens of columns that incorporated grand stairways on either side. The entrance, as built, leads into a rather cramped vestibule with doorways to the hall, and small passages like rabbit holes leading to stairways in the corners of the building. But this was the price to be paid for the tower that gives this building its unique character, a piece of high Victorian Baroque. It was not universally admired, and, as Linstrum has pointed out, Ruskin considered it 'an abortion ... upon a town hall of fair Roman composite architecture'.[15] Today it is easier to see it as a remarkably assured and individualistic design which has no obvious precedents (10.2). A square tower with six columns a side rises from a podium with two tiers of panelled ornaments. Above this a concave clock stage is topped by a dome, square in plan but elliptical in outline. This is pure Brodrick, and so successful is it here that versions were devised by several later architects at Morley, Bolton, Portsmouth and even as far afield as Melbourne in Australia.

Not that the tower was the only addition. The plain cornice of the contract design was enriched with vases, finely conceived from a distance, but inelegantly balanced on a parapet that had to be thickened to support them (10.3). It was not until the work was well up that Brodrick ordered trial ornaments to be fitted, and only after that did he approach the Council with a request for the extra work to be allowed.[16] Brodrick was evidently the sort of architect who had no qualms about asking for additional sums to make his building even more perfect; and he was fortunate that there was a majority on the Council as eager as he to see their town hall built to the highest standards. Not that the relationship was entirely smooth. The very practical matter of heating and ventilating the building and its great hall had to be allowed for; and it is interesting that Haden, the contractor, visited the building early in 1854.[17] Later Brodrick ordered that the ventilating shafts be enlarged to 10 feet square; but when these started to sprout from the roof there was immediate concern on the

12. Journal [note 7], Thursday 30 Nov 1854.

13. *Ibid.*, Friday 23 March 1855.

14. There is some evidence that Brodrick had already conceived a tower for his design. See Linstrum [note 2], p. 20.

15. E.T. Cook and A. Wedderburn (eds), *The Works of John Ruskin*, London, 1903-1912, vol. XXXIV, p. 725, quoted in Linstrum [note 2], p. 26.

16. Journal [note 7], 29 May 1856 and Town Hall Committee minutes, 17 Oct 1856.

17. *Ibid.*, Thursday 2 March 1854.

10.4: Leeds, Town Hall, tower and ventilation turret from the north-west (Cuthbert Brodrick, 1853-8).

Council. There were even complaints from owners of neighbouring properties. Brodrick was ordered to stop the work, and to see how other similar buildings were ventilated, though one presumes that he must have decided on the system at a much earlier stage in the building.[18] The towers were resumed and are another part of this building's strongly Victorian picturesque but practical character (10.4).

18. Town Hall Committee Minutes, 16 Nov 1855 and Town Hall Visiting Sub-committee Minutes, 12 Jan 1856.

10.5: Leeds, Town Hall, half section through hall roof showing the laminated beam, contract drawing, 25 July 1853. (*WYASL, LLD/1/4/42/2/1/16.*)

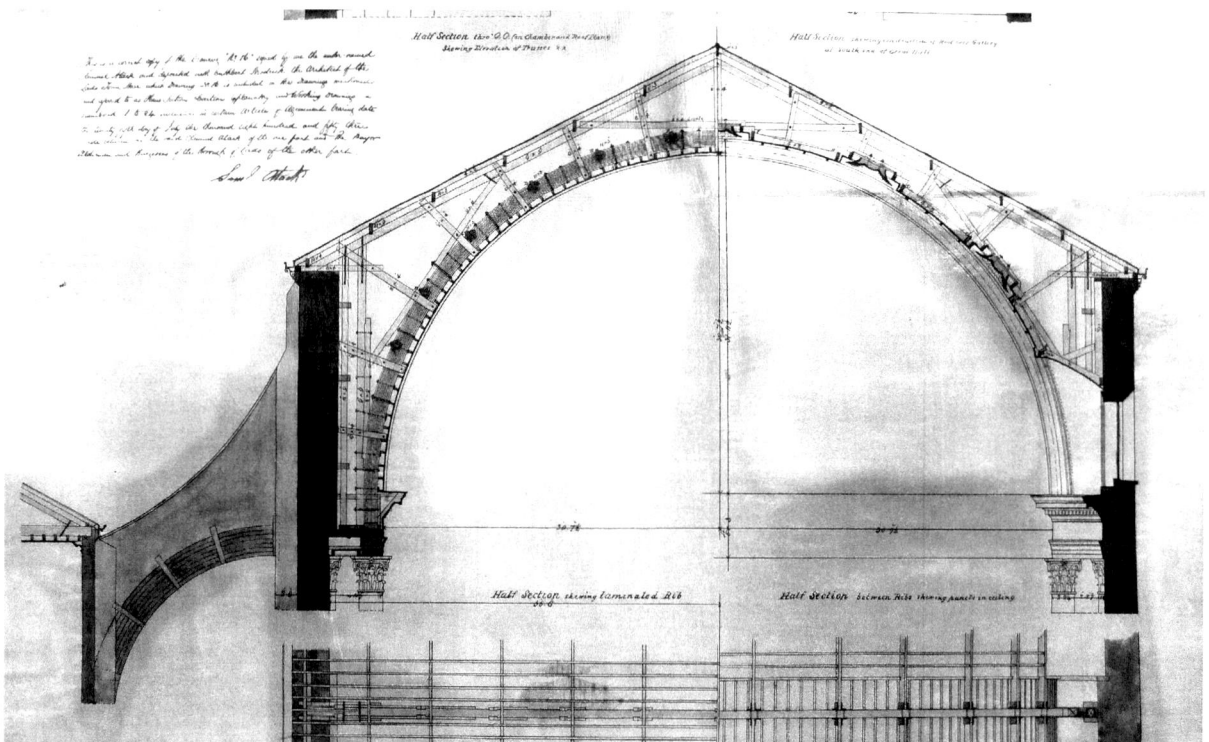

At the time the complaints were lost in yet one more difficulty, the bankruptcy of the contractors. It seems they were overwhelmed by the sheer size of the commission and had not calculated on Brodrick's passion for detail. Another factor may also have been the construction. In addition to his genius as a designer, Brodrick was also interested in bold new techniques. From the start he planned a novel roof for his great hall (10.5). The span, a clear sixty one feet from the capitals of the great columns that adorn the hall[19] is bridged by a single semicircular rib made up of a dozen, one and a half inch thick, planks held together by a series of fifty bolted clasps. This laminated timber is simply bent into a vast semicircle and fitted into a cast iron shoe atop the columns. It is a staggeringly bold structure and was used here for only the third time in Britain. Brodrick would undoubtedly have seen the first examples in the transepts of the Crystal Palace and over the train shed at Kings Cross,[20] and it says a good deal about his aims as an architect that he set out to use this new industrial roofing in a municipal palace. New to Leeds and new for Brodrick, its installation was not without problems. The contract drawing shows a single rib to each bay of the hall; but there were modifications, possibly at the suggestion of Sir Charles Barry. In the spring of 1855, when the walls were almost ready for the roof the Clerk of Works noted 'Sir Charles Barry & Son on the ground ... & went to the office of Mr Brodrick to see the designs for the proposed alterations & improvements of roof of large hall.'[21] A week later Brodrick ordered the roof to proceed to a modified plan and at considerable extra expense with two ribs per bay.[22] The novel structure was duly installed and remains to this day, probably the only surviving example of this type of roof. But the ribs were sufficiently straight to be used for the centring of the elaborate plaster

19. The columns project into the space; and the overall dimensions of the hall are 75 x 75 x 162ft.

20. Brodrick claimed that the system was the invention of a French engineer.

21. Journal [note 7], Saturday 14 April 1855.

22. *Ibid.*, Friday 20 April 1855. The roof evidently excited some interest among architects, for in the same week Donaldson noted that 'Mr Hardwick of London' visited and 'expressed himself much satisfied'.

10.6: Leeds, Town Hall, detail of plaster ceiling of great hall. (*Author, 1973.*)

ceiling that enriches the hall (10.6). The whole structure showed little sign of stress, needing only to be tightened once under the architect's supervision. Unseen but impressive it is the final touch of genius in this breathtaking building.

Its decoration was also the very best to match the structure. The hall was fitted with a splendid organ by Gray and Davison; and John Gregory Crace was summoned from London to devise a scheme of decoration. There was a good deal of marbling and gilding with the columns painted to look like *Rosso Antico* on a base of *Verde Antique*. The walls were of olive green with dark green fret ornament and the frieze was of 'deep violet' with a series of appropriate mottoes such as '*Labor Omnia Vincit*';[23] and the ceiling was a light vellum colour with ornaments of bronze and gold outlined in lime green and grey – an extravagantly Victorian splendour.[24] It was all most certainly extravagant. The original estimate had been £39,000, but the final cost was around £125,000. Yet Leeds, soon to become a city, found it had made an excellent investment and happily celebrated its new centrepiece. To mark the completion of the great work the British Association for the Advancement of Science was persuaded to hold its 1858 meeting in the hall, and there was a grand music festival for which Sterndale-Bennett composed The May Queen especially. Finally the Town Hall was opened by the Queen in person on 11 September 1858 and Albert, climbing the still incomplete tower alongside the architect, told him 'when I first saw the building, Mr Brodrick, I said to the Queen "Magnificent! Magnificent! Beautiful proportion"'.

With this achievement behind him one might have assumed that a successful career as an architect was in front of 'Town Hall Brodrick'.

23. 'Hard work conquers all'. Other mottoes were 'Forward' and 'Except The Lord Build The House'.

24. The present scheme of decoration is based on a redecoration of the hall by Crace's son John Diblee Crace in the 1890s. A portion of the original decoration survives in the lost space beneath the gallery that was added in 1890.

10.7: Leeds, no 7, Alma Road, Headingley (Cuthbert Brodrick, 1859). (*Ruth Baumberg*.).

He was not yet forty and could expect to be approaching the peak of his career. He was well established in Leeds. He was a member of the prestigious Leeds Club, indeed had been since 1853. He had designed and built a substantial mansion at No 7. Alma Road, and there may well have been others[25] (10.7). Moorland Terrace was about to begin and he had completed a handful of works in the East and West Ridings. But so far another great prize had eluded him. In March 1856, along with forty other hopefuls, he had submitted designs for the Lille Cathedral competition that had an initial cost limit of £120,000. Given the machinations surrounding that competition, and the setting aside of the winner, he may not have been too disappointed not to be selected. But he must have had better hopes in his submission for the Manchester Assize Courts in 1859. Had he not just completed the building that was shortly to house the West Riding Assizes? Again he was beaten, this time by the young Alfred Waterhouse whose career was beginning in a remarkably similar pattern to Brodrick's. Being ten years younger, however, Waterhouse, unlike Brodrick, was more in tune with the coming fashion for Gothic. In fact in the five years following the completion of his Leeds masterpiece, poor Brodrick failed to win no less than seven significant competitions. And there were to be a further eight failures during the last decade of his architectural career.[26] The fact that he chose to preserve the fine presentation drawings for so many of these schemes suggest that he thought a great deal of them. Another failure, though it seems this was not an unsuccessful competition entry, was his design for the Cotton Exchange in Bombay in 1866. Only one design survives for a structure over 970 feet in length that would presumably have stood with the other great buildings of *Urbs Prima in Indis* facing Bombay Green.[27] The design was commissioned at just the moment when Bombay's textile industry was taking off into dramatic growth. Sadly it was never to be built to stand alongside Scott's University or the great Gothic Law Courts by General James Fuller (it would have been 300 feet longer than even that enormous pile). Brodrick was certainly aiming high, but the chances of winning competitions were always slim. Nonetheless, one imagines a growing sense of disappointment as he found his designs increasingly out of tune with the clients and assessors. There can be no certainty as to the reasons for his lack of success; but some issues may be important. Competition entries were strictly anonymous, but there were regular complaints about breaches of regulations and pre-selection of winners. Even with a fair competition there was always the possibility that assessors might know the drawing style of a given competitor. Certainly the extent of Brodrick's failures suggests that he was more than usually unlucky, unless we are to see him as simply pig-headed in entering competitions where the odds were against success in any case and there was a good chance of losing time and money in preparing designs that

25. See note 1.

26. The competitions were: Manchester Assize Courts (1859); St Mary, Scarborough, font (1860); St Martin, Scarborough (1861); Sydney Houses of Parliament (1861); Leeds Queens Hotel (1862); Liverpool Exchange Buildings (1863); Bolton Town Hall (1863). Later failures were London, Natural History Museum; Hull, Dock Offices; Manchester, Exchange; London, National Gallery; Leeds, Wesleyan Theological College; Manchester, Town Hall; Castle Howard, monument; London, Corn Exchange.

27. The drawing survives in the RIBA Drawings & Archives Collection (SC 35/14). Linstrum suggests that it may have been the estimated cost (£270,000) that precluded the building of this fantastic palace. However, if it was really intended to stand on Bombay Green that would have created immediate difficulties since the harbour in Back Bay, the other side of the peninsula, was the one being developed. The present Bombay Cotton Exchange stands at Sewri, close to Back Bay.

would never be wanted. And, competitions apart, it is also true that the rest of his *oeuvre* reveals that direct commissions did not come flooding in on the back of the Leeds Town Hall job.

So what sorts of reasons might there be for his unpopularity? It may be that stylistically he was behind the times, though some of the surviving designs show an amazing inventiveness. But he was able and willing to design in a Gothic mode as well as a Classical. His Headingley Hill Congregational Church of 1864, in fact his only built church, is a demonstration of his competence in a Gothic that is both individual and muscular (10.8). Gothic also is his submitted design for Manchester Town Hall with its extraordinary and dramatic circular tower. The thing is like no medieval Gothic building, but it is certainly eye-catching and could only have been designed in the nineteenth century. So it is probably unjust to believe that it was stylistic distance that made his designs unattractive.

There is evidence of a deep commitment to the form and appearance of his buildings on their sites.[28] He had shown this clearly with his modifications to the design at Leeds. And the whole experience of building Leeds Town Hall demonstrated his passion for quality workmanship which should, surely, have enhanced his reputation with clients. Then the novel roof was a triumph of modern engineering; and that, too, was the sort of thing to impress a confident Victorian clientele. His design for Manchester Town Hall demonstrates this interest in daring engineering once again. He offered a great tower to the main facade that rose above a vaulted atrium five stories in height. The vault in turn was the base for two massive girders five foot deep which in turn supported both a bell frame and a spiral staircase rising a further five stories into the tower! Had he, perhaps, seen Barry's amazing spiral stair in the Victoria tower of the Palace of Westminster?

10.8: Leeds, Congregational Church, Headingly Hill (Cuthbert Brodrick, 1864). (*Ruth Baumberg.*)

28. On what appears to be his earliest sketch for the Manchester Town Hall competition, there is an interesting note that indicates this (RIBA Drawings & Archives SB51/9/13). He draws a Beaux Arts composition with a central dome flanked by towers, which he then abandons in favour of increasingly dramatic Gothic designs with circular towers. His note, presumably a reflection on the appropriateness of his sketch, reads: 'a square is not good for this [front] of Building [illegible] a proper space in front would necessitate ... too thick for the sharp angle of either side and would show up the awkward angle of building instead of smoothing them down as a round one would do'.

10.9: Leeds, Mechanics Institute, Cookridge Street, initial design (Cuthbert Brodrick, 1860-5). (**Building News**, *7, 1861, p. 965.*)

10.10: Leeds, Mechanics Institute, Cookridge Street (Cuthbert Brodrick, 1860-5). (*Author.*)

Either way it does not seem that Brodrick's designs can have been rejected because he was not reliable where quality was concerned or that he was insufficiently up to date.

Two weaknesses seem to me to be likely candidates for unpopularity with the newly powerful commercial elites of industrial Britain. First, the cost overruns of the town hall must have been fairly widely known in Leeds, even if not more widely. However, the fact that he did win further major commissions in Leeds suggests that this was not the chief reason why his designs might not be preferred. There remains his skill as a planner, which, it must be admitted, was relatively modest. The planning of the town hall is straightforward, but not entirely successful. The redesign of the vestibule to accommodate the tower, for instance, left but a poor entrance to anything other than the great hall. It could certainly be argued that there was little scope in his building for the grandeur of mayoral comings and goings. Nor is there much evidence that this aspect of architecture interested Brodrick greatly. His later commission for the Corn Exchange in Leeds required only the simplest of plans. The Mechanics Institute was almost as straightforward. Yet, as the century progressed, there was an increasing demand for complex buildings where skill in planning would make or mar the final outcome. Here, I think, we have to admit that Brodrick was no leader.

However, his buildings are the abiding monuments to his creativity and daring as a designer, and the remaining two great Leeds commissions must be allowed to sum up his contribution as a Leeds architect. Both followed swiftly after the town hall, being commissioned in 1860; and in both cases Brodrick was the beneficiary of local competitions. The most notorious of these was for the Mechanics Institute[29] in Cookridge Street (10.9) where his design was

29. Erected as the Mechanics Institute, the building was converted into the Civic Theatre and more recently has been converted again, this time into the Leeds City Museum. As well as the theatre it was also used by LCAD for teaching.

chosen without professional advice, and there were predictable complaints from other architects such as W.H. Crossland, a former pupil of Scott, and from Henry Garling a close friend of Brodrick as well as a fellow-competitor. There was even, it appears, an attempt to have the decision set aside. Almost as though an act of poetic justice, work on the building was delayed until 1865, but it was Brodrick's design that was built. The building consisted of a large circular lecture theatre with other spaces slotted around it. Once again Brodrick's interest in engineering is evident in the lecture theatre that *The Builder* described as having 'an ornamental coved ceiling, a roof of somewhat novel construction, with windows immediately below it'.[30] The tapered base and the simple rhythm of arched windows, together with the characteristically solid decorative details give this Mechanics Institute a status that lifted it well above the norm for such buildings (10.10). The stone facade seems much more in keeping with a civic theatre or city museum, particularly when one remembers that mechanics institutes were often humble buildings, as indeed was the predecessor of this one. There is a hint that Brodrick may have been aware of this in his alternative design which has the wall surface coloured pink. Could it be that he was prepared to build it of brick like the side facades? As it is, the building, with its great flight of steps leading up and into the arched entrance, has a tremendous dignity. Contemporary criticisms, that the absence of windows in the upper wall would give an unfortunate appearance of heaviness, seem to me only a different view of the formal grandeur of this structure.

30. *The Builder*, 25, 1867, p. 698, quoted in Linstrum [note 2].

10.11: Leeds, Mechanics Institute, Cookridge Street, detail of carved stone work (Cuthbert Brodrick, 1860-5). (*Author.*)

10.13: Leeds, Corn Exchange, (Cuthbert Brodrick, 1860-2). (*Engraving, 1860, Leeds Library and Information Services.*)

The Corn Exchange, Leeds

The Mechanics Institute certainly made a dramatic contribution to the streetscape of Cookridge Street in what effectively became an enclave of Brodrick's work. Two other commissions, one sadly demolished, stood close by. Two shops demonstrate the simplicity of which he was capable while at the same time creating an idiosyncratic and striking facade in the Gothic style (10.12). The sad loss, however, was Brodrick's most unusual building, and one that testified to his ability to play the game with stylistic costume. The Cookridge Street Baths was an extravagant essay on the 'Moorish' style, with a minaret acting as its chimney and roofed with no less than seven domes of different sizes and shapes. Its bold facade of stripey brick will have amazed passers-by until 1882, when it was concealed behind a dreary Gothic facade. It was demolished in 1969. But there were to be relatively few other great buildings, in Leeds or elsewhere; and only the enormous swagger of the Grand Hotel in Scarborough (1862) does anything to stamp Brodrick's character on other towns.

The final monument to him in Leeds was commissioned in the same year as the Mechanics Institute, but built more swiftly and completed in 1862 (12.13). It was initiated through yet another competition organised by the Council which aroused deep suspicion among architects, and which resulted in a first prize for Brodrick, second for William Hill, another Leeds architect, and third for Lockwood & Mawson, by now the leading architects in Bradford. It is even less of a surprise that the builders were Addy & Nichols, who had only just finished the tower on the Town Hall. The Corn Exchange is even simpler in concept than the Town Hall, but in every way as dramatic. Linstrum has pointed out its stylistic closeness to Béranger's roofing of the *Halle au Blé* in Paris; but it makes an impact on the townscape more

10.12: Leeds, nos 49-51, Cookridge Street (Cuthbert Brodrick, 1864). (*Ruth Baumberg.*)

10.14: Leeds, Corn Exchange, interior (Cuthbert Brodrick, 1860-2). (*Author*.)

akin to Rome's Pantheon. A simple ring of offices on two floors surround a huge oval Exchange space measuring almost 90 x 140 ft.[31] This is covered by a spectacular lightweight iron roof (10.14). Externally there is the simplest rhythm of round headed windows. Most amazingly the entire wall surface, above a basic podium with two beefy string courses, is shaped as diamond rustication, giving a vital sense of variety to this vast upturned pudding bowl. The extreme simplicity of the basic form (the two porches are merely blips on the outside) makes an unforgettable element in the townscape. It was also huge in comparison with what was there already. The Leeds White Cloth Hall of 1770 is dwarfed by the new structure (10.16). If the architectural press of the day was critical of the architecture of Leeds, apart from the Town Hall, as unworthy of this wealthy town, this was emphatically the answer.

The completion of the Corn Exchange was achieved before the final touches had been put to the Town Hall. There, a programme of modifications had been in place since the opening.

The enclosure of the entry to the Police station and the bold lions by William Keyworth were not even commissioned till 1866. Barely fifteen years had elapsed since Brodrick won that competition; and the three great buildings he had already designed, and almost built, were

31. In the published design, the ground floor offices formed a horseshoe, leaving an open extension to the main space. See *The Builder*, 19, 1861, p. 651.

10.16: Leeds,Corn Exchange (Cuthbert Brodrick, 1860-2) dominating the White Cloth Hall (*c.*1770). (*Author.*)

10.15: Leeds, Corn Exchange, detail of walling and cornice (Cuthbert Brodrick, 1860-2). (*Author.*)

quite enough to secure his reputation. Although not the last to be built, the Corn Exchange can stand as a summing up of Brodrick's contribution to the architecture of mid-Victorian Leeds. Within ten years of its completion he had abandoned architecture and retired to France, moving first to Paris. This was Paris at the collapse of the Second Empire, and Brodrick somehow had to avoid the bloody siege of Paris and the traumas of the Commune. Yet he did weather the storm, and took up residence in a substantial modern house in Le Vésinet, near St Germain-en-Laye, by 1876. There he lived for a further nineteen years, first with his mistress or partner Marguerite, and then in the care of one of his nieces until 1905. One probably does not need to read any sense of embittered failure into his abandonment of architecture. After all, he had achieved four or five major buildings in one city, and he had evidently earned enough to allow him to live like a gentlemen. It was a perfectly respectable, even enviable, pattern of life for a successful professional gentleman. James Fergusson, for instance, whom he very likely knew through his Bombay design, had done the same by the age of twenty eight; Brodrick had to wait until he was fifty. The buildings he left behind are quite enough to speak of the dramatic genius of this Leeds architect. Each of his buildings has a wonderfully massive character. Each is different. But all are carefully, even sparingly, enriched with bold ornament. Above all traditional styles, immaculate construction and the very latest in daring engineering are the hallmarks of his work. The Town Hall, Corn Exchange and Mechanics Institute are individually unforgettable, but also inseparable from what makes Leeds a unique city. And they are Brodrick's contribution to that.

Catalogue

From Linstrum [note 2], pp. 143-4, unless another source is given.

HULL, General Cemetery, 1846, dem.

HULL, Christ Church Schools, 1847.

HESSLE, EY, layout for villa residences for Hull Charterhouse, 1847.

HULL, 4, 5 and 6 Silver Street for Hull Charterhouse, 1848.

HULL, Royal Flower Pot Hotel, 1848, dem.

SIGGLESTHORNE, EY, Sigglesthorne Hall, enlargement, 1850.

HESSLE, All Saints, restoration, 1852.

HULL, Royal Institution, c.1852-4, dem. (*LM*, 11 Dec. 1852.)

BEVERLEY, 'a mansion', c.1853. (*LM*, 18 June 1853.)

LEEDS, Town Hall, 1852-8.

LUND, EY, All Saints, rebuilding except chancel, 1853.

LEEDS, St Mark, Woodhouse, font, 1853-4. (*LM*, 5 Nov 1853.)

DRIFFIELD, EY, National School, 1853-4. (*LM*, 6 May 1854.)

WITHERNSEA, EY, Queens Hotel, c.1853-4. (*LM*, 8 Oct 1853.)

ILKLEY, Wells House Hydropathic Establishment, c.1854. (*LI*, 6 May 1854.)

GRAINSBY, Lincs, Grainsby Hall, rebuilding, c.1854. (*LM*, 27 May 1854.)

WITHERNSEA, EY, layout of terraces, 1854.

DRIFFIELD, EY, 51 Market Place, bank, 1854.

PAULL, EY, vicarage, now Manor, 1857.

THORPE BASSETT, EY, vicarage, now The Lowlands, 1857.

CHERRY BURTON, EY, Cherry Burton Hall, remodelling, 1857.

WITHERNSEA, EY, St Nicholas, restoration, 1858. (*LM*, 5 June 1858.)

LEEDS, 7 Alma Road, Headingley, 1859.

LEEDS, Poor Law Offices, East Parade, unsuccessful comp. entry, 1859. (*LI*, 11 June 1859.)

LEEDS, Moorland Terrace, Woodhouse, 1859. (*L1*, 21 Jan 1860.)

LEEDS, house, lodge, gates etc at Weetwood, c.1860-1. (*LI*, 20 Oct 1860.)

LEEDS, Corn Exchange, 1860-2. (*LI*, 8 Dec 1860.)

LEEDS, Mechanics Institute, 1860-5.

BEVERLEY, EY, St Mary, unspecified work, 1860.

LEEDS, dwelling-house, stables and lodge, Weetwood, c.1861 [possible the same project as the one advertised on 20 Oct 1860]. (*LI*, 23 Feb 1861.)

HULL, Town Hall, 1861-2, dem. (*LM*, 31 May 1862.)

LEEDS, unspecified woollen warehouse, alterations and additions, c.1861. (*LM*, 29 June 1861.)

BEVERLEY, EY, 37-39 North Bar Within, 1861. (*LI*, 27 July 1861.)

SCARBOROUGH, Grand Hotel, 1862-7. (*LI*, 1 Aug 1863.)

LEEDS, 3 warehouses in King Street, 1862, dem. (*LI*, 25 Jan 1862.)

SALTBURN, NY, 'a mansion', c.1863. Could this be Rushpool Hall? (*LI*, 14 March 1863.)

HULL, St John, remodelling, 1864, dem.

LEEDS, 49-51, Cookridge Street, 1864.

LEEDS, Headingley Hill Congregational Church, 1864.

LEEDS, Oriental Baths, Cookridge Street, 1866, dem. (*LM*, 23 July 1864.)

YOKEFLEET, EY, Yokefleet Hall, for J.H. Empson, 1867-8. (*LM*, 2 Nov 1867.)

11. *Chorley and Connon, and their partners*

JANET DOUGLAS

Charles Chorley

Charles Chorley (1830-1912) was a member of a well-known Leeds family of woollen merchants and medical practitioners; for over thirty years his grandfather, Thomas Chorley, was a distinguished surgeon at the Infirmary and two of Thomas' sons followed in their father's footsteps.[1] Charles' father, Thomas Chorley junior, however, became 'a teacher of languages' and died in 1836, leaving a widow and two small children living at 5, Alfred Place in Little London.[2] According to the 1841 census Charles and his brother Francis Weeks Chorley were at school in Pontefract whilst their mother Margaret, still at Alfred Place, was described as 'a governess'. It may be a fanciful notion but around the corner from Alfred Place was Robert Chantrell's (*q.v.*) home, Oatlands and perhaps Margaret or Charles himself was persuaded that architecture would make a fine profession for a young man of limited financial means. Charles was articled to William Perkin and Elisha Backhouse (*q.v.*) in 1847 and after his five-year apprenticeship, remained with the firm for a further three years as an assistant. In 1855 he formed a partnership with the older local architect Jeremiah Dobson (*q.v.*) that continued until the latter's retirement in 1870.[3] Their offices were at 19, Park Row. Remaining in Park Row until 1906, for fifteen years Charles Chorley practised independently, becoming a fellow of the RIBA in 1881. In 1861 Charles was still living in Little London with his mother and brother who was now a curate at St Matthew's Church. After Charles' marriage in 1866 to Mary

1. Thomas Chorley, Charles Chorley's grandfather was involved in the famous Mary Bateman case, 'the Yorkshire Witch' who was hanged in 1809. His great uncle, Francis Chorley, a partner in the woollen firm of Chorley and Uppleby, opened a woollen mill in 1818 in Little Woodhouse where Chorley Lane commemorates the family's connection with the district. Initially the family worshipped at St Paul's, Park Square and when the church was demolished in the early twentieth century, a number of Chorley memorial tablets were removed to Holy Trinity, Boar Lane.

2. *White's Directory for the West Riding of Yorkshire*, William White, 1837.

3. Linstrum, *WYAA* must surely be wrong when he refers to a partnership between John Dobson and Charles Chorley. No such name appears in the Leeds Directories for the period and the address cited by the author was occupied by Jeremiah Dobson.

Sutton of Congleton, Cheshire, the couple made their home first in Ashwood Villas, Headingley, and then from 1881 they lived in a larger house at 9, Spring Road.

Chorley's partnership with Connon began in 1885. Now in late middle age, he may have felt the need for assistance but additionally, Connon's background, interests and specialisms usefully complemented those of Chorley. Whereas the latter was a devout Anglican and a Conservative, Connon – the son of a Wesleyan minister – became a member of the Mill Hill Unitarian chapel, was an active member of the Liberal Party and was already experienced in school and hospital design. Connon was far more 'clubbable' than the older Chorley whose only outside interests seemed to have revolved around Leeds Parish Church – where he was a church warden[4] – and angling. His son Harry Sutton Chorley (1869-1939) entered the firm of Chorley and Connon as a pupil in 1891 and two years later was made a partner. All three men were at times presidents of the Leeds and Yorkshire Architectural Society: John Connon (1885-6), Charles Chorley (1886-7) and Harry Chorley (1906-8). Charles Chorley retired in 1903 and left Leeds to live in the Malvern Hills. He was buried in Leeds Parish Church where a brass tablet in the north aisle records that he was 'a churchwarden of this church for forty years, 1864-1904'.

John Wreghitt Connon

John Wreghitt Connon (1849-1921) was born in Whitehaven. Between 1863-4 he attended Wolverhampton and Newcastle Schools of Art, and in 1865 joined his eldest brother who was a doctor in Dewsbury, where he was articled to Henry Holtom and George Butler. After travelling in France during 1869, he returned to Dewsbury and continued in Holtom's employment, becoming a partner in the firm in 1875. In association with Holtom, Connon designed a number of schools and in 1873 was granted a patent for 'an improved seat and desk for use in schoolrooms'. In 1876 he moved to Horsforth and from 1880 worked alone in Leeds; a year later was elected a fellow of the RIBA.

Connon was an active Liberal and secretary of the Leeds Liberal Club since its foundation in 1880. He was also on the board of directors of the Hotel Metropole, Leeds Ltd, and both these connections were to lead to major commissions for the partnership as we shall see. He also published papers on such varied topics as 'The Legal Registration of Architects'[5] and 'A Guide to Kirkstall Abbey'. He was a director of the Gildersome Fever Hospital and for ten years a committee member of the Leeds Hospital for Women and Children.[6] His wife Rhoda Annie was also involved in public life as a member and one time president of the Leeds Women's Liberal Society. She was also

4. Not only was Charles Chorley's brother a Church of England vicar but two of his sons also entered the ministry.

5. Quoted in *LM*, 3 Dec 1887.

6. W.T. Pike, *A Dictionary of Edwardian Biography: the West Riding of Yorkshire*, Peter Bell, 1986, p. 364.

a member of the Leeds Corporation Education Committee and a Governor of the Leeds Girls High School. A keen suffragist, she became president of Leeds branch of the National Union of Women's Suffrage Societies in 1913.[7] Both Connon and his wife were buried in All Hallows Church, Bardsey, a village eight miles north of Leeds where they had lived for several years and where in 1909 he had restored the parish church. There are also memorial plaques to the couple in Leeds' Mill Hill Chapel.

The practice and some of its major patrons

The third son of Charles Chorley, Harry Chorley, was educated at Leeds Grammar School and read history at Trinity College, Oxford, before joining his father's practice as a pupil in 1891. He became an associate of the RIBA in 1896 and the following year a partner in Chorley and Connon. Following his father's retirement in 1903 he continued in partnership with Connon, obtaining his fellowship of the RIBA in 1906. Having been brought up in Headingley, for most of his adult life Harry lived in genteel Burley in Wharfedale, fifteen miles north-east of Leeds.[8] Although this volume is not concerned with post-First World War architects and architecture, for the sake of completeness, it should be noted that following Connon's death in 1921, Harry Chorley remained sole partner, practising as H.S. Chorley until the mid-1920s when he formed a partnership with B.R. Gribbon and G.H. Foggitt. Chorley was appointed Advisory Architect to the City Council and oversaw the first council housing estates built under the Addison Act. In 1923 the council dispensed with his services when under the Chamberlain Act responsibility for the design of estates passed to the Engineer's Department. He continued the family involvement with the Church of England for forty years, acting as Diocesan Surveyor for the Ripon Diocese. He largely retired from business in 1931 and died a few days before the outbreak of the Second World War.[9]

A practice (or more correctly a series of practices) that lasted for well over fifty years would not be expected to show much architectural continuity but surprisingly there are some common themes. Despite the spectacular growth in the Leeds tailoring trade, I can find no examples of the firms' involvement in factory design of any kind and their commercial work was rather limited although Harry Chorley is said to have designed many branch banks all over the north of England for the Yorkshire Penny Bank, as well as some for Beckett's Bank and later the Westminster Bank.[10] Their portfolio of work focused on four building types: residences that ranged from suburban middle class dwellings to country houses; Anglican churches with just a single Nonconformist commission in Charles Chorley's design for a Unitarian

7. E. Crawford, *The Women's Suffrage Movement: a Reference Guide 1866-1928*, Routledge, 2000, p. 45.

8. N.R. Paxton, 'Harry Sutton Chorley' in *Journal of the West Yorkshire Society of Architects*, 20 February 1934.

9. http://www.flickr.com/ photos/25393012@NO4/2445738745/in/ set-7215760441202346

10. Beckett's Bank became part of the Westminster Bank in 1921.

Chapel in Holbeck; public buildings such as shops (1.14), schools and hospitals and lastly hotels and clubs – Chorley and Connon's best known work in Leeds is the Leeds and County Liberal Club (1889-90 – now Quebec's Hotel) and the neighbouring Hotel Metropole (1897-8). In terms of architectural style, the firms' repertoire was impressive: Classical or Italianate – although examples are relatively infrequent after the 1860s – Gothic for both ecclesiastical and early domestic commissions, Jacobean and Domestic Revival and, from the late 1890s, Neo-Baroque.

The partnership exhibited drawings in a number of locations, presumably to enhance its status, including the Royal Academy[11] and the Glasgow International Exhibition.[12] However, its triumphs remained close to home. All successful architects need strong patronage and a wealthy and influential patron can establish a young architect's credentials; in Leeds, the mighty James Kitson (1807-1885), owner of the Airedale Foundry, was to play such a role in the career of Charles Chorley. Kitson, one of the pioneer locomotive builders, had come from humble beginnings as the son of a tavern keeper in Camp Road, but rose to become one of the richest men in the town. His prestige was recognised and confirmed by a variety of public appointments, for example between 1858-68, he was a Liberal alderman and twice served as mayor between 1860-2.[13] After living in a variety of rented homes in Woodhouse and Little Woodhouse, he decided that he needed a country mansion commensurate with both his wealth and his newly found social standing. In 1864 he purchased sixty-five acres of land for £18,000 from the Nicholson's Roundhay Park estate (see Chapter 5) in Roundhay – a small village not yet incorporated into Leeds – and commissioned Dobson and Chorley to design a grandiose Italianate villa. There is no obvious rationale for Kitson's architectural patronage: Dobson was essentially a 'middle order' Leeds designer and Chorley

11. *LM*, 1 May 1888.

12. *LM*, 26 May 1888.

13. For details of the Kitson family, see J. Ashley Miller, *Call Back Yesterday*, Strathmore Publishing 2007, pp. 33-83, and R.J. Morris, The Rise of James Kitson: Trades Unions and the Mechanics Institute, Leeds 1826-1851, *Proceedings of The Thoresby Society* Vol. LIII, Part 3, No.118, 1972, pp. 179-200.

11.1: Leeds, Elmete Hall, Roundhay (Dobson and Chorley, 1865). (*Ruth Baumberg*.)

would have been too inexperienced to account for the commission. A sales brochure of 1900 describes how Elmete Hall (11.1) was 'built without regard to cost'. It was clearly intended to impress but despite the money lavished on it, the design is not entirely successful and it lacks any sense of over-all cohesion.[14] The entrance façade to the west contains a central canted bay which projects almost as a complete octagon and which once rose above the roofline to form a two-storey tower. Within the central bay, above the open pediment of the doorway, is a carved shield and motto flanked by putti. The coat of arms appears to have been filched from the Kytsons of Hengrave Hall in Suffolk,[15] whilst the Latin tag, perhaps appropriately, translates 'Let him who has merited the palm [of victory] wear it'. The irregular south front divides into four sections corresponding to the rooms behind it: the projecting south-west section contains a large canted bay window, the next bay is set back with round-arched windows, even further back a narrow unit contains a bay window and finally there is a slightly projecting end bay at the south-east corner crowned by a pyramidal tower. The first and last sections of the facade are topped by stone balustrades. The vast interior was fitted out with fine woodwork, plaster ceilings and marble fireplaces, but at the heart of the house – and its finest feature – is an impressive top-lit circular staircase hall with cantilevered stone stairs, elaborate cast-iron balustrade and moulded handrail. There are round-headed recesses to the hall, on the staircase and first floor. The glazed dome is filled with delicate petal patterns in pink, blue and cream painted glass. Further east is a second staircase hall treated very differently, with a Jacobean-style fireplace and panelling, moulded plaster ceiling and cornice, staircase with twisted balusters and wooden arched screen and balustrade at landing level.

In 1874 Elmete Hall was followed by another prestigious commission when Arthur Wilson, the richest of the Hull shipping magnates engaged Charles Chorley to design a country mansion in Anlaby, near Hull. Tranby Lodge is a three-storey, nine bay Italianate house of yellow brick with stone dressings, complete with a 72 ft. balustraded corner tower.[16] To the left is an imposing projecting stone porch with pilasters, its interior covered in elaborate plasterwork. At the centre of the front façade is a large square bay window at ground floor level with pilasters, frieze and balustraded parapet, the window above is crowned with a segmental pediment. Further right is a canted bay window rising through the three storeys of the house. The interior is characterised by lavish and costly decoration in a vaguely Neoclassical style to provide a fitting setting for visits from the Prince of Wales to pursue his amorous encounters with Lily Langtry.[17] A large two-storey stable block to the north-west – Wilson was the Master of the Holderness Hounds – also dates from 1874, and was built in similar yellow brick with red brick detailing and an ornate clock tower.

14. It has been suggested that the reason for this awkwardness is due to the incorporation of earlier fabric.

15. Dr David Boswell, private communication.

16. Tranby Lodge was also known as Tranby Croft. Since 1944 it has been the home of the Hull High School for Girls.

17. E. Gillet & K. Macmahon, *A History of Hull*, Hull UP, 1980, pp. 335, 392.

The connections between Chorley and the Kitson family were to continue over the next thirty years, passing from James Kitson senior to his second son, Sir James Kitson, later Lord Airedale (1835-1911), and even to the third generation when Harry Chorley was one of the those who proposed another of Kitson's sons, the architect Sidney Kitson for full membership of the RIBA. Between 1877-8 Charles Chorley enlarged Spring Bank, Headingley Lane for James Kitson junior and a year later he designed offices for the Airedale Foundry in Hunslet and a stable block at the Monkbridge Iron Works (1886) owned by the Kitson family. Although James Kitson II remained involved with the family business, his role in public life was far more extensive than that of his father: he was chairman of the Infirmary Board at the time of its rebuilding, Chairman of the Leeds Musical Festival Committee, from 1880 President of the Leeds Liberal Association and President of the National Liberal Federation between 1883-90 and the first Lord Mayor of Leeds in 1896-7. Defeated in the parliamentary election in Leeds in 1886, he represented Colne Valley between 1892-1907. A necessary adjunct to a successful political career was hospitality on a scale that outstripped the facilities of a suburban villa in Headingley so in 1885, the year before he was knighted, Kitson bought Gledhow Hall (2.8) and its 150 acres of woods and gardens – just beyond the north-east fringe of the town – creating the largest and grandest house of those belonging to the Leeds entrepreneurial elite. This substantial mid-eighteenth century house, attributed to John Carr of York (see Chapter 2), needed enlargement to suit Kitson's purposes. The family's relationship with Chorley had now been cemented by his partnership with Connon who, as we have seen, was actively involved Liberal Party politics.

Between 1885-90 the firm added two projecting wings at the rear of the house, to the left a large service block whilst the other three-storied wing provided a billiard room and large sitting room with additional bedrooms above. A new entrance (11.2) was sited on the east façade with two pairs of decorated Ionic columns *in antis* forming an enclosed porch with a white marble floor; the doorway has a carved scroll to the entablature and shallow pediment with a winged cherub bearing a shield inscribed 'SALVE', and a pair of partially glazed and panelled doors – the stained glass depicting fruit and butterflies has unfortunately been damaged. The entrance hall within has a fine mosaic floor with a scrolled pattern in black and brown, and a cantilevered stone stairs with cast iron scrolled balustrade and mahogany handrail. The stair well contains eight lunette windows each with brilliantly coloured stained glass of foliage, flowers and fruit framing a central skylight with painted decorative borders. What many local people know about, but few have seen, is the remarkable bathroom (11.3) completely tiled in hand-painted Burmantoft's faience

11.2: Leeds, Gledhow Hall, Chapel Allerton, entrance (Chorley and Connon, 1885-90). (*Ruth Baumberg.*)

11.3: Leeds, Gledhow Hall, Chapel Allerton, bathroom (Chorley and Connon, 1885-90). (*From S. Lasdun, The Victorians at Home, p. 142.*)

in shades of greenish-blue and cream with chestnut mouldings designed by Chorley and Connon in 1885, reputedly for a visit from the Prince of Wales.[18] The practice was also responsible for alterations to the stable block, various farm buildings and additions to the lodge. They may have designed the early twentieth century motor house with its glazed roof with cast-iron trusses. As will be discussed later in this chapter, the Kitson clan were also connected with the firm's most celebrated buildings in Leeds' centre, the Leeds and County Liberal Club and the Hotel Metropole.

Another important Leeds family, the Luptons were also patrons of Charles Chorley. Whereas the Kitsons represented new industrial wealth, the Lupton family were prominent woollen merchants in the eighteenth century. The two families must have known each other, for

18. The Prince of Wales' visit never materialised. For details of Gledhow Hall and its famous bathroom, see *The Builder*, 49, July 1885 and S. Lasdun, *Victorians at Home*, Weidenfeld and Nicholson, 1981.

11.4: Leeds, *Penraevon*, St Mary's Road, Chapeltown (Chorley and Connon, 1881). (*Ruth Baumberg.*)

both worshipped at Mill Hill Unitarian Chapel and Beechwood, one of the Lupton family homes, was located close to Elmete Hall.[19] Just as Earl Cowper in the 1820s had sought to augment his fortune by establishing a New Town in the area we now know as Chapeltown, so in the more propitious 1870s Darnton and Francis Lupton embarked on a speculative building venture, laying out an exclusive residential estate on the west side of Chapeltown Road at the southern corner of the grounds of Newton Hall, their family home.[20] Initially, in 1871 the Lupton brothers appointed the eminent local architect George Corson to draw up plans, but for whatever reason these were not proceeded with and the estate was built under the auspices of the Newton Park Building Club,[21] engaging Chorley in 1879 to produce new drawings and build a number of houses. The layout is geometrical. An imposing gateway on Chapeltown Road, with pedestrian entrances to each side, marks the beginning of the principal street, St Mary's Road which leads to the largest house on the estate, *Rockland*. A broad street lined with trees, it is bisected by Oak Road and further west by Laurel Mount. The earliest building on the estate was St Martin's Church (1879-81), although again for unknown reasons to job went to the architects Adams and Kelly (*q.v.*). A second place of worship, a Congregational chapel, was built sometime before 1888.[22] Virtually all the nineteenth century houses have been attributed either to Chorley, or to Chorley and Connon, with the exception of nos.1-10 St Mary's Road (1894) where the architects were Smith and Tweedale (*q.v.*).[23] Chorley's (and later Chorley and Connon's) stone terraces and semi-detached villas are

19. Newton Hall was demolished in the 1920s though the lodge of 1856 survives in Chapeltown Road next to St Martin's Church.

20. The Luptons and the Kitson did not inter-marry until 1890; possibly the Luptons regarded the Kitsons as *parvenus*.

21. There appear to be no extant details of the Newton Park Building Club, but perhaps Francis Lupton established the Club as a way of raising additional capital.

22. In 1887 Archibald Neil designed the Union Chapel, a joint venture between the Congregational and the Baptist denominations and the earlier chapel became the Congregational Hall. The chapel has recently been badly burnt and will probably be demolished.

23. *The Chapeltown Conservation Appraisal for Leeds City Council*, 2003.

pleasant, albeit humdrum, in terms of their design. However, there are four residences in the Domestic Revival style which are exceedingly striking. *Penraevon* (11.4) on Laurel Mount is probably the best of these: built in stone in 1881 with a half-timbered gable above an oriel window, leaded lights and a pretty timber porch.[24] *Eltonhurst* and *Oakfield* (1885) on St Mary's Road, remain as spectacular as the illustration in *The Builder* (11.5) suggests:[25] a cavalcade of fishscale tiling, half-timbering and decorated plaster coving below large gables, with their roofs continuing as catslides to the ground floor and with wooden porched entrances to the sides. The largest house on the estate is the twin-gabled *Rockland* of 1886, built for Francis Lupton with the same recipe of stone, render, hung tiles and tall brick chimneys (now capped), to the left is an oriel window with a plaster frieze of swirling foliage. In 1887 Chorley and Connon also designed a house in Headingley for another member of the family, Henry Lupton. *Lyndhurst* on North Grange Road has similar Domestic Revival features as those they employed in Newton Park. The house is now the home of the Roman Catholic Bishop of Leeds.

Whilst engaged at Gledhow Hall and Newton Park, Chorley and Connon were also employed by another member of the Leeds political

24. Behind *Penraevon* are stables and row of cottages which predate the house.

25. http://two.archiseek.com

11.5: Leeds, *Eltonhurst* and *Oakfield*, St Mary's Road, Chapeltown (Chorley and Connon, 1885). (*http://two.archiseek.com*)

SEMI-DETACHED HOUSES. NEWTON PARK ESTATE. LEEDS. *Messrs Chorley & Connon.* Architects 15 Park Row. LEEDS.

elite, Sir Andrew Fairbairn (1828-1901) on the construction of Askham Grange (1886) which dominates the village green of Askham Richard, south-west of York and some twenty miles from Leeds. Son of Sir Peter Fairbairn who had founded a prestigious engineering firm in Leeds, Andrew Fairbairn was mayor of the town between 1866-8, Chairman of the Leeds School Board from 1870 to 1878 and a Liberal MP for the Eastern division of the West Riding (1880-5) and for Otley (1885-6).[26] In the 1870s Fairbairn had leased Goldsborough Hall from the Lascelles family but as he began to detach himself from the affairs of his home town he – like so many of the wealthiest Leeds merchants from the eighteenth century onwards – sought the life of a country gentleman, and he began to buy up land in Askham Richard, becoming the largest landowner in the neighbourhood. Designed in a Domestic Revival idiom, the house has been described by Peter Leach as 'Fussily Old English, with various gables and bay windows, bits of half-timbering and pargetted eaves, a turret and an oriel'.[27] This description suggests a riot of ill-thought out features, although an equally persuasive interpretation would detect an order within its irregularity, the blending of different textures and colours, and a balance between the low, long frontage and a roofline pierced by pointed eaves, a pyramid tower and a plethora of tall brick chimneys. Fairbairn was not particularly concerned about stylistic details but was deeply interested in the house's efficiency and it was equipped with the most up-to-date arrangements for central heating, ventilation and drainage; the latter included an automatic flushing device. It remained in the ownership of Fairbairn family until the Second World War when it was presented to the government, becoming a women's open prison in 1947.

Ecclesiastical commissions

Ecclesiastical work was the bread and butter of the various architectural practices which involved Charles Chorley, Wreghitt Connon and Harry Chorley, and the Chorleys' personal Anglican connections explain why, with one exception,[28] these commissions came from the Church of England. Much of the work was fairly mundane: repairs, the laying of new floors and the like, and there were substantial restorations carried out at St Mary's, Swillington (1884), All Hallows, Bardsey (1909) and St Mary's, Kippax (1920), along with a range of church schools, mission halls and vicarages, largely in Leeds. In 1861, for example, Dobson and Chorley supervised the repairs and alterations to Leeds Parish Church including the insertion of three new windows in the transepts. The fact that Chantrell (*q.v.*) was not consulted about this work led to angry letters in *The Builder*.[29] In total, the Chorleys and Connon were responsible for the design of at least ten churches, mostly in Yorkshire and all Gothic ranging from High Victorian to Free Gothic. The first

26. Details of the life of St Andrew Fairbairn in Pike [note 6], p. 406.

27. Pevsner, *WY*, p. 105.

28. A Unitarian domestic mission to Holbeck was first established in 1844 financed in part by the Lupton family. Eight years later a small building which served as both a chapel and a school was erected and in 1881 Charles Chorley designed a chapel in Domestic Street in a classical style with a tall semi-circular portico reaching up into a broken pediment.

29. C. Webster, *R.D. Chantrell (1793-1872)*, Spire Books, 2010, p. 158.

11.6: Leeds, Church of the Holy Name, Woodhouse (Charles Chorley, 1881.) (*Leodis.*)

church designed wholly by Charles Chorley was the Church of the Holy Name (1881) (11.6) in Woodhouse, a daughter church of All Souls, Blackman Lane, and built at a cost of £4000. Demolished in the 1960s, the church occupied an awkward triangular site hemmed in by working class terraces. From surviving photographs, the design was unusual, certainly for Leeds: the church had a tower with a helm roof, tall lancets in the tower, east and west ends, and a nave with a series of projecting gabled chapels to both sides separated by buttresses. A year later, Connon won the competition to design St John, Crossens, near Southport, Lancs, a handsome Gothic work in yellow sandstone with red sandstone dressings. Its outstanding feature is a north-west tower with angled buttresses, a corbel table, embattled parapet and polygonal vyse to half the height of the tower.

A comparison between St Michael and All Angels, Farnley (1885) and Harry Chorley's St James the Great (1911-1914) at Manston, charts the Gothic shift from a concern with 'correctness' and elaborate decoration to a bold and unadorned austerity. Externally both churches share a certain simplicity, neither were well-funded and as a consequence both were not completed according to their original design.[30] St Michael and All Angels (11.7) has a four-bay nave with north and south aisles, a gabled southern transept with a small bellcote and two-bay chancel, lancet windows throughout except for an elaborate five-light east window. Inside slender octagonal columns with moulded capitals and chamfered arches lead up to a high and wide chancel arch. Within the chancel are corbel angels with musical

11.7: Farnley, WY, St Michael's and All Angels (Chorley and Connon, 1885). (*Ruth Baumberg.*)

instruments and scrolls, and a timber barrel-vaulted roof. St Michael's is known as 'the terracotta church' since £1,000 of the building costs of £3,900 was given by the Farnley Iron Company which also produced fireclay products: there are terracotta tiles lining the walls of the porch and the interior walls below the windows are ornamented with bands of moulded terracotta with a floral design in deep relief. The first church of St James the Great at Manston had been designed by Perkin and Backhouse (*q.v.*) between 1846-7 at a time when Charles Chorley began his pupilage with the firm. Sixty years later, the decision to build a new church (11.8) was taken partly because of an increase in the local population and also because the shallow chancel of the old church no longer accorded with the Anglo-Catholic liturgical practices of the Revd H.H. Malleson who had been appointed in 1898. Initially only three bays of the nave, the chancel, the lady chapel and south aisle were built and then the money ran out. The remaining three bays of the nave were not added until 1957. Financial difficulties may well explain the simplicity of the present church but for modern sensibilities, severity has its attraction. The plainness of the exterior with its simple lancets and chunky buttresses is relieved only by the Decorated tracery of the east window and the chapels of the south aisle that break through the eaves to form three gables. Lacking distracting decorative features, the interior exudes a calmness which undoubtedly for some is an aid to spirituality, but architecturally allows for a focus on the muscular, unadorned columns and the bold stone transverse arches set between a timber roof. At the east end, the rockface stonework provides a perfect setting for the delicate tracery of the large window, since 1963 filled with stunning stained glass depicting Christ in Glory.

11.8: Leeds, St James the Great, Manston (Connon and Chorley, 1911-14). (*Ruth Baumberg.*)

Schools and public buildings

Like their churches, the schools designed by Charles Chorley as well as by Chorley and Connon employed the Gothic style, although Dobson and Chorley's Leeds Parish Church School (1856) (19.20) might more properly be called Tudoresque, an idiom which Chorley replicated when he was employed to build the Leeds Church Middle Class School (1876) (11.9). By 1869 the number of pupils in the top class of the Parish Church Day School was almost a hundred and this prompted the church authorities to open a new school to cater for older children. The school taught such modern subjects as the sciences, languages and commerce and was one of the first schools in the country to have a properly equipped laboratory.[31] The advent of the twentieth century and Harry Chorley's arrival brought about stylistic changes. The little school built for St James the Great in Manston was in a Queen Anne style and the new building for Leeds Girls High School, where Mrs Connon was a governor, adopted the increasingly popular Neo-Georgian. The High School first opened in 1876 in an eighteenth century merchant's residence in Woodhouse Lane and moved to Headingley Hill in 1905-6 where they occupied Rose Court, a fine 1842 Neo-classical house attributed to John Clark (*q.v.*), but they also

31. To us the nomenclature of the school seems deliberately exclusionary but it was not until the very end of the nineteenth century that a small minority of working class pupils remained at school beyond the statutory leaving age. The Middle Class School did admit girls. In 1908, the building became Leeds Girls Modern School and following its removal to Lawnswood in 1931, was the College of Housecraft or in more popular parlance, 'the Pud School'. See L. O'Connell, *A Century of Teacher Training in Leeds 1875-1975,* Leeds Metropolitan University, 1994, p. 192.

11.9: Leeds, Leeds Middle Class School, Woodhouse (Charles Chorley, 1874-6). (*Ruth Baumberg.*)

HOME FOR WAIFS AND STRAYS. MEANWOOD. LEEDS.

11.10: Leeds, The Beckett Home for Waifs and Strays, Meanwood (Chorley and Connon, 1885). (*http:/archiseek.com*)

11.11: Leeds, The Ida Hospital, Cookridge (Chorley and Connon, 1887-8). (*Ruth Baumberg.*)

required additional accommodation. It was Harry Chorley rather than Connon, who produced a long two-storey block with an attic, of six bays in brick with stone dressings. Divided by brick pilasters with stone caps, the projecting end bays have open pediments. The tall, thin multi-

11.12: Leeds, The Hospital for Women and Children at Leeds (Chorley and Connon, 1887-8), dem. (*From A. Claye,* A Short History of the Hospital For Women at Leeds 1853-1953, *p. 2.*)

32. The Waifs and Strays Society was formed in 1881 by Edward de Montjoie under the auspices of the Church of England to provide homes and training for vagrant and abandoned children. Miss Mary Beckett and her sister, Elizabeth lived at Meanwood Hall and were major benefactors to the village. In 1935 the orphanage became a home for babies and was later taken over by the City Council as the Beckett Nursery. It has now been converted into flats.

33. John Thomas North (1842-96) was born in Leeds and travelled to South America as a representative of the Leeds Steam Plough Co. Setting up on his own, he made a vast fortune out of nitrates and returned to England making his home at Avery Hill in Kent. In 1888 he purchased Kirkstall Abbey for the people of Leeds and in 1891 was made a freeman of the city. See W. Emundson, *The Nitrate King: a biography of 'Colonel' John Thomas North,* Palgrave-Macmillan, 2011.

paned windows are spaced close together and the lower section of the building is embellished with banded brickwork. The interior was planned round a central two-storey hall with galleries giving access to the classrooms.

In 1885 Chorley and Connon designed the Anglican Beckett Home for Waifs and Strays (11.10) in Meanwood. Although a brick building had been planned, numerous villagers signed a petition to Miss Beckett requesting that the building be faced in stone, something which added £200 to the original estimates.[32] Set on 'a most precipitous hill' called Greenwood Mount, the house rises up like a small picturesque manor house with half-timbered gables, mullioned windows and a tiled roof, less elaborate but not dissimilar to the some of the houses the partnership were designing for the Newton Park Estate. The Domestic Revival theme also informed the Ida Convalescent Hospital (1886-8) (11.11), erected next to Norman Shaw's Cookridge Hospital of 1868-9. The convalescent hospital was financed by John Thomas North, 'the Nitrate King', in memory of his daughter, Ida, and cost £6000.[33] A single-storey, half-butterfly plan (an early use) built in stone, it provided for a mixture of large and small wards opening onto sun verandas (now bricked up) with half-timbering in eight rendered gables. At the centre is a three-storey, three-bay block with twin half-timbered gables. The ground floor, built of stone, has arched windows with rendering at the first floor and a central oriel window. For a convalescent hospital set in the countryside on the edge of Leeds, a picturesque style was deemed appropriate but when, ten years later, the architects came to design the Leeds Women and Children's Hospital (11.12) on a site close to both the city centre and Scott's Infirmary, a more austere style influenced by Northern Renaissance architecture was selected. The Hospital for Women had first been established in 1853 in former domestic premises in East Parade and in 1860 moved to the Springfield Lodge estate where a new hospital was built. In the late 1890s an anonymous gift of £8000 facilitated a new building programme.[34] Connon was already a member of the hospital committee but resigned when the competition for the new hospital was announced; nevertheless Chorley and Connon were awarded the commission. Their design was for an L-shaped building, a two storey block of open wards ending with a angled tower and turret; above the wards were tumbled gables. Smaller wards and the hospital entrance were located in a slightly projecting block with pointed gables whilst the out-patients department and associated services were set at right angles to the main building with an arcade of large arched

34. A.M. Claye, *A Short History of the Hospital for Women in Leeds, 1853-1953* (other bibliographical details are not available). The hospital was demolished in the 1980s.

11.13: Leeds, Leeds and Yorkshire Liberal Club, Quebec Street (Chorley and Connon, 1889-90). (The Builder, *48, May 1890, p. 402.*)

11.14: Leeds, Leeds and Yorkshire Liberal Club, entrance (Chorley and Connon, 1889-90). (*Ruth Baumberg.*)

windows. An early photograph of the building shows porthole windows in the undercroft of the building to allow for the free circulation of air.

Chorley and Connon's finest and best-known buildings in the centre of Leeds are the Leeds and County Liberal Club and the Hotel Metropole. Both structures were intended to be noticed and were financed accordingly, and both projects take us back to the Kitson connection. James Kitson's role in local and national politics has already been addressed and as the *Morning Post* commented in 1886, for a short time 'Leeds would seem to be the new Liberalism; what Manchester was to the reformers of 1832; what Birmingham was to the Radicals of 1880'.[35] To celebrate Leeds' new-found national ascendancy it was felt that the Liberal Club, established in 1880 and housed in rented accommodation in Park Row, was no longer sufficiently large or prestigious, a situation no doubt aggravated by the lavish rebuilding of the Conservative Club in South Parade.[36] In 1888 Connon, the club's secretary since its foundation, called a special general meeting to discuss the construction of new purpose-built premises to be financed by the establishment of a limited liability company (the building cost £25,000) and thus 'remove the impropriety of the dominant political party in Leeds being constrained to house its club in hired premises'.[37] The site selected for the new Leeds and County Liberal Club (11.13; 11.14) was in Quebec Street, close to the town's railway stations; its foundation stone was laid by James Kitson on 15 March 1890, an event celebrated by a huge plaque within entrance porch. The architects furnished an impressive four-storey design in a Free Renaissance style in faience, but they rejected the more muted colour range of the faience produced by the local Burmantofts Fireclay Company and instead visited the Ruabon works in North Wales specifically to obtain a fiery-red terracotta. The exterior of the building remains virtually unchanged, its eleven bay façade ends with a turret and open balcony 'from which a crowd below may be addressed on occasions of political excitement', though it was also pointed out any crowd gathered to listen to the political speeches would be well away from the Club's main entrance which was situated at the other end of the building. The entrance is flanked by Corinthian columns with an elliptical arch above ornamented spandrels and moulded scroll consoles; its splendid wrought iron gates were made by Francis Skidmore of Birmingham. The entire frontage is richly ornamented: the decorative terracotta blocks were hand-finished to emphasise their high relief and the twin Dutch gables bear the coats of arms of Leeds and Yorkshire.

The splendid interior, although much changed, continues to dazzle and contains one of the hidden treasures of the city, now known as the Oak Room, on the top floor. The entrance hall was described by the *Leeds Mercury* as 'one of the finest of the features of the club'.[38] The drama of its sweeping staircase with large lion newel posts carved in

35. *Morning Post*, quoted in *LM*, 3 Nov 1886.

36. The work of Smith and Tweedale.

37. The records of the Leeds Liberal Club including prospectuses and annual reports are in the Family and Local Studies Department of Leeds Central Library. William Gladstone accepted the presidency of the new Club when he visited the town in 1881; the vice-presidents included James Kitson, Sir Andrew Fairbairn, and John Barran. The published membership list includes many members of the Barran, Kitson and Lupton families. Wreghit Connon continued as the Club's secretary.

38. *LM*, 1 Oct. 1889 and *LM*, Supplement 15 March 1890 and 21 February 1891. The building was also described and illustrated in *The Builder* 31 May 1890 and its fame even reached the USA where an account of the club appeared in *American Architect and Architecture*, vol. 37-8, 1892, p. 22.

oak and carrying ornate gilded lamps is matched by the large jewel-like heraldic landing window made by Powell Brothers and displaying the coats of arms of various Yorkshire towns. Most of the original club rooms have long disappeared: at ground floor level along the street frontage was a large smoking room with marble columns and gilded capitals, and a billiard room; on the first floor was the club dining room to seat 150 people which ran the full length of the façade and led out to the corner balcony. The sumptuousness of the interior fittings can still be savoured in the Oak Room, once a private dinning room with a table to seat forty diners, which has plain oak panelling with balusters to fireplace level, followed by bands of Renaissance carving in a variety of designs reminiscent of the seventeenth century oak woodwork in St John's, Briggate. Below the plaster ceiling divided into lozenge patterns with flowers and foliage, is a deep strapwork plaster frieze with spirals, rosettes and sun motifs. The Liberal Club closed just after the Second World War and the building was occupied by the National Employers Federation until the late 1990s when it was converted into a hotel. The new owners are responsible for the extremely effective exterior lighting scheme which highlights the exuberant façade.

The Hotel Metropole (1896-1899) (11.15; 11.16) was financed by a consortium of local businessmen led by Grosvenor Talbot, the brother-in-law and close college friend of Sir James Kitson. Kitson's nephew, Frederick Kitson, and Connon both had shares in the company, floated with a capital of £80,000. The appointment of

11.15: Leeds, Hotel Metropole, King Street (Chorley and Connon, 1896-9). (*Ruth Baumberg.*)

11.16: Leeds, Hotel Metropole, King Street, detail of the entrance (Chorley and Connon, 1896-9). (*Ruth Baumberg.*)

Chorley and Connon as architects for the new venture is another indication of the continuing importance of family and personal connections to architectural patronage in Leeds. Until the opening of the Metropole, Leeds had two large hotels – the Queen's Hotel of 1863 and the Great Northern which opened five years later – but both were soot-laden dreary buildings owned by railway companies and as the *Leeds Mercury* noted in September 1896, the construction of a new hotel 'in some measure will place the city on a level with other great towns in the country with regard to hotel accommodation'.[39] Both the Queen's and the Great Northern were undeniably grand, but since the 1880s – thanks to the influence of Cesar Ritz – hotel planning was changing: sophistication rather than splendour, quality rather than quantity, and more modern conveniences particularly bathrooms were increasingly the order of the day. Talbot was a seasoned innovator. He began life as a stuff merchant but in the 1880s became a great advocate of the benefits of electricity, forming the first electricity company in Leeds in 1891. The name selected for the new hotel, Hotel Metropole, with its inversion of normal English usage signified its modernity as well as its Continental associations.

The site selected for the new hotel was the redundant White Cloth Hall of 1868 in King Street, close to the city's railway stations, tailoring warehouses and the Liberal Club. Again Chorley and Connon used an orangey-red faience from Ruabon, marking the connections between the two buildings but for the Hotel Metropole, the architects chose what Nikolaus Pevsner described as 'undisciplined French Loire taste'.[40] The busyness of the design – either loved or hated today (the lack of taste of the plutocrat!) – must have added a touch of glamour to the blackened streetscapes of Leeds. The distinctive three-storey bowed central section of the hotel has its entrance marked by four chunky columns with a frenzy of swirling ornamentation. To each side are paired oriel windows with moulded cherubs which rest on enormous moulded consoles. Dutch gables and a small turret rise above the building and perched on this extravaganza of red and buff faience is the stone cupola which once graced the White Cloth Hall. Another remnant of the Cloth Hall can be found to the side of the building where a large Leeds coat of arms is placed over a service entrance to the hotel. . Beyond the hotel entrance is an inner porch with a plaster ceiling decorated with thistles which in turn leads into a large rectangular reception hall. This and the hotel's other rooms have been remodelled on a number of occasions so that it is difficult discern their original features. The reception hall retains its pilasters and arched divisions but the domed ceiling, mosaic floor, wooden wall panelling and much of the stained glass have disappeared. A glazed screen with double doors still leads to a large hall with giant columns and a partially glazed, coved ceiling that was once the hotel's dining room. It also had

39. *LM*, Supplement, 12 Sept. 1896 and 1 July 1899. The Hotel Metropole was also reported in *The Builder*, 15 July 1899.

40. N. Pevsner, *The Buildings of England, Yorkshire: the West Riding,* Penguin Books 1959, p. 319.

11.17: Leeds, unsuccessful entry in Leeds Municipal Buildings competition (Holtom and Connon, 1876). (Building News, *5 January 1877.*)

a small bar, something which distinguished it from the Liberal Club next door where temperance allegiances prevented the selling of alcohol. To the right of the hall are two small rooms that retain their original moulded plaster ceilings. On the left, at the end of the reception hall, is a wide, cantilevered staircase with an elaborate bronze balustrade. Lit throughout by electricity (the many advertisements which appeared in the national and local press emphasised that there was no additional charge for lighting in the bedrooms), and with one of the earliest hydraulic lifts in Leeds, the Hotel Metropole graphically revealed how stylistic extravagance might be combined with practical modernity, enhancing the city's reputation for go-ahead enterprise.

Catalogue

Dobson and Chorley commissions (1855-70) are listed under Dobson in Chapter 19

Charles R. Chorley (1870-85)

LEEDS, Oaklands, Long Causeway, Adel for John Crofts, *c.*1869. dem. (Sales Particulars, WCL59 233 Am 233 series.)
BINGLEY, unidentified residence, 1871 (*Bradford Observer*, 21 Jan 1871.)
LEEDS, Church Middle Class School, Vernon Road, Woodhouse, 1874-6. (Linstrum, *WYAA*, p. 374.)
HULL, Tranby Lodge, mansion for Arthur Wilson, 1874-6. (http://www.imagesofengland.org.uk)

LEEDS, Spring Bank, Headingley, alterations for James Kitson 1877-8. (Linstrum, *WYAA*, p. 374.)
LEEDS, Holbeck Unitarian Chapel, Domestic Street, 1881, dem. (Linstrum, *WYAA*, p. 374.)
LEEDS, Church of the Holy Name, Servia Street, Woodhouse, 1881, dem. (Linstrum, *WYAA*, p. 374.)
LEEDS, offices for the Airedale Foundry, Hunslet for James Kitson, 1881. (*LM*, 11 Nov 1881.)
LEEDS, laboratory for Leeds Grammar School, *c.*1881. (*LM*, 11 Nov 1881.)
SWILLINGTON, restoration of St Mary's Church, 1884. (Pevsner, *WY*, p. 727.)

Holtom and Connon c.1874-80)

DEWSBURY, St Luke's Church, *c.*1874 (http://archiseek.com)
DEWSBURY, Methodist New Connexion Chapel, 1875. (Linstrum, *WYAA*, p. 379.)
SOOTHILL, four Board Schools at Earlsheaton, Mill Lane, East Ardsley and St Mary's, Savile Town, 1875 (Linstrum, *WYAA*, p. 379.)
PUDSEY: Board School, 1876 (http://archiseek.com)
LEEDS, unsuccessful entry for Leeds Municipal Buildings competition, 1876. (*Building News*, 5 Jan 1877.)
SOUTHOWRAM, Board School, *c.*1876. (http://archiseek.com)
THORNE, South Yorks, Board School, *c.*1876. (http://archiseek.com)

WAKEFIELD, unsuccessful entry for Wakefield Town Hall competition, illustrated in *The Architect*, xvii, 1877.

DEWSBURY, St Philips Church, 1878 (Linstrum, *WYAA*, p. 379.)

HOLMFIRTH, Board School, 1878 (Linstrum, *WYAA*, p. 379.)

John Wreghitt Connon (1880-5)

HORSFORTH, cemetery chapels, 1881. (*LM*, 11 Nov 1881.)

CROSSENS, St John's Church 1882 (Roger Harper, *Victorian Architectural Competitions*, 1983, p. 204.)

LEEDS, LICS emporium and People's Hall, Albion Street 1883-4, dem. (*LM*, 21 July 1884; G. J. Holyoak, *Leeds Co-operative Society: Jubilee Celebration*, 1897.)

LEEDS, Mill Hill Chapel, oak and walnut table, 1884 (*Furniture Gazette*, 1884, p. 45.)

Chorley and Connon (1885-1903)

LEEDS, estate layout and houses at Newton Park, Chapeltown for Francis and Darnton Lupton, 1879-86 (Linstrum, *WYAA*, p. 374.)

LEEDS, Shops etc, Call Lane, for the Charitable Uses Trust, c.1885. (*The Architect*, 28 Aug 1885.)

ASKHAM RICHARD, Askham Grange, for Sir Andrew Fairbairn, 1885-6. (http://en.wikipedia.org/wiki/Andrew Fairbairn_(politician).)

LEEDS, Gledhow Hall, Chapel Allerton, extensions and alterations to house, lodge and various outbuildings for James Kitson 1885-90 (Linstrum, *WYAA*, p. 374.)

LEEDS, St Michael and All Angels Church, Lawns Lane, Farnley, 1885. (*LM*, 27 Jan 1886.)

LEEDS, Home for Waifs and Strays, Meanwood, 1885-7. (*LM*, 21 Dec 1885; 10 Aug 1887.)

LEEDS, stables for the Monkbridge Iron Company owned by James Kitson, 1886 (Linstrum, *WYAA*, p. 374.)

LEEDS, offices for the Yorkshire Post, Albion Street, 1886, dem.. (Linstrum, WYAA, p. 374.)

RETFORD, Notts, Beckett's Bank in the Market Place, 1887. (Private communication from Ruth Harman.)

LEEDS, *Lyndhurst*, North Grange Road, Headingley, for H. Lupton 1887 (Linstrum, *WYAA*, p. 374.)

LEEDS, Ida Convalescent Hospital, Cookridge, 1887-8 (*LM*, 12 Nov 1887.)

LEEDS, Parish Church Mission Room, 1888. (Linstrum, *WYAA*, p. 374.)

LEEDS, stables for *Hawkhills*, Gledhow, 1888. (Linstrum, *WYAA*, p. 374.)

OULTON, additions to Oulton Hall for E. Calverley, 1888-91. (Linstrum, *WYAA*, p. 374.)

LEEDS, extensions to Headingley National School, 1889 & 1893 (Pevsner, *Leeds*, p. 256.)

LEEDS, Leeds and County Liberal Club, Quebec Street, 1889-91. (*LM*, 1 Oct 1889; 5 Oct 1889; 20 Feb 1891.)

LEEDS, alterations to Union Infirmary, Beckett Street, 1890. (*LM*, 3 June 1890.)

HULL, third prize in competition for Hymers College, 1890. (*LM*, 7 June 1890.)

LEEDS, alterations to Kirkstall Grange for Sir Ernest Beckett, *c.*1890 (Pevsner, *WY*, p. 491.)

LEEDS, parish hall and school room for St Aidan's, Elford Place,1890. (*LM*, 15 Feb 1890.)

LEEDS, Clergy House, Parish Church, 1894. (*LM*, 6 Nov 1894.)

LEEDS, Hotel Metropole, King Street, 1896-9. (*LM*, 9 July 1896; 9 Sept 1896.)

LEEDS, Women and Children's Hospital, Woodbine Place, 1897-9, dem. (Linstrum *WYAA*, p. 374.)

WHITBY, Metropole Hotel, West Cliff, 1897-8. (http://www.hello-yorkshire.co.uk)

Chorley, Connon and Chorley (1893-1903)

LEEDS, gallery to the Leeds Library, 1900 (Pevsner, *Leeds*, p. 121.)

LEEDS, choir vestry at Leeds Parish Church, 1901. (J. Sprittles, *Leeds Parish Church*, n.d.)

HARROGATE, Police Convalescent Home, 1900. (Roger Harper, *Victorian Architectural Competitions*, Mancell, 1983, p. 201.)

LEEDS, St James the Great School, Sandbed Lane, Manston, 1901. (http:// www.leodis.org)

Connon and Chorley (1903-21)

LEEDS, Holy Trinity, Armley Hall, repairs and reseating, 1904-5. (www.churchplansonline.org)

LEEDS, School Buildings for Leeds Girls High School, Headingley Lane, 1905-6. (Pevsner, *Leeds*, p. 256.)

HELLIFIELD, St Aidan's Church, Main Street 1905-6 (Pevsner, *WY*, p. 330.)

BEN RHYDDING, St John's, 1905-12 (Pevsner, *WY*, p. 340.)

LEEDS, cemetery chapels at Harehills and Bramley, 1907-8. (*Leeds and Yorkshire Architects Society Green Book*, 1907-8.)

LEEDS, Sunday School, Silver Royd Hill Primitive Methodist Chapel, Tong Road Wortley, 1907-8 (*Leeds and Yorkshire Architects Society Green Book*, 1907-8.)

GUISELY, unidentified rectory, 1907. (*Leeds and Yorkshire Architects Society Green Book*, 1907-8.)

EAST FERRY, Lincs, chapel of ease, 1907. (Leeds and Yorkshire Architects Society Green Book, 1907-8.)

RIPON, Ripon High School, 1909-10. (www.yorksj.ac.uk/library/learning cent/special collection/plans)

WILDSWORTH, Lincs, additions to St John's Church for Hon F.A. Meynell, 1908-9. (*Leeds and Yorkshire Architects Society Green Book*, 1908-9.)

LEEDS, Tramway Depot, Swinegate, 1908-10. (J. Soper, *Leeds Transport,* vol 2.)

LEEDS, vicarage for St Edward's, Holbeck, 1908. (Linstrum, *WYAA,* p. 374.)

LEEDS, St Hugh's Church, Armley Lodge Road, 1908-9. (*Yorkshire Post,* 17 Dec. 1908.)

THORP ARCH, Marguerite Home Hospital for Children for the Leeds Invalid Children's Society (1909-10) (*Leeds and Yorkshire Architects Society Green Book*, 1909-10.)

POOL IN WHARFEDALE, Wesleyan Chapel, 1909-10. (*Leeds and Yorkshire Architects Society Green Book*, 1909-10.)

RODLEY, unidentified Sunday School, 1909-10. (*Leeds and Yorkshire Architects Society Green Book,* 1909-10.)

BARDSEY, All Hallows, restoration, 1909. (Linstrum, *WYAA*, p. 374.)

SHEFFIELD, The Grand Hotel, 1909-10, dem. (http://flicka.com/photosa/25393012@NO4/2445738745/in/set-721576044102348)

ASKRIGG, St Oswald, vicarage, 1912 (http://www.thedales.org.uk/HistoryOfStOswaldsAskrigg)

LEEDS, St James the Great, Manston, 1911-14. (Colin Wright, *The Parish of St James the Great, Manston,* 1997.)

WINKSLEY, St Cuthbert and St Oswald, a gift of Lady Furness of Grantley Hall, 1914-17. (Pevsner, *WY*, pp. 756-7.)

LEEDS, St Luke, Beeston Hill, reredos, 1914-15. (E. Beety, *Our Church,* 2004.)

Note: Perhaps because the alliteration of the names 'Chorley and Connon' which trip off the tongue and often the pen, even in published sources, work is often ascribed to the partnership which predate its actual formation. In most cases buildings in Leeds erected before 1885 are by Charles Chorley when he was in independent practice.

12. Thomas Ambler (1838-1920)

JANET DOUGLAS

Background and early life

Thomas Ambler was born in Holbeck, Leeds in 1838. His father, Joseph Ambler, was described in the 1841 Census as a 'machine maker' and was sufficiently prosperous to educate his son at Priest Hill College at Spofforth, outside Wetherby. Thomas was articled to the Leeds architect and builder George Smith and attended classes at the Leeds School of Design where he was awarded a Gold Medal by the Department of Science and Art in 1858. Certainly by 1861, and still living in Holbeck, he was describing himself as an architect with offices at 10, Park Row. A year later he married Ann Lucas, the daughter of Joseph Lucas, another local machine maker, at the Queens Street Independent Chapel and by 1871 the couple were living at *Woodsley Lodge*, a detached villa in Clarendon Road, with their four children and two living-in servants. A year before Ann's death in 1888, the family – which now consisted of five daughters and two sons – moved to *Broomhill*, Harrogate Road, in the Leeds suburb of Moortown, which Ambler rented until his death in 1920. *Broomhill* was a substantial c.1838 villa, probably designed by Chantrell (*q.v.*), set in huge grounds.

By 1867 Ambler's practice had become so successful that that he was able to move to larger offices at 9, Park Place – in the heart of the town's professional quarter – where he occupied a substantial three-storey Georgian house. Here he remained until the early twentieth century when he moved to 29, Cookridge Street, but by that time the practice was winding down and it probably closed in 1910. One of

Ambler's earliest assistants was Daniel Dodgson who subsequently worked independently on the design of villas in the Old Gardens Estate, Cardigan Road, in the early 1870s. Walter Braithwaite (*q.v.*) was articled to Ambler and returned to the office after working for a time with John Winn and Sons, builders, before establishing his own practice in 1880. Following Braithwaite's departure, Ambler was joined by Frederick Bowman who became a partner in 1891, leaving nine years late to be replaced by Ambler's only surviving son, Herbert.

Ambler, politics and social reform

Ambler's career involved more than architecture. From the early 1860s he was active in the movement for the improvement of working class housing through the Leeds Permanent Benefit Building Society, and produced designs for model housing. On a number of occasions he served as vice-president and president of the society. For many years he held official positions with the Leeds, Skyrac and Morley Savings Bank, another philanthropic venture aimed at working class improvement. Between 1884 and 1893 Ambler was a Liberal Borough Councillor (the first architect to be elected to the corporation), representing the Brunswick Ward which until Ambler's election has always returned a Conservative. During this period newspaper reports reveal his presence at many Liberal Party meetings: he was a member of the Executive Committee of the Liberal Club and even designed the platforms for the monster Woodhouse Moor demonstration of 1884 in favour of an extension of the franchise. As a supporter of the temperance movement, he lined up with the teetotal cabal that dominated the Council in the 1870s and 1880s, although Ambler was never a slavish party man. Despite being a supporter of the free market like other members of the burgeoning professional class, he was not always in favour of 'small government'. He was a member of the municipal Gas Committee which bungled the Gas Workers' Strike of 1890 by bringing in four hundred and twenty blacklegs from Manchester. Perhaps more congenially, he was also a member of the Library Committee that was responsible for establishment of the City Art Gallery in 1888. On an issue which split the Liberal Group in 1894, Ambler supported an increase in the Library rate in order provide additional funds for the gallery, a proposal that was defeated by a temporary coalition between more economy-minded Liberals and the Conservatives, but by this time, Ambler was moving towards a Liberal Unionist position as were a number of other elite members of the Liberal Party in Leeds. Ambler's participation in Liberal Party networks undoubtedly brought with it professional advantages: he now mixed with 'the great and good' of the town and certainly a number of his commissions derived from these contacts. He probably left politics because of a *contretemps* that took place in March 1894. Seeing William White, a mason employed on the construction of new Post Office, coming out of nearby Liberal Club, Ambler presumed that the man had been drinking and in public called him 'a thief' for stealing his employer's time. White pressed charges against Ambler and the architect was brought before the magistrates for using 'abusive language' and fined twenty shillings.[1] Ambler was active in the affairs of the Leeds Architectural Association and elected its Vice-President in 1880; he was also a member of the Zetland Masonic Lodge.

When introducing Ambler at a Liberal election meeting in 1883, Edwin Gaunt, the hat and cap manufacturer, told his audience that 'Mr Ambler was a man who had risen to a respectable position in his profession as a result of his own exertions'.[2] The wealth that facilitated his upward social mobility from Holbeck to Moortown derived not solely from the design of buildings. Throughout his career, he was retained as a valuer for the Corporation, and moreover on his own behalf built up a varied portfolio of land and property interests both in the town centre and the outer suburbs. For example, in 1874 Ambler purchased Lot 3 of the Headingley Glebe Estate when it came on the market and proceeded to lay out Hollin Lane and Glebe Terrace. The former was divided into half-acre plots that Ambler intended to sell to purchasers willing to build houses to his design. This venture in property development appears not to have been entirely successful as he is known to have designed only two pairs of large semi-detached villas in Hollin Lane but in Glebe Terrace he designed smaller houses which he retained and rented out to tenants. In 1874, Ambler also paid £12,000 for the site of the Scarborough Hotel, in Ludgate, and held

1. *LM*, 24 March 1894.

2. *LM*, 12 Nov 1894.

12.1: Leeds, Beeston Hill, designs for model housing (Thomas Ambler, 1860). (*Leeds Permanent Building Society*, A Survey of One Hundred Years, *Leeds PBS, 1948, p. 16*.)

on to the land and premises for twenty years until the Corporation acquired it for a road-widening scheme.

Although Ambler's career is notable for the design of town-centre commercial and industrial buildings, most memorably the exotic Moorish factory erected in Park Square for John Barran, his earliest commission – in 1860, the year he probably set up in practice – was for ten through houses in Coupland Street, Beeston Hill (12.1), for the Model Cottage Society.[3] This voluntary society was an example of what the housing historian, Jennifer Tarn has called 'Five percent Philanthropy',[4] and sought to demonstrate that decent working class housing was not incompatible with market provision. Ambler's houses were simple in their design, with small front gardens and steps to front doors which led directly into a front parlour with a kitchen behind, a staircase from the kitchen led to three bedrooms at first floor level, and to a pantry in the basement. The ends of the terrace were dignified by ornamental Dutch gables with a smaller gable in the centre. Each house cost £150; the occupier paid a small deposit and was supplied with a mortgage by the Leeds Permanent Benefit Building Society. Ambler designed a similar row of eighteen houses for the Model Cottage Society in Meadow Lane in 1863, and much of his early work involved working class housing.

3. C.J. Higenbottam, 'Thomas Ambler (1838-1920), architect of Leeds' in *The Victorian Society West Yorkshire Journal*, 8, 1988, pp. 5-22.

4. J. Tarn, *Five percent Philanthropy: an account of housing in urban areas 1840-1914*, Cambridge University Press, 1973. See also 'Better Houses for the Working Men of Leeds' in *LM*, 18 Nov 1862 and the editorial in *LM*, 15 Oct 1863, both of which mention Ambler.

12.2: Leeds, warehouse at 30, Park Place, for N.P. Nathan (Thomas Ambler, *c.*1863). (*Ruth Baumberg.*)

Early architectural commissions

A year after the Coupland Street commission, Ambler was at work on something far grander: in 1861 he designed *Weetwood Grove* for Thomas Wolryche Stansfeld, a Leeds woollen merchant and partner in a Bradford worsted company. It was a richly ornamental Gothic design with stepped gables, a large crenellated canted bay, rose window and lancets. The porch has columns with elaborately carved capitals and above the door a tympanum bears the date 1861 and the monogram TWS. The house was extended to the rear in the 1880s and half-timbering added, but it is not known if this was Ambler's work. Gothic was also the preferred style for another early Ambler design, 30 Park Place (12.2), a warehouse built for N.P. Nathan, a shipping merchant. Park Place had first been developed as genteel Georgian terraces in the 1770s with houses on the north side only, giving the residents a clear view over the fields to the River Aire, but from the mid-nineteenth century what were once the gardens of Park Place were in-filled with commercial buildings attracted to the district because of its proximity to the town's railway stations along Wellington Street. As was usual with warehouses of this period, the focus of the design was on the ground floor, particularly on a handsome entrance intended to impress buyers visiting the premises. At Park Place, Ambler provided a slightly raised ground floor to provide maximum light for the firm's show rooms, the ground floor is richly ornamented with stone carving, with two pointed arched windows with plate tracery placed to each side of the projecting columned porch and a circular window above the door protected by a decorative wrought iron grill. The upper floors of brick with stone dressings are far less ornate with a mixture of round-arched and trabeated windows. The building was later extended on the left by three bays in an identical style, altering the balance of the façade.

Thomas Ambler and John Barran

Ambler's professional success was to be yoked to that of his major patron and later friend, John Barran (1821-1905), who has been credited with introducing the ready-made clothing trade to Leeds.[5] Born in London, the son of a gun-maker, Barran set up as a tailor and clothes dealer in Leeds in 1842 with premises in Briggate. By the mid-1850s, he had accumulated sufficient resources as a retailer to establish a small factory in Alfred Street, off Boar Lane, using between 20-30 sewing machines. Crucial to his business success as a manufacturer was the employment of new technology, the sewing machine and the band-knife, and the introduction of organisational innovations based on a complex division of labour in the production process. He opened a new shop at 1, Boar Lane, and by 1871 had moved to larger factory

5. Ambler is referred to as 'a friend' of Barran's at the opening of the Drinking Fountain in Roundhay Park. (*LM*, 4 April 1882.)

premises in the Commercial Buildings, Park Row. The origins of Ambler's association with Barran remain unknown, although both were Nonconformists (Barran was a Baptist), both were supporters of the temperance cause and the two men shared similar political beliefs. Barran became a Liberal Borough Councillor in 1867, was mayor of Leeds between 1870-1 and served as Liberal MP for the town between 1876-85. He represented Otley between 1886-95 and in the latter year was knighted for his public services. Following the 1866 Leeds Improvement Act, it was Barran who spearheaded the Council's Boar Lane Improvement Scheme which widened what had been a medieval street from 21 feet to 64 feet by the demolition of all the existing properties on the its south side. The objective was two-fold: to provide for the major increase in traffic generated by urban expansion and to promote the grandeur of Leeds by constructing a prime shopping street linking the railway stations with Briggate, the ancient heart of the town.

Initially the Borough Council considered imposing a uniform design but such municipal interference with the rights of property owners and market freedom was very much against the spirit of the age; instead we have a grand sweep of tall varied frontages built between 1869-76 whose architectural style embraces both the Italianate and the Gothic and gives the street what Susan Wrathmell refers to as 'a delightful skyline of moulded parapets, dormers, statuary and spiky turrets'.[6] Numbers 1-13 were sold to John Barran and a syndicate of gentlemen

6. Pevsner, *Leeds*, p. 93.

12.3: Leeds, Victoria Buildings, Boar Lane (Thomas Ambler, *c*.1872). (*Ruth Baumberg.*)

12.4: Leeds, Griffin Hotel, Boar Lane (Thomas Ambler, *c.*1872). (*Ruth Baumberg.*)

for the construction of the Treveyan Temperance Hotel,[7] a building with shops on the ground floor (one of which Barran retained for his own retail premises) and offices and hotel facilities above, the latter included seventy bedrooms. The building cost £65,000 and Ambler was engaged as architect, the first of his many commissions for Barran. Amber's design in brick and stone is a dignified exercise in an Italianate-Second Empire style with dormers and mansard roofs piercing the roof-line of the thirteen-bay frontage. Although the ground floor is much altered, it retains the two original entrances with their carved pediments with cornucopia and two carved heads, possibly Shakespeare and Milton. The widening of Boar Lane lead to a tremendous increase in land values along the street which encouraged those who purchased plots from the Council to ensure that the buildings they erected were of matching quality. As virtually all the buildings on the south side have been attributed to Ambler,[8] a brief description of their facades demonstrates the architect's stylistic versatility and skill in handling very differently-sized plots. Next to the Trevelyan Hotel is a narrow Venetian Gothic building with ornate ogee tracery to the third storey, a style which appears nowhere else in the city centre. The block ends with another Gothic design in brick with stone detailing and gargoyles on end finials. Ambler's sequence of designs continues with Nos 15 and 16 Boar Lane which combine Italianate and Gothic features in a single block: the central three bays are highly ornamental whilst the end elements austerely Gothic; Nos 19-21 form a three-storey Italian

7. Sir Walter Trevelyan was President of the UK Temperance Alliance, and there were Trevelyan Hotels in London and Manchester as well as numerous Temperance Halls and reading rooms bearing his name. For a discussion of the architecture of the Temperance Movement, see A. Davison (2010),'Worthy of the Cause': the Buildings of the Temperance Movement, in G. Brandwood (ed), *Living, Leisure and Law: eight building types in England 1800-1914*, Spire Books, 2010, pp. 9-32.

8. Pevsner, *Leeds*, p. 93.

palazzo. The much admired bank building on the corner of Alfred St was not designed by Ambler but is the work of Wilson and Bailey, and next a sliver of a building in a Neo-Jacobean style which once swept round into New Station Street, a street opened in 1873 for the newly extended railway station. On the opposite corner of New Station Street are the Victoria Buildings (12.3), the first new building opened in Boar Lane built for Masser's, the printers, a Classical design with, at its corner, a bust of the Queen in a pedimented niche. Adjoining Victoria Buildings is the former Saracen's Head Hotel, another Italianate design with an elaborate corner pediment to Mill Hill. In contrast on the opposite corner stands the lavishly Gothic Griffin Hotel (12.4) with finely carved stone details, cast-iron cresting, oriel windows, pinnacles and gargoyles. Its entrance on Mill Hill has stone columns with carved capitals, tall flanking pinnacles and a sharply pointed arch above the now blocked doorway with a carved griffin and decorative panels. The corner of the building has an oriel window and a clock with the letters 'Griffin Hotel' instead of the customary numbers.

Although in this chapter there will be few details of Ambler buildings which have been demolished, an exception must be made for a remarkable shop and warehouse of 1873 (12.5) which, until forty years ago, stood on the corner of Basinghall Street and the north side of Boar Lane.[9] John Barran, the purchaser of the site, insisted that every inch of the limited plot must be used and that the outer walls should cover no more than six inches. Ambler's solution was to design a four-storey, cast-iron Gothic building beneath a conventional roof with a corner spire. The public facades were filled with large plate glass windows that included tracery heads filled with stained glass. In order to relieve the front and give light and shade, a balcony abutted from the third floor supported by ornamental cast-iron brackets.[10] Cast-iron was rarely used in building façades in the Victorian period: even Peter Ellis' much admired Oriel Chambers in Liverpool (1864) has a composite façade of iron framing and stone facing. Despite its Gothic details, Ambler's project pointed to the future with its realisation that massive external walls were unnecessary and as the *Building News* pointed out, such a method of construction was inexpensive and not incompatible with a handsome design.[11]

The continued success of Barran's clothing business necessitated another move in 1878 which was to produce Ambler's most famous building in Leeds, St Paul's House (12.6). Initially a multi-purpose structure located between Park Square and St Paul's Street it housed two hundred sewing machines, cutting and pressing rooms, warehouse facilities and show rooms. The decision to produce a design in a Venetian-Saracen style seems to have been Ambler's own, and the art historian, John Sweetman declares the building 'a triumph and a genuinely creative adaptation of Islamic form to a building with a

12.5: Leeds, shop and warehouse, corner of Basinghall Street and Boar Lane (Thomas Ambler, 1873). (Building News, *xxv, 19 Dec 1873.*)

9. The building was illegally demolished during the weekend before the official publication of its listing. The site is now part of the Bond Street Shopping Centre.

10. Working drawings for the novel façade construction were published in *The British Architect*, 4, 1875, p. 48.

11. *Building News*, 19 Dec 1873.

The factory in St Pauls Street

12.6: Leeds, St Paul's House, Park Square, for John Barran, entrance and south side (Thomas Ambler, 1877-8). (*Drawing by David Knight, from D. Ryott*, John Barran's of Leeds 1851-1951, *1951, p.9.*)

modern purpose'.[12] Ambler's inspiration is usually attributed to Owen Jones' measured drawings of the Alhambra published in 1842-6, although there was an exemplar nearer to home: Cuthbert Brodrick's Oriental Baths in Cookridge Street, built in 1866. St Paul's House is constructed in red and pink brick and Doulton terracotta (the first application of the firm's architectural products). The ground and mezzanine floors are united beneath mighty segmental-arched windows, and the first and second floors linked by a trabeated frame with the addition of an intermediate transom and pretty Islamic colonettes as mullions. The windows of the smaller third floor have triple Moorish-styled arches and above is a brick and terracotta parapet pierced by quatrefoil openings. At the corner of Park Square East and St Paul's Street the canted entrance was set beneath a tall scalloped arch with greenish-blue moulded tiles above, and magnificent wrought-iron

12. J. Sweetman, *The Oriental Obsession*, Cambridge University Press, 1987.

gates by Francis Skidmore. At the five corners of the building were brick and terracotta minarets, the one at the north-west corner serving as a chimney and flue for the boilers of the hot water heating system. It is difficult to believe now that it was intended to demolish this jewel in Ambler's crown. The minarets and parapet had already been removed before the local authority intervened. The missing features had to be replaced by fibre-glass copies and a new terracotta parapet produced by Shaw's of Darwin. The restoration and remodelling of the interior was the work of Booth, Shaw and Partners and the building that Leeds so nearly lost, was re-opened by Nikolaus Pevsner in 1976. At the south-west corner of Park Square stands a later warehouse designed in 1891 by Ambler for Barran, functional in its appearance except for giant pilaster strips; the building is linked to St Paul's House by a subway. Ten years after the opening of St Paul's House, the manufacture of clothing moved to Hanover Lane and between 1888-1904, Ambler designed a huge factory complex, including a new warehouse and offices (12.7) erected in Chorley Lane in 1904. The whole site covered five acres and housed three thousand workers. The complex was strictly utilitarian except for the Chorley Lane range where the main business entrance – the workers had their own humbler entrance on Hanover Lane – sits beneath a deep segmental arch and the rusticated ground floor contains heavily moulded window openings with huge keystones.

Other commissions from John Barran included the Golden Lion Hotel located on the corner of Briggate and Swinegate along with accompanying shops in Blayds Yard in 1879. During his mayoralty, Barran had been instrumental in the controversial purchase of the Roundhay Park Estate to form a public park for the town. Even ten years later the controversy was still raging and special criticism was

12.7: Leeds, offices and warehouse, Chorley Lane (Thomas Ambler, 1888-1904). (*From a drawing by David Knight.*)

12.8: Roundhay, Leeds, drinking fountain, Roundhay Park, for John Barran (Thomas Ambler, 1882). (Fine Art Photographs of Leeds, *Rock Bros, n.d., p. 31.*)

12.9: Roundhay, Leeds, *Parcmont*, for John Barran II (Thomas Ambler, 1883). (*Leodis website.*)

aimed at Barran personally with the park sometimes publicly referred to as 'Barran's Folly'. In 1881 Barran tried to fend off further hurtful criticism by addressing one of the public's many complaints, the lack of drinking water. He commissioned Ambler to design a drinking fountain for the park (12.8). The architect produced a Classical rotunda supported by eight Corinthian columns. Inside the dome was the inscription 'Presented to the Leeds Corporation by John Barran, M.P. 3rd April 1882'. Twenty taps each with a bronze cup attached on a chain, were connected to the town's water supply with four red granite basins beneath to capture any spilt water. The fountain had cost Barran £3000 but it was not until the construction of an electric tramway in 1891, when Roundhay Park became easily accessible, that it became widely popular with the Leeds masses and the criticisms gradually died away. Ambler's relationship with the Barran family extended to the next generation when he designed a villa for John Barran junior – Parcmont (12.9) – close to Roundhay Park. Here again the architect demonstrated his stylistic versatility by an exercise in the Old English style with steeply pitched roofs, half timbering in the gables and tall chimneys.

Ambler's industrial buildings

The dramatic growth of the ready-made clothing trade – by 1901 there were 104 clothing businesses in Leeds – provided rich pickings for the town's architects. Ambler was responsible for at least three more tailoring factories: in 1881 he designed a factory for Arthur and Sons at 34-5 Park Square which J.B. Fraser, the President of the Leeds

Architectural Association, described as having 'a striking principal front – polychromatic brick, the carving over the central entrance is excellent and there is a good example of wrought iron work in the panels'.[13] A year later he built a factory for Joshua Buckley at 2-5 Greek Street, in brick with polychromatic decoration and a Gothic-styled entrance to the side of the front elevation with attached granite columns on tall stone bases and cast-iron cresting above. The third factory, built in 1888 for Stewart and Macdonald, was situated between Park Street and Chariot Street. All these buildings have been demolished.

Another of Ambler's industrial designs, currently (2010) undergoing conversion into offices, is the Crown Point Printing Works built between 1878-81 for Alf Cooke (1842-1902), a political colleague of the architect. The son of a printer, Cooke opened his first business in 1866 and became a pioneer of art colour printing, known for producing 'art for the millions'. Following a fire at his works near Crown Point Bridge, he engaged Ambler to design a new factory on the west side of Hunslet Road (12.10). Its grand façade in red brick with stone dressings is composed of three storeys with a different window design to each floor. On the ground floor segmental arched windows alternate with projecting bays with gabled canopies and semi-circular arched windows. The first floor is arcaded with elliptical arches and pilasters whilst the third storey has two-light round-headed windows with slender columns between. The thirty bay façade finishes at a canted corner entrance and ornate doorway with pilasters and a broken segmental pediment with scrolls and the monogram, AC. The entrance hall within was adorned with hanging baskets of flowering

13. J.B. Fraser, president of the Leeds Architectural Association, *Annual Report*, quoted in *LM*, 11 Nov 1881.

12.10: Leeds, Crown Point Printing Works, Hunslet Lane, for Alf Cooke (Thomas Ambler, 1878-81). (*Ruth Baumberg*.)

12.11: Leeds, Crown Point Printing Works, Hunslet Lane, for Alf Cooke, interior (Thomas Ambler, 1878-81). (*P. Brears*, Images of Leeds, Breedon Books, 1992, p. 157.)

plants and cages of singing birds. In plan the ground floor interior (12.11) was a vast open space with a limited number of enclosed offices, the only interruption being the cast-iron columns bearing the initials AC which supported galleries at first and second floors. Access to these is by two spiral staircases or conventional stairs at one corner. The New Crown Point Works were claimed to be the 'largest, cleanest, healthiest and most completely fitted printing works in the world',[14] housing three hundred chromo-litho and other machines and employing six hundred men. Following another fire in 1894, the factory was rebuilt with the addition of a domed clock tower above the corner entrance.

The streetscape of central Leeds

Probably after Cuthbert Brodrick and George Corson (see Chapters 10 and 14), no single architect working in the town has contributed more than Ambler to the built-environment of nineteenth century central Leeds. St Paul's House is now recognised nationally as a stunning design, but Ambler was also responsible for a diverse range of eye-catching buildings and handsome streets that augment the Victorian legacy so important to the city's identity. Although his work was not exclusively in Leeds, it was here that overlapping political, religious and temperance networks provided a steady stream of commissions. His connections with the temperance movement accounted for his involvement with the erection of St James Hall (1877) (12.12), New York Street, close to the town's markets. The patron here was W.J. Armitage of the Farnley Iron Company. An emblematic piece of bourgeois philanthropy, its purpose was to provide a counter-attraction to the public houses and disreputable lodging houses which clustered

14. Quoted in Hunslet Remembered http://hunslet.org/industry_page_2.html

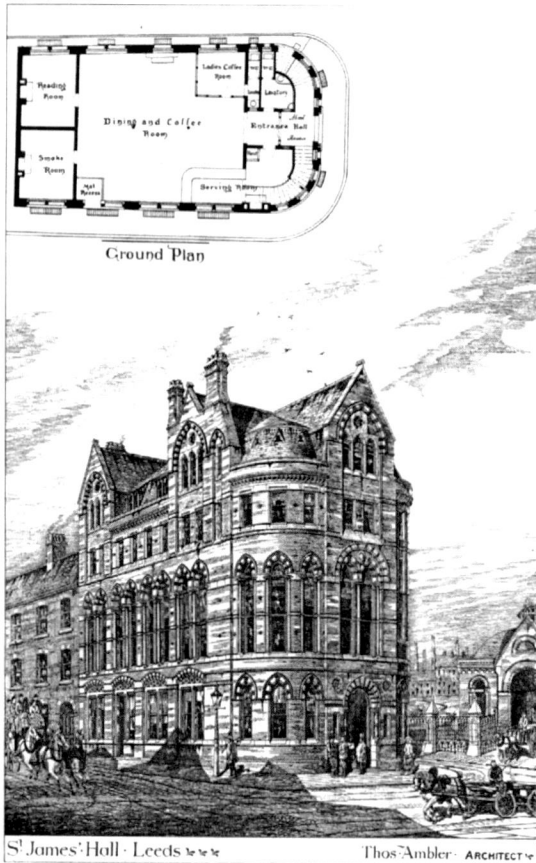

St. James' Hall · Leeds ·&·&·&·   Thos. Ambler · ARCHITECT ·&·

12.12: Leeds, St James Hall, New York Street, (Thomas Ambler, 1877-8). (Building News, *xxiii, July-Dec 1878.*)

in this part of the town. Ambler provided a simple Gothic design in brick relieved by stone dressings and polychromatic brickwork. The ground floor accommodated a large dining room, coffee and cocoa rooms, a smoke room and reading room, no doubt filled with edifying reading matter. To each side were staircases leading to a large first floor lecture room and gallery lit by tall lancet windows and capable of seating four hundred and fifty people. The next level contained private apartments for the manager of the hall and two club rooms for meetings of friendly societies and trade unions 'so many of which have now to assemble in public houses'.[15] Above, the attic floor was divided into twenty eight sleeping compartments where strangers to the town and homeless working men could stay without have to resort to rough lodging houses. In the basement were kitchens and a classroom for 'gutter children'. In 1884, the building was extended by Amber and Thorp, and given a new Gothic crocketed entrance. Now known as Westminister Buildings, appropriately many of the city's social and charitable organisations, such as the Citizens Advice Bureau and the Leeds Credit Union, still have their offices here.

15. *Building News,* 17 March 1876.

12.13: Leeds, Tunstall's Buildings, Duncan Street (Thomas Ambler, 1882). (*Ruth Baumberg*.)

In 1882 work began on the widening of Duncan Street. As with Boar Lane ten years earlier, Ambler was to play a major role in the rebuilding of its south side, something acknowledged by the *Building News*: 'Fortunately for the appearance of the street, the greater portion of the undertaking has been in the hands of one architect (Mr Thomas Ambler, Park-place), and he has striven as far as possible to make the buildings a harmonious whole'.[16] On the corner of Briggate and Duncan Street, he designed a building for Thomas Kirk, a Leeds pawnbroker, consisting of shops on the ground floor and living accommodation above. Gothic-inspired with an octagonal corner turret and spire and Burmantofts faience decoration, the building was demolished in the 1930s. However, Ambler's other building adjacent to Kirk's survives and has been recently restored. A long, Classical seven-bay block, it was constructed for William Tunstall in 1882 (12.13). Symmetrical with a central wagon arch, the six ground floor shops have pilastered windows; offices were situated on the first floor and a large open warehouse on the upper storey. Access to the latter was through the central archway – with a magnificent carving of the town's coat of arms – into Hirst's Yard. The Whip Inn, located in the yard, has a Neo-Tudor entrance also by Ambler. As in Boar Lane, here again we have evidence of Ambler's ability to make use of a whole range of architectural styles in order to meet his own or his clients' preferences.

One of the largest of Ambler and Bowman's commercial projects – Bowman was made a partner in 1891 – was the Victoria Arcade (1898) named in honour of Queen Victoria's Diamond Jubilee (12.14). The work was carried out for F.W. Dawson who owned several dilapidated properties fronting Lands Lane and the Upper Headrow that produced little rental income. Cashing in on the late Victorian boom in domestic consumption, Dawson commissioned an L-shaped arcade of twenty-six large shop units with showrooms on the ground floor and work rooms above defined by three windowed bays. The entrance on Lands

16. Quoted in Higenbottam [note 3], p. 11.

12.14: Leeds, Victoria Arcade, the Headrow, entrance showing Lands Lane to the left (Thomas Ambler, 1897-8). (*P. Brears*, Images of Leeds, *Breedon Books, 1992, p. 93.*)

Lane was carefully positioned to form a virtual continuation of Thornton's Arcade and led to an large octagon under a great glass dome; from this space emerged the second arm of the arcade which linked to the Headrow entrance thus creating a covered shopping way between Woodhouse Lane and Briggate. The eclectically-styled elevations were of red brick and faience with great glazed arched entrances flanked by tall turrets, and ornate pediments which had spandrels filled with stained glass. The Headrow entrance contained a faience cameo image of Queen Victoria. The entrance gates were similarly ornate, and could be lowered into the basement. The floor of the arcade was made of marble mosaic and the shops fitted out with highly polished woodwork. Snowden Schofield, a draper, occupied one of the shops facing the Headrow and gradually more and more of the arcade was to be taken over by what became Schofield's department store and in 1959 the arcade was demolished to make way for a purpose-designed store, itself now demolished. If the Victoria Arcade had survived it would been one of Ambler's most notable buildings and would have undoubtedly become a site for 'bijou' shopping to rival the County Arcade (now part of the Victoria Quarter).

Religious and domestic work

Although best known for its commercial work, the Ambler practice extended to a range of other building types though strangely not schools, despite this being a period when the Leeds School Board were calling on the services of a number of the town's other architects.[17] The firm's religious commissions were also relatively limited but included Burley Road Baptist Chapel (1874), Oak Road Congregational Chapel,

17. The Leeds School Board initially organised open competitions for the design of schools with the result that they were constructed in a variety of styles. After 1873 they appointed Richard Adams (*q.v.*) as architect to the Board. In 1886 in response to a letter from Leeds and Yorkshire Architectural Association, the Board reverted to open competitions but problems regarding fees led them to return to the system of a single Board Architect, a position held by William Landless between 1889-1892 and Walter Braithwaite (*q.v.*) from 1896-1903.

New Wortley (1876), Prospect United Methodist Chapel, Holbeck (1880-1), and Clowes Primitive Methodist Chapel, Meanwood Road (1893-4), all located in working class districts. Again we see the same stylistic versatility that marks Ambler's other work. Burley Road Baptist Chapel and Oak Road Congregational Chapel were Gothic designs; the former cost £3,300 with accommodation for six hundred and fifty worshippers, whilst the more expensive Oak Road cost £7000 and could seat 900. Both have been demolished but Ambler's other two have survived: the Prospect Chapel has a grand Baroque Revival front in ashlar attached to a plain brick building and is now a carpet warehouse, whilst Ambler and Bowman's Primitive Methodist Chapel remained loyal to chapel Classicism. It cost £2,862 and since 1978 has been used by the Seventh Day Adventist Church. Despite its somewhat ill-proportioned exterior, it retains a fine interior with some original pews, a gallery with cast-iron columns, the original organ case and entrance screens.

During his career, Ambler spanned the whole spectrum of housing design from mansions, large detached and semi-detached suburban villas, to brick terraced houses and even back-to-backs. As we have seen in the biographical section of this chapter, Ambler appears to have been genuinely concerned about the question of affordable houses for the working classes, also – in a way that we might find hypocritical today – he had his own pecuniary interests in the provision of such houses. Working for builders, development companies and sometimes on his own behalf, he probably designed hundreds of houses in working class districts like Armley, Woodhouse and south Headingley.[18] None of his surviving middle class housing is particularly distinguished, usually four-square villas such as Newport House (12.15), in brick with stone dressings. One of the aberrations and great puzzles of Ambler's career is how Sir Richard Wallace, who had resided in Paris until the Revolution of 1871, came to commission Ambler to redesign Hertford House in Manchester Square to accommodate his vast art collection. The original five-bay house had been built in 1776 by the Duke of Manchester but was fundamentally altered by Ambler between 1872-82 by the construction of a vast *porte cochère* with giant Doric columns, end bays to extend the façade along with further additions constructed around a central courtyard. A new smoking room lined with Minton tiles was created at the rear of the house. Commentators have been universally critical of Ambler's efforts, one even doubted if 'another man could be found who would make almost as many mistakes with a Doric entablature as Ambler has made with his stuck-on pilasters'.[19] Wallace must have been pleased with the result, for he paid Ambler £900 in four instalments between 1873 and 1875, gave him a marble console table and perhaps more importantly, a further commission in 1880 to design Castle House in Lisburn, Northern Ireland, a town

18. Trowell, TS.

19. http://wallacecollection.org/the collection/history of the collection/hertfordhousethebuilding

12.15: Leeds, *Newport House*, Cardigan Road (Thomas Ambler, 1870). (*Ruth Baumberg.*)

which he represented in the House of Commons. Indeed Castle House looks like a smaller version of Hertford House.

When Thomas Ambler died at the beginning of January 1920, the *Yorkshire Post's* obituary stated that 'it is probably safe to say that the hand of Mr Ambler, more than other architect, can be traced in lines of buildings that form one of the chief streets of Leeds'.[20] A reference presumably to Boar Lane, but Ambler left his mark on numerous streets in the centre of town, designing or remodelling many premises in Briggate, Commercial Street, Duncan Street and Cookridge Street. His busy life in architecture had made him a relatively wealthy man; he travelled widely and along with John Barran in his younger years, followed the Bramham Hunt whilst his latter years appear to have been devoted to golf. At some point in his life, he transferred his religious allegiance to the Anglican church and both Canon Longbottom of St John's, Briggate, and the Vicar of Moor Allerton, officiated at his funeral. He was buried at the private cemetery in Woodhouse.

20. *Yorkshire Post*, 14 Jan 1920.

Catalogue

LEEDS, Coupland Street, Beeston Hill, ten through working class houses for the Leeds Model Cottages Society, 1860, dem. (Higenbottam [note 3].)

LEEDS, Burley, pairs of semi-detached houses, c.1860. (*LM*, 14 April 1860; *LM*, 21 April 1860.)

LEEDS, Hunslet, 20 houses, c.1860. (*LM*, 28 April 1860.)

LEEDS, Caledonia Road, 3 houses, c.1860. (*LM*, 23 June 1860.)

LEEDS, 'extensive houses and shop, Waterloo Road, Hunslet', c.1860. (*LM*, 4 Aug 1860.)

LEEDS, '4 houses at Ward End, Hunslet Road', c.1860. (*LM*, 8 Sept 1860.)

LEEDS, 9 houses at Quarry Hill, c1860. (*LM*, 22 Sept 1860.)

LEEDS, 4 houses at Sheepscar Street, c.1860. (*LM*, 20 Oct 1860.)

LEEDS, 4 houses in Headingley-cum-Burley, c1860-1. (*LM*, 3 Nov 1860.)

LEEDS, warehouse in Guildford Street for T. Fotherby and Son, c.1860-1. (*LM*, 8 Dec 1860.)

LEEDS, *Weetwood Grove*, Weetwood Lane, for T.W. Stansfeld, 1861. (Pevsner, *WY*, p. 517.)

LEEDS, house, shop and furniture warehouse, Hunslet Rd, c.1861. (*LM*, 2 Feb 1861.)

LEEDS, 6 houses, Burmantofts, c.1861. (*LM*, 9 Feb 1861.)

HUNSLET, 8 houses, Ward Street, c.1861. (*LM*, 9 March 1861.)

LEEDS, 2 houses, Hilary Street, c.1861. (*LM*, 23 March 1861.)

LEEDS, alt. to house in Halton, c.1861. (*LM*, 13 April 1861.)

LEEDS, a good house nr Woodhouse Moor, c.1861. (*LM*, 20 April 1861.)

LEEDS, 2 semis, Lloyd Estate, Woodhouse Moor, c.1861. (*LM*, 20 April 1861.)

LEEDS, house in Victoria Rd, Headingley Hill, c.1861. (*LM*, 29 June 1861.)

LEEDS, Particular Baptist chapel, Sunny Bank, c.1861. (*LM*, 13 July 1861.)

LEEDS, 4 houses nr Woodhouse Moor, c.1861. (*LM*, 30 July 1861.)

LEEDS, 8 houses nr Green Rd, c.1861. (*LM*, 14 Sept 1861.)

LEEDS, house at Hyde Park, c.18612. (*LM*, 16 Nov 1861.)

LEEDS, mill in Shannon Street, c.1861-2. (*LM*, 23 Nov 1861.)

LEEDS, 8 'improved houses' for Soc. for the Erection of Improved Dwellings for the Working Classes, c. 1861-2. (*LM*, 30 Nov 1861.)

LEEDS, warehouse in Park Place, c.1862. (*LM*, 2 Jan 1862.)

LEEDS, 6 houses near St George's church, c.1862. (*LM*, 25 Jan 1862.)

LEEDS, pair of semi-detached houses near Chapeltown Road, c.1862. (*LM*, 8 Feb 1862.)

LEEDS, 10 houses and 2 shops, York Road, c.1862. (*LM*, 8 Feb 1862.)

LEEDS, house in Burmantofts, c.1862. (*LM*, 1 March 1862.)

LEEDS, 3 houses, Wortley, c.1862. (*LM*, 29 March 1862.)

LEEDS, public houses and shop, Hunslet Road, c.1862. (*LM*, 29 March 1862.)

LEEDS, house and shop, Great George Street, c.1862. (*LM*, 5 April 1862.)

LEEDS, det. house, nr Chapeltown Road, c. 1862. (*LM*, 12 April 1862.)

LEEDS, house at Carlton Hill, c. 1862. (*LM*, 19 April 1862.)

SHADWELL, nr Leeds, alterations and additions to Shadwell Old Hall, c.1862. (*LM*, 26 April 1862.)

LEEDS, 2 houses, Caledonian Road, c.1862. (*LM*, 17 May 1862.)

LEEDS, 12 model cottages, Messrs Longley's estate, New Wortley, c.1862. (*LM*, 7 June 1862.)

LEEDS, house on the Lloyd Estate, Woodhouse Moor, c.1862. (*LM*, 2 Aug 1862.)

LEEDS, house, Wortley, c.1862. (*LM*, 2 Aug 1862.)

LEEDS, 12 'good houses' on Messrs Eastwood's estate, Woodhouse Moor, c.1862. (*LM*, 16 Aug 1862.)

LEEDS, 15 houses, Langham Street, New Wortley, for Soc. for the Erection of Improved Dwellings for the Working Classes, c.1862. (*LM*, 18 Oct 1862.)

LEEDS, warehouse, St Paul's Street, c.1862-3. (*LM*, 29 Nov 1862.)

HARROGATE, det. villa res., c. 1862-3. (*LM*, 13 Dec 1862.)

LEEDS, Leeds Club, Albion St, supervised the remodelling of a pair of Georgian houses, 1863. (http://www.threealbionplace.co.uk /history)

LEEDS, 30 Park Place, warehouse for N.P. Nathan, c1863 (Linstrum, *WYAA*, p. 370.)

THWAITE, Swaledale, Congregational chapel, 1863. (*The Builder,* 21, 1863, p. 625.)

LEEDS, Meadow Lane, eighteen through working class houses for the Leeds Model Cottages Society, 1863, dem. (*LM,* 15 Oct 1863.)

LEEDS, alterations to offices, Park Row, c.1864. (*LM*, 10 Sept 1864.)

LEEDS, 'a good house in Belle Vue-road', c.1865. (*LM*, 7 Jan 1865.)

LEEDS, 9 houses in Kirkstall, c.1865. (*LM*, 18 Feb 1865.)

LEEDS, 4 houses and shops, Holbeck, c.1865. (*LM*, 18 March 1865.)

LEEDS, 18 houses and 2 shops, Cemetery Road, Beeston Hill, c.1865. (*LM*, 24 June 1865.)

LEEDS, 'a good houses in Burley Road', c.1865. (*LM*, 22 July 1865.)

LEEDS, house and shop, top of Cookridge Street, c.1865. (*LM*, 26 Aug 1865.)

LEEDS, extensive clothier's warehouse, Park Row, c.1865. (*LM*, 23 Sept 1865.)

LEEDS, St Mark's Road, Woodhouse, two villa houses. (*LM,* 10 Jan 1866.)

RIPON, The Crescent, two semi-detached houses. (*LM,* 14 April 1866.)

LEEDS, house and farm buildings, Thorner Road, Skelton Grange, for W.T. Smith, c.1866. (*LM*, 2 June 1866.)

LEEDS, 5 houses in Chapeltown, c.1866. (*LM*, 9 June 1866.)

LEEDS, Armley Hall Day and Sunday Schools for Queen Street Chapel, 1866, dem. (*LM*, 30 Aug 1866.)

LEEDS, villa, Headingley, c.1867. (LM, 5 Jan 1867.)

LEEDS, police stations in Wellington Road, York Road and New Wortley, c.1867. (*LM*, 12 Jan 1867; 19 Jan 1867.)

LEEDS, 4 houses and shops, Great George Street, c.1867. (*LM*, 16 March 1867.)

LEEDS, 'a house near Woodhouse Moor', c.1867. (*LM*, 13 April 1867.)

LEEDS, warehouse, York Place, c.1867. (*LM*, 20 April 1867.)

LEEDS, 'detached villa at St Marks, Woodhouse Lane', c.1867. (*LM*, 25 May 1867.)

LEEDS, '2 houses near St Andrew's church', c.1867. (*LM*, 13 July 1867.)

LEEDS, various projects in Boar Lane, commenced in 1867. (*LM*, 17 July 1867; 24 Aug 1867; 21 Jan 1868.)

LEEDS, villa and stables, coach house etc, Burley for John Briggs, c.1867. (*LM*, 24 Aug 1867.)

LEEDS, 2 houses in Fenton Street, c.1867-8. (*LM*, 9 Nov 1867.)

LEEDS, 6 houses at Beeston Hill, c.1867-8. (*LM*, 23 Nov 1867.)

LEEDS, Baptist school, Upper Hollis Street, Burley Road, c.1867-8. (*LM*, 21 Dec 1867.)

HORSFORTH, Leeds, villa, Scotland Lane, c.1867-8. (*LM*, 28 Dec 1867.)

LEEDS, 'extensive buildings, 4 storeys high, Buslingthorpe, c.1868. (*LM*, 18 Jan 1868.)

LEEDS, alterations to house and new stables, Middleton Grange, c.1868. (*LM*, 11 April 1868.)

LEEDS, 2 warehouses in Park Place, c.1868. (*LM*, 11 April 1868.)

LEEDS, Boar Lane, 11 shops, restaurant, etc for John Barran, after 1868. (*LM*, 5 May 1868.)

LEEDS, Wesleyan Mission Chapel and school, Henrietta Street, c.1868. (*LM*, 9 May 1868.)

LEEDS, 2 semi-detached villas, St John's Hill, c.1868. (*LM*, 4 July 1868.)

ILKLEY, new wing for Hydropathic Establishment, Wells Road, c.1868. (*LM*, 31 Oct 1868.)

LEEDS, Young Men's Christian Association, South Parade, conversion from dwelling house, 1868, dem. (*LM*, 2 Dec 1868.)

LEEDS, Boar Lane, Treveleyan Temperance Hotel, and various shops, offices and warehouses, 1869-76 (Linstrum, *WYAA*, p. 370.)

ILKLEY, Parish Gill Road, semi-detached villas, 1869. (*The Builder*, 11 Feb 1869.)

LEEDS, *Newport House*, Cardigan Road, Headingley, villa for Henry Williamson, 1870. (Trowell, TS.)

LEEDS, Bridge End, shops and chambers, c.1870 (Pevsner, *Leeds*, p. 139.)

ILKLEY, Woodbank for T.P. Muff, 1871, dem. (Linstrum, *WYAA*, p.370.)

LONDON, Hertford House, Manchester Square, town house for Sir Richard Wallace, 1872-82. (http:// www.wallacecollection.org)

LEEDS, 1 Boar Lane/ 46 Basinghall Street, warehouse, 1873, dem. (*Building News*, 19 Dec 1873.)

LEEDS, Burley Road Baptist Chapel, 1874, dem. (*British Architect*, 31 July1874.)

LEEDS, Basinghall Street, printing works for McCorquodale and Co., 1874, dem. (*LM*, 14 Nov 1874.)

LEEDS, Hollin Lane and Glebe Terrace, Far Headingley, 1874-1877. (Trowell, TS.)

LEEDS, Oak Road Congregational Church., Wortley, 1876, dem. (*Bradford Observer*, 5 Sept 1874.)

LEEDS, Layout of the Royal Park housing estate for Thomas Hattersley, 1875 (Trowell, TS.)

LEEDS, Cleveland House, Cardigan Road, Headingley, villa for William Sugden, 1875 (Trowell, TS.)

LEEDS, York Street, St James's Public Hall, Temperance Hotel and Dining Rooms, 1877-8 (*Building News*, XXXIII, 1877.)

LEEDS, Park Square, St. Paul's House, clothing factory and warehouse for John Barran, 1878 (*Building News*, XXXVI, 1879.)

LEEDS, Golden Lion Hotel, Briggate, 1879 for John Barran (Pevsner, *Leeds*, p. 92.)

LEEDS, Whingate, Armley, twelve back-to-back houses 1879 dem. (Trowell, TS.)

LISBURN, N. Ireland, Castle House, a town house for Sir Richard Wallace, 1880. (http://www.wallacecollection.org)

LEEDS, Hill Top Estate, Burley, working class houses for the Yorkshire Land, Building and Investment Co. 1880 (Trowell, TS.)

LEEDS, 34-5 Park Square, clothing factory for Arthur and Sons 1881, dem. (*LM*, 11 Nov 1881.)

LEEDS, Prospect UMFC, Domestic Street, Holbeck, 1880-1. (*LM*, 16 April 1881.)

LEEDS, Leeds Library, Commercial Street, 1881-2, alterations, including new entrance and staircase. (Pevsner, *Leeds*, p. 121.)

LEEDS, Hunslet Road, Crown Point Printing Works for Alf Cooke, 1878-81 Rebuilt after a fire in 1894 (*The Builder*, XLI, 1881; *LM*, 7 Oct 1894.)

LEEDS, Briggate/Duncan Street, shops and house for Thomas Kirk, 1881. (Higenbottam [note 3].)

LEEDS, Duncan Street, shops, offices and warehouse for William Tunstall, 1882. (*Building News*, XL, 1883.)

LEEDS, Greek Street, Clothing factory for J. Buckley and Sons, 1882, dem. (*LM*, 22 Sept 1888.)

ROUNDAY, Leeds, Roundhay Park, Rotunda Drinking Fountain presented by John Barran, 1882. (*LM*, 4 Apr 1882.)

ROUNDHAY, Leeds, *Parcmont* for John Barran II, 1883. (Linstrum, *WYAA*, p. 370.)

HUNSLET, Leeds, offices and warehouse for Peter Gilston, 1884, dem. (*LM*, 7 Oct 1884.)

LEEDS, Hanover Lane/Chorley Lane, factory, warehouse, offices for John Barran 1888-1904. (Pevsner, *Leeds*, p. 21.)

LEEDS Park Street/Chariot Street, clothing factory for Stewart and Macdonald, 1888, dem. (*LM*, 22 Sept. 1888.)

LEEDS, National Provincial Bank, 2 Park Row, 1890-2, dem. (A. Luty and Leeds Civic Trust *Catalogue of Exhibition of Leeds Architecture*, 1968.)

LEEDS, Park Square, warehouse for John Barran, 1891. (Higenbottam [note 3].)

LEEDS, American Screw Co., Kirkstall Rd., adapted plans devised in USA, 1892, dem. (*LM*, 13 Oct 1892.)

LEEDS, Clowes PM, Meanwood Road, now Seventh Day Adventist, but probably by Bowman, 1893-4. (*The Builder*, 4 Nov 1893.)

LEEDS, Victoria Arcade, Lane Lane, 1897-8, dem. (*Building News*, LXXVII, 1899.)

LEEDS, 19-21 Cookridge Street, shop fronts, 1890 to former warehouse of 1840-7 for William Smith (Pevsner, *Leeds*, p. 151.)

LEEDS, Briggate/ Albion Place, shop for Charles Kirkless, 1902. (Pevsner, *Leeds*, p. 159.)

13. George Corson
1829–1910

SUSAN WRATHMELL

Biography

George Corson came to Leeds, aged twenty, in 1849 and remained until his death in 1910, establishing the town's leading practice of the last third of the century. He was born in Dumfries, the fourth son of James Corson[1] and Janet, née Reid. His mother's family was, since the mid-eighteenth century, from Kirkennan, Kirkcudbrightshire. George's father was Provost from 1831 to 1833 but died suddenly in 1836 when George, the youngest of his six children, was seven. *Cassylands House* and *Stakeford* near Dumfries were the family homes until 1848.

He was educated at Dumfries Academy and in about 1844 followed his brother William Reid Corson as an apprentice to the Dumfries architect Walter Newall (1780-1863), the most accomplished of the local practitioners. His 1829 design for Alton farmhouse and steading, Carronbridge, was published in Loudon's influential *Cottage and Village Architecture*,[2] (1833 with many later editions). By the 1840s he preferred picturesque Gothic to Greek Revival and George may have worked with him on various manses including Gillesbie at Boreland and Granton House at Moffat.[3]

Perhaps George and his brothers felt that England offered better opportunities for advancement; James moved to Manchester to work in the cotton trade, while William moved to Leeds in the mid-1840s where he established a partnership with Edward la Trobe Bateman at 3, Albion Place.[4] By 1849 George had completed his articles in Dumfries and joined William in Leeds, where they lived at 10, Lyddon

1. Corson is a common name in Dumfries and derived from Acorsone or Ap Corsane, names of British or Celtic origin. T.B. Wilson, *Two Leeds Architects: Brodrick and Corson*, Leeds, 1937, suggested that the name derived from the Italian architect, Corsini, builder of Sweetheart Abbey and Devorgilla's Bridge in Dumfries. He tells us that a John Corsane or Corson was Provost of Dumfries in 1618; 'Corson House' in the town – baronial with crow-stepped gables and dated 1622 – was pulled down shortly before 1840.

2. J. Gifford, *The Buildings of Scotland: Dumfries and Galloway*, Penguin, 1996, p.162.

3. Colvin, p. 740-2.

4. Charleton and Archdeacon's *Leeds Directory*, 1849-50, p. 433. Dictionary of Scottish Architects (www.scottisharchitects.org.uk) William Reid Corson had formed a brief partnership with William La Trobe Bateman after they had worked for Owen Jones in 1847 on Little Woodhouse Hall.

Terrace, and took a post as an assistant with the short-lived Latrobe-Corson partnership. Subsequently, the brothers worked together for ten years[5] – although the firm seems always to have used the style 'W.R. Corson' – and George, a skilled artist, travelled, sketched[6] and continued his architectural studies. Among his early jobs was the supervision of *Hawkhurst* – a country house in Kent which the brothers designed – where he spent the winter of 1854-5 as clerk of works, perhaps as a means of gaining greater understanding of building construction and site management. He went to the Great Exhibition in 1851, the year that the Leeds Improvement Society was founded with the intention of transforming the 'squalid and unbeautiful town' of Leeds. The decision to build Brodrick's magnificent Town Hall in 1852 was an early response to the Society's condemnation and a mark of a growing awareness of the way in which a town could be dignified *via* its architecture; Corson had arrived at an opportune moment in the development of what would be, by the end of his career, one of the country's great provincial cities.

The brothers worked diligently, quickly building up the thriving practice which included town centre shops, an inn and mill-owners' warehouses near the new railway termini (13.1). However, in 1860 William moved to Manchester, leaving George to run the Leeds office in South Parade.[7] He remained there until 1872 when he moved to 13, Cookridge Street.[8] In the early '60s George designed the elaborate Gothic auction house and offices for Hepper and Son in East Parade. It did much to establish his reputation, especially as it was illustrated in *The Builder* (13.2). This, along with the patronage by prominent individuals in the academic and business spheres[9] – notably Dr Heaton

5. George was initially an Income Tax Inspector in Headingley-cum-Burley before becoming a full-time architect.

6. Wilson [note 1], p. 47, states that 'a number of his sketches still exist of buildings in the neighbourhood of Leeds, some of which are dated 1850'.

7. W.R.G.'s move to Manchester, and thus G.C.'s status, is not altogether clear. The *Directories* for 1851, 1853 and 1856 name the practice as 'Wm Reid Corson' at 5, South Parade. The 1857 *Post Office Directory* again refers to Wm Reid Corson, but this time lists the address as '5, South Parade and 20 Cooper Street, Manchester'. At no point does the practice appear to have been listed as 'Corson and Corson' or similar. From 1861 onwards, the *Directories* list George Corson – with no mention of W.R.C. – still with the 5, South Parade office.

8. The move was announced in *LM*, 11 May 1872.

9. Corson became a member of the Leeds Library in June 1857 and relinquished his share in 1901 (*ex inf.* Geoffrey Forster, the Librarian). He joined the Leeds Club in 1864.

13.1: Leeds, 17 and 19 Wellington Street, exterior (William and George Corson, 1859-60). *(Ruth Baumberg)*.

and the Tetley family – ensured the development of George's practice. His work encompassed every type of Leeds building: houses and villas, warehouses and offices, schools, churches, the massive School Board offices, the Municipal Buildings and the Grand Theatre and Opera House. In all these, the decorative detailing and range of craftsmanship reflected Corson's artistic skills and interest in all aspects of the work. In 1863 he made the first use of Peterhead granite at Hepper's auction house and produced richly detailed porticoes elsewhere such as at the Scottish Widows offices in Park Row (1869) (13.3; 13.4), just as G.G. Scott was establishing Gothic as the popular Leeds style (18.12). The practice was also responsible for laying out new roads (from about 1868), parkland and a major cemetery.

In 1882 he was married in Bath to Harriot Mary Gough, the daughter of Alexander Reid, a Surgeon-Major in the Bengal Army. They had three sons, Frederick, Eric and Douglas, but none followed their father's profession. As well as a comfortable Leeds house, *Dunearn* in Wood Lane (13.5), Corson was wealthy enough to have a country house in Scotland, *Carn Dreag* at Gairlock, Wester Ross, which he had built in 1880. As his family grew it was, apparently, a much loved and regularly visited holiday home. In 1897 he sold *Dunearn*,[10] moving to *Ballamona* in Shire Oak Road, Headingley, where he and his wife lived until 1908, when they moved to 14, Woodland Park Road, Wood Lane, Headingley, remaining there until George's death in 1910.

Corson and the practice of architecture

As well as his work at the drawing board, Corson made an important contribution to the establishment of the profession in Leeds. His public pronouncements about architecture and the architect's responsibilities provide a useful context for an examination of his buildings to which we shall turn later. In 1876 he was a founder member of the Leeds Architectural Association and was elected as its first president in January 1877.[11] There were 80 members and in his first presidential address, delivered on 31 October that year he made four points: 'some regard should be had to [neighbouring buildings] in designing the one between. They ought to be connected in their horizontal lines … and so designed as to group with them', as he had done at Wormald's in Great George Street (13.6); avoid the 'poverty-stricken look' of shallow reveals to windows and doors; make walls a little thicker and joists a little stronger as 'one never knows what may be required of a building … there is nothing so destructive of it as poverty of construction'; shop windows require arches to the ground floor, 'abandon the idea of the absence of all support for the superincumbent weight'. He went on to work for the Society for twenty-five years, a well-known and respected[12] figure, committed to architectural education and improving the status

10. Demolished

11. The new society was planned in 1874 with W.H. Thorp at a meeting at the Mechanics Institute. (K.A. Jones, 'The West Yorkshire Society of Architects, 1876-1976' in *Yorkshire Architect*, 1976, pp. 8-9.)

12. Jones [note 11]. Jones took much of his information from the Society's Minute books and concluded Corson was 'shrewd and talkative'.

13.2: Leeds, auction house and offices for Hepper and Son, East Parade (G. Corson, c.1863). (The Builder, *21, 1863, p. 425.*)

13.5: Leeds, Headingley, *Dunearn*, Wood Lane, (George Corson, 1873). (*From a drawing by T.B. Wilson, 1937.*)

13.4: Leeds, two 'Corsonian' porches: Hepper's Auction Rooms, (1863) and Scottish Widows' offices, (1869). (*Ruth Baumberg*).

of the profession. At society meetings in 1896 he read three papers written by brother William who, by this time, was living in Santa Monica, California.[13]

Leeds was made a city in 1893 and just four years later Corson was again elected president of the society, although by this time it had changed its name to the Leeds and Yorkshire Architectural Society and had a membership that numbered 115. In addresses during this second presidency he revealed his visions for Leeds's future in which its recently elevated status would be reflected in its architectural monuments. He spoke passionately about the positive impact that good design could have on its surrounding area and quoted the example of the recently completed City Square which he admired and which had 'enhanc[ed] the value of the surrounding property'; the city was increasing its rates and would 'reap the advantage'. He welcomed the street improvements and new buildings: 'judicious improvements always pay for themselves'. He regretted the spread of hoardings covered with advertising bills, and the itinerant hawkers selling goods in the streets. He was also outspoken about the Corporation's apathy in clearing back-to-back houses.[14]

At the Society's twenty-first anniversary dinner at the Queen's Hotel in 1898, Corson replied to Alderman Gordon's speech with a reminder of the advantages produced by the street improvements of thirty years before,[15] and he welcomed the projected widening of Lands Lane. He proposed the replacement of back-to-back houses with 'dwellings on double the area of land and put one family on the ground floor and another family in the upper storey, which would be approached by a separate staircase'. To ease housing congestion in the east end of the

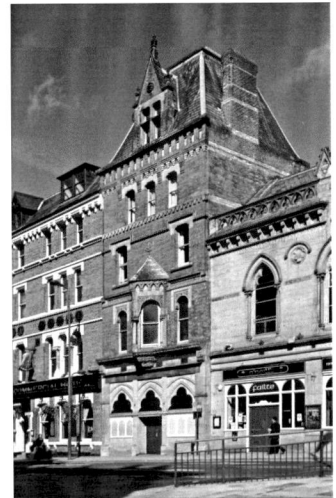

13.6: Leeds, Great George Street, premises for Wormald, photographer (George Corson, 1865). (*Ruth Baumberg*).

13. The papers were: 'The acoustic properties of rooms', 'Masons' marks', and 'The use of practical geometry in designing rooms'. (Wilson [note 1], p. 71.)

14. Minute Books, quoted in Jones [note 11], p. 8.

13.7: Leeds, 14 Commercial Street, chemist's shop, exterior (George Corson, 1868), showing the building before ground floor alterations. (*From Wilson [note 1].*)

13.8: Leeds, Sun Building, Park Row (George Corson, 1877) dem. (*From Wilson [note 1].*)

15. The 1869 Improvement Act.

16. Now the premises of the Yorkshire Archaeological Society.

17. *Building News*, xviii, 1860, p. 552. The building was also mentioned in *LM*, 1 Nov 1876.

city land should be purchased a few miles out of Leeds and suburban villages built for the working classes as a healthier alternative. The residents 'by means of the great railway facilities of Leeds would be able to travel to and from their work conveniently'. He proposed the clearance of old, undistinguished buildings crowding the Town Hall – 'one of the noblest buildings in England' he believed – and the creation of a worthy setting. He also argued for the erection of law courts and an art gallery 'more befitting the dignity of Leeds than the present'. Finally, he appealed for the independent status of the architect to be recognized, and believed that the position of architects in a public office and under the city engineer was not acceptable.

On the issue of architectural style, Corson was adept at using most of the fashionable alternatives. No doubt early in his career he was seduced by the possibilities of Venetian Gothic, so eloquently set out in Ruskin's *The Stones of Venice* (first editions 1849-53), and *via* professional publications like *The Builder* or *Building News,* he was able to remain fully conversant with metropolitan stylistic developments. He would have taken a keen interest in the work of London luminaries like Scott who brought to Leeds the very latest possibilities for a modern, secular Gothic in buildings like the new Infirmary (1862-8) and Beckett's Bank, Park Row (1863-7). Corson's remarkable chemist shop for Harvey and Reynolds in Commercial Street (1868) (13.7) thus very much belonged to the stylistic avant-garde. He was also adept at using Romanesque – for instance in the Sun Buildings, Park Row (13.8) – Italian *Palazzo* (13.3) and Scottish Baronial – no doubt a style close to his heart – and he often combined styles in his commercial buildings with novel results.

George Corson's practice

In the 1850s, the brothers initially took on a number of modest commissions but soon attracted the attention of more influential clients. One was Dr Heaton, physician and a co-founder of the Yorkshire College, for whom in 1856 George added a porch and bay windows to his house, *Claremont* in Clarendon Road.[16] Other early patrons were the Lupton brothers, influential mill owners for whom the Corsons designed wool warehouses in Wellington and King Streets (1859-60) (13.1), close to the railway stations. Here they provided offices, display rooms, packing and store-rooms under one roof behind an exotic façade which blended Italianate and Gothic idioms applauded in the *Building News*: 'seemingly discordant elements blend most harmoniously together'.[17] The Luptons passed the plans and costings of their Wellington Street warehouse to the firm of D. and J. Cooper who planned to build on the adjacent plot, no. 15. The Luptons' generosity had a condition: the Coopers had to employ the Corsons –

what greater confidence could a patron lavish on his architects?[18] This new type of building, demanded by mill owners and other industrialists with factories outside the town, had to be both functional and impressive, ideally with an elaborate carved entrance detailing and a lavish display of architectural embellishment, an appropriate prelude to the latest textile products within.[19]

In 1860, William[20] left for Manchester leaving the Leeds office to George. The first reference to George's independence comes in February when he invited tenders for new houses in Far Headingley,[21] although the partnership seems not to have been formally severed as instances of collaborations continued for some years. For instance, for 'Mr Metcalf', a brewer from Pateley Bridge, WY, the brothers designed *Castlestead*, a house on the River Nidd, as well as a school and new brewery, all in 1867. The drawings were issued from Manchester but details were drawn in the Leeds office.[W.R.] Corson and Aitken of Manchester also designed George Metcalfe's nearby Glasshouses mill settlement between 1861 and 1875.[22]

18. 'Recollections and Traditions of William Lupton & Co. Leeds', 1927. (Leeds Library, Beckwith Collection.)

19. The 'beauty and originality' of the doorways was noted in *LM*, 1 Nov 1876.

20. William Reid Corson designed buildings in Scotland, including Auchencairn House for Ivie Mackie the former Lord Mayor of Manchester in 1860. *The Dictionary of Scottish Architects* attributes the winning design of the Glasgow Municipal Buildings (1880) to him.

21. *LM*, 11 Feb 1860.

22. Walter Evan Jones, quoted in Wilson [note 1], p. 50; Pevsner, *WY*, p. 280.

13.9: Leeds, brewery for Joshua Tetley (George Corson, 1862). (*From a Corson drawing illustrated in Wilson [note 1].*)

Following the separation, warehouses in Wellington and King Streets were continued, and in 1860, George provided a design for alterations to a chemist's shop in Kirkgate, a plain brick building which he enriched with stone and cement detailing, a mosaic plaque and Minton tiles.[23] His reputation was made in 1862 when he was commissioned to design *Fox Hill* for Francis Tetley of the prominent Leeds brewing family. Crucially, this led to the extensive rebuilding at the vast brewery complex on the south side of the River Aire (1862-72) (13.9). His association with the company lasted until 1904 – Corson's final professional commitment – and the huge industrial building, with all its structural and functional complexities, established Corson in this specialised and lucrative sector of professional practice.

The practice also built small shops and business premises in the centre of Leeds during the '60s, and in a number of instances, houses in the Leeds suburbs for the same clients soon followed, e.g. *Clareville* for John Hepper (1868). Among the best of the early commercial schemes are Hepper & Sons' auction house in East Parade, and Harvey & Reynold's chemist's shop at 14, Commercial Street, both in George's favoured modern Gothic style. In the latter example, the ground floor arches with red granite shafts, now sadly missing, were adorned with carvings of medicinal plants including foxgloves and dandelions. Corson considered that the shop displays should be framed by the architecture, and later in his career criticized alterations to produce plate-glass fronts. By the late 1860s the practice was increasingly involved with suburban middle-class housing as the pattern of migration from the town centre continued, as it had been doing for half a century. Corson had a hand in the continuation of Clarendon Road between Hanover Square and Fairbairn House, forming an important access road from Burley Road at one end to Hyde Park and Headingley at the other. On the new section of road he designed detached villas in a variety of Scottish Baronial and Gothic styles for clients that included clergy, mill owners and engineers, notably number 12 for Herbert Rayner, an importer of valonia.[24] He also designed his first church in the rapidly developing northern suburb of Chapeltown, St Clement (1868) (13.10), quickly followed by St Silas in Hunslet (1869).

The development of both his practice and his style is reflected in his large Italian *palazzo*-style office block in Park Row for the Scottish Widows Fund, 1869, now St Andrew's Chambers (13.3). The design acknowledged P.C. Hardwick's stately Bank of England (1861) on the opposite side of the street, while the Peterhead granite paired columns of the surviving porch – there was another at the south end – are notably larger and more conspicuous than Mr Hepper's of a few years earlier. The use of Yorkshire sandstone over a millstone grit foundation, combined with granites from Scotland and Ireland and some fine

23. *Building News*, 6 Jan 1860.

24. Valonia is Levantine evergreen oak acorn cups used for tanning, dyeing and ink production.

13.10: Leeds, Chapeltown, St Clement
(George Corson, 1868) dem.

carving (including thistles) display the architect's confidence and wide
business contacts. Interestingly, he subsequently added a similar porch
to the Bank of England.

1870 was a turning point for his practice, as churches, shops, offices
and substantial houses were completed in a rich variety of styles from
modest Dutch in ancient Swinegate to elaborate Gothic near the
railways stations. His striking brick warehouses and offices at 37-41
York Place have much stone detailing and strongly moulded facades
with clearly defined basement store-rooms, ornate stone entrances and
reception rooms/ display areas on the raised ground floor, with less
ornate windows to workshops and offices on the second and third
floors.

An indication of the expanding practice is Heugh, Dunlop and Co's Scottish Baronial premises at 46 Peckover Street, Bradford (1871). Such was his success that year that he took time to design and build his own home, *Dunearn* in Wood Lane (13.5). He lavished on it a variety of materials from local sandstone to clay tiles and half-timbered gables and a motto over the porch: 'Keep within compass so shall ye be sure'. Here and in all his houses there was careful attention to the services: second floor servants' quarters and a basement wash-house and heating chamber. Sketches of this modest but picturesque house were published in the *British Architect's* influential series 'Architects' Homes'.[25]

Between 1870 and 1873, much of Corson's time and talent were directed towards the production of designs for board schools in Leeds, a highly competitive field. Prior to Richard Adams' (*q.v.*) 1873 appointment as the board's architect, designs were chosen by competition and Corson secured several of the jobs; his plans for Green Lane School were selected from fifty-two entries. In 1878, he was appointed to build the School Board Offices facing the town hall, one of his most memorable additions to Leeds and a building we shall address shortly, and which included rooms for the board's architect.

With fewer school jobs to occupy him, Corson turned his attention to securing more prestigious projects and a whole string of notable buildings punctuated the mid-1870s, the most successful part of his career. The first was in Roundhay. In 1873, John Barran, a wealthy clothier and local politician, acquired the Roundhay Park estate for the town and began developing it for public use. Corson won the competition to landscape it, providing chalets and croquet lawns[26] (9.6), and in 1874-5 he designed luxurious villa-style homes on the edge of the park, although development was slow. He was also involved the creation of the Newton Park estate for the Lupton family, for whom he had designed warehouses at the start of his career.[27]

25. Corson's house was No 6 in the series, appearing in the edition of 11 Jan 1874, ii, p. 378.

26. A review of the designs was published in *The Builder*, xxxi, 1873, p.739. See also Linstrum, *WYAA*, p. 122.

27. The houses at Newton Park were designed by Chorley & Connon in 1879.

13.11: Leeds, Municipal and School Board Offices, Calverley Street, competition winning design (George Corson, 1876). (The Builder, *35, 1877, p. 811*.)

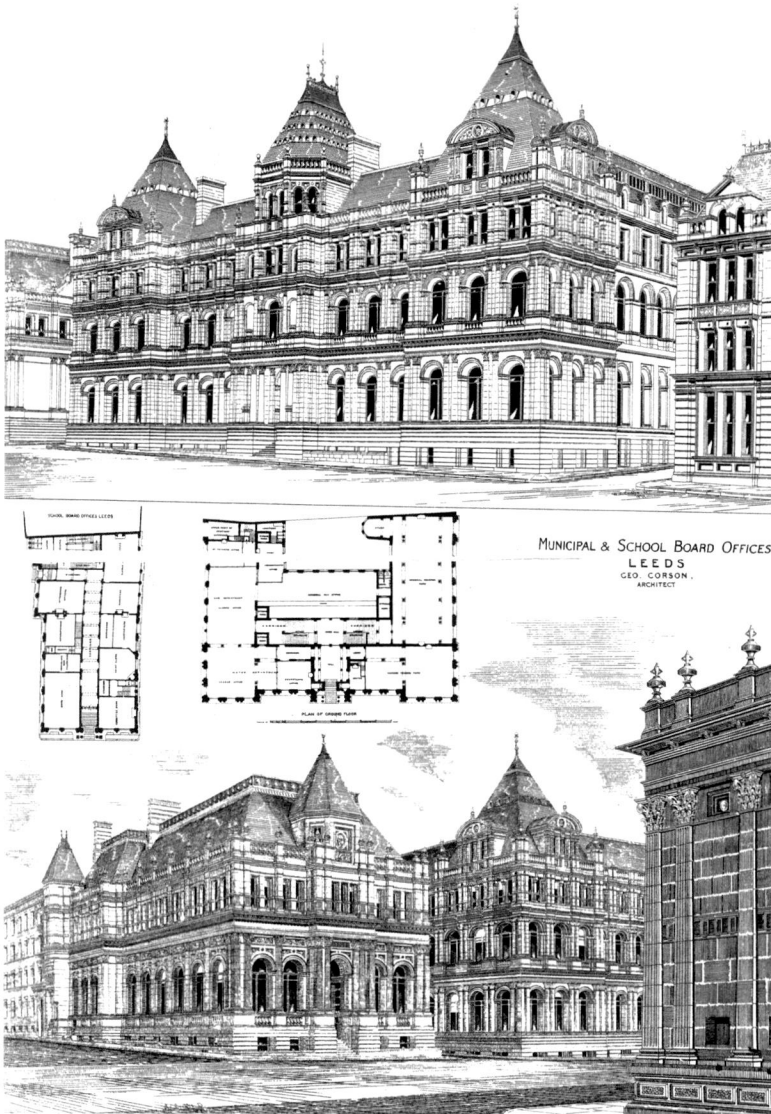

13.12: Leeds, Calverley Street, Municipal and School Board Offices, revised design, 1877 (George Corson, 1876-84). (Building News, *1 August 1879.*)

28. *Building News,* 1 Aug 1879. See *Building News,* xxxii, 1877, p. 36 for the first design and *British Architect,* xxi, 1884, pp. 40, 54 for a full description.

Perhaps as a result of his School Board work, he had formed a firm bond with the corporation's Engineer's Department; Lawnswood Cemetery with its Corson buildings (opened in 1875), was one likely outcome. Much more significantly, in 1876 as 'Crayon' he won the competition for the School Board and Municipal Buildings, facing the Town Hall in Calverley Street, his largest work, completed in 1884. Although the first version was considered 'heavy and uninteresting' by *The Builder* (13.11), the amended design, separating the Board School offices and retaining the line of Alexander Street, was highly regarded,[28] and rightly so (13.12; 13.13; 13.14). The building provided accommodation for the finance, gas, water and sanitary departments in addition to the school board, as well as a public library and reading room. That such a building was needed was a mark of the rapid increase in the provision of public services in the quarter century since Brodrick planned his majestic town hall. The Calverley Street site flanked the Brodrick masterpiece and the issue of an appropriate style for the new structure must have exercised Corson. He considered it 'should be similar in style to the town hall, but not identical ... I think a certain extent of variation of that building would be to the advantage of the effect of both'.[29] Corson chose what might best be described as a mixed Classical style, less assertive than its neighbour, but no less original. Interestingly, at least one of his competitors for the job, Holtom and Connon, felt Gothic offered the best solution, despite its proximity to the Town Hall (11.17). 'More Venetian palace than corporate building' was to be the *British Architect's* assessment of Corson's scheme,[30] although it is difficult to detect any obvious Venetian references. The *Building News's* 'Palladian, but freely treated'[31] seems marginally more appropriate. The separate School Board Offices followed two years later in a similar style, making this, in Linstrum's sound assessment 'the noblest (though short) street in Leeds'.[32]

To appreciate its full splendour, the Public Library should be entered from Calverley Street, past Mr Jones' iron gates and railings with paired owls standing to attention. The entrance and staircases are richly carved with posturing dogs and lions in the style of William Burges, using

13.13: Leeds, Calverley Street, Municipal Buildings now Public Library, exterior (George Corson, 1878-84). (*Ruth Baumberg*).

13.14: Leeds, Calverley Street, Leeds School Board Offices (George Corson, 1878-81). (*Ruth Baumberg.*)

29. Quoted, without acknowledgement, in Linstrum, *WYAA*, p. 356.

30. *British Architect,* 21, 1884, p. 54.

31. *Building News*, 37, 1879, p. 122.

32. Linstrum, *WYAA*, p. 358.

13.15: Leeds, Calverley Street, Municipal Buildings, (George Corson, 1878-84). Entrance hall roundel carved 1884 by J.W.Appleyard whose name, with that of George Corson, is being inscribed in the open book. (*Ruth Baumberg*).

Devonshire marble, Caen and Hopton Wood stone. There is also tiling and terracotta in abundance. The ground floor Reading Room (now the 'Tiled Hall') has relief portraits of literary giants sculpted by 'Mr Creswick of London',[33] and a fire-proof vaulted ceiling[34] of coloured bricks made by the local Farnley Iron Company. Above the tax office entrance (now the lending library) a carved stone boss, appears to show Leeds' owl overlooking medieval figures happily handing over and receiving taxes – perhaps a reference to Corson's first job in Leeds – but the seated figure is, in fact, inscribing the names 'George Corson, architect' and 'J.W. Appleyard, sculptor' (13.15). 'Incandescent electric lights' were introduced as the building neared completion. A reporter at the opening ceremony on 17 April was amazed, calling it, 'The Leeds Municipal Palace' and a cartoon captured the pomp and splendour of the day.[35] It shows the architect, with drawings under his arm, in procession behind the mayor as he crossed the road from the Town Hall at the opening (13.16).

At the same time his practice provided the city with the Grand Theatre and Opera House (1876-78).[36] The complex included, in addition to the stunning auditorium, the Assembly Room, connecting supper room and six shops (1.13). Corson was commissioned by a limited company to provide the town with 'a noble temple of drama' which provided seats for 2,600 and standing room for 200 in a curved auditorium with pit, stalls, three tiers of circles and a gallery. An eclectic Gothic façade and an even more remarkable mixed-Gothic interior reflected the styles of Paris and Vienna, using 'carton pierre'[37] for lavish moulded decoration and a drop scene painted with a view of Kirkstall Abbey. The theatre was opened on 18 November 1878 to wide acclaim for its comfort and convenience,[38] although it seems likely that much of the design was actually the work of Corson's chief assistant James Watson. Corson's architectural drawings of the 'Theatre and Opera

33. Probably Benjamin Creswick (1853-1946).

34. Initially developed to fire-proof textile mills.

35. *The Yorkshireman*, 19 and 26 April 1884.

36. Illustrated in *Building News*, 26 May 1876.

37. A development from *papier maché* which used the quick setting of gypsum with the flexibility of paper. It was developed in France in 1817 and Corson perhaps saw it at the Great Exhibition in 1851. It was painted to imitate stone, and gilded. It was used in many theatres by the later nineteenth century and later in early cinemas.

38. See: *The Builder*, xvii, 1859, p. 275; *Yorkshire Post*, 20 Nov 1876; *The Builder*, xxxvi, 1878. Edwin Sachs in his seminal *Modern Opera Houses and Theatres*, 1896, noted the Grand as the earliest of the provincial theatres that he discussed. He considered it noteworthy for 'the breadth of its conception' and concluded its architectural quality was 'above the average'. (Quoted in Linstrum, *WYAA*, pp. 272-3.)

13.16: The Mayoral procession crossing Calverley Street from the Town Hall to open the Municipal Buildings, George Corson carries his drawings. (The Yorkshireman, *26 April 1884, Leeds Library and Information Services.*)

13.17: Leeds, Otley Road, 'Spenfield'
(George Corson, 1875). (*Ruth Baumberg.*)

House' and 'Selected Design for the proposed Municipal and School Board Offices, Leeds' were shown at the Royal Academy in 1878.[39]

Further recognition of his expertise as a provider of impressive public buildings came with victory in the 1880 competition for the Glasgow Municipal Buildings – and a premium of £750 – a collaboration with his brother William.[40] The prize was, perhaps, the justification for Corson building his house in Wester Ross and perhaps he would have returned permanently to Scotland had not the Glasgow project been aborted, 'one of the most frustrating architectural competitions ever held'.[41]

The mid-1870s also saw him working on his most splendid house, *Spenfield* (13.17), a fine residence on Otley Road for the banker J.W. Oxley, son of the first Lord Mayor and a director of the Midland Railway. It has an impressive but sombre exterior with opulent interior using a wide range of decorative materials including marble columns with carved capitals, tiles, brasswork, carved wood and stained glass. Corson displays all the building skills available in his day in rooms intended to reflect the owner's private art collection. The drawing room was decorated in 1888 with furniture by John Faulkner Armitage and in 1890 a billiard room and linking gallery were added. The floor of marble mosaic and semi-circular arches is in the style of the Alhambra.

The 1880s saw Corson involved in various domestic developments including the laying out of Shire Oak Road in Headingley (1883-86), on land sold by the Earl of Cardigan's estates in the early '70s. Half-acre plots were provided and the practice intended to design the homes of purchasers, but development there was slow and other architects were often employed. An unusual design is the Early Gothic style Parish Institute in Bennett Road, Headingley (1883) with its heavy ornate

39. *LM*, 18 May 1878.

40. For a description of the design, see *LM*, 3 Sept 1880.

41. A. Gomme and D. Walker, *Architecture of Glasgow*, Lund Humphries, 1987, p. 192, which includes an account of the competition.

porch and dramatic sculpture of St George and the Royal arms. Further afield, the practice designed a house in Keswick and a bank extension in York during the '80s. In 1886 his Reading Room in the Municipal Buildings, was converted into a sculpture gallery.[42]

The 1890s are marked by less innovative but skilful work, in particular his extension to Leeds General Infirmary of 1891-92 where he exactly matched the front block to Scott's 1863-'69 original and provided a linking passage. It was another competition victory; this time against eighteen opponents, fifteen of whom were from Leeds.[43] The new buildings included a large outpatients' waiting hall and dispensary with consulting rooms set behind, a pathology department and additions to the nurses home. For the building's principal elevation, he exactly matched the 1860s work, sending one of his assistants, A.E. Dixon, climbing ladders to measure Scott's work before drawing up mouldings and other details full size, an apparently 'long and tedious task'.[44] More innovative was the clerestoried out-patients' hall, with a barrel-vaulted roof and curved steel trusses springing from corbels. It was to be Corson's last great public commission.

The office, partners and staff

Information about the Corson's office and its staff has survived to a remarkable degree. It is not only one of the best documented of any provincial office in this period, but reveals in extraordinary detail the extent to which Leeds architects might train with one architect, be an assistant elsewhere and finally enter a partnership with a third.

42. Now the Tiled Hall. A detailed description was published in *British Architect* [note 30].

43. *The Builder*, lxiii, 2 July 1892, p. 18.

44. Wilson [note 1], p.70. Corson's connection with the Infirmary ceased in 1898 and W.H. Thorp subsequently built the new nurses' home.

13.18: Leeds, Wellington Street, warehouse and offices for Crowe & Co. (W. Evan Jones and George Corson, with Perkin & Bulmer, 1903). (*Ruth Baumberg.*)

By 1853 the Corsons' office was at 5, South Parade where it remained until 1871 when George moved to larger premises at 13, Cookridge Street. He moved again in 1876 to 25 Cookridge Street in order to accommodate the growing number of staff – there were at least eight in the office by 1878. He remained there until his retirement from full-time work in 1901 – when he was 72 – and the practice was taken over by Walter Evan Jones, Corson's former pupil, under the name of Corson and Jones, moving to 7, Cookridge Street. With Perkin & Bulmer, they worked on Crowe & Co.'s drapery warehouse and offices[45] in Wellington Street together, a late flowering of the now traditional warehouse using a steel frame and pink terracotta. In 1904 Corson retired as architectural adviser to the Tetley brewery which effectively marked the end of his career.

Of the office staff, the earliest known is James Robinson Watson (1839/40-1887) who arrived in 1859. He was born in Dumfries and probably trained as a surveyor.[46] Inexplicably, he acquired a detailed knowledge of theatre construction, including safety and stage requirements. He was promoted to Chief Assistant by 1877, and oversaw much of the construction and decoration of the Grand.[47] In the 1870s, George Bertram Bulmer (1851-1915) was an assistant prior to becoming a partner in Perkin & Bulmer in 1877.[48] Bulmer was subsequently president of the Leeds & Yorkshire Architectural Society in 1891-92 and 1904-05. T.B. Wilson conveniently recorded those in the office in 1878.[49] Then, alongside Corson and Watson were: James Corson,[50] William Carr Crofts,[51] H.P. Downer, Walter Evan Jones,[52] James Henry Martindale,[53] Harry Watkins Wild,[54] C.H. Young. Jones was one of five pupils, but Wilson did not record the names of the two assistants, although it seems likely Martindale was one. A.E. Dixon was an assistant in 1892. He was educated at Leeds Grammar School and the Leeds College of Art, and had been articled to J.W. Connon, subsequently of Chorley & Connon (q.v.). Charles F. Gurney entered the office as a pupil, aged 16, in 1899.

Corson had less formal links to a number of Leeds architects or practices. William Gay, designer of Undercliffe Cemetery, Bradford, assisted the practice in the design for Lawnswood Cemetery (1874-75). Chorley & Connon (q.v.) had business links with the Corson practice for many years. They designed houses in Corson's Newton Park estate in 1879, and one of Corson's assistants was articled to Connon who, from 1892, worked on extensions and alterations including, possibly, the General Infirmary. In 1900 H.F. Chorley's cast iron gallery for the New Room at Leeds Library was designed with the assistance of Corson. Around 1900, he also had dealings with W.A. Jones (q.v.). Thomas Butler Wilson (1859-1942) had a long association with Corson. In 1884 he was in practice in Leeds and London and designed large houses with well-detailed interiors in Headingley (e.g. Wheatfield

45. Now Apsley House.

46. *Dictionary of Scottish Architects*, www.scottisharchitects.org.uk

47. He was responsible for the bills of quantity and on 20 March 1879 he read a paper entitled 'Theatre Construction' before the Leeds Architectural Association, showing working drawings of the new theatre.

48. Dictionary [note 46].

49. Wilson [note 1], p. 63.

50. He was Corson's nephew and lived at Corson's house before returning to his home in Bath.

51. He was an Oxford graduate and is known to have prepared the perspective drawings for the Municipal Buildings and Board School offices in 1879.

52. Educated at Leeds Grammar School. Following pupilage with Corson, he became an assistant in Nottingham and then practiced in California, (possibly with William Corson who traveled to Santa Monica later in his career). He returned to Leeds in 1898 to become Corson's partner. Jones added the north-east wing and tower to Corson's Hartlington Hall in 1900 and was elected a member of the Leeds & Yorkshire Architectural Society, but subsequently became 'a worsted yarn spinner in Haworth'. (Wilson [note 1], p. 76.)

53. Afterwards elected FRIBA and Diocesan Architect for Carlisle.

54. He became a wallpaper designer and joined Arthur Sanderson & Sons. His house at Chilham was restored by W.Baillie Scott.

Lodge and Castle Grove) and Harrogate. He was a tireless worker for improved standards of architectural education, President of the WYAS 1901-04 and wrote one of the earliest studies of any provincial architects in 1937: *Two Leeds Architects*[55] which dealt with Brodrick – whom he know by reputation – and his associate Corson.

Of his site staff, K.J. Osborne acted as Clerk of Works for the Municipal Buildings (1878-84). He had overseen the building of Manchester Town Hall. Drawings were signed by Thomas Corson, Emily E. Nicholson, Marshall Nicholson and Thomas Winn; the last went on to have a respected independent practice. He appointed staff with expertise in structural engineering, especially useful in the construction of fire-proof textile mills (13.18). He employed highly-skilled local craftsmen and artists, and was happy to engage with local stone-masons and manufacturers to obtain the best local building materials.

Conclusion

George Corson died on 17 November 1910 and was buried in Lawnswood cemetery, the headstone a plain Celtic cross. His obituary in the York*shire Weekly Post* described him as someone 'for whom everyone entertained a high feeling of respect', having qualities of 'native shrewdness, diligence and artistic merit … He always displayed an active interest in the development of his art, and showed himself very helpful in his attitude to younger members of his profession.'[56] T.B. Wilson's words sum up his philosophy: 'The dignity of his profession was a matter very near to his heart. Anything he could do to uphold the status of architects, he in his determined yet genial and pleasant way did'.[57] He might have added that Corson's glittering career produced a succession of memorable buildings in his adoptive city and he was, undoubtedly, the best Leeds architect of his generation.

55. Linstrum, *WYAA*, p.386.

56. *Yorkshire Weekly Post*, 26 Nov 1910. It is notable that Sidney Kitson made no mention of Corson's death in his 1910 presidential address to the Leeds & Yorkshire Architectural Association. He referred to the year as 'not an important one' and he observed, '…happy is the Society which has no history, and the object of this Society is not to make history … '

57. Wilson [note 1], p. 76.

Catalogue

(In the list below, Wilson refers to
T. Butler Wilson [note 1] in the text of
this chapter.)

W.R. Corson (with G. Corson)

LEEDS, premises for W.Lupton & Co,
Wellington Street, 1850-51.
(Wilson, p. 48.)

LEEDS, Queen Street Chapel,
alterations, c.1851. (*LM*, 19 April
1851.)

LEEDS, new brewery buildings for
Messrs Tetley, c.1853. (*LM*, 19
March 1853.)

LEEDS, Phoenix Inn, corner of York
Street and Kirkgate, c.1853-4. (*The
Builder*, xii, 1854, p. 171; *Building
News*, vi, 10 Feb 1860, p. 94.)

LEEDS, Woodhouse, 23, Clarendon
Road, added porch and bay
windows, and internal works after
1856. (Pevsner, *Leeds*, p. 191.)

LEEDS, Poor Law Offices, East Parade,
unsuccessful comp. entry, 1859. (*LI*,
11 June 1859.)

LEEDS, nos. 17-19 Wellington Street,
1859-60. (*Building News*, xviii,
1860, p. 552; *LM*, 1 Nov 1876.)

LEEDS, Far Headingley, three houses,
1860. (*LM*, 11 Feb 1860.)

LEEDS, Chemist's shop, probably
no.116 Kirkgate, 'decorative features
superimposed on the old work'
(*Building News*, vi, 6 Jan 1860, p.
11.)

GREENHOW HILL, near Pateley
Bridge, parsonage, c.1861. (*LM*, 6
April 1861.)

George Corson

LEEDS, warehouse, 52, Wellington
Street and 1-3 King Street, c.1860-
61. (*The Builder*, xix, 1861, p. 357.)

LEEDS, 2 shops with houses, Great
George Street, c.1861. (*LM*, 30
March 1861.)

LEEDS, Little London, St Matthew's
church, c.1862-8. (*LM,* 2 April
1862.)

WEETWOOD, Leeds, *Foxhill*, 1862.
(Wilson, p. 49.)

LEEDS, Hepper House, 17a East
Parade, c.1863. (*The Builder*, xxi,
1863, p. 425.)

LEEDS, New brewery complex
including Crown Point Maltings for
Joshua Tetley & Son, 1864-c.72;
architect for the brewery 1864-1904.
(Wilson, p. 48.)

LEEDS, 28, Great George Street,
premises for Edmund and Joseph
Wormald, photographers, 1865.
(Wilson, p. 50.)

LEEDS, Leeds Medical School, Park
Street, 1865, dem. (Wilson, p.50.)

LEEDS, steam printing and lithography
works, 33 Bond Street, for Henry
Inchbold, c.1865. (*LM*, 21 Oct
1865.)

LEEDS, saw mill, Queen Street, for
Messrs Illingworth, c.1866. (*LM*, 14
April 1866.)

LEEDS, Chapeltown, St Clement,
1866-8. (Wilson, p. 48; *LM*, 8 Nov
1866.)

PATELEY BRIDGE, WY, *Castlestead*,
Metcalfe's Brewery and Church
Schools, c.1867-74. (Wilson, p. 50;
LM, 7 June 1873.)

LEEDS, warehouse or workshop,
Swinegate, c.1868. (*LM*, 8 Feb
1868.)

LEEDS, warehouse opp. Kirk Ings
Wharf, the Calls, c.1868. (*LM*, 25
April 1868.)

LEEDS, 14 Commercial Street,
chemist's shop for Harvey and
Reynolds, 1868. (Wilson, p. 50.)

LEEDS, Headingley, *Clareville*, 43
Cardigan Road and Spring Road, for
John Hepper, 1868. (Wilson, p. 51.)

LEEDS, nos. 21-23, Park Row, offices of
Scottish Widows' Fund and St
Andrew's Chambers,1868-69.
(Wilson, p. 52.)

LEEDS, *Hyde Gardens*, 12, Clarendon
Road, for George Herbert Rayner,
1869. (Wilson, p. 51.)

LEEDS, Chapeltown, St Clement's
Parish Room and Sunday School,
1869. (Linstrum, *WYAA*, p. 375.)

LEEDS, Hunslet, St Silas, 1868-9. (*LM*,
14 March 1868; Wilson, p. 52.)

LEEDS, Meanwood, *St Ives*, Wood
Lane, house and school for Miss
Ledman, 1869. (Wilson, p. 53.)

LEEDS, Mill Hill United Reformed
Church, Sunday School and
Institute, 1870s. (Trowell.)

LEEDS, nos. 14 and 16 Swinegate,
shops and offices for J.D.Heaton,
1870. (Wilson, p. 53.)

LEEDS, nos 34-35, 37, 39, 40, 41 and
44 York Place, c.1870. (Wilson,
p. 53.)

LEEDS, 54, Wellington Street, addition
to Ledgard's premises, 1870.
(Wilson, p. 53.)

LEEDS, nos. 51-55 North Street, shops
and offices for Major Hartley, 1870.
(Wilson, p. 53.)

BRADFORD, Peckover Street,
warehouse for John Heugh of
Manchester and Walter Dunlop of
Bingley, 1870-71. (*LM*, 14 June
1870.)

LEEDS, laid out the Newton Park Estate
for Messrs Lupton, 1871. (Wilson,
p. 54.) (Houses by Chorley &
Connon, c.1879.)

LEEDS, St Simon's vicarage, 1871.
(Wilson, p. 53.)

LEEDS, Chapeltown, St Clement's
vicarage and schools, 1871. (Wilson,
p. 54.)

LEEDS, Bewerley Street Board School,
c.1871-5. (LM, 1 Aug 1872.)

LEEDS, New Wortley, Green Lane
Board School, c.1871-3. (*LM*, 7
June 1873.)

LEEDS, no 12, Park Row, music rooms
for Archibald Ramsden, 1871.
(Wilson, p. 54.)

LEEDS, *Dunearn*, Wood Lane, 1871.
(*LM,* 6 Jan 1875; *British Architect*, 2,
1874, p. 374.)

LEEDS, Hunslet, St Silas, National
School, c.1872. (*LM*, 24 Feb 1772.)

RODLEY, nr Leeds, house, c.1872.
(*LM*, 8 June 1872.)

LEEDS, Roundhay Park, winner of competition to landscape the former Nicholson estate for John Barran as a public amenity, 1873. (*The Builder*, xxxi, 1873, p. 739.)

LEEDS, Hunslet, St Silas, parsonage, c.1874. (*LM*, 14 March 1874.)

LEEDS, 3 houses in Lee's Yard, Meadow Lane, c.1874. (*LM*, 26 March 1874.)

LEEDS, New Briggate, premises for Messrs. Pearson Brothers, 1875. (*LM*, 6 Jan 1875; 1 Nov 1876.)

LEEDS, warehouses and other premises, York Place, c.1875. (*LM*, 28 April 1875.)

LEEDS, Lawnswood, cemetery landscaping, mortuary chapels and lodge, c.1875. (*LM*, 12 July 1875.)

LEEDS, Saville Green School, 1875. (Linstrum, *WYAA*, p. 375.)

LEEDS, Weetwood, *Spenfield*, Otley Road, for James Walker Oxley, 1875-77. (Wilson, p. 55.)

LEEDS, Richmond Hill, St Edmund, Providence Street, 1875-6. (*LM*, 30 March 1875.)

LEEDS, Headingley, laid out Shireoak Road between Otley Road and Wood Lane as a building estate, 1876. (Wilson, p. 56.).

LEEDS, Kirkstall Grange, St Chad's, parish room and additions to vicarage, 1876. (Wilson, p. 65.)

LEEDS, 28A, York Place, repository for Hepper & Sons, 1876. (Wilson, p. 56.)

LEEDS, Commercial Street, bank premises refitted for Wm. Williams, Brown & Co., c1876. (Wilson, p. 56.)

LEEDS, New Briggate, Grand Theatre and Opera House, 1876-8. (*Building News*, 26 May 1876; *Yorkshire Post*, 20 Nov 1876; *The Builder*, xxxvi, 1878.)

LEEDS, Municipal Buildings, Calverley Street,1876-84. (Contract with floor plans, sections, elevations, West Yorkshire Archives, LC/Wks 1878;

first design: *The Builder*, 31, 25 Nov and 2 Dec 1876, *The Builder* xxxii, 1877, p. 36; *Building News*, 12 Jan 1877; *Building News*, 1 Aug 1879; full description: *British Architect*, 21, 1884, pp. 40,54.)

LEEDS, 15, Park Row, Headland Buildings, later Sun Buildings, 1877. (Wilson, p. 60.)

LEEDS, Headingley, Parochial Institute, Bennett Road, 1877-80. (Wilson, p. 61.)

RIPON, Hob Green, additions to residence of F. Reynard, 1878. (Wilson, p. 64.)

LEEDS, Methley, Board School, 1878. (WT.B.W. *op.cit.*, p.64).

LEEDS, General Infirmary, Nurses' Home, 1878-80. (*LM*, 5 Sept 1878; 15 Jan 1880.)

LEEDS, Leeds School Board offices, Calverley Street, 1878-81. (*British Architect*, 21, 1884, pp. 40, 54.)

LEEDS, 9, 11 and 13 Hyde Terrace, 1878-9. (*LM*, 12 Oct 1878.)

LEEDS, Town Hall, proposed alterations inc removal of mayor's chambers to increase court space, 1879. (*LM*, 22 Feb 1879.)

GAIRLOCH, Wester Ross, *Carn Dreag*, 1880. (Wilson, p. 68.)

GLASGOW, Municipal Buildings, with William Corson, competition, first prize. 1880, not executed. (LM, 3 Sept 1880.)

LEEDS, Kirkstall Lane, St Ann's Towers, entrance lodge, 1880. (Trowell.)

WORTLEY, Bethel Congregational Church, attrib., 1880. (*ex inf.* Colin Dews.)

KESWICK, Cumberland, House for John Douglas at Lairthwaite, c.1881. (LM, 23 Aug 1881.)

YORK, alterations to Messrs Beckett & Co.'s bank, 1881. (Wilson, p. 66.)

LEEDS, Shire Oak Road, *St Michael's Mount*, 1883. (Wilson, p. 67.)

LEEDS, 31, Lyddon Terrace, for William Woodham Best, solicitor, 1883. (Wilson, p. 67.)

LEEDS, Shire Oak Road laid out with half-acre plots, 1884-6. (Pevsner, *Leeds*, p. 248.)

LEEDS, 21 and 23, Shire Oak Road, 1884-6. (Pevsner, *Leeds*, p. 249.)

LEEDS, Shireoak Road, semi-detached houses, *Bellamona* and *Ravenstone*, 1887. (Wilson, p. 69.)

LEEDS, Headingley, lodge to *St Michael's Mount*, Shire Oak Road, 1887. (Wilson, p. 69.)

LEEDS, All Hallows, Hyde Park Road, supervised installation of new east window, 1887. (*LM*, 30 May 1887.)

LEEDS, *West Mount*, 51, Clarendon Road, n.d., before 1888. (LM, 30 June 1888.)

RIPON, Grammar School, additions, 1888. (Wilson, p. 69.)

LEEDS, Otley Road, *Spenfield*, addition of gallery and billiard room, 1890. (Wilson, p. 69.)

LEEDS, General Infirmary, wards, outpatients' waiting hall, consulting rooms, 1891-92. (*The Builder*, 63, 2 July 1892, p. 18.)

APPLETREEWICK, near Skipton, Hartlington Hall, 1894. (Wilson, pp. 71, 76.)

LEEDS, St Clement, parish room and Sunday school, 1896. (Wilson, p. 71.)

RIPON, additions to Melmerby Hall for J.T. Pearson, 1896. (Wilson, p. 71.)

LEEDS, General Infirmary, addition of clinical lecture theatre and operating theatre, 1896-7. (Wilson, p. 77.)

RIPON, Victoria Clock Tower, 1898. (Pevsner, *WY*, p. 673)

LEEDS, designs for suburban villas on the edge of Roundhay Park, 1900. (Pevsner, *Leeds*, p. 293.)

LEEDS, Leeds Library, New Room gallery, with H.F. Chorley, 1900. (Leeds Library, unclassified papers.)

LEEDS, Wellington Street, Apsley House, with W. Evan Jones, 1900-3; Perkin & Bulmer associate architects. (Wilson, p. 76.)

14. Walter Samuel Braithwaite (1854-1922)

PAULA JACKMAN

Walter Samuel Braithwaite was born in Leeds on 6 January 1854, the son of James Ellis Braithwaite and his wife Sarah. Records indicate that his father was a bricklayer or builder,[1] and Walter took the not uncommon step for a builder's son towards the profession of architect. He received his education at Darley Street Wesleyan Day School – an early sign of life-long links with Methodism. His professional training began in the office of Thomas Ambler (*q.v.*) where he was a pupil, before spending a spell in the office of John Winn and Son, builders, where he gained practical knowledge of building work.[2] Following this he returned to Ambler's office rising to the position of chief assistant at a time when Ambler would have been working on one of the city's most distinctive buildings – the 1879 clothing manufactory and warehouse in St Paul's Street.

Braithwaite set up practice on his own in 1880 in offices at 6 South Parade.[3] At this time, and in fact to this day, this part of the city was the heart of the business and professional community. The practice remained there for many years, and the building which now stands at this address was built in the 1930s for Legal and General Assurance to designs by Braithwaite and Jackman.[4] In 1916 W.S. Braithwaite shared this address with mercantile offices, three accountants, a loan office, an elocutionist, a hairdresser and a manufacturer's agent.[5] In 1919, towards the end of his life, Braithwaite was joined by Harry Jackman and the firm became Braithwaite and Jackman. In Harry's later years Herbert Waddington became a partner. The Jackman family continued the practice when Harry's son Brian joined his father in the early 1950s,

1. 1891 Census.

2. W. Herbert Scott, *The West Riding of Yorkshire at the Opening of the Twentieth Century*, 1902, p. 363

3. Linstrum, *WYAA*, p. 372

4. Braithwaite and Jackman archives.

5. *Kelly's Directory of Leeds*, 1916.

and subsequently Louis Tinker also became a Partner. Brian in turn handed the practice on to his daughter Paula and her husband Colin Straw. The firm continues to this day, the only one of the practices discussed in this book to do so.

In Braithwaite's time at South Parade, Leeds had three Walter Braithwaites: Walter Samuel (the architect); Walter (artist of 26 Victoria Chambers, South Parade); and Walter (photographer of 8 Monkbridge Road).[6] Watercolours of Victorian Leeds which have sometimes been accredited to Braithwaite are, in fact, the work of his neighbour, the artist.

The section on 'Contemporary Biographies – Architects and Surveyors' in W. Herbert Scott's *The West Riding of Yorkshire at the opening of the Twentieth Century* includes an informative summary of Braithwaite's life and work together with a rather severe portrait . He married twice – first to Emily Ward at Woodhouse Lane MNC chapel on 11 September 1877.[7] The 1881 census shows the family living at 61, Grosvenor Terrace with 2 sons: Robert Ward aged 2 and James Ellis aged 10 months together with one servant. By 1891 the household included a third son and two daughters (aged 8, 6 and 4) as well as Braithwaite's parents James and Sarah, but in the intervening years the family had suffered the loss of both their mother Emily and eldest son Robert. Mortality rates among young children as well as mothers in childbirth were many times higher than now, but that is not to say that the affect on the family was any easier to bear. His second marriage to Annie Wildblood, daughter of John Wildblood of Wildblood and Ward printers, took place on 22 October 1892,[8] also at Woodhouse Lane MNC, further strengthening his links to the chapel's community. In 1895, the second Mrs Braithwaite became Honorary Treasurer of the Leeds Unmarried Women's Benevolent Institution.[9] By 1911 the family was at *May House*, St Mark's Villas, Woodhouse Lane, together with six children and a servant. The census of this year records James Ellis (age 30) occupation 'Architect and Surveyor', evidence of his proudly following his father into the profession. Sadly, his career was shortlived; he served with the West Yorkshire Regiment (Prince of Wales's Own) 1st/5th Batallion, was wounded and subsequently died in a French hospital on 4 October 1916. He is buried in the Wimereux Communal Cemetery.[10]

Although Leeds was growing rapidly in the mid-nineteenth century, the areas of Woodhouse and Headingley remained distinct villages and were not amalgamated into the urban conurbation until the end of the century. The middle classes favoured suburbs such as these to the north-west of the city, away from the smoke of the industrial areas. However, new roads and the tram system improved transport and links with the city, and enabled the working classes to set up home in these areas too. The Woodhouse of Braithwaite's day demonstrates clearly many of his

6. *Robinson's Leeds Directory*, 1902-3.

7. *LM*, 13 Sept 1877.

8. *LM*, 29 Oct 1892.

9. *LM*, 8 Jan 1895.

10. Commonwealth War Graves Commission.

interests and beliefs. The area had early links with Methodism, having a Methodist chapel on Woodhouse Street as early as 1756, some 70 years before a parish church was built there. Religion played an influential part in the strong community life, and Sunday schools of the time taught not only religion but also the 3Rs. The community also had its own library and by the 1880s its own savings bank.[11]

Braithwaite's time in practice saw extensive building programmes for both schools and churches as well as cemeteries and it is his work in these areas for which he is best known. A member of the Methodist New Connexion, he attended Woodhouse Lane chapel and was involved in its musical life, being an organist and also lecturing on musical topics. He was also active in both the public and cultural life of late-nineteenth century Leeds. In politics a Liberal, he was Chairman of the North West Ward Liberal Association, served on the Committee of the YMCA with the Primitive Methodist and Liberal architect, Thomas Howdill, and was a member of the Leeds Sunday School Union. He was a committee member of the Thoresby Society, being elected to the society in 1892, and was an original member of the Society of Architects in London. In 1896 he was joint secretary for the Micklefield Colliery Disaster.

The Leeds and Yorkshire Architectural Society met at the time in offices above the Liverpool and London and Globe Insurance Company in Albion Street which housed a lecture hall, museum of building appliances and library. It was open to the public as a centre of information. Its objectives were described in the *Building News* on 14 December 1883 as 'to promote the technical education of architectural students, … to foster a fraternal feeling amongst architects, … gaining the aid and sympathy of those outside their profession who were interested in their work' – objectives which the profession would do well to achieve in present times. Braithwaite was an active member, serving on the Council and becoming Vice-President in 1896-7.[12]

Braithwaite's interest in social housing can be clearly seen in his lecture entitled 'The Housing of the Working Classes' delivered on 29 January 1898 to the Leeds and County Liberal Club. In this he referred in detail to the various steps which had been taken in Leeds to deal with insanitary and overcrowded areas.[13] He described an area in which 12,000 people dwelt which the medical officer had condemned as unhealthy. Braithwaite advocated not wholesale demolition but rather the removal of some buildings in order to admit light, air and ventilation into confined yards and courts. He goes on to describe his preference that the local authority should provide new dwellings in the form of tenements rather than those 'technically known as flats', questioning whether those dwellings were desirable. In this, Braithwaite shared the view of some members of the then Leeds Insanitary Areas Committee.

11. W. Gill, *Woodhouse in Leeds*, D & J Thornton, 1984, p. 25

12. Scott [note 2], p. 363

13. *The Builder*, 5 Feb 1898.

Cemeteries

Living conditions for much of the population in nineteenth century Leeds were crowded and of a poor standard. The lack of awareness of the link between dirty conditions and the spread of disease contributed to the high mortality rates at the time. The century saw enormous changes in medicine, but not before diseases had ravaged the population, including cholera, tuberculosis and smallpox. With the high level of deaths came a need to increase burial provision which was met by establishing new cemeteries throughout the country. The need stemmed in part from the rapid growth in population, insufficient remaining plots in churchyards and high death rates due to the cholera epidemics at this time.[14] Victorian cemeteries were a focal point for the culture of commemoration which was expressed through elaborate funerals, family monuments and mausolea, and hence the overall design and the architecture of the resulting buildings held great importance.

Following the Leeds Burial Act of 1842 which allowed the corporation to levy rates for internment of the dead, a number of cemeteries were set up in the town on land bought for the purpose by the corporation. Open competitions were often held for the layout of cemeteries founded by the burial boards through advertisements in *The Builder*, and Braithwaite's design for East Morley was placed second in the competition reported in the *Building News* on 9 November 1883.

'The burial board for Morley, Yorkshire, recently received 31 sets of designs, in response to offers of prizes of 20 and 10 guineas respectively for designs for a cemetery chapel and lodge, and laying out grounds. The first premium has been awarded to "Truth" by Mr J. Sykes of Morley, and second to "Economy" by Mr W.S. Braithwaite, Park Square, Leeds.'

Among Braithwaite's earliest works are the twin lodges at Beckett Street cemetery, completed in 1880 – of undistinguished design, but of interest for being perhaps his earliest known work and part of one of the first municipal cemeteries.[15] Then known as the Leeds Burial Ground, it was opened in 1845. As was usual at the time, half was for Anglicans and half for Dissenters and each had its own gates, lodge, chapel, staff and registers. Little space remained by the end of the First World War and although the cemetery has not been closed, maintenance at the site has been a continuing difficulty. In Braithwaite's day the site had a rural setting among the fields and brick kilns of Burmantofts – very different from the dense urban setting it has become. However, the north lodge was recently restored following an arson attack, and plans for the proposed tram route, which would have destroyed both lodges, have been abandoned.[16]

Of greater interest than Beckett Street is Braithwaite's later work at Lawnswood where a cemetery had been set up further away from the

14. 'The Register of Parks and Gardens of special historic interest in England: Cemeteries', English Heritage website, www.english-heritage.org.uk/content/imported-docs/p-t/cemeteries.pdf .

15. Pevsner, *Leeds*, p. 223.

16. N. Chilton, *The Story of Beckett Street Cemetery*, www.beckettstreetcemetery.org.uk, 2005.

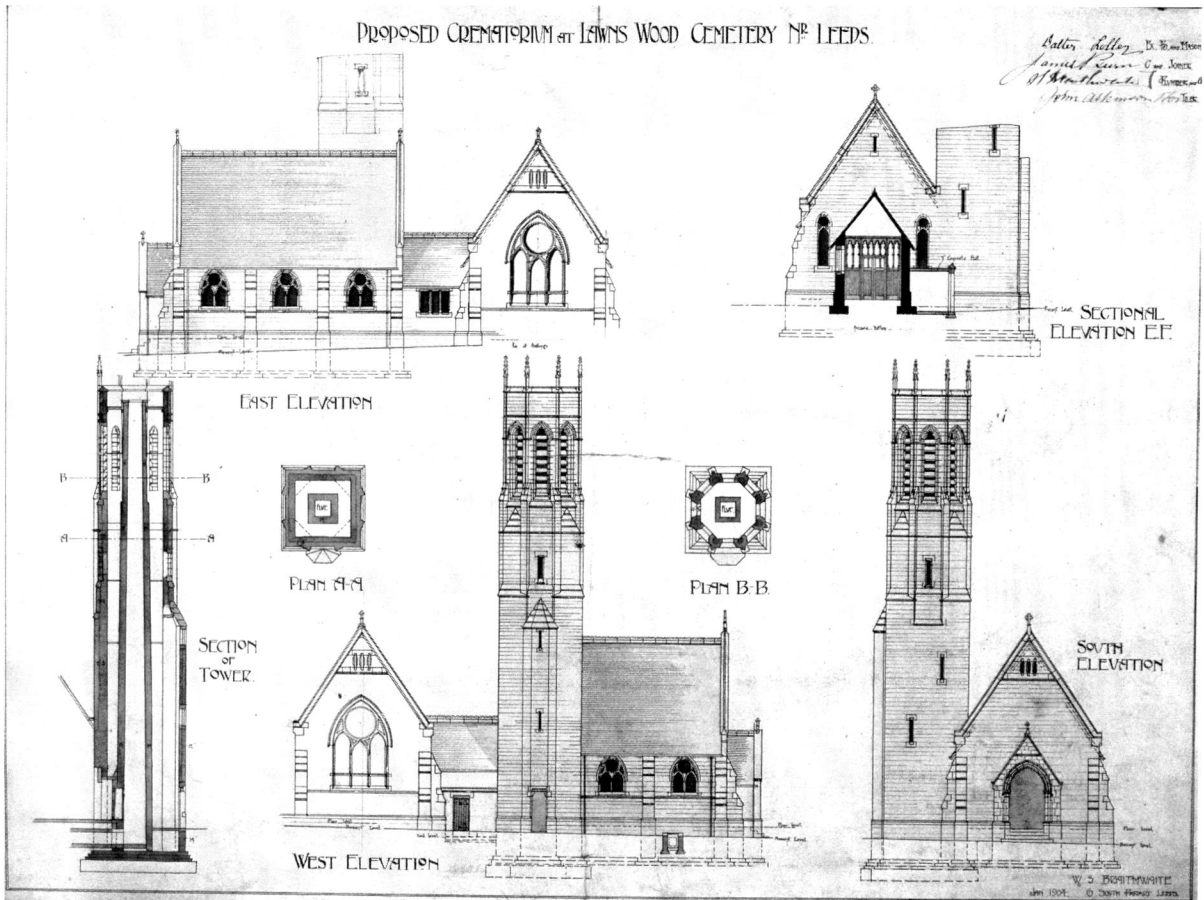

14.1: Lawnswood crematorium (W.S. Braithwaite, 1905). (*Braithwaite and Jackman archive.*)

city centre reflecting the population's growth through Headingley and Far Headingley to the north-west of the city. It is a picturesque layout (perhaps drawing inspiration from Paris's Pere Lachaise of 1804). Breaking the mould of the grid plan which by this time was the main model for cemetery design, it was laid out to an informal design by the landscape gardener William Gay with buildings by George Corson (*q.v.*) and opened in 1875. Subsequently, Braithwaite prepared designs for a number of buildings, most notably the crematorium of 1905 which was attached to the south end of Corson's group of chapel buildings of 1870-6 (14.1). This is important as an early example of a crematorium and as a composition, it is an especially distinguished example of the new building type. A plaque in the basement indicates it was the first of its kind in the country, using a gas cremator under the guidance of French engineers who had developed the method.[17] The building is sympathetic to Corson's design and culminates in a tall square tower with the chimney subtly disguised as an octagonal belfry. The turn of the century saw the move towards simpler funerals and the gradual increase in cremation. However it was not until after the Second World War that the practice became widely used.

17. Pevsner, *Leeds*, p. 294.

14.2: Designs for the columbarium at Lawnswood cemetery (W.S. Braithwaite, 1914). (*Braithwaite and Jackman archive.*)

Braithwaite also prepared a series of four finely executed designs for the columbarium at Lawnswood, none of which were built. The drawings, in pencil, ink and watercolour are retained in Braithwaite and Jackman's archives (14.2, 14.3). The present building is attributed to Kirk and Tomlinson and was not completed until 1933. The archive also includes drawings for alterations in 1907 to Corson's lodge or Registrar's house of *c.*1876 sited at the main gate.

Schools and the Leeds School Board

Braithwaite is probably known best for his work on schools. The majority of these were carried out for the Leeds School Board and in 1895 he was appointed Architect to the Board, (succeeding William Landless) – a post he held until 1903 when the Board was disbanded and schools came under the responsibility of the Local Education Authority. The improvement in education of children in Victorian Leeds resulted directly from the efforts of this board, and its importance should not be underestimated. Braithwaite's work for the board is, arguably, his single most significant professional achievement.

The Leeds School Board was created following the Elementary Education Act of 1870, and was set up to run schools providing elementary education for the town. Members were elected, usually every three years, and income came in part from the ratepayers with additional funding from government loans. The board's work ranged from finding and buying sites to the design and construction of the schools, as well as all aspects of running and maintaining the buildings. Its work is well documented in *Year Book*s and minutes of meetings for both the main board and the various committees. Braithwaite would no doubt have prepared detailed reports regarding the progress on each project, as well as the quality of materials and workmanship. It is clear that his designs were discussed at meetings, and sometimes changes requested prior to the board granting approval, though the detailed reports are not included. Following approval of a design, tenders were obtained for separate trades. These are described in detail in Leeds School Board records held at WYASL and in a typical example included 'Excavator brick and mason, Carpenter and joiner, Plumber and glazier, Smith and founder, Girder work, Slater, Painter, Plasterer, and Concretor'.

14.3: Designs for the columbarium at Lawnswood cemetery. (W.S. Braithwaite, 1914). (*Braithwaite and Jackman archive.*)

By 1895, when Braithwaite was appointed, the board had completed fifty-six schools and had a further ten projects underway. Braithwaite was assisted in the Sites and Buildings Department by two clerks of works, an architect's draughtsman and a tracing clerk, and it is recorded that Braithwaite did not devote the whole of his time to the board's service. He was also required to prepare bills of quantities for new works, though the board required that this was done as part of his private practice and the minutes of 4 March 1895 state 'that it be understood that this work shall not be allowed to interfere with the Architect's ordinary duties, or delay the preparation of plans, specifications etc required by his engagement with the board'. At the same meeting it was agreed the committee were 'empowered to employ Mr W.H. Wood [Hoffman Wood] as Quantity Surveyor'.[18] In 1895, Braithwaite's salary as the board's architect was increased from £200 to £250 per annum.

The work undertaken was varied and included preparing sketch designs for schools on vacant sites purchased by the board, priority being given to those sites in rapidly growing districts. Approved projects were taken forward through detailed design, specification, tender and construction stages. Once completed, schools continued to be altered and improved by the board with projects often following soon after the original buildings were opened. The process of negotiating for the purchase of sites and all aspects of the erection and maintenance of school buildings, whether owned or rented by the board, was handled by the nine members of the Sites and Buildings Committee.

18. WYASL, Leeds School Board Minutes, 4 March 1895.

14.4: Leeds, Gipton School, for the Leeds School Board (W.S. Braithwaite, 1897). (*Leeds Central Library.*)

14.5: Leeds, Gipton School, for the Leeds School Board (W.S. Braithwaite, 1897). (*Leeds Central Library.*)

Whereas Braithwaite was appointed by the board to design all the Leeds schools, elsewhere the competition process was widely used. It is a mark of the expertise he amassed in this specialised area of construction that he was regularly appointed as the assessor for competitions organised by boards outside Leeds.

Among the first new schools completed following Braithwaite's appointment in Leeds were Gipton Board School on Harehills Road (14.4, 14.5), and Brudenell School on Welton Road (14.6), which were completed in 1897. Brudenell has been replaced by new buildings on a nearby site and the original buildings demolished, but Gipton remained in use as a school until 1986. Having stood empty for almost twenty years, it has been refurbished and re-opened as the 'Shine' business hub for the community, retaining many of the original features of Braithwaite's building. Both demonstrate well the features by which Leeds Board Schools of the time – and Braithwaite's schools in particular – can be recognised. These include symmetrical front elevations usually of brick with ashlar and carved stone details in a Renaissance Revival style arranged in a series of bays often culminating in Dutch or Elizabethan style gables. Unlike his predecessor Landless and Richard L. Adams (*q.v.*), the previous architect to the board, Braithwaite did not use one particular architectural style, but instead drew on the range of fashionable alternatives which could be adapted to suit his requirements. The symmetry of his schools allowed for the provision of separate entrances for boys and girls in projecting bays which contained stairs and cloakrooms together with towers to conceal ventilation shafts. The accommodation usually comprised large central

14.6: Leeds, Brudenell School for the Leeds School Board (W.S. Braithwaite, 1897). (*WYASL*.)

halls surrounded by lofty and well lit classrooms which opened directly from it.[19] Other facilities included a manual workshop, a cookery kitchen, and in some cases a swimming bath. Considerable attention was paid to the provision of good ventilation and the later schools were lit by electricity.

By 1898 it is clear that the workload was too great for one architect, and Braithwaite sought to share it. At this time the board had taken the somewhat controversial decision to buy land in Great George Street, adjacent to the Central Higher Grade School, intending to erect a Pupil Teachers College, a decision reported in the *Yorkshire Post* as 'the most momentous which had ever come before the Board'.[20] The resulting building is widely attributed to Braithwaite, presumably because it is recognised as among the most important of the board's projects during his tenure. It was therefore disappointing to discover in the Minutes of 8 June that, when the question of relieving the Architect's Department was considered, it was agreed that 'Architectural work of the Pupil Teachers School and the Southern Higher Grade School be placed in the hands of Mr J.M. Bottomley'.[21] Bottomley's services are again described in his letter of appointment of 7 July. Alongside Bottomley,

19. The central hall plan had been introduced to the Leeds School Board by Landless who, by the early 1890s, was aware of its earlier development by the London School Board and its architects.

20. *Yorkshire Post*, 22 April 1898, reporting the board's meeting of the previous day.

21. WYASL, Leeds School Board Minutes, 8 June 1898.

Braithwaite was asked to prepare sketch plans for the Junior and Infants departments. It seems surprising that he should have delegated these rather than other less prestigious projects. However, despite its initial importance, the Pupil Teachers College was short-lived. In 1908 Braithwaite worked on alterations to Central Higher Grade School to form a new entrance, stair and toilets,[22] and in 1909 it was joined with the adjoining college to become Thoresby High School. In 1994-5, the building was converted to offices for Leeds City Council by Leeds Design Consultancy.

The three most important events in Braithwaite's time as Architect to the Board are recorded in *The Souvenir of the Leeds School Board 1870 – 1903* as the erection of the School and Home for Blind and Deaf Children (1899), the erection of the Pupil Teachers College (1901), and the opening of the Cockburn School (1902), originally named the Southern Higher Grade School for the south side of the city, described as 'the finest and best equipped the Board has built'. The school was named after the last Chairman of the Board, George J. Cockburn. The facilities provided at the school were extensive and included rooms specially fitted out for art, dressmaking and cookery as well as laboratories for chemical, physical, electrical and mechanical engineering, lecture theatres, workshops for both woodwork and

22. WYASL, Schools Portfolio.

14.7: Leeds, Blenheim Home for Blind and Deaf Children for the Leeds School Board (W.S. Braithwaite, 1899). (*WYASL.*)

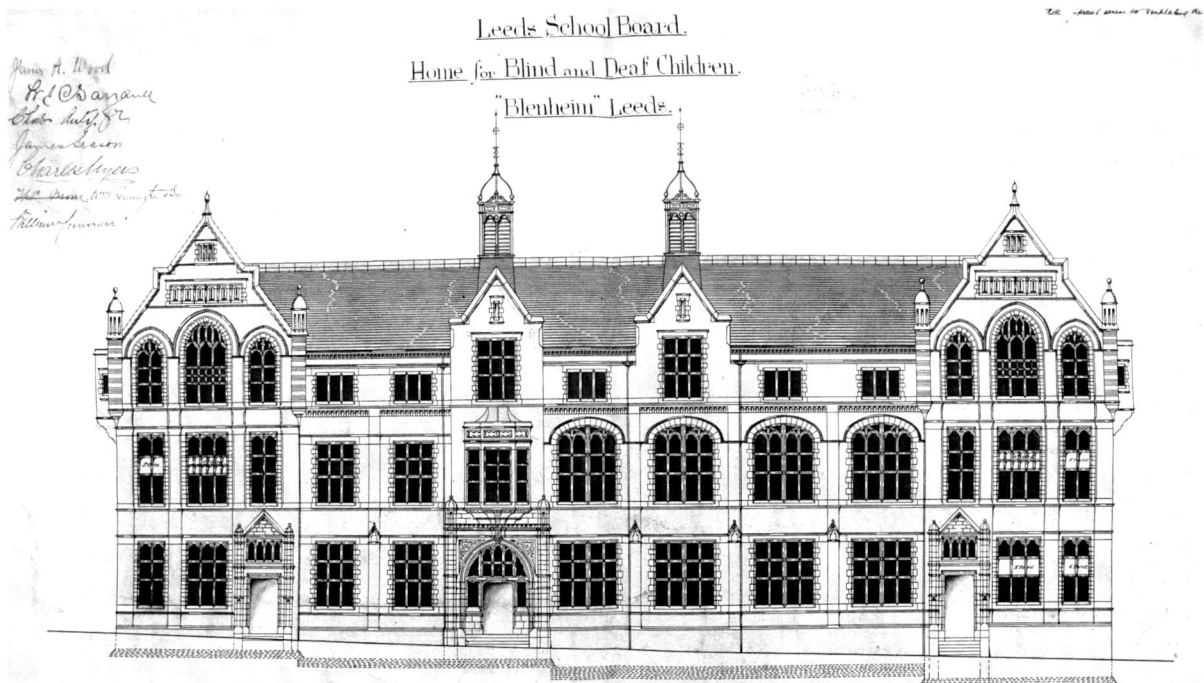

Leeds School Board.
Home for Blind and Deaf Children.
"Blenheim" Leeds.

metalwork, as well as a spacious gymnasium. Portfolios were kept for each school and often included drawings. Large numbers of drawings from Braithwaite's time are held at WYAS in Leeds. With the exception of Brudenell School, which is catalogued under Braithwaite, these form part of their extensive Leeds School Board archive.

Among the special schools created following the Elementary Education (Blind and Deaf Children) Act of 1893 was the Blenheim Home for Blind and Deaf Children which was opened in 1899 (14.7). Early stage pencil elevations show a finely detailed three-storey building with a central entrance and gables at both ends.[23] The symmetry of the front elevation was not reflected in the layout behind, which, because of the specialist nature of the establishment was quite different from the other schools. Separate accommodation, (including dormitories) was provided for 208 blind and deaf children, and separate entrances and cloakrooms for boys and girls. The school included a swimming bath in the basement.

In 1900, newly completed schools included Armley Park Board School on Stanningley Road. The description held in the WYASL records tells of a building which provided accommodation for 1180 children including babies, infants and the 'Mixed Department' with classrooms of up to 70 children. Once again the importance of good lighting, heating, fresh air and ventilation was emphasised and the school had the luxury of 'latrines placed in convenient positions … arranged on the most modern system, with … automatic flushing cisterns'. The school, described as 'elegant and competently handled Neo-Jacobean',[24] was converted to offices in the late-twentieth century (14.8, 14.9, 14.10, 14.11). Meanwhile, the new infant school in

23. WYASL, Schools Portfolio, LC/ED Acc 3204 22.

24. Pevsner, *Leeds*, p. 214.

14.8: Leeds, Armley Park School, for the Leeds School Board (W.S. Braithwaite, 1900). (*Paula Jackman*.)

14.9: Leeds, Armley Park School, for the Leeds School Board (W.S. Braithwaite, 1900). (*Paula Jackman.*)

Hunslet Hall Road included, according to *The Builder*,[25] a series of 'rooms for babies', each containing accommodation for a staggering 120 little souls.

The Souvenir of the Leeds School Board 1870 – 1903 describes the work of the Board with typical Victorian pride, noting that 'many of its school buildings, especially those erected in recent years [ie Braithwaite's] are ornaments to the City'. The souvenir concluded that 'it is a matter for rejoicing that the children of the present day are taught in such commodious and well-appointed buildings.'

25. *Builder,* 19 Feb 1898.

14.10: Leeds, Armley Park School, for the Leeds School Board, entrance detail (W.S. Braithwaite 1900). (*WYASL.*)

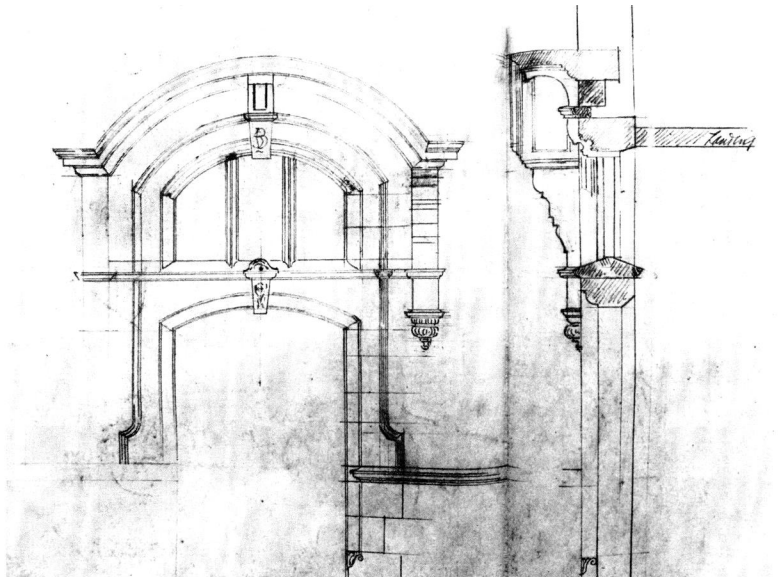

14.11: Leeds, Armley Park School, for the Leeds School Board (W.S. Braithwaite, 1900). (*WYASL.*)

Between 1870 and 1903 the population of Leeds almost doubled. In the same period the number of children registered at a school increased fourfold and attendance increased from 64% to 89%. The community came to recognise its responsibility and provided not only for the ordinary child, but also for 'the children of exceptional ability, for the blind and deaf, for the feeble minded, and for the waifs and strays'. Whereas before, a parent was under no legal obligation to send a child to school, by 1903 no child in Leeds could go to work before the age of 12, nor leave school altogether before the age of 14 unless he had passed the seventh standard.[26] The *Souvenir* concludes with a tribute to 'the Board, the Teachers and the Parents – for their hearty co-operation. The difference between the condition of schools at the time the Board entered on its task and their condition today is like a change from darkness to light'. No mention is made, or credit given to the architect or those involved in the design and construction of schools, with the exception of a single line – the thirteenth of fourteen Leeds School Board Officers mentioned on the final page of the publication: 'Architect – WS Braithwaite'.

26. *Souvenir of the Leeds School Board 1870-1903*, Leeds City Council, 1903.

14.12: Leeds, New Methodist Free Church, Victoria Road, Headingley (W.S. Braithwaite, 1886). (*Colin Straw.*)

As the city's most experienced school architect, it s not surprising that his services were regularly called upon by the new Education Committee, and continued to be so until shortly before his death.

Among the members of the final Leeds School Board was John W. Jackman, a printer and bookbinder of Basinghall Street. Jackman would therefore have known Braithwaite well during their years together at the Board, and it is likely that this connection led to his son Harry joining Braithwaite in practice after the first World War.

Chapels and the Methodists

Given his MNC background it is not surprising that Braithwaite was the architect of some of their chapels. An early example was the Ebenezer chapel on Bachelor Lane, Horsforth (1882), 'in the Classic style, simply treated to accommodate the growing congregation.'[27] The building endeavours of the Nonconformists were usually reported in the *Leeds Mercury* which provided detailed accounts whenever foundation stones were laid, new buildings opened or existing ones extended. All were events attended by large numbers of local worthies and all were recorded in the usual language of Victorian pride. One such occasion was the opening of the new United Methodist Free Church in Victoria Road, Headingley (1886). A bazaar was held in Leeds Town Hall to raise funds for a building described as 'a beautiful structure in the decorated Gothic style as a chapel ... school premises below, and minister's residence and chapel-keeper's house adjoining'.[28] The chapel, 'a violently Gothic interjection'[29] slotted into the streetscape of terrace houses opposite the former LGHS site, is now the Bethel United Church (14.12). The growing numbers attending the city's first MNC chapel at Zion Street led to its being replaced by a new chapel on land at Clark Lane (1894), a site selected for its proximity to the new workmen's cottages which the North-Eastern Railway Company were soon to build there;[30] again Braithwaite was employed.

Chapels were often combined with schools or Sunday schools and examples include new Sunday schools at the Ventnor Street MNC chapel (1898)[31] and at Tempest Road, Beeston Hill (1906), which provided accommodation for about 500.[32] In Armley, a new Methodist chapel and school were built at Hall Lane, in 1897 – the year in which the MNC celebrated its centenary.[33] Built in brick, with stone dressings, the chapel contained an organ gifted by Joseph Hepworth.

Commercial Work

Probably it was *via* Braithwaite's Methodist connections that several of his commercial projects arrived in his office. These include his work for the Pettys, a United Methodist Free Church family. His work for

27. *LM*, 12 June 1882.

28. *LM*, 25 Nov 1886.

29. Pevsner, *Leeds*, p. 254.

30. *LM*, 2 Jan 1894.

31. *The Builder*, 7 May 1898.

32. *The Builder*, 3 Nov 1906.

33. *The Builder*, 13 Feb 1897.

them at their printing business on Whitehall Road began around 1891.[34] From this time onwards the buildings have undergone an extensive programme of continuing expansion, new build and alterations, but they remain on this site to this day as part of the Polestar business, and Braithwaite and Jackman remain their architects. His Methodist links are again evident in work for the Hepworth family, also members at Woodhouse Lane, who provided much of the funding

34. Braithwaite and Jackman Archive, Letter Book.

THE BUILDING NEWS, MAR. 21, 1884.

MESSRS. J. HEPWORTH & SON CLOTHING FACTORY. WELLINGTON. STREET. LEEDS.

W.S. Braithwaite Architect Leeds

14.13: Leeds, Wellington Street, Clothing factory for Messrs J. Hepworth & Sons (W.S. Braithwaite, 1884). (The Building News, *21st March 1884*.)

14.14: Leeds, Albion Street, west side, New Premises for the Leeds Industrial Co-operative Society (W.S. Braithwaite, 1891). 'The business transacted at the existing headquarters of the society [Connon's 1883-4 building (see 1.14)] has long outgrown all reasonable demands, and this new structure is one of many buildings and new stores the society is erecting in various parts of the borough'. (Building News, *25 March 1892.*)

for the new chapels. He worked on alterations to *Longfield* on Victoria Road in Headingley for N.R. Hepworth,[35] and in 1884, J. Hepworth & Son's new clothing factory on Wellington Street was completed to Braithwaite's design.[36] (14.13)

By 1892 the Leeds Industrial Co-operative Society had outgrown its headquarters and was expanding with new stores in various parts of Leeds. Braithwaite's Albion Street building housed the furniture and draper's stores approached through a large central entrance. Provision was made for the loading and unloading of goods, and for storage at

35. *Ex inf.* Colin Dews

36 *Building News*, 21 March 1884.

basement level. *Building News* noted the particular attention paid to the provision of '… electric light, special heating and ventilation apparatus … The rooms will be lofty, and will be carried on iron girders and iron columns, and all made fireproof',[37] and includes a fine illustration (14.14). Accommodation also included space for the educational department of the society.

Among the later records of his work are bills of quantities prepared in 1915 for extensions to the Leeds Meat Markets.[38] (14.15) It seems these were again extended in 1921 at which time some drawings show W.S. Braithwaite as architect and others refer to Braithwaite and Jackman.[39]

Architects at this time often provided services as valuers and surveyors and Braithwaite was no exception. He undertook a considerable number of survey reports and valuations on a range of buildings from houses to commercial property, and also prepared bills of quantities.[40] These include those for a hotel in Carlisle. He also acted for the Leeds Corporation in valuing a great part of the insanitary area it was proposing to demolish.

As might be expected, commissions for the 1914-18 period are few compared with Braithwaite's earlier prolific output. To some extent, this can be explained by the impact of the war, but by its end Braithwaite would have been 64 years old and nearing the end of his life. With the death of his son James, any hopes of keeping the practice in the family were dashed and perhaps he never recovered his enthusiasm for the profession in which he had once achieved so much. My grandfather Harry Jackman became his partner in 1919 and took the practice forward as Braithwaite and Jackman.

The large scale programme of housing estates built by private enterprise which followed the war soon spread to the fields of the Meanwood Valley near Braithwaite's home. The description by Walter Gill in his publication *Woodhouse in Leeds* is apt: 'The catastrophic World War 1 dislocated social and religious life. The effects in Woodhouse were long-term and things never did get back to normal'.

Braithwaite's career did not include any outstanding buildings, but he ran a busy, well regarded practice that produced a broad range of buildings in an equally broad range of styles. His principal contribution to Leeds is his many schools, the best of which are impressive and all were thoughtfully designed and intended as prominent landmarks in their communities, despite usually tight budgets. The Leeds School Board was paralleled by similar organisations in other major towns and cities, and the architectural patronage of these boards represents a not insignificant chapter in the story of late-nineteenth and early-twentieth century architectural practice. Beyond his educational work, the study of Braithwaite's career reveals an illuminating picture of the career of one of the age's diligent, but essentially unremarkable, workhorses.

37. *Building News*, 25 March 1892.

38. Archives [note 4].

39. Leodis photographic archive.

40. Archives [note 4].

Brought forward   £

mold to pedi-
ment, with
one end hav-
ing external
and internal
mitres returned
to main cornice,
thus:-

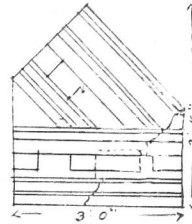

N°. 1.   D°. 3'-0" x 3'-3" x 3'-5"
and   d°. d°.
with mitred,
returned and
moulded end
and joint to
main cornice.

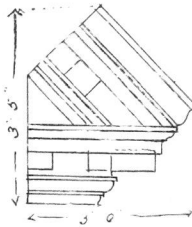

" 1.   D°. 3'-0" x 3'-5" x 3'-5" and d°. d°. d°.

" 2.   D°. 3'-0" x 4'-8" x 3'-5"
molded and sunk
on face as before
and mitred and
returned 2'-0" deep
with internal mitre
and portion circu-
lar moulded, thus:-

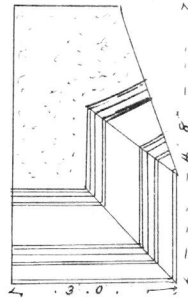

" 4.   Footstones 2'-2" x 2'-10" x 1'-4" molded
and sunk on
face with one end
mitred, returned &
stopped to wall, thus:-

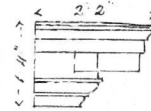

" 2.   D°.   2'-2" x 3'-0" x 1'-4" and d°. d°.

" 2.   Apex stones 3'-10" x 3'-3" x
3'-0" molded, mitred
and sunk,
thus:-

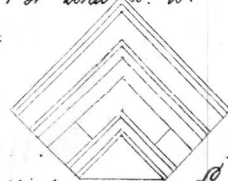

Builder.

Carried forward £

/2.

14.15: Leeds, York Street, from Bills of Quantities for Extensions to the Meat Markets (W.S. Braithwaite, 1915). (*Braithwaite and Jackman archive.*)

Catalogue

Unless another source is given,
the following list is taken from the Braithwaite and Jackman Archive,
held at the practice's office in Leeds.

LEEDS, Beckett Street Cemetery, twin lodges, c.1880. (*LM*, 6 July 1880.)

LEEDS, Ebenezer MNC, Bachelor Lane, Horsforth, c.1882. (*LM*. 12 June 1882.)

LEEDS, Blackman Lane, 2 dwelling houses, c.1882. (*LM*, 15 April 1882.)

LEEDS, Hanover Square, 2 houses with coach houses and stables, c.1882. (*LM*, 15 April 1882.)

LEEDS, competition design for cemetery buildings, East Morley, 1883. (*Building News,* 27 July and 9 Nov 1883.)

LEEDS. Messrs J Hepworth & Sons clothing factory, Wellington Street, c.1884. (*Building News.* 21 March 1884.)

HEADINGLEY, Leeds, New Methodist Free Church, Victoria Road, c.1886. (*LM*, 29 July 1886.)

LEEDS, Holy Trinity Sunday School, Armley Hall (with C.D. Swale), c.1887. (*LM*, 25 April 1887.)

LEEDS, layout of estate in Meanwood Road, 1888. (*LM*, 29 September 1888.)

LEEDS, Abattoir, Gelderd Road, 1890.

LEEDS, new premises for the Leeds Industrial Co-operative Society, Albion Street, 1891/2.

HEADINGLEY, Leeds, additions to *Longfield*, Victoria Road, for N.R. Hepworth, 1892. (*Ex inf.* Colin Dews.)

LEEDS, new auxiliary stores for LICS, Albion Street, 1894. (G.J. Holyoake, *The Jubilee History of the Leeds Industrial Co-operative Society from 1847 to 1897,* Central Co-operative Offices, Leeds, (?)1897.)

LEEDS, Zion Methodist New Connexion Chapel, Clark Lane, 1894. (*LM,* 21 Nov 1894.)

LEEDS, St Luke's National School, Beeston Hill, 1894 (*LM,* 5 November 1894.)

LEEDS, St Lukes National School, Beeston Hill, new Infants School, c.1895. (*LM*, 25 May 1895.)

LEEDS, Hunslet Lane Board School, 1895, dem. (*LM*, 16 March 1895.)

LEEDS, Burmantofts Board School, 1896. (Leeds School Board Yearbooks, WYASL.)

LEEDS, Bramley Town Street Board School, 1896. (Leeds School Board Yearbooks, WYASL)

LEEDS, Burley Lawn Board School, 1896. (Leeds School Board Yearbooks, WYASL.)

LEEDS, Whingate Road Board School, 1896. (Leeds School Board Yearbooks, WYASL.)

LEEDS, Hunslet Carr Board School, 1896. (Leeds School Board Yearbooks, WYASL.)

LEEDS, Hall Lane MNC Chapel, Armley, 1897-8. (*The Builder*, 13 Feb 1897.)

LEEDS, Green Lane Board School, New Wortley, 1896. (*LM*, 9 April 1896.)

LEEDS, Methodist Chapel and School, Armley, 1897.

LEEDS, Gipton Board School, Harehills Road, 1897 (later Harehills Middle School, now 'Shine').

LEEDS, Brudenell Board School, 1897-9. (WYASL.)

LEEDS, Hunslet Hall Road Infant School, 1898 (*The Builder,* 19 Feb 1898.)

LEEDS, Kepler Board School, 1898. (Linstrum, *WYAA*, p. 372)

LEEDS, Ventnor Street MNC Sunday School, 1898. (*The Builder*, 7 May 1898.)

LEEDS, Blenheim Home for Blind and Deaf School, 1899 (*LM*, 11 May 1899.)

LEEDS, Ivy House Estate, off York Road, purchased Lots 9 and 10 (?)for development. (*LM*, 14 April 1899.)

LEEDS, Armley Park Board School, Stanningley Road, 1900. (WYASL.)

LEEDS, Bramley Board School, Broad Lane, 1900. (Leeds School Board Yearbooks, WYASL.)

LEEDS, Lovell Road Board School, 1901. (Linstrum, *WYAA*, p. 372)

LEEDS, Pettys printing factory, Whitehall Road, 1901.

LEEDS, Lawnswood Crematorium, 1905.

LEEDS, Sunday School, Tempest Road, Beeston Hill, 1906.

KIRKBURTON, Storthes Hall Asylum, 1907-8.

LEEDS, Tempest Road Methodist New Connexion Chapel, 1907-8. (*The Builder,* 23 Nov 1906.)

CASTLEFORD, Castleford Secondary School, 1909. (Linstrum, *WYAA*, p. 372)

BRIGHOUSE, Methodist New Chapel.

HALIFAX, Elland and District Secondary School, (now the Brooksbank Sports School College), 1911. (Plan at WYAS, Halifax.)

LEEDS, Series of designs for Columbarium buildings at Lawnswood, 1914.

LEEDS, Lawnswood Cemetery, additions to Corson's Main Lodge, 1915.

LEEDS, Wholesale Meat Market, New York Street, extensions 1915 and 1921.

15. *Thomas Howdill (1840-1918) & Charles Barker Howdill (1863-1940)*

D. COLIN DEWS

Thomas Howdill

Thomas Howdill (1840-1918) – hereafter Thomas – was born at the Manor House, Tadcaster, into one of the town's old yeomanry families, and attended Tadcaster Grammar School.[1] His religious conversion on 1 January 1858 brought him into the Primitive Methodism of his mother and with hindsight this event would not only shape his religious commitments, including appointment to Connexional office – i.e. to a committee with a national responsibility – but also the direction he would take professionally. In 1859 his name was placed on the Tadcaster Primitive Methodist Circuit plan as a local preacher. Then on the death of his father in 1861, Thomas, by then a joiner and cabinetmaker, left the town to find employment first in Lancashire and then in Leeds. His cabinet making skills would emerge over thirty years later when with his son, Charles Barker Howdill, he would make and present the president's chair to the Primitive Methodist conference when it met in Leeds in 1898.[2]

Thomas's credentials as a local preacher were transferred to the Leeds III Circuit in August 1863 where he joined Rehoboth PM, Park Lane, and it was among this denomination that he would receive his earliest architectural work. Within the Rehoboth congregation, a small group, mainly of a similar age, seems to have shaped his professional career. Given that in the early 1870s Joseph Wright (1818-85), a Primitive Methodist and leading Hull architect, was living in Leeds and in membership at Rehoboth, one might speculate that he influenced

1. Much of the information on the Howdill family and some of their commissions was provided by Miss Madge Howdill (1905-2000), granddaughter of Thomas and daughter of Charles. During the 1970s, she generously shared with the author her extensive knowledge of her architect relations.

2. The Primitive Methodist President's Chair is currently on display at the Englesea Brook Chapel & Museum of Primitive Methodism, Cheshire.

Thomas's move into the profession. Thomas emerges as an architect in 1873 and only three years later was a founder member of the Leeds Architects' Association, later the Leeds & Yorkshire Architects' Association. Certainly, his first chapel, Ebenezer PM, Kirkstall (1874), seems to coincide with Wright returning to Hull. Also in membership at Rehoboth at the time Thomas's arrival in Leeds was William Beckworth (1840-1911), a Hull-born local preacher who had moved to Leeds in 1857 to work in a tannery and who would eventually became a leading and influential Connexional officer. Another family associated with Rehoboth were the Walmsleys. William Walmsley (1843-1914) came to Leeds in the early 1870s and his brother Benjamin (1845-1910), another local preacher, arrived in 1872. As builders they developed large estates in such places as Harrogate, Leeds, Normanton and Scarborough. Subsequently, the Walmsleys commissioned Thomas to design houses for them, to which we will return later.

Charles Barker Howdill

Charles Barker Howdill (1863-1941) – hereafter Charles – Thomas's only child, followed his father into the profession. Having attended Leeds Modern School, he joined his father's practice in 1879 as a pupil and at the same time took a course at the Leeds School of Art. In 1883 he too became a member of the Leeds and Yorkshire Architectural Society, and was appointed an auditor in 1885. Also in 1885, the Society awarded him a three-guinea prize for Construction Design, following his submission of drawings of roof bindings, although there were only two entries.[3] He was now showing considerable academic promise and other awards followed. In 1885 he was awarded the National Silver Medal for a measured drawing of the chancel screen of St. John's, New Briggate, Leeds, and then in 1887 he was the first Leeds School of Art student to win the coveted National Gold Medal for his scheme for a Post Office. He also received the Queen's Prize in a national competition held at the South Kensington Museum for a design for a village institute.[4] Following his five-year pupilage, in 1884 he was promoted to an assistant in his father's office and five years later, in 1889, he was appointed the Assistant Architect to the Leeds School Board, working under the direction of its principal architect William Landless (b.1847), also engaged by the board in 1889. While in the Board's office, he continued to study part-time at the Leeds School of Art, an institution where he would later be a governor. Again, we might speculate that William Beckworth used his influence to get Charles appointed to the Board; at a time when political connections could be crucial for professional advancement, Beckworth – for a time the Liberal councillor for the Headingley Ward – had also been a member

3. This information was derived from the *Annual Reports* of the Leeds and Yorkshire Architectural Society.

4. *LM*, 31 July 1888.

of the first Leeds School Board from 1870. The period during which Charles was with the Board was a time when Leeds was facing an acute shortage of school accommodation and as a result he was responsible for £70,000 worth of capital works. He was involved in the design of many of its buildings, such as Harehills Board School (1891) the Industrial School, Czar Street, Holbeck (1891) and Queens Road Board School (1892), and may have been solely responsible for some of these designs as Landless left Leeds in 1892. On 13 June 1892, W.H. Thorp, G.B.Bulmer and E.J. Dodgshun proposed Thomas for RIBA membership, all three having Leeds connections. He joined his father's practice as a partner in 1893, and continued to run the practice after the latter's death in 1918. Of the two, Charles seems to have been the more able and innovative architect, and his influence can be detected in the changes emerging in their chapel designs after 1893. He undertook several Continental excursions where he noted current architectural trends,[5] although it is not clear to what extent these had an impact on his own compositions.

5. The information comes from Howdill [note 1], although she was not able to provide more specific information about dates or itineraries.

15.1: Skipton, Gargrave Road PM (Thomas Howdill, 1878-9). (*Author.*)

The practice and its work

Thomas's first commission, Ebenezer PM, Kirkstall (1874), came from the Leeds III PM Circuit, in which Rehoboth was the main society. This was a modest structure and the first of his chapels to have a gallery was probably that at Garforth (1876-7). His first large chapel was Rehoboth PM, West Bowling, Bradford (1877-8), which had similarities to two of Joseph Wright's PM chapels in Hull. Of Thomas's early work, typical examples are Rehoboth PM, West Bowling, Bradford, and Gargrave Road PM, Skipton (1879) (15.1), where galleried chapels were built over a basement schoolroom. The main façades had flanking towers for the gallery stairs and the triple entrances were approached by a flight of steps. A further example of this arrangement was at Bourne PM, Hollinwood, Lancs (1884), where a new Italianate façade was added to an existing chapel. A similar arrangement was used at Salem PM, Holdforth Street, New Wortley, Leeds (1879-80) (15.2). However, here Thomas was faced with an unusual problem in that the site had a street frontage wider than it was deep; rather than put the main entrances facing the street – Thomas's usual arrangement – he placed them in what was the shorter, side elevation but still placed the twin towers in the street elevation, even though they no longer framed the doorways.

15.2: New Wortley, Leeds, Holdforth Street PM (Thomas Howdill, 1879-80). (*Author.*)

This model typified the large Primitive Methodist chapels of this period, at least in the north, and another architect to use it was Hull's William Freeman (fl.1872-90). His Ebenezer, Spring Bank PM (1878) and Hessle Road PM (1881) similarly had flanking towers but in these cases the towers also served as entrances.[6] Later variations of the Howdills' use of the flanking tower plan were at Silver Royd Hill PM, Leeds (1901) and Portland Place Memorial PM, Lincoln (1905-6), both in the Renaissance style. The Howdills used a similar arrangement at St. George's PM, Bristol (1903), but this time clothed it in Gothic, complete with buttresses and a flèche. In contrast, many of Thomas's chapels at this period were quite small, modest, brick structures, with plain pilasters on the side façades creating recesses for the windows, as for example at Far Royds PM, Beeston, Leeds, and Providence PM, Durkar, Wakefield (both 1878).

The favoured style for Thomas's early chapels is best described as Italianate but there were two early exceptions, both with Gothic features: Kirkstall PM (1874) and Wetherby PM (1874-5). Cardigan Road PM's school/chapel (1883) was also mildly Gothic with lancet windows and when, in 1894, a more substantial chapel was added at the site, it too was Gothic, but of a much more robust strain, replete with buttressed aisles and clerestory, and what appears externally as a chancel. This was the first 'churchy' Primitive Methodist chapel in Leeds; as Charles had become a partner by this time, to what extent did Cardigan Road represent his influence? Although built in two stages, might the whole complex have been designed in 1883, or was the chapel a new design of a decade later?[7]

6. For the Hull chapels see: D. Neave, *Lost Churches and Chapels of Hull,* Hull City Museums and Hutton Press, 1991.

7. W. Beckworth, *A Book of Remembrance, being records of Leeds Primitive Methodism,* 1910, p. 262 reproduces the architects' drawing of the chapel and school, with the inscription 'Thos. Howdill; Chas. B. Howdill ARIBA'. Does this imply that the chapel was designed separately but in the same style as the schoolroom?

15.4: Kilburn, London, College Park PM
(T. & C.B. Howdill, 1897). (*Author.*)

The Cardigan Road plan was repeated in a number of other Gothic chapels, including Hunter Street PM, Chester (1898) which had a very distinctive clerestory designed to let in maximum light, spire, and a schoolroom on the ground floor. Northwood PM, Middlesex (1902-3) also had a clerestory with a fleche over the gable of the main façade, while the Gothic idioms at Millsbridge WM, Spen Valley, WY (1903-4) (15.3), with a spire and chancel, were ever more ecclesiastical. This basic plan could be adopted to any of the stylistic alternatives to Gothic and was easily adapted for an arrangement with a central hall and flanking vestries in the 'aisles'; interestingly, it was a plan which had much in common with School Board's favoured arrangement of assembly hall surrounded by classrooms. College Park PM, Kilburn, North London (1897) (15.4) and Zion PM, Dean Park, Ferryhill, Co Durham (1907), both in a Free Renaissance style, and Jubilee PM, Woodhouse, Leeds (1902-3), in a late Gothic style, were all based on the 'school board' design. This evolution in chapel planning and greater stylistic variety – especially the use of Gothic and seventeenth century English Renaissance idioms – coincided with Charles' arrival in the office.

Although Thomas's practice was known primarily for its chapels, there was certainly domestic work as well, although it seems all of the latter was small-scale, functional and economical. It is known he designed houses in Normanton (1874), Stanley (1875) and Leeds (1886). There were also some houses in the Hyde Park area of Headingley, Leeds.[8] And the Walmsley family, builders, Primitive Methodists, and developers mainly of back-to-back houses in the Headingley area, also exploited Thomas's architectural talents. However, the Walmsleys often sold plots for other builders to develop

8. Towell, TS, p. 116 records 14 dwellings in 1893 by T. Howdill and a further one in 1910 by T & C.B. Howdill.

– using their own architects – and it is thus difficult to ascertain precisely the extent of Walmsley-Howdill collaborations. Meanwhile, back in 1873, Thomas – still described as a joiner – became a member of a practical committee of the Industrial Co-operative Society to assist members build houses.[9] Alterations to his own house at 14 Hanover Square[10] included the addition of a rear bedroom on the half-landing. It is further suggested that Charles designed a house at Horsforth for the Cryer family who attended Rehoboth and were related by marriage. In contrast to a succession of substantial chapels, domestic work may have been only a minor part of the Howdill output, but it is likely that many Howdill houses await identification.

The practice also produced industrial buildings. A major example – thought to be from the drawing board of Charles without his father's assistance – was the Viaduct Tannery, Leeds (1892) (15.5), for William Beckworth. It is also known that the Howdills designed a tannery in Southwark, London,[11] again probably for Beckworth.[12] Prior to owning his own business, Beckworth worked for the Nichols family, who owned the Joppa Tannery, Kirkstall Road, Leeds, and there is reason to believe Thomas undertook some work here too. Family tradition[13] states that Taylor's Drug Co premises, Burley Hill, Leeds, were also by the Howdills. Certainly, the excellent Art & Craft style lettering on the building is typical of Charles' work and W.B. Mason, a local preacher and Sunday school superintendent at Oxford Place Wesleyan Chapel, owned the business.

Of office staff, little is known although one of Thomas's assistants was Frederick Mitchell (b. 1863), son of, Henry Mitchell, also an

9. G.J. Holyoake, *The Jubilee History of the Leeds Industrial Co-operative Society, from 1847 to 1897,* LICS, 1897, p. 91.

10. Originally 41 Hanover Square until renumbered.

11. *Ex inf.* Miss Howdill [note 1].

12. At the time, this part of London was an important centre for the leather industry and the Howdill commission might have been at any one of a number of tanneries.

13. See [note1].

15.5: Leeds, Viaduct Tannery, Canal Road, for William Beckworth (C.B. Howdill, possibly without Thomas, 1892). (*Ruth Baumberg*.)

architect. Subsequently Mitchell was an assistant with John Kirk & Sons, Huddersfield and then from 1887 to 1897 was in partnership with C.D. Swale in Leeds, before opening an office of his own in 1897.[14]

That it has not been possible to identify any Howdill chapels after 1910 perhaps points to the practice undertaking few if any commissions after this date. One might speculate that Charles became more interested in architectural education as well as experimenting with photography. In the wider context, this decade was also the last flourish of Victorian chapel building, brought almost to a halt with the First World and followed, soon after, by the post-war economic depression. There was an added factor in that in the first decade of the new century, Primitive Methodism enthusiastically marked its centenary with a peofusion of schemes for new or enlarged places of worship, initiatives which exhausted the funds as well as the energies of many chapel-building committees. If expansion did not quite come to a halt, after the war ambitions were certainly moderated. In addition, the new century brought a new face to the Leeds architectural scene: W.G. Smithson. Smithson was ambitious and also had Primitive Methodist connections, and secured chapel commissions that might, otherwise, have been destined for the Howdill office.[15] After Thomas's death in 1918, Charles continued the practice under his own name until his own death in 1941. However, the last known job was Guisborough PM (1907) and it seems Charles' interests lay outside the office.

Charles had a strong interest in education and taught construction at Leeds and Dewsbury Technical Colleges (1886-1903), Huddersfield Technical School (1914-1941) and Batley Technical School (1928-1941) as well as at the Leeds School of Art, where he was also a governor. That he was still working aged 78 confirms his commitment to architectural education, although it was also a reflection of the teacher shortages during both wars. His pedagogical interests passed to his son, Norman (b.1898), who taught at Hammersmith School of Building and Arts and Crafts, subsequently retiring as Principal of East Ham Technical College. Charles also developed an interest in photography, taking it up in his early twenties. He was a friend of the Leeds-born Frank Meadow Sutcliffe (1853- 1941) who from 1875 was based in Whitby and who subsequently achieved considerable fame. Charles was a pioneer of colour photography and in 1900 he was experimenting with the Sango Shepherd three colour printing process.[16] He lectured on colour photography and it has been claimed that he was the first in the country to attempt to illustrate a lecture on an architectural theme with the aid of colour photographs. He was also an expert on Yorkshire's medieval cathedrals and a member of the Yorkshire Archaeological Society as well as Leeds & Yorkshire

14. Towell, TS, p. 109.

15. W.G. Smithson, a local preacher, came to Leeds from Bingley in 1904; in 1901 he moved to Crossgates and by 1932 seems to have retired to Scarborough. His chapels include: Leeds, Bramley Back Lane PM Mission vestries, 1901 – possibly not built (WYASL; architect's drawings); Whitby, Church Street PM, 1902 (*PMA Mag*, 1903); Barmby Marsh PM, 1902 (Neave [note 7]); Leeds, Beeston Hill PM, Lady Pit Lane, 1902 (Beckworth [note 8]); Market Weighton PM, 1902 (Neave [note 6]); Featherstone, Featherstone Lane PM, 1903 (*Diamond Jubilee Brochure*, 1963); Thorne, Centenary PM, 1907-8 (*Jubilee Brochure*, 1957); Heage PM, 1908 (*The Builder*, 8 August 1908).

16. *The [Adelade] Advertiser*, 24 April 1914.

Architectural Society. He exhibited at various photographic exhibitions, including six of the Royal Photographic Society's shows between 1901 and 1913, and among his exhibits was a photograph of W.T. Stead, taken on the *Titanic*.[17]

Patronage

Thomas's early chapels are all close to Leeds where he could capitalise on family connections. And with the exception of Wetherby in the Tadcaster PM Circuit, all are within the Leeds PM circuits. Rehoboth PM, West Bowling (started 1877), was the first of a number of commissions in the Bradford & Halifax PM District, which included work from a number of circuits in Bradford. There were also jobs from within the Brighouse & Greetland, Clayton West, and Skipton circuits. With this solid core of satisfied clients, his reputation grew and soon he was working over a much wider geographical area; by the mid-1880s, he secured two commissions on the Isle of Man – at Ramsay (1886) and Castletown (1890) – followed by Swindon, Wiltshire (1895) and Boston, Lincs (1897). The expansion of the practice coincided with Charles' arrival and it is likely that his middle-class upbringing, more thorough training and greater awareness of current architectural thinking made him more adept than his father at courting

17. Walter Thomas Stead (1849-1912), son of the Congregationalist manse, pioneer of investigative journalism and editor of the *Pall Mall Gazette*, drowned in the disaster. The photograph was held by the family.

15.6: Northwood, Middlesex, High Street PM (T. & C.B. Howdill, 1902-3). (1896-1946, Jubilee Souvenir, *1946*.)

potential clients. However, Thomas' contribution should not be overlooked and the web of connections that he had developed from being a delegate from the Leeds and York PM District to Conference, and also serving as the Treasurer of the Connexional General Chapel Fund[18] – a committee with a remit to serve the whole country – were surely important in the practice's growth. Was this, perhaps, the explanation for the firm obtaining work in and around London, for instance at College Park PM, Kilburn (1898) and at Northwood (15.6, 15.7)?

So successful were the Howdills that they secured jobs from other Methodist bodies, for instance the United Methodist Free Churches and the Wesleyans, although all the identifiable examples are near Leeds. The extent of the practice's ecclesiastical output can be measured by the claim that by the late 1880s Thomas Howdill had undertaken a hundred commissions and could include Anglicans alongside his Nonconformist clients, although research has failed to substantiate the claim and perhaps many within this total were very minor alterations.

Another aspect of the Howdills' work, perhaps reflecting Thomas's origins as a joiner, are the bench pews provided at Skelmanthorpe PM, WY, in 1887. These were built to the Howdill 'pew patent',[19] designed to give a greater level of comfort than the standard straight-backed seating. A further attention to detail was found at Woodhouse Hill PM, Leeds (1901-2), where, unusually, provision was made in the brickwork on either side of the church's central entrance for notices and displays.

When it comes to studying the distribution of a particular architect's commissions at this period, the provision of the public transport needs to be considered. By the time Thomas began his practice what is now West Yorkshire was well served by a railway network and a copy of *Bradshaw's Railway Timetable* was, from a business perspective, even more important than a copy of the weekly *Primitive Methodist Leader* or *The Builder*. Many of the early commissions, for example, were accessible via the Midland Railway from Leeds, including Ilkley (also *via* the North Eastern Railway) Methley Junction, Normanton; Garforth and Wetherby *via* the North Eastern Railway; Durkar, Hollinwood, and probably Hightown *via* the Lancashire & Yorkshire Railway. Where the local station was a distance away from the station, a cab would be taken to the building site. Within Leeds from 1871 there was a growing tramway network, with Kirkstall being part of the original network. Originally horse drawn, from the 1880s steam trams were also used and then from 1896 work began on electrifying the system. This network enabled the Howdills not only to develop their practice from a very small one in Leeds in a way an earlier generation of architects would have found more difficult, but it also fostered the efficient supervision of projects *via* regular inspections.

15.7: Northwood, Middlesex, High Street PM, interior (T. & C.B. Howdill, 1902-3). (1896-1946, Jubilee Souvenir, *1946*.)

18. *LM*, 17 June 1887.

19. Reference to the patent comes from a number of sources, but all are vague about its precise form. It seems that it involved an angled back-rest for greater comfort, although for a patent to have been granted, it must have included rather more of an innovation than this. I am indebted for this information to the late Tom Wainwright, a member at Skelmathorpe who had been taught by C.B. Howdill at Huddersfield Technical School.

An assessment

How then should the Howdills be assessed as architects? Rarely were their chapels monumental or innovative, but then Primitive Methodism was not a particularly wealthy church nor one prone to architectural pretension. Pevsner is one of the few critics to comment on them; Pickering, he concluded, was 'in a terrible Italianate style' and Guisborough 'unforgivable'.[20] However, such dismissal should be tempered with Pevsner's well known hostility to most Nonconformist chapels. Stell[21] fails even to notice their work. Leach's 'makes skilful use of its corner site'[22] for Armley is as near as we come to praise.

The Howdills of Leeds were not in the first flight of architects. Few buildings were outstanding and many were insignificant, but on occasions they could produce accomplished designs as at Armley in Leeds (15.8), and at Lincoln (15.9). Certainly their story, which interweaves worship, patronage and practice, is an instructive one in the context of middle-order practitioners. Yet from modest beginnings, by the end of the century the practice could reasonably claim a national importance in Nonconformity. Among the Primitive Methodists, their reputation for reliability as providers of solid, economical chapels was

20. N. Pevsner, *The Buildings of England; the North Riding* (1966). pp. 180, 284.

21. C. Stell, *Nonconformist Chapels and Meetinghouses*, HMSO, 4 vols, 1986-2002.

22. Pevsner, *WY*, p. 564.

15.8: Armley, Leeds, Branch Road PM (T. & C.B. Howdill, 1905). (*Author.*)

15.9: Lincoln, Portland Place Memorial PM, now Central PM (T. and C.B. Howdill, 1905-6). (*Early twentieth century postcard.*)

secure. Towards the end of his life, Thomas could reflect on a meteoric rise from carpenter to luminary in the world of chapel building. With his son, he had designed PM chapels in Ferryhill and Guisborough to the north, York and Scarborough to the east, Boston and Lincoln in Lincolnshire, London and Swindon in the south, Bristol to the south–west, Brownhills in the West Midlands, Chester and Hollinwood to the west, as well as on the Isle of Man. It was a not inconsiderable record.

Catalogue

LEEDS, 14 (formerly 41) Hanover Square, nd, alterations to family home including additional bedroom. (Howdill [note 1].)

KIRKSTALL, Leeds, Ebenezer PM, 1874. (Beckworth [note 7], p.194.)

BOTTOMBOAT, Wakefield, PM, 1874. (Howdill [note 1].)

MORLEY, Brunswick PM, 1874. (W. Smith, *The History and Antiques of Morley*, 1876, p. 191.)

ROTHWELL, WY, Marsh Street PM, 1874-9. (J. Batty, *The History of Rothwell*, 1877, p. 256.)

NORMANTON, three houses for William Eastwood, 1874-5. (Howdill [note 1].)

WETHERBY, North Street PM, 1874-5. (WYASL, trust records.)

STANLEY, nr Wakefield, houses for Winterburn, 1875. (Howdill [note 1].)

HIGHTOWN PM, nr. Heckmondwike, 1875-6. (Howdill [note 1].)

METHLEY, WY, Methley Junction PM, 1875-6. (www.bomfi.co.uk/archive/mt/mt118.htm)

ARMLEY, Leeds, Branch Road PM school-chapel, 1876. (Howdill [note 1].)

LEEDS, 'Through Houses', c.1876. (*LM*, 18 Nov 1886.)

GARFORTH, Central PM, 1876-7. (Howdill [note 1].)

LEEDS, Lady Pit Lane PM, laying out the site for a tin tabernacle, 1877. (WYASL, chapel records.)

LEEDS, Temple Vue PM, 1877. (WYASL, trust minute book.)

BRADFORD, West Bowling, Rehoboth PM, 1877-8. (*LM*, 24 Aug 1878; T.A. Fairweather and Percy Ackroyd, *Fifty Years of Primitive Methodism in West Bowling*, 1928, p. 18.)

BEESTON, Leeds, Far Royds PM, 1878. (Howdill [note 1].)

BRADFORD, Tyersal PM, Bury Street, 1878. (Howdill [note 1].)

CASTLEFORD, Temple Street PM, 1878. (WYASW, circuit records.)

DURKAR, nr Wakefield, PM, Crigglestone Road, 1878. (Howdill [note 1].)

ILKLEY, Leeds Road PM, 1878. (*LM*, 25 March 1878.)

LEEDS, Oulton Street PM, 1878. (Howdill [note 1].)

FERRYBRIDGE, SY, PM, 1878. (Howdill [note 1].)

MORLEY, Ebenezer PM, Fountain Street, school-chapel, 1878. (Howdill [note 1].)

PUDSEY, nr Leeds, PM, Sunday school, 1878-9. (Howdill [note 1].)

SKIPTON, Gargrave Road PM, 1878-9. (*Lancaster Gazette & General Advertiser*, 23 Nov 1878.)

CASTLEFORD, Bradley Street PM, additions and new gutters, 1879. (*LM*, 22 Feb 1879.)

LEEDS, Cardigan Road PM, tin tabernacle, 1879. (Howdill [note 1].)

MANNINGHAM, Bradford, Heaton Road PM, 1879. (*LM*, 25 Feb 1879.)

WOODHOUSE HILL PM, nr Leeds, school-chapel, 1879. (Beckworth [note 7], p. 238.)

LEEDS, New Wortley, Holdforth Street PM, 1879-80. (Beckworth [note 7], p.185.)

BRADFORD, Manningham PM, c.1879. (*LM*, 25 Feb 1879.)

BRADFORD, Tennyson Place PM, 1879-80. (*LM*, 6 Sept 1880.)

WETHERBY, 4 houses, c.1881. (*LM*, 15 Oct 1881.)

LEEDS, Tabernacle UMFC, Meadow Road, Sunday school, 1881-2. (WYASL, Sunday school records.)

BRADFORD, Dirkhill PM, All Saints Road, 1882. (Howdill [note 1].)

CARLTON, nr Rothwell, WY, Carlton PM, Sunday School, 1882 (Howdill [note 1].)

MOSSLEY, Cheshire, PM, Waggon Road, 1882. (*LM*, 22 March 1882.)

WINTERWELL, nr Wath-on-Deane, SY, PM chapel, 1882. (*Sheffield & Rotherham Independent*, 15 May 1882.)

LOWER WORTLEY, nr Leeds, boundary and retaining wall alongside beck, 1882. (*LM*, 5 Aug 1882.)

RAWCLIFFE, nr Goole, PM, 1882-3 (*York Herald*, 12 May 1882.)

LEEDS, Cardigan Road PM, Sunday school, 1883. (Beckworth [note 7], p. 262.)

EASINGWOLD, NY, PM, restoration, 1884. (*York Herald*, 21 June 1884.)

LOWER WORTLEY, Leeds, Bull Ring PM, extension to include porch, 1884. (WYASL: trust minutes; *LM*, 25 Aug 1884.)

MORECAMBE, Parliament Street PM, 1884. (Howdill [note 1].)

HOLLINWOOD, nr Oldham, Lancs, Bourne Street PM, façade added to existing chapel, 1884. (*LM*, 12 April 1884.)

LEEDS, Eleven Lanes End PM, Sunday school, 1884-5. (WYASL: trust minutes.)

LOWER WORTLEY, Leeds, Rehoboth UMFC, 1884-5. (*LM*, 1 March 1884.)

PICKERING, NY, Potter Hill PM, 1885. (*LM*, 21 June 1884.)

HOLBECK, nr Leeds, Princes Field PM, refurbishment and porch added 1885 to chapel of 1837 by James Simpson. (*LM*, 13 July 1885).

KNARESBOROUGH, Gracious Street WM, alterations, 1885. (*LM*, 15 Aug 1885.)

DENBY DALE, Miller Hill PM, extension and alterations, c.1886. (architect's drawing, WYAS, Kirklees.)

LEEDS, Atack Street, off Greystone Street, conveniences for W.H. Milton, 1886-7. (Howdill [note 1].)

SKELMANTHORPE PM, Sunday school, Pilling Lane, 1886-7. (*Ex inf.* Tom Wainwright.)

LEEDS, renovations and roof alterations to a tan yard, 1887. (*LM*, 12 March 1887.)

BATLEY, Whittaker Street, houses, c.1888. (*LM*, 4 Aug 1888.)

NOT SPECIFIED, 'alterations to shops and houses in various locations', c.1888. (*LM*, 15 Sept 1888.)

STAIRFOOT, nr Barnsley, School Street PM, 1888. (*LM*, 15 March 1888.)

BRIGHOUSE, WY, Lane Head PM, 1888-9. (*LM*, 29 September 1888; *Huddersfield Chronicle & West Yorkshire Advertiser*, 4 August 1888.)

HEADINGLEY, Leeds, houses in the Ashville streets, part of the Walmsley development, 1889. (Trowell.)

ROUNDHAY, Leeds, Park Avenue, detached villa and stables for George Hatton. 1889. (*LM*, 4 Feb 1889.)

FISHLAKE, nr Doncaster, PM, 1890. (*The Builder*, 1890.)

HIGH HOYLAND nr Barnsley, PM, 1890. (*LM*, 29 Nov 1890.)

LEEDS, six houses off Queen's Road, 1890-1. (*LM*, 6 Dec 1890.)

CASTLETOWN, Isle of Man, PM, Malew Street, 1890-3. (attribution, Howdill [note 1].)

IDLE, Bradford, Idle PM, Sunday school, 1892. (*LM*, 11 April 1892.)

LEEDS, Viaduct Tannery, Canal Road, for William Beckworth, 1892, possible only by Charles Barker Howdill. (Howdill [note 1].)

HEADINGLEY, Leeds, 14 houses on the Walmsley development, from 1892. Estate. (Trowell.)

RAMSAY, Isle of Man, Parliament Street PM, 1892. (*The Builder*, 27 Feb 1892; *Isle of Man Times*, 20 Feb 1892.)

SNOWGATEHEAD PM, nr Holmfirth, 1893. (*Ex inf.* Tom Wainwright.)

ROTHERHAM, Masborough, 1893-4. (*Sheffield & Rotherham Independent*, 20 June 1893; *LM*, 8 July 1893.)

HEADINGLEY, Leeds, a house on the Walmsley development, post 1894. (Trowell.)

LEEDS, Cardigan Road PM, chapel, 1894-5. (*The Builder*, 28 September 1895; (Howdill drawing reproduced in Beckworth [note 7], p. 262.)

LOWER WORTLEY, Leeds, Bull Ring PM, Sunday school and vestries, 1897. (WYASL: trust minutes.)

SWINDON, Wilts, Regent Street PM, Sunday School, 1894-5. (*Bristol Mercury & Daily Post*, 31 March 1894.)

BROWNHILLS, Staffs, Mt Zion PM, High Street, 1895. (*Birmingham Daily Post*, 16 April 1895.)

MIDDLETON, Leeds, Middleton PM, 1896. (*The Builder*, 21 April 1896.)

BOSTON, Lincs, West Street PM, 1897-8. (*The Builder*, 23 Jan 1898.)

KILBURN, London, College Park PM, 1897. (Howdill [note 1].)

STOURTON, Leeds, Wakefield Road WM, 1897. (Howdill [note 1].)

CHESTER, Hunter Street PM, 1897-8 (*Cheshire Observer*, 23 October 1897; *The Builder*, 3 May 1898.)

GUISBOROUGH, NY, Chapel Street PM, alterations and extension, c.1898, unexecuted. (S. Crossman and B. Preston, *Southside Story: the first 100 years 1907-2007*, 2010, pp. 17-18, including illustration.)

WATFORD, Herts, St. Alban's Road PM, 1899. (Howdill [note 1].)

HORBURY, WY, Highfield UMFC, 1899-1900. (*The Builder*, 1899.)

YORK, Albany PM, Leeman Road, 1900. (*LM*, 17 May 1900.)

LEEDS, Stanningley, Eleven Lane Ends PM, extension, 1901-2. (WYASL, trust minutes.)

LEEDS, Silver Royd Hill PM, chapel, 1901-2. (Beckworth [note 7], p. 305.)

LEEDS, Woodhouse Hill PM, chapel, 1901-2. (*The Builder*, 4 Jan 1902; foundation stone inscription.)

MANOR PARK, nr Illford, Essex, Sixth Avenue PM, 1901-2. (*The Builder*, 1901.)

LEEDS, Woodhouse, Jubilee PM, 1902-3. (*The Builder*, 23 & 30 Aug 1903.)

NORMANTON, WY, Beckridge PM, 1902-3. (Inscription on foundation stone mallet.)

NORTHWOOD, Middlesex, High Street PM. 1902-3 (*1896-1946, Jubilee Souvenir*, 1946, p. 5.)

BRISTOL, Salem, St. George's PM, m, Church Road. 1903 (*The Builder*, 20 June 1903.)

HECKMONDWYKE, WY, Millbridge WM, Leeds Road, 1903-4. (*The Builder*, 19 Dec 1903 & 12 Nov 1904; Wesleyan Methodist Annual Chapel Report, 1905.)

HARROW, Middlesex, Wheldon Crescent PM, 1904. (Foundation stone inscription.)

ARMLEY, Leeds, Branch Road PM, 1905. (*Primitive Methodist Leader*, 2 Nov 1905.)

LINCOLN, Portland Place Memorial PM, now Central Methodist, 1905-6. (*Primitive Methodist Leader*, 24 May 1906.)

STOURTON, Leeds, Wakefield Road WM, band room, 1905. (Foundation stone mallet.)

RODBOURNE CHERRY, nr Swindon, Wilts, PM, chapel, 1906. (Howdill [note 1].)

FERRYHILL, Co Durham, Zion PM, Dean Bank. 1907 (*The Builder*, 4 May 1907.)

GUISBOROUGH, NY, South Side PM, 1907. (S. Crossman and B. Preston, *Southside Story: the first 100 years 1907-2007*, 2007.)

Other works that are possibly by the Howdills:

HORSFORTH, house for the Cryer family. (*Ex inf.* Ian Howdill.)

LEEDS, Joppa Tannery, Kirkstall Road, alterations. (Howdill [note 1].)

LEEDS, Timothy White & Taylor's premises, Burley Hill. (Howdill [note 1].)

SELBY, chapel, c.1887. (Ambiguous reference in *LM*, 22 March 1887.)

SHEFFIELD, chapel, c.1887. (Ambiguous reference in *LM*, 22 March 1887.)

SOUTHWARK, London, tannery, possibly for William Beckworth. (Howdill [note 1].)

WOMBWELL, SY, Henry Adam Memorial PM, Barnsley Road, 1902. (Howdill [note 1].)

16. The Bedford and Kitson practice (1892-1914)

DAVID BOSWELL

The formation of the partnership and the organisation of their practice

1. Until projected publications appear, reference may be made to D.M. Boswell, 'The Kitsons and the Arts', unpublished D. Phil. thesis, University of York, 1995, specifically to Chapter 4, Appendix 1 which lists details of all the commissions from 1892-1920s, and a substantial bibliography of the published work of the practice. In 2009 Roger Shaw, the last senior partner, privately printed a review of the practice from 1892-1994 which includes much material on subsequent partners and some later work, *A History of Kitson and Partners, Chartered Architects, Leeds, 1892-1994*. Both authors provided data included in Pevsner, *Leeds*, and Pevsner, *WY*. This author would like to acknowledge the help and information from the late Professor Derek Linstrum, Roger Shaw FRIBA, the late Elisabeth and Barbara Kitson, Mrs Margaret Bedford and the staff of several institutions and citizens of Leeds. The relevant documents and drawings have subsequently been bequeathed to or deposited in the WYASL, Leeds City Art Gallery, the RIBA, and the Cecil Higgins Museum and Art Gallery in Bedford.

2. C. Holme (ed), 'Modern British domestic architecture and decoration' in *The Studio*, 8 Feb. 1901, pp. 35-8; L. Weaver, *Country Life*, 8 Feb. 1913, pp. 7-8, 11.

When Sydney Kitson (1871-1937) returned to Leeds in 1896 he joined Francis Bedford (1866-1904), who had already set up independently in 1892, and, when the latter left shortly before his death in 1904, he continued with assistants, several of whom became partners as the practice flourished until its dissolution in 1994. In the creative years before the First World War, it made major contributions to domestic architecture in Leeds, the remodelling and modernising of country houses in Yorkshire and elsewhere, the design of banks, offices and public houses, and a variety of public buildings for educational and medical usage. This high quality work continued through and after the war.[1]

Regularly featured in the architectural press from 1897, their country house for R.D. Pullar of Perth, *Brahan*, was selected for the *Studio's* special supplement in 1901, and in 1913 Lawrence Weaver included Kitson's own home, *Hillside*, in *Country Life's* 'A smaller country house of yesteryear'.[2] Significant foreign recognition came in 1904-5 in Hermann Muthesius's *Das Englische Haus*:

'Leeds has … a firm of very promising young architects who have recently built a number of country houses which are among the best of recent years. Their exteriors are more or less traditional in design, but inside they experiment in more independent ways, though without becoming fantastic, and create rooms that are striking for their comfort and their pleasant appointments and furniture and give an impression of quiet refinement. To judge from their work to date we can expect much of them.'[3]

Francis W. Bedford and Sydney D. Kitson were both younger sons of successful entrepreneurs: James Bedford of the Wood and Bedford Dyeworks in Kirkstall and James Kitson I of Kitson's locomotive works and foundry in Hunslet. The architects' eldest brothers shared this commercial flair and played a major role in civic affairs. James E. Bedford served on the Leeds Institute's council and the city corporation, becoming Lord Mayor in 1914-15, and he was an active member of the Geological Society of London. James Kitson II, Lord Airedale, also played a significant part in local affairs, being a governor of the Yorkshire College, Leeds' first Lord Mayor in 1896-7, and as Chairman of the National Liberal Federation he held the city's support for Gladstone after the party split over the Irish Home Rule.

In 1883 Francis Bedford was articled to the Leeds architect William H. Thorp (1852-1944) (*q.v.*) before entering the London office of Ernest George and Peto, arguably the country's leading training practice where Herbert Baker (1862-1946), Guy Dawber (1861-1938) and briefly Edwin Lutyens (1869-1944) were just a few of many who gained expertise from its extensive town and country house work.[4] Like George (1839-1922), Bedford was a fine draughtsman and painter in watercolours. While in that office he studied at the Westminster School of Art, the Royal Academy and at the Architectural Association Schools. He was awarded the silver medal in the Soane competition and in 1890 the Ashpital prize – coupled with an Owen Jones studentship – enabled him to undertake an extensive architectural study and sketching tour of Sicily, Italy and Spain in 1890-1. Some of the resulting drawings were published in *The Builder* and in his subsequent article, 'Colour in Architecture', in the second volume of *The Architectural Review* in 1897; twenty-seven of them were exhibited at the R.A.[5]

Bedford opened his office in Leeds in 1892, providing perspective drawings for Thorp and others, industrial buildings for his family's works, designs for notable interior decorators, particularly Marsh, Jones and Cribb, as well as a home for his brother, and semi-detached houses on Headingley sites owned by his father. By April 1895, he was recording visits to Rufus D. Pullar at Perth, the first of several commercial companies for which the practice was to build or remodel branches in northern England. He became Hon. Treasurer of the Leeds and Yorkshire Architectural Society in 1894 and its Hon. Secretary in 1895-1901, and also local Secretary of the Arts and Crafts Exhibition Society.[6]

Sydney Kitson was the younger son of his father's second marriage. When the latter died, the family left Elmet Hall to stay with their Clark cousins in Cambridge and live in Scarborough. From Charterhouse he followed his cousin Edwin Kitson Clark to Trinity College, Cambridge,

3. H. Muthesius, (D. Sharp ed.), *The English House*, Crosby, Lockwood, Staples, 1904-5, 1908-11, (trans. 1979), p. 58 and fig. 355.

4. For George and Peto see H.J. Grainger, 'The architecture of Sir Ernest George and his partners c.1860-1922', unpublished Ph.D. thesis, University of Leeds, 1985; Hilary J. Grainger, *The Architecture of Sir Ernest George*, Spire Books, 2011.

5. See Boswell [note 1], pp. 47-8.

6. See e.g. *West Yorkshire Society of Architects' Green Book*, 1935-6, 60th session pp. 20-2 and 1936-7, 61st session, pp. 8-11.

and read History. Among several close friends maintained in his later social and professional life was H.M. Fletcher (1870-1953) who from 1892 was articled to Mervyn Macartney (1853-1932), a founding member of the Art Workers' Guild and its master in 1899, and editor of the *Architectural Review* from 1906-20. Harry Fletcher was to join the London practice of Smith and Brewer, became president of the Architectural Association in 1917, and was actively involved in the development of architectural education.[7]

Two of the country's leading practices of the late nineteenth century were those of Norman Shaw and Ernest George, and Bedford and Kitson were perfectly placed to exploit this pair's innovations: Kitson served in the office of E.J. May (1853-1941), Norman Shaw's assistant and architect of the Bedford Park development from 1880-85, notable for its brick and terra-cotta 'Queen Anne' houses; Bedford was well acquainted with picturesque tile-hung and half-timbered designs from his time in George's office. Such features provided the core ingredients for Bedford and Kitson's early houses, bringing to Leeds the most fashionable London idioms. And throughout his career, Kitson's many sketchbooks demonstrate his close attention to the details of laying brick and stone, the construction of wooden staircases, doorways and panelling, and the craft of wrought ironwork, all central features of current metropolitan architectural thinking at the end of the century.[8]

In 1895 Kitson visited Naples and Rome, returning the next February to Milan and Venice. He then joined Harry Fletcher to start a grand architectural tour of the Veneto, Dalmatia, and the Ionian Islands before reaching the British School in Athens for whom they made a survey of 'Churches of Melos'.[9] Their tour was curtailed when Kitson fell seriously ill, was brought back to Italy and collected by his mother. He recovered and was subsequently employed as the clerk of works – widely seen as the ideal way to gain practical experience of a building site – during construction of St. Stephen's Nottingham, for W.D. Caroe (1857-1938), the senior architect to the Ecclesiastical Commissioners. By 1 November 1897 he had formed his partnership with Francis Bedford which lasted until the latter moved to London late in 1903. He began building his own house at Cobham, Surrey, but died of typhoid fever a few months later aged only 38.

Bedford was elected a fellow of the RIBA in 1900, and Harry Chorley (*q.v.*) proposed Kitson for election in 1906. From 1910-12, as President of the West Yorkshire Society of Architects, Kitson served on the RIBA council and after retiring to Kidlington, Oxon, he was its Hon. Secretary from 1928-34, busy years that included the passage of the Architects' Registration Act of 1931 and the building of the RIBA's new headquarters in Portland Place. In Leeds he was a co-opted member of the Art Gallery's sub-committee from 1911-34, the Hon.

7. H. Begenal, and H.M. Fletcher, *Some architectural writings of Harry Martineau Fletcher and H.M.Fletcher: a memory and a portrait*, London, privately printed, 1957.

8. The majority of these sketchbooks were donated to the RIBA, but a few later ones were retained by Kitson's daughters.

9. H.M. Fletcher and S.D. Kitson, *Journal of the British School*, Vol.II, Athens, 1895-6, p. 155.

Curator of the Philosophical and Literary Society's museum, and he gave active support to the development of architectural education at the Leeds School of Art which his practice had designed in 1901-3.[10]

The partnership's office was initially in East Parade, moving to Greek Street Chambers in 1904, and in 1908 to the Vicar Lane Chambers over their client Lloyd's Bank, where it remained, despite the rebuilding required to implement Sir Reginald Blomfield's plan for the Headrow in 1928-29, until its dissolution in 1994. By 1901 both partners were drawing an income of about £1200 annually and employing a draughtsman and /or clerk of works on their larger residential site developments, and for their public works.

From 1901-04 Martin Shaw Briggs (1882-1977) served his time as a pupil for which his clergyman father paid annual fees of £25. He spent two and a half days each week studying antique and life drawing. When he left for London with his school contemporaries – Thorp's son Ralph and John C. Procter (1882-1941) – he joined Ernest George (by now in partnership with Alfred Yeates) but 'some terrific commission for a titled client fell through', so he was laid off and set out to tour Calabria and Lecce and wrote the book that launched his career as an architectural historian.[11]

James Parish joined as an assistant in 1902 after attending the Building College and night school where he learnt technical draughtsmanship and quantity surveying. He became project architect for the tram depots built at Beckett Street and Guiseley in 1912-13, and the first new partner in June 1914. He effectively 'held the fort' after Kitson volunteered and was posted Provost-Marshal in the 10th Yorkshire Hussars to a succession of different camps in England after the 1918 armistice, and helped to organise demobilization transport in France.[12]

10. These classes were held in the premises of the former Methodist Chapel adjoining the School in Woodhouse Lane.

11. M.S. Briggs, *In the heel of Italy*, London, 1910, and see Boswell [note 1], p. 69. Procter, a brother of the painter Ernest Procter, went on to establish an avant-garde practice in Leeds where he designed a series of fine modernist houses and remodelled halls of residence for the University between the wars. He redesigned Victoria Square, in Leeds city centre, as the setting for his completely new Art Gallery and Library, to replace those of Thorp (*q.v.*) and Corson (*q.v.*). This became a casualty of the slump and the Second World War, and remained unbuilt.

12. For Parish see Shaw [note 1], pp. 6-10. Pevsner, *WY*, p. 421, notes the similarity of the Edwardian Baroque Leeds Tramways Head Offices (now Malmaison Hotel), of 1915 in Swinegate Street, to Kitson's surviving Guiseley Tram Depot, of 1914, but none of the surviving ledgers or letterbooks substantiate this plausible attribution although no other architect has been proposed.

16.1: Leeds, *Arncliffe*, Shire Oak Road, Headingley, for James E. Bedford, perspective and ground floor plan drawn by Bedford, (F.W. Bedford, 1892-4). (The Architect and Contract Reporter, *vol. 52, 25 July 1894, ff. p. 57*.)

Kitson had reduced the office after Bedford's departure but work picked up by 1909 when he employed Charles Gascoyne to draw the perspective for the Doncaster Bank and Offices that was published in *The Builder* and exhibited at the R.A. in 1912 (16.9). A gifted draughtsman like Francis Bedford and also a winner of the RIBA's Owen Jones travelling studentship, Gascoyne was to form a partnership with George Nott and in 1913 they won the second prize in a Harrogate school competition for which Kitson was the assessor; in 1915 they were one of the ten finalists for the Board of Trade Offices competition won by Vincent Harris. Gascoyne became a close family friend, and it was a bitter blow when he died of wounds as a prisoner of war in Germany late in 1917.[13]

The domestic designs of Bedford and Kitson

Francis Bedford's first important designs impressively indicate the range and versatility achieved by the joint practice over the next twenty years. *Arncliffe,* designed for his elder brother, at the top of Shire Oak Road, Headingley, is set back in a deep plot looking west over the gardens of the other houses (16.1). Built in brick with substantial decorative chimneys resembling a 'small Tudor manor house', it has a dark-panelled hall flanked by a white drawing room, both with bold plaster friezes by George Bankart of the Bromsgrove Guild, and an oak-panelled dining room with a ceiling based on the *Plantin Haus* in Antwerp. The half-butterfly plan was presaged by Norman Shaw at Chesters in 1890 and followed by several Arts and Crafts architects in the next decade. The lower service courtyard, half-timbered coach house and Dutch-garden gazebo recall works by Ernest George such as Rousden in Devon with their picturesque composition and colourful use of different building materials.

George and Peto had designed several asymmetrical and therefore freely-planned semi-detached houses in the 1880s, and these became characteristic of Bedford and Kitson's developments in Shire Oak, North Hill and Cardigan roads on land acquired by George Corson (*q.v.*), Norris Hepworth and others. The first, of 1892-4, in The Old Gardens, resembles one large house composed of a variety of tile-hung and half-timbered gables with prominent bays and latticed casements. The second is quite different, appearing to be an axially-planned 'Queen Anne' villa, nos. 2-3 (now 4-6) Shire Oak Road, in scale with adjacent large detached houses by Corson and Thorp. In fact the central door of its balanced front leads into one of the two houses, and the other has the front door at the side with its rooms placed differently but of similar dimensions.[14] Both these pairs were speculative developments for Bedford's father.

13. See Boswell [note 1], p. 69; G. Stamp, *The Great Perspectivists*, Trefoil Books, 1982, pp. 16,19, 94-5, 101.

14. Published respectively in *The Architect and Contract Reporter*, vol. 52, 25 July 1894, p. 57 and *The Builder*, vol. 70, 4 Jan. 1897, p.149.

Bedford's first major external commission was on G.W. Brown's site for the engineer Hartley Wicksteed, at *Weetwood Croft* in 1896-98, adjacent to Thorp's *Quarry Dene.* The large but low stone house is set in wide gardens with a spacious panelled stair-hall, stained glass casements, ingle-nooked reception rooms, a decorative porch and chimneys, arranged on an L-shaped plan with service wing. This follows a well-tried model for Arts and Crafts residences. However, in 1897 Bedford produced an innovative plan for Rufus Pullar's agent's house, *Dalguire*, in Harrogate. Although the tile-hung and timbered gables over a stone ground floor look familiar, they are jettied out between chimney stacks that articulate a shift in orientation between the three reception rooms, which have different garden prospects, linked by a small circulation hall – a sophisticatedly simple free-style plan.[15]

Work expanded after Kitson joined the practice but not with new commissions from his family who tended to live in older, often rented, properties that only required alterations. More recent manufacturers and a few successful professional men formed their clientele. In 1901 Shire Oak Road again provided a site for *Redhill*, built for Joseph Nicholson as a wedding present for his daughter and extended for his son-in-law in 1911. It represents the apogee of Bedford and Kitson's Home-Counties gabled and tile-hung vernacular with superbly decorated interiors. The white-painted and plastered drawing room, dark panelled hall and dining room, each have inglenooks. These fireplaces have subtly crafted repoussé copper over-mantles and fittings, as well as central heating added beneath the window seats.[16] Contrasting white and dark-panelled reception rooms may be found in many British Arts and Crafts houses as well as the Art Nouveau residences of Brussells and other northern European cities (16.2).

15. *The Builder* [note 14], p. 609.

16. See G. Stamp and A. Goulancourt, *The English House 1860-1914: the flowering of English Domestic Architecture*, Faber and Faber, 1986, pp. 216-7.

16.2: Leeds, *Redhill*, Shire Oak Road, Headingley, for Joseph Nicholson (Bedford and Kitson, 1901). (*Author*.)

16.3: Leeds, *The Red House (Gledhow Manor)*, Gledhow Lane, Chapel Allerton, for Major Bernal Bagshaw (Bedford and Kitson, 1903-4). (*Ruth Baumberg.*)

The practice had already embarked on designing at least six large houses – which necessitated the appointment of a clerk of works – in 1902-4 on land acquired by W.J. Cousins in Allerton Drive (now Allerton Park Road), Leeds. Some, like *The Rookery* and *Webton Court* were built in stone with tile-hung or half-timbered upper floors and panelled stair-halls in the picturesque manorial vernacular already perfected by Bedford. Others were in red brick with stone dressings and 'Queen Anne' fenestration that Kitson had adopted for his brother-in-law at St Aidan's Vicarage off the Roundhay Road in 1900.[17] These were the kind of spacious, well-fitted and refined residences that captured the attention and praise of Hermann Muthesius in 1904-5.

At *Hillside*, Kitson remodelled and enlarged the house below Gledhow Hall that his brother had given him when he married in 1903 in ways that Lawrence Weaver was to commend as 'a very successful and agreeable adaptation of not very promising materials'.[18] The gallery/drawing room had a moulded-plaster ceiling, Georgian furniture, paintings of Italy by David Roberts and Edward Lear, and an exquisitely embroidered hanging, worked by Kitson's mother from a design by Sir Robert Lorimer (1864-1929).

The Red House (1903-4, now *Gledhow Manor*), on the opposite bank of the valley by Allerton Drive, Leeds, provided the opportunity for a totally new design on 'Wrenaissance' lines. Major Bernal Bagshawe, the chairman of Leeds Forge Co., wanted to entertain and to exhibit his large collection of Bartolozzi portrait prints. This grander manner of Edwardian Baroque was becoming general in public buildings and accompanied a greater architectural respect for early Georgian work. The practice used Hopton Wood stone for the plinth and portico columns, red Woodville brick from Leicester, and Ancaster stone dressings with sash windows (16.3). The symmetrical garden fronts are differentiated from the service wing by a change at roof-level from a

17. Now demolished but echoed on a smaller scale in 1902 at All Hallows Vicarage in Hyde Park, Leeds, where the bulls-eye rear window comes straight from Kitson's 1892-93 Sketchbook.

18. Weaver [note 2].

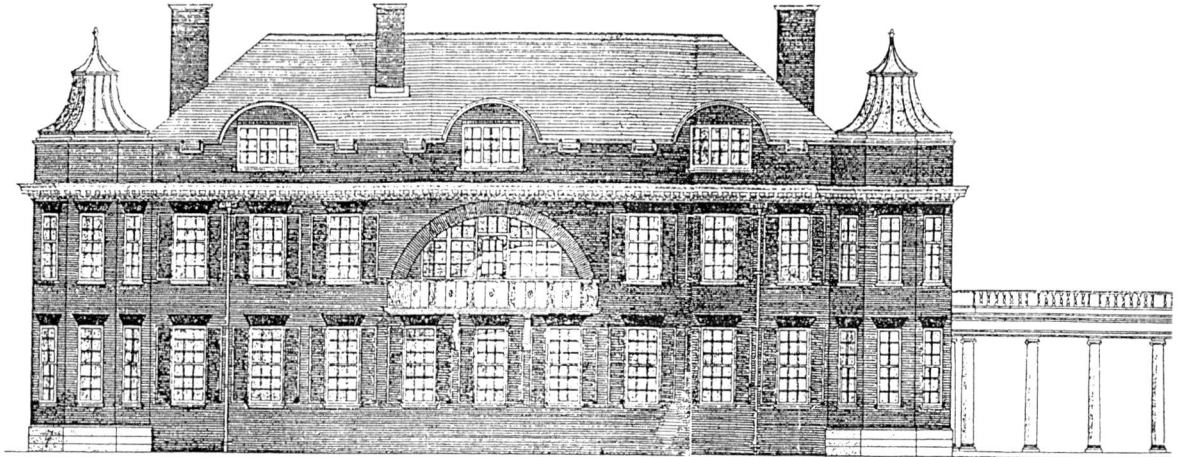

EAST ELEVATION

dentilled cornice to guttering supported by the kind of tendril-brackets used by Charles Voysey and his contemporaries. The stable block and motor-house has an even more characteristically sweeping Art Nouveau arch.

The plan provides for a rather grand effect inside. From the spacious portico and vestibule one enters a great stained glass and galleried atrium with a massive fireplace of colourful Derbyshire marbles. The main rooms on the ground floor lead out under carved over-doors and are furnished with fine fireplaces of polished woods, and marbles or painted relief panels. Opposite the entrance an imperial staircase mounts to a tall window before breaking into two flights to the gallery through a colonnaded screen with the bedroom corridors on each side. All the roseate-bowered glass is probably by George Walton of Glasgow. Turquoise tiles line the bathroom walls. It is superbly crafted inside and out.[19]

Redcourt (1899-1902), a large brick and stone-dressed seaside mansion, had already established this opulent style for the practice on the esplanade at Scarborough, graced with Baroque turrets and a double colonnaded loggia around the formal garden (16.4). It was built for the foundry proprietor and engineer Colonel F.W. Tannett Walker of Leeds, for whom Bedford and Kitson were also altering and extending *Carr Manor* in Stonegate Road, Leeds, which Professor E.S. Prior (1852-1932) had designed in 1881 for Dr T.C. Albutt, in Yorkshire stone.[20]

The versatility and sensitivity of the practice to new ideas in design is well exemplified by the history of *Brahan,* their country house for Rufus Pullar at Perth. Bedford's first project in 1896 was an Arts and

16.4: Scarborough, *Redcourt*, The Esplanade, (Bedford and Kitson, 1899-1902). (The Builder, *86, 5 March 1904, ff. p. 297.*)

19. *Architectural Review,* vol. 16, 1904, pp. 216, 219-222. However Talbot-Griffiths recalled Allerton Drive in the 1920s as 'profiteers' park'.

20. *The Builder,* vol. 86, 5 March 1904, pp. 256-257. Carr Manor was further remodelled by Kitson in 1914-15 for Sir Berkeley, later Lord, Moynihan, F.R.S. and columns re-erected in the garden were from a demolition site for Lloyd's Bank in Stockton.

Crafts Tudor stone-built mansion, with extensive store and service wings, but a symmetrical garden front of bay-windowed main rooms flanking a transverse hall of similar size, a compact version of Batsford Park where Bedford had assisted Guy Dawber for George and Peto.[21] Yet within two years he had totally revised both the plan and elevations. Coursed stone walls and mullions gave way to white harled walls, wide bands of windows and half-timbered gables. The main rooms were now arranged along the garden fronts served by a central circulation hall to their rear. Marsh, Jones and Cribb provided the panelling and George Walton and other Scottish craftsmen the stained glass and metalwork. Both designs were published and the results critically assessed in *The Studio* and by Muthesius.[22] They had achieved one of the finest Scottish interiors, exemplifying the co-ordinated combination of architectural design and craftsmanship for which Robert Lorimer and C.R. Mackintosh have become renowned (16.5, 16.6).

This significant development in the practice's approach to house design is also marked by two Leeds houses in North Hill Road: *Lincombe* (1898-9), built for H.M. Hepworth, the clothing chain retailer and later chairman of the City Art Gallery's sub-committee; and *High Garth* (1901-2). They demonstrate the impact of Voysey and Baillie Scott's published designs and buildings. Bedford collaborated with Mrs. Currer Briggs in arranging Arts and Crafts exhibitions and would have been familiar with *Broadleys* which Voysey had just built for her above Windermere. Both are rendered with deep eaves over their emphatic lines of windows. *Lincombe* has a green-stone slate roof and stone mullions (16.7). The white wooden framed windows of *High Garth* were repeated in Bedford's last house, *Headingley*, when he removed to Cobham in Surrey, and there he totally abandoned a four-square plan in favour of a single row of reception and bedrooms on the

21. *The Builder,* vol. 76, 11 Feb 1899, p.145 and vol. 86, 14 May 1904, p. 524. See also [note 2]. It was demolished in the 1960's. For Batsford Park, see Grainger [note 4]; J. Franklin, *The Gentleman's Country House and its Plan, 1835-1914*, RKP, 1981, pp. 181-11.

22. See [notes 1 and 2].

16.5: Perth, *Brahan*, for Rufus D. Pullar, garden-front perspective for the second and executed design drawn by Bedford (Bedford and Kitson, 1898.) (The Builder, *14 May 1904, ff. p. 524.*)

south (garden) front with hall/gallery and services behind them on Voyseyan lines.[23] Kitson used rather similar elevations for the houses he designed for Henry Barran in West Park Crescent in 1907 and 1909 on some of the land retained after his client had acquired Roundhay Park for the public use of the city. Their restrained and apparently simple lines may be compared with those of Ernest Newton and other leading London architects reviving Georgian vernacular domestic designs at this time.

The commercial work of the practice.

Almost all the industrial premises for the Bedford's dyeworks and the Kitsons' iron foundry at Monkbridge have been demolished as has Chorley and Connon's (*q.v.*) locomotive works for Kitsons at Hunslet. For over seventy years the main stays of the practice were the branch banks for the Yorkshire Banking Company and Tetley's tied public houses still to be seen over the north of England. However, many of these were alterations to existing buildings and their carefully designed interiors have subsequently been stripped out, so that one can no longer appreciate the unified composition of their bold polished wooden counters, metal lights and screen-fittings, and floor mosaics.

Within six months of Kitson's arrival one notes work for the Yorkshire Banking Company with which his family had been closely associated for three generations, and which was soon to merge with the Midland Bank. From 1901 came similar commissions for Lloyd's Bank, and then Martin's Bank. Kitson published three designs for banks, offices and shops in *The Architect* and *The Builder* which illustrate this kind of work. In 1909 a shop with offices were designed for the Indian

16.6: Perth, *Brahan*, billiard room inglenook with carving by Hayes of Edinburgh (Bedford and Kitson, 1898.) (*C. Home (ed.),* Modern British Domestic Architecture and Decoration: Studio special number, *1901, ff. p. 32.*)

23. *The Builder,* vol. 85, 29 Aug 1903, p. 228; *Architectural Review,* vol. 18, 1905, pp. 84-8.

16.7: Leeds, *Lincombe*, 7 North Hill Road, Headingley, for H.M. Hepworth (Bedford and Kitson, 1899). (*Kitson and partners' archive, c.1900.*)

rubber manufacturer, Thornton and Co. in Briggate, Leeds, extended to match in 1922. The advantage of a faience facing was the relative ease with which it shed the sooty deposits for which the city had become notorious (16.8).

In 1912 a bank with office chambers above was designed for Colonel Somerville which was taken by Lloyd's in Doncaster High Street, and another for Lloyd's in Keighley. Each had a Burmantoft's faience or a stone curtain front on a steel-framed structure. In August 1910 *The Builder* devoted its monthly engineering review to technical drawings of the Coignet system skeleton that Kitson had used for the Post Office House above Tetley's Cloth Hall Tavern in Infirmary Street, Leeds, and applauded his use of traditional materials for cladding 'until an appropriate and pleasing architectural style has been evolved for reinforced buildings'.[24] Each was given a symmetrical Classical façade, with a rusticated ground floor surmounted by a giant order of engaged columns and an entablature supporting an attic parapet and inscribed tablet. The doors at either side led to the chambers above or a banking hall furnished with broad mahogany counters, decorative fittings and a mosaic floor. There is a well-proportioned balance and logic in these Neoclassical designs which is demonstrated in Charles Gascoyne's masterly perspective wash drawing for the Doncaster premises (16.9).

Kitson's marriage to Winifred Tetley, the elder daughter of the chairman of Joshua Tetley and Sons, brought in the other major commercial client which was embarking on the expansion of the brewery to supply its increasing chain of public houses that the practice

24. *The Builder,* vol. 99, 1910, pp. 243-44.

16.8: Leeds, Thornton and Co., India Rubber Manufacturers, Briggate (Bedford and Kitson, 1909-10 and 1922), with later ground floor windows. (*Ruth Baumberg.*)

16.9: Doncaster, Lloyd's Bank and Chambers, High Street, perspective drawing by Charles Gascoyne (S.D. Kitson, 1912.) (The Builder, *102, 29 May 1912, p. 604.*)

was commissioned to remodel and maintain. Their Tudorbethan pubs with convivial-huntsmen signs may still be seen but Kitson's neo-Georgian industrial plant has gone, commended by *The Builder* as showing 'how architectural character can be given to a building fulfilling simple practical requirements.'[25] His last building design was the Queen's Arms on the Harrogate Road of 1926, for which he was recalled by Tetley to enhance Chapel Allerton with a roadhouse in this neo-Georgian style. He had already provided a Caroline extension to George Corson's (*q.v.*) *Foxhill* for his father-in-law's home in 1913 15. An echo of the brewery buildings may be found in the turreted garage, now a bar, of the Ripon Spa Hydro Hotel of 1906. The offset residential wings splay out from the reception core of the main building which has Kitson's characteristic volutes flanking each dormer window.

25. *The Builder*, vol. 100, 1911, p. 495.

The whole design pleasantly presages the post-war lidos of the Modern Movement with the garage providing a playful point on the roadside front.

The public commissions of the practice

Despite the widespread use of competitions in this period in the selection of architects for public buildings, Bedford and Kitson entered only a handful, such as those in 1899 for Bradford's Cartwright Hall (1899) and for Leeds's Armley Library, in neither of which were they successful. However, those they won were for substantial local buildings of significance. Since 1896 they had remodelled buildings for the Blind Institute and the Poor Law Overseers in Leeds, and in 1901 they built the first of several structures at Carlton Barracks. But, like the creation of the Leeds Maternity Hospital from two large villas in Hyde Terrace, they are not of architectural note. Three new commissions placed them in a higher category: the Dewsbury Road Library, Police and Fire Stations (1901) for Leeds City Corporation; the School of Art for the Leeds Institute of Science, Art and Literature (1901-3); and the Leeds Public Dispensary which was won in a limited competition in 1902.

Dewsbury Road provided a corner site with one long frontage like those in Woodhouse and Chapeltown which Thorp had filled with more elaborately decorated, similarly multipurpose, buildings. At Dewsbury Road, the main brick and stone front is articulated by the gabled corner and the carved and pedimented library entrance which is glazed with civic owls in George Walton's style. After the Great War a sense of place was added when Kitson's War Memorial Cross was

16.10: Leeds, library with police and fire stations, Dewsbury Road, remodelled internally for the library and probation office, c.1993. (Bedford and Kitson, 1901-3). Kitson's War Memorial was erected opposite in 1922. (*Ruth Baumberg.*).

erected between the library and St. Peter's church in 1922. As in their houses, the subtle details of the cut stonework which give different levels of emphasis to the various doorways and the colourful brickwork tied into a coherent composition by the dressed stone banding, gives distinction to an otherwise modest set of functions (16.10).

The Leeds School (now College) of Art (16.11) extended the range of technical educational facilities offered by the Leeds Institute in competition with the Leeds School Board, both of which were soon to be incorporated in the city's Department of Education when the 1902 Education Act was implemented. A committee, led by W.H. Thorp and J.E. Bedford, inspected several schools that incorporated craft with art training including Glasgow, Birmingham and the Central School in London. As at Dewsbury Road, Bedford and Kitson used Accrington

16.11: Leeds, School (now College) of Art, Vernon Street, studio north front and entrance (Bedford and Kitson, 1901-3; mosaic by Professor Gerald Moira). (*Ruth Baumberg.*)

brick banded and dressed with Ancaster stone, but a functional emphasis is given to the Vernon Street front by its vertical studio lights with their riveted metal frame exposed to view. The lower panes of the tall lights were ingeniously redirected to add light to the lower floors and even the round window between the studios had a specific function – to illuminate the models' changing cubicle! The Gibbsian doorcase of the main entrance is surmounted by a gold-backed mosaic of 'Painting and Sculpture' by Gerald Moira, professor at the recently reformed Royal College of Art. Made of Rust's vitreous mosaic, this was later adopted by Frank Brangwyn for his great apse commission from R.H. Kitson at St. Aidan's Church, Leeds, dedicated in 1916.[26]

The site available for the Public Dispensary charity presented an even greater challenge than the constricted ex-playground for the Art School. North Street was being redeveloped by the clothing industry, many of whose poor and often immigrant workers lived nearby. The dispensary needed to provide consulting rooms and staff quarters as well as In- and Out-patient facilities. The main street frontage was short so the bulk of the building would have to be between the narrow lanes on the hill behind (16.12). They designed a five-storeyed residential and office block at the front with the Baroque *gravitas* of contemporary metropolitan work by Belcher, Gotch and Blomfield. The long floors of the medical wards and waiting rooms reduce in number as the hill

26. See D.M. Boswell, 'Arts and Crafts: a new School of Art for Leeds' in C. Miller (ed.) *Behind the Mosaic: one hundred years of art education,* Leeds City Art Gallery, 2003, pp. 17-43; D.M. Boswell, 'Frank Brangwyn and his patrons' in L. Horner and G. Naylor (eds), *Frank Brangwyn 1867-1956,* Leeds Museums and Galleries, 2006, pp. 156-85.

16.12: **Leeds, Public Dispensary, North Street (Bedford and Kitson, 1902-4).** (*Ruth Baumberg.*)

rises so the casualty department was situated at the bottom entered near North Street, and the outpatients above with their entrance at the top of the lane overseen by an accomplished sculpture of 'Hygeia', probably carved by Caldwell Spruce who was to work on later public buildings for the practice. The way in which the whole design is articulated as if in separate blocks is explained by the fact that its great length was originally viewed up the narrow roads on each side and not, as now, across the cavities of the ring road as if this side was the main front.[27]

The Public Dispensary was by far their largest commission, so it was probably on the strength of this, and his published house designs, that Bedford left for London. A decade later Kitson designed two more large and equally enduringly serviceable buildings for public authorities, both of which became involved in the war effort. Although G.W. Atkinson (1860-1950) won the commission to build the educational block and one hostel for the Leeds Education Department's teacher training college at Beckett Park in 1909, Kitson designed both the men's Cavendish and Fairfax Halls in 1911-15, for which Caldwell Spruce carved their stone embellishments. These were commandeered to become the 2nd Northern General Hospital for military casualties for the duration of the Great War, which delayed the completion of work on the King Edward VII Memorial Wing of wards, begun in 1915, as the first major departure from G.G. Scott's remarkable Gothic Revival design for the Leeds General Infirmary (see Chapter 18). Here Kitson relied on a stripped 'Wrenaissance' style of brick with some stone dressings and long, open wards that have since been easily adaptable for the use of different categories of patient. However it fits rather bleakly between the rich ornament of Scott and the refined twirls of the hospital's Brotherton Wing, a much later post-war building of the practice.[28]

The decorative and ecclesiastical work of the practice

Bedford and Kitson both took a scholarly interest in architecture with an attention to detail revealed in their sketches and note-books, and in Bedford's article on Baldassare Peruzzi (1481-1536).[29] He transformed the interior decoration of St. James's, Cross York Street, Leeds in 1894[30] and the furnishing of Brodrick's Congregational Church on Headingley Hill in 1903-4. Kitson undertook much ancillary work at St. Aidan, Roundhay Road (designed by the Newcastle architects R.J. Johnson and A. Crawford Hick, 1891-4) which included the vicarage, Clayton Halls, side chapel rails, and the wrought-iron font cover (16.13) made by Silas Paul of the School of Art in 1914, all but the last recently demolished. The impressive feature of both the original furnishings by Crawford Hick, and subsequent presentations like the lectern, font and

27. *Architectural Review*, vol. 15, Dec 1904, p.276.

28. See various chapters in L. Beckett (ed.), *City of Leeds Training College: Continuity and Change 1907-2007*, Leeds Metropolitan University, 2007; M. Parsons, *The General Infirmary at Leeds: a Pictorial History*, William Sessions, 2003.

29. *Journal of the RIBA*, vol. ix, third series, 1902, pp.165-86.

30. The building was erected in 1793 and demolished in 1952. (see T. Friedman, *Church Architecture in Leeds, 1700-1799*, PTS, 1997, pp. 157-63.) Bedford's father had earlier worshipped in this octagonal Classical chapel where the partnership carried out an acclaimed restoration which included the elaborate plaster ceiling.

16.13: Leeds, St Aidan, Roundhay Road, font cover, made by Silas Paul (S.D. Kitson, 1914). (*Author.*)

cover, is that they all adopt a bold, grand scale appropriate in such a great, spacious basilica.

For St Matthew, Chapel Allerton, Leeds, Kitson also designed chapel furnishings and the Parish Hall above Woodland Road of 1913, a lively building topped with urns and a cupola. But he only designed one church, St Wilfrid, Harehills, Leeds (1906), and that remained unbuilt until 1927-32, and on a reduced scale, by James Parish. The Great War resulted in a demand for war memorials throughout Leeds and West Yorkshire. Kitson responded with at least thirteen: finely detailed obelisks and crosses in white limestone outside churches – and tablets inside them – as well as personal memorials like the carved font cover for St John's, Adel in 1921.[31]

The partners were regularly commissioned to alter, refit and decorate the large suburban villas and country houses rented or bought by the Bedford, Kitson and Tetley family members and their friends, the Barran family, as well as other local industrialists and professional men, but few were published. Some notable examples represent this significant element of Kitson's work.

Dumbleton Hall near Evesham is a neo-Jacobean mansion designed by G.S. Repton(1780-1858) in 1830, for which the practice was commissioned to undertake major works for Miss Eyres, later Lady Monsell, the heiress of a Leeds stuff-mill fortune, from 1903. In addition to the richly plastered rooms by George Bankart, these included a group of estate cottages so beautifully built in Cotswold stone as to earn the critical soubriquet 'The Palaces' from their client, as well as a dairy, the neatly refurnished parish church at the gates, and the installation of electricity (16.14). In 1905 Wormington Grange was altered to become this client's dower house.[32]

Kitson became an authority on the Georgian York architect John Carr (1723-1807) through commissions to remodel and modernise several of his country houses. In 1909-10 he altered Hazlewood Castle near Tadcaster for the Leeds solicitor, E.O. Simpson, levelling the Jacobean wing, revealing the Gothic window embrasures in Carr's otherwise Classical great hall, and installing a buffet in the dining room. It is difficult to detect how many of Carr's moulded doorcases and other decorative features may in fact have been restored by Kitson to this and other houses, such as Brandsby Hall for R.S. Pearson in 1914-15. At Lord Airedale's homes, Gledhow Hall and 3, Cadogan Place in London, he introduced a finely panelled library and other Georgian-style Classical fittings and plasterwork in 1911[33] (16.15).

Such work culminated in the prestigious and lucrative commission to restore and refit Goldsborough Hall, near Knaresborough, for Viscount Lascelles and Princess Mary following their marriage in 1922. Robert Adam had preceded Kitson in converting a great-chambered Jacobean manor into a Georgian mansion, so Kitson proceeded to

31. e.g. The cross in Dewsbury Road, the obelisk at the Shire Oak, and the tablet in St.Michael's, Headingley, of 1921-2. Extensive searches have failed to find who carved the Adel font cover but the unexplained attribution since 1960 to Eric Gill must be discounted.

32. See Boswell [note 1], pp. 67-8; D. Verey and A. Brooks, *Glousectershire 2: The Vale and Forest of Dean*, Yale, 2002, pp. 342-4.

33. e.g. S.D. Kitson, 'Carr of York', *Journal of the RIBA*, vol xviii, 3rd series, no. 6, 1910, pp. 241-66.

16.14: Dumbleton Hall, Glos. '*The Palaces*', four stone cottages for Miss Eyres, later Lady Monsell (Bedford and Kitson, 1903). (*Author.*)

restore some of both these aspects outside and in the rooms' decoration, including fitted furniture for the princess's bedroom and her husband's dressing room, and a nursery suite over the concealed vault of the old great chamber.[34]

Princess Mary's enthusiastic gratitude encouraged Kitson to remove his family to London and open an office there but the onset of severe tuberculosis ended his hope for such a development of the practice. Despite remaining active as senior partner until 1931, he designed few more buildings although he continued as architectural adviser to Wakefield and other dioceses, and played an important role in the development of the RIBA and its library's collection of drawings. This last was a by-product of Kitson's research into the life and work of eminent late-Georgian watercolour painter, John Sell Cotman (1782–1842). Following Kitson's retirement, under Parish, Ledgard, Pyman and later partners, the practice still had sixty-three productive years ahead.[35]

An assessment of the practice.

The practice introduced the main national developments in domestic design to Leeds – a robust and colourful type of hitherto Home-Counties vernacular housing, a freely-planned form of asymmetrical semi-detached villas, and a holistic Arts and Crafts approach to interior decoration and fitted furnishing, which was taken up by the architectural press, as was the work of their counterparts in other British cities such as Chamberlain and Bidlake in Birmingham, and Edgar Wood in Huddersfield and Middleton, Lancs. 'Queen Anne' brickwork was followed in the new century by a more opulent and spacious

16.15: Leeds, Gledhow Hall, library doorcase with Kitson Arms, for Lord Airedale, the architects' eldest half-brother, carver unknown (S.D. Kitson, 1911). (*Kitson and Partners' Archive, c.1911.*)

34. Kitson had come to know Viscount Lascelles on the hunting field. He treasured Princess Mary's letters. By the time she and Lord Harewood moved into Harewood House, he had retired from active practice and it was Herbert Baker, Bedford's friend from the George and Peto days, who restored it for their use.

35. S.D. Kitson, *The Life of John Sell Cotman,* Faber and Faber, 1937, reprinted by Rodart Reproductions, 1982. See also Boswell, D.M. and Millar, C. (1992) *Cotmania and Mr Kitson,* Leeds City Art Galleries, 1992; Shaw [note 1].

'Wrenaissance' style, with stone dressings and carving which Kitson continued into the Great War and Noel Pyman thereafter.

This was also the style adopted for most of their major public works. Rolled-steel-joists, long used industrially, made free planning possible, and in Leeds School of Art they were used in a demonstrative and almost decorative way. Their banks, office blocks, shops and substantial medical buildings also used the available patent reinforced concrete frameworks clad in Neoclassical screens of tiles and faience, brick or stone. These facades were delicately detailed with clearly defined lines that enhance their use of colourful materials and the play of light across their dressed stone elements and the occasional use of stained glass or mosaic.

Care was taken in the functional design of their buildings, which is obvious not only in the wide range of their different plans, but from the few letter-books surviving from the period of the war and the later 1920's. The materials used and the fittings installed have withstood a century of constant private and public use. At *The Red House* and *Redhill* the central heating radiators are still working well as are the casement latches and door fittings. This attention to detail and robust craftsmanship is as apparent as the comfortable spaciousness of their designs. Although less remains of the variety but co-ordinated unity of their decorative interiors, one can appreciate Bedford and Kitson's reputation as architects of some of the finer smaller houses of their day, catering for affluent and discriminating families of taste. Once the war was over, this was also applied to their design of the large public housing estate at Hawksworth Wood, above Kirkstall, Leeds. Here they incorporated stone and brick houses, terraces and groups of flats, a shopping centre and a church designed by W.D. Caroe with whom Kitson had begun his architectural career.[36] The partners' wealth of historical, material and technical architectural knowledge, combined with a practical response to their clients' functional requirements, and an attention to detail in both design and craftsmanship, has given an enduring quality to Bedford and Kitson's houses and their various public and other buildings.

36. The first of these 'Homes for Heroes' date from 1919 with St Mary's church only following in 1932-5. It is not clear whether the house and flat plans were designed by the practice or adopted from recommended models. See Shaw [note 1], p. 9; Pevsner, *WY*, p. 512.

Catalogue

The following is a select list of major works. A full list of the practice's 254 substantial commissions, accompanied by dates, clients, contractors and sources, can be found in Boswell [note 1].

The Bedford and Kitson partnership lasted from 1896 to 1904. Earlier projects (listed below) are by Bedford working alone, while those after 1904 are the sole responsibility of Kitson.

LEEDS, *Arncliffe*, Shire Oak Road, 1892-4.
LEEDS, *The Old Gardens*, Cardigan Road, 1892-4.
PERTH, Perth and Kinross, *Brahan*, 1895-1902.
LEEDS, *Weetwood Croft*, Weetwood, 1896-8.
HARROGATE, *Dalguire*, 1897.
LEEDS, *Lincombe*, North Hill Road, 1898-9.
THIRSK, Yorkshire Bank, 1898-1900.
SCARBOROUGH, *Redcourt*, 1899-1902.
LEEDS, St. Aidan's vicarage, off Roundhay Rd, 1900.

LEEDS, *Redhill*, Shire Oak Road, 1901 and 1911.
LEEDS, *High Garth*, North Hill Road, 1901-2.
LEEDS, *Hillside*, Gledhow, 1901-2.
LEEDS, free library with police and fire stations, Dewsbury Road, 1901-3.
LEEDS, Leeds School of Art, Vernon Street, 1901-3.
LEEDS, *Webton Court*, Allerton Park Road, 1901-3.
LEEDS, Public Dispensary, North Street, 1902-4.
LEEDS, *Red House*, Gledhow Lane, 1903-4.
LEEDS, All Hallow's vicarage, Hyde Park. 1903-4
LEEDS, Congregational Chapel, Headingley Hill, organ case and furnishings, 1903-4.
DUMBLETON HALL, Gloucestershire, alterations, cottages, dairy and church furnishings, 1903-4.
RIPON, Spa Hydro Hotel, 1906-7.
LEEDS, St. Wilfrid, Harehills, 1906 and 1927.
TADCASTER, Hazlewood Castle, staircase hall and other alterations, 1909-10.

LEEDS, premises for Thornton and Co., 50 Briggate. 1909 and 1922.
LONDON, 3 Cadogan Place, alterations, 1910.
LEEDS, Gledhow Hall, alterations and internal fittings, 1911.
LEEDS, St Matthew, Chapel Allerton, panelling and side chapel work with paintings by Charles Gascoyne, 1911.
DONCASTER, Lloyd's Bank, 1911-12.
LEEDS, Beckett's Park Teacher Training College, Cavendish and Fairfax Halls, 1911-14.
LEEDS, Parish Hall, Chapel Allerton, 1913.
LEEDS, *Foxhill*, Weetwood, alterations, 1913-15.
LEEDS, Beckett Street Tram Depot, 1914.
GUISELEY, nr Leeds, tram depot, 1914.
BRANDSBY HALL, nr Easingwold, NY, alterations, 1914-19.
LEEDS, General Infirmary, King Edward VII Memorial Wing, 1915-21.
KNARESBOROUGH, Goldsborough Hall, alterations, 1923.
LEEDS, The Queen's Arms, Harrogate Road, Chapel Allerton, 1926–7, built 1931–3.

17. *Percy Robinson (1869-1950)*

JANET DOUGLAS

Today Percy Robinson is best remembered for his books, *Relics of old Leeds* (1896)[1] and *Leeds: old and new* (1926), because the sketches he drew to illustrate these texts are frequently reproduced in other historical publications as well as being sold as prints in their own right. Yet Robinson was a talented architect with a mission 'to beautify' the city of his birth. A number of his impressive commercial buildings continue to make a major contribution to the streets of the city centre but often go unnoticed because their ground floors have been 'modernised' in line with retailing fashions.

Published sources on Percy Robinson are sparse and are intriguingly vague about his background. The 1861 Census reveals that his mother, Emily, was a milliner, the daughter of a tailor who lived in West Street, a poor neighbourhood that has largely disappeared under the new road system around Westgate. Later that year she married Daniel Robinson, an assistant in his father's grocer's shop on the Upper Headrow, but two years after the birth of Percy – their only child – in 1869, Emily was back living with her parents in West Street and was still working as a milliner. Daniel died in 1876 and the following year Emily married Tom Carter Moxon, a publican at the Castle Inn, Lisbon Street. By 1891 widowed for a second time, Emily and Percy Robinson were living on Park Lane, and Percy was described in the census as 'an architect'. He had trained in Leeds with William Henry Beevers (1855-1933) and during his apprenticeship attended art classes at the Wortley Mechanics Institute where he was awarded first prizes in government-sponsored examinations in freehand and model drawing.[2] On the

1. *Relics of Old Leeds* was dedicated to Edmund Wilson, the founder of the Thoresby Society of which Robinson was a member. He explained in his preface to the book that its purpose was 'to serve as a record of some of the landmarks of Leeds which are gradually disappearing before the ever advancing tide of modern improvements and requirements'.

2. *LM*, 15 Aug 1885.

completion of his pupilage, Robinson worked for two years in the office of Thomas Winn (d.1908) and for a year with the Batley architect Harry Bagshaw Buckley before setting up his own practice at 72 Albion Street in 1890. Between 1905-1914 Robinson was in partnership with William Alban Jones (1875-1960) with an office in Yorkshire Post Chambers, Albion Street, and then with the little-known John James Birkinshaw; in the late 1920s he was with William Whitehead.

Art, Architecture and Robinson's Architectural Philosophy

With an underprivileged childhood spent in the squalid streets of the West End, it is difficult to know from whom or where Percy Robinson acquired the cultural capital that was to manifest itself in an amazing range of interests. A member of the Leeds Practical Naturalists Club, he edited the club's magazine and it was probably there that he met Edmund Bogg (1850-1933), the owner of an artists' materials shop and prolific author of North Country guidebooks, many of them with illustrations by Robinson.[3] It was Bogg who founded the bohemian Leeds Savage Club – sometimes known as the Attic Art Club – in 1897, bringing together 'the best local talent in the city' in the fields of art, music and literature.[4] Robinson was a founder member of the club as were the sculptor Edward Caldwell Spruce (1849-1923), the artists Mark Senior (1862-1927) and Owen Bowen (1873-1967), and the famous Leeds cartoonist, Kester (J.H. Dodgson, d.1953). Robinson's future partner, 'Billy' Alban Jones was also 'a Savage'. Under their leader 'Big Chief' Bogg, the Savages met in their American Indian head-gear for 'pow-wows' in various cafes, pubs and members' homes where they consumed great bowls of stews, drank plenty of 'firewater' and smoked innumerable 'pipes of peace'. A coterie of members rented the top floor of a house in South Parade for twice-weekly life classes, whilst weekends were often spent at their 'attic abode', a picturesque cottage in Barwick in Elmet, or tramping the countryside, sketching the landscape and camping out of doors. Organising musical evenings and public concerts formed a regular part of their activities – Robinson himself had a fine voice and on at least one occasion sang after the Leeds and Yorkshire Architects Society AGM.[5]

There was some over-lapping membership between the Savage Club and the Leeds Arts Club established in 1903 by Alfred Orage (1873-1934) and Holbrook Jackson (1874-1948): Robinson, Caldwell Spruce, Mark Senior, 'Kester' and Billy Jones were members of both clubs. The Arts Club according to the cultural historian Tom Steele was 'one of the most interesting sites of radical thought and experimental art outside of London. It popularised the introduction of Nietzschean thought, cradled the early formation of Guild Socialism, exhibited impressionist and post-impressionist painting …'.[6] Amongst

3. The first of these books 'A Thousand Miles in Wharfedale' was published in 1892. In 1895, a group of Robinson's drawings were shown at the Royal Academy.

4. Various papers relating to the Savage Club are located in the Family and Local Studies Library, Leeds Central Library at SRQ 367 L517.

5. Leeds and Yorkshire Architects Society, *Green Book 1906-7*. Percy Robinson's wife, Elizabeth whom he married in 1892, was a member of the Leeds Amateur Operatic Company.

6. Tom Steele, *Alfred Orage and the Leeds Arts Club*, Scolar Press, 1990, p. 98. In 1905 Robinson was the Club chairman and remained on its management committee until 1909.

the intellectual celebrities who visited the Club was George Bernard Shaw who, in February 1905, told his audience that 'Art is a thing that can finally make you believe that Leeds as it exists at present is a very intolerable place, that it is a place where no decent individual ought to live and that you individually have no right to be alive at all. It even has the power, finally, of driving you, under certain provocation, to burn down your town'. Shaw's cynicism apart, his insistence on the social responsibility of art and its capacity to inspire action was not lost on Robinson when two months later he gave his own lecture to the Arts Club entitled 'Street Architecture and its Defects'.

Despite the avant-garde intellectualism of the Leeds Arts Club, part of its purpose was to make cultural interventions in the life of the city that might have practical outcomes. For members, notions of citizenship were bound up with creating 'The City Beautiful', a dialectic process in which beautiful cities sprang from beautiful ideas and would in turn produce beautiful people.[7] Campaigning on a non-partisan basis, they sought to influence the city council, those who commissioned new buildings and the local architectural profession. In 1904 for example, the club organised an exhibition of architects' designs for houses, and there were a number of talks about the Arts and Crafts Movement, and garden cities.[8] Such themes informed Robinson's talk to the club on 'Street Architecture and its Defects' in which he blamed the lack of arts education and lack of 'a collective appreciation of art' for the unplanned ugliness of British cities. Buildings, according to Robinson, should straightforwardly and simply express their purpose, whilst at the same time relating to the general streetscape in terms of height and scale. Like some architects before and many afterwards, Robinson criticised the City Council for its lack of vision and the petty restrictions that hampered the development of the profession. His talk did, however, end on a more optimistic note: the advent of electricity would allow factories to decentralise with the result that the city centre would become a cleaner and more colourful place.

Robinson was twice elected president of Leeds and Yorkshire Architects Society (1908 and 1909) and in his 1909 and 1910 presidential addresses, he reiterated and further developed many of these arguments. Unlike the rather bland addresses of previous presidents, in 1909 – for example – he appealed for a closer relationship between architects, painters, sculptors and craftsmen, and welcomed the Housing and Town Planning Act. A year later, he gave members an account of a lecture he had delivered to the Health Congress that had recently taken place in Leeds. Speaking on the subject of 'Town Planning and its Relation to Health', he had urged that 'due consideration be given to the artistic side of all city developments, pointing out the relationship or interdependence of beauty and health

7. Notions of urban beautification shaping behaviour and inspiring civic loyalty were key elements in the American City Beautiful Movement of the 1890s and early twentieth century. A City Beautiful conference was held in Liverpool in 1907.

8. LYAS, *Green Book 1904-5*.

and the influence of the environment upon the mind and life of the people.' Returning to the theme of the need for urban planning, Robinson recounted how 'Leeds like many other cities, has grown in a haphazard fashion without a definite plan of development … We have dog-legged streets wandering about in an apparently aimless fashion and leading to nowhere in particular. We have our public buildings scattered about in all directions and cramped up on ill-considered sites. Our Library and Art Gallery are in a back street …', and with an uncanny prescience he observed that 'Civic Architecture has even a commercial value apart from the influence on the lives of the citizens. This fact is usually lost sight of by the man absorbed in business pursuits. He fails to realise that it pays to have beautiful streets and beautiful cities, a fact which, if Leeds is to become the shopping centre of the North as is the ambition of our trades people, it is well they should bear in mind.'[9]

17.1: Leeds, Firemen's Flats, Park Street (Percy Robinson, 1909) dem.

If some of Robinson's ideas chime with urban Modernism, so far as his own architectural practice was concerned, he had a living to make and without wealthy patrons could not stray too far from the aesthetic conventions of the day; nor was there in Edwardian Leeds the money for the *Beaux-Arts* monumentality associated with the American City Beautiful Movement. His work embraced a range of architectural styles: Gothic, Renaissance, Arts and Crafts and Baroque, sometimes combined in the same façade in an engaging eclecticism that enlivened the streetscape of the city centre. Of all the architects working in Leeds in the early years of the twentieth century, Robinson was the one most given to Art Nouveau motifs – particularly in his treatment of windows and decorative detailing – whilst his design for the little parochial hall at Halton (1908), and the tower of the Firemen's Flats in Park Street, designed a year later, might well have sprung from the drawing board of some Vienna Secession architect (17.1).

Early Architectural Career

The earliest record of buildings by Robinson was for two houses and shops erected in 1896 in south Leeds, and humdrum work of this kind dominated his early practice. According to Frank Trowell, Robinson designed 63 houses between 1896-1901.[10] His professional breakthrough was to come in 1900 when he won a competition for the first purpose-built library in the city[11] (17.2). Surely still the most attractive library in Leeds, it stands on the corner of Stocks Hill and Wesley Road in the drab working-class neighbourhood of Armley. Its Flemish Renaissance style and contrasting red brick and buff stonework exemplify Robinson's ideas about adding beauty and colour to the lives of ordinary people. The dominant feature of the building is the wonderful curved entrance loggia on the corner with its three round

9. See Steele [note 6] for details of Robinson's talk to the Leeds Art Club and his presidential addresses are to be found in the LYAS *Green Books* for 1908-9 and 1909-10. The Library and Art Gallery were situated in Centenary Street with a row of factory buildings and courtyards in front of them until the latter were cleared as part of the creation of the Headrow Scheme.

10. Trowell, 18, p. 117.

11. Leeds adopted the Public Libraries Act in 1868. A branch library was established in Armley in 1874 but like other branch libraries this was located in an existing building.

17.2: Leeds, Armley Public Library, Stocks Hill (Percy Robinson, 1900-2). (*Ruth Baumberg.*)

arches set on short columns, richly carved spandrels and carved frieze above. One arch furnishes a porch whilst the other two shelter the steps leading up to the library entrance. Above is a brick tower with stone quoins, a clock set in diagonal square panels and a louvred cupola with a lead dome and finial. On each return elevation are shaped gables with a date stone and the city's coat of arms. Restored in 2002-3, the interior retains many of its original features including a mosaic floor, glazed wooden screen with leaded Art Nouveau glass, more coats of arms and a glazed dome with moulded ribs and transoms framing leaded glass panels.

Shopping and the City

The advent of mass consumption in the latter part of the nineteenth century represented a pivotal moment in spatial re-organisation of city centres. As the 1909 *Leeds Shopping Guide* noted, 'no city in England can boast a more wonderful transformation than that witnessed in Leeds during the past two or three decades. The centre of Leeds has been practically re-carved and polished'.[12] Although the consumer revolution was never an exclusively female or bourgeois arena, the construction of the middle-class female consumer who shopped partly for pleasure had profound implications for the design of retailing

12. S. Burt and K. Grady, *An Illustrated History of Leeds*, Breedon Books, 1994, p. 195.

outlets: attractive shop fronts, refined decorative details to appeal to the female gaze and large plate glass windows often on two floors for the display of goods to entice the customer inside. The premier example of this retailing revolution was the shopping complex of the Leeds Estates Company (1900-1904, now the Victoria Quarter), a swaggering design in faience by Frank Matcham that included two hundred shops, cafes, tea rooms and a theatre (1.15). Although nothing designed by Robinson was quite as lavish or ostentatious, he was responsible for six relatively large retailing outlets in the city centre. Probably the earliest was at 26, Lands Lane (17.3) built following the Lands Lane Improvement Scheme of 1902, and occupied by a fancy draper. It is a striking and advanced (probably steel-framed) four-storey design contained within a tall moulded brick arch, and with a shallow pediment above, and short octagonal turrets to the sides. The arch is virtually entirely glazed with wooden framed canted bay windows on the first and second floors and a semi-circular window with glazing bars to the third floor. The ground floor is modern.

The municipal council's contribution to the consumer revolution was largely limited to street widening schemes, though for the Leeds Estate Company's project, the local authority did compulsorily purchase some buildings, and in the case of Robinson's next city centre project, it had extended the line of Albion Place so that it joined Briggate, the city's main shopping street.[13] 13 and 14 Albion Place (17.4) were built for Eveleigh Bishop, 'stationer, printer, fancy goods importer, jeweller and silversmith'. Its eight bays stretch along Albion Place with an angled corner bay and a single bay on Briggate. An elegant mixture of building materials – stone, red brick, buff, white and green faience – enhance this Baroque design that deserves to be more widely appreciated.[14] There are four storeys with attics and a different treatment to each floor. A canted bay window in the centre of the Albion Street façade extends through two floors; at first floor level the window is flanked by large plate glass windows with small panes above organised in patterns which borrows from Art Nouveau design, while the second floor has recessed bays with pilasters between. Above, running the length of the building, is a frieze of shields and swirling foliage and stylised flowers. The sash windows of the third floor are separated by green faience columns. Above the parapet is a variegated array of elaborate dormers. Two large end gables contain Diocletan windows; on the left the window has a triangular pediment whilst that at the right end gable has a segmental pediment and large stone-carved lion. At the far left is a blocked carriage entrance and doorway with porthole windows above and an Art Nouveau decorated panel, while at roof level there is an amazing white faience temple-like structure with a large central arch, columns with festoons and a pretty wrought iron balustrade. There are canted bay windows at the eastern

17.3: Leeds, 26 Lands Lane, shop (Percy Robinson, 1902). (*Ruth Baumberg.*)

13. Part of the Leeds Estates Company scheme was constructed on the site of the Old Shambles, an area of narrow courts and yards crammed with butchers' shops and abattoirs – clearly not desirable properties so close to the city's shopping district. Albion Place previously ended at Land's Lane and in 1903, the municipal authority cleared two of yards behind Briggate and demolished four properties on the west side if Briggate to create a through street from Albion Street to Briggate.

14. Again the ground floor shops bear no relationship to the original building design and because of the relative narrow width of Albion Place, it is difficult to view the whole length of the façade.

17.4: Leeds, 13-14 Albion St., shop for Eveleigh Bishop (Percy Robinson, 1903-4). (*Ruth Baumberg.*)

corner and the Briggate bay repeats the Albion Street façade with a carved lion in the gable.

In 1893 the large Central Market (1824-7) on Duncan Street was destroyed by fire which facilitated a further street widening in 1900 and the opulent rebuilding of the north side.[15] On the corner for Hepworth's the tailors (17.5), Robinson designed another Baroque

15. The Central Market was designed by Francis Goodwin (see Chapter 4). Duncan Street had already been widened in the 1880s.

17.5: Leeds, 4 Duncan St., shop for Hepworths the Tailors (Percy Robinson, c.1904). (Changing Leeds, *Yorkshire Post, n.d., p. 90.*)

tour-de-force which uses some of the detailing already seen in Albion Street. Four storeys with attics in cream terracotta, the four bays on Briggate and three bays on Duncan Street are treated similarly, though not identically. Here remnants of the original ground floor have survived, with rusticated pilasters at the bay divisions which are carried up to the eaves level. On the Duncan Street façade, canted bay windows in round arched recesses repeat the treatment of the corner bay though the circular window at the corner has been replaced by the sash windows and pilasters. At roof level is an elaborate scrolled parapet and lines of dormers, some with circular windows and above the corner bay rises an octagonal turret with a dome. There is lots of moulded decoration to the sill levels, the sides of the windows and within the spandrels including a panel of draped female figures cradling the circular windows. These are reputedly by the sculptor Edward Caldwell Spruce who was a friend of Robinson's from the Savage Club and was chief modeller for the Burmantofts Fireclay Company.[16] Unusually on both this building and the one on Albion Street, the name 'Percy Robinson' is stamped on one of the faience blocks. Further along at 5-9 Duncan Street (17.6), Robinson produced a more symmetrical design of seven bays with rusticated pilasters and canted bay windows. In the centre, the bays are carried through two floors with a recessed window. In the central gable there are squat columns and a pediment. The outer bays are crowned by square turrets with attached columns, a parapet

16. For a photograph of Spruce at work, see P. Brears, *Images of Leeds*, Breedon Books, 1992, p. 128.

17.6: Leeds, 7, Duncan St., shop and offices for Messrs Rawcliffe. (Percy Robinson, c.1904). (*Ruth Baumberg*.)

with swags and huge faience globes resting on large scrolled brackets. The design of Exchange Buildings, 137, Briggate, (1907) (17.7), began as a scheme for ground floor shops but was adapted to provide accommodation for the Post Office with a post and telegraph office, telephone boxes, letter boxes and lockers. Above was a grocery exchange with reading and writing rooms and the two upper two floors were devoted to office space. The building cost £6000. In terms of style, the rows of round arched windows and particularly the upper storey with its arcade of round arched columns and recessed windows, suggest a Renaissance idiom rather than Robinson's more familiar Neo-baroque. The central bay however has the canted bay windows that feature in many of Robinson's other city centre buildings. Above the first and second floors, are bands of moulded decoration with Art Nouveau figures, swags and foliage. Massive cylindrical columns with roll mouldings survive inside the building. The top storey of the building was added in the 1920s when Woolworth's first occupied the building.

Robinson in the Suburbs

Robinson's stylistic versatility is demonstrated in his ability to handle both spectacle and simplicity. If the spectacular dominates his city-centre buildings, the simple can be seen in a clutch of buildings scattered around the city. Between 1900-1 he designed the Children's Central Home, Street Lane, Moortown (17.8) for the Leeds Board of Guardians to accommodate up to forty pauper children. The scheme included administrative offices for 'the scattered homes system' which placed children in family groups in suburban homes under the care of

17.7: Leeds, Exchange Buildings, 137, Briggate, former post office, grocers exchange and offices (Percy Robinson, 1907). (*Ruth Baumberg*.)

17.8: Leeds, Central Children's Home, Street Lane (Percy Robinson, 1900-1) (Ruth Baumberg)

a house mother, and a detached superintendent's house. The home cost £7000. Designed in an Arts and Crafts idiom in brick and white render with half-timbered gables, pretty dormer windows and tall chimneys, it was light, airy and far removed from the forbidding orphanages of the previous century. The conversion of the building into apartments has involved only minor changes; it retains its large front gardens but has lost the two covered playgrounds which once projected as two wings attached to the front of the home. A year later Robinson was responsible the design of St Martin's Institute, Chapeltown (17.9), a Perpendicular-styled building in coursed-faced gritstone which served as the parochial hall for St Martin's Church, Chapeltown. The church itself was by Adams and Kelly (1879-81) and served the community

17.9: Leeds, St Martin's Institute, St Martin's View, Chapeltown (Percy Robinson, 1902)

17.10: Collingham, Leeds, house for
Owen Bowen (Percy Robinson, 1905).
(The Studio Magazine, *vol 35.*)

of the exclusive Newton Park Estate (for details see Chapter 11). In 1905 *The Studio Magazine* devoted an article to the house that Robinson designed for Owen Bowen, the artist and fellow member of the Savage Club, to demonstrate how 'modern' houses might be built for even those with limited financial means.[17] (17.10; 17.11)

Robinson and Jones, and National Architectural Competitions

Alongside Robinson and Bowen in the Savage/Attic Club was William Alban Jones (*q.v.*), usually known as Billy. After working as an assistant

17. *Studio Magazine,* vol. 35, 1905, pp. 148-51.

17.11: Collingham, Leeds, house for
Owen Bowen (Percy Robinson, 1905).
(The Studio Magazine, *vol 35.*)

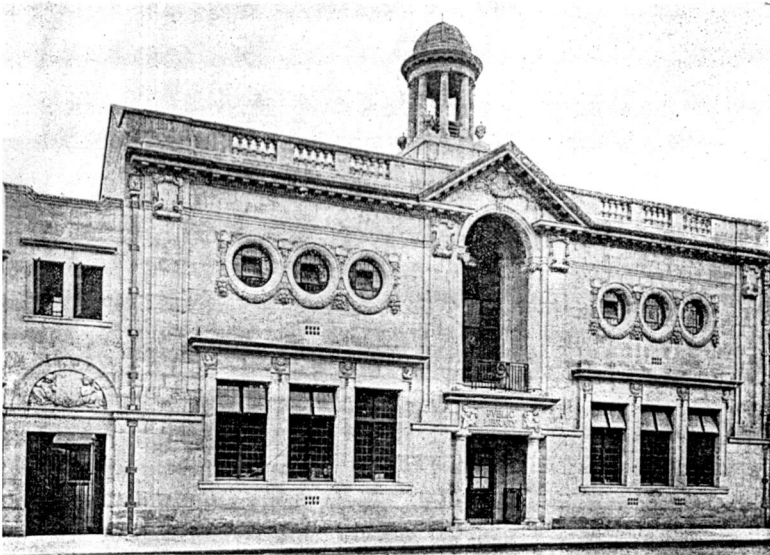

17.12: Hove, Sussex Public Library, Church Road (Robinson and Jones, 1905-8) photographed in 1908. (*C. Mason-Jones.*)

for William Bakewell (*q.v.*), in 1904 Jones established his own practice. As an exceptionally gifted artist, Jones supplemented his fee income by producing perspective drawings – and sometimes whole designs – for other architects and it seems the Robinson-Jones partnership started in this way, even though Robinson's own artistic skills were not inconsiderable. By 1907, a more formal partnership existed between them – with Robinson not unreasonably, the senior partner – and in March that year, the men signed a formal document in which they agreed to divide any work that came *via* competitions two-thirds, one-third, with Robinson responsible for all expenses.[18] It was a remarkably successful collaboration.

Robinson's reputation in Leeds today would be far greater if it were widely known that, in the early years of the twentieth century, he and Jones won a string of competitions, including three very prestigious ones which were widely reported and illustrated in the professional journals – the Bethnal Green design was shown at the Royal Academy – and they brought the partnership to national prominence. The first was for Hove Public Library (1907-9) (9.14; 17.12). Seventy-one designs were submitted and the assessor was John Belcher, President of the RIBA. What appears now as a Baroque revival building was originally – according to a design published in *Academy Architecture* and the *Architectural Review*[19] – rather more English Renaissance, featuring a Gothicky central bay with a pointed tower that was subsequently replaced by a central pediment with round arched opening carried on Ionic columns, and containing a tall round-topped window fronted by a wrought-iron balcony. To each side are three circular windows with carved festoons and ribbons and on the ground floor, three square-headed windows that have now lost their small

18. The hand written document is dated 26 March 1907, and used a sheet of the partnership's headed paper giving the office address as Yorkshire Post Chambers, Albion Street. A copy of this document, and much other valuable information about the partnership is in a biography of Jones by his grandson. (C. Mason-Jones, 'William Alban Jones: a Life in Architecture', unpublished B.Arch dissertation, University of Newcastle, 1986.) I am grateful to Mr Mason-Jones for allowing me access to this material.

19. *Academy Architecture and Architectural Review*, 1906 p. 23. The Library and its fittings cost £12,900.

leaded panes. A carved panel over the entrance is inscribed 'Public Library' with accompanying carved cherubs. To the east is a service entrance with carved cherubs set within a semi-circular panel. The cupola which was carried by eight Ionic columns was removed in 1967. Much of the interior plan and many of the features remain intact. The vestibule leads to an octagonal hall with Tuscan columns and lit by a glazed dome with a wrought-iron balustraded steps leading to the first floor. To the west and east of the hall are reading rooms and radiating south is the large semi-circular space of the lending library divided into bays with large windows above. Lighting and surveillance were key elements in the design of early libraries and the semi-circular lending library allowed the library staff to survey the whole area from a centrally placed counter. Many of the original oak bookcases have survived though the original painted texts advocating Economy and the acquisition of Knowledge have been removed. On the first floor, reference and special collections rooms were located above the reading rooms and the rotunda and the adjacent rooms served as a museum.

17.13: London, Bethnall Green Town Hall, winning competition entry (Robinson and Jones, 1907-10). (The Architect, *20 Dec 1907*.)

GROUND FLOOR.

The Architect Dec 20th 1907

BETHNAL GREEN MUNICIPAL BUILDINGS.
P A ROBSON Architect

17.14: London, Bethnal Green Town Hall, as built (Robinson and Jones, 1907-10). (Academy Architecture, *1909*.)

Beyond was a semi-circular open air reading room or smoking gallery enclosed in 1928. The library cost £12,900, most of the finance coming from the Andrew Carnegie Trust. This gem of a building has been much appreciated by local residents but not always by the local authority. Crumbling away, the Council decided to close the library because of high cost of its repair and build a new library, a decision met by a storm of protest and one which the Council eventually rescinded, carrying out a full restoration in 2006. In 2009 a centenary exhibition was held in the library and ironically Robinson is now probably better known in Hove than he is in Leeds.

In the same year that Robinson and Jones won the competition for Hove Public Library, they were also successful in the competition for Bethnall Green Town Hall, (17.13; 17.14). Since the beginning of the twentieth century a number of London metropolitan boroughs including those in the East End had opened new town halls built in the grand manner of Edwardian public buildings.[20] Succumbing to inter-borough rivalry and in a rare exercise in civic pride, the Bethnall Green Council erected, at a cost of £20,000, a showy, rather bombastic Edwardian Baroque town hall in Portland stone intended to outshine local rivals. The three-bay front façade has a cupola, open pediment and a tall arched recess above the entrance. Over the doorway, a large sculptural group of Prosperity by Henry Poole (1873-1928) depicts a mother caring for two young children each carrying cornucopia representing the blessings conferred on the local residents by a caring borough council. The north elevation has a centrally placed pediment and Diocletian window with another sculpture by Poole of Justice.[21]

20. Shoreditch (1901), Lambeth (1905), Deptforth (1905).

21. A 19-bay extension to the east was built in the Inter-War period.

The interior retains much of its original splendour: veined marble floors, a wealth of oak panelling, armorial glass and a glazed dome. Committee rooms and the mayor's parlour were located along the front elevation, while the council chamber, richly ornamented with plaster figures by Poole representing Truth, Happiness, Industry and Temperance, was behind. Having been disused for fifteen years and placed on English Heritage's Buildings at Risk Register, the Town Hall has recently been converted into a bijou hotel.

The third of their national successes was on the Isle of Man. Resisting what Robinson called 'the hybrid restless character of many seaside buildings',[22] for their competition entry for a Kursaal (17.15) commissioned by Douglas Corporation, Jones and Robinson produced a restrained Classical building set in eight acres of specially laid out gardens with lawns, a backdrop of mature trees to the north and a view of the Douglas Bay to the south. Again to quote from Robinson, what they had in mind were 'the old stuccoed Italian private palaces, which, with their wide overhanging roofs and deep cool shadows form reposeful features set amidst the luxurious gardens of the Continent'. The gardens were not actually completed until 1931 but Jones and Robinson did design a bandstand in the Chinese style which is now demolished. A rather austere Classical temple entrance with two open pavilions to the sides leads to a large octagonal auditorium (now called the Royal Hall) designed for orchestral concerts. Around seven sides of the octagon runs a balcony supported by plain columns and behind the balcony, the wall is punctured by large arched openings, some with doorways and others with handrails so that those promenading around

22. *The Manx Quarterly,* 13, 1913.

17.15: Douglas, Isle of Man, Villa Marina Kursaal (Robinson and Jones, 1911-14). (*C. Mason-Jones.*)

17.16: Leeds, South Parade, Headingley, Baptist School (Robinson and Jones, 1908-9).

South Parade Baptist Church, Headingley, 1909
exterior and interior

the upper ambulatory might view the concerts. The coffered ceiling lacks embellishment except for fluted semi-circular panels just below the lantern whilst the lantern itself is detailed with dog-tooth decoration. On three sides of the Royal Hall were lounges, cafes, reading and writing rooms. Over the whole of the surrounding rooms were a series of roof gardens, promenades and two summerhouse pavilions serving refreshments. The main roof with a hundred foot span was built from ferro-concrete on the Kahn System and was reputedly the largest roof of its kind in England without any internal support.[23]

Of the less prominent successes, perhaps the most attractive design is the one they produced in 1908 for South Parade Baptist chapel and

23. The Kahn system was invented at the beginning of the twentieth century by the American civil engineer, Julius Kahn to facilitate long span construction associated with early US car plants.

school in Headingley, a bold, free Gothic composition with prominent stone dressings.[24] (17.16) As was the Baptist custom, school-rooms were opened before the erection of chapel buildings and the three-storey tower which was part of the 1908-9 plan was to furnish a link with the chapel, eventually built between 1924-7.

Always an inventive architect capable of working within small or large budgets, after the successes of the Edwardian period, Robinson's career appears to have petered out following the First World War. Although he was only in his early 50s and according to his obituary in the *Yorkshire Post* worked until the late 1940s,[25] it has proved impossible with two exceptions to trace any of his work: he designed one of the city's early council estates,[26] and in 1928-30 refurbished a rare survival of a group of late Georgian shops on the corner of The Headrow and Briggate adding cement stucco rustication and a pediment. The mystery is compounded by the fact that when the Baptists at South Parade erected their church in the mid-1920s, they selected Jones as their architect – by then in partnership with J.E. Stocks – rather than Robinson. The beginnings of a sea change in architectural history was underway which included a revulsion against the excesses of Edwardian architecture with which Robinson may have been associated, in favour of greater simplicity. In financially straitened times, the few large projects that were available in Leeds tended to go to architects from outside the city, often ones with more 'modernist' inclinations. The localism which had nurtured the profession in Leeds for over a hundred years was increasingly being replaced by large London-based practices or national organisations with their own in-house architects designing 'branded' buildings to promote public recognition in different urban locations. Maybe with his Arts and Crafts background, Robinson returned to domestic work, but the architects of the thousands of suburban homes built in Leeds in the Inter-War period, have largely gone unresearched.

24. 'South Parade' was the name of the Baptist congregation's city centre chapel which was sold in 1905 and which financed the construction of their premises in Headingley and Harehills.

25. *Yorkshire Post,* 12 Jan 1950.

26. Unidentified but it must have been before 1923 because thereafter estates were designed by the Borough Engineers Department.

Catalogue

Percy Robinson

LEEDS, two houses and shops, Dewsbury Road, 1896. (*LM*, 26 Sept 1896.)

LEEDS, Armley Branch Library, Stocks Hill, 1900-2. (Pevsner, *Leeds*, p. 209.)

LEEDS, St Columba's Mission Church, Burley Road, 1900. (*LM*, 12 May 1900.)

LEEDS, offices for the Bramley Board of Guardians, 1900. (*LM*, 20 June 1900.)

LEEDS, Leeds Union Central Children's Home and Superintendent's house, Street Lane, for the Board of Guardians, 1900-1901. (http://users.ox.ac.uk/~peter/workhouse/Leeds/Leeds.shtml)

LEEDS, shop, 26, Lands Lane c.1902. (English Heritage Listing).

LEEDS, St Martin's Church Institute, St Martin's View, Chapeltown, 1902. (Pevsner, *Leeds*, p. 231.)

LEEDS, shop and offices, Briggate/Albion Place, for Eveleigh Bishop, 1903-4. (Pevsner, *Leeds*, p. 159.)

LEEDS, Shop and offices for Messrs Hepworth, 4 Duncan Street, c.1904. (Pevsner, *Leeds*, p. 97)

LEEDS, Victoria Memorial Institute, Potternewton, 1903-4. (*The Builder*, 86, 4 Feb 1904.)

LEEDS, Shop and Offices, Duncan Street c.1904. (Pevsner, *Leeds*, p. 97.)

LEEDS, Boar Lane, shop for Messrs Rawcliffe, 1905. (Linstrun, *WYAA*, p. 383.)

COLLINGHAM, near Leeds, house for Owen Bowen, 1905. (*The Studio Magazine* vol. 35, pp. 148-51.)

WAKEFIELD, block of shops, Bull Ring/Cross Square, 1906. (K. Taylor (ed.), *Wakefield District Heritage*, Vol. 1, 1976.)

CHAPEL ROW, Berks, detached house, 1906. (*Academy Architecture and Architectural Review*, 60, 1906, p. 160.)

LEEDS, Embo Leather Works for W.H. Miers, 390-92, Dewsbury Road, 1906-7, dem. (Leeds & Yorkshire Architects Society, *Green Book, 1906-7.*)

LEEDS, Leeds Exchange Building, Briggate, 1907. (Linstrum, *WYAA*, p. 383.)

WAKEFIELD, unidentified clothing factory 1907-8 (Leeds and Yorkshire Architects Society, *Green Book, 1907-8.*)

Robinson and Jones, winning competition entries

HOVE, Public Library, Church Road 1905-8, cupola removed, 1967. (*British Architect*, 15 Dec 1905; *Hove Gazette and Brighton and County Graphic*, 11 July 1908.)

OSSETT, WY, elementary school, design prepared for W.A. Kendall of Ossett, 1906. (Mason-Jones [note 18].)

BETHNALL GREEN, London, Town Hall, Cambridge Heath Road, 1907-10. (*Building News*, 18 Oct 1907.)

LEEDS, South Parade Baptist Sunday School, Headingley, 1908-9. (Pevsner, *Leeds*, p. 252.)

LEEDS, City of Leeds Training College, Macaulay Hall, 1911. (*Yorkshire Post*, 12 Jan 1950.)

DOUGLAS, Isle of Man, Villa Marina Kursaal, The Promenade, 1911-14. (*Engineering*, 21 Nov 1913, pp. 688-90.)

HORBURY, nr Wakefield, public hall, design prepared for W.A. Kendall of Ossett, 1913. (Mason-Jones [note 18].)

Percy Robinson

LEEDS, Extensions to the Fire Station and Firemen's Flats, Park Lane, 1909, dem. (Linstrum, *WYAA*, p. 383.)

LEEDS, Parochial Hall, Halton, 1908. (J. Gilleghan, *Halton*, 2004, p. 166.)

DONCASTER, Masonic Hall, 1913. (*ex inf.* Ruth Harman.)

CONISBOROUGH, nr Doncaster, Conisborough and Mexborough Hospital, 1913. (Mason-Jones [note 18].)

LEEDS, shops, 88-89 Briggate/The Headrow, cement stucco rustication and pedimented north gable added to a late-Georgian block, 1928-30. (Pevsner, *Leeds*, p. 169-70, which records the architects as Robinson and Whitehead.)

18. The Work of London Architects in Leeds

KENNETH POWELL

In the eighteenth century, Leeds had largely looked to York, as the regional centre of taste, for architects – John Carr for the Infirmary, for example, William Etty for Holy Trinity church. However, during the late-Georgian and Victorian periods the local profession developed, forming the subject of this book. With twenty-three architectural practices operating there as early as 1853, Victorian Leeds hardly lacked local talent, yet throughout the period under discussion, a succession of London-based men secured some – but by no means all – of the best jobs. This chapter will examine a selection of these buildings but also explore a patron's likely motives for eschewing the Leeds practices.

Industrialisation drove the growth of Leeds and equally reduced the isolation of the town from the capital. Eighteenth-century stagecoach travellers faced a journey of two or three days from London to Yorkshire. The advent of the railway – the Leeds-Selby line opened in 1834 – changed everything. By 1850 it was possible to travel to London by train in as little as six and a half hours, a timing almost halved by 1900. Train travel made it possible for London architects to supervise projects across the country. A.W.N. Pugin 'hurtled to and fro' across England.[1] George Gilbert Scott spent a considerable part of his working life on trains. So, as the Leeds architectural community grew apace, so did the involvement of London architects in Leeds projects. Before the railway, only the very wealthy engaged architects from the capital – Robert Adam recast Harewood House for the hugely rich Lascelles family. The industrial magnate Benjamin Gott's commission to Robert Smirke to rebuild Armley House produced a Greek Revival building

1. R. Hill, *God's Architect: Pugin & The Building of Romantic Britain*, Penguin, 2007, p. 251.

18.1: Leeds, Armley House, Armley, for Joseph Gott (remodelled by Robert Smirke, c.1818).

fully in line with advanced metropolitan taste (18.1). The great German architect Karl Friedrich Schinkel judged it 'magnificent ... in the best style both inside and out'.[2] The flax manufacturer John Marshall's Temple Mills, with architecture by Joseph Bonomi Jnr framing a technically advanced structure by engineer James Combe, was an equally sensational act of patronage (18.2). Such commissions clearly proclaimed the wealth – and the informed taste – of clients. Improved communications made it possible for London architects to work nationally. Architectural journals, such as *The Builder* and *Building News* – first published in the 1840s and '50s respectively – and popular journals such as *Punch* and the *Illustrated London News* featured the works of London practitioners and doubtless won them clients far beyond the capital. Together, the railway and the national press broke

2. D. Bindman & G. Riemann (eds.), *Karl Friedrich Schinkel: The English Journey*, Yale UP, 1993, p. 145.

18.2: Leeds, Temple Mills, Holbeck, for John Marshall (James Combe and Joseph Bonomi Jun., 1838-43). The mill complex is an extraordinary collaboration between Combe, a local engineer, and Bonomi, a London-based Egyptologist and curator of the Soane Museum. It is a diligent copy of the Temple of Horus at Edfu, and 'one of the architectural splendours of the Industrial Revolution'. (Pevsner, *Leeds*, p. 554.) (*Leeds Library and Information Services.*)

down the isolation of the provinces. In architecture, as in other areas, fashions emanated from London and were taken up across the land. London practices equally had the resources to handle the demand for new types of buildings – hotels, office blocks, department stores, railway stations, and hospitals. Although small by twenty-first century standards, Scott's office, for instance, with up to forty assistants, was one of the largest of its day – the Leeds architect Edward Birchall worked there for a time while his sometime partner, John Kelly, had spent three years working for G.E. Street, also a major London practitioner. Pupilage was thus another way in which the London architectural world extended its hold on the provinces.

In 1852 Leeds turned, however, not to a London architect but to Cuthbert Brodrick of Hull for the design of that supreme monument of civic pride, the Town Hall. The competition won by Brodrick was judged by Charles Barry, architect of the new Palace of Westminster, for which project he had been knighted. Barry had been engaged with major alterations to Harewood House in 1843-50, including a reconstruction of the south front. In adjudicating the Town Hall competition Barry 'had to meet with considerable efforts of local interest on behalf of other competitors ... but he stood firm in what he considered to be his duty'.[3] Barry's biographer, his son Alfred, was headmaster of Leeds Grammar School between 1854 and 1862. In 1857 the commission for the new school buildings close to Woodhouse Moor went to his architect brother, Edward Middleton Barry – one of

3. A. Barry, *The Life and Works of Sir Charles Barry*, John Murray, 1867, p. 318.

18.3: Leeds, former Leeds Grammar School (E.M. Barry, 1858-9, chapel to the left of the photograph, 1862-3). (*Leeds Library and Information Service*.)

18.4: Leeds, St Andrew, Cavendish Street (G.G. Scott, 1842-5) dem. (*Leeds University Library, Special Collections.*)

his first significant projects. The new buildings, which included a chapel, were in the Gothic style (18.3). By the 1850s Gothic had become the almost universal style for new Anglican churches. The Ecclesiological Society, founded, as the Cambridge Camden Society, in 1839, took its inspiration from Pugin, but succeeded in purging Gothic of its Romanist associations and making it the preferred style of the Established Church. At the same time, the Ecclesiologists were merciless in condemning those church architects and their patrons who

18.5: Leeds, St John, Little Holbeck (G.G. Scott, 1847-50) dem. (*Leeds University Library, Special Collections.*)

failed to follow its rigorous prescriptions concerning the medieval arrangements and details that should be followed. One outcome was that church work quickly became a specialised activity which could no longer be safely entrusted to the local jobbing architect, no matter how reliable he was when asked to provide a market hall or mechanics' institute. It is not surprising that among the commissions that went to London, churches appear prominently. George Gilbert Scott was a key figure in this process. Although inspired by Pugin and the Ecclesiologists, Scott was able to cater for the tastes of what he called 'the multitude' – the broad mass of Anglicans beyond the advanced Tractarian party, which took its name from the *Tracts for the Times* published in Oxford in the 1830s and which were widely seen as the beginnings of the movement to push Anglicanism closer to Roman Catholicism and away from Evangelicalism. Scott's early work, done in partnership with W.B. Moffatt, consisted largely of workhouses. His first major church, St Giles, Camberwell, was begun in 1842. Scott's first Leeds commission came in the same year. The church of St Andrew, Cavendish Street (18.4), was described by Pevsner as 'dull, with lancet windows, and only a SW turret instead of a tower'.[4] Even so, it was a landmark project, reflecting the influence of the Ecclesiological movement and far more 'correct' in style than Taylor's St Mary (5.15) or Clark's St George (7.15). More significant, however, was St John, Little Holbeck (18.5), another inspired commission by the Marshalls of Temple Mills. Consecrated in 1850, the church, intended for use by the firm's employees, was described by the Revd R.V. Taylor, drawing on an account of the church in *The Builder,* as 'perhaps the only modern church which is vaulted in stone throughout its whole extent, a distinction which renders its internal aspect peculiarly striking and novel'.[5] A drawing of the building – ' a special work', said Scott – was shown at the Royal Academy in 1851. The church, inspired by the Temple Church in London, attracted some criticism because of its use of the Early English style instead of the 'Middle Pointed' favoured by the Ecclesiologists – the style seems to have been imposed by the client. St John's was demolished in the 1930s, along with the nearby church of St Barnabas and most of the surrounding district, and no photographs of it appear to exist. The pioneering enthusiast for Victorian architecture H.S. Goodhart-Rendel wrote movingly of it:

when the vaulted choir of the beautiful Temple Church in London had met its doom in the last war, I felt it consoling to reflect that Sir Gilbert Scott's copy of it in the slums of Leeds would display the beauty of its form to future generations. When, the other day, I hunted for it, map in hand, it had gone; effaced, not, I was told, by enemy action, but by its guardians, who had no further use for it. If

4. N. Pevsner, *The Buildings of England, Yorkshire, The West Riding*, Penguin, 1967, p. 323. A note by Enid Radcliffe adds that the church had been demolished since Pevsner's visit.

5. R.V. Taylor, *The Ecclesiae Leodienses, or Historical and Architectural Studies of the Churches of Leeds and Neighbourhood*, Simpkin, Marshall and Co., 1875, p. 381.

18.6: Leeds, St Thomas, The Leylands
(W. Butterfield, 1849-52) dem.
(*Gavin Stamp*.)

the choir of the Temple Church had not risen again, the copy, although having had little value while the original was standing, would have been a treasure of the second order.[6]

Scott was to make his mark on Leeds with a number of other projects, but other major Gothic Revival architects were also to work on church projects there. The appointment of Walter Farquhar Hook as Vicar of Leeds in 1837 was hugely significant in this respect. Hook was a High Churchman of the old school, sympathetic to the Oxford Movement but not to the 'ritualism' which grew out of it. The parish of Leeds was vast, extending far beyond the township of Leeds and with a population of around 150,000 – but only one parish church. Outlying districts, such as Armley, Headingley and Chapel Allerton, were served by modest chapels of ease and even lacked accommodation for resident clergy. Recent church building in Leeds consisted of 'three large and ugly Peel churches, which proved to be total failures.'[7] Having rebuilt the Parish Church to Chantrell's designs, Hook turned to the provision of new churches across the old parish, which was sub-divided to form new parishes – in total, some twenty-four new churches were built at Hook's behest. Not all were buildings of architectural distinction, but Hook's High Church leanings led to commissions to some leading Tractarian architects. William Butterfield, whose All Saints, Margaret Street, London, was to be seen as the model Tractarian church, was the architect of St Thomas, The Leylands, Leeds, completed in 1852 and a pioneering example of the use of 'structural polychromy' (18.6). Described, when new, as 'standing in a squalid waste, strewed with heaps of rubbish', the church was another victim

6. H.S.Goodhart-Rendel, 'Victorian Conservanda' in *Journal of the London Society,* Nov 1958, p. 45. I owe this reference to Prof. Gavin Stamp.

7. W.R.W. Stephens, *The Life and Letters of Walter Farquhar Hook,* Richard Bently, 1880, p.377. The churches were Atkinson & Sharp's St Mark, Woodhouse, Thomas Taylor's St Mary, Quarry Hill, and Christ Church, Meadow Lane, designed by Chantrell – Hook's architect for the new Parish Church. The churches were certainly not 'failures' and Stephen's assessment can be explained as his attempt to inflate the reputation of his father-in-law's endeavours.

18.7: Leeds, St Michael, Headingley (J.L. Pearson, 1884-6). (*Keith Gibson.*)

8. Cited in P. Thompson, *William Butterfield*, Routledge, 1971, p. 239.

9. N. Yates, *Leeds and the Oxford Movement*, PTS, 55, 1975, p. 21.

of inter-war slum clearance. The architectural historian Henry-Russell Hitchcock, who saw it shortly before demolition, thought it something of a masterpiece, with an 'exquisitely balanced' use of colour and a notable 'harmony of tone' internally.[8] St Thomas's appears never to have been a 'ritualistic' church, but Leeds was to become – in contrast, for example, to nearby, largely Evangelical Bradford – a centre of Anglo-Catholicism. The pioneering church in this respect was St Saviour's, paid for, as a mission to the slums of 'The Bank' district, by Dr E.B. Pusey, one of the leaders of the Oxford Movement. Designed by the Oxford-based, Irish-born architect John McDuff Derick, the church was enriched with stained glass by Pugin and later in the century with a reredos and other adornments by G.F. Bodley. Hook initially welcomed the foundation of the church but was subsequently alienated by its 'extreme' liturgical practices. His own moderation notwithstanding, many of the curates attached to the Parish Church were thoroughgoing Tractarians. One of them was F.J. Wood, who, after a twenty-five year curacy, became first vicar of the new parish of Headingley in 1881. Some in the parish were suspicious of his views – 'no need is there – God forbid it may be done at Headingley! – for the Lord's Table to be raised on a dais to resemble an altar', wrote one parishioner.[9] But in 1884-86 the new St Michael's church (18.7), the third on the site, was constructed to designs by J.L. Pearson, another London architect associated with the Anglo-Catholic movement in the Church of England. (Pearson, also responsible for St Margaret's, Horsforth, had launched his independent career with a series of churches in the East Riding of Yorkshire.) Another of Hook's former curates, R.R. Kirby, appointed to Chapel Allerton in 1871,

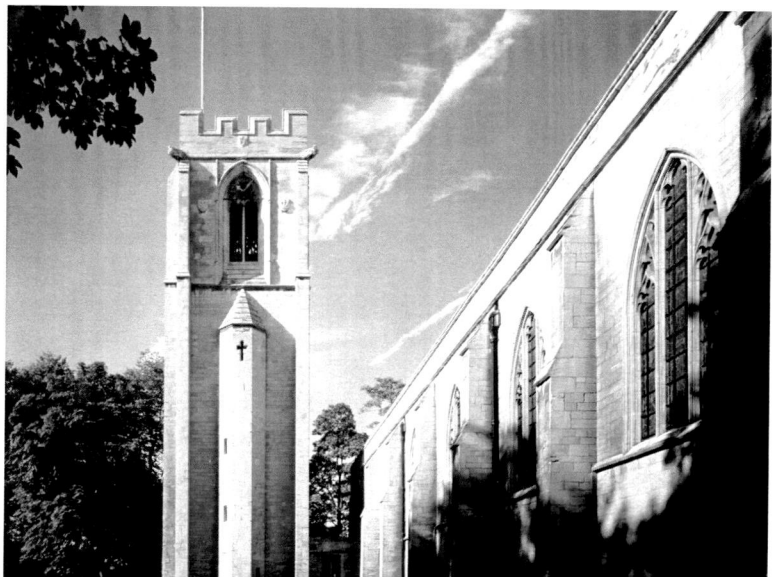

18.8: Leeds, St Matthew, Chapel Allerton (G.F. Bodley, 1897-9). (*Keith Gibson.*)

commissioned designs for a new church there from George Edmund Street (1874) but they remained unrealised. (Street's other work in Leeds included the restoration of Adel church and reordering of the sanctuary at Leeds Parish Church.) Hook left Leeds in 1859 to become Dean of Chichester but his memory was cherished in the town. After his death, a shrine-like monument to him was erected in the Parish Church to designs by Scott. His son, Cecil Hook, a firm Anglo-Catholic, became first vicar of the church of All Souls, Blackman Lane – the Hook Memorial Church – a major late work by Scott, completed after his death by his son John Oldrid Scott.

The provision of a new church at Chapel Allerton had to wait until the last years of the nineteenth century, when the new St Matthew's was constructed (18.8). Its architect, George Frederick Bodley, a pupil of Scott, was much favoured in late-Victorian Anglo-Catholic circles, though St Matthew's was never a particularly 'high' church. (The lead in appointing Bodley seems to have been taken by the local MP, W.L. Jackson, who chaired the building committee. He wrote to the vicar in 1896 that Bodley was 'an interesting man, evidently an artist, and knows his work, but you have to be careful with him as regards definite information as to costs'.)[10] Bodley had a major patron in the Leeds area in the person of Emily Meynell Ingram, sister of the 2nd Lord Halifax (the leading Anglo-Catholic layman) and chatelaine of Temple Newsam in succession to her husband Hugo. As a memorial to the latter, who died in 1871 as a result of a hunting accident, Mrs Meynell Ingram commissioned Bodley and his then partner Thomas Garner to design the exquisite church of the Holy Angels on her estate at Hoar Cross, Staffs. At Temple Newsam, she brought in Bodley in 1877 to create a private chapel in the former library. Bodley's chapel, tragically dismantled in the 1940s, was a masterly exercise in sensitive conversion – the bookshelves, for example, were left in place and simply panelled over. An organ was slotted into the chimney recess. The reredos was of black and white marble, Classical in style, in keeping with its setting and (it has been suggested) a dry run for the huge reredos Bodley later designed for St Paul's Cathedral. Bodley's supervision extended even to the choice of fabric for the cassocks of the choirboys singing at the dedication service on 14 September 1877 – the architect loathed strident colours.[11] Mrs Meynell Ingram took an active interest in parish life in the Leeds area. Disliking the regime at Whitkirk church, the parish church for Temple Newsam, with its 'dreariness, want of life, & indevoutness of the people & choir', she acquired the advowson, appointed a sympathetic incumbent and got Bodley to remodel the east end.[12] Bodley was the natural choice as architect for the new church Mrs Meynell Ingram planned to build in Holbeck. In 1898, she wrote to him recommending a visit to some of the great brick churches of northern Germany – 'then if the necessity arose for my building a

10. I owe this reference to Mr Michael Hall, who is writing a major study of Bodley's work.

11. C. Gilbert, 'The Victorian Chapel at Temple Newsam' in *Leeds Arts Calendar*, 62, 1968, pp. 5-9; M. Hall, 'Emily Meynell Ingram and Holy Angels, Hoar Cross, Staffordshire: a Study in Patronage' in *Architectural History*, 47, 2004, pp. 284-328.

12. Hall [note 11], p. 317.

18.9: Leeds, St Hilda, Cross Green (J.T. Micklethwaite, 1876-82), early twentieth century photograph.

church in Leeds, which is not off the cards, we might do something rather good in brick'.[13] St Edward King & Martyr, Brown Lane, was completed soon after Emily Meynell Ingram's death in 1904. Simple in plan, the church, always a centre of advanced Anglo-Catholicism, was a container for exquisite fittings, most of which were salvaged after its tragic and unnecessary demolition in 1984. Mrs Meynell Ingram was also supportive of the construction of another Anglo-Catholic mission, St Hilda's, Cross Green, designed by J.T. Micklethwaite – 'on many occasions she would stop her carriage at the door of St Hilda's and go inside to look at something that was new – the windows or the screen or the altar candlesticks'. The construction of St Hilda's, initially as an offshoot of St Saviour's, began in 1878 (18.9). Wakefield-born Micklethwaite, a former assistant of Gilbert Scott, was at the time in a London partnership with George Somers Clarke junior but he seems to have taken sole charge of the St Hilda's project, having 'met Mr Collins (vicar of St Saviour's since 1859) in 1872 and heard from him about his scheme to build a church in his growing parish'.[14] In the 1890s Micklethwaite, a supporter of William Morris's Society for the Protection of Ancient Buildings, was in charge of repairs to the ruins of Kirkstall Abbey – Gilbert Scott, in a report of 1873, had recommended reroofing the monastic church and bringing it back into use for worship.

The continuing programme of church building in Leeds in the last decades of the nineteenth century produced another monumental project in the form of St Aidan's, Roundhay Road, designed by the Tyneside practice of R.J. Johnson (a pupil of Scott, responsible for many of the fittings in All Souls church and for the adjacent clergy house) and A. Crawford Hick, and completed in 1894. One of the submissions in the competition held in 1891 to secure a design was

13. Hall [note 11], p. 317.

14. S. Savage & C. Tyne, *The Labours of Years,* Leeds (?)1974, p. 60; J.S. Willimott, *The Story of St Hilda's, Leeds,* Leeds, 1932, p. 18.

18.10: Leeds, St Margaret, Cardigan Road (Temple Moore, designed 1901, a reduced scheme was built 1907-9). (Academy Architecture, *26, 1904, p. 10, courtesy of Geoff Brandwood.*),

that from Temple Lushington Moore, who had trained with George Gilbert Scott junior. Resident in Hampstead, Moore had spent some of his formative years in Yorkshire, where he was to complete some of his finest work. Moore's introduction to Leeds came via the Scott family – the Rev. John Scott, a cousin of Gilbert Scott, moved from Hull to become vicar of St John's, Leeds, in 1883. St John's, a rare example of a church built during the reign of Charles I, had been threatened with demolition in the mid-1860s – to be replaced by a new church designed by the local practice of Dobson and Chorley (*q.v.*). Gilbert Scott was at the time completing the new Infirmary and took it upon himself to oppose the demolition proposals. The building was in need of extensive repairs, he concluded, but remained 'an object worthy of preservation'. The Bishop of Ripon was impressed by the views of 'the highest authority we have on Church Architecture'. Dobson and Chorley were paid off and the young Norman Shaw given the job of restoring the church, a task he himself later admitted that he had carried out with too much severity, stripping the plaster from the walls and rearranging or removing quantities of Stuart woodwork. John Scott's aim was 'reparation', undoing the damage done nearly twenty years earlier – fortunately much of the woodwork thrown out by Shaw had survived. Moore continued his work at St John's into the 1900s.[15] His other works in Leeds included the Clergy School Chapel (1895-96), the Hostel of the Resurrection, Woodhouse (1907-10), a reredos for St Michael, Headingley (1903), and various embellishments at St Saviour's, as well as the church of St Margaret, Cardigan Road (1907-09)

15. J. Douglas & K. Powell, *St John's Church, Leeds, A History*, Redundant Churches Fund, (?)1982, pp. 15-18.

18.11: Leeds, Mount St Mary's, The Bank (nave, J. Hansom and W. Wardle, 1853-7; chancel, E.W. Pugin, 1866). (*Keith Gibson*.)

(18.10). Though the projected west tower was never built, St Margaret's (now in secular use) is a masterly exercise in Moore's preferred early Gothic style, with all of the power of the medieval Yorkshire abbeys Moore had studied in his youth.[16]

Large-scale Irish immigration into Leeds from the early nineteenth century onwards reinvigorated the local Roman Catholic community, given new confidence by Catholic Emancipation. The new churches of St Anne and St Patrick were designed by the local architect John Child but the Oblates of Mary Immaculate (OMI), a French missionary order, looked further afield when they resolved to build a large new church, Mount St Mary's, on The Bank in east Leeds (18.11). William Wardell was responsible for the nave of the church, begun in 1857, but the far more impressive east end (1864-66) was the work of Edward Welby Pugin, who had already completed several projects for the OMI. The compulsory purchase (for road widening) of St Anne's church – elevated to cathedral status in 1878 – provided the opportunity for the Leeds Diocese to build a new and far more dignified cathedral. An obvious choice for the commission was Yorkshire-born John Francis Bentley, by this time indisputably the preeminent Roman Catholic architect in Britain. Bentley, however, was preoccupied with work on Westminster Cathedral and the Leeds job went to Leeds-born, London-based John Henry Eastwood. Assisted by S.K. Greenslade, Eastwood produced a building, completed in 1904, outstanding both for its innovative plan and its inventive details.

Bentley (who had designed a pulpit for the old St Anne's as well as a handsome organ case for the Anglican church of St Clement, Sheepscar) had worked in Leeds as long ago as the 1860s when he assisted his friend Matthew Ellison Hadfield with the interiors of the Great Northern Hotel, attached to the Central Station.[17] The hotel was a forceful exercise in the secular Gothic style, which George Gilbert Scott was instrumental in popularising, not least with the new Leeds General Infirmary, constructed in 1863-68 (18.12) and prefiguring in many respects Scott's designs for the Midland Grand Hotel at St Pancras, which he won in competition in 1865. Planned on the most up to date lines, the Infirmary, like the St Pancras hotel, made extensive use of iron construction, with a central winter garden engineered by Rowland Mason Ordish (later one of the designers of the train shed at St Pancras). Concurrent with the Infirmary, Beckett's Bank on Park Row (completed 1867) broke the Classical hold on Leeds' principal business artery – William Beckett was a key member of the committee which selected Scott for the new Infirmary. The polychromatic Gothic style, using brick as the basic raw material, found favour in Leeds, which became, unlike Bradford and Halifax, 'a multi-coloured town'.[18] It certainly influenced the architecture of local board schools and warehouses. By the 1870s, however, the Gothic Revival was in retreat,

16. G.Brandwood, *Temple Moore: An Architect of the Late Gothic Revival*, Paul Watkins, 1997), *passim*.

17. See P. Howell, 'Letters from J.F. Bentley to Charles Hadfield' in *Architectural History*, 23, 1980, pp. 105,119.

18. Linstrum, p. 22.

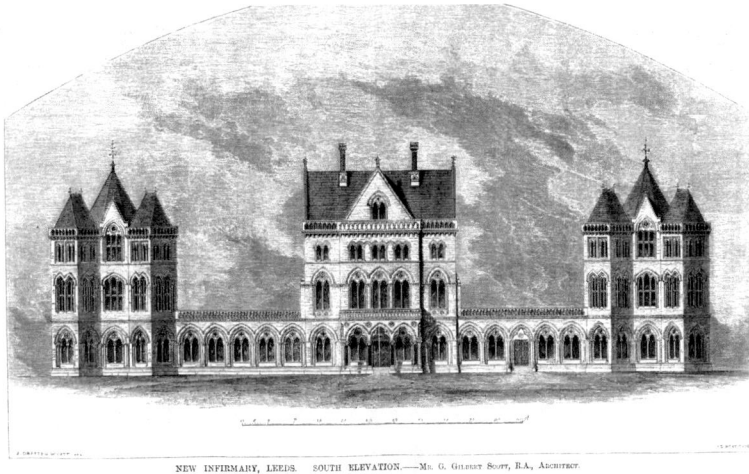

18.12: Leeds, General Infirmary, Great George Street (G.G. Scott, 1863-9). (The Builder, *22, 1864, p. 117.*)

NEW INFIRMARY, LEEDS.   SOUTH ELEVATION.——Mr. G. Gilbert Scott, R.A., Architect.

corralled back into the field of church design. A key figure in this sea change was Londoner Richard Norman Shaw, who had begun his career as a Goth – his first major work was the church of Holy Trinity in Bingley (1866-68). Shaw's connections with the Heatons of Leeds and Bingley doubtless led to his commission at St John's, Leeds and certainly to that for the new convalescent hospital at Cookridge, built 1868-69 (18.13), where the leading figure on the building committee was John Metcalfe Smith, a close friend of the manufacturer and designer John Aldam Heaton. The plan of Cookridge took inspiration from Scott's new Infirmary but the architectural style was very different. As Andrew Saint comments, 'it is Kentish vernacular, unashamedly transferred to Yorkshire to cheer the city convalescents up among the bracken and pure suburban air'.[19] A few years later, Shaw was again in Leeds, completing interiors at Meanwood Towers (18.14), the extraordinary Gothic mansion designed by E.W. Pugin for the manufacturer T.S. Kennedy – Pugin had been declared bankrupt. Shaw's brilliant pupil, Edward Schroeder Prior, obtained the commission for nearby Carr Manor in 1880 after acting as Shaw's clerk of works for the fine church of St Margaret, Ilkley (completed in 1879). Shaw, it appears, was recommended to the client, Dr (later Sir) Thomas Clifford Allbutt MD (1836-1925) by Kennedy. In 1879, however, Shaw's health had collapsed, probably as a result of overwork, and he passed on the job to Prior – it was the latter's first project. Carr Manor, which integrated an existing seventeenth century house, was another exercise in the vernacular manner – but on this occasion the vernacular is that of the Pennines and Dales, not Kent. The house was much extended after 1903 to designs by the Leeds practice of Bedford and Kitson. Allbutt, like Prior, was an alumnus of Gonville & Caius College, Cambridge, and both client and architect went on to hold chairs at the University of Cambridge.[20]

19. A.Saint, *Richard Norman Shaw,* Yale U.P., 2010, p. 79; for the Heatons, see B. and D. Payne (eds.), *Extracts from the Journals of John Deakin Heaton MD, of Claremont, Leeds,* PTS, 53 (2), 1971.

20. I owe much of this information to Dr Lynne Walker, whose 1978 London Ph.D. thesis is the major source for Prior's life and work.

18.13: Cookridge, Leeds, Cookridge Hospital, entrance lodge (Norman Shaw, 1868-9). (*Ruth Baumberg.*)

18.14: Leeds, Meanwood Towers, Meanwood for Thomas Kennedy (E.W. Pugin, 1867). The upper sections of the tower and chimneys have been removed. (*Ruth Baumberg.*)

Shaw and the other promoters of the 'Queen Anne' style moved domestic architecture decisively away from Gothic and towards what became the neo-Georgian. By the later 1870s, the severe Gothic of Adel Grange, the mansion designed by Alfred Waterhouse, for the Ford family and completed in 1866, must have seemed very dated – what did William Morris, who often stayed there, make of it? The Fords, like the Waterhouses, were Quakers. Alfred Waterhouse was soon to achieve national fame with Manchester Town Hall, although he had already moved his office to London by 1866. From there he ran a remarkably successful national practice. His association with the

18.15: Leeds, Leeds University Great Hall (Alfred Waterhouse, 1890-4). (*Ruth Baumberg.*)

Prudential Assurance Company began in 1877 and produced 27 buildings across the country – Waterhouse pioneered the idea of architectural branding, later exemplified in the inter-war stores of Burton's and Marks & Spencer. The Prudential's building on Park Row, Leeds, was completed in 1894 and included lettable offices and a restaurant as well as accommodation for the 'Pru'. (Defaced in the 1960s, when its roofline was shaved off, it was cleverly restored in 1989-90.) His appointment to design Owen's College, Manchester, made him an obvious choice for the new buildings of the Yorkshire College, later the University of Leeds. Appointed in 1877, Waterhouse worked there up to the time of his death in 1902, with his son Paul succeeding him. Waterhouse's most significant building on the campus, the Great Hall (1890-94), gave the college a memorable landmark (18.15). Internally, Waterhouse used locally-produced Burmantofts faience. To progressive thinkers, the Gothic Revival may have seemed moribund by the 1890s but Waterhouse gave it a new lease of life, creating a style indelibly associated with the 'Redbrick' universities. Waterhouse completed another commercial building in Leeds, for William Brown & Co., Bankers, on Park Row in 1898. Local practices, however, were responsible for the majority of warehouses, office buildings and shops which transformed the centre of Leeds in the second half of the nineteenth century. Most public commissions, including the new Board schools built as a result of the 1870 Education Act, were equally the preserve of local practitioners – Richard Adams designed no fewer than 35 schools. Exceptions were the small number of buildings commissioned by the government. The County Court building (1870)

18.16: Leeds, former Bank of England, Park Row (P.C. Hardwick, 1862-4). (*Ruth Baumberg.*)

in Albion Place, for instance, was designed by Thomas Charles Sorby (1836-1924), County Court Surveyor and architect of a number of similar buildings across the country (and of several police stations in London). Some years earlier, P.C. Hardwick had been responsible for the Bank of England's branch at the northern end of Park Row (1862-4) (18.16) – a building lacking the gravitas of C.R. Cockerell's work for the Bank in Liverpool and Manchester. Henry Tanner (1835-1924) became chief architect to the Office of Works in 1884 – previous to this, he had spent two years working for the Office in Leeds. Tanner designed a series of head post offices across the country, including that in Leeds, completed in 1896. Tanner's preferred style, often referred to as 'Northern Renaissance', was applied regardless of context, but the Leeds Post Office (now converted to other uses) gives real dignity to City Square and could be mistaken for a major municipal building (9.13). That such a significant project should go to an outsider was probably a cause of annoyance to Leeds architects – Tanner's designs were 'generally disapproved of as inadequate and unworthy by the press, the architectural profession and the town council'.[21]

The growing hold of London practices on certain categories of work, and the trend towards specialisation characteristic of the later-Victorian period, are reflected in the field of theatre design. Frank Matcham (1854-1920) is credited with building or rebuilding more than 150 theatres across Britain. When the Empire Palace in Briggate opened in 1898 the *Leeds Mercury* declared it 'the handsomest of its kind in the country', its internal decor 'a triumph of artistic skill'.[22] The auditorium, lavishly decorated, seated 2500 , with provision for another 1000 standing. Designed, like Matcham's London Coliseum, for music hall and musical theatre, the Empire Palace was part of a larger development, including the King Edward Restaurant, elaborately decorated in marble, mosaic and mahogany, which represented 'the apotheosis of the music hall'.[23] Matcham was commissioned by the Leeds Estates Company to design a comprehensive redevelopment of an entire block between Briggate and Vicar Lane containing the town's abattoir and meat market. Two new streets were created, along with the County and Cross arcades, the whole complex in a free Baroque style, with ample use of Burmantofts faience and the arcades richly decorated with marble columns and mosaics (1.15). The Empire Palace, which provided a vivid contrast to the more severe style of Corson & Watson's Grand Theatre (1.13), was demolished in the 1960s. (A banal commercial development replaced it – Harvey Nichols store now stands on the site.) The remainder of the Matcham scheme survived and, magnificently restored in the late 1980s, has been rebranded as the Victoria Quarter.

It was the continued vigour of Leeds' economy in the Victorian and Edwardian period which provided plenty of work for a flourishing local

21. *Building News,* 24 July, 1891, cited in J. Oxley, *Post Office Architecture,* London, 2010, p. 22.

22. B.M. Walker (ed.), *Frank Matcham: Theatre Architect,* Blackstaff, (?)1980, p. 161.

23. Linstrum, *WYAA,* p. 280.

architectural profession and ample scope for outsiders, most of them from London, to make their mark. The architectural culture of Leeds was reinforced by the establishment of the Leeds Society of Architects and of a school of architecture, part of a national move towards a regulated system of professional training. The mixed economy of Leeds allowed the city to weather the inter-war depression better than other industrial towns in the region and its continuing dynamism fuelled major building projects by leading London practitioners, including Sir Reginald Blomfield, Lanchester & Lodge, W. Curtis Green, and E. Vincent Harris. Despite the vitality of the local scene, it was London that set the pace for new architecture in the city. The triumph of modernism in the years after 1945 opened the way for a new dialogue – and for the destruction of too much of the rich heritage of Victorian Leeds.

✤

PART TWO

THE DIRECTORY

19. The Directory

Richard Life Adams (1840-1883)

Adams was born in Wisbech, Cambridgeshire, the son of an architect and surveyor, William Adams. Little is known of Richard Adams' background and one presumes that he received his training in his father's office. In 1864 he was married in Peterborough and by 1865 was living in Leeds where he formed a partnership with John Kelly

19.1: Leeds, Church Institute, Albion Place (Adams and Kelly, 1866-8). (The Builder, *1867, p. 60-1*.)

1. *LM*, 14 March 1873.

2. Linstrum's extensive list of Board School commissions appears to come from D. Williams, Leeds School Board and its Architecture, unpublished B.Arch thesis, Leeds Polytechnic, 1875.

(*q.v.*). The first notice of the practice was their unsuccessful entry in the competition for the New Dispensary in Leeds in May 1865. Although one of the most prolific firms in the town in the second half of the nineteenth century, neither Adams nor his partner appears to have had any association with the RIBA. Their professional relationship was cemented by their marriages to wives from the same small village in Cambridgeshire (possibly relatives?) and both families were close neighbours in Newton Grove, Chapeltown, Leeds. Between 1869-72, John Leeming – later of the Halifax firm of Leeming and Leeming – worked as their assistant. In March 1873, Adams was appointed architect to the Leeds School Board at a salary of £400 per year,[1] selected from twenty-one applications and a shortlist of three that included Edward Birchall (*q.v.*) and S.E. Smith (*q.v.*). He designed at least thirty-five schools for the Board[2] and retained his post until his early death in 1883. Most of the schools appeared under Adams' name alone, although some were listed as being by the partnership.

ABOVE
19.2: Leeds, Emmanuel Church, Woodhouse Lane (Adams and Kelly, 1877-80). (*Ruth Baumberg.*)

LEFT TOP
19.3: Leeds, Armley Road Board School (Adams and Kelly, 1878). (*Ruth Baumberg.*)

LEFT BOTTOM
19.4: Leeds, St Martin, Chapeltown (Adams and Kelly, 1879-81). (*Ruth Baumberg.*)

The practice achieved some early prominence from its well-regarded Church Institute in Leeds, but a long succession of schools, alongside some unmemorable churches, came to dominate the firm's output.

The firm's office was initially at 18 Park Row, in April 1876 they moved to 20 Park Row and in January 1880 they were at the Commercial Buildings, Park Row.

Adams and Kelly

LEEDS, St John the Baptist Church, New Town (now called Chapeltown), 1866-68, demolished (*LM*, 25 Jan 1866.)

LEEDS, The Church Institute, Albion Place, 1866-8 (*LM*, 14 Aug 1866; *Builder*, 1867, pp. 60-1.)

LEEDS, Shannon St., houses for the Leeds Industrial Dwellings Co., 1867, dem. (Linstrum, *WYAA.*)

LEEDS, St Mary the Virgin, Beeston, 1867. (ICBS, file 06664.)

GATESHEAD, Christ Church, 1868-73. (ICBS, file 06751.)

HULL, St Matthews, Anlaby Rd, 1868-71. (ICBS, file 06824; *LM*, 22 Aug 1868.)

LEEDS, Christ Church and Schools, Upper Armley, 1869-72. (*LM*, 2

Oct 1869; 16 April 1870; 20 Jan 1872; ICBS, file 07018.)

BATLEY, St Mary of the Angels Church, 1869-70. Additions by Kelly, 1884. (Linstrum, *WYAA*.)

LEEDS, St Luke, Beeston Hill, 1870-2. (*LM*, 6 Feb 1872; ICBS, file 07104.)

LEEDS, Holy Trinity, Armley Hall, 1870-2. (*LM*, 10 Feb 1872.)

LEEDS, nine shops and houses in Chapeltown for J.J. Cousins, 1871. (*Yorkshire Post*, 1 July 1871.)

SOUTH ACTON, Middlesex, All Saints Church, 1872. (*LM*, 3 Oct 1872; ICBS, file 07299.)

LEEDS, Meanwood C of E school, Green Lane, (1840), additions, 1872, (Pevsner, *WY*.)

LEEDS, St Mark, Woodhouse, restoration, 1873. (*LM*, 6 Jan 1873.)

Near LEEDS, unidentified vicarage, 1872-3. (*LM*, 11 Jan 1873.)

HUNSLET, Leeds, Jack Lane Board School, 1872-3, dem. (*LM*, 14 Feb 1873.)

GILDERSOME, St Peter, 1873, dem. (Linstrum, *WYAA*.)

ALTOFTS, nr Wakefield, St Mary Magdalene, 1873-90. (Linstrum, *WYAA*.)

LEEDS, Saville Green Board School, 1874, dem. (Linstrum, *WYAA*.)

LEEDS, Cross Stamford Street. Board School, 1875, dem, (Linstrum , *WYAA*.)

LEEDS, Sheepscar Board School, 1875, demolished (Linstrum, *WYAA*.)

RODLEY, Rodley Board School, 1876. (*LM*, 20 May 1876.)

LEEDS, Burley Lawn Board School, 1876. (Linstrum, *WYAA*.)

LEEDS, Farnley Board School, 1876, dem. (Linstrum, *WYAA*.)

HUNSLET, Leeds, Hunslet Carr Board School, 1876, dem. (Linstrum, *WYAA*.)

LEEDS, Leylands Board School, 1876, dem. (Linstrum, *WYAA*.)

LEEDS, Upper Wortley Board School, Ashley Rd., 1876. (Pevsner, *WY*.)

LEEDS, Lower Wortley Board School, Lower Wortley Rd., 1876. (Linstrum, *WYAA*.)

LEEDS, Woodhouse Board School, 1876. (Linstrum, *WYAA*.)

LEEDS, Bramley Board School, 1876-7. (Linstrum, *WYAA*.)

LEEDS, Ellerby Lane Board School, 1877. (Linstrum, *WYAA*.)

LEEDS, Park Lane Board School, 1877, dem. (Linstrum, *WYAA*.)

BOSTON SPA, alterations to house and new stabling for Col. Wombwell, 1877. (*LM,* 14 July 1877.)

SHADWELL, Leeds Industrial School, Shadwell Lane, 1877-9. (*LM*, 9 May 1877.)

LEEDS, St Peter's Square Board School, 1877, dem. (*LM*, 2 Aug 1877.)

LEEDS, York Rd. Board School, 1877, dem. (Linstrum, *WYAA*.)

LEEDS, Emmanuel Church, Woodhouse Lane, 1877-80. (*LM*, 10 Feb 1877; 10 Jan 1880.)

LEEDS, St Martin, Chapeltown Rd, 1879-81. (LM, 24 Nov 1877, 3 Feb 1880.)

STOCKTON on TEES, St Peter Church, 1878-81. (churchplansonline.org)

LEEDS, Armley Board School, 1878. (Linstrum, *WYAA*.)

HUNSLET, Low Rd. Board School, 1878, dem. (Linstrum, *WYAA*.)

HULL, St Andrew, Holderness Rd, 1878. (Pevsner and Neave, *Yorkshire: York and the East Riding*, Penguin, 1996, p. 504.)

LEEDS, Roundhay Rd. Board School, 1878, (Linstrum, *WYAA*.)

LEEDS, Sweet St. Board School, 1878, dem. (Linstrum, *WYAA*.)

LEEDS, Blenheim Board School, 1879, dem. (Linstrum, *WYAA*.)

LEEDS, Chapeltown Board School, 1879. (Linstrum, *WYAA*.)

LEEDS, Park Lane, St Ann's Catholic Schools, 1880-1, dem. (LYAS, *Annual Report,* 1880-1.)

LEEDS, Leeds Bridge, The People's Café, 1880-1. (LYAS, *Annual Report,* 1880-1.)

LEEDS, Beeston Hill Board School,
1880. (Linstrum, *WYAA*.)

LEEDS, Little Holbeck Board School,
1880, dem. (Linstrum, *WYAA*.)

LEEDS, Old Farnley Board School,
1880, dem. (Linstrum, *WYAA*.)

LEEDS, St Mary, Tong Rd, New
Wortley, 1881-5. (*LM*, 1 Sept.
1881; 25 April 1885; LYAS *Annual
Report*, 1885.)

BRAMHOPE, WY, St Giles, 1881.
(Pevsner, *WY*.)

LEEDS, Campfield, Holbeck, mission
chapel and schools, 1881-2. (LYAS
Annual Report, 1881-2.)

LEEDS, Headingley Board School,
1882. (Linstrum, *WYAA*.)

LEEDS, Kirkstall Board School, 1882.
(Linstrum, *WYAA*.)

LEEDS, elaborate decorations for the
Catholic Church Bazaar in the
Victoria Hall devised by John Kelly,
1882. (*LM*, 26 Jan 1882.)

STANNINGLEY, Leeds, Board School,
1882. (Linstrum, *WYAA*.)

LEEDS, Belle Vue Board School, 1883.
(Linstrum, *WYAA*.)

LEEDS, Castleton Board School, 1883.
(Linstrum, *WYAA*.)

LEEDS, Dewsbury Rd. Board School,
1883. (Linstrum, *WYAA*.)

LEEDS, Meanwood Rd. Board School,
1883, dem. (Linstrum, *WYAA*.)

LEEDS, St Bartholomew, Armley,
pulpit, 1884. (Pevsner, *Leeds*.)

LEEDS, Whitehall Rd. Board School,
1884. (Linstrum, *WYAA*.)

LEEDS, New Wortley Board School,
Kildare Terrace, 1884. (Pevsner,
WY.)

LEEDS, Beckett St. Board School,
1885. (Linstrum, *WYAA*.)

LEEDS, Burley Road School, c.1885.
(*LM*, 2 May 1885.)

LEEDS, Quarry Mount Board School,
Woodhouse, 1885. (Linstrum,
WYAA.)

LEEDS, Whingate Rd. Board School,
Armley 1886 (Linstrum, *WYAA*.)

LEEDS, church and school, Sheepscar,
c.1885. (*LM*, 30 May 1885.)

Thomas Ambler (1838–1920)
See Chapter 12

Elisha Backhouse (c.1810-1894)

Elisha Backhouse was born in Leeds,
probably in 1810.[3] He enrolled as a
pupil of the minor architect/surveyor/
estate agent Benjamin Jackson who
practised in Leeds from c.1818 to 1836.
The *Intelligencer* of 17 January 1835
announced they had formed a
partnership, based at Jackson's office at
18 Guildford Street. However, it was
short-lived as Jackson died in 1836 and
in October that year, Backhouse
announced he was carrying on the
practice alone.[4] Nothing is known of his
independent design work – it seems
estate agency occupied much of his time
– in the period before he joined Perkin
in late 1838 or early '39. The first
indication of that partnership came in
March 1839, in an advertisement
announcing the sale of building land in
Camp Road, Leeds,[5] an activity much
closer to Backhouse's usual business than
Perkin's. However, their fortunes quickly
changed and they went on to have the
leading Leeds practice in the period
before Brodrick was established, and
even after that they continued to secure
important jobs. The partnership was
dissolved in July 1864[6] after which
Backhouse carried on alone, but
maintained the partnership's office.
However, it seems he built relatively
little of importance after he and Perkin
parted company. He died aged 84 in
1894.

*An account of the Perkin and
Backhouse partnership and list of work
can be found under William Perkin.*

Elisha Backhouse

LEEDS, 12 houses, New Wortley,
c.1865. (*LM*, 4 Feb 1865.)
STANNINGLEY, Leeds, parsonage,
c.1865. (*LM*, 4 Feb 1865.)
ARMLEY, Leeds, 2 blocks of model
dwellings, Armley Hall Estate,
c.1865. (*LM*, 11 March 1865.)

3. The Register of Deaths notes his age as 84
when he died in March 1894.

4. *LI*, 22 Oct 1836.

5. *LI*, 9 March 1839.

6. *London Gazette*, 5 July 1864.

LEEDS, Leeds Steam Printing Works
for Messres Baines and Sons,
c.1865. (*LM*, 15 July 1865.)

LEEDS, 3 shops, Briggate, on site of
former Beckett's Bank, c.1867. (*LM*,
21 Sept 1867.)

LEEDS, new shop for J.T. Beer, Boar
Lane 'Improvement', c.1868. (*LM*,
17 March 1868.)

LEEDS, house, Clarendon Road,
c.1868. (*LM*, 13 June 1868.)

William Bakewell (1839-1925)

Bakewell was born in Hampstead, the
son of Frederick C. Bakewell, an author.
He was articled to the London architect
Henry Astley Derbyshire (1825-99) in
1852, aged 13, and remained there until
1857. He enrolled at the RA schools in
1856. He moved on to be an improver
in the office of Sir Charles Barry and
then with Carpenter and Slater, a
prominent firm of church designers.
He was an assistant in the offices of E.R.
Robson – subsequently famous as the
London School Board architect – John
Douglas in Chester, Hunt and
Stephenson in London, and finally
William Henry Crossland in Leeds,
presumably his entrée to the town.[7]
It was a remarkably wide-ranging
apprenticeship: each master differed
from the other in his expertise, but all
were at the very top of their respective
fields.

By 1869 he was in partnership with
George Mallinson using the style
Mallinson and Bakewell of Leeds and
Dewsbury, but by the following year
Bakewell was on his own with an office
in 12, East Parade. He was at 30 Park
Square by 1883. In 1891 Bakewell's
former pupil W.A. Jones (*q.v.*) was taken
on as an assistant and nine years later
was promoted to Chief Assistant. Jones
left in 1904.

Bakewell was a Major in the 2nd West
Yorks Volunteer Royal Engineers,[8] and
was regularly referred to as 'Major
Bakewell', suggesting he took his army
position seriously; certainly he gained
several commissions through military
connections. He also secured several
large jobs like the hospitals in Wakefield
and Halifax, but despite his London
experience, few of his buildings are

19.5: Leeds, Coliseum, Cookridge Street
(William Bakewell, 1882-5). (*Ruth Baumberg.*)

7. Information about Bakewell's training
comes from Felstead, pp. 42-3.

8. *LM*, 19 Aug 1889.

LEFT TOP
19.6: Holbeck, Leeds, design for Holbeck Public Library (William Bakewell, c.1900). (*Academy Architecture, 1902, pt 1, p. 40.*)

LEFT BOTTOM
19.7: Bramley, Leeds, design for Bramley Baths (William Bakewell, c.1902). (*Academy Architecture, 1903, pt 1, p. 22.*)

ABOVE
19.8: Leeds, Pearl Assurance Building, The Headrow/East Parade (William Bakewell, c.1910). (*Academy Architecture, 1912, pt 1, p. 102.*)

notable. An exception is the Leeds Coliseum with its remarkable Gothic façade. According to Jones, it was he who was responsible for some of Bakewell's best late work. He retired to the Kent seaside where he died in 1925.

Bakewell exhibited at the RA on four occasions between 1872 and 1903. He was elected FRIBA in 1892, and was a member of the committee for the Leeds International Exhibition in 1890.[9] His obituary appeared in *The Builder*, 128, 1925, p. 229.

Mallinson and Bakewell

LEEDS, hotel, Boar Lane, for Yorkshire Investment Company, winning competition entry, 1869. (Harper, pp. 77, 260.)

BRADFORD, Town Hall, unsuccessful competition entry, 1869. (Harper, p. 260.)

ROTHERHAM, Rotherham Hospital and Infirmary, c.1869-70. (*LM*, 8 May 1869.)

William Bakewell

ARTHINGTON, nr Leeds, 2 semi-detached vills, c.1870. (*LM*, 21 May 1870.)

LEEDS, 'Lot 6, Boar Lane', shop, c.1870. (*LM*, 21 May 1870.)

HALIFAX, Unitarian chapel and school, c.1870-1. (*LM*, 21 May 1870.)

HALIFAX, Assembly Rooms, alterations to form extra accommodation for Infirmary, c.1870. (*LM*, 18 May 1870.)

HALIFAX, Infirmary, c.1871-3. (Harper, p. 183.)

LEEDS, Masonic Hall, Carlton Hill, 1872. (Linstrum, *WYAA*, p. 371.)

9. *LM*, 18 March 1890.

LEEDS, Coloured Cloth Hall, alterations to accommodate musical performances at the Yorkshire Exhibition, c.1874-5. (*LM*, 26 Dec 1874; 30 Jan 1875.)

LEEDS, St Anne's Buildings, New Briggate, c.1875. (*LM*, 6 Jan 1875.)

LEEDS, Market Hotel, York Street (on site of York Tavern) for Leeds Borough Council, c.1876. (*LM*, 29 April 1876.)

WAKEFIELD, Clayton Hospital, c.1876-9. (Harper, p. 183.)

LEEDS, Cookridge Street Baths, alterations to Brodrick's Oriental Baths, 1881-2. (*LM*, 24 Dec 1881; 1 May 1882.)

LEEDS, Coliseum, Cookridge Street, 1882-5. (*LM*, 7 Aug 1882; 12 Aug 1882; 13 July 1885.)

ILKLEY, Heber's Ghyll Hydropathic Establishment, c.1883-4. (*LM*. 13 Oct 1883.)

MORLEY, Leeds, alterations to Morley Hall, c.1885. (*LM*, 25 April 1885.)

LEEDS, Gibralter Barracks, Claypit Lane, c.1889. (*LM*, 19 Aug 1889.)

LEEDS, Athenaeum Buildings, Park Lane, c.1890. (Linstrum, *WYAA*, p. 371.)

LEEDS, Birmingham and Midland Bank, Kirkgate, opposite Central Market, c.1890-91. (*LM*, 18 Oct 1890.)

LEEDS, offices for Leeds Safe Deposit Box Company Ltd, 69-71 Albion Street, c.1891. (*LM*, 24 March 1891.)

LEEDS, headquarters for Leeds Artillery Corps, Fenton Street, c.1892-3. (*LM*, 12 Nov 1892.)

LEEDS, Engineers' Ground, Camp Road, central hall for the Yorkshire International Exhibition, 1895. (*Building News*, 28, 1895.)

LEEDS, layout of City Square, c.1896. (*LM*, 20 May, 8 Oct, 9 Dec 1896.)

LEEDS, Tower Works, Globe Road, additions for T.W. Harding, c.1899. (Linstrum, *WYAA*, p. 371.)

HOLBECK, Leeds, library, c.1901. (Drawings exhibited RA, 1902.)

BRAMLEY, Leeds, public baths, c.1903. (*Academy Architecture,* 23, 1903, p. 22.)

(Probably) DIDSBURY, Manchester, Warburton Clock Tower, c.1904. (*Academy Architecture*, 24, 1904, p. 140.)

SOUTH MILLFORD, WY, school, c.1904. (*Academy Architecture*, 1904, pt 2, p. 90.)

ILKLEY, library, hall and civic offices (with W.A. Jones), c.1904-8. (*British Architect*, 9 Sept 1904.)

LEEDS, Pearl Assurance offices, East Parade, c.1911. (*Builder*, 128, 1925, p. 229.)

Francis Beford (1866–1904)
See Chapter 16

Edward Birchall (1838-1903)

Edward Birchall was the youngest son of Samuel Jowitt Birchall, a wealthy Quaker wool stapler and was brought up at Springfield House, Leeds. He was articled to William Perkin (*q.v.*) and went to work in George Gilbert Scott's London office in 1860 before returning to Leeds and establishing his own practice in 1864. It was Scott who proposed his associate membership of the RIBA in 1863. He became a Fellow in 1871 when Alfred Waterhouse was among his proposers. Walter Hobson (1854-1910) was one of Birchall's pupils.

Birchall, according to W.H. Thorp (*q.v.*), who worked in Birchall's office for three years, was 'possessed of ample means, he did not push his practice but carried it on in an old-fashioned, leisurely manner'. On occasions he collaborated with John Kirk of Huddersfield where Birchall had family connections, through the Brooks of Meltham Mills, and between 1883-1893 he was in partnership with John Kelly (*q.v.*). Birchall was President of the LYAS in 1883-4 but was forced to resign from the Society in 1887 for his part in a price-cutting war amongst architects with regard the design of Leeds Board schools. Aspects of his private life can be found in the diary of his brother Dearman Birchall, edited by David Verey, '*The Diary of a Victorian Squire*', Alan Sutton, 1983.

LEEDS, Friends Meeting House, Woodhouse Lane, 1866-8 (now part of Leeds Metropolitan University) (*LM*, 24 March 1866.)

BRADFORD, House of Recovery, invited to submit a design, unex, 1867. (*LM*, 23 Dec 1867.)

LEEDS, schools, committee rooms and outbuildings in connection with New Meeting House, Carlton House Estate, 1867. (*LM*, 16 Feb 1867.)

ENDERBY, Leicestershire, St John the Baptist Church for the Brook family (relatives of Birchalls), 1866-7. (*Leicester Chronicle,* 29 June 1867.)

LEEDS, warehouse, Wellington Street, c.1867. (*LM*, 5 Aug 1867.)

MELTHAM MILLS, Huddersfield, convalescent home built by the Brook family, 1866-7. (*Bradford Observer,* 29 Oct 1868.)

RYLSTONE, WY, Scale House, Italianate additions to a former Quaker Meeting House, 1866. (Pevsner, *WY*, p. 678.)

LEEDS, warehouse, 60,Wellington Street for Walter Stead, 1868. (Linstrum, *WYAA.*)

GLOUCESTERSHIRE, alterations, extensions and stables for Bowden Hall for his brother, Dearman Birchall 1869-72. (D. Verey, *Diary of a Victorian Squire.*)

LEEDS, Cardigan House, 84,Cardigan Road, for Joseph Poulter Webb (the partner of Dearman Birchall), 1870. (Linstrum, *WYAA.*)

WRATH, St Mary's Church 1874-5 (*York Herald,* 3 Feb 1875.)

LEEDS, Blind, Deaf and Dumb Institute, Albion St., 1875-6, dem. (*LM*, 5 May 1877.)

TADCASTER, NY, St Mary, rebuilding of medieval church, 1875-7. (*York Herald,* 16 Jan 1877.)

LEEDS, The Friends Sabbath and Mission Room, Great Wilson Street, 1877, dem. (*LM*, 25 June 1877.)

LEEDS, Basinghall St., premises for Marsh, Jones and Cribb, 1877-8, dem. (LYAS, *Annual Report*, 1877-8.)

19.9: Leeds, former Friends' Meeting House, Woodhouse Lane (Birchall 1866-8). (*Ruth Baumberg.*)

19.10: Leeds, St Agnes, Stony Rock Road (Birchall and Kelly, 1886-7). (*Ruth Baumberg.*)

TADCASTER, NY, Board School and master's house, Station Road, 1877-8. (D. Verey, *Diary of a Victorian Squire.*)

MELTHAM, Huddersfield, *The Mount,* 1878, with John Kirk. (Linstrum, *WYAA.*)

ALMONDBURY, WY, additions to St Bartholomew, additions, 1878, with John Kirk. (Charles Hulbert, *Annals of the Church and Parish of Almondbury,* Longmans, 1882.)

SAWLEY, WY, St Michael, 1878-9. (Pevsner, *WY.*)

WINCHFIELD, Hants, Tylney Hall for Charles E. Harris (a relative), 1879. (English Heritage Listing.)

SELBY, school and chapel competition, 3rd prize. (Harper, p. 190.)

LEEDS, Woodhouse Lane, shop for Mr Wood, 1881-2. (LYAS, *Annual Report,* 1881-2.)

LEEDS, alterations to Holy Trinity Church, Meanwood, 1882. (Pevsner, *WY.*)

LEEDS, St Mary of Bethany, New Wortley, 1885-6, dem. The church was begun by Adams and Kelly and completed by Birchall and Kelly. (ICBS, file 08994.)

Note: Verey mentions the following unidentified works as completed by Birchall before 1886: house in Harrogate for Thomas Hattersley, house at Ilkley for H. Richardson, house at Scarborough for Joseph Poulter Webb , house at Durker Roods for Captain Armitage (a family member); schools at Leicester, Otley, Selby and Leeds; Police Courts at Kirby Lonsdale.

Birchall and Kelly

LEEDS, St Matthias, Burley, extension, c.1886. (*LM,* 12 June, 15 Nov 1886.)

LEEDS, All Hallows Church, Regent Road, Woodhouse, 1886, dem. (Leodis Photographic Archive.)

LEEDS, church, Tong Rd, New Wortley, 1886. (*LM,* 25 Oct 1886.) [see also St Mary, Tong Rd, under Adams and Kelly.]

LEEDS, St Agnes, Stoney Rock Road, Burmantofts, 1886-7. (Pevsner, *WR.*)

SHIRESHEAD, Lancs, St James, 1887-90. (churchplansonline.org)

LEEDS, Central Higher Grade School, Woodhouse Lane, 1887-9. (Linstrum, *WYAA.*)

POOL-IN-WHARFEDALE, WY, vicarage, 1887. (*LM*, 1 Aug 1887.)

TADCASTER, NY, Girls Middle Class School and schoolmistress's house, 1888. (*LM*, 28 Feb 1888.)

LEEDS, extensions to Bramley Board School, 1888. (*LM*, 13 July 1888.)

KINGSTON UPON THAMES, St Luke, Gibbon Rd, 1888. (Cherry and Pevsner, *London 2: South*, Penguin, 1999, p. 313.)

HULL, St Luke, Gibbon Road, 1888-91. (English Heritage listing)

LEEDS, York Road, St Patrick RC, 1889–91. (*The Builder*, 86, 1904, p. 641)

LEEDS, Sacred Heart, Burley, 1890, enlarged by Kelly, 1893. (Linstrum, *WYAA*.)

LEEDS, Richmond Hill Board School, 1890, dem. (*LM*, 12 June 1890.)

LEEDS, St Anne RC Cathedral, extension, 1890, dem. (*LM*, 27 June 1890.)

LEEDS, work premises, Basinghall St., for Marsh, Jones and Cribb Ltd., 1890, dem. (Linstrum, *WYAA*.)

LEEDS, Bethlehem Creche, The Bank, 1890. (*LM*, 1 Sept 1890.)

LEEDS, All Hallows Sunday school and parochial hall, Woodhouse, 1892. (*LM*, 30 May 1892.)

Birchall

HUDDERSFIELD, St Joseph, 1894. (Linstrum, *WYAA*.)

LEEDS, Holy Family, 1894-5. (Linstrum, *WYAA*.)

LEEDS, St Francis of Assisi, Holbeck, 1896, dem. (Linstrum, *WYAA*.)

Philip Boyce (fl. 1846-59)

Boyce was, probably, C.W. Burleigh's (*q.v.*) assistant and only appears in the *Directories* in independent practise from 1856 – after Burleigh's early retirement – interestingly, working from 40, Albion Street, Burleigh's old office. St James, Horsforth, seems to have been a joint enterprise. Boyce did not stay long after

Burleigh's departure and in the late 1850s moved to Cheltenham where he continued to practise, although he seems to have produced little there. He was a member of the Cambridge Camden Society by 1853.[10]

LEEDS, All Saints, York Road, c.1846-7. (*LI*, 31 Oct. 1846.)

BARNSLEY, St John, 1853-8. (ICBS, file 04985.)

LONDON, St Botolph, Aldgate, enlargement, 1854. (ICBS, file 04794.)

HUNSLET, Leeds, St Jude's Vicarage, 1856-7. (WYASL WYL 555/24.)

LLANABER, Wales, St Bodfan, 1857-9. (ICBS, file 05350.)

MALTBY, SY, St Bartholomew, 1858-9. (R. Dixon and S. Muthesius, *Victorian Architecture*, Thames an Hudson, 1978, p. 253.)

HORTON, Gloucestershire, National School, 1859-60. (D. Verey and A. Brooks, *The Buildings of England Gloucestershire 1: The Cotswolds*, Yale U.P., 2002, p. 419.)

Cuthbert Brodrick (1821-1905)
See Chapter 10

Walter Braithwaite (1854–1922)
See Chapter 14

Charles Walklett Burleigh (c.1819-84)

C.W. Burleigh was born in Kirtlington, about 8 miles north of Oxford, in 1818 or '19,[11] the son of Benjamin Burleigh.[12] By 1841, Burleigh – by then around twenty-two – was in London.[13] He described himself as 'architect', and was probably working as an assistant to an established architect, or perhaps completing his pupilage.

He first appears in Leeds in 1845,[14] although there is no indication of what brought him to the town. Throughout his stay, his office was at 40, Albion

10. G. Brandwood, 'A Camdenian Roll-call' in C. Webster and J. Elliott, '*A Church as it Should be*', The Cambridge Camden Society and its Influence, Shaun Tyas, 2000, p. 374.

11. Different census returns give slightly different ages for him, but 1819 seems the most likely. I am most grateful to Gwen Brown for her research on Burleigh's family history.

12. Benjamin married Mary, née Walklett at Kirtlinton in 1807. IGI Marriage Index, Oxford Marriages, 1538-1837, online.

13. The 1841 census has him in what was probably a lodging house in the parish of All Hallows, London Wall, sharing accommodation with his brother Benjamin, described as a 'civil engineer'. For Benjamin, see Felstead, p. 137.

14. See Catalogue. He does not appear in the 1845 *Directory* – perhaps compiled in 1844 – but is listed in that for 1847: White's, p. 162.

RIGHT
19.11: Leeds, St Matthew, Little London, design with bellcote (C.W. Burleigh, 1848-54). (*Leeds Library and Information Services*.)

ABOVE
19.12: Leeds, St Matthew, Little London, design with tower (C.W. Burleigh, 1848-54). (*Leeds Library and Information Services*.)

Street. It seems he never married and had lodgings in Ellerby Place, Leeds.[15] Although his career started promisingly, he left Leeds in the mid-1850s, still in his 30s, returned to Oxfordshire to live with his widowed mother and unmarried sister, and retired. He acquired a share in the Leeds Library in 1847 and relinquished it in May 1853, which perhaps indicates his precise departure from Leeds. He is not listed in the *Directory* for 1853. The 1861 census records him in Rotherfield Greys, near Henley, as 'architect not in practice'. He died there in September 1884. He joined the Cambridge Camden Society in 1847[16] and was a member of the Yorkshire Architectural Society by 1850.[17]

Despite Burleigh's modest output, he managed to gain national recognition in the pages of *The Ecclesiologist*, although this probably came about as a result of Burleigh contacting the journal rather than from his fame having spread to London. The edition of February 1846 noted: 'We have seen a wood-engraving of [St James, Woodside, Horsforth] from

the north-west ... The design has considerable merits', although as anyone familiar with this journal will know, it could never conclude a review without some criticism and in this case felt the chancel was 'perhaps unnecessarily lofty [but] it seems of very good length ... Upon the whole we are well satisfied, and hope to meet Mr Burleigh again.'[18] This was praise indeed and readers did not have long to wait for another 'meeting'. Eleven months later, in an article about the design of schools, it included 'a pretty plan for Farnley National School, which has been sent to us.' It discussed it in detail and while it is not altogether enthusiastic about the arrangement, thought 'economy might seem to demand it' and concluded, 'nevertheless, this is a very pretty building, and does credit to the architect, Mr Burleigh of Leeds.'[19]

Burleigh seems to have been a talented artist and produced the plates of the medieval church at Nun Monkton that accompanied the final part (in 1848) of *The Churches of Yorkshire*, a publishing venture inaugurated by Revd

15. 1851 census lists him lodging with Mr and Mrs Mallorie.

16. G. Brandwood, 'A Camdenian Roll-call' in C. Webster and J. Elliott, '*A Church as it Should be*', *The Cambridge Camden Society and its Influence*, Shaun Tyas, 2000, p. 378.

17. *YAS Reports and Papers*, 1850. This is the first published membership list.

18. *Ecclesiologist*, n.s. 2, Feb. 1846, p. 82.

19. *Ecclesiologist*, n.s. 4, Jan. 1847, pp. 3-4.

G.A. Poole and the antiquary J.W. Hugall in 1844. Alongside his artistic skills, he had ambitions as a writer too and 'in future [*The Churches of Yorkshire* series will] be edited by Mr Burleigh',[20] announced *The Ecclesiologist*, although nothing seems to have come of this venture.

It appears that on occasions Burleigh worked with Philip Boyce (*q.v.*); certainly this was the case for St James, Woodside. However, Boyce also did independent jobs.

LEEDS, Superintendent Registrar's Office, Lady Lane, 1845. (*LI*, 26 April 1845.)

LEEDS, Industrial School competition, unsuccessful entrant, 1846. (*LI*, 9 May 1846.)

FARNLEY, nr Leeds, school and master's house, 1846. (*LI*, 11 April 1846.)

LEEDS, National School, York Road District, 1846-7. (*LI*, 9 May 1846.)

LEEDS, National School and house for master and mistress, New Town of Leeds, 1846-7. (*LI*, 1 Aug. 1846.)

HORSFORTH, nr Leeds, St James, Woodside, 1846-8. (*LI*, 5 Dec. 1846.)

KIRK SANDAL, nr Doncaster, rectory, 1847. (*LI*, 29 May 1847.)

LEEDS, St Mary's School, Quarry Hill, added upper floor and master's house, 1848. (*LI*, 13 May 1848.)

NEW WORTLEY, Leeds, school and master's house, 1848. (*LI*, 27 May 1848.)

LEEDS, '8-roomed house at St Saviour's', The Bank, 1848. (*LI*, 26 August 1848.)

BRAMLEY, Leeds, school and master's house, 1848-9. (*LI*, 4 Nov. 1848.)

LEEDS, 'St Matthew's District', new church, (prob. St Matthew, Camp Rd), 1848-54. (*LI*, 4 Nov. 1848.)

HORSFORTH, nr Leeds, National School and master's house, Woodside, 1849-50. (*LI*, 3 March 1849.)

HORSFORTH, nr Leeds, Horsforth Chapel (C of E), roof repairs and new ceiling, 1849. (*LI*, 1 Sept 1849.)

HORSFORTH, nr Leeds, parsonage house for St James, Woodside, 1850. (*LI*, 2 Feb. 1850.)

BINGLEY, WY, St Matthew, c.1850-1. (*LI*, 16 Aug 1851.)

KILDWICK IN CRAVEN, S. of Skipton, school and master's house, 1851. (*LI*, 29 March 1851.)

LEEDS, 'St Paul's District', school and master's house, 1850. (*LI*, 18 May 1850.)

THIRSK, NY, parsonage, 1851. (*LI*, 17 May 1851.)

HUNSLET, Leeds, St Jude, 1852-3. (*LI*, 17 July 1852; ICBS, file 04451.)

BUSLINGTHORPE, Leeds, St Michael, 1852-4. (*LI*, 4 Sept 1852; ICBS, file 04375.)

Robert Dennis Chantrell (1793-1872)

See Chapter 6.

John Child (c.1790[21]-1868)

Child probably started out in one of the building trades and by the 1820s obtained employment as a clerk of works, first for Taylor (*q.v.*) at Hanging Heaton church, Dewsbury (1823-5), for which he was paid £76,[22] and then for Clark (*q.v.*) during the construction of the massive Commercial Buildings in Leeds (1825-9). He first appears in the Leeds *Directories* in 1830, using the Commercial Buildings as his address, but by 1834 his office was at 36, Boar Lane. Later offices were at Park Row (c.1839-45), Guildford Street (c.1845-c.1860) and Wormald's Row (c.1860-5). Around 1855 Child moved to Knaresborough and ran a second office from his home address, Tenter Lodge, Knaresborough, for the rest of his career. By 1845, he was joined by his son Henry Paul Child (1823/4-1898).

Child was probably a RC as several of his early commissions were for this

20. *Ecclesiologist*, n.s. 5, Dec. 1847, p. 186.

21. This is estimated from the fact that his wife was born in 1789. (*LM*, 30 April 1867.)

22. CBC, Minute Book 30, p. 119.

denomination, although he also obtained work from a variety of other denominations. However, it was the impressive St Anne RC church in Leeds (**4.3**) that really established his reputation. He also designed several substantial houses, for instance Headingley Castle (1843-6) (**4.7**), and he might have been responsible for other nearby Tudor villas that repeat elements of the Castle's façade, for instance Ashwood House. He probably designed his own house, The Priory, Cumberland Road.

The Knaresborough office – astutely placed in an area with little competition – brought the partnership much employment in that town and its neighbours in the 1850s and '60s. In the early-1840s, Child senior served as a surveyor for the Leeds Improvement Act.

KNARESBOROUGH, WY, RC church, 1831. (Pevsner, *WY*, p. 377.).

LEEDS, St Patrick RC, 1831-2. (Linstrum, *WYAA*, p. 374.)

PUDSEY, Leeds, vicarage, 1831. (Pevsner, *WY*, p. 626.)

LEEDS, Workhouse, unsuccessful competition entry, 1835. (*LI*, 14 March 1835.)

LEEDS, ST Anne RC, Park Terrace, c.1836-8. (*LI*, 22 Sept 1838.)

HEADINGLEY, Leeds, Headingley Castle for Thomas English, 1843-6. (Inscription in stained glass window to the castle's staircase.)

LEEDS, Mill Hill chapel, unexecuted design, c.1845. (A. Petford, 'Unitarians and Ecclesiology in the North', *Chapels and Chapel People*, The Chapel Society, 2010, p. 36.)

Child and Son

EAST ARDSLEY, nr Wakefield, parsonage, c.1845. (*LI*, 12 April 1845.)

HEADINGLEY, Leeds, town school and master's house, c.1846. (*LI*, 4 April 1846.)

LEEDS, girls' school at St Anne's, Park Terrace, c.1848. (*LI*, 10 June 1848.)

HEADINGLEY, Leeds, 7 four-storey houses, c.1849. (*LI*, 14 April 1849.)

CHESTERFIELD, Derbyshire, alterations to lace manufactory to form ale and porter brewery, c.1851. (*LM*, 26 July, 1851.)

ARTHINGTON, WY, inn or hotel, c.1852. (*LI*, 17 July 1852.)

CASTLEFORD, WY, malthouse, c. 1852. (*LI*, 14 Aug 1852.)

ALDBOROUGH, WY, house and offices, c.1854. (*LI*, 25 March 1854.)

BOROUGHBRIDGE, NY, works at Ellingthorp Hall and lodge, c.1855. (*LM*, 7 April 1855.)

KNARESBOROUGH, WY, houses or houses in Park Place, c.1856. (*LM*, 12 July 1856.)

KILLINGHALL, WY, alterations and additions to house, c.1856. (*LI*, 1 March 1856.)

ASKERN, parsonage, c.1857. (*LI*, 9 May 1857.)

CASTLEFORD, malt kiln for Messrs Austin, c.1857. (*LI*, 30 May 1857.)

KILLINGHALL, WY, house and out-offices, c.1857. (*LI*, 18 July 1857.)

KNARESBOROUGH, WY, banking house for Knaresborough and Claro Banking Co., c.1857. (*LI*, 18 July 1857.)

LEEDS, house, Chapeltown Road, c.1859. (*LI*, 26 March 1859.)

LECKBY, nr Boroughbridge, NY, farmhouse and buildings, c.1859. (*LI*, 19 Feb 1859.)

MORTON FLATTS, nr Northalerton, NY, farmhouse and buildings, c.1859. (*LI*, 19 Feb 1859.)

LEEDS, malt kiln and perim. walls, Accommodation Road, c.1859. (*LI*, 9 April 1859.)

STARBECK, nr Harrogate, house, stables etc, c.1859. (*LI*, 16 April 1859.)

LEEDS, malt house kiln and engine house, c.1859. (*LI*, 4 June 1859.)

LEEDS, St Joseph RC Hunslet, church and priest's residence, 1859-60. (*LI*, 19 Nov 1859.)

HEADINGLEY, Leeds, '3 good houses', c.1860. (*LI*, 5 May 1860.)

LEEDS malt house, stores etc, Melbourne Street, c.1860. (*LI*, 18 Aug 1860.)

FARNHAM nr Knaresborough, house, stables, coach ho. for Fred. Oates, 1860. (*LM*, 7 Jan 1860.)

HARROGATE, *Hollins House*, alterations for James Powell, c.1860. (*LM*, 31 March 1860.)

LEEDS, 4 shops and accomm., Woodhouse, c.1860. (*LM*, 7 April 1860.)

LEEDS, 3 good houses, Headingley, c.1860. (*LM*, 5 May 1860.)

LEEDS, 6 houses and other accomm., Holbeck, c.1860. (*LM*, 21 July 1860.)

LEEDS, malt-kiln, Melbourne Street, c.1860. (LM, 1 Sept 1860.)

LEEDS, enlargement of *Prospect House*, Moor Allerton, c.1860. (*LM*, 22 Dec 1860.)

LEEDS, malt house, Burley, c.1861. (*LI*, 25 May, 15 June 1861.)

LEEDS, schools 'attached' to St Joseph, Hunslet, c.1861. (*LM*, 22 June 1861.)

TOCKWITH, WY, large malthouse for Rob. Brogden, c.1861. (*LM*, 20 April 1861.)

KNARESBOROUGH, WY, Town Hall, 1861-2. (*LM*, 31 Aug 1861.)

HARROGATE, villa and out-offices 'near Harrogate', c.1861. (*LM*, 12 Oct 1861.)

WAKEFIELD, weaving shed and other works, c. 1863. (*LM*, 1 Aug 1863.)

PATELY BRIDGE, NY, Nidd Valley Brewery, brewery and malthouse, c.1864. (*LM*, 23 July 1864.)

KNARESBOROUGH, 2 houses near the gas-works, c.1865. (*LM*, 8 Sept 1865.)

KNARESBOROUGH, WM chapel, c.1867. (*LM*, 9 April 1867.)

Charles Chorley (1830–1912)
See Chapter 11

John Clark (1798-1857)
See Chapter 7

John Wreghitt Connon (1849–1921)
See Chapter 11

George Corson (1829-1910)
See Chapter 12

Joseph Cusworth (1788 or 9-1844)

In June 1817, Joseph Cusworth 'Respectfully inform[ed] the Public that he proposes residing at Mr Wilson's, Mill Hill Leeds, where he will be happy to receive the Commands of those who may have Occasion for his professional Services. During a Period of Nine Years Practice with the late Mr Thomas Johnson, of Leeds, and since that Time Five Years with Messrs Atkinson [Peter Atkinson jnr] and Phillips of York, he trusts he has been enabled to gain Experience in every Thing necessary and useful in the *Profession of an Architect*, and hope[d] by his Diligence and Attention to Business, to ensure the Patronage and Support of his Employers'.[23]

23. *LI*, 2 June 1817, repeated 16 June.

19.13: Leeds, Holy Trinity, Boar Lane, gallery and organ case (Joseph Cusworth, 1822). (*WYASL*.)

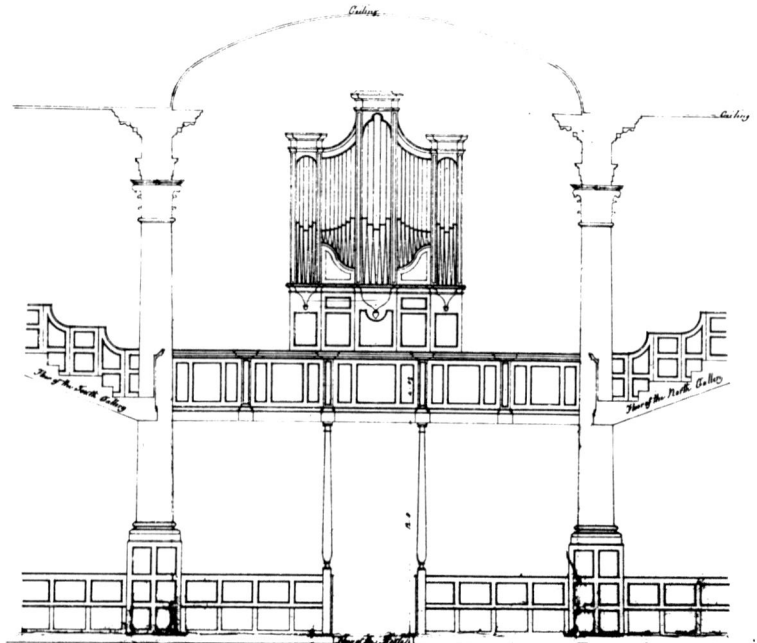

Subsequently, he had an office in Leeds for around twenty-six years, initially at Mill Hill then at Kirkgate (from 1818), at 5 Albion Street (from 1822), and finally in Albion Square (from 1826).

A total of fourteen years with Johnson and then Atkinson and Phillips – two of the county's principal firms of the early-nineteenth century – was an impressive credential for independent practice. However, what we know of his career would suggest he never rose beyond the middle order of practitioners, and seems to have occupied himself with a series of alterations, surveys and letting properties. Surviving drawings suggest he was a competent draughtsman and his 'elegantly drawn'[24] scheme for Holy Trinity's organ case and gallery is an attractive ensemble.

In 1824 he married Elizabeth Pearson of the Union Inn, Leeds,[25] and his death, aged 55, was announced in the *Mercury* of 20 July 1844.

LEEDS, the Leeds Library, report on the library's roof, 1818. (Unclassified papers at the Leeds Library.)
LEEDS, Public Baths, unsuccessful competition entry, 1819. (WYASL DB 276.)
LEEDS, Chapel Allerton Chapel, alterations, 1819. (T. Friedman, *Church Architecture in Leeds, 1700-1799*, PTS, 1997, p. 105.)
LEEDS, Holy Trinity, new west gallery and organ case, 1822. (Friedman, *op. cit.*, p. 100-1.)
LEEDS, John Atkinson's estate, Little Woodhouse, garden buildings and other work, 1822-3. (WYASL DB5/59.)
LEEDS, Albion Street Methodist Chapel, enlargement, 1823. (*LI*, 20 March 1823.)
LEEDS, Holy Trinity, new stone steps in steeple, 1823. (WYASL RDP35/35.)
LEEDS, Upperheadrow north side, proposed line of shops and houses for Leeds Highways Charity, 1828, unexecuted. (WYASL DB 197/241.)

LEEDS, unspecified work for Leeds Highway Estate account, 1829, 1830 and 1834. (WYASL DB197/2.)
LEEDS, unspecified work for Leeds Free School Estate account, 1834. (WYASL DB197/2.)
LEEDS, Mill Hill, proposed alterations to street for Leeds Improvement Commissioners, 1837-8. (WYASL Leeds Improvement Act, committee minutes.)

George Francis Danby (1845-1929)

Danby was born in Leeds, the son of Francis Danby, a cabinetmaker and upholsterer, and committed Wesleyan. He was educated at Leeds Grammar School and then spent nine years with William Hill (*q.v.*), initially as a pupil and then as an assistant, [25A] before commencing his own practice in Leeds in 1872. By 1886 he had offices in the former Masonic Hall in Great George Street.

A significant part of Danby's work was for the Wesleyans: chapels, schools and associated buildings. The majority were close to Leeds, but several were in East Yorkshire – especially for the Pocklington circuit – and some in North Yorkshire. Most were modest in scale but competently designed. He developed an efficient 'Nonconformist Gothic' style which he seems to have favoured, but could turn his hand to the Classical tradition too. His most impressive work was the Baroque re-fronting (1890-1902) of Simpson's (*q.v.*) Oxford Place Chapel, Leeds, carried out in collaboration with W.H. Thorp (*q.v.*). It has often been assumed the two men were in partnership, but the *Directories* confirm they continued separate practices with separate offices throughout the lengthy construction at Oxford Place. For some of his later chapels he worked with John Simpson, possibly the son of James Simpson (*q.v.*).

24. T. Friedman, *Church Architecture in Leeds, 1700-1799*, PTS, 1997, p. 100.

25. *LI*, 23 Oct 1824.

25A. W.T. Pike (ed.), *The West Riding of Yorkshire, at the opening of the twentieth century*, Brighton, 1902, p. 365.

19.14: Leeds, Oxford Place WM and Oxford Place Chambers (Danby and Thorp, 1896-1903). (*Ruth Baumberg*.)

He retired around 1910 and died in Knaresborough, NY, in 1929, aged 84.

He exhibited 'New Congregational Church, Leeds' at the RA in 1901, and did not join the RIBA.

HEADINGLEY, Leeds, houses on the Royal Park Estate, nd. (Trowell.)

HEADINGLEY, Leeds, house in Kensington Terrace, c.1873-8. (Trowell.)

LEEDS, workshop, boiler-house and chimney for Leeds Forge Co Ltd, Armley Road, c.1874. (*LM*, 9 May 1874.)

LEEDS, Woodhouse Carr WM, 1874. (Kelly's *Leeds Directory*, 1893.)

HEADINGLEY, Leeds, Woodhouse Moor WM, 1874, assistant to the Liverpool architect, C.O. Ellison (1832-1904). (Trowell.)

THORNER, nr Leeds, WM, 1876-8. (*LM*, 17 June 1876; T. Morris, *Thorner Methodist Church, 1754-2004*, 2004, p. 14.)

LEEDS, warehouse, Accommodation Rd, Hunslet, c.1877. (*LM*, 23 June 1877.)

HEADINGLEY, Leeds, *Broomfield House* on the Chapel Lane Estate for Robert Slater, plumber, 1878. (Trowell.)

SCHOLES, nr Leeds, WM, 1878-9, attrib., similar to Crossgates WM, see below. (*Scholes Methodist Church Centenary, 1879-1979*, p. 15.)

CROSSGATES, nr Leeds, WM school-chapel, , 1878-82. (*LM*, 30 March 1878; S.H. Young, *Cross Gates Wesleyan Methodist Church; fifty year's record*, 1932, p. 5.)

LEEDS, Roscoe Place WM Sunday school, 1880-2. (*LM*, 22 July 1882; 21 July 1891.)

HEADINGLEY, Leeds, villa and stables, North Hill Road, c.1880. (*LM*, 28 Feb 1880.)

ROUNDHAY, Leeds, villa and stables, Park Lane, c.1880. (*LM*, 28 Feb 1880.)

ROUNDHAY, Leeds, WM Sunday school, c.1884. (*LM*, 5 July 1884.)

HEADINGLEY, Leeds, four through houses, Queens Road, 1884. (Trowell.)

HEADINGLEY, Leeds, Woodhouse Moor WM, caretaker's house, 1885. (Trowell.)

LEEDS, mission room for Hanover WM Soc., c.1885-6. (*LM*, 10 Nov 1885.)

WOODHOUSE GROVE, WY, WM, 1887(?), attrib.

LEEDS, Dewsbury Road WM, 1887-8, chapel. (*LM*, 3 Oct 1887; *The Builder*, 22 Sept 1888.)

LEEDS, Lincoln Fields WM, Sunday school, 1887-8. (*LM*, 30 April 1888; J.E. Ellison (ed.), *History of Lincoln Fields Wesleyan Methodist Sunday School*, 1895, plan facing p. 54.)

LEEDS, Lincoln Fields WM, chapel, c.1890. (J.E. Ellison (Ed.), *History of Lincoln Fields Wesleyan Methodist Sunday School*, 1895, p. 57, citing the *Yorkshire Post*.)

EAST KESWICK, nr Leeds, WM chapel and school, c.1890. (*LM*, 8 Feb 1890.)

LEEDS, Trinity Wesleyan school, Rounhay Rd, c.1890. (*LM*, 19 May 1890.)

LEEDS, Eldon WM, 1890, scheme not fully completed. (*LM*, 12 Nov 1890; *The Builder*, 29 Nov 1890.)

LEEDS, Oxford Place WM, Chapel and Chambers, alterations, new front and extension, with W.H. Thorp, built in stages, 1890-1902. (*LM*, 25 Oct 1892; B.L. Austick, H.B. Jobbings, *A Century – Not out!… Oxford Place Chapel Leeds, 1835 to 1935*, 1935, passim.)

HUNSLET, Leeds, Moor End WM Mission, 1891. (*The Builder*, 5 Nov 1891.)

LEEDS, Dewsbury Road WM, schoolroom, c.1891. (*LM* 20 April 1891; *The Builder*, 18 July 1891.)

LEEDS, Hanover Place WM, schoolroom, 1891. (*LM*, 21 June 1890; *The Builder*, 24 Oct 1891.)

LEEDS, Woodhouse (Street) WM, Sunday school, 1891-2. (*The Builder*, 1891.)

19.15: Leeds, Woodhouse Lane Congregational Church (G.F. Danby, 1898-1901). (Building News, *1901*.)

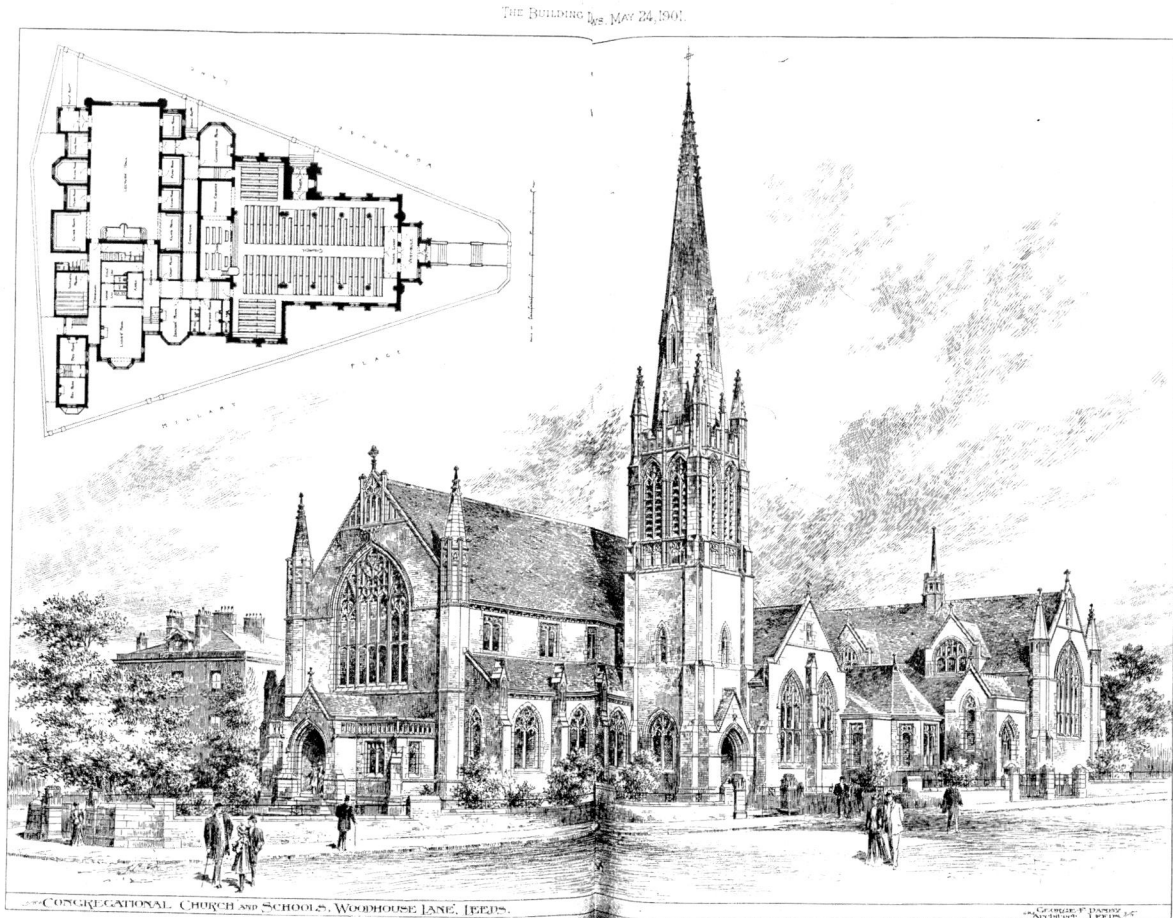

CROSSGATES, nr Leeds, WM church, 1892-3. (S.H. Young, *Cross Gates Wesleyan Methodist Church; fifty year's record,* 1932, p. 9.)

LEEDS, Woodhouse (Street) WM, alterations to chapel of 1840 by James Simpson, including organ chamber and external porches, 1891-2. (*The Builder,* 1893)

SHADWELL, nr Leeds, WM, 1892. (*LM*, 27 Feb 1892; *Scholes Methodist Church Centenary, 1879-1979*, p. 15.)

LEEDS, Roseville Road WM, Charlie Coulson Memorial, 1893-4. (*The Builder,* 27 April 1893.)

LEEDS, Brunswick WM, repairs and alterations, 1893-4. (*LM*, 22 Feb 1894.)

LEEDS, Trinity WM, Roundhay Road, chapel, 1894. (WYASL, mss church records.)

LEEDS, Richmond Hill WM Sunday school, 1894-5. (*LM*, 27 Oct 1894; *The Builder,* 24 Oct 1891.)

BURLEY WM, nr Leeds, chapel and ancillary premises, 1896-8. (Pevsner, *WY*, p. 486.)

LEEDS, New Blackpool WM, 1896-7. (*The Builder,* 28 November 1896.)

LEEDS, Lady Pit Lane WM, c.1898. (*The Builder*, 9 April 1898.)

BARWICK IN ELMET, WM, William Dawson Memorial, 1898-9. (*LM*, 4 April 1899; *The Builder*, 30 March 1895.)

LEEDS, Woodhouse Lane, Trinity Congs [later Trinity-St. David's URC], 1898-1902. (C. Binfield, *So Down to Prayers,* 1977, p. 98.)

ELVINGTON, EY, WM, 1899. (D. & S. Neave, *East Riding Chapels and Meeting Houses* , EYLHS, 1990, p. 49.)

MELBOURNE, EY, WM, 1899, alterations (D. & S. Neave, *op. cit.,* p. 61.)

CATTON, EY, WM, 1900 (D. & S. Neave, *op. cit.,* p. 48.)

LEEDS, Woodsley Road Congs, 1900. (*The Builder,* 10 Feb 1900.)

MILLINGTON, EY, WM, 1900. (D. & S. Neave, *op. cit.,* p. 54.)

SEATON ROSS, EY, WM, 1900. (D. & S. Neave, *op. cit.,* p. 56.)

BISHOP WILTON WM, alterations, 1990-1. (D. & S. Neave, *op. cit.,* p. 46.)

BRAMLEY, Leeds, Brunswick WM, internal alterations including porch, 1900-1. (WYASL, trust minutes.)

NEWTON-ON-DERWENT, EY, WM, 1901. (D. & S. Neave, *op. cit.,* p.54.)

SHIPLEY, WY, Hall Royd WM, school chapel, 1901. (*The Builder,* 1 June 1901.)

BRADFORD, Westgate Hill WM, plans presumably not implemented as W.J. Morley of Bradford was the architect. (*The Builder,* 1 June 1901.)

OTLEY, WY, WM, Later Trinity Meth. Sunday school, 1902-5.Danby & Simpson competitor winners. (*Centenary Brochure,* 1975.)

CAYTON, nr Scarborough, WM, 1903. (*Wesleyan Methodist Annual Chapel Department Report,* 1903)

GREEN HAMERTON, NY, WM, 1903. (NYCRO, architect's drawings.)

ILKLEY, Wells Road WM Sunday School, 1903, plans submitted unsuccessfully in the competition. (WYASB, church records.)

STARBECK, nr Harrogate, WM, 1904, but as the chapel was built in 1888 it is uncertain what these plans were for. (NYCRO, plans.)

LEEDS, Burley WM, Cardigan Lane, Sunday school, Sunday school [by Danby & Simpson], 1904-5. (Pevsner, *WY*, p. 486.)

LEEDS, Dewsbury Road Congs, 1906, scheme not completed. (*ex inf.,* John Minnis.)

LEEDS, Park WM, Cross Flatts, 1906-7, scheme not fully completed. (*The Builder,* 19 May 1900.)

WORTLEY, Leeds, Bethel Congs Institute, Upper Wortley Road, 1908. (*The Builder,* 10 Oct 1908.)

HEADINGLEY, Leeds, WM, school and lecture hall, 1909. (*The Builder*, 6 Nov 1909.)

19.16: Monument to Christopher Beckett, Leeds Parish Church (designed by Jeremiah Dobson, 1847). (*Leeds Library and Information Services.*)

Jeremiah Dobson (fl. 1845-70)

The first notice of Dobson comes with the announcement of his partnership with Thomas Shaw (*q.v.*) in 1845 when their office was at 19 Park Row.[26] This was short lived and by 1847 Dobson was working alone, although he kept the office in Park Row. By 1856 he was in partnership with C.R. Chorley, (*q.v.*) an arrangement that lasted until Dobson's retirement in 31 March 1870.[27]

Although among his commissions were many modest ones, he also produced several well-designed churches. His 1847 monument to Christopher Beckett in Leeds Parish Church was much admired and securing second place in the competition for Bradford's St George's Hall was commendable. Chorley's arrival seems to have taken the practice to a slightly higher level. Their offices for the Old Gas Company was deemed by *The Architect* to be one of the 'handsomest buildings' in the newly-widened Boar Lane,[28] when its reviewer came to assess the town's recent buildings.

Dobson was a member of the Leeds Library from 1856-65.[29] He might have been the Jeremiah Dobson that died in Ripon in 1873, aged 59.

Dobson and Shaw (1845-7)

LEEDS, Free School, unexecuted proposal for enlarging school, c.1845. (WYASL 197/30.)
LEEDS, Mill Hill Chapel, submitted design, c.1845. (A. Petford, 'Unitarians and Ecclesiology in the North' in *Chapels and Chapel People*, The Chapel Society, 2010, p. 36.)
LEEDS, house in Headingley Lane, c.1845-6. (*LI*, 29 Nov. 1845.)
YEADON, nr Leeds, Yeadon Gaslight and Coal Company works, c. 1845. (*LI*, 14 June 1845.)
LEEDS, school in Darley Street, c.1846. (*LI*, 6 June 1846.)
LEEDS, Woodhouse Grove School, alteration, c.1846-7. (*LI*, 12 Dec. 1846; WYASL, Nettleton Papers.)

Jeremiah Dobson (1847-55)

LEEDS, Leeds Parish Church, designed monument to Christopher Beckett, c.1847. (Maynall, *Annals of Yorkshire* vol I, p. 535-6.)

19.17: Gomersal, WY, St Mark (Jeremiah Dobson, c.1849-51). (*Leeds University Library, Special Collections.*)

26. *LI*, 22 Feb. 1845.

27. Felstead, p. 170.

28. Quoted in *LM*, 1 November 1876.

29. Unclassified papers at the Leeds Library.

ROBERTTOWN, WY, National School
and master's house, c.1849-50. (*LI*,
16 June 1849.)

LEEDS, organ case at St George's, 1849-
50. (*LM*, 16 Feb. 1850.)

GOMERSALL, WY, St Mary, c. 1849-
51 (*LI*, 6 Oct. 1849; 1 Feb. 1851.)

GOMERSALL, mechanics' Institute,
c.1850. (*LM*, 26 Oct. 1850.)

BRADFORD, second prize in
competition for St George's Hall,
1851. (*LI*, 15 Feb. 1851.)

LEEDS, eight unidentified almshouses,
c.1850. (WYASL, Free School
Accounts.)

LEEDS, Harrison Almshouses, Wade
Lane, c.1850. (WYASL, Free School
Accounts.)

LEEDS, Charity School, repairs, c.1851.
(WYASL, 160/197/8.)

LEEDS, St John the Baptist, New
Wortley, c. 1852-4. (*LI*, 24 July
1852.)

LEEDS, St Philip's school, masters
house and 'new west window' [?for
church], 1852. (*LI*, 31 July 1852.)

LEEDS, additions to White Horse
hotel, c.1853. (*LI*, 13 Aug. 1853.)

LEEDS, St Stephen, Burmontofts,
c.1853-4. (*LI*, 3 Dec. 1853; Boyne,
vol V, no. 60.)

LEEDS, Whitkirk church, repewing,
1855. (WYASL, RDP 106/65.)

LEEDS, parsonage for St Philip's,
c.1855. (*LI*, 20 Jan. 1855.)

19.18: New Wortley, Leeds, St John the
Baptist (Jeremiah Dobson, 1852-4).
(*Leeds University Library, Special
Collections.*)

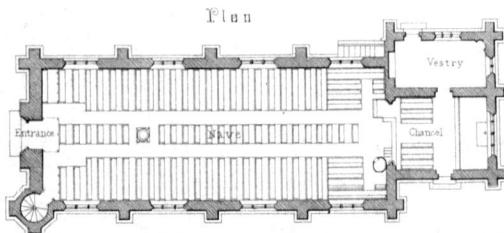

19.19: Leeds, St Stephen, Burmantofts
(Jeremiah Dobson, c.1855). (*Leeds
Library and Information Services.*)

LEEDS, parsonage for St Michael's, Buslingthorpe, c.1855. (*LI*, 20 Jan. 1855.)

KIRKSTALL, Leeds, eleven houses and three shops, c.1855. (*LI*, 27 Jan. 1855.)

LEEDS, parsonage for St Stephen, Burmantofts, c.1855. (*LM*, 10 Feb 1855.)

LEEDS, alterations to St Mary, Whitkirk, c.1855. (*LI*, 19 May 1855.)

LEEDS, house and offices, Clarendon Road, c.1855. (*LI*, 21 April 1855.)

GOMERSAL, WY, parsonage for St Mary's, c.1855. (*LI*, 17 Feb. 1855.)

Dobson and Chorley (1856-70)

LEEDS, parsonage for St John, Wortley, c.1856. (*LI*, 12 April 1856.)

LEEDS, school and master's residence at Leeds Parish Church, c.1856-7. (*The Builder*, 1856, 14, pp. 662-3; *LI*, 23 Aug 1856.)

LEEDS, monument in St Mark, Woodhouse, c.1856. (*LM*, 18 Oct 1856.)

LEEDS, five houses in Far Headingley, c.1856. (*LI*, 7 Feb 1857.)

LEEDS, two villa residences in Hilary Place, c.1857. (*LI*, 18 April 1857.)

GOATHLAND, NY, offices, manager's house, engine house etc for Goathland Iron Works, c.1857. (*LI*, 25 July 1857.)

LEEDS, Leeds Library, proposed alterations, 1858. (Unclassified papers at Leeds Library.)

LEEDS, St Thomas's School, c.1858. (*LI*, 16 Jan 1858.)

HALIFAX, two villa residences at Pickle Bridge, c.1859. (*LI*, 26 Feb 1859.)

LEEDS, boys school at St Matthew's, 1859-60. (*LI*, 24 Sept. 1859; 21 July 1860.)

LEEDS, St Stephen's School, Burmantofts, c.1859-60. (*LI*, 15 Oct 1859.)

LEEDS additional buildings at St George's School, c.1859-60. (*LI*, 12 Nov 1859.)

LEEDS, warehouse, Wellington Street, c.1860-1. (*LI*, 29 Dec 1860.)

LEEDS, internal alterations to Leeds Parish Church, 1861. (*LM*, 31 Aug 1861.)

LEEDS, board room, steward's office, shops for Committee of Charitable Uses, c.1861. (*LI*, 11 May 1861.)

19.20: Leeds, St Peter's Parish Church Schools (Dobson and Chorley, c.1856-7). (The Builder, *14, 1856, p. 663*.)

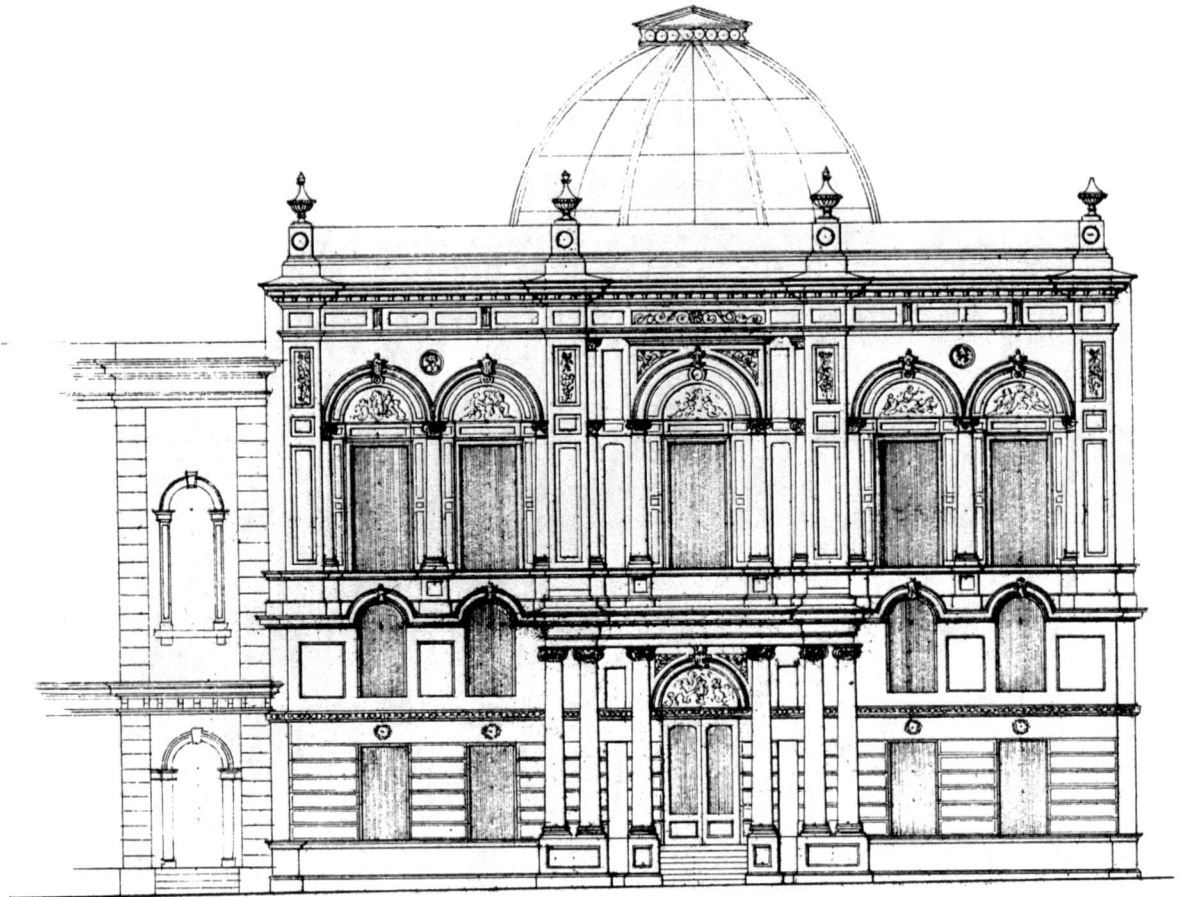

19.21: Leeds, unexecuted design for new premises for the Leeds Library, Albion Place (Dobson and Chorley, 1858). (*The Leeds Library.*)

LEEDS, St John, Briggate, unexecuted plans for new church, 1861. (*ex inf.* Janet Douglas.)

LEEDS, alterations and additions to Philosophical Hall, 1861-2. (*LI*, 25 May 1861; 17 Dec. 1862.)

NORTHALERTON, NY, alterations and additions to Pepper Hall, *c.*1861. (*LI*, 31 Aug 1861.)

WAKEFIELD, Calder Vale Iron Works, c.1862. (*LI*, 12 April 1862.)

LEEDS, 2 houses De Grey Road, Woodhouse Lane, c. 1862. (LI, 17 June 1862.)

LEEDS, 8 houses Love Lane, Camp Road, c.1862. (*LI*, 6 Sept 1862.)

LEEDS, additions to master's residence, Leeds Grammar School, c.1863. (*LI*, 21 March 1863.)

LEEDS, warehouse for Messrs Constantine, Cookridge Street, c.1863. (*LI*, 4 April 1863.)

LEEDS, New Wortley Cemetery, chapels, lodges etc, 1863-4. (*LI*, 7 Feb. 1863; 16 July 1864.)

LEEDS, warehouse for Charles Roadhouse, Cookridge Street, c.1863-4. (*LM*, 19 Dec 1863.)

LEEDS, additions to St John's School, New Wortley, c.1864-5. (*LI*, 26 Nov 1864.)

LEEDS, St John the Baptist, Spence Lane, New Wortley 1864-5, dem. (Wortley Local History Group, *Wortley Churches and Chapels*, 1995.

LEEDS, Elmete Hall, Roundhay, for James Kitson senior, 1865 (Pevsner, *WY.*)

19.22: Banbury, Oxon, Corn Exchange
(William Hill, 1857). (*Christopher
Webster.*)

PONTEFRACT, 2 villas, Charlton Park
Estate, *c.*1865. (*LM*, 10 June 1865.)

ROUNDHAY, Leeds, alterations to
Oakwood House, *c.*1865-6. (*LM*,
11 Nov 1865.)

LEEDS, St John, report, 1865. (*LM*, 23
Dec 1865.)

BISHOP MONKTON, NY, parsonage,
*c.*1866. (WYASL 555/3.)

LEEDS, warehouse for Messrs
Constantine, South Parade, c.1866,
[but see entry for 1863]. (*LM*, 27
Jan 1866.)

PONTEFRACT, alterations to Red
Lion Estate for Leeds and Co Bank
Ltd, c.1866. (*LM*, 27 Jan 1866.)

LEEDS, Leeds and County Bank, 1866.
(*LM*, 16 Feb 1866.)

BISHOP MONKTON, nr
Boroughbridge, NY, parsonage,
c.1866. (*LM*, 3 March 1866.)

LEEDS, Old Gas Co offices corner of
Boar Lane and Alfred Street, *c.*1867-
8. (*LM*, 27 March 1868.)

LEEDS, monument to William Beckett,
Leeds Parish Church, 1867-8. (*LM*,
22 Feb 1868.)

LEEDS, 'building for parochial purposes
in The Calls, for Leeds Parish
Church', c.1868. (*LM*, 18 April
1868.)

GOOLE, bank and 3 shops for Leeds
and County Bank Ltd., c.1868-9.
(*LM*, 5 Dec 1868.)

William Hill (1827 or 8-1889)

Hill was educated at the West Riding
Proprietary School, Wakefield and
subsequently studied under Perkin &
Backhouse (*q.v.*). In 1850 – aged just
twenty-two – he announced the opening
of his office with 'A Card' in the
Intelligencer;[30] his office was at 59 Albion
Street. He was elected a Fellow of the
RIBA on 4 December 1871, proposed
by T. Oliver, H.J. Paull[31] and his former
master, Perkin. He was in partnership
with Salmon L. Swann from 1868 until
at least 1877 and this seems to coincide
with the practice having a Sheffield

office, presumably run by Swann.
However, not all of the firm's work in
this period carries both names. By 1875
the Leeds office had moved to 11 Park
Square. William Longfield Hill (1864-
1927), his son and winner of the
Queen's Prize and Silver Medal, trained
in his father's office and took over the
practice on his father's death. Amongst
William Hill's other pupils was George
Danby (*q.v.*), later Hill's assistant until
1872 when he established his own
practice. Another was Stephen Ernest
Smith (*q.v.*), son of John Wales Smith,
a Leeds undertaker, who went on to
work in partnership with John Tweedale
(*q.v.*).[32]

During his time with Perkin and
Backhouse, that partnership was
extremely busy with a number of
substantial public buildings, especially
ones associated with the provisions of
the Poor Law and welfare systems:
workhouses and hospitals. Hill's
experience with them would prove most
useful later.

In 1856 he joined the Lodge of
Fidelity in Leeds,[33] a lodge popular with
the architect community. In 1874 he
moved to *The Heath*, Adel, Leeds, a
Gothic house he had designed and
where he remained for the rest of his
life.[34] He and his wife Elizabeth are
interred in Adel churchyard; the
monument, designed by Hill and
sculpted by Hodgson, consists of a cross
under a Norman arch flanked by angels.

Hill's early designs were for modest
structures, mainly small groups of

30. *LI,* 8 June 1850. His office was at 59
Albion Street.

31. London, RIBA nomination files quoted
in Felstead, p. 445.

32. W.T. Pike (ed.), *The West Riding of
Yorkshire, at the opening of the twentieth
century,* Brighton, 1902, pp. 365, 367, 373.

33. A. Scarth & C.A. Bain, *History of the
Lodge of Fidelity,* Beck and Inchbold, 1894,
p. 224.

34. His obituary is in *The Builder,* 56, 1889,
p. 34.

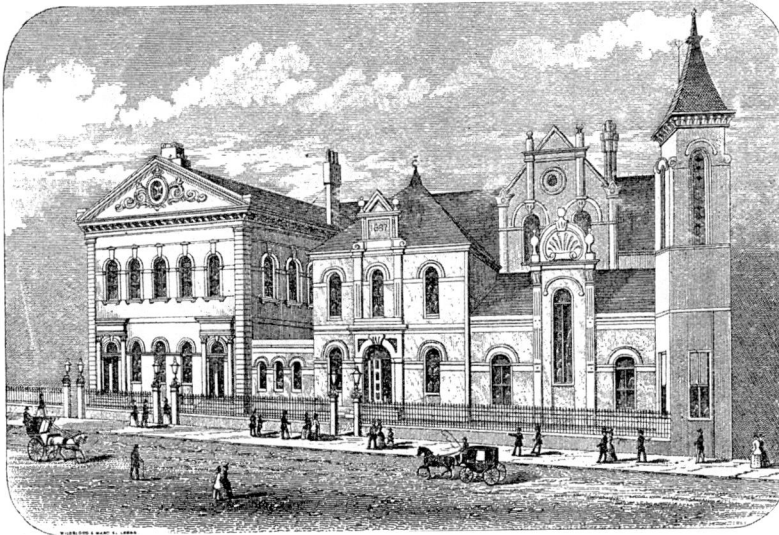

19.23: Leeds, Woodhouse Lane MNC, chapel on left (William Hill, 1858); school on right (William Hill, 1887). (*Colin Dews.*)

labourers' cottages and some villas, but his MNC associations soon produced a string of chapel commissions, including some substantial buildings like the one in Woodhouse Lane, Leeds (1853-8) – which he attended – and, significantly, the Connexion's ministerial training establishment, Ranmoor College, Sheffield (1862-4), a Gothic composition. Here the financial support and influence of the Firth family of steel manufactures, leading members of the Connexion in Sheffield, were important and soon after, in 1869, Hill was appointed the architect for the town's Firth Almshouses. A number of influential New Connexion families gave Hill private commissions, including the Hepworth tailoring family of Leeds and, perhaps, John Whittaker, a very successful MNC cotton spinner from Hurst, near Manchester.

From the 1860s Hill was the architect of many of the MNC's main chapels especially in the industrial West Riding but also in places as far apart as Cumbria, Birmingham, Bury, Hull, Jarrow and Stockport. By his forties William Hill was their leading northern architect, although there were others within the Connexion such as A.H. Goodall of Nottingham, a son of the manse, who also designed a number of MNC chapels.[35] A measure of Hill's importance within the Connexion came with his being awarded the prestigious commission for Christ Church MNC, Abbey Road, Barrow-in-Furness, 1874-5. A Gothic design, the church had a capacity of over 850 and cost £8,500. The land was given by the Duke of Devonshire – on condition that a structure of some dignity was erected – so the entire budget was spent on the

35. Goodhall, for example, was the architect of Rose Street MNC and Sycamore Street MNC school-chapels Nottingham, both 1895 (*MNC Mag.* 1895, pp. 274 & 403) as well as the earlier Beeston MNC, 1875 (*MNC Mag.*, 1875, p. 40) and Kimberley MNC, 1884 (*MNC Mag*, 1895, p. 115).

19.24: Bolton, Lancs, Town Hall (**William Hill, 1863-73). (The Builder, *31, 1873, pp. 446-7.*)

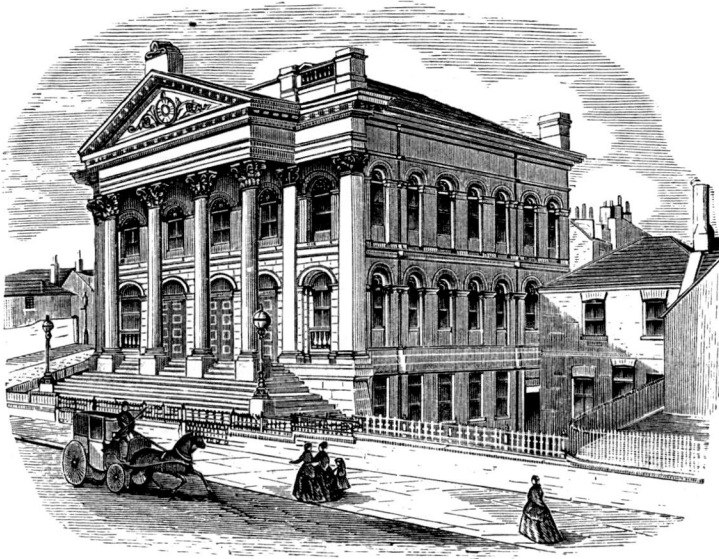

MOUNT TABOR, STOCKPORT

19.25: Stockport, Cheshire, Mount Tabor MNC (William Hill, 1865-8) (*Colin Dews.*)

building which made it one of the most expensive in the Connexion. It was also the largest Nonconformist chapel in the town.

By the end of his career, Hill could count at least forty-five Nonconformist chapels for a variety of denominations, plus a host of alterations and associated

Sunday schools. Yet despite this enviable record of chapel work, clearly Hill had grander ambitions – and the energy to pursue them – and secured victories in a number of competitions around the country for modest public buildings, including the Corn Exchanges in Banbury, Oxfordshire (**19.22**) and Devizes, Wiltshire, both in 1857. He produced cemeteries for Salford (1856) and Chichester (1857-8), and there were other competitions he entered but failed to win, for instance for Spurgeon's New Tabernacle, Newington, London (1859) and the Mechanics Institute and County Museum in Lincoln (1861). In both of these he was placed second.

However, it is for two great town halls that Hill is best remembered, both far from Leeds, but with an obvious link to the town as we shall see. His first town hall appointment was announced in 1854, for a new building in Preston, although the project came to nothing[36] and in 1867 G.G. Scott was employed. Nearby in Bolton, the council also desired a fine town hall and in 1863, sent a committee to examine recently erected edifices around the country. Its favourite was Brodrick's in Leeds. Soon a competition was held and Hill, knowing

19.26: Leeds, 'Old' Dispensary, Vicar Lane (William Hill, 1865-7). The entrance front was originally symmetrical, but the left hand side was altered to accommodate road widening. (*Ruth Baumberg.*)

36. C. Cunningham, *Victorian and Edwardian Town Halls*, RKP, 1981, pp. 82-3.

what the good folk of Bolton admired most, set out to give them just what they wanted: a scaled down version of Leeds. Ironically, Brodrick also entered the competition with a pastiche of his Leeds essay, but it was Hill who emerged as victor (**19.24**). Hill's other great town hall was in Portsmouth (1886-90), completed by his son (**9.15**). It was another version of Brodrick's masterpiece.

Hill was adept at composing in all the fashionable styles, although arguably weakest with Gothic. His best chapels and civic buildings are Classical and where the budget was generous, he could rise to the occasion with a monumental essay. He also impressed with some smaller Classical schemes, for instance the 'old' dispensary in Leeds (**19.26**) and the Corn Exchange in Banbury. The practice, substantially but not totally northern, reached its climax with Bolton and Portsmouth Town Halls, two buildings which established Hill as a figure of national importance.

His obituary (*The Builder*, 56, 1889, p. 34) reported that 'during the past thirty-seven years [he] has held a leading position among the architects of the town' and alongside a short list of his major public buildings, includes 'mansions at Ranmore [Sheffield] and in the neighbourhood of Leeds … [and] upwards of 100 chapels and schools.'

HEADINGLEY, Leeds, *Longfield*, Victoria Road, additions for Norris R. Hepworth, nd (Trowell.)

LEEDS, 9 dwellinghouses 'in the immediate neighbourhood of Leeds', c.1850. (*LM*, 23 Nov 1850.)

SHEFFIELD, dwelling house, c.1852. (*LM*, 7 Feb 1852.)

IDLE, Bradford, 2 dwelling houses and shops c.1853. (*LI*, 13 Aug 1853.)

LEEDS, 'near the Burley Road', 8 dwelling houses c.1853. (*LM*, 5 Feb 1853.)

LEEDS, 6 houses fronting Virginia Street, Beech Grove, c.1853. (*LM*, 28 May 1853.)

19.27: Leeds, warehouses, Aire Street (**William Hill, 1868-9**). (*Ruth Baumberg.*)

LEEDS, Woodhouse Lane MNC, 1853-8. (*LM*, 17 Oct 1857.)

LEEDS, Burley Road, 5 houses and a shop, c.1854. (*LM*, 20 May 1854.)

LEEDS, Woodhouse Lane, tobacco mill with stabling and sheds with 6 houses and shops, c.1854. (*LM*, 25 Feb 1854.)

ROTHWELL, Windmill Field, between Rothwell and Carlton, 4 houses and other works, c.1854. (*LI*, 15 April 1854.)

LEEDS, Harehills Lane, villa residence and outbuildings, c.1854-5. (*LM*, 20 Oct 1854.)

LEEDS, new Workhouse, unsuccessful competition entry, 1855. (*LM*, 6 Feb 1855.)

PRESTON, new Town Hall, 1855, probably unexecuted. (*LM*, 17 March 1855.)

SALFORD, cemetery, mortuary chapel, lodge and entrance, c.1856. (*LM*, 23 Feb 1856.)

HOLMFIRTH, WY, Flood Almshouses, 1856. (*LI*, 1 March 1856.)

HOLMFIRTH, WY, villa residence, c.1856-7. (*LM*, 20 Sept. 1856.)

DEVIZES, Wilts, Corn Exchange, 1856-7. (*LM*, 18 Oct 1856.)

BANBURY, Oxon, Corn Exchange, 1857. (English Heritage Listing Description.)

CHICHESTER, cemetery buildings, c.1857-8. (*LM,* 17 Nov 1857.)

HECKMONDWIKE, WY, Upper Chapel, Congs, day and Sunday schools, c.1858. (*LM,* 6 March 1858.)

LEEDS, Sheepscar, Belgrave Street Congs, mission schools, c.1858-9. (*LM,* 26 June 1858.)

HERTFORD, Corn Exchange, c.1858-9. (*LM,* 26 June 1858.)

LEEDS, Clarendon Road, 2 houses, c.1858-9. (*LM,* 23 Oct 1858.)

BANBURY, Oxon, 3 houses, Bath Crescent, c.1859. (*LM* 1 Jan 1859.)

BANBURY, Oxon, pair of semi-detached villas, Broughton Road, c.1859. (*LM,* 1 Jan 1859.)

HOLBECK, Leeds WM day schools and master's house, Holbeck. c1859. (*LM* 14 May 1859; *LI,* 24 Dec 1859.)

LONDON, Newington, Spurgeon's New Tabernacle competition, second premium, c.1858-9. (*LI,* 19 Feb 1859.)

FARNLEY, Leeds, burial ground, new Episcopalian chapel, lodge and walls, c.1859-60. (*LI,* 30 July 1859.)

LEEDS, stalls for Woodhouse Lane MNC Bazaar, Leeds Town Hall, 1859 (*MNC Mag.,* 1859, p. 336.)

LEEDS, house in Blenheim Terrace, c.1859-60. (*LI,* 24 Sept 1859.)

LEEDS, Poor Law Union Offices, East Parade, 1859-60. (*LI,* 19 Feb 1859.)

WARCOP, Cumbria, National School and master's house, c.1860. (*LM,* 5 May 1860.)

PUDSEY, WY, Unit., 1860-1. (*LM,* 22 Dec 1860.)

LEEDS, Corn Exchange competition, second place, 1860. (Pevsner, *Leeds,* p. 68.)

HARROGATE, 2 houses nr Brunswick Hotel, c.1860-1. (*LM,* 10 Nov 1860.)

LEEDS, Burley Road, 3 dwelling houses, c.1860-1. (*LM,* 8 Dec 1860.)

HOLBECK, Leeds, St. Matthew, spire and additions to church, 1860-1. (*LI,* 31 March 1860; 4 May 1861.)

WEETWOOD, nr Leeds, villa residence, stables, lodge etc, c.1861. (*LI,* 6 April 1861.)

LEICESTER, St. Paul's MNC, London Road, 1861. (*LM,* 22 Sept 1860.)

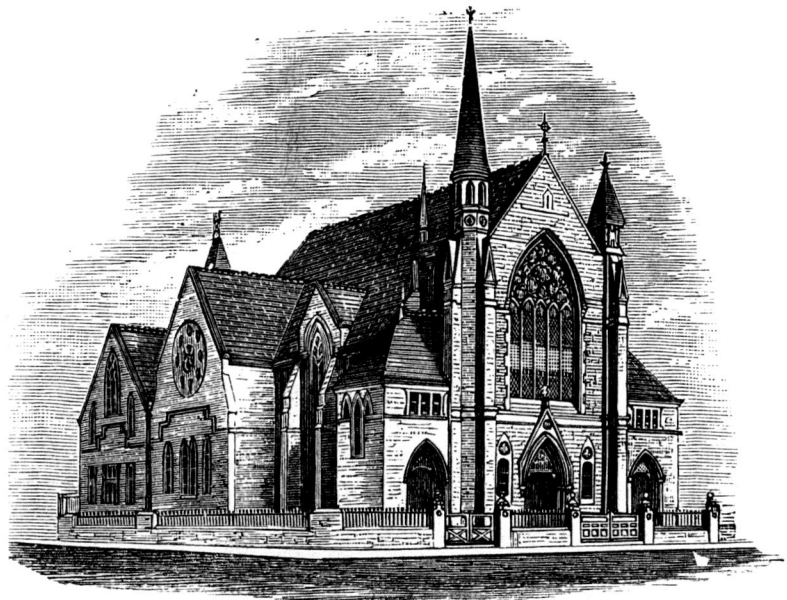

19.28: Barrow in Furness, Christ Church MNC (William Hill, 1873-5). (*Colin Dews.***)**

19.29: Adel, near Leeds, *The Heath* (William Hill, 1874), Hill's own house. (*Colin Dews.*)

BEESTON, Leeds, villa res. and stabling, c. 1861. (*LM*, 22 June 1861.)

LINCOLN, Mechanics Institute and County Museum competition, second premium, 1861. (*LI*, 12 Oct 1861.)

LEEDS, Dewsbury Road MNC, later West Hunslet Central Mission, 1861-3. (Linstrum, *WYAA*, p. 378.)

LEEDS, Woodhouse Moor, 2 dwelling houses, c.1862. (*LI*, 26 April 1862.)

LEEDS, 4 houses, De Grey Road, c.1862. (*LM*, 21 June, 12 July 1862.)

LEEDS, Blenheim Bapt, plans submitted but rejected, 1862. (*Ex inf.* Janet Douglas.)

LEEDS, 3 shops and houses, Cookridge Street, c.1862-3. (*LM*, 5 Dec 1862.)

HURST, nr. Ashton-under-Lyne, 'mansion', possibly Hurst Hall for John Whittaker, MNC cotton spinner, c.1862-3. (*LI*, 13 Dec 1862.)

SHEFFIELD, Ranmoor College, MNC, ministerial training institute, 1862-4. (Kelly's *West Riding Directory*, 1897.)

HUNSLET, Leeds, workhouse, enlargement, c.1863. (*LI*, 25 July 1863.)

BOLTON, Lancs, Town Hall, 1863-73. (*The Builder*, 31, 1873, pp. 446-7.)

CHIDSWELL, nr Dewsbury, Mount Tabor MNC, 1863-4. (*MNC Mag.*, 1864, p. 776.)

DEWBURY, Salem MNC, Northgate, 1863-4. (*LI,* 28 Feb 1863; *MNC Mag.,* 1864, p. 767.)

HOLBECK, Leeds, Union Workhouse, 1864. (*LI,* 7 March 1863.)

LEEDS, Salem Cong. School, Hunslet Road, c.1864. (*LI*, 20 Feb 1864.)

BEESTON HILL, Leeds, Cong chapel, 1864-5. (*LM*, 21 May 1864; architect's drawing at Beeston Hill Free Church.)

HOLBECK, Leeds, Marshall Street Cong Chapel, alterations, 1864-5. (John Mayhall, *Annals of Yorkshire,* nd.)

HUDDERSFIELD, High Street MNC, 1864-7. (*MNC Mag,* 1864, p. 581; *Bradford Observer,* 17 April 1864.)

SHEFFIELD, villa at Ranmoor, c.1865. (*LM*, 4 Feb 1865.)

LONDON, chapel at Forest Hill, c.1865. (*LM*, 18 Feb 1865.)

WAKEFIELD, chapel, c.1865. (*LM*, 18 March 1865.)

SHEFFIELD, Andover Street MNC, now Seventh Day Adventist, 1865. (*MNC Mag,* 1864, p. 588.)

SHEFFIELD, Fulwood, WM, c.1865. (*LM,* 6 May 1865.)

BLYTH, Northumberland, chapel and school, c.1865. (*LM*, 20 May 1865.)

DRIGHLINGTON, nr Leeds, WM, 1865. (*Bradford Observer*, 15 June 1865.)

SHEFFIELD, Broomhill WM, c.1865. (*LM*, 17 June 1865.)

MANCHESTER, chapels and schools, Piercy Street, c.1865. (*LM*, 19 Aug 1865.)

BEESTON, Leeds, Wesley Street WM, 1865-6 (*LM*, 21 July 1866.)

BEESTON HILL, Leeds, WM, 1865-7. (*LM*, 11 Sept 1865.)

LEEDS, Public Dispensary, later Chest Clinic, New Briggate, 1865-7. (*LM*, 6 May 1865.)

LEEDS, Lincoln Fields WM Sunday School, 1865-6. (*LM*, 7 Nov 1865; 3 May 1866;

STOCKPORT, Mount Tabor MNC, Wellington Road South, 1865-8. (*LM*, 7 Dec 1865.)

LEEDS, house and stables, Woodhouse Lane, c.1866. (*LM*, 13 Jan 1866.)

LEEDS, 2 houses and shops, Woodhouse Lane, c.1866. (*LM*, 10 Feb 1866.)

RAVENSTHORPE, Dewsbury, chapel, c.1866. (*LM*, 10 Feb 1866.)

LEEDS, WM school, Lincoln Field, c.1866. (*LM*, 3 March 1866.)

CHAPEL ALLERTON, Leeds, 4 houses, c.1866. (*LM*, 17 March 1866.)

HUNSLET, Leeds, villa, Woodhouse Hill, 1866. (*LM*, 21 April 1866.)

BARNSLEY, MNC chapel, c.1866. (*LM*, 9 June 1866.)

LEEDS premises in Kirkgarte, enlargement, c.1866. (*LM*, 23 June 1866.)

HUNSLET, Leeds, temporary hospital for the Hunslet Guardians of the Poor, 1866. (*LM*, Aug 1866.)

HUNSLET, new hospital for Hunslet Workhouse, c.1866. (*LM*, 1 Sept 1866.)

SHEFFIELD, villa for J.H. Andrews, Tapton, 1866. (*LM*, 27 Oct 1866.)

HOLBECK, Leeds. Bethel UMFC, Meadow Road, 1866. (stylistic attribution, *cf* Hunslet Carr MNC.)

LEEDS, Blenheim Bapt, Woodhouse Lane, 1866, organ case. (*LM*, 18 Oct 1866.)

WAKEFIELD, Grove Road MNC, 1866. (stylistic attribution, *cf* Hunslet Carr MNC.)

BOLTON, Lancs, town hall, 1866-73. (*LM*, 16 June 1866.)

HUNSLET, Leeds, villa, Woodhouse Hill, c.1867. (*LM*, 2 March 1867.)

RIPON, pair of semi-detached villas, c.1867. (*LM*, 6 April 1867.)

STOCKPORT, MNC chapel, c.1867-8. (*LM*, 6 April 1867.)

LEEDS, 4 cottages, Woodhouse Carr, 1867. (*LM*, 25 May 1867.)

LEEDS, 'rebuilding of premises in Kirkgate and Briggate', c.1867-8. (*LM*, 30 Nov 1867.)

STALYBRIDGE, Cheshire, Chapel Street MNC, Sunday school, 1868. (*MNC Mag.*, 1869.)

HOLBECK, Leeds, Isle Lane WM, alterations to include new entrance, 1868. (WYASL, Trust Accounts.)

HULL, Stepney MNC, Beverley Road, 1868-9. (*MNC Mag*, 1869.)

Hill and Swann

SHEFFIELD, MNC chapel, Attercliffe, c.1868. (*LM*, 25 April 1868.)

LEEDS, 30-34 Aire Sreet, 4 warehouses, 1868-9. (*LM*, 20 Oct 1868.)

SHEFFIELD, Firth Almshouses, 1868-9. (*LM*, 26 May 1868; *MNC Mag.*, 1869.)

HUDDERSFIELD, villa at Lindley, c.1868. (*LM*, 17 Oct 1868.)

LEEDS, pair of semi-detached villas, Headingley Hill, c.1868-9. (*LM*, 12 Dec 1868.)

LEEDS, 3 warehouses, Aire Street, c.1868-9, [same as above?]. (*LM*, 19 Dec 1868.)

ILKLEY, Parish Hill Road, villa, 1869. (*LM*, 13 May 1869.)

SHEFFIELD, Glossop Road Bapt, unsuccessful competition entry, 1869. (*Sheffield and Rotherham Independent*, 17 March 1869.)

19.30: Barnsley, Mechanics' Institute (William Hill, 1878). (The Builder, *36*, *1878, p. 242.*)

SHEFFIELD, *Moordale*, now Fulwood Inn, Fulwood Road, 1869, for James Nicholson of the Mowbray Steel Works, 1869, attributed. (Harman & Minnis, *Sheffield*, p. 271.)

RAVENSTHORPE, Dewsbury, MNC, c.1869. (*MNC Mag.*, 1869.)

SHEFFIELD, Castle Mount, now Kersal Mount Nursing Home, Manchester Road, for Joseph B. Jackson of Spear & Jackson, 1869. (Harman & Minnis, *Sheffield*, p. 254.)

LIVERPOOL, St Domingo MNC, Everton, 1870-1. (Pevsner, *South Lancashire*, 1969.)

SHEFFIELD, Clarkehouse Road, villa, 1870. (*LM*, 13 Aug 1870.)

TREBORTH, nr Bangor, mansion for Richard Davies MP, c.1870. (*Baner ac Amserau Cymru*, 20 April 1870.)

LEEDS, Woodhouse Lane MNC, organ case, 1871. (*MNC Mag.*, 1871, p. 169.)

WEST HARTLEPOOL, Wesley WM. Victoria Road, 1871-3. (Julian Orbach, *Blue Guide to Victorian Architecture in Britain,* 1987, p. 78.)

HALIFAX, Salem MNC, 1871-4. (*MNC Mag.*, 1871, p. 613.)

HUNSLET, Leeds, Union Workhouse, school and dormitories, 1872. (Linstrum, *WYAA*, p. 378.)

LEEDS, Aire Street, commercial premises for Watson Brothers, 1872. (Linstrum, *WYAA*, p. 378.)

BARNSLEY, Ebenezer MNC, 1872-3. (J.E. Vero, *History of the Methodist New Connexion, Barnsley Circuit, 1797-1907*, 1907.)

LEEDS, Ventnor Street MNC, 1872-3. (*LM*, 26 Feb 1872.)

PORTWOOD nr Stockport, MNC, alterations, 1873-4. (*MNC Mag.*, 1873, p. 290; 1874, p. 290.)

BIRMINGHAM, Ladywood MNC, 1873-4. (*MNC Mag,* 1874, p. 487.)

BARROW, Christ Church MNC, Abbey Road, 1873-5. (*Lancaster Gazette & General Advertiser,* 11 Oct 1873; *MNC Mag.,* 1874, p. 569.)

LEEDS, Beckett Street WM, 1873-5. (*LM,* 5 April 1873.)

ADEL, nr Leeds, *The Heath*, Dunstan Lane, 1874, for himself (V. Compton, *History of Adel,* 2010, p. 85.) A request for tenders (*LM,* 5 April 1873) for a villa in Adel might refer to this.

HEADINGLEY, Leeds, Grove Terrace, Grove Road, 1874. (*ex inf.* Janet Douglas)

SEACROFT, nr Leeds, WM, new façade, 1874. (Stylistic attribution.)

HEADINGLEY, Leeds, *Oak Lea* and *Burton Grange*, Burton Crescent, post 1874. (Trowell.)

ARMLEY, Leeds, Southfield PM, Wesley Road, 1874-5. (Beckworth, 1910, p. 195.)

HULL, Bethel MNC, restoration, 1875. (*MNC Mag.,* 1876, pp. 286-7.)

MIDGLEY, Halifax, MNC, plans not implemented, 1876. (H.W. Harwood, *History of Methodism in Midgley, near Halifax,* 1933, p. 43.)

HUNSLET, Leeds, Hunslet Carr MNC, 1876-8. (*MNC Mag.,* 1878.)

BRADFORD, Mannville MNC, Great Horton Road, later the Bradford College, Grove Library, 1875. (Pevsner, *WY,* p. 191.)

LEEDS, Beckett Street WM, 1875. (Kelly's *Leeds Directory,* 1893; *The Builder,* Jan 1875.)

BURY, Lancs, Heywood Street MNC, 1876-7. (*MNC Mag,* 1874; *LM,* 30 Dec 1876.)

HALIFAX, Queens Road MNC, 1877. (*MNC Mag.,* 1877, p. 363.)

BARNSLEY, Mechanics Institute, 1878. (*The Builder,* 9 March 1878.)

ADEL, nr Leeds, house, lodge and stables, c.1879. (*LM,* 3 May 1879.)

ELLAND, WY, Bethesda MNC, 1879-80. (*LM,* 16 Nov 1878.)

YEADON, WY, Mechanics Institute, now Town Hall, 1879-80. (*LM,* 2 Nov 1878.)

MEANWOOD, Leeds, WM, 1880-1. (*LM,* 14 Feb 1880; A. Hopwood & S. Rose, *Sequicentenary Story: 150 Years of Meanwood Methodism,* 1961, p. 17.)

Location not stated, weaving shed, warehouse and works, 1882. (*LM,* 1 July 1882.)

DURHAM, Bethel MNC, North Road, 1883, interior remodelling of 1853-4 chapel by E.R. Robson. (G. Potts, 'Methodist Chapels and Gothic Revival', *Proceedings of the Wesley Historical Society,* 41, 1991-2.)

ADEL, nr Leeds, St. John the Baptist Graveyard, monument to Eliza and William Hill, 1884. (V. Compton, *History of Adel,* 2010, p. 82.)

JARROW, Co Durham, Park MNC, Bede Burn Road, 1884-5. (*MNC Mag.*, 1885, p. 447.)

HOLBECK, Leeds, Holbeck Union Workhouse infirmary, 1886, possibly not built (*LM,* 22 May 1886.)

MEANWOOD, Leeds, WM, extension to chancel, 1886-7. (A. Hopwood & S. Rose, *Sequicentenary Story; 150 Years of Meanwood Methodism,* 1961, p. 19.)

PORTSMOUTH, Guildhall, 1886-90, completed by W.H. Hill. (Linstrum, *WYAA,* p. 378.)

HANLEY, Staffs, Bethesda MNC, alterations to include gallery extensions for an enlarged organ, 1887. (J. Leigh *et al, Bethesda Methodist Chapel, Hanley, Stoke-on-Trent: a history and guide,* 2009, p. 8.)

LEEDS, Woodhouse Lane MNC, Sunday School, 1887-8. (*LM,* 13 June 1887; Kelly's *Leeds Directory,* 1893.)

ROTHERHAM, market Rotherhm, no date given. (*Builder,* 56, 1889, p. 34.)

HUNSLET, Leeds, workhouse and school, no date given. (*Builder,* 56, 1889, p. 34.)

Thomas Howdill (1840-1918)
See Chapter 15

Charles Barker Howdill (1863-1940)
See Chapter15

Lawrence Ingham (fl. 1814-17)

In 1814, an advertisement announced, 'Lawrence Ingham, Architect, begs leave most respectfully to solicit of the Nobility, Gentry and Others in this neighbourhood, in the above Profession, and on account of the Death of Mr Johnson, for those Friends who have employed him in that Line, he would be glad to finish any Plans not executed by him; and their further Favours would also be most gratefully acknowledged.' His address was given as '1, Trinity Lane'.[37] The wording is ambiguous; had Ingham been a pupil or assistant of Johnson, or simply an ambitious tradesman who had heard of Johnson's death and identified an opportunity? He appears in the 'Architects' section of an 1816 directory, based at Boar Lane, and in that for 1817 with an office at 4, Church Row. However, not a single job of any sort undertaken by him is known. Should he be in a book like this? Arguably not, yet he provides an interesting dimension to our study of the Leeds profession: anyone could aspire to the status that the style 'architect' implied. At a time when this could be achieved without any training or qualifications, the cost of an advertisement and listing in a directory must have seemed a modest financial speculation. For some, it led to a comfortable living although not, apparently, for Ingham.

Benjamin Jackson (fl. c.1814-36)

Jackson illustrates a common practice of the early nineteenth century: despite producing almost no designs for buildings, and running an office whose principle function involved what today would be termed estate agency, he always signed himself 'architect'. Indeed, he was probably the town's principal estate agent – literally dozens of advertisements appeared in the newspapers selling, renting or

auctioning land and buildings – but to be known as an architect implied a higher status. Perhaps the two callings complemented each other: probably he could more easily sell a building plot if he could also supply a rudimentary design for the finished house. He also offered services more usually associated with surveyors: building repairs and road widening.

In 1814, his office was at 1, Kirkgate, by 1826 he had moved to 70, Kirkgate and by 1830 he was at 18, Guildford Street. At the beginning of 1835, he took into partnership his former pupil Elisha Backhouse[38] (q.v.), perhaps intending to undertake more architectural work. Jackson died the following year leaving Backhouse to practise alone[39] and the latter, interestingly, soon abandoned the estate agency side of the business.

LEEDS, payments for unspecified work listed in Leeds Parish Church, wardens' accounts, 1820 and 1824. (WYASL RDP68/71)

LEEDS, 'superintended' new building at rear of Leeds Library, 1823. (Leeds Library, unclassified papers)

HUNSLET, Leeds, Hunslet Chapel, new roof, repairs and extension, 1823-6. (ICBS, file 00742)

LEEDS, plan for widening Bond Street for Borough of Leeds, 1829. (WYASL DB/197/254)

LEEDS, St Mark's Terrace, uniform fronted houses. (LI, 31 May 1832)

LEEDS, Workhouse, unsuccessful competition entry (with Backhouse), 1835. (LI, 14 March 1835)

Thomas Johnson (1762-1814)
See Chapter 3

William Alban Jones (1875-1960)

Jones was born on 21 may 1875 in London, the son of a telegraph clerk. His father James died in c.1880 and the family moved to Leeds where an uncle

37. *LI*, 15 August 1814.

38. *LI*, 17 Jan. 1835.

39. *LI*, 22 Oct. 1836.

---

lived. Jones attended Winton Street Higher Grade School, but left in 1887, aged 12, to assist his mother in her grocery shop. A talent for drawing prompted him to seek work in an architect's office and in 1888 he went as a junior to William Bakewell (q.v.). Soon after he enrolled at evening classes at Leeds School of Arts, Science and Technology. In 1891, although still only 15, he was promoted to 'assistant' by Bakewell. In 1892 he won the National Silver Medal for Original Architectural Design, a prize presented annually by the Royal College of Art. His design, for a pair of labourer's cottages, was illustrated in the *Carpenter and Builder*, December 1892. Eleven months earlier, the journal had illustrated his 'Design for a Gentleman's Cottage', an impressive composition if hardly a 'cottage', and a precocious drawing for a 16-year-old. He also won the Silver Medal in 1893 and was beginning to be noticed in Leeds. Although offered work in London and the opportunity to enter the Royal Academy Schools, he felt unable to leave his widowed mother and younger sister. In 1894 he began publishing cartoons in the Yorkshire journal *Round the Town* – using the

pseudonym 'Silam' – and in 1895 he was a founder member of Ye Attic Art Club (discussed in Chapter 17). In 1900 he was promoted to Bakewell's chief assistant and given considerable responsibility for the entries for several competitions in which second place was achieved; in 1904 they secured first premium in the Ilkley Free Library and Municipal Offices competition (**19.31**) with a design Jones claimed was his 'but was spoilt in execution through unsympathetic detailing by Bakewell'.[40] Jones also maintained that Bakewell's design for the 'Giotto' tower at the Tower Works, Globe Road, was actually his. Despite the offer of a junior partnership from Bakewell in 1904, Jones decided to leave and establish his own practice, with an office in Albion Place.

By now an artist of exceptional skill, Jones supplemented his fee income by producing competition entries – along with seductive drawings – for a variety of local architects and in 1905 teamed up with his friend from the Attic Club, Percy Robinson (q.v.). Following their victory in the Hove public Library competition in 1905, in 1907 the two entered a formal arrangement whereby

40. C. Mason-Jones, 'William Alban Jones: a life in architecture', unpublished B.Arch dissertation, University of Newcastle, 1986. I am grateful to Mr Mason-Jones for access to his dissertation which contains a perspective view of the Ilkley building, taken from *The British Architect*, annotated with this quotation.

19.31: Ilkley, Town Hall and Library (William Bakewell and W.A. Jones, 1904-6). (*Drawing by T. Raffles Davison*, The British Architect, *9 Sept 1904*.)

the fees from competition successes would be divided one third, two-thirds in Robinson's favour, but with Robinson responsible for all expenses. There followed successes with Bethnal Green Town Hall, London (1907), Headingley Baptist Church and school (1908), Leeds Training College hostel, Headingley (1911) and finally the Villa Marina in Douglas, Isle of Man (1911). They also provided W.A. Kendall of Ossett, WY, with winning designs for several less prestigious competitions.

The arrangement with Robinson came to an end in 1914 and, it seems, Jones struggled to find other employment during the war. He spent some time as an assistant for the Huddersfield surveyors Abbey and Hanson, and in 1915 unsuccessfully entered the competition for Stepney Town Hall. He was elected to the Council of the LYAS in 1916. Subsequently, he formed a partnership with John E. Stocks – another of Bakewell's former assistants – using the style Jones and Stocks with an office in Prudential Buildings. After the war, the firm went on to produce a number of large-scale local authority housing schemes including ones at Kippax, nr Leeds (from 1919), Rothwell, nr Leeds (from 1919) and Bramley, Leeds (from 1920). More interesting was an estate of private houses in Bardsey, nr Leeds (from 1925). In the inter-war period Jones was responsible for much of the village of Linton, nr Wetherby – 'one of the outstanding examples of good rural development in England'[41] – as well as work on the Harewood estate, and a number of substantial individual houses. In all of these he was able to develop his Arts and Crafts sympathies from the 1890s.

He was president of the LYAS in 1924-6, he produced a 'highly interesting scheme' for the Leeds University competition in 1927[42] and in the same year, completed the South Parade Baptist Church in Headingley (started 1908), a particularly accomplished example of late Arts and Crafts Gothic. His reputation rested on his fondness for traditional materials and construction, and for his exceptional drawing skills, exploited with equal felicity for both the serious or the humorous.

Stocks died in 1951 and Jones retired around the end of 1952, although the firm continued until 1997, overseen by Jones' son Denis Mason Jones (1918-2010) who joined in 1952. Denis inherited many of his father's accomplishments, and became famous for his drawings of architectural landmarks and after-dinner speeches, as well as for several major buildings in Leeds.

DESIGN for a gentleman's cottage, 1892. (*Illustrated Carpenter and Builder*, 26 Jan 1862.)
DESIGN for a pair of labourer's cottages, 1892, silver medal competition winner. (*Illustrated Carpenter and Builder*, 9 Dec 1892.)
DESIGN for the Barrett Browning Institute and Clock Tower, c.1892-3. (*Illustrated Carpenter and Builder,* 27 Jan 1893.)
DESIGN for a small shooting box, c.1893. (*Illustrated Carpenter and Builder*, 3 March 1893.)
LEEDS, Tower Works, Globe Road, 'Giotto' tower, c.1900, with William Bakewell. (*ex inf.* Denis Mason-Jones.)
ILKLEY, library, public offices and assembly hall, 1904, with William Bakewell. (Mason-Jones, dissertation.)
OSSETT, WY, elementary school, 1906-9, design produced for W.A. Kendall. (Mason-Jones dissertation.)
HOVE, Sussex, public library, 1905-9, with Percy Robinson. (*Building News*, 6 July 1906.)
CASTLEFORD, WY, secondary school, winning design by not built, 1908, with Percy Robinson. (Mason-Jones, dissertation.)

19.32: Headingley, Leeds, South Parade Baptist Chapel (Percy Robinson and W.A. Jones, 1908-10). (*Drawing by Jones, Academy Architecture, 1912, pt 1, p. 112.*)

41. Report of the 1959 National town Planning Conference, quoted in Mason-Jones, dissertation, p. 49.

42. Illustrated in *Architect and Building News*, Jan 1927.

19.33: Petersham, Richmond, Surrey, All Saints (John and Claude Kelly, 1899). (Academy Architecture, *1911, pt 1, p. 69.*)

HEADINGLEY, Leeds, South Parade Baptist Church and school, 1908-10 (with Percy Robinson), completed 1927 by Jones and Stocks. (*Academy Architecture*, 1912, pt 2, p. 112.)

BETHNAL GREEN, Town Hall, 1907-11, with Percy Robinson. (*Building News*, 18 Oct 1907.)

HEADINGLEY, City of Leeds Training College, Macaulay Hall, 1911-13, with Percy Robinson. (*Yorkshire Post*, 12 Jan 1950.)

DOUGLAS, Isle of Man, Villa Marina, 1911-14, with Percy Robinson. (*Engineering*, 21 Nov 1913.)

HORBURY, nr Wakefield, public hall for Horbury D.C., 1913-14, design produced for W.A. Kendall. (Mason-Jones, dissertation.)

John Kelly (1840-1904)

John Kelly spent his early years in Dewsbury where his Irish-born father was a carpenter and his mother an inn-keeper. One of a large Roman Catholic family, the Kellys moved to Scarborough in about 1847 and John was articled to the Scarborough architect, John Petch. Following his pupilage, he worked in Kington in Herefordshire and then for James Medland Taylor in Manchester.

Subsequently Kelly spent three years with the eminent London architect G.E. Street working alongside J.D. Sedding. In 1865, in his mid-twenties, he formed a partnership with Richard Adams (*q.v.*) – although it is not clear how the men met – and 'at the request of Mr Adams'[43] they chose Leeds for their base. Following the latter's death in 1883, he established a partnership with Edward Birchall which continued until 1893. Subsequently he took his son Claud into the practice and worked until his death in 1904.

Kelly's obituary refers to him 'head of the firm of John Kelly and Son, London' and it seems in the mid-1890s he left Leeds for the capital. Perhaps surprisingly, he succeeded in securing a number of prestigious ecclesiastical jobs in and around London, despite his provincial background. In his lifetime, it is said that he designed over fifty churches, not exclusively for the Roman Catholic church though the scarcity of Catholic architects brought commissions in many parts of the country.

Kelly's obituary appeared in *The Builder*, 86, 1904, p. 641.

Adams and Kelly's work is listed under Adams

Birchall and Kelly's work is listed under Birchall

19.34: Roundhay, Leeds, house (John and Claude Kelly, c.1900. (Academy Architecture, *1904, pt 1, p. 143.*)

43. *The Builder*, 86, 1904, p. 641.

John and Claud Kelly

LONDON, St Patrick RC, Soho Square, 1891-3 (E. Jones & C. Woodward, *A Guide to the Architecture of London,* 1983.)

RICHMOND ON THAMES, Sacred Heart, RC, Kingston Road, 1893. (Cherry and Pevsner, *London 2: South*, Penguin, 1999, p. 535.)

KINGSTON upon THAMES, St Agatha, RC, 1899, dem. (*The Builder*, 86, 1904, p. 641.)

RICHMOND upon THAMES, All Saints, Petersham, 1899. (*The Builder,* 86, 1904, p. 641.)

HOVE, St Peter's Hall, Tamworth Rd., 1902 (originally served as the church) (*English Heritage Review of Diocesan Churches,* 2005.)

FOULRIDGE, LANCS, St Michael's and All Angels, 1903-5 (*Murray's Lancashire Architectural Guide,* 1955.)

LEEDS, St Anthony of Padua, RC, Beeston, 1904. (J. Minnis, *Religion and Place in Leeds,* English Heritage, 2007, p. 15.)

CHISWICK, London, Our Lady of Grace and St Edward, RC, 1904. (Cherry and Pevsner, *London 3: North West,* Yale, 1994, p. 394.)

SOUTH ACTON, All Saints, no date given. (*The Builder*, 86, 1904, p. 641.)

KINGSTON ON THAMES, St Luke, no date given. (*The Builder*, 86, 1904, p. 641.)

Sydney Kitson (1871–1937)
See Chapter 16

William Belton Perkin (c.1809-74)

Perkin was the son of William Perkin, a master mason in Wakefield.[44] In 1833 he collaborated with the landscape gardener Josuah Major to enter the competition for the General Cemetery in Leeds – for which they won the second prize – and probably in 1834 he submitted an unsuccessful entry for the Exeter Market competition.[45] The following year he entered the Leeds Workhouse competition for which he was awarded first prize but, apparently, a plan by a 'favourite candidate' was approved by the parish authorities, and he was denied the commission,[46] although nothing seems to have been built. (Elisha Backhouse – still at this time with Jackson – also entered the competition.[47]) In 1835, '36 and '37, Perkin was elected one of the surveyors for the Leeds Improvement Commission and produced road-widening schemes for West Bar, Mabgate and Swinegate.[48] Around this time he moved from Wakefield to settle in Leeds. In 1838,

44. Felstead, p. 709.

45. In 1839 he exhibited 'A Design for a Market at Exeter', probably an entry for the 1834 competition held there. (*Catalogue of the Leeds Public Exhibition, 1839.*)

46. Perkin at least brought his name to the national stage by setting out the facts in a letter to the *Architectural Magazine*, 2, 1835, pp. 484-5. The unnamed favourite appears to have been Clark he was paid various sums for plans. (*LI*, 19 March 1836.)

47. *LI*, 14 March 1835.

48. *LM*, 11 Nov 1865.

19.35: Leeds, Moral and Industrial Training Schools, Beckett Street (Perkin and Backhouse, 1845-8). (*Leeds Library and Information Services.*)

19.36: Leeds, House of Recovery, Beckett Street (Perkin and Backhouse, 1846). (*Leeds Library and Information Services.*)

he entered the competition for the Leeds Oddfellows Hall, but was not successful. His entries in several competitions over a wide geographical area suggest he was ambitious, and his capacity for self-publicity is confirmed by several drawings in the Leeds Public Exhibition of 1839.[49] In 1839 he formed a partnership with Elisha Backhouse (*q.v.*) and although, like Backhouse, his pre-1839 work was unremarkable, together they formed an exceptionally successful team. A huge amount of work passed through the office and they had the town's busiest practice in the middle decades of the century.

It is of interest that the firm's title put Perkin before Backhouse, whereas the reverse might have been expected on alphabetical grounds, and also because it seems it was Perkin who came to join Backhouse, rather than the other way around. However, perhaps Perkin was the slightly older of the two or injected more capital into the partnership; given what we know of their work before and after the partnership, Perkin seems to have been much the more talented. He also seems to have been astute. In 1836 he gave 5 gns to the recently formed charity which aimed at encourage additional church places – a very substantial donation from a young man – and made it known he would gratuitously design new churches or alterations.[50] This public display of philanthropy was soon repaid and three months later he was designing galleries for Taylor's (*q.v.*) St Mary, Quarry Hill. Thereafter, many commissions for churches, parsonages and schools flooded in.

Perkin and Backhouse built up an exceptionally successful practice specialising in modest houses and small-scale public buildings. However, they also produced some very substantial structures like the various Poor Law buildings (1845-c.1863) that subsequently made up the core of

49. As well as the Exeter design, he also exhibited his Oddfellows' Hall design. (*Catalogue of the Leeds Public Exhibition, 1839.*)

50. *LI*, 12 March 1836.

19.37: Leeds, Burley National School (Perkin and Backhouse, 1846). (*Leeds Library and Information Services.*)

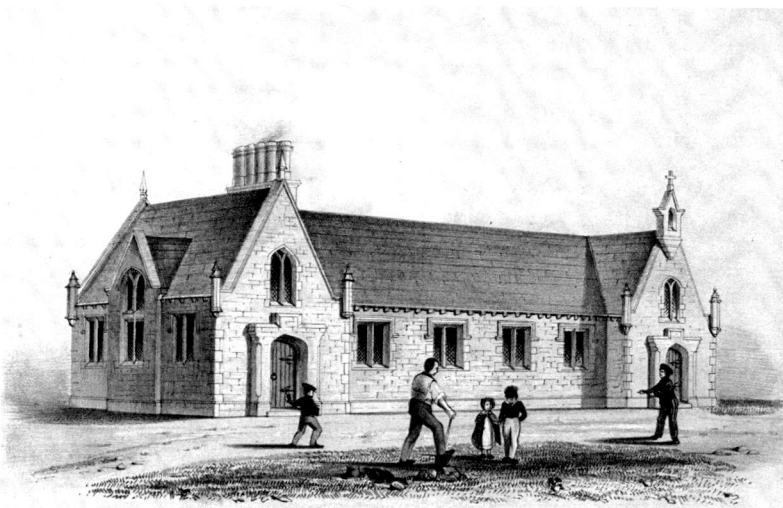

19.38: Morton, Bingley, WY, St Luke (Perkin and Backhouse, 1849-51). (*Leeds University Library, Special Collections.*)

St James Hospital (**19.35, 19.36**), as well as Armley Gaol (1843-7) (**4.14**) which had a huge budget of £40,000. They designed several attractive churches (**19.40**), altered mansions and one of their last projects was the acclaimed Queen's Hotel, Leeds. Perhaps better than any other in the town, the practice usefully illustrates the way architects with talent and ambition – but lacking the benefits of a London training – could, in the space of only a few years, elevate themselves from the prosaic world of surveying and estate agency, to the status of eminent architects.

In the unsavoury business of the Leeds Gaol commission – in which Perkin and Backhouse were appointed to execute Hurst and Moffatt's winning design[51] – they maintained a dignified silence. However, following their announcement as victors in the Leeds Moral and Industrial School competition (1846) the firm entered into a protracted correspondence in the pages of the *Intelligencer* with John Clark (*q.v.*) – one of the unsuccessful entrants – on the vexed issue of the conduct of architectural commissions.[52]

In 1842 Perkin was a churchwarden at St Mary's[53] and in the same year offered his services as a surveyor to the Leeds Improvement Commissioners.[54] In 1846 he joined the Lodge of Fidelity,[55] just in time to enjoy Chantrell's company there before the latter left for London. Perkin and Backhouse were described as 'surveyors to the Great North of England, and Yorkshire and Glasgow Union Railway' in 1845,[56] and in 1853 as 'architects for the Leeds New Gas Company.'[57]

A number of men who later became important Leeds architects trained in their office including William Hill (*q.v.*) (pupil, c.1845-50) and C.R. Chorley (*q.v.*) (pupil 1847-52, assistant then chief assistant, 1852-5.)[58] The partnership was dissolved in July 1864[59] with the *Mercury* of 5 July 1864 carrying two separate advertisements announcing the two new practices: Backhouse kept the partnerships old office at 5, Pease Buildings, South Parade while Perkin formed a partnership with his son W.J.B. Perkin at 10, East Parade. In August 1866 the Perkins moved to 2, East Parade and in 1871 another son, Henry (1847-1925) joined the practice.[60] The family firm closed in 1874 when William died. At this point W.J.B. Perkin appears to have retired while Henry moved on to a Leeds partnership with George Bulmer.[61]

51. LI, 11 Nov 1843.

52. *LI*, 14 Nov 1846. The spat with Clark continued in *LI*, 3 March 1848; 18 March 1848.

53. *LI*, 8 Oct 1842.

54. WYASL, L/WYAS 3067.

55. A. Scarth and C.A. Braim, *A History of the Lodge of Fidelity, Leeds*, Beck and Inchbold, 1894, p. 222.

56. *LM*, 18 Oct 1845.

57. *Sheffield and Rotherham Independent*, 9 March 1853.

58. Felstead, p. 170.

59. The dissolution was announced in *LI*, 2 July 1864.

60. Felstead, p. 709.

61. Felstead, p. 709.

William Perkin

Leeds, General Cemetery competition, second prize, in collaboration with Josuah Major, 1833. (LUL SC MS 421/33.)

LEEDS, Workhouse competition, first prize (unexecuted), 1835. (*LI*, 14 March 1835.)

LEEDS, prepared plans for widening Boar Lane, 1835. (*LI*, 13 June 1835.)

LEEDS, St Mary, 3 galleries, other alterations and gas lighting,1836. (*LI*, 4 June 1836.)

LEEDS, 'improvements', almost certainly including building, at Quebec, for Leeds Improvement Commissioners, 1836. (WYASL, L/WYAS 3067.)

LEEDS, requested to value property by Improvement Commissioners, 1837. (WYASL L/WYAS 3067.)

LEEDS, tabernacle for the Wesleyan Association, Meadow Lane, 1837. (*LI*, 18 March 1837.)

LEEDS, St Mary, Quarry Hill, installation of clock, 1842. (*LI*, 8 Oct. 1842.)

Perkin and Backhouse

LEEDS, Oddfellows' Hall, design, pre-1839. (*Catalogue of the Leeds Public Exhibition*, 1839.)

ARMLEY, Leeds, Wesleyan Association chapel, 1839. (*LI*, 23 March 1839.)

LOFTHOUSE, nr Wakefield, Christ Church, 1839-40. (*LI*, 15 June 1839.)

HECKMONDWYKE, Blanket Hall, 1840-1. (*LI*, 1 Feb. 1840.)

LEEDS, Commercial Buildings, proposed alterations to dining room, 1840. (*LI*, 8 Feb 1840.)

LEEDS, St Luke, North Street, 1840-1. (*LI*, 21 March 1840.)

HECKMONDWYKE, parsonage, 1840. (*LI*, 11 April 1840.)

GUISELEY, parochial school, 1840. (*LI*, 26 Sept 1840.)

WAKEFIELD, Primrose Hill, 8 dwelling houses with out-offices, 1840-1. (*LI*, 10 Oct. 1840.)

LOFTHOUSE, nr Wakefield, parsonage, 1840-1. (*LI*, 24 Oct. 1840.)

19.39: Leeds, West Riding Penitentiary, Burmantofts (Perkin and Backhouse, c.1852-3). (*Leeds Library and Information Services*.)

BRADFORD, Mechanics Institute, 1839-41. (K. Grady, *Georgian Public Buildings*, PTS, 1989, p. 154.)

HUDDERSFIELD, Highfield Chapel, Congregational, 1843-4. (*LI*, 8 April 1843.)

LEEDS, Gaol, 1843-7. (*LI*, 11 Nov. 1843.)

CULLINGWORTH, nr Bradford, National School, 1843-4. (*LI*, 4 Nov 1843.)

HEADINGLEY, Leeds, school and master's house, 1844. (*LI*, 9 March 1844.)

ADDINGHAM, nr Ilkley, National School and master's house, 1844. (*LI*, 16 March 1844.)

ROYSTON, nr Barnsley, National School and master's house, 1844. (*LI*, 23 March 1844.)

MORTON, parish of Bingley, National School, 1844. (*LI*, 24 Aug. 1844.)

LOFTHOUSE, nr Wakefield, National School and master's house, 1844. (*LI*, 7 Sept. 1844.)

HEADINGLEY, Leeds, four dwelling houses and out-offices, 1844. (*LI*, 5 Oct. 1844.)

MENSTON, nr Otley, church and parsonage, 1844-7. (*LI*, 23 May 1846.)

COTTON STONES, nr Halifax, church, 1845-6. (*LI*, 10 May 1845.)

LEEDS, Court House, alterations, 1845. (*LI*, 17 May 1845.)

LEEDS, Industrial Schools, 1845-8. (*LI*, 9 May, 12 Sept. 1846.)

LEEDS, House of Recovery, Beckett Street, c.1845-6. (Leeds Central Library, Boyne's illustrations of Leeds, vol. 5, pl. 19.)

SHADWELL, nr Leeds, school and master's house, c.1846. (WYASL, Nettleton Papers.)

BURLEY, Leeds, school and master's house, 1846. (*LI*, 6 June 1846.)

MORTON BANKS, parish of Bingley, church, 1846-7. (*LI*, 7 Nov. 1846.)

MIRFIELD, villa, 1845. (*LM*, 10 May 1845.)

OTLEY, National School, 1845-6. (*LM*, 30 Aug. 1845.)

LEEDS, St George's Terrace, Camp Rd, uniform fronted houses, c.1847. (*LI*, 27 April 1847.)

LEEDS, 'temporary sheds' next to convalescent home, Camp Road, 1847. (*LI*, 5 June 1847.)

LEEDS, 'Medical Office', Grantham Street, baths and washhouse, 1847. (*LI*, 5 June 1847.)

MANSTON, Leeds, St James, 1846-7. (*LI*, 6 Nov 1847.)

KILLINGBECK, Leeds, alterations to 'a mansion', 1847. (WYASL, Nettleton Papers.)

CALVERLEY, Leeds, detached dwelling house and out-offices, 1847-8. (*LI*, 27 Nov 1847.)

ADDINGHAM, nr Ilkley, villa, 1848. (*LI*, 25 March 1848.)

SHADWELL, Leeds, parsonage, 1848. (*LI*, 3 June 1848.)

LEEDS, Weetwood, ten houses, 1848. (*LI*, 23 Sept 1848.)

FARSLEY, Leeds, National School, 1848. (*LI*, 14 Oct 1848.)

SOWERBY, nr Halifax, parsonage, 'St Mary's district', 1848-9. (*LI*, 25 Nov 1848; plans WYASL 555/53.)

RIPON, parsonage for Trinity church, 1849. (*LI*, 27 Jan 1849.)

LEEDS, two houses in Cowper Street, New Leeds, 1849. (*LI*, 17 May 1849.)

BARDSEY, nr Leeds, vicarage, 1849. (*LI*, 16 June 1849.)

KIRK DEIGHTON, nr Wetherby, church, restoration, 1849. (WYASL, RD/AF/2/2a/22; *LI*, 21 June 1849.)

LEEDS, Leeds Club, Albion Place, alterations, 1849-50. (*LI*, 21 July 1849; 19 Jan, 26 Jan 1850.)

MORTON, nr Bingley, St Luke, 1849-51. (*LI*, 25 Aug 1849; 15 March, 26 April 1851.)

LEEDS, parsonage for St Luke's church, 1849-50. (*LI*, 29 Dec 1849.)

BRADFORD, 'new building on south side of Kirkgate', 1850. (*LI*, 23 Feb 1850.)

SOWERBY, nr Halifax, National School and master's house, 1850-1. (*LI*, 27 April 1850; 26 April 1851.)

19.40: Hunslet, Leeds, St Mary (Perkin and Backhouse, c.1862-4). (*Leeds Library and Information Services.*)

RIPON, Dispensary and Fever Hospital, 1850. (*LI*, 25 May, 29 June 1850.)

OULTON, Leeds, Oulton Hall, reconstruction following fire, from 1850. (G. Worsley, 'Oulton Hall' in *Country Life*, 17 Sept. 1987.)

HOLBECK, Leeds, parsonage, 1850. (*LI*, 24 Aug. 1850; plans WYASL 555/22.)

INGROW, nr Keighley, parsonage, c.1850. (plans, WYASL 555/24.)

LEEDS, parsonage at St Luke, Skinner Lane, c.1850. (WYASL 555/33.)

KEIGHLEY, parsonage 'near Keighley', 1850-1 (probably Ingrow, see above). (*LI*, 9 Nov 1850.)

STANNINGLEY, Leeds, Richardshaw church, 1851. (*LI*, 11 Jan 1851.)

ARMLEY, Leeds, parsonage, 1851. (*LI*, 15 Feb 1851.)

LEEDS, brick tank, Meadow Lane, for New Gas Company, 1851. (*LM*, 8 March 1851.)

RIDDLESDEN, nr Keighley, St Mary, 1851. (*LI*, 15 March 1851.)

BINGLEY, Grammar School, 1851-2. (*LI*, 2 Aug 1851.)

CULLINGWORTH, nr Keighley, church, 1851-2. (*LI*, 16 Aug 1851.)

LEEDS, parsonage at Christ Church, Meadow Lane, c.1851. (*LI*, 3 May 1851; plans WYASL 555/30.)

LEEDS, Female Penitentiary, Burmantofts, c.1852-3. (*LI*, 6 Nov 1852.)

LEEDS, St Matthias, Burley, c.1852-4. (*LI*, 11 Dec 1852.)

LEEDS, three shops with houses, Briggate, c.1853. (*LI*, 16 April 1853.)

RIPON, National School, c.1853. (*LI*, 23 April 1853.)

RIPON, Union [Work] House, c.1853. (*LI*, 4 June 1853.)

LEEDS, five houses and offices, nr Woodhouse Moor, c. 1853. (*LI*, 23 July 1853.)

KEIGHLEY, bank and dwelling house, c.1853. (*LI*, 23 July 1853.)

KEIGHLEY, church, c.1853-4. [probably St Mary the Virgin, Eastwood]. (*LI*, 12 Nov 1853; 4 March 1854.)

CHAPEL ALLERTON, Leeds, St Matthew's, new tower, c.1853-4. (*LI*, 31 Dec 1853.)

LEEDS, 'two beautiful villas for sale in Springfield Mount'. (*LI*, 10 Sept 1853.)

LEEDS, seven cottage dwellings, Low Wortley, c.1854. (*LI*, 4 Feb 1854.)

ILKLEY, Hydro competition, second premium, 1854. (Harper, p. 277.)

GOMERSAL, WY, rebuilding of Gomersal Hall, c. 1854. (*LI*, 22 April 1854.)

BRAMHAM, WY, church, restoration, c.1854. (*LI*, 6 May 1854.)

LEEDS, four houses on Kirkstall Road, c.1854. (*LI*, 20 May 1854.)

THORP ARCH, nr Wetherby, Residence and School Premises [Thorp Arch Grange], c.1854-5. (*LI*, 5 Aug 1854.)

TONG, nr Bradford, parsonage, c.1854. (*LI*, 26 Aug 1854.)

LEEDS, parsonage for St Mathias, Burley, c.1855. (*LI*, 7 April 1855.)

MASHAM, NY, repairs to church, 1855. (WYASL, Masham Parish Papers.)

MASHAM, NY, Riddell Memorial Mechanics Institute, c.1855-6. (*LM*, 24 Nov 1855.)

LEEDS, organ factory, c.1855-6. (*LM*, 8 Dec 1855.)

SOWERBY BRIDGE, nr Halifax, town hall, c.1856. (*LI*, 12 Jan 1856.)

LEEDS, residence in Victoria Place, Camp Road, c.1856. (*LI*, 1 March 1856.)

LEEDS, Guardian Asylum, additions, c.1856. (*LI*, 12 April 1856.)

LEEDS, parsonage for Holy Trinity, c.1856. (*LI*, 19 April 1856.)

KEIGHLEY, school and master's house, c.1857. (*LI*, 14 Feb 1857.)

MASHAM, NY, alterations to National School, 1858. (WYASL, Masham Parish Papers.)

HARROGATE, Prospect House, enlargement and alterations, c.1858. (*LM*, 21 Jan 1858.)

LEEDS, schools and residences, Ventnor Street, c.1858. (*LI*, 13 Feb 1858.)

LEEDS, school and master's house attached to St Luke's, Skinner Lane, c.1858. (*LI*, 20 March 1858.)

LEEDS, Workhouse, 1857-60. (*LI*, 20 March, 15 May 1858.)

MASHAM, Healey Parsonage, c.1858. (*LI*, 20 March 1858.)

HARROGATE, Prospect House Hotel, unspecified work, c.1858. (*LI*, 18 Sept. 1858.)

KEIGHLEY, workhouse, Holycroft, c.1858-9. (*LM*, 16 Oct 1858.)

LEEDS, Workhouse, infirmary and chapel, c.1858-9. (*LI*, 11 Dec 1858.)

SEACROFT, nr Leeds, enlargement of school and master's house, c.1859. (*LI*. 16 April 1859.)

BARNSLEY, burial ground, chapels, lodge, gates etc, c.1859-60. (*LI*, 10 Sept 1859; *LM*, 11 Feb. 1860.)

LEEDS, [Queen's] hotel at Midland Railway Station, c.1859-64. (*LI*, 24 Sept 1859, 29 March 1862, 7 May 1864.)

CHAPEL ALLERTON, nr Leeds, house and outbuildings, c.1860. (*LI*, 11 Feb 1860.)

LEEDS, Leeds [prob. Queen's] Hotel, c.1860. (*LI*, 10 March 1860.)

LEEDS, Mechanics Institute competition, second prize, 1860. (Harper, p. 277.)

HEATH, nr Wakefield, gent's res., c.1860. (*LM*, 19 May 1860.)

LEEDS, synagogue, Belgrave Street, c.1860. (*LI*, 30 June 1860.)

ILKLEY, Bath's Charity hospital, c.1860-1. (*LM*, 17 Nov 1860.)

LEEDS, Stock Exchange, Albion Street, alterations inc. removal of columns, c.1860-1. (*LM*, 22 Dec 1860.)

BRAMLEY, Leeds, church, 1861-3. (*LI*, 5 Jan, 23 March 1861.)

LEEDS, detached house, Woodhouse Cliff, c.1861. (*LI*, 12 Jan 1861.)

LEEDS, house at Mount Preston, c.1861. (*LI*, 26 Jan 1861.)

LEEDS, conversion of Springfield Lodge to Women and Children's Hospital, c.1861. (*LI*, 9 Feb 1861.)

HARROGATE, villa residence(s) in Victoria Park, c.1861. (*LI*, 23 March, 27 April 1861.)

HUNSLET, Leeds, school attached to St Jude's, c.1861. (*LI*, 27 April 1861.)

HUNSLET, Leeds three cottages and a shop, Glass House Street, c. 1861. (*LI*, 27 April 1861.)

LEEDS, school, Silver Royd Hill, Wortley, c.1861. (*LI*, 29 June 1861.)

LEEDS, Blenheim Baptist Chapel, unsuccessful competition entry, 1862. (*ex inf.* Janet Douglas.)

HUNSLET, Leeds, St Mary, c.1862-4. (*LI*, 25 March 1862, 23 July 1864.)

LEEDS, Workhouse, additional wards, c.1862. (*LI*, 11 Oct 1862.)

LEEDS, Industrial Schools, drying house, c. 1862-3. (*LI*, 13 Dec 1862.)

ROTHWELL, nr. Leeds, school and master's residence, c.1863. (*LI*, 7 Feb 1863.)

KIRKSTALL, Leeds, St Stephen, 'extensive alterations', 1863-4. (*LI*, 7 Feb 1863, 13 Aug 1864.)

ALLERTON BYWATER, WY, church, c.1863. (*LI*, 6 June 1863.)

LEEDS, Park Row, demolition and excavation for new Beckett's Bank, c.1863. (*LI*, 6 June 1863.)

KIRKSTALL, Leeds, mill shed, c.1863. (*LI*, 1 Aug 1863.)

LEEDS, chapel in St George Street, demolition and removal for rebuilding on new site, c.1863-4. (*LI*, 12 Dec 1863.)

LEEDS, supervised erection of G.G. Scott's bank for Messrs Beckett and Co., Park Row, 1863-4. (*LI*, 19 Dec 1863.)

LEEDS, Wortley Cemetery, two chapels, lodge and gates, c.1864. (*LI*, 23 Jan 1864.)

LEEDS, Masonic Hall, Great George Street, 1864-5. (*LI*, 9 April 1864.)

Perkin and Son (1864-74)

LEEDS, New West Riding Club, Bond Street, c.1864. (*LI*, 3 Sept 1864.)

SELBY, parsonage 'near Selby', c.1864-5. (*LM*, 25 Oct 1864.)

LEEDS, lodge to a gentleman's house, 'near Leeds', c.1864-5. (*LM*, 25v Oct 1864.)

SHEFFIELD, Bierlaw Union Workhouse, boundary walls etc, c.1865. (*LM*, 15 May 1865.)

HARROGATE, wine merchant's store, c.1865. (*LM*, 27 May 1865.)

RURAL LOCATION, enlargement of gent's res. 'in the country', c.1865. (*LM*, 27 May 1865.)

NORMANTON, WY, inn and stabling, 'near railway station', c.1865. (*LM*, 4 Nov 1865.)

HUNSLET MOOR, church, near toll bar, c.1866. (*LM*, 10 Feb 1866.)

ALLERTON BYWATER, WY, parsonage, c.1866. (*LM*, 21c April 1866.)

LEEDS, stabling, offices and 2 lodges for gent's res., c.1866. (*LM*, 22 May 1866.)

LEEDS, 4 houses, Lofthouse Place, Carlton Hill, c.1866. (*LM*, 22 May 1966.)

HUGGATE, nr Pocklington, EY, house for Glebe Farm, c.1866. (*LM*, 22 May 1866.)

KIRKSTALL, Leeds, mill and engine shed, c.1866. (*LM*, 10 June 1866.)

LEEDS, new White Cloth Hall, Infirmary Gardens, Wellington Street, c.1866-7. (*LM*, 25 Aug 1866.)

LEEDS, new hospital for Borough Gaol, c.1866-7. (*LM*, 24 Nov 1866.)

LEEDS, house at Chapeltown, c.1867. (*LM*, 2 March 1867.)

ARDSLEY, nr Wakefield, house near railway, c.1867. (*LM*, 4 May 1867.)

ALTOFTS, near Wakefield, National School, c.1867. (*LM*, 4 May 1867.)

ALLERTON BYWATER, near Castelford, schoolmaster's house, c.1867. (*LM*, 1 June 1867.)

HARROGATE, stabling etc at Prospect Hotel, c.1867-8. (*LM*, 21 Dec 1867.)

LEEDS, Boar Lane Improvement, restaurant for D. Harrison, c.1868. (*LM*, 16 May 1868.)

LEEDS, extension of 58, Briggate for C. Pegler, c.1868. (*LM*, 6 June 1868.)

WOODLESFORD, near Leeds, church, c.1868. (*LM*, 15 Aug 1868.)

LEEDS, junction of Upper Headrow and Briggate, commercial buildings for H.B. Legg, including clock tower, c.1868, probably unexecuted. (*LM*, 10 Dec 1868.)

ROUNDHAY, Leeds, WM chapel, 1873-4. (*Roundhay Methodist Church, Ladywood, Centenary 1874-1974*, 1974.)

Percy Robinson (1869–1950)
See Chapter 17

Thomas Shaw (fl. 1839-68)

Shaw would have had experience in one of the building trades and in 1838 was chosen by R.D. Chantrell to be his clerk of works on the huge Leeds Parish Church rebuilding project (1837-41). He must have impressed as Chantrell used him as something of an assistant on various minor jobs elsewhere at this time. Shaw also secured at least two commisions in his own name. In 1842, he formed a partnership with Chantrell's son John, an arrangement that seems to have been promoted by Chantrell senior as a means of establishing a career for his son. Although the practice notionally produced a number of buildings, it is likely that the majority – and certainly the major churches – were actually designed by Chantrell senior. In 1845, the partnership was dissolved, somewhat acrimoniously, with R.D. Chantrell claiming Shaw had made 'blunders' in the execution of several of 'his' churches. Given that Shaw went on to enjoy a solid if unremarkable career and John Chantrell did almost nothing on his own account, perhaps Chantrell senior's criticism was not entirely objective.[62]

Shaw immediately formed a partnership with Jeremiah Dobson (*q.v.*),[63] taking over the office at 19 Park Row formerly occupied by Chantrell and Shaw. This partnership was also short-lived and by 1847 Shaw was

62. See C. Webster, *R.D. Chantrell (1793-1872) and the architecture of a lost generation*, Spire Books, 2010, pp. 169-72.

63. *LI*, 22 Feb 1845.

19.41: Embsay, NY, St Mary (Thomas Shaw, 1852-3). (*Leeds University Library, Special Collections.*)

working alone at 15 Park Row.[64] His son Henry joined the firm in 1860 when it was known as Shaw and Son, and from mid-1863 it used the style Thomas and Henry Shaw with an office at 2, Belgrave Square. Thomas retired in 1868, leaving Henry to carry on the business.

Shaw secured third place in the Leeds Mechanics Institute competition in 1860, and executed an impressive quantity of work which included churches, chapels, houses as well as industrial buildings. His church at Embsay is a competent essay and his Gothic Baptist chapel in St George Street, Leeds is distinguished.

Thomas Shaw

LEEDS, paid £5 in 1839 by Leeds Improvement Commissioners, possibly for numbering houses. (WYASL, minutes.)
LOTHERSDALE, nr Skipton, parsonage, c.1839-40. (WYASL BDP 72 4/2/1.)

Chantrell and Shaw

HEADINGLEY, Leeds, unidentified house, c.1842. (*LI*, 25 June 1842.)

LEEDS, 2 unidentified houses in Woodhouse Lane, c.1842. (*LI*, 23 July 1842.)
DEWSBURY, Church of England School, Daisy Hill, c.1842-3. (*LI*, 10 Sept 1842.)
ROBERTTOWN, WY, All saints, 1843-5. (CBC, Roberttown file, 16067.)
LEEDS, Beckett's Street Cemetery, chapel, lodge, entrances, c.1844-5. (*LM*, 11 May 1845.)
HUNSLET, Leeds, cemetery, chapel, lodge, entrances, c.1844-5. (*LM*, 11 May 1845.)

Thomas Shaw

LEEDS, *Elmfield* and *Spring Hill*, Cumberland Road, Headingley Lane, c.1846. (LU, Deeds, 44 and 59.)

Dobson and Shaw
See under Dobson

Thomas Shaw

FREESLAND, [where?] Christ Church, c.1849-50. (*LI*, 23 June 1849.)
LEEDS, Woodhouse Grove, school and master's house, c.1849-50. (*LI*, 1 Sept. 1849.)

64. *LI*, 22 May 1847.

LEEDS, Baptist chapel, Great George Street, 1849-50. (Boyne, vol. V, no. 20.)

HARROGATE, Leeds Terrace, Low Harrogate, c.1849-50. (*LI*, 15 Dec. 1849.)

LEEDS, retaining wall etc for footbridge over the Aire at Armley, c.1850. (*LM*, 27 April 1850.)

HALIFAX, 13 houses at Heathfield, c.1850. (*LM*, 4 May 1850.)

SKIPTON, 'inn near the railway station', c.1850. (*LI*, 6 July 1850.)

HARROGATE, additions and alterations to Binn's Hotel, 1850. (*LM*, 12 Oct 1850.)

OTLEY, parish church, alterations, c.1850-1. (*LI*, 9 Nov 1850.)

LEEDS, rebuilding shop and house in Briggate, c.1850-1. (*LM*, 7 Dec 1850.)

LEEDS, house in Clarendon Road, c.1850-1. (*LM*, 14 Dec 1850.)

EMBSAY, nr Skpton, St Mary, 1851-3. (*LI*, 11 Oct 1851.)

LEEDS, West Street, five shops, c.1851-2. (*LI*, 15 Nov 1851.)

LEEDS, villa res, stables, coach house etc, Gledhow, c.1851. (*LM*, 17 May 1851.)

BRADFORD, 6 houses at Eccleshill, c.1851-2. (*LM*, 6 Dec 1851.)

LEEDS, house n Little Woodhouse, c.1851-2. (*LM*, 13 Dec 1851.)

19.42: Leeds, Baptist church, Great George Street (Thomas Shaw, c.1855). (*Leeds Library and Information Services.*)

DENHOLME GATE, nr Keighley, inn and outbuildings, c.1852. (*LM*, 3 Jan 1852.)

LEEDS, 'neighbourhood of', house, stabling, outbuildings, c.1853. (*LM*, 30 April 1853.)

HARROGATE, villa res. in Low Harrogate, c.1853. (*LM*, 17 Sept 1853)

HARROGATE, villa res., c.1853. (*LM*, 22 Oct 1853.)

HEADINGLEY, Leeds, house and outbuildings, c.1853. (*LI*, 9 Jan 1853.)

LEEDS, Woodhouse Grove School, enlargement, c.1853. (*LI*, 12 Feb 1853.)

LEEDS, 4 houses, c. 1853-4. (*LM*, 29 Oct 1853.)

LEEDS, warehouse in West Street, c.1853-4. (*LM*, 5 Nov 1853.)

LEEDS, 5 houses in Meanwood Road, c.1854-5. (*LM*, 9 Dec 1854.)

LEEDS, entrance lodge, Leeds Royal Gardens, c.1855. (*LM*, 3 Feb 1855.)

PONTEFRACT, house, stabling, coach ho., c.1855. (*LM*, 10 March 1855.)

LEEDS, 5 shops with houses, Kirkstall Rd, c.1855. (*LM*, 2 June 1855.)

OTLEY, alterations and additions to Independent Chapel, c.1855. (*LM*, 16 June 1855.)

HARROGATE, house, outbuildings etc, c.1855. (*LM*, 30 June 1850.)

LEEDS, Baptist church, Great George Street, c.1855, dem 'after only a few years' for site of LGI. (Leeds Central Library, Boyne's History of Leeds, vol. 5, pl. 20.)

LEEDS, 9 cottages nr Kirkstall Rd, c.1855. (*LM*, 30 June 1855.)

GOOLE, 12 houses, c.1856. (*LM*, 3 May 1856.)

GOOLE, boring of a well, c.1856. (*LM*, 30 Aug 1856.

HUNSLET, Leeds, fireproof warehouse, c.1856. (*LI*, 24 May 1856.)

HEADINGLEY, Leeds, villa, stables, lodge etc, c.1856-7. (*LM*, 1 Nov 1856.)

LEEDS, weaving shed, Abbey Mills, Kirkstall, c.1857. (*LM*, 10 Jan 1857.)

OTLEY, toll bar house, c.1857. (*LM*, 2 May 1857.)

OTLEY, parish church, internal alterations inc. re-seating, c.1858. (*LM*, 5 June 1858.)

LEEDS, alterations to Castleton Lodge, Wortley, c.1858-9. (*LM*, 20 Nov 1858.)

LEEDS, 5 houses, Woodhouse Cliff, c.1858-9. (*LM*, 4 Dec 1858.)

LEEDS, alterations to villa, Kirkstall, c.1859. (*LM*, 14 May 1859.)

LEEDS, unsuccessful entry for new Poor Law Office, East Parade, 1859. (*LI*, 11 June 1859.)

LEEDS, villa, stabling, coach ho., Headingley, c.1859. (*LM*, 5 Nov 1859.)

HUNSLET, Leeds, fireproof warehouse, c.1859. (*LI*, 26 Mar 1859.)

LEEDS, lodge, gatehouse, garden walls etc for villa residence in Headingley, c.1859. (*LI*, 19 Oct 1859.)

KIRSKSTALL, Leeds, Villa residence with stables, coach house etc., c.1859. (*LI*, 19 Nov 1859.)

BRAMHOPE, nr Leeds, cemetery chapels, lodge etc, c. 1859-60. (*LI*, 26 Nov 1859, 21 April 1860.)

LEEDS, house and shop, c.1859-60. (*LI*, 10 Dec 1859.)

Thomas Shaw and Son; from mid 1863, Thomas and Henry Shaw

LEEDS, alterations and additions to villa in Armley, c. 1860. (*LM*, 4 Feb 1860.)

HEADINGLEY, Leeds, villa, stables, coach house etc, c.1860. (*LI*, 7 April 1860.)

LEEDS, Inn and 4 shops, c.1860. (*LM*, 8 Sept 1860.)

METHLEY, nr Leeds, additions to school, 1860-1. (*LI*, 26 May 1860, 7 April 1861.)

LEEDS, taking down Broomfield House, Hunslet Lane, c.1860. (*LI*, 1 Sept 1860.)

HUNSLET, Leeds, warehouse, c. 1860-1. (*LI*, 8 Sept. 1860.)

THORNE, SY, Brook's Carity, school and master's house, c.1860-1. (*LM*, 15 Dec 1860.)

HEADINGLEY, Leeds, villa residence, c.1861. (*LI*, 2 March 1861.)

LEEDS, eight first class houses adjoining Leeds Grammar School, c.1861. (*LI*, 13 April 1861.)

LEEDS, 6 shops and houses, c.1861. (*LM*, 20 April 1861.)

KEIGHLEY, school and master's house at Riddlesden, c.1861. (*LI*, 8 June 1861.)

LEEDS, house nr Woodhouse Bar, c.1861. (*LM*, 22 June 1861.)

LEEDS, 2 houses, Hunslet Lane, c.1862. (*LM*, 11 Jan 1862.)

LEEDS, 26 houses and 4 shops, Armley Road, c.1862. (*LM*, 8 March 1862.)

LEEDS, 2 shops and warehouses, Cookridge Street, c.1862. (*LM*, 24 May 1862.)

LEEDS, 5 houses, Headingley Hill, c.1862. (*LM*, 28 June 1862.)

LEEDS, 2 houses, Potternewton, c.1862. (*LM*, 26 July 1862.)

LEEDS, 10 houses, Chapeltown Road, c.1862. (*LM*, 27 Sept 1862.)

GILDERSOME, nr Leeds, engine house and dye house, c.1862-3. (*LM*, 29 Nov 1862.)

METHLEY, nr Leeds, inn for Earl of Mexborough, c. 1863. (*LI*, 28 Feb 1863.)

LEEDS, two houses in New Leeds, c. 1863. (*LI*, 4 July 1863.)

LEEDS highways depot next to River Aire, incl. Lodge, sheds etc, c.1863. (*LI*, 6 June 1863.)

METHLEY, nr Leeds, Whitwood church, c.1864. (*LI*, 13 Feb 1864.)

LEEDS, Tower Works, Globe Road, entrance range and Italianate chimney, 1864-6. (Pevsner, *Leeds*, pp. 129-31.)

LEEDS, 5 houses, Victoria Road, Headingley Hill, c.1865. (*LM*, 8 July 1865.)

HUNSLET, additions and alterations to mill, c.1865. (*LM*, 29 July 1865.)

HORSFORTH, villa, c.1865. (*LM*, 28 Oct 1865.)

BRAMHOPE, WY, villa, c.1866. (*LM,* 17 Feb 1866.)

BEESTON HILL, Leeds, villa, coach house etc, c.1866. (*LM,* 24 March 1866.)

LEEDS, house, Victoria Street, c.1866. (*LM,* 14 April 1866.)

LEEDS, 12 houses and 2 shops, Kirkstall Road, c.1866. (*LM,* 9 June 1866.)

LEEDS, saw mill, boiler house etc, c.1867. (*LM,* 22 June 1867.)

BROMPTON, near Northallerton, weaving shed, preparing rooms, engine houses, chimney etc, c.1867. (*LM,* 20 July 1867.)

KIRKSTALL, 3 houses, Butler's Spring, c.1867. (*LM,* 5 Oct 1867.)

LEEDS, Kensington Terrace, Headingley, five through houses for Thomas Clapham, 1868. (Trowell.)

LEEDS, double villa, Hilary Place, c.1868. (*LM,* 4 April 1868.)

James Simpson (1792-1864)
See Chapter 8

Stephen Ernest Smith (1845-1925)

Stephen Smith was the son of John Wailes Smith, a Leeds tailor and woollen draper. After attending Bramham College, he was articled to William Hill (*q.v.*) in 1864, staying three years. Subsequently, he studied at the RA, and then went as an improver to the London office of G. Somers Clarke before working in the office of another London architect, Joseph Douglas Matthews in 1867-8. He travelled in France, Italy and Germany and in 1868 opened his Leeds office in Park Row. Nine years later, he took into partnership his former pupil, John Tweedale (*q.v.*). Smith became an ARIBA in 1867 and was elected FRIBA in 1881. He was a vice-chairman of the LYAS and a vice-chairman of the Leeds and County Conservative Club. Apparently, he continued to work until around 1919, thus completing half a century of practice in Leeds, although

nothing is known after 1900. He died on 11 April 1925.

His obituary appeared in *The Builder,* 32, 1925, p. 619.

LEEDS, public house, 2 shops, Henrietta Street, c.1868. (*LM,* 11 Jan 1868.)

LEEDS, 2 warehouses, York place, c.1868-9. (*LM,* 31 Oct 1868.)

LEEDS, *Torridon,* Headingley Lane for Henry Ludolf, 1869, dem. (Trowell.)

LEEDS, Imperial Insurance Co. offices, Park Row, 1870-1. (*LM,* 30 Sept 1870.)

LEEDS, *Buckingham Villas,* Headingley Lane, 1870 (Pevsner, *Leeds.*)

LEEDS, warehouse 1-2 York Place for G. R. Portway, 1872. (Pevsner, *WY.*)

MENSTON, nr Leeds, unidentified villa, 1873. (*LM,* 31 May 1873.)

LEEDS, cabinet-making factory, Cross Park St. for Hummerston Bros. 1873 (*LM,* 28 June 1873.)

LEEDS, millinery shop 6, New Briggate, 1874. (Linstrum, *WYAA,* p. 384.)

LEEDS, 3 houses collectively known as *Oak Bank,* Shaw Lane, Headingley, 1875. (*LM,* 6 Jan 1875.)

ADEL, *Adel Towers* for J.A. Hirst c.1875, dem. (Linstrum, *WYAA,* p. 384.)

Smith and Tweedale

LEEDS, synagogue, Belgrave St., 1877, dem. (*LM,* 6 Jan 1877.)

LEEDS, Imperial Fire & Life Assurance Co., Bond St. 1877, dem. (*LM,* 16 April 1877.)

LEEDS, cricket pavilion, Leeds Grammar School, 1878, dem. (LSA *Annual Report,* 1877-8.)

LEEDS, four warehouses, York Place, 1879. (*LM,* 3 May 1879.)

LEEDS, Kirkstall Congregational Church, Commercial Road, 1880. (Linstrum, *WYAA,* p. 384.)

LEEDS, Backwell House, shops and warehouse 22-24 New Market St, 1880. (Pevsner, *Leeds.*)

LEEDS, shops on Park Lane/Somers St., c.1880-1. (LAS *Annual Report, 1880-1.*)

LEEDS, Grace St., cap and clothing factory for Messrs Brook and Co., c.1880. (LAS *Annual Report,* 1880-1.)

LEEDS, Meanwood Road Baptist School, 1881. (*LM,* 11 Nov 1881.)

LEEDS, *St Chad's Villas,* Otley Road for S.E. Smith and the solicitor John Tweedale. (*LM,* 11 Nov 1881.)

LEEDS, Billiard Room at, *North Hill House,* North Grange Mount, Headingley, for J. Wilkinson, 1881. (Linstrum, *WYAA,* p. 384.)

LEEDS, Bramma St., Mission Room, 1881-2. (LAS *Annual Report,* 1881-2.)

LEEDS, unidentified houses at Wrangthorn, Woodhouse, c.1881. (LAS *Annual Report,* 1881-2.)

LEEDS, detached house, Bainbrigge Road, Headingley, 1883. (Trowell.)

GARFORTH, St Mary, alterations, 1884. (*LM,* 26 Feb 1884.)

HARROGATE, two houses, West Park, 1884. (*LM,* 1 March 1884.)

LEEDS, chambers, South Parade, 1884. (*LM,* 13 Sept 1884.)

LEEDS, remodelling of Leeds and County Conservative Club, South Parade, 1885, dem. (Linstrum, *WYAA,* p. 384.)

ROUNDHAY, *Woodbourne,* house, stables and lodge for Richard Buckton, 1885. (Linstrum, *WYAA,* p. 384.)

LEEDS, premises, Albion St., 1885. (*LM,* 20th June 1885.)

LEEDS, *St Chad's Gardens,* Far Headingley, 1885. (D. Hall, *Far Headingley,* Far Headingley Village Soc., 2000.)

LEEDS, annex to St George's Schools, Clarendon Road, 1887. (*LM,* 18th June 1887.)

POOL in WHARFDALE, house, 1887. (*LM,* 19 Nov 1887.)

LEEDS, extensions to St Matthias' School, Burley, 1888. (*LM,* 25th June 1888.)

LEEDS, extensions to clothing factory for Eastwood Bros., Parliament St., 1888. (*LM,* 25 June 1888.)

LEEDS, villa, 19, Bainbrigge Road, Headingley, for Benjamin Ward, 1888. (Trowell.)

LEEDS, estate surveyor and design of houses on Cardigan Road, 1888-91. (Trowell.)

MEANWOOD, Leeds, St Oswald, Highbury Mt, 1889-90. Extended 1900. (F. Casperson, *Centenary Booklet.*)

LEEDS, Wilkinson Memorial School, Kirkstall, 1890. (*LM,* 9 May 1890.)

LEEDS, St Bartholomew's mission room, Parliament St., Armley, 1890. (*LM,* 25 Aug 1890.)

LEEDS, cricket pavilion, Headingley, for the Leeds Cricket, Football and Athletic Co. (Tweedale's brother was one of the directors) 1890, dem. (*The Builder,* 32, 1925, p. 619.)

LEEDS, plans for the Sandfield House Estate, Monkbridge Road, Headingley, 1891. (E. Bonsor, *Printed Maps and Plans of Leeds.*)

LEEDS, temporary church of St Margaret of Antioch, Cardigan Road, 1891. (G. Brandwood, *Temple Moore,* Paul Watkins, 1997, p. 98.)

LEEDS, March Institute, Cathcart St., Woodhouse, 1892. (*The Builder,* 132, 1925, p. 619.)

LEEDS, York City and County Bank, Park Row, 1892. (*The Builder,* 88, 1905, p. 576.)

LEEDS, 1-10, St Mary's Road, for the Newton Park Estate, 1894. (Pevsner, *Leeds.*)

LEEDS, St Luke's School, Skinner Lane, 1894. (*LM,* 13 Oct 1894.)

LEEDS, additions to Christ Church School, Theaker Lane, Armley, 1895. (*The Builder,* 88, 1905, p. 576.)

LEEDS, St John the Baptist Church School, Newtown, 1895. (*LM,* 27 Feb 1895.)

LEEDS, Grand Arcade, New Briggate, 1896-7. (Linstrum, *WYAA,* p. 385.)

19.43: **Leeds, Baptist school, Meanwood (Smith and Tweedale, 1881).** (*Ruth Baumberg.*)

19.44: **Leeds, Grand Arcade, New Briggate (Smith and Tweedale, 1896-7).** (*Ruth Baumberg.*)

19.45: **Leeds, York City and County Bank, Park Row (Smith and Tweedale, 1892).** (The Builder, *54, 1896, p. 576.*)

19.46: Leeds, library and police station, Woodhouse (W.H. Thorp, 1901.) (*Ruth Baumberg*)

LEEDS, former Yorkshire Penny Bank, corner of Kirkgate and New York St., 1899. (Pevsner, *WY*, p. 433.)

LEEDS, St Luke's Day School, St Luke's Grove, Beeston, 1896. (Linstrum, *WYAA*, p. 385.)

GARFORTH, Manor Farm, extensive agricultural college buildings, 1900. (*The Builder*, 32, 1925, p. 619.)

Tweedale's obituary in The Builder *lists the following buildings by the partnership without giving dates.*

LEEDS, 'large block of shops facing New Briggate and Cross Belgrave Street' [possibly the Grand Arcade block].

LEEDS, a warehouse in Whitehall Road.

Thomas Taylor (1777 or '8-1826)
See Chapter 5

William Henry Thorp (1852-1944)

Thorp's father was a local builder who may have worked with R. Norman Shaw on his Yorkshire commissions. In 1868 Thorp was articled to A.M. Fowler who was in private practice as well as being Leeds Borough Surveyor (1865-72). Subsequently, Thorp spent three years with Edward Birchall (*q.v.*). By 1876 he was an assistant in the architects' office in Leeds School Board which had been established under the 1870 Education Act. 1876 was also the year Thorp set up his own practice and promoted the scheme which led to the foundation of the Leeds Architectural Association in 1877, with Corson *(q.v.)* as its first president and Thorp as joint secretary with Joseph Hall. Thorp was himself president in 1890-2.

Despite a relatively modest number of commissions, Thorp succeeded in giving Leeds a series of memorable landmark buildings. Not only are they of the highest quality, but they display a remarkable stylistic range. The most

prominent is Oxford Place Methodist Church and Chambers (1890-1903) (**19.14**), a rare example of two independent architects working together on a single job.[65] The project involved a major remodelling of James Simpson's (*q.v.*) 1830's chapel, adding a substantial office block on its north side and giving the whole complex a noble Baroque façade. The result is an impressive composition to close the western side of the *piazza* in front of the Town Hall, and a building capable of standing up to Brodrick's masterpiece.

His other important city-centre building is the Art Gallery (1886-8), commissioned as a cheaper alternative to the scheme proposed by Corson who had just completed the Municipal Buildings and Library to which it is attached. It was originally built behind the structures then fronting the Headrow, and was not intended to have any prominence; it was revealed only after their demolition but then encased half a century later by the Henry Moore Sculpture Gallery. Several of the galleries were subsequently altered so that now only the Queen's Room and imperial staircase indicate Thorp's capabilities as a designer of public spaces.

The School of Medicine of 1894 (**frontispiece**), beside Leeds General Infirmary, is an attractive Arts and Crafts Tudor building, which 'includes a richly decorated entrance hall in Burmantofts faience unusually cool in tone'.[66] Thorp's ability with yet another stylistic alternative comes with the YMCA in Albion Place (1900) where, in a highly innovative composition, he successfully blended English Renaissance, Wren and Early Georgian motifs. However, perhaps no two buildings better reveal his fondness for variety than the library/police station buildings at Woodhouse Moor (1901) (**19.46**) and Chapel Allerton (1904) (**19.47**). The first is Italian Baroque, complete with dome, broken pediments and coupled columns, the other is one of Leeds' most delightful buildings, an elegantly

65. For some time it was thought Danby (*q.v.*) and Thorp were in partnership, but the Leeds *Directories* confirm that the two men continued to have their own offices and addresses.

66. Linstrum, *WYAA*, p. 264.

detailed, sensitively handled essay in Cotswolds Arts and Crafts, quite different from his earlier Medical School and a radical alternative to the Woodhouse Moor block, despite the similar functions.

In the 1880's Thorp undertook a series of commissions to design substantial new houses and remodel existing ones in Weetwood, several of which subsequently became Leeds University halls of residence. The most notable are the Jacobethan *Quarry Dene* of 1881-6 built for John Rawlinson Ford with which Francis Bedford may have assisted. *Woodlands*, the huge mansion for Charles Barran in West Avenue, Roundhay, is another important example. In the early years of the new century he designed several commercial buildings – shops with a temperance hotel in Vicar Lane and, in 1906, a great warehouse for Hotham and Whiting in Wellington Street. His last public commission came from Cleckheaton after winning the competition in 1908 to design the town's first Secondary and Technical School for boys and girls under the new Education Act. It was opened in 1910 on Whitcliffe Mount, a long, stone columned, late Tudor front with three wings to the rear.

Thorp played an active role in the organization of most of Leeds' artistic institutions. He was on the Leeds Institute's sub-committee that worked out the brief for the new School of Art in 1900, and for many years the deputy chairman of the sub-committee of the City Art Gallery, which he had designed. In 1904 he chaired the Arts and Crafts exhibition arranged jointly with the Leeds Arts Club and, for the latter, mounted an exhibition of modern domestic architecture including the work of C.A. Voysey, Baillie Scott, E.J. May, Basil Champneys and others. He and Francis Bedford (*q.v.*) were both working resident members of the Leeds Fine Arts Club, founded in 1874, and Thorp was a founding member of the Leeds Art Collection Fund in 1912.

His son, Ralph, became an architect and joined his father for some years before the First World War but from 1919, Thorp senior was in partnership with G.H. Foggitt. Like Thorp's son, Foggitt (born 1887) began his architectural training at Leeds School of Art alongside his lifelong friend, Piet de Jong (1887-1967). They both won prizes that enabled them to travel and study together in Italy.

When Thorp retired in 1923, he moved to Bristol to be near other family members. In recognition of his services to the architectural profession in Leeds, he was elected the first life member of the West Yorkshire Society of Architects, presented with an illuminated address and a donation of £50. Foggitt, in 1926, went into partnership with Harry Chorley, whose father Charles (*q.v.*) had died in 1914.

In 1884 Thorp published *An Architect's sketchbook at home and abroad*, a large book of his drawings of buildings in Yorkshire, Belgium and Germany, produced with the assistance of many prominent Leeds and other subscribers, on the lines of those published by Ernest George, but in this case dedicated to

19.47: Chapel Allerton, Leeds, library and police station (W.H. Thorp, 1904). (*Ruth Baumberg*.)

Richard Norman Shaw. He also published 'Villas and gardens of Rome, Tivoli and Frascati' in *Journal of the R.I.B.A.*, 14, 1907, pp. 585-604, which he had earlier read to the Leeds and Yorkshire Architectural Society. He exhibited at the Royal Academy four times between 1884 and 1893. Francis Bedford (*q.v.*) was one of his pupils.

An obituary appeared in *The Builder*, 166, 1944, p. 98. In it he is referred to as 'one of the best known architects in the North of England'.

LEEDS, *The Hollies,* Mill Lane, Weetwood, 1864. (*ex inf.* David Boswell.)

HEADINGLEY, Leeds, Home for Orphan Girls, Cliff Road, c.1873 and 1876. (*LM*, 1 Sept 1873.)

RAWDON, nr Leeds, Boys Wing, Friends School, c.1877. (*LM*, 27 March 1877.)

SELBY, 2 shops and residences, c.1880. (*LM*, 3 July 1880.)

ROUNDHAY, Leeds, *Woodlands,* West Avenue, early 1880's. (*ex inf.* David Boswell.)

LEEDS, *Weetwood Villa* (now Oxley Hall), Weetwood Lane, extensive alterations, 1880s. (Pevsner, *WY*, p. 517.)

LEEDS, *Quarry Dene*, Weetwood, 1881-6. (Linstrum, *WYAA*, p. 385.)

HEADINGLEY, Leeds, pair of houses, Burton Crescent, c.1882. (*LM*, 19 Aug 1882.)

LEEDS, St James Hall, New York Street, extension, 1884. (*LM*, 5 Nov 1884.)

LEEDS, City Art Gallery, 1886-8. (*LM*, 12 Feb 1887.)

FAR HEADINGLEY, Leeds, 4, St Chad's Gardens, c.1886. (*LM*, 24 April 1886.)

GOOLE, WY, villa, Clifton Gardens, c.1886. (*LM*, 12 June 1886.)

WEETWOOD, Leeds, Weetwood Hall, new north wing, 1887. (Pevsner, *WY*, p. 517.)

FELIXTOWE, Suffolk, The Gables, c.1889. (*Academy Architecture*, 1889, p. 75.)

LEEDS, Jewish Synagogue, Merrion Street, c.1890. (*LM*, 9 Jan 1890.)

LEEDS, Friends' Adult School, Denison Street, Burley, 1890. (*LM*, 31 March 1890.)

LEEDS, Town Hall, south balcony in Victoria Hall, 1890. (Pevsner, *WY*, p. 413.)

LEEDS, School of Medicine, Leeds General Infirmary, 1890-4. (*LM*, 4 Oct 1894.)

19.48: Burnley, Lancs, unexecuted design for Technical Institute (W.H. Thorp, c.1900). (Academy Architecture, *1902, pt 2, p. 15.*)

LEEDS, Oxford Place, Chapel and Chambers, WM, with George Danby (*q.v.*), alterations, new front and extension, 1890-1903. (*LM*, 11 Sept 1896.)

LEEDS, Stables Memorial Nurses' Home, Leeds General Infirmary, 1897-8. (Linstrum, *WYAA,* p. 385.)

BURNLEY, LANCS, Technical Institute, unexecuted design, 1900. (*Academy Architecture*, 1902, pt 2. p. 15.)

LEEDS, library and police Station. Woodhouse Lane, 1901. (Pevsner, *WY*, p. 470.)

LEEDS, 58-62 Vicar Lane, temperance hotel, shops and offices, c.1902. (Pevsner, *WY*, p. 445.)

CHAPEL ALLERTON, library and police station, 1904. (Linstrum, *WYAA*, p. 385.)

LEEDS, Hotham and Whiting warehouse, Wellington Street. 1906. (Linstrum, *WYAA*, p. 385.)

LEEDS, police station, Meadow Lane, 1907. (Linstrum, *WYAA*, p. 385.)

LEEDS, YMCA, Albion Place, c.1908. (Pevsner, *WY*, p. 442.)

CLECKHEATON, WY, Whitcliffe Mount Secondary and Technical School, 1909-10. (A.L. Mowat, A.L. (ed.), *Whitcliffe Mount School,* privately published, 1957.)

John Tweedale (1853-1905)

Tweedale was born in Dewsbury, the son of James Smithies Tweedale, a woollen merchant. He was educated at Batley Grammar School and Leeds Grammar School. In 1871 he was articled to S.E. Smith (*q.v.*) and subsequently spent 1874-5 as an assistant to Sir Robert William Edis in London. While in London he enrolled at the South Kensington Art School. In 1876 he spent seven months travelling in France, Switzerland and Northern Italy. In 1877 he returned to Leeds and entered partnership with Smith, his former master, using the style Smith and Tweedale. This lasted until 1903 when

he retired and moved to the Isle of Man. He died there two years later, aged 51.

He became an ARIBA in 1881 and was elected a Fellow in 1889. He served as a vice-president of the LYAS. For nine years he was a Liberal member of Leeds Borough Corporation, chairman of its Gas Committee and deputy chairman of the Art Gallery Committee. For many years he was also a member of the executive committee of the Leeds Music Festival and secretary of the Leeds Philharmonic Society.

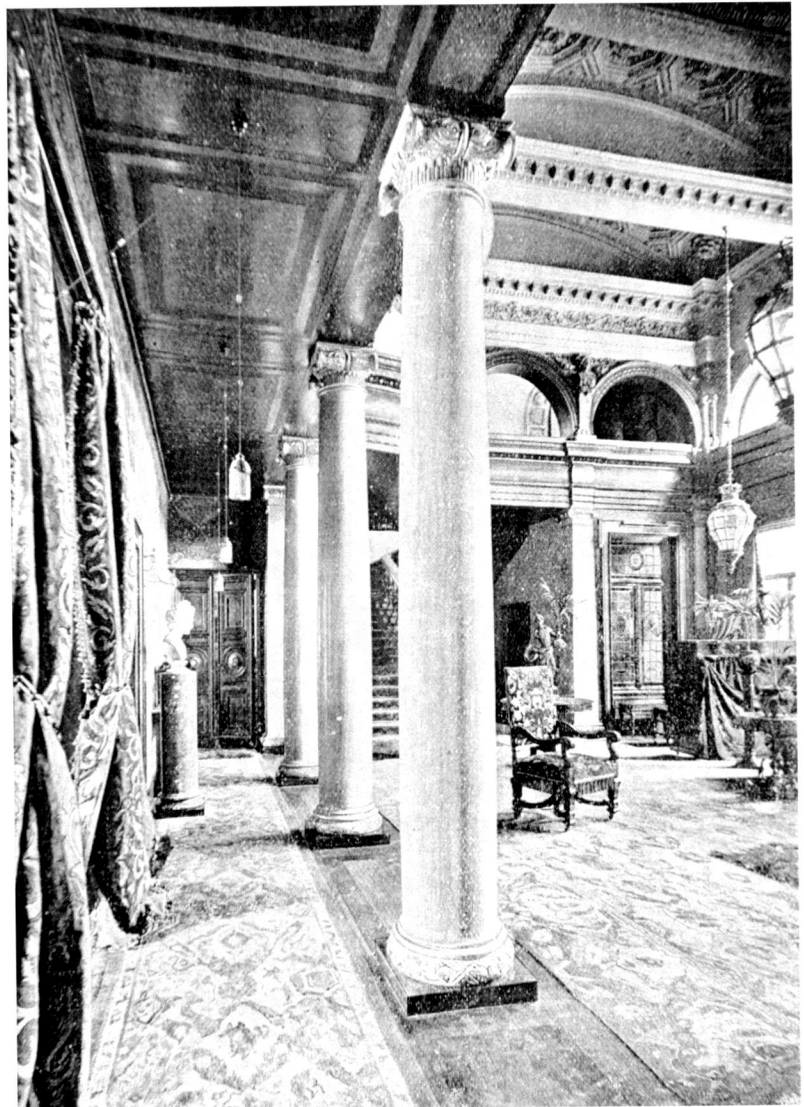

19.49: Headingley, Leeds, Castle Grove (T. Butler Wilson, c.1896). (Academy Architecture, *1903, pt 1 p. 92.*)

19.50: Halifax, *Tourelle* (Wilson and Oglesby, c.1900). (*Academy Architecture, 1900, pt 1, p. 19.*)

67. Apparently he also enrolled at the Yorkshire College in Leeds and King's College, London. Biographical information – not always consistent – can be found in Felstead, Linstrum, *WYAA* and in his obituaries.

68. Linstrum (*WYAA*, p. 386) records they also had a London office, but this is not mentioned in other sources.

Obituary: *The Builder*, 88, 1905, p. 576.

The work of Smith and Tweedale is listed under Stephen Smith

Thomas Butler Wilson (1859-1942)

Wilson was the son of James Wilson jnr (1837-1912), a man with some architectural work to his credit, but one more usually recorded as an ornamental plasterer with a large and successful business. The family were devout Wesleyans. He was educated at Leeds Grammar School and was articled to his father in 1877. The following year he enrolled at the Leeds School of Art, and later at the Architectural Association in London.[67] He spent 1878-80 travelling through France, Belgium and Holland and in 1881 was an improver in the London office of Charles Bell (1846-99), also a Wesleyan. In 1882 he returned to work in his father's office and in 1884 opened his own practice in Leeds at 12, East Parade, essentially taking over his father's architectural business. Three years later, he opened a second office in Harrogate at Central Chambers,[68] and in 1889 formed a partnership with Robert Parr Oglesby (1863-1914), using the style Butler Wilson and Oglesby.

The practice had a reputation for designing large houses with comfortable, well-detailed interiors, often published in professional journals, and through his Wesleyan connections came a succession of chapel commissions. He also designed some minor public buildings. However, he is best remembered for his contributions to the various professional debates about architectural practice, registration and education (discussed in Chapter 9), and in 1904 he published, at his own expense, a 'draft Bill for the Statutory Registration of Architects'. He was elected FRIBA in 1893 and served on the RIBA's Council 1896-7, 1901-4, 1924-8. He also sat on its Board of Architectural Education, the Board of Examiners and was a member of the Practice, Science and Registration Committees. In Leeds he joined the LYAS in 1886, was its President from 1901-4 and continued as a member of its council over many years. At the time of his death he was the Hon. Treasurer. Through his interest in education he was largely responsible for the formation of the Leeds School of Architecture in 1902, and he maintained an active interest in its students up to his death. He was a member of the Advisory Committee of the school for many years.

According to his *Builder* obituary, he was 'one of the Society's best after-dinner speakers and was a great raconteur. His fine memory enabled him to recall and describe vividly many events in the history of Society and the RIBA, and his numerous and informative speeches were a popular feature of the meetings of the Society and the School.'

In 1897 he published *Modern House Interiors* and 1937 *Two Leeds Architects: Cuthbert Broderick and George Corson.* .

An extensive but largely un-catalogued collection of Thomas Butler Wilson's papers and scrapbooks are located in the Archive Collections of Leeds Metropolitan University. Obituaries appeared in *The Builder*, 162, 1942, p. 366 and *RIBA Journal*, 49, 1942, p. 125.

James Wilson Jnr

LEEDS. Hyde Park Road WM, 1869. (*Kelly's Leeds Directory*, 1888)
HEADINGLEY, Leeds, *Beech Grove* and *Ormond House*, Bainbrigge Road, 1872. (Trowell, TS.)
HARROGATE, Oatlands Mount WM, 1883. (Centenary brochure, 1983.)

James Wilson & Son

SOUTH ELMSALL, WY, Trinity WM, 1884-5. (Centenary brochure, 1985.)

T. Butler Wilson

DARRINGTON, nr Pontefract, Wesleyan Chapel, 1883-4. (Butler Wilson Papers.)

SCARBOROUGH, Wesleyan Church, South Cliff, 1884. (Butler Wilson Papers.)

LEEDS, extension to the Meanwood Institute, Green Lane, 1885. (Butler Wilson Papers.)

BROUGH, near Newark, Wesleyan Chapel 1885. (Butler Wilson Papers.)

HELPERBY, near Boroughbridge, Wesleyan Chapel and School, 1887. (*LM*, 31 May 1887.)

METHLEY, WY, two semi-detached houses, 1887. (*LM*, 9 July 1887.)

METHLEY, WY, WM chapel and schools 1887. (*LM*, 31 May 1887.)

LEEDS, extensions and refitting of Headingley Methodist Chapel, 1887. (*LM*, 31 May 1887.)

HUNSLET, Leeds, WM Sunday school, Waterloo Rd. 1887. (*LM*, 28 Dec 1887.)

LEEDS, Business Premises and Manager's House, Claypit Lane, for Henry Clarkson, 1888, dem. (http://archiseek.com/2009/1888)

STARBECK, near Harrogate, Wesleyan Chapel, 1888. (*LM*, 14 Aug 1888.)

HARROGATE, Wesley WM School, Cheltenham Parade 1888 (NYCRO: plans of propos alterations.)

LEEDS, Claypit Lane, house and business premises, 1888. (*Architecture News and Views* on web site)

STARBECK, The Avenue WM, 1888-9. (*Starbeck Methodist Jubilee Brochure*, 1981.)

LEEDS, clothing warehouse, c.1888. (Drawings exhibited Glasgow Int. Exhib, *LM*, 26 Aug 1888.)

STARBECK, Harrogate, The Avenue WM, 1888-9. (*LM*, 2 March 1889.)

HARROGATE, Bilton Bar Wesleyan Chapel, 1889. (*LM*, 2 Mar 1889.)

RIPON, 2 semi-detached villas, Crescent Parade, 1889. (*LM*, 9 March 1889.)

HARROGATE, remodelling of *Grove House*, Skipton Rd for Sampson Fox, c.1890-1900. (Pevsner, *WY*, p. 318.)

LEEDS, additions to Wesleyan Schools, Vivian St, New Wortley, 1891. (*LM*, 19 May 1891.)

HEADINGLEY, Leeds, additions and alterations to *Whinfield*, Headingley for F.L. Hepton, 1891. (*LM*, 29 Dec 1891.)

LEEDS, Skilbeck Street WN, New Wortley, extensions to schoolroom, 1891. (*LM*, 19 May 1891.)

LEEDS, The Mint WM, Moor View, Holbeck, chapel and school, 1891-2. (*The Builder*, 26 Dec 1891.)

HARROGATE, Craven Lodge, Victorian Ave. for Major J. Cooper Eddison, 1892. (Butler Wilson Papers.)

LEEDS, additions and stable block, *Wheatfield Lodge*, Alma Rd., Headingley for Joseph Nicholson, 1892. (Pevsner, *Leeds* p. 250.)

ALTOFTS, near Normanton, four through houses, George St, 1892. (*LM*, 23 July 1892.)

HARROGATE, Claremont Hotel, alterations and additions, 1893-4. (*LM*, 9 Dec 1893.)

HARROGATE, Clarendon Drive, det. res., c.1894. (*LM*, 9 June 1894.)

LEEDS, Extensions and lavish interior decoration and remodelling for Castle Grove, Moor Rd, Headingley for John Kirk, 1894-6. (*Academy Architecture*, 1900, pt 1, p. 151.)

HARROGATE, *Godolphin House*, Clarence Drive, 1894. (*LM*, 9 Jun 1894.)

HARROGATE, Alterations to Selbourne House, 1894-5. (Butler Wilson Papers.)

LEEDS, interior decoration of the premises of the Leeds Engineer Volunteers, 1895, (*LM*, 21 Dec 1895.)

LEEDS, Additions to the Poor Law Offices, East Parade, 1897. (Butler Wilson Papers.)

LEEDS, alterations to *Moorbank*, Shire Oak Rd, Headingley for Joseph Pickersgill, 1898. (Butler Wilson Papers.)

HARROGATE, club house for Harrogate Golf Club, 1899. (*LM,* 25 May 1899.)

HALIFAX, house at 19, Tourelle, c.1900. (*Academy Architecture,* 1900, pt 1, p. 19.)

LEEDS, premises for City Printing and Publishing Works, Cookridge St, for Fred Sparks, 1900-1. (*LM,* 4 Sept 1900.)

LEEDS, Royal Exchange Club, 1904. (Butler Wilson Papers.)

HALIFAX, three houses, Queensgate, Saville Park, 1905. (Butler Wilson Papers.)

Also listed in the Butler Wilson papers are the following executed projects, but without dates.

HARROGATE, extensions and stable block, *Foxholme,* Queen's Rd., for Thomas Hargraves.

LEEDS, 41, Park Square, Leeds, alterations.

HARROGATE, det. res., St James' Park, for Major F.A. Johnson.

HARROGATE, house and studio, Bracken Edge.

HARROGATE, det. res., Woodside, Harrogate, for G.W. Chapman.

SHADWELL, nr Leeds, WM chapel.

CATTAL, nr York, WM chapel.

SOUTH EMSALL, nr Wakefield, WM chapel.

MIDDLETON, Leeds, extension to WM school.

RIPON, alterations and additions to girls' National School.

ROUNDHAY, Leeds, alterations and additions to Asket Hall, for Thomas Green, ironmaster.

LEEDS, 7 shops, Clark Lane.

HARROGATE, Town Mission and missioner's res., Mayfield Grove, Strawberrydale.

HEADINGLEY, Leeds, 2 shops and house, Otley Rd, for John Rayton.

APPERLEY BRIDGE, nr Leeds, laundry building for Woodhouse Grove School.

LEEDS, Wellington Street, alterations to business premises for Messrs Eastwood.

LEEDS, houses and shops, Ellerby Terrace, for J.T. Pearson.

LEEDS, alterations to General Assurance Building, East Parade.

SCARBOROUGH, business premises, Newborough St.

SOUTH EMSALL, nr Wakefield, house and shop.

MEANWOOD, Leeds, 2 det. houses, Monkbridge Rd., for Benjamin Rowley.

HEADINGLEY, Leeds, shop, residence and smithy, Moor Rd.

HEADINGLEY, Leeds, additions to Beech Villa, Shaw Lane, for James Walker.

OUTWOOD, nr Wakefield, St Mary Magdalene Parochial Institute.

LEEDS, mission church, Roundhay Rd., for Leeds Church Extension Society.

HEADINGLEY, Leeds, *The Cedars,* addition of morning room, for Bernal Bagshaw.

Notes on the Contributors

Authors

Dr David Boswell read history at Christ's College, Cambridge, and has a Ph.D from the University of Manchester and a D.Phil. from the Institute for Advanced Architectural Studies at York. He has published on a range of topics including John Sell Cotman, the Leeds College of Art, and the patronage of Sir Frank Brangwyn. He is currently preparing research into the Bedford and Kitson architectural practice for wider publication.

Dr Colin Cunningham was for many years Senior Lecturer and Reader in Architectural History at the Open University. While in that post he wrote and presented numerous television programmes on architecture. Among his publications is *Victorian and Edwardian Town Halls* and he was co-author of the biography of Alfred Waterhouse which won the Alice Davis Hitchcock Medallion. He also prepared the RIBA catalogue of the drawings of Alfred Waterhouse. He was a former Chairman of the Society of Architectural Historians of Great Britain and of the Victorian Society. This essay is Colin's final publication, completed shortly before his untimely death in 2011.

Colin Dews trained as a teacher at Southlands College of Education, Wimbledon, and until retirement was first a lecturer and then Health and Safety Officer at Park Lane College of Further Education, Leeds.

He was awarded an M.Phil from the University of Bradford for his researches on Methodism in Leeds and has written a number of chapel histories and related articles. Currently he is the Leeds Methodist District Archivist and Secretary of the Wesley Historical Society (Yorkshire).

Janet Douglas was formerly a Principal Lecturer in Politics at Leeds Metropolitan University and for over thirty years a member of the West Yorkshire Group of the Victorian Society as well as being Convenor of its Conservation Committee. She is the author of a wide range of publications on the history of Leeds, the most recent of which is 'Cranes over the city: the city centre, 1980-2008' in *Sport, Leisure and Culture in the post-Modern City*.

Dr Terry Friedman, retired Principal Keeper of Leeds City Art Gallery and the Henry Moore Centre for Studies in Sculpture, is an architectural historian based in Leeds. He is the author of *James Gibbs* and *The Eighteenth Century Church in Britain* (Yale University Press, 2011), and has written widely on Yorkshire 18th century buildings.

Dr Kevin Grady is Director of Leeds Civic Trust (the city's built environment and heritage trust), having formerly been a lecturer in Economic History at Exeter and Leeds Universities. He has researched, written and lectured extensively on the history of Leeds and the West Riding of Yorkshire. His publications include books on the building development of the West Riding in the Georgian period, and *The Illustrated History of Leeds* (1994 and 2002) which is the standard work on the history of the city.

Paula Jackman read Architecture at Newnham College, Cambridge, and has been a practising Chartered Architect for the last 25 years, initially in Cambridge where projects included work for Kings College, the Old Palace at Ely and the University of Cambridge's first building providing accommodation for disabled students. She has exhibited drawings in the Architecture Room at the Royal Academy Summer Exhibition and was recently commissioned to provide a series of watercolours for a Parliamentary Report on future strategy for the Houses of Parliament. Since 1993 she has been a Partner in the family business of Braithwaite and Jackman in Leeds.

Hugh Kerrigan retired after a career in industry. He is currently engaged in a number of research projects which exploit the rich resources of the libraries in Leeds but trawling through the newspapers seeking information about architects and their businesses has brought a new dimension to his work.

Kenneth Powell is an architectural critic and historian based in London and Leeds. He has worked in the field of conservation as Secretary of SAVE and Director of the Twentieth Century Society, and has served on the London DAC and the Historic Churches Committee of the Diocese of Leeds. A member of Council of the Architectural Association and Honorary Fellow of the RIBA, he is the author of many books and as a journalist has been architecture correspondent of the *Daily Telegraph* and contributor to numerous magazines and journals.

Ian Serjeant is the conservation officer for the Methodist Church and is responsible for the management of its Ecclesiastical Exemption system throughout the UK. He is currently a member of English Heritage's Places of Worship Forum, is on the steering group of the SPAB's Faith in Maintenance project and serves on the Diocese of Blackburn's DAC. He has published numerous articles and, with K E Street, is co-author of *Heritage and Mission,* Methodist Publishing House (2000).

Christopher Webster returned to Leeds after a career at Staffordshire University. He has published widely on English architecture in the first half of the nineteenth century including *R.D. Chantrell and the architecture of a lost generation*, on provincial practice, post-Waterloo church design and the influence of the Cambridge Camden Society.

Susan Wrathmell is the Senior Listed Buildings Officer for the Yorkshire Dales National Park and has recently completed research for English Heritage into the historic buildings of Skipton town centre. After undertaking listed building reviews of Leeds and Yorkshire textile mills she wrote (with contributions) the *Pevsner Architectural Guide* to Leeds, published by Yale in 2005.

Project Photographer and Picture Editor

Ruth Baumberg read mathematics at Somerville College, Oxford, and spent her working life in the computer industry. She has an interest in late Victorian Art Pottery and has published articles on Burmantofts pottery. She is a member of the Victorian Society, enjoys looking at buildings and has always had an interest in photography.

Project Administrator

Peter Hirschmann was formerly Consultant Dental Radiologist at Leeds Dental Institute and editor of *DentoMaxilloFacial Radiology*. He is chairman of the West Yorkshire Group of the Victorian Society and since retirement has been able, when not on his allotment, to devote more of his time to cultural causes, in particular the historic and built environment.

Index

Architects are designated with *
prior to their name.